Modern C++ Programming Cookbook

Second Edition

Master C++ core language and standard library features, with over 100 recipes, updated to C++20

Marius Bancila

BIRMINGHAM - MUMBAI

Modern C++ Programming Cookbook

Second Edition

Producer: Ben Renow-Clarke
Acquisition Editor – Peer Reviews: Suresh Jain
Project Editors: Carol Lewis and Tom Jacob
Content Development Editor: Alex Patterson
Copy Editor: Safis Editing
Technical Editor: Saby D'silva
Proofreader: Safis Editing
Indexer: Priyanka Dhadke
Presentation Designer: Sandip Tadge

First published: May 2017
Second Edition: September 2020

Production reference: 1090920

Published by Packt Publishing Ltd.
Livery Place
35 Livery Street
Birmingham B3 2PB, UK.

ISBN 978-1-80020-898-8

www.packt.com

Contributors

About the author

Marius Bancila is a software engineer with almost two decades of experience in developing solutions for the industrial and financial sectors. He is the author of *The Modern C++ Challenge* and coauthor of *Learn C# Programming*. He works as a software architect and is focused on Microsoft technologies, mainly developing desktop applications with C++ and C#, but not solely. He is passionate about sharing his technical expertise with others and, for that reason, he has been recognized as a Microsoft MVP for C++ and later developer technologies since 2006.

I would like to thank all the people at Packt that worked on this project and helped to make a better book updated with the latest C++ changes. To Carol, Alex, Tom, and Saby for their efforts and coordination of the project. And to my family for their support during the time spent writing this book.

About the reviewer

Steve Oualline wrote his first program at age 11. He's been programming ever since. He has worked at a variety of programming jobs since then.

Table of Contents

Preface

C++ is one of the most popular and most widely used programming languages, and it has been like that for three decades. Designed with a focus on performance, efficiency, and flexibility, C++ combines paradigms such as object-oriented, imperative, generic, and functional programming. C++ is standardized by the **International Organization for Standardization** (**ISO**) and has undergone massive changes over the last decade. With the standardization of C++11, the language has entered into a new age, which has been widely referred to as modern C++. Type inference, move semantics, lambda expressions, smart pointers, uniform initialization, variadic templates, and many other recent features have changed the way we write code in C++ to the point that it almost looks like a new programming language. This change is being further advanced with the release of the C++20 standard that is supposed to happen during 2020. The new standard includes many new changes to the language, such as modules, concepts, and coroutines, as well as to the standard library, such as ranges, text formatting, and calendars.

This book addresses many of the new features included in C++11, C++14, C++17, and the forthcoming C++20. This book is organized in recipes, each covering one particular language or library feature, or a common problem that developers face and its typical solution using modern C++. Through more than 130 recipes, you will learn to master both core language features and the standard libraries, including those for strings, containers, algorithms, iterators, streams, regular expressions, threads, filesystem, atomic operations, utilities, and ranges.

This second edition of the book took several months to write, and during this time the work on the C++20 standard has been completed. However, at the time of writing this preface, the standard is yet to be approved and will be published later this year.

More than 30 new or updated recipes in this book cover C++20 features, including modules, concepts, coroutines, ranges, threads and synchronization mechanisms, text formatting, calendars and time zones, immediate functions, the three-way comparison operator, and the new `span` class.

All the recipes in the book contain code samples that show how to use a feature or how to solve a problem. These code samples have been written using Visual Studio 2019, but have been also compiled using Clang and GCC. Since the support for various language and library features has been gradually added to all these compilers, it is recommended that you use the latest version to ensure that all of them are supported. At the time of writing this preface, the latest versions are GCC 10.1, Clang 12.0 (in progress), and VC++ 2019 version 14.27 (from Visual Studio 2019 version 16.7). Although all these compilers are C++17 complete, the support for C++20 varies from compiler to compiler. Please refer to `https://en.cppreference.com/w/cpp/compiler_support` to check your compiler's support for C++20 features.

Who this book is for

This book is intended for all C++ developers, regardless of their experience level. The typical reader is an entry- or medium-level C++ developer who wants to master the language and become a prolific modern C++ developer. The experienced C++ developer will find a good reference for many C++11, C++14, C++17, and C++20 language and library features that may come in handy from time to time. The book consists of more than 130 recipes that are simple, intermediate, or advanced. However, they all require prior knowledge of C++, and that includes functions, classes, templates, namespaces, macros, and others. Therefore, if you are not familiar with the language, it is recommended that you first read an introductory book to familiarize yourself with the core aspects, and then proceed with this book.

What this book covers

Chapter 1, Learning Modern Core Language Features, teaches you about modern core language features, including type inference, uniform initialization, scoped enumerations, range-based for loops, structured bindings, class template argument deduction, and others.

Chapter 2, Working with Numbers and Strings, discusses how to convert between numbers and strings, generate pseudo-random numbers, work with regular expressions and various types of string, as well as how to format text using the C++20 text formatting library.

Chapter 3, Exploring Functions, dives into defaulted and deleted functions, variadic templates, lambda expressions, and higher-order functions.

Chapter 4, Preprocessing and Compilation, takes a look at various aspects of compilation, from how to perform conditional compilation, to compile-time assertions, code generation, and hinting the compiler with attributes.

Chapter 5, Standard Library Containers, Algorithms, and Iterators, introduces you to several standard containers, many algorithms, and teaches you how to write your own random-access iterator.

Chapter 6, General-Purpose Utilities, dives into the `chrono` library, including the C++20 calendars and time zones support; the `any`, `optional`, `variant`, and `span` types; and type traits.

Chapter 7, Working with Files and Streams, explains how to read and write data to/from streams, use I/O manipulators to control streams, and explores the `filesystem` library.

Chapter 8, Leveraging Threading and Concurrency, teaches you how to work with threads, mutexes, locks, condition variables, promises, futures, atomic types, as well as the C++20 latches, barriers, and semaphores.

Chapter 9, Robustness and Performance, focuses on exceptions, constant correctness, type casts, smart pointers, and move semantics.

Chapter 10, Implementing Patterns and Idioms, covers various useful patterns and idioms, such as the pimpl idiom, the non-virtual interface idiom, and the curiously recurring template pattern.

Chapter 11, Exploring Testing Frameworks, gives you a kickstart with three of the most widely used testing frameworks, Boost.Test, Google Test, and Catch2.

Chapter 12, C++20 Core Features, introduces you to the most important new additions to the C++20 standard—modules, concepts, coroutines, and ranges.

To get the most out of this book

The code presented in the book is available for download from `https://github.com/PacktPublishing/Modern-Cpp-Cookbook-Second-Edition`, although I encourage you to try writing all the samples by yourself. In order to compile them, you need VC++ 2019 16.7 on Windows and GCC 10.1 or Clang 12.0 on Linux and Mac. If you don't have the latest version of the compiler, or you want to try another compiler, you can use one that is available online.

Although there are various online platforms that you could use, I recommend Wandbox, available at `https://wandbox.org/`, and Compiler Explorer, available at `https://godbolt.org/`.

Download the example code files

You can download the example code files for this book from your account at `http://www.packtpub.com`. If you purchased this book elsewhere, you can visit `http://www.packtpub.com/support` and register to have the files emailed directly to you.

You can download the code files by following these steps:

1. Log in or register at `http://www.packtpub.com`.
2. Select the **SUPPORT** tab.
3. Click on **Code Downloads & Errata**.
4. Enter the name of the book in the **Search** box and follow the on-screen instructions.

Once the file is downloaded, please make sure that you unzip or extract the folder using the latest version of:

- WinRAR / 7-Zip for Windows
- Zipeg / iZip / UnRarX for Mac
- 7-Zip / PeaZip for Linux

The code bundle for the book is also hosted on GitHub at `https://github.com/PacktPublishing/Modern-CPP-Programming-Cookbook-Second-Edition`. We also have other code bundles from our rich catalog of books and videos available at `https://github.com/PacktPublishing/`. Check them out!

Download the color images

We also provide a PDF file that has color images of the screenshots/diagrams used in this book. You can download it here: `https://static.packt-cdn.com/downloads/9781800208988_ColorImages.pdf`.

Conventions used

There are a number of text conventions used throughout this book.

`CodeInText`: Indicates code words in text, database table names, folder names, filenames, file extensions, pathnames, dummy URLs, user input, and Twitter handles. For example: "The geometry module was defined in a file called `geometry.ixx/.cppm`, although any file name would have had the same result."

A block of code is set as follows:

```
static std::map<
  std::string,
  std::function<std::unique_ptr<Image>()>> mapping
{
  { "bmp", []() {return std::make_unique<BitmapImage>(); } },
  { "png", []() {return std::make_unique<PngImage>(); } },
  { "jpg", []() {return std::make_unique<JpgImage>(); } }
};
```

When we wish to draw your attention to a particular part of a code block, the relevant lines or items are highlighted:

```
static std::map<
  std::string,
  std::function<std::unique_ptr<Image>()>> mapping
{
  { "bmp", []() {return std::make_unique<BitmapImage>(); } },
  { "png", []() {return std::make_unique<PngImage>(); } },
  { "jpg", []() {return std::make_unique<JpgImage>(); } }
};
```

Any command-line input or output is written as follows:

```
running thread 140296854550272
running thread 140296846157568
running thread 140296837764864
```

Bold: Indicates a new term, an important word, or words that you see on the screen, for example, in menus or dialog boxes, also appear in the text like this. For example: "Select **System info** from the **Administration** panel."

Warnings or important notes appear like this.

Tips and tricks appear like this.

Get in touch

Feedback from our readers is always welcome.

General feedback: Email `feedback@packtpub.com`, and mention the book's title in the subject of your message. If you have questions about any aspect of this book, please email us at `questions@packtpub.com`.

Errata: Although we have taken every care to ensure the accuracy of our content, mistakes do happen. If you have found a mistake in this book we would be grateful if you would report this to us. Please visit, `packtpub.com/support/errata`, selecting your book, clicking on the Errata Submission Form link, and entering the details.

Piracy: If you come across any illegal copies of our works in any form on the Internet, we would be grateful if you would provide us with the location address or website name. Please contact us at `copyright@packtpub.com` with a link to the material.

If you are interested in becoming an author: If there is a topic that you have expertise in and you are interested in either writing or contributing to a book, please visit `http://authors.packtpub.com`.

Reviews

Please leave a review. Once you have read and used this book, why not leave a review on the site that you purchased it from? Potential readers can then see and use your unbiased opinion to make purchase decisions, we at Packt can understand what you think about our products, and our authors can see your feedback on their book. Thank you!

For more information about Packt, please visit `packtpub.com`.

1

Learning Modern Core Language Features

The C++ language has gone through a major transformation in the past decade with the development and release of C++11 and then, later, with its newer versions: C++14, C++17, and C++20. These new standards have introduced new concepts, simplified and extended existing syntax and semantics, and overall transformed the way we write code. C++11 looks like a new language, and code written using the new standards is called modern C++ code.

The recipes included in this chapter are as follows:

- Using `auto` whenever possible
- Creating type aliases and alias templates
- Understanding uniform initialization
- Understanding the various forms of non-static member initialization
- Controlling and querying object alignment
- Using scoped enumerations
- Using `override` and `final` for virtual methods
- Using range-based for loops to iterate on a range
- Enabling range-based for loops for custom types
- Using explicit constructors and conversion operators to avoid implicit conversion
- Using unnamed namespaces instead of static globals

- Using inline namespaces for symbol versioning
- Using structured bindings to handle multi-return values
- Simplifying code with class template argument deduction

Let's start by learning about automatic type deduction.

Using auto whenever possible

Automatic type deduction is one of the most important and widely used features in modern C++. The new C++ standards have made it possible to use `auto` as a placeholder for types in various contexts and let the compiler deduce the actual type. In C++11, `auto` can be used for declaring local variables and for the return type of a function with a trailing return type. In C++14, `auto` can be used for the return type of a function without specifying a trailing type and for parameter declarations in lambda expressions. Future standard versions are likely to expand the use of `auto` to even more cases. The use of `auto` in these contexts has several important benefits, all of which will be discussed in the *How it works...* section. Developers should be aware of them, and prefer `auto` whenever possible. An actual term was coined for this by Andrei Alexandrescu and promoted by Herb Sutter—**almost always auto** (**AAA**).

How to do it...

Consider using `auto` as a placeholder for the actual type in the following situations:

- To declare local variables with the form `auto name = expression` when you do not want to commit to a specific type:

```
auto i = 42;          // int
auto d = 42.5;        // double
auto s = "text";      // char const *
auto v = { 1, 2, 3 }; // std::initializer_list<int>
```

- To declare local variables with the `auto name = type-id { expression }` form when you need to commit to a specific type:

```
auto b  = new char[10]{ 0 };            // char*
auto s1 = std::string {"text"};         // std::string
auto v1 = std::vector<int> { 1, 2, 3 }; // std::vector<int>
auto p  = std::make_shared<int>(42);    // std::shared_ptr<int>
```

- To declare named lambda functions, with the form `auto name = lambda-expression`, unless the lambda needs to be passed or returned to a function:

```
auto upper = [](char const c) {return toupper(c); };
```

- To declare lambda parameters and return values:

```
auto add = [](auto const a, auto const b) {return a + b;};
```

- To declare a function return type when you don't want to commit to a specific type:

```
template <typename F, typename T>
auto apply(F&& f, T value)
{
  return f(value);
}
```

How it works...

The `auto` specifier is basically a placeholder for an actual type. When using `auto`, the compiler deduces the actual type from the following instances:

- From the type of expression used to initialize a variable, when `auto` is used to declare variables.
- From the trailing return type or the type of the return expression of a function, when `auto` is used as a placeholder for the return type of a function.

In some cases, it is necessary to commit to a specific type. For instance, in the first example in the previous section, the compiler deduces the type of `s` to be `char const *`. If the intention was to have an `std::string`, then the type must be specified explicitly. Similarly, the type of `v` was deduced as `std::initializer_list<int>`. However, the intention could be to have an `std::vector<int>`. In such cases, the type must be specified explicitly on the right side of the assignment.

There are some important benefits of using the `auto` specifier instead of actual types; the following is a list of, perhaps, the most important ones:

- It is not possible to leave a variable uninitialized. This is a common mistake that developers make when declaring variables specifying the actual type. However, this is not possible with `auto`, which requires an initialization of the variable in order to deduce the type.
- Using `auto` ensures that you always use the correct type and that implicit conversion will not occur. Consider the following example where we retrieve the size of a vector to a local variable. In the first case, the type of the variable is `int`, though the `size()` method returns `size_t`. This means an implicit conversion from `size_t` to `int` will occur. However, using `auto` for the type will deduce the correct type; that is, `size_t`:

```
auto v = std::vector<int>{ 1, 2, 3 };
```

```
// implicit conversion, possible loss of data
int size1 = v.size();

// OK
auto size2 = v.size();

// ill-formed (warning in gcc/clang, error in VC++)
auto size3 = int{ v.size() };
```

- Using `auto` promotes good object-oriented practices, such as preferring interfaces over implementations. The fewer the number of types specified, the more generic the code is and more open to future changes, which is a fundamental principle of object-oriented programming.
- It means less typing and less concern for actual types that we don't care about anyway. It is very often the case that even though we explicitly specify the type, we don't actually care about it. A very common case is with iterators, but there are many more. When you want to iterate over a range, you don't care about the actual type of the iterator. You are only interested in the iterator itself; so, using `auto` saves time used for typing possibly long names and helps you focus on actual code and not type names. In the following example, in the first `for` loop, we explicitly use the type of the iterator. It is a lot of text to type; the long statements can actually make the code less readable, and you also need to know the type name that you actually don't care about. The second loop with the `auto` specifier looks simpler and saves you from typing and caring about actual types:

```
std::map<int, std::string> m;
for (std::map<int, std::string>::const_iterator
  it = m.cbegin();
  it != m.cend(); ++it)
{ /*...*/ }

for (auto it = m.cbegin(); it != m.cend(); ++it)
{ /*...*/ }
```

- Declaring variables with `auto` provides a consistent coding style with the type always in the right-hand side. If you allocate objects dynamically, you need to write the type both on the left and right side of the assignment, for example, `int* p = new int(42)`. With `auto`, the type is specified only once on the right side.

However, there are some gotchas when using `auto`:

- The `auto` specifier is only a placeholder for the type, not for the `const`/`volatile` and references specifiers. If you need a `const`/`volatile` and/or reference type, then you need to specify them explicitly. In the following example, `foo.get()` returns a reference to `int`; when the variable `x` is initialized from the return value, the type deduced by the compiler is `int`, not `int&`. Therefore, any change made to `x` will not propagate to `foo.x_`. In order to do so, we should use `auto&`:

```
class foo {
  int x_;
public:
  foo(int const x = 0) :x_{ x } {}
  int& get() { return x_; }
};

foo f(42);
auto x = f.get();
x = 100;
std::cout << f.get() << '\n'; // prints 42
```

- It is not possible to use `auto` for types that are not moveable:

```
auto ai = std::atomic<int>(42); // error
```

- It is not possible to use `auto` for multi-word types, such as `long long`, `long double`, or `struct foo`. However, in the first case, the possible workarounds are to use literals or type aliases; as for the second, using `struct`/`class` in that form is only supported in C++ for C compatibility and should be avoided anyway:

```
auto l1 = long long{ 42 }; // error

using llong = long long;
auto l2 = llong{ 42 };     // OK
auto l3 = 42LL;            // OK
```

- If you use the `auto` specifier but still need to know the type, you can do so in most IDEs by putting the cursor over a variable, for instance. If you leave the IDE, however, that is not possible anymore, and the only way to know the actual type is to deduce it yourself from the initialization expression, which could mean searching through the code for function return types.

The auto can be used to specify the return type from a function. In C++11, this requires a trailing return type in the function declaration. In C++14, this has been relaxed, and the type of the return value is deduced by the compiler from the return expression. If there are multiple return values, they should have the same type:

```
// C++11
auto func1(int const i) -> int
{ return 2*i; }

// C++14
auto func2(int const i)
{ return 2*i; }
```

As mentioned earlier, auto does not retain const/volatile and reference qualifiers. This leads to problems with auto as a placeholder for the return type from a function. To explain this, let's consider the preceding example with foo.get(). This time, we have a wrapper function called proxy_get() that takes a reference to a foo, calls get(), and returns the value returned by get(), which is an int&. However, the compiler will deduce the return type of proxy_get() as being int, not int&. Trying to assign that value to an int& fails with an error:

```
class foo
{
  int x_;
public:
  foo(int const x = 0) :x_{ x } {}
  int& get() { return x_; }
};

auto proxy_get(foo& f) { return f.get(); }

auto f = foo{ 42 };
auto& x = proxy_get(f); // cannot convert from 'int' to 'int &'
```

To fix this, we need to actually return auto&. However, this is a problem with templates and perfect forwarding the return type without knowing whether it is a value or a reference. The solution to this problem in C++14 is decltype(auto), which will correctly deduce the type:

```
decltype(auto) proxy_get(foo& f) { return f.get(); }
auto f = foo{ 42 };
decltype(auto) x = proxy_get(f);
```

The `decltype` specifier is used to inspect the declared type of an entity or an expression. It's mostly useful when declaring types are cumbersome or not possible at all to declare with the standard notation. Examples of this include declaring lambda types and types that depend on template parameters.

The last important case where `auto` can be used is with lambdas. As of C++14, both lambda return types and lambda parameter types can be `auto`. Such a lambda is called a *generic lambda* because the closure type defined by the lambda has a templated call operator. The following shows a generic lambda that takes two `auto` parameters and returns the result of applying `operator+` to the actual types:

```
auto ladd = [] (auto const a, auto const b) { return a + b; };
struct
{
  template<typename T, typename U>
  auto operator () (T const a, U const b) const { return a+b; }
} L;
```

This lambda can be used to add anything for which the `operator+` is defined, as shown in the following snippet:

```
auto i = ladd(40, 2);            // 42
auto s = ladd("forty"s, "two"s); // "fortytwo"s
```

In this example, we used the `ladd` lambda to add two integers and to concatenate to `std::string` objects (using the C++14 user-defined literal `operator ""s`).

See also

- *Creating type aliases and alias templates* to learn about aliases for types
- *Understanding uniform initialization* to see how brace-initialization works

Creating type aliases and alias templates

In C++, it is possible to create synonyms that can be used instead of a type name. This is achieved by creating a `typedef` declaration. This is useful in several cases, such as creating shorter or more meaningful names for a type or names for function pointers. However, `typedef` declarations cannot be used with templates to create template type aliases. An `std::vector<T>`, for instance, is not a type (`std::vector<int>` is a type), but a sort of family of all types that can be created when the type placeholder `T` is replaced with an actual type.

In C++11, a type alias is a name for another already declared type, and an alias template is a name for another already declared template. Both of these types of aliases are introduced with a new `using` syntax.

How to do it...

- Create type aliases with the form `using identifier = type-id`, as in the following examples:

```
using byte     = unsigned char;
using byte_ptr = unsigned char *;
using array_t  = int[10];
using fn       = void(byte, double);

void func(byte b, double d) { /*...*/ }

byte b{42};
byte_ptr pb = new byte[10] {0};
array_t a{0,1,2,3,4,5,6,7,8,9};
fn* f = func;
```

- Create alias templates with the form `template<template-params-list> identifier = type-id`, as in the following examples:

```
template <class T>
class custom_allocator { /* ... */ };

template <typename T>
using vec_t = std::vector<T, custom_allocator<T>>;

vec_t<int>          vi;
vec_t<std::string>  vs;
```

For consistency and readability, you should do the following:

- Not mix `typedef` and `using` declarations when creating aliases
- Prefer the `using` syntax to create names of function pointer types

How it works...

A `typedef` declaration introduces a synonym (an alias, in other words) for a type. It does not introduce another type (like a `class`, `struct`, `union`, or `enum` declaration). Type names introduced with a `typedef` declaration follow the same hiding rules as identifier names. They can also be redeclared, but only to refer to the same type (therefore, you can have valid multiple `typedef` declarations that introduce the same type name synonym in a translation unit, as long as it is a synonym for the same type). The following are typical examples of `typedef` declarations:

```
typedef unsigned char   byte;
typedef unsigned char * byte_ptr;
typedef int             array_t[10];
typedef void(*fn)(byte, double);

template<typename T>
class foo {
  typedef T value_type;
};

typedef std::vector<int> vint_t;
```

A type alias declaration is equivalent to a `typedef` declaration. It can appear in a block scope, class scope, or namespace scope. According to C++11 paragraph 7.1.3.2:

> *"A typedef-name can also be introduced by an alias declaration. The identifier following the using keyword becomes a typedef-name and the optional attribute-specifier-seq following the identifier appertains to that typedef-name. It has the same semantics as if it were introduced by the typedef specifier. In particular, it does not define a new type and it shall not appear in the type-id."*

An alias declaration is, however, more readable and clearer about the actual type that is aliased when it comes to creating aliases for array types and function pointer types. In the examples from the *How to do it...* section, it is easily understandable that `array_t` is a name for the type array of 10 integers, while `fn` is a name for a function type that takes two parameters of the type `byte` and `double` and returns `void`. This is also consistent with the syntax for declaring `std::function` objects (for example, `std::function<void(byte, double)> f`).

It is important to take note of the following things:

- Alias templates cannot be partially or explicitly specialized.
- Alias templates are never deduced by template argument deduction when deducing a template parameter.
- The type produced when specializing an alias template is not allowed to directly or indirectly make use of its own type.

The driving purpose of the new syntax is to define alias templates. These are templates that, when specialized, are equivalent to the result of substituting the template arguments of the alias template for the template parameters in the type-id.

See also

- *Simplifying code with class template argument deduction* to learn how to use class templates without explicitly specifying template arguments

Understanding uniform initialization

Brace-initialization is a uniform method for initializing data in C++11. For this reason, it is also called *uniform initialization*. It is arguably one of the most important features from C++11 that developers should understand and use. It removes previous distinctions between initializing fundamental types, aggregate and non-aggregate types, and arrays and standard containers.

Getting ready

To continue with this recipe, you need to be familiar with direct initialization, which initializes an object from an explicit set of constructor arguments, and copy initialization, which initializes an object from another object. The following is a simple example of both types of initialization:

```
std::string s1("test");   // direct initialization
std::string s2 = "test";  // copy initialization
```

With these in mind, let's explore how to perform uniform initialization.

How to do it...

To uniformly initialize objects regardless of their type, use the brace-initialization form {}, which can be used for both direct initialization and copy initialization. When used with brace-initialization, these are called direct-list and copy-list-initialization:

```
T object {other};   // direct-list-initialization
T object = {other}; // copy-list-initialization
```

Examples of uniform initialization are as follows:

- Standard containers:

  ```
  std::vector<int> v { 1, 2, 3 };
  std::map<int, std::string> m { {1, "one"}, { 2, "two" }};
  ```

- Dynamically allocated arrays:

  ```
  int* arr2 = new int[3]{ 1, 2, 3 };
  ```

- Arrays:

  ```
  int arr1[3] { 1, 2, 3 };
  ```

- Built-in types:

  ```
  int i { 42 };
  double d { 1.2 };
  ```

- User-defined types:

  ```
  class foo
  {
    int a_;
    double b_;
  public:
    foo():a_(0), b_(0) {}
    foo(int a, double b = 0.0):a_(a), b_(b) {}
  };

  foo f1{};
  foo f2{ 42, 1.2 };
  foo f3{ 42 };
  ```

- User-defined POD types:

```
struct bar { int a_; double b_;};
bar b{ 42, 1.2 };
```

How it works...

Before C++11, objects required different types of initialization based on their type:

- Fundamental types could be initialized using assignment:

```
int a = 42;
double b = 1.2;
```

- Class objects could also be initialized using assignment from a single value if they had a conversion constructor (prior to C++11, a constructor with a single parameter was called a *conversion constructor*):

```
class foo
{
  int a_;
public:
  foo(int a):a_(a) {}
};
foo f1 = 42;
```

- Non-aggregate classes could be initialized with parentheses (the functional form) when arguments were provided and only without any parentheses when default initialization was performed (call to the default constructor). In the next example, `foo` is the structure defined in the *How to do it...* section:

```
foo f1;           // default initialization
foo f2(42, 1.2);
foo f3(42);
foo f4();         // function declaration
```

- Aggregate and POD types could be initialized with brace-initialization. In the following example, `bar` is the structure defined in the *How to do it...* section:

```
bar b = {42, 1.2};
int a[] = {1, 2, 3, 4, 5};
```

A **Plain Old Data** (**POD**) type is a type that is both trivial (has special members that are compiler-provided or explicitly defaulted and occupy a contiguous memory area) and has a standard layout (a class that does not contain language features, such as virtual functions, which are incompatible with the C language, and all members have the same access control). The concept of POD types has been deprecated in C++20 in favor of trivial and standard layout types.

Apart from the different methods of initializing the data, there are also some limitations. For instance, the only way to initialize a standard container (apart from copy constructing) is to first declare an object and then insert elements into it; `std::vector` was an exception because it is possible to assign values from an array that can be initialized prior using aggregate initialization. On the other hand, however, dynamically allocated aggregates could not be initialized directly.

All the examples in the *How to do it...* section use direct initialization, but copy initialization is also possible with brace-initialization. These two forms, direct and copy initialization, may be equivalent in most cases, but copy initialization is less permissive because it does not consider explicit constructors in its implicit conversion sequence, which must produce an object directly from the initializer, whereas direct initialization expects an implicit conversion from the initializer to an argument of the constructor. Dynamically allocated arrays can only be initialized using direct initialization.

Of the classes shown in the preceding examples, `foo` is the one class that has both a default constructor and a constructor with parameters. To use the default constructor to perform default initialization, we need to use empty braces; that is, `{}`. To use the constructor with parameters, we need to provide the values for all the arguments in braces `{}`. Unlike non-aggregate types, where default initialization means invoking the default constructor, for aggregate types, default initialization means initializing with zeros.

Initialization of standard containers, such as the vector and the map, also shown previously, is possible because all standard containers have an additional constructor in C++11 that takes an argument of the type `std::initializer_list<T>`. This is basically a lightweight proxy over an array of elements of the type `T const`. These constructors then initialize the internal data from the values in the initializer list.

The way initialization using `std::initializer_list` works is as follows:

- The compiler resolves the types of the elements in the initialization list (all the elements must have the same type).
- The compiler creates an array with the elements in the initializer list.
- The compiler creates an `std::initializer_list<T>` object to wrap the previously created array.
- The `std::initializer_list<T>` object is passed as an argument to the constructor.

An initializer list always takes precedence over other constructors where brace-initialization is used. If such a constructor exists for a class, it will be called when brace-initialization is performed:

```
class foo
{
  int a_;
  int b_;
public:
  foo() :a_(0), b_(0) {}

  foo(int a, int b = 0) :a_(a), b_(b) {}
  foo(std::initializer_list<int> l) {}
};

foo f{ 1, 2 }; // calls constructor with initializer_list<int>
```

The precedence rule applies to any function, not just constructors. In the following example, two overloads of the same function exist. Calling the function with an initializer list resolves to a call to the overload with an `std::initializer_list`:

```
void func(int const a, int const b, int const c)
{
  std::cout << a << b << c << '\n';
}

void func(std::initializer_list<int> const list)
{
  for (auto const & e : list)
    std::cout << e << '\n';
}

func({ 1,2,3 }); // calls second overload
```

This, however, has the potential of leading to bugs. Let's take, for example, the `std::vector` type. Among the constructors of the vector, there is one that has a single argument, representing the initial number of elements to be allocated, and another one that has an `std::initializer_list` as an argument. If the intention is to create a vector with a preallocated size, using brace-initialization will not work as the constructor with the `std::initializer_list` will be the best overload to be called:

```
std::vector<int> v {5};
```

The preceding code does not create a vector with five elements, but a vector with one element with a value of `5`. To be able to actually create a vector with five elements, initialization with the parentheses form must be used:

```
std::vector<int> v (5);
```

Another thing to note is that brace-initialization does not allow narrowing conversion. According to the C++ standard (refer to paragraph 8.5.4 of the standard), a narrowing conversion is an implicit conversion:

> "- *From a floating-point type to an integer type.*
>
> *- From long double to double or float, or from double to float, except where the source is a constant expression and the actual value after conversion is within the range of values that can be represented (even if it cannot be represented exactly).*
>
> *- From an integer type or unscoped enumeration type to a floating-point type, except where the source is a constant expression and the actual value after conversion will fit into the target type and will produce the original value when converted to its original type.*
>
> *- From an integer type or unscoped enumeration type to an integer type that cannot represent all the values of the original type, except where the source is a constant expression and the actual value after conversion will fit into the target type and will produce the original value when converted to its original type.*"

The following declarations trigger compiler errors because they require a narrowing conversion:

```
int i{ 1.2 };              // error

double d = 47 / 13;
float f1{ d };             // error
```

To fix this error, an explicit conversion must be done:

```
int i{ static_cast<int>(1.2) };

double d = 47 / 13;
float f1{ static_cast<float>(d) };
```

A brace-initialization list is not an expression and does not have a type. Therefore, `decltype` cannot be used on a brace-init-list, and template type deduction cannot deduce the type that matches a brace-init-list.

Let's consider one more example:

```
float f2{47/13};           // OK, f2=3
```

The preceding declaration is, however, correct because an implicit conversion from `int` to `float` exists. The expression `47/13` is first evaluated to integer value `3`, which is then assigned to the variable `f2` of the type `float`.

There's more...

The following example shows several examples of direct-list-initialization and copy-list-initialization. In C++11, the deduced type of all these expressions is `std::initializer_list<int>`:

```
auto a = {42};   // std::initializer_list<int>
auto b {42};     // std::initializer_list<int>
auto c = {4, 2}; // std::initializer_list<int>
auto d {4, 2};   // std::initializer_list<int>
```

C++17 has changed the rules for list initialization, differentiating between the direct- and copy-list-initialization. The new rules for type deduction are as follows:

- For copy-list-initialization, auto deduction will deduce an `std::initializer_list<T>` if all the elements in the list have the same type, or be ill-formed.
- For direct-list-initialization, auto deduction will deduce a `T` if the list has a single element, or be ill-formed if there is more than one element.

Based on these new rules, the previous examples would change as follows (the deduced type is mentioned in comments):

```
auto a = {42};   // std::initializer_list<int>
auto b {42};     // int
auto c = {4, 2}; // std::initializer_list<int>
auto d {4, 2};   // error, too many
```

In this case, `a` and `c` are deduced as `std::initializer_list<int>`, `b` is deduced as an `int`, and `d`, which uses direct initialization and has more than one value in the brace-init-list, triggers a compiler error.

See also

- *Using auto whenever possible* to understand how automatic type deduction works in C++
- *Understanding the various forms of non-static member initialization* to learn how to best perform initialization of class members

Understanding the various forms of non-static member initialization

Constructors are places where non-static class member initialization is done. Many developers prefer assignments in the constructor body. Aside from the several exceptional cases when that is actually necessary, initialization of non-static members should be done in the constructor's initializer list or, as of C++11, using default member initialization when they are declared in the class. Prior to C++11, constants and non-constant non-static data members of a class had to be initialized in the constructor. Initialization on declaration in a class was only possible for static constants. As we will see here, this limitation was removed in C++11, which allows the initialization of non-statics in the class declaration. This initialization is called *default member initialization* and is explained in the following sections.

This recipe will explore the ways non-static member initialization should be done. Using the appropriate initialization method for each member leads not only to more efficient code, but also to better organized and more readable code.

How to do it...

To initialize non-static members of a class, you should:

- Use default member initialization for constants, both static and non-static (see `[1]` and `[2]` in the following code).
- Use default member initialization to provide default values for members of classes with multiple constructors that would use a common initializer for those members (see `[3]` and `[4]` in the following code).
- Use the constructor initializer list to initialize members that don't have default values, but depend on constructor parameters (see `[5]` and `[6]` in the following code).
- Use assignment in constructors when the other options are not possible (examples include initializing data members with the pointer `this`, checking constructor parameter values, and throwing exceptions prior to initializing members with those values or self-references of two non-static data members).

The following example shows these forms of initialization:

```
struct Control
{
  const int DefaultHeight = 14;                                  // [1]
  const int DefaultWidth  = 80;                                  // [2]

  TextVerticalAligment   valign = TextVerticalAligment::Middle;  // [3]
  TextHorizontalAligment halign = TextHorizontalAligment::Left;  // [4]

  std::string text;

  Control(std::string const & t) : text(t)       // [5]
  {}

  Control(std::string const & t,
    TextVerticalAligment const va,
    TextHorizontalAligment const ha):
    text(t), valign(va), halign(ha)              // [6]
  {}
};
```

How it works...

Non-static data members are supposed to be initialized in the constructor's initializer list, as shown in the following example:

```
struct Point
{
  double X, Y;
  Point(double const x = 0.0, double const y = 0.0) : X(x), Y(y)  {}
};
```

Many developers, however, do not use the initializer list, but prefer assignments in the constructor's body, or even mix assignments and the initializer list. That could be for several reasons—for larger classes with many members, the constructor assignments may look easier to read than long initializer lists, perhaps split on many lines, or it could be because they are familiar with other programming languages that don't have an initializer list. It also could also happen, unfortunately, for various reasons they don't even know about it.

It is important to note that the order in which non-static data members are initialized is the order in which they were declared in the class definition, and not the order of their initialization in a constructor initializer list. On the other hand, the order in which non-static data members are destroyed is the reversed order of construction.

Using assignments in the constructor is not efficient, as this can create temporary objects that are later discarded. If not initialized in the initializer list, non-static members are initialized via their default constructor and then, when assigned a value in the constructor's body, the assignment operator is invoked. This can lead to inefficient work if the default constructor allocates a resource (such as memory or a file) and that has to be deallocated and reallocated in the assignment operator. This is exemplified in the following snippet:

```
struct foo
{
  foo()
  { std::cout << "default constructor\n"; }
  foo(std::string const & text)
  { std::cout << "constructor '" << text << "\n"; }
  foo(foo const & other)
  { std::cout << "copy constructor\n"; }
```

```
  foo(foo&& other)
  { std::cout << "move constructor\n"; };
  foo& operator=(foo const & other)
  { std::cout << "assignment\n"; return *this; }
  foo& operator=(foo&& other)
  { std::cout << "move assignment\n"; return *this;}
  ~foo()
  { std::cout << "destructor\n"; }
};

struct bar
{
  foo f;

  bar(foo const & value)
  {
    f = value;
  }
};

foo f;
bar b(f);
```

The preceding code produces the following output, showing how the data member `f` is first default initialized and then assigned a new value:

```
default constructor
default constructor
assignment
destructor
destructor
```

Changing the initialization from the assignment in the constructor body to the initializer list replaces the calls to the default constructor, plus the assignment operator, with a call to the copy constructor:

```
bar(foo const & value) : f(value) { }
```

Adding the preceding line of code produces the following output:

```
default constructor
copy constructor
destructor
destructor
```

For those reasons, at least for types other than the built-in types (such as `bool`, `char`, `int`, `float`, `double`, or pointers), you should prefer the constructor initializer list. However, to be consistent with your initialization style, you should always prefer the constructor initializer list when possible. There are several situations when using the initializer list is not possible; these include the following cases (but the list could be expanded for other cases):

- If a member has to be initialized with a pointer or reference to the object that contains it, using the `this` pointer in the initialization list may trigger a warning with some compilers that it is used before the object is constructed.
- If you have two data members that must contain references to each other.
- If you want to test an input parameter and throw an exception before initializing a non-static data member with the value of the parameter.

Starting with C++11, non-static data members can be initialized when declared in the class. This is called *default member initialization* because it is supposed to represent initialization with default values. Default member initialization is intended for constants and for members that are not initialized based on constructor parameters (in other words, members whose value does not depend on the way the object is constructed):

```
enum class TextFlow { LeftToRight, RightToLeft };

struct Control
{
  const int DefaultHeight = 20;
  const int DefaultWidth = 100;

  TextFlow textFlow = TextFlow::LeftToRight;
  std::string text;

  Control(std::string t) : text(t)
  {}
};
```

In the preceding example, `DefaultHeight` and `DefaultWidth` are both constants; therefore, the values do not depend on the way the object is constructed, so they are initialized when declared. The `textFlow` object is a non-constant non-static data member whose value also does not depend on the way the object is initialized (it could be changed via another member function); therefore, it is also initialized using default member initialization when it is declared. `text`, on the other hand, is also a non-constant non-static data member, but its initial value depends on the way the object is constructed.

Therefore, it is initialized in the constructor's initializer list using a value passed as an argument to the constructor.

If a data member is initialized both with the default member initialization and constructor initializer list, the latter takes precedence and the default value is discarded. To exemplify this, let's again consider the `foo` class mentioned earlier and the following `bar` class, which uses it:

```
struct bar
{
  foo f{"default value"};

  bar() : f{"constructor initializer"}
  {
  }
};

bar b;
```

The output differs, in this case, as follows:

```
constructor 'constructor initializer'
destructor
```

The reason for the different behavior is that the value from the default initializer list is discarded, and the object is not initialized twice.

See also

- *Understanding uniform initialization* to see how brace-initialization works

Controlling and querying object alignment

C++11 provides standardized methods for specifying and querying the alignment requirements of a type (something that was previously possible only through compiler-specific methods). Controlling the alignment is important in order to boost performance on different processors and enable the use of some instructions that only work with data on particular alignments.

For example, Intel **Streaming SIMD Extensions** (**SSE**) and Intel SSE2, which are a set of processor instructions that can greatly increase performance when the same operations are to be applied on multiple data objects, require 16 bytes of alignment of data. On the other hand, for **Intel Advanced Vector Extensions** (or **Intel AVX**), which expands most integer processor commands to 256 bits, it is highly recommended to use 32 bytes alignment. This recipe explores the `alignas` specifier for controlling the alignment requirements and the `alignof` operator, which retrieves the alignment requirements of a type.

Getting ready

You should be familiar with what data alignment is and the way the compiler performs default data alignment. However, basic information about the latter is provided in the *How it works...* section.

How to do it...

- To control the alignment of a type (both at the class level or data member level) or an object, use the `alignas` specifier:

```
struct alignas(4) foo
{
  char a;
  char b;
};
struct bar
{
  alignas(2) char a;
  alignas(8) int  b;
};
alignas(8)   int a;
alignas(256) long b[4];
```

- To query the alignment of a type, use the `alignof` operator:

```
auto align = alignof(foo);
```

How it works...

Processors do not access memory one byte at a time, but in larger chunks of powers of two (2, 4, 8, 16, 32, and so on). Owing to this, it is important that compilers align data in memory so that it can be easily accessed by the processor. Should this data be misaligned, the compiler has to do extra work to access data; it has to read multiple chunks of data, shift and discard unnecessary bytes, and combine the rest.

C++ compilers align variables based on the size of their data type. The standard only specifies the sizes of `char`, `signed char`, `unsigned char`, `char8_t`, and `std::byte`, which must be 1. It also requires that the size of `short` must be at least 16 bits, the size of `long` must be at least 32 bits, and that the size of `long long` must be at least 64 bits. It also requires that 1 == `sizeof(char)` <= `sizeof(short)` <= `sizeof(int)` <= `sizeof(long)` <= `sizeof(long long)`. Therefore, the size of most types are compiler-specific and may depend on the platform. Typically, these are 1 byte for `bool` and `char`, 2 bytes for `short`, 4 bytes for `int`, `long`, and `float`, 8 bytes for `double` and `long long`, and so on. When it comes to structures or unions, the alignment must match the size of the largest member in order to avoid performance issues. To exemplify this, let's consider the following data structures:

```
struct foo1    // size = 1, alignment = 1
{              // foo1:    +-+
  char a;      // members: |a|
};

struct foo2    // size = 2, alignment = 1
{              // foo2:    +-+-+
  char a;      // members  |a|b|
  char b;
};

struct foo3    // size = 8, alignment = 4
{              // foo3:    +----+----+
  char a;      // members: |a...|bbbb|
  int  b;      // . represents a byte of padding
};
```

`foo1` and `foo2` are different sizes, but the alignment is the same—that is, 1—because all data members are of the type `char`, which has a size of 1 byte. In the structure `foo3`, the second member is an integer, whose size is 4. As a result, the alignment of members of this structure is done at addresses that are multiples of 4. To achieve this, the compiler introduces padding bytes.

The structure foo3 is actually transformed into the following:

```
struct foo3_
{
  char a;        // 1 byte
  char _pad0[3]; // 3 bytes padding to put b on a 4-byte boundary
  int  b;        // 4 bytes
};
```

Similarly, the following structure has a size of 32 bytes and an alignment of 8; that is because the largest member is a double whose size is 8. This structure, however, requires padding in several places to make sure that all the members can be accessed at addresses that are multiples of 8:

```
struct foo4     // size = 24, alignment = 8
{               // foo4:    +--------+--------+--------+--------+
  int a;        // members: |aaaab...|cccc....|dddddddd|e.......|
  char b;       // . represents a byte of padding
  float c;
  double d;
  bool e;
};
```

The equivalent structure that's created by the compiler is as follows:

```
struct foo4_
{
  int a;         // 4 bytes
  char b;        // 1 byte
  char _pad0[3]; // 3 bytes padding to put c on a 8-byte boundary
  float c;       // 4 bytes
  char _pad1[4]; // 4 bytes padding to put d on a 8-byte boundary
  double d;      // 8 bytes
  bool e;        // 1 byte
  char _pad2[7]; // 7 bytes padding to make sizeof struct multiple of 8
};
```

In C++11, specifying the alignment of an object or type is done using the alignas specifier. This can take either an expression (an integral constant expression that evaluates to 0 or a valid value for an alignment), a type-id, or a parameter pack. The alignas specifier can be applied to the declaration of a variable or a class data member that does not represent a bit field, or to the declaration of a class, union, or enumeration.

The type or object on which an `alignas` specification is applied will have the alignment requirement equal to the largest, greater than zero, expression of all `alignas` specifications used in the declaration.

There are several restrictions when using the `alignas` specifier:

- The only valid alignments are the powers of two (1, 2, 4, 8, 16, 32, and so on). Any other values are illegal, and the program is considered ill-formed; that doesn't necessarily have to produce an error, as the compiler may choose to ignore the specification.
- An alignment of 0 is always ignored.
- If the largest `alignas` on a declaration is smaller than the natural alignment without any `alignas` specifier, then the program is also considered ill-formed.

In the following example, the `alignas` specifier has been applied to a class declaration. The natural alignment without the `alignas` specifier would have been 1, but with `alignas(4)`, it becomes 4:

```
struct alignas(4) foo
{
  char a;
  char b;
};
```

In other words, the compiler transforms the preceding class into the following:

```
struct foo
{
  char a;
  char b;
  char _pad0[2];
};
```

The `alignas` specifier can be applied both to the class declaration and the member data declarations. In this case, the strictest (that is, largest) value wins. In the following example, member `a` has a natural size of 1 and requires an alignment of 2; member `b` has a natural size of 4 and requires an alignment of 8, so the strictest alignment would be 8. The alignment requirement of the entire class is 4, which is weaker (that is, smaller) than the strictest required alignment and therefore it will be ignored, though the compiler will produce a warning:

```
struct alignas(4) foo
{
  alignas(2) char a;
```

```
    alignas(8) int  b;
};
```

The result is a structure that looks like this:

```
struct foo
{
    char a;
    char _pad0[7];
    int b;
    char _pad1[4];
};
```

The `alignas` specifier can also be applied to variables. In the following example, variable `a`, which is an integer, is required to be placed in memory at a multiple of 8. The next variable, the array of 4 longs, is required to be placed in memory at a multiple of 256. As a result, the compiler will introduce up to 244 bytes of padding between the two variables (depending on where in memory, at an address multiple of 8, variable `a` is located):

```
alignas(8)   int a;
alignas(256) long b[4];

printf("%p\n", &a); // eg. 0000006C0D9EF908
printf("%p\n", &b); // eg. 0000006C0D9EFA00
```

Looking at the addresses, we can see that the address of `a` is indeed a multiple of 8, and that the address of `b` is a multiple of 256 (hexadecimal 100).

To query the alignment of a type, we use the `alignof` operator. Unlike `sizeof`, this operator can only be applied to type-ids, and not to variables or class data members. The types it can be applied to can be complete types, an array type, or a reference type. For arrays, the value that's returned is the alignment of the element type; for references, the value that's returned is the alignment of the referenced type. Here are several examples:

Expression	**Evaluation**
`alignof(char)`	1, because the natural alignment of `char` is 1.
`alignof(int)`	4, because the natural alignment of `int` is 4.
`alignof(int*)`	4 on 32-bit, 8 on 64-bit, the alignment for pointers.
`alignof(int[4])`	4, because the natural alignment of the element type is 4.
`alignof(foo&)`	8, because the specified alignment for the class `foo`, which is the referred type (as shown in the previous example), was 8.

The `alignas` specifier is useful if you wish to force an alignment for a data type (taking into consideration the restriction mentioned previously) so that variables of that type can be accessed and copied efficiently. This means optimizing CPU reads and writes and avoiding unnecessary invalidation from cache lines. This can be highly important in some categories of applications where performance is key, such as games or trading applications. On the other hand, the `alignof` operator retries the minimum alignment requirement of a specified type.

See also

- *Creating type aliases and alias templates* to learn about aliases for types

Using scoped enumerations

Enumeration is a basic type in C++ that defines a collection of values, always of an integral underlying type. Their named values, which are constant, are called enumerators. Enumerations declared with the keyword `enum` are called *unscoped enumerations*, while enumerations declared with `enum class` or `enum struct` are called *scoped enumerations*. The latter ones were introduced in C++11 and are intended to solve several problems with unscoped enumerations, which are explained in this recipe.

How to do it...

When working with enumerations, you should:

- Prefer to use scoped enumerations instead of unscoped ones
- Declare scoped enumerations using `enum class` or `enum struct`:

```
enum class Status { Unknown, Created, Connected };
Status s = Status::Created;
```

The `enum class` and `enum struct` declarations are equivalent, and throughout this recipe and the rest of this book, we will use `enum class`.

Because scope enumerations are restricted namespaces, the C++20 standard allows us to associate them with a `using` directive. You can do the following:

- Introduce a scoped enumeration identifier in the local scope with a `using` directive, as follows:

```
int main()
{
  using Status::Unknown;
  Status s = Unknown;
}
```

- Introduce all the identifiers of a scoped enumeration in the local scope with a `using` directive, as follows:

```
struct foo
{
  enum class Status { Unknown, Created, Connected };

  using enum Status;
};

foo::Status s = foo::Created; // instead of
                              // foo::Status::Created
```

- Use a `using enum` directive to introduce the enum identifiers in a `switch` statement to simplify your code:

```
void process(Status const s)
{
  switch (s)
  {
    using enum Status;
    case Unknown:   /*...*/ break;
    case Created:   /*...*/ break;
    case Connected: /*...*/ break;
  }
}
```

How it works...

Unscoped enumerations have several issues that create problems for developers:

- They export their enumerators to the surrounding scope (for which reason, they are called unscoped enumerations), and that has the following two drawbacks:
    a. It can lead to name clashes if two enumerations in the same namespace have enumerators with the same name, and
    b. It's not possible to use an enumerator using its fully qualified name:

    ```
    enum Status {Unknown, Created, Connected};
    enum Codes {OK, Failure, Unknown};   // error
    auto status = Status::Created;       // error
    ```

- Prior to C++ 11, they could not specify the underlying type, which is required to be an integral type. This type must not be larger than `int`, unless the enumerator value cannot fit a signed or unsigned integer. Owing to this, forward declaration of enumerations was not possible. The reason for this was that the size of the enumeration was not known. This was because the underlying type was not known until the values of the enumerators were defined so that the compiler could pick the appropriate integer type. This has been fixed in C++11.
- Values of enumerators implicitly convert to `int`. This means you can intentionally or accidentally mix enumerations that have a certain meaning and integers (which may not even be related to the meaning of the enumeration) and the compiler will not be able to warn you:

    ```
    enum Codes { OK, Failure };
    void include_offset(int pixels) {/*...*/}
    include_offset(Failure);
    ```

The scoped enumerations are basically strongly typed enumerations that behave differently than the unscoped enumerations:

- They do not export their enumerators to the surrounding scope. The two enumerations shown earlier would change to the following, no longer generating a name collision and being possible to fully qualify the names of the enumerators:

    ```
    enum class Status { Unknown, Created, Connected };
    enum class Codes { OK, Failure, Unknown }; // OK
    Codes code = Codes::Unknown;               // OK
    ```

- You can specify the underlying type. The same rules for underlying types of unscoped enumerations apply to scoped enumerations too, except that the user can explicitly specify the underlying type. This also solves the problem with forward declarations since the underlying type can be known before the definition is available:

```
enum class Codes : unsigned int;

void print_code(Codes const code) {}

enum class Codes : unsigned int
{
  OK = 0,
  Failure = 1,
  Unknown = 0xFFFF0000U
};
```

- Values of scoped enumerations no longer convert implicitly to `int`. Assigning the value of an `enum class` to an integer variable would trigger a compiler error unless an explicit cast is specified:

```
Codes c1 = Codes::OK;                       // OK
int c2 = Codes::Failure;                    // error
int c3 = static_cast<int>(Codes::Failure);  // OK
```

However, the scoped enumerations have a drawback: they are restricted namespaces. They do not export the identifiers in the outer scope, which can be inconvenient at times. For instance, if you are writing a `switch` and you need to repeat the enumeration name for each case label, as in the following example:

```
std::string_view to_string(Status const s)
{
  switch (s)
  {
    case Status::Unknown:   return "Unknown";
    case Status::Created:   return "Created";
    case Status::Connected: return "Connected";
  }
}
```

In C++20, this can be simplified with the help of a `using` directive with the name of the scoped enumeration. The preceding code can be simplified as follows:

```
std::string_view to_string(Status const s)
{
  switch (s)
  {
    using enum Status;
    case Unknown:   return "Unknown";
    case Created:   return "Created";
    case Connected: return "Connected";
  }
}
```

The effect of this `using` directive is that all the enumerator identifiers are introduced in the local scope, making it possible to refer to them with the unqualified form. It is also possible to bring only a particular enum identifier to the local scope with a `using` directive with the qualified identifier name, such as `using Status::Connected`.

See also

- *Creating compile-time constant expressions* in *Chapter 9, Robustness and Performance* to learn how to work with compile-time constants

Using override and final for virtual methods

Unlike other similar programming languages, C++ does not have a specific syntax for declaring interfaces (which are basically classes with pure virtual methods only) and also has some deficiencies related to how virtual methods are declared. In C++, the virtual methods are introduced with the `virtual` keyword. However, the keyword `virtual` is optional for declaring overrides in derived classes, which can lead to confusion when dealing with large classes or hierarchies. You may need to navigate throughout the hierarchy up to the base to figure out whether a function is virtual or not. On the other hand, sometimes, it is useful to make sure that a virtual function or even a derived class can no longer be overridden or derived further. In this recipe, we will see how to use the C++11 special identifiers `override` and `final` to declare virtual functions or classes.

Getting ready

You should be familiar with inheritance and polymorphism in C++ and concepts such as abstract classes, pure specifiers, virtual, and overridden methods.

How to do it...

To ensure the correct declaration of virtual methods both in base and derived classes, but also that you increase readability, do the following:

- Prefer to use the `virtual` keyword when declaring virtual functions in derived classes that are supposed to override virtual functions from a base class.
- Always use the `override` special identifier after the declarator part of a virtual function's declaration or definition:

```
class Base
{
  virtual void foo() = 0;
  virtual void bar() {}
  virtual void foobar() = 0;
};

void Base::foobar() {}

class Derived1 : public Base
{
  virtual void foo() override = 0;
  virtual void bar() override {}
  virtual void foobar() override {}
};

class Derived2 : public Derived1
{
  virtual void foo() override {}
};
```

The declarator is the part of the type of a function that excludes the return type.

To ensure that functions cannot be overridden further or that classes cannot be derived any more, use the `final` special identifier:

- After the declarator part of a virtual function declaration or definition to prevent further overrides in a derived class:

```
class Derived2 : public Derived1
{
  virtual void foo() final {}
};
```

- After the name of a class in the declaration of the class to prevent further derivations of the class:

```
class Derived4 final : public Derived1
{
  virtual void foo() override {}
};
```

How it works...

The way `override` works is very simple; in a virtual function declaration or definition, it ensures that the function is actually overriding a base class function; otherwise, the compiler will trigger an error.

It should be noted that both the `override` and `final` keywords are special identifiers that have a meaning only in a member function declaration or definition. They are not reserved keywords and can still be used elsewhere in a program as user-defined identifiers.

Using the `override` special identifier helps the compiler detect situations where a virtual method does not override another one, as shown in the following example:

```
class Base
{
public:
  virtual void foo() {}
  virtual void bar() {}
};
```

```
class Derived1 : public Base
{
public:
  void foo() override {}
  // for readability use the virtual keyword

  virtual void bar(char const c) override {}
  // error, no Base::bar(char const)
};
```

Without the presence of the `override` specifier, the virtual `bar(char const)` method of the `Derived1` class would not be an overridden method, but an overload of the `bar()` from `Base`.

The other special identifier, `final`, is used in a member function declaration or definition to indicate that the function is virtual and cannot be overridden in a derived class. If a derived class attempts to override the virtual function, the compiler triggers an error:

```
class Derived2 : public Derived1
{
  virtual void foo() final {}
};

class Derived3 : public Derived2
{
  virtual void foo() override {} // error
};
```

The `final` specifier can also be used in a class declaration to indicate that it cannot be derived:

```
class Derived4 final : public Derived1
{
  virtual void foo() override {}
};

class Derived5 : public Derived4 // error
{
};
```

Since both `override` and `final` have this special meaning when used in the defined context and are not, in fact, reserved keywords, you can still use them anywhere else in the C++ code. This ensured that existing code written before C++11 did not break because of the use of these names for identifiers:

```
class foo
{
  int final = 0;
  void override() {}
};
```

Although the recommendation given earlier suggesting using both `virtual` and `override` in the declaration of an overridden virtual method, the `virtual` keyword is optional, and can be omitted to shorten the declaration. The presence of the `override` specifier should be enough to indicate to the reader that the method is virtual. This is rather a matter of personal preference and does not affect the semantics.

See also

- *Static polymorphism with the curiously recurring template pattern* in *Chapter 10, Implementing Patterns and Idioms* to learn how the CRTP pattern helps with implementing polymorphism at compile time

Using range-based for loops to iterate on a range

Many programming languages support a variant of a `for` loop called `for each`; that is, repeating a group of statements over the elements of a collection. C++ did not have core language support for this until C++11. The closest feature was the general-purpose algorithm from the standard library called `std::for_each`, which applies a function to all the elements in a range. C++11 brought language support for `for each` that's actually called *range-based for loops*. The new C++17 standard provides several improvements for the original language feature.

Getting ready

In C++11, a range-based for loop has the following general syntax:

```
for ( range_declaration : range_expression ) loop_statement
```

To exemplify the various ways of using range-based for loops, we will use the following functions, which return sequences of elements:

```
std::vector<int> getRates()
{
  return std::vector<int> {1, 1, 2, 3, 5, 8, 13};
}

std::multimap<int, bool> getRates2()
{
  return std::multimap<int, bool> {
    { 1, true },
    { 1, true },
    { 2, false },
    { 3, true },
    { 5, true },
    { 8, false },
    { 13, true }
  };
}
```

In the next section, we'll look at the various ways we can use range-based for loops.

How to do it...

Range-based for loops can be used in various ways:

- By committing to a specific type for the elements of the sequence:

```
auto rates = getRates();
for (int rate : rates)
  std::cout << rate << '\n';
for (int& rate : rates)
  rate *= 2;
```

- By not specifying a type and letting the compiler deduce it:

```
for (auto&& rate : getRates())
  std::cout << rate << '\n';

for (auto & rate : rates)
  rate *= 2;

for (auto const & rate : rates)
  std::cout << rate << '\n';
```

- By using structured bindings and decomposition declaration in C++17:

```
for (auto&& [rate, flag] : getRates2())
  std::cout << rate << '\n';
```

How it works...

The expression for the range-based for loops shown earlier in the *How to do it...* section is basically syntactic sugar as the compiler transforms it into something else. Before C++17, the code generated by the compiler used to be the following:

```
{
  auto && __range = range_expression;
  for (auto __begin = begin_expr, __end = end_expr;
  __begin != __end; ++__begin) {
    range_declaration = *__begin;
    loop_statement
  }
}
```

What `begin_expr` and `end_expr` are in this code depends on the type of the range:

- For C-like arrays: `__range` and `__range + __bound` (where `__bound` is the number of elements in the array).
- For a class type with `begin` and `end` members (regardless of their type and accessibility): `__range.begin()` and `__range.end()`.
- For others, it is `begin(__range)` and `end(__range)`, which are determined via argument-dependent lookup.

It is important to note that if a class contains any members (function, data member, or enumerators) called `begin` or `end`, regardless of their type and accessibility, they will be picked for `begin_expr` and `end_expr`. Therefore, such a class type cannot be used in range-based for loops.

In C++17, the code generated by the compiler is slightly different:

```
{
  auto && __range = range_expression;
  auto __begin = begin_expr;
  auto __end = end_expr;
```

```
    for (; __begin != __end; ++__begin) {
      range_declaration = *__begin;
      loop_statement
    }
  }
```

The new standard has removed the constraint that the `begin` expression and the `end` expression must be the same type. The end expression does not need to be an actual iterator, but it has to be able to be compared for inequality with an iterator. A benefit of this is that the range can be delimited by a predicate. On the other hand, the `end` expression is only evaluated once, and not every time the loop is iterated, which could potentially increase performance.

See also

- *Enabling range-based for loops for custom types* to see how to make it possible for user-defined types to be used with range-based for loops
- *Iterating over collections with the ranges library* in *Chapter 12, C++20 Core Features*, to learn about the fundamentals of the C++20 ranges library
- *Creating your own range view* in *Chapter 12, C++20 Core Features*, to see how to extend the C++20 range library's capabilities with user-defined range adaptors

Enabling range-based for loops for custom types

As we saw in the preceding recipe, range-based for loops, known as `for each` in other programming languages, allow you to iterate over the elements of a range, providing a simplified syntax over the standard `for` loops and making the code more readable in many situations. However, range-based for loops do not work out of the box with any type representing a range, but require the presence of a `begin()` and `end()` function (for non-array types) either as a member or free function. In this recipe, we will learn how to enable a custom type to be used in range-based for loops.

Getting ready

It is recommended that you read the *Using range-based for loops to iterate on a range* recipe before continuing with this one if you need to understand how range-based for loops work, as well as what code the compiler generates for such a loop.

To show how we can enable range-based for loops for custom types representing sequences, we will use the following implementation of a simple array:

```
template <typename T, size_t const Size>
class dummy_array
{
  T data[Size] = {};

public:
  T const & GetAt(size_t const index) const
  {
    if (index < Size) return data[index];
    throw std::out_of_range("index out of range");
  }

  void SetAt(size_t const index, T const & value)
  {
    if (index < Size) data[index] = value;
    else throw std::out_of_range("index out of range");
  }

  size_t GetSize() const { return Size; }
};
```

The purpose of this recipe is to enable writing code like the following:

```
dummy_array<int, 3> arr;
arr.SetAt(0, 1);
arr.SetAt(1, 2);
arr.SetAt(2, 3);

for(auto&& e : arr)
{
  std::cout << e << '\n';
}
```

The steps necessary to make all this possible are described in detail in the following section.

How to do it...

To enable a custom type to be used in range-based `for` loops, you need to do the following:

- Create mutable and constant iterators for the type, which must implement the following operators:
    - `operator++` (both the prefix and the postfix version) for incrementing the iterator
    - `operator*` for dereferencing the iterator and accessing the actual element being pointed to by the iterator
    - `operator!=` for comparing it with another iterator for inequality
- Provide free `begin()` and `end()` functions for the type.

Given the earlier example of a simple range, we need to provide the following:

1. The following minimal implementation of an iterator class:

```
template <typename T, typename C, size_t const Size>
class dummy_array_iterator_type
{
public:
  dummy_array_iterator_type(C& collection,
                            size_t const index) :
  index(index), collection(collection)
  { }

  bool operator!= (dummy_array_iterator_type const & other)
const
  {
    return index != other.index;
  }

  T const & operator* () const
  {
    return collection.GetAt(index);
  }
  dummy_array_iterator_type& operator++()
  {
    ++index;
    return *this;
  }
```

```
    dummy_array_iterator_type operator++(int)
    {
      auto temp = *this;
      ++*temp;
      return temp;
    }

  private:
    size_t   index;
    C&       collection;
  };
```

2. Alias templates for mutable and constant iterators:

```
  template <typename T, size_t const Size>
  using dummy_array_iterator =
    dummy_array_iterator_type<
      T, dummy_array<T, Size>, Size>;

  template <typename T, size_t const Size>
  using dummy_array_const_iterator =
    dummy_array_iterator_type<
      T, dummy_array<T, Size> const, Size>;
```

3. Free `begin()` and `end()` functions that return the corresponding begin and end iterators, with overloads for both alias templates:

```
  template <typename T, size_t const Size>
  inline dummy_array_iterator<T, Size> begin(
    dummy_array<T, Size>& collection)
  {
    return dummy_array_iterator<T, Size>(collection, 0);
  }

  template <typename T, size_t const Size>
  inline dummy_array_iterator<T, Size> end(
    dummy_array<T, Size>& collection)
  {
    return dummy_array_iterator<T, Size>(
      collection, collection.GetSize());
  }

  template <typename T, size_t const Size>
```

```
inline dummy_array_const_iterator<T, Size> begin(
  dummy_array<T, Size> const & collection)
{
  return dummy_array_const_iterator<T, Size>(
    collection, 0);
}

template <typename T, size_t const Size>
inline dummy_array_const_iterator<T, Size> end(
  dummy_array<T, Size> const & collection)
{
  return dummy_array_const_iterator<T, Size>(
    collection, collection.GetSize());
}
```

How it works...

Having this implementation available, the range-based for loop shown earlier compiles and executes as expected. When performing argument-dependent lookup, the compiler will identify the two `begin()` and `end()` functions that we wrote (which take a reference to a `dummy_array`) and therefore the code it generates becomes valid.

In the preceding example, we have defined one iterator class template and two alias templates, called `dummy_array_iterator` and `dummy_array_const_iterator`. The `begin()` and `end()` functions both have two overloads for these two types of iterators.

This is necessary so that the container we have considered can be used in range-based for loops with both constant and non-constant instances:

```
template <typename T, const size_t Size>
void print_dummy_array(dummy_array<T, Size> const & arr)
{
  for (auto && e : arr)
  {
    std::cout << e << '\n';
  }
}
```

A possible alternative to enable range-based for loops for the simple range class we considered for this recipe is to provide the member `begin()` and `end()` functions. In general, that will make sense only if you own and can modify the source code. On the other hand, the solution shown in this recipe works in all cases and should be preferred to other alternatives.

See also

- *Creating type aliases and alias templates* to learn about aliases for types
- *Iterating over collections with the ranges library* in *Chapter 12, C++20 Core Features*, to learn about the fundamentals of the C++20 ranges library

Using explicit constructors and conversion operators to avoid implicit conversion

Before C++11, a constructor with a single parameter was considered a converting constructor (because it takes a value of another type and creates a new instance of the type out of it). With C++11, every constructor without the `explicit` specifier is considered a converting constructor. Such a constructor defines an implicit conversion from the type or types of its arguments to the type of the class. Classes can also define converting operators that convert the type of the class to another specified type. All of these are useful in some cases but can create problems in other cases. In this recipe, we will learn how to use explicit constructors and conversion operators.

Getting ready

For this recipe, you need to be familiar with converting constructors and converting operators. In this recipe, you will learn how to write explicit constructors and conversion operators to avoid implicit conversions to and from a type. The use of explicit constructors and conversion operators (called *user-defined conversion functions*) enables the compiler to yield errors—which, in some cases, are coding errors—and allow developers to spot those errors quickly and fix them.

How to do it...

To declare explicit constructors and explicit conversion operators (regardless of whether they are functions or function templates), use the `explicit` specifier in the declaration.

The following example shows both an explicit constructor and an explicit converting operator:

```
struct handle_t
{
  explicit handle_t(int const h) : handle(h) {}
```

```
  explicit operator bool() const { return handle != 0; };
private:
  int handle;
};
```

How it works...

To understand why explicit constructors are necessary and how they work, we will first look at converting constructors. The following class, `foo`, has three constructors: a default constructor (without parameters), a constructor that takes an `int`, and a constructor that takes two parameters, an `int` and a `double`. They don't do anything except print a message. As of C++11, these are all considered converting constructors. The class also has a conversion operator that converts a value of the `foo` type to a `bool`:

```
struct foo
{
  foo()
  { std::cout << "foo" << '\n'; }
  foo(int const a)
  { std::cout << "foo(a)" << '\n'; }
  foo(int const a, double const b)
  { std::cout << "foo(a, b)" << '\n'; }

  operator bool() const { return true; }
};
```

Based on this, the following definitions of objects are possible (note that the comments represent the console's output):

```
foo f1;              // foo()
foo f2 {};           // foo()

foo f3(1);           // foo(a)
foo f4 = 1;          // foo(a)
foo f5 { 1 };        // foo(a)
foo f6 = { 1 };      // foo(a)

foo f7(1, 2.0);      // foo(a, b)
foo f8 { 1, 2.0 };   // foo(a, b)
foo f9 = { 1, 2.0 }; // foo(a, b)
```

The variables `f1` and `f2` invoke the default constructor. `f3`, `f4`, `f5`, and `f6` invoke the constructor that takes an `int`. Note that all the definitions of these objects are equivalent, even if they look different (`f3` is initialized using the functional form, `f4` and `f6` are copy initialized, and `f5` is directly initialized using brace-init-list). Similarly, `f7`, `f8`, and `f9` invoke the constructor with two parameters.

In this case, `f5` and `f6` will `print foo(l)`, while `f8` and `f9` will generate compiler errors because all the elements of the initializer list should be integers.

It may be important to note that if `foo` defines a constructor that takes an `std::initializer_list`, then all the initializations using `{}` would resolve to that constructor:

```
foo(std::initializer_list<int> l)
{ std::cout << "foo(l)" << '\n'; }
```

These may all look right, but the implicit conversion constructors enable scenarios where the implicit conversion may not be what we wanted. First, let's look at some correct examples:

```
void bar(foo const f)
{
}

bar({});             // foo()
bar(1);              // foo(a)
bar({ 1, 2.0 });     // foo(a, b)
```

The conversion operator to `bool` from the `foo` class also enables us to use `foo` objects where Boolean values are expected. Here is an example:

```
bool flag = f1;                  // OK, expect bool conversion
if(f2) { /* do something */ }  // OK, expect bool conversion
std::cout << f3 + f4 << '\n';  // wrong, expect foo addition
if(f5 == f6) { /* do more */ } // wrong, expect comparing foos
```

The first two are examples where `foo` is expected to be used as a Boolean. However, the last two with addition and test for equality are probably incorrect, as we most likely expect to add `foo` objects and test `foo` objects for equality, not the Booleans they implicitly convert to.

Perhaps a more realistic example to understand where problems could arise would be to consider a string buffer implementation. This would be a class that contains an internal buffer of characters.

This class provides several conversion constructors: a default constructor, a constructor that takes a `size_t` parameter representing the size of the buffer to preallocate, and a constructor that takes a pointer to `char` that should be used to allocate and initialize the internal buffer. Succinctly, the implementation of the string buffer that we use for this exemplification looks like this:

```
class string_buffer
{
public:
  string_buffer() {}

  string_buffer(size_t const size) {}

  string_buffer(char const * const ptr) {}

  size_t size() const { return ...; }
  operator bool() const { return ...; }
  operator char * const () const { return ...; }
};
```

Based on this definition, we could construct the following objects:

```
std::shared_ptr<char> str;
string_buffer b1;            // calls string_buffer()
string_buffer b2(20);        // calls string_buffer(size_t const)
string_buffer b3(str.get()); // calls string_buffer(char const*)
```

The object `b1` is created using the default constructor and thus has an empty buffer; `b2` is initialized using the constructor with a single parameter where the value of the parameter represents the size in terms of the characters of the internal buffer; and `b3` is initialized with an existing buffer, which is used to define the size of the internal buffer and copy its value into the internal buffer. However, the same definition also enables the following object definitions:

```
enum ItemSizes {DefaultHeight, Large, MaxSize};

string_buffer b4 = 'a';
string_buffer b5 = MaxSize;
```

In this case, `b4` is initialized with a `char`. Since an implicit conversion to `size_t` exists, the constructor with a single parameter will be called. The intention here is not necessarily clear; perhaps it should have been `"a"` instead of `'a'`, in which case the third constructor would have been called.

However, `b5` is most likely an error, because `MaxSize` is an enumerator representing an `ItemSizes` and should have nothing to do with a string buffer size. These erroneous situations are not flagged by the compiler in any way. The implicit conversion of unscoped enums to `int` is a good argument for preferring to use scoped enums (declared with enum class), which do not have this implicit conversion. If `ItemSizes` was a scoped enum, the situation described here would not appear.

When using the `explicit` specifier in the declaration of a constructor, that constructor becomes an explicit constructor and no longer allows implicit constructions of objects of a `class` type. To exemplify this, we will slightly change the `string_buffer` class to declare all constructors as `explicit`:

```
class string_buffer
{
public:
  explicit string_buffer() {}

  explicit string_buffer(size_t const size) {}

  explicit string_buffer(char const * const ptr) {}

  explicit operator bool() const { return ...; }
  explicit operator char * const () const { return ...; }
};
```

The change here is minimal, but the definitions of `b4` and `b5` in the earlier example no longer work and are incorrect. This is because the implicit conversions from `char` or `int` to `size_t` are no longer available during overload resolution to figure out what constructor should be called. The result is compiler errors for both `b4` and `b5`. Note that `b1`, `b2`, and `b3` are still valid definitions, even if the constructors are explicit.

The only way to fix the problem, in this case, is to provide an explicit cast from `char` or `int` to `string_buffer`:

```
string_buffer b4 = string_buffer('a');
string_buffer b5 = static_cast<string_buffer>(MaxSize);
string_buffer b6 = string_buffer{ "a" };
```

With explicit constructors, the compiler is able to immediately flag erroneous situations and developers can react accordingly, either fixing the initialization with a correct value or providing an explicit cast.

This is only the case when initialization is done with copy initialization and not when using functional or universal initialization.

The following definitions are still possible (and wrong) with explicit constructors:

```
string_buffer b7{ 'a' };
string_buffer b8('a');
```

Similar to constructors, conversion operators can be declared explicit (as shown earlier). In this case, the implicit conversions from the object type to the type specified by the conversion operator are no longer possible and require an explicit cast. Considering `b1` and `b2`, which are the `string_buffer` objects we defined earlier, the following are no longer possible with an explicit conversion `operator bool`:

```
std::cout << b4 + b5 << '\n'; // error
if(b4 == b5) {}               // error
```

Instead, they require explicit conversion to `bool`:

```
std::cout << static_cast<bool>(b4) + static_cast<bool>(b5);
if(static_cast<bool>(b4) == static_cast<bool>(b5)) {}
```

The addition of two `bool` values does not make much sense. The preceding example is intended only to show how an explicit cast is required in order to make the statement compile. The error issued by the compiler when there is no explicit static cast, should help you figure out that the expression itself is wrong and something else was probably intended.

See also

- *Understanding uniform initialization* to see how brace-initialization works

Using unnamed namespaces instead of static globals

The larger a program, the greater the chances are you could run into name collisions when your program is linked to multiple translation units. Functions or variables that are declared in a source file, and are supposed to be local to the translation unit, may collide with other similar functions or variables declared in another translation unit.

That is because all the symbols that are not declared static have external linkage and their names must be unique throughout the program. The typical C solution for this problem is to declare those symbols as static, changing their linkage from external to internal and therefore making them local to a translation unit. An alternative is to prefix the names with the name of the module or library they belong to. In this recipe, we will look at the C++ solution for this problem.

Getting ready

In this recipe, we will discuss concepts such as global functions and static functions, as well as variables, namespaces, and translation units. We expect that you have a basic understanding of these concepts. Apart from these, it is required that you understand the difference between internal and external linkage; this is key for this recipe.

How to do it...

When you are in a situation where you need to declare global symbols as static to avoid linkage problems, you should prefer to use unnamed namespaces:

1. Declare a namespace without a name in your source file.
2. Put the definition of the global function or variable in the unnamed namespace without making them `static`.

The following example shows two functions called `print()` in two different translation units; each of them is defined in an unnamed namespace:

```
// file1.cpp
namespace
{
  void print(std::string message)
  {
    std::cout << "[file1] " << message << '\n';
  }
}
void file1_run()
{
  print("run");
}

// file2.cpp
namespace
```

```
{
  void print(std::string message)
  {
    std::cout << "[file2] " << message << '\n';
  }
}

void file2_run()
{
  print("run");
}
```

How it works...

When a function is declared in a translation unit, it has external linkage. This means two functions with the same name from two different translation units would generate a linkage error because it is not possible to have two symbols with the same name. The way this problem is solved in C, and by some in C++ also, is to declare the function or variable as static and change its linkage from external to internal. In this case, its name is no longer exported outside the translation unit, and the linkage problem is avoided.

The proper solution in C++ is to use unnamed namespaces. When you define a namespace like the ones shown previously, the compiler transforms it into the following:

```
// file1.cpp
namespace _unique_name_ {}
using namespace _unique_name_;
namespace _unique_name_
{
  void print(std::string message)
  {
    std::cout << "[file1] " << message << '\n';
  }
}
void file1_run()
{
  print("run");
}
```

First of all, it declares a namespace with a unique name (what the name is and how it generates that name is a compiler implementation detail and should not be a concern). At this point, the namespace is empty, and the purpose of this line is to basically establish the namespace. Second, a `using` directive brings everything from the `_unique_name_` namespace into the current namespace. Third, the namespace, with the compiler-generated name, is defined as it was in the original source code (when it had no name).

By defining the translation unit local `print()` functions in an unnamed namespace, they have local visibility only, yet their external linkage no longer produces linkage errors since they now have external unique names.

Unnamed namespaces also work in a perhaps more obscure situation involving templates. Prior to C++11, template non-type arguments could not be names with internal linkage, so using static variables was not possible. On the other hand, symbols in an unnamed namespace have external linkage and could be used as template arguments. Although this linkage restriction for template non-type arguments was lifted in C++11, it is still present in the latest version of the VC++ compiler. This problem is shown in the following example:

```
template <int const& Size>
class test {};

static int Size1 = 10;

namespace
{
  int Size2 = 10;
}

test<Size1> t1;
test<Size2> t2;
```

In this snippet, the declaration of the `t1` variable produces a compiler error because the non-type argument expression, `Size1`, has internal linkage. On the other hand, the declaration of the `t2` variable is correct because `Size2` has external linkage. (Note that compiling this snippet with Clang and GCC does not produce an error.)

See also

- *Using inline namespaces for symbol versioning* to learn how to version your source code using inline namespaces and conditional compilation

Using inline namespaces for symbol versioning

The C++11 standard has introduced a new type of namespace called *inline namespaces*, which are basically a mechanism that makes declarations from a nested namespace look and act like they were part of the surrounding namespace. Inline namespaces are declared using the `inline` keyword in the namespace declaration (unnamed namespaces can also be inlined). This is a helpful feature for library versioning, and in this recipe, we will learn how inline namespaces can be used for versioning symbols. From this recipe, you will learn how to version your source code using inline namespaces and conditional compilation.

Getting ready

In this recipe, we will discuss namespaces and nested namespaces, templates and template specializations, and conditional compilation using preprocessor macros. Familiarity with these concepts is required in order to proceed with this recipe.

How to do it...

To provide multiple versions of a library and let the user decide what version to use, do the following:

- Define the content of the library inside a namespace.
- Define each version of the library or parts of it inside an inner inline namespace.
- Use preprocessor macros and `#if` directives to enable a particular version of the library.

The following example shows a library that has two versions that clients can use:

```
namespace modernlib
{
  #ifndef LIB_VERSION_2
  inline namespace version_1
  {
    template<typename T>
    int test(T value) { return 1; }
  }
  #endif
```

```
  #ifdef LIB_VERSION_2
  inline namespace version_2
  {
    template<typename T>
    int test(T value) { return 2; }
  }
  #endif
}
```

How it works...

A member of an inline namespace is treated as if it was a member of the surrounding namespace. Such a member can be partially specialized, explicitly instantiated, or explicitly specialized. This is a transitive property, which means that if a namespace, `A`, contains an inline namespace, `B`, that contains an inline namespace, `C`, then the members of `C` appear as they were members of both `B` and `A` and the members of `B` appear as they were members of `A`.

To better understand why inline namespaces are helpful, let's consider the case of developing a library that evolves over time from a first version to a second version (and further on). This library defines all its types and functions under a namespace called `modernlib`. In the first version, this library could look like this:

```
namespace modernlib
{
  template<typename T>
  int test(T value) { return 1; }
}
```

A client of the library can make the following call and get back the value 1:

```
auto x = modernlib::test(42);
```

However, the client might decide to specialize the template function `test()` as follows:

```
struct foo { int a; };

namespace modernlib
{
  template<>
  int test(foo value) { return value.a; }
}
```

```
auto y = modernlib::test(foo{ 42 });
```

In this case, the value of y is no longer 1 but 42 because the user-specialized function gets called.

Everything is working correctly so far, but as a library developer, you decide to create a second version of the library, yet still ship both the first and the second version and let the user control what to use with a macro. In this second version, you provide a new implementation of the test() function that no longer returns 1, but 2. To be able to provide both the first and second implementations, you put them in nested namespaces called version_1 and version_2 and conditionally compile the library using preprocessor macros:

```
namespace modernlib
{
  namespace version_1
  {
    template<typename T>
    int test(T value) { return 1; }
  }

  #ifndef LIB_VERSION_2
  using namespace version_1;
  #endif

  namespace version_2
  {
    template<typename T>
    int test(T value) { return 2; }
  }

  #ifdef LIB_VERSION_2
  using namespace version_2;
  #endif
}
```

Suddenly, the client code will break, regardless of whether it uses the first or second version of the library. This is because the test function is now inside a nested namespace, and the specialization for foo is done in the modernlib namespace, when it should actually be done in modernlib::version_1 or modernlib::version_2. This is because the specialization of a template is required to be done in the same namespace where the template was declared.

In this case, the client needs to change the code, like this:

```
#define LIB_VERSION_2

#include "modernlib.h"

struct foo { int a; };
namespace modernlib
{
  namespace version_2
  {
    template<>
    int test(foo value) { return value.a; }
  }
}
```

This is a problem because the library leaks implementation details, and the client needs to be aware of those in order to do template specialization. These internal details are hidden with inline namespaces in the manner shown in the *How to do it...* section of this recipe. With that definition of the `modernlib` library, the client code with the specialization of the `test()` function in the `modernlib` namespace is no longer broken, because either `version_1::test()` or `version_2::test()` (depending on what version the client is actually using) acts as being part of the enclosing `modernlib` namespace when template specialization is done. The details of the implementation are now hidden to the client, who only sees the surrounding namespace, `modernlib`.

However, you should keep in mind that the namespace `std` is reserved for the standard and should never be inlined. Also, a namespace should not be defined inline if it was not inline in its first definition.

See also

- *Using unnamed namespaces instead of static globals* to explore anonymous namespaces and learn how they help
- *Conditionally compiling your source code* in *Chapter 4*, *Preprocessing and Compilation*, to learn the various options for performing conditional compilation

Using structured bindings to handle multi-return values

Returning multiple values from a function is very common, yet there is no first-class solution in C++ to make it possible in a straightforward way. Developers have to choose between returning multiple values through reference parameters to a function, defining a structure to contain the multiple values, or returning an `std::pair` or `std::tuple`. The first two use named variables, which gives them the advantage that they clearly indicate the meaning of the return value, but have the disadvantage that they have to be explicitly defined. `std::pair` has its members called `first` and `second`, while `std::tuple` has unnamed members that can only be retrieved with a function call, but can be copied to named variables using `std::tie()`. None of these solutions are ideal.

C++17 extends the semantic use of `std::tie()` into a first-class core language feature that enables unpacking the values of a tuple into named variables. This feature is called *structured bindings*.

Getting ready

For this recipe, you should be familiar with the standard utility types `std::pair` and `std::tuple` and the utility function `std::tie()`.

How to do it...

To return multiple values from a function using a compiler that supports C++17, you should do the following:

1. Use an `std::tuple` for the return type:

   ```
   std::tuple<int, std::string, double> find()
   {
     return std::make_tuple(1, "marius", 1234.5);
   }
   ```

2. Use structured bindings to unpack the values of the tuple into named objects:

   ```
   auto [id, name, score] = find();
   ```

3. Use decomposition declaration to bind the returned values to the variables inside an `if` statement or `switch` statement:

   ```
   if (auto [id, name, score] = find(); score > 1000)
   {
     std::cout << name << '\n';
   }
   ```

How it works...

Structured bindings are a language feature that works just like `std::tie()`, except that we don't have to define named variables for each value that needs to be unpacked explicitly with `std::tie()`. With structured bindings, we define all the named variables in a single definition using the `auto` specifier so that the compiler can infer the correct type for each variable.

To exemplify this, let's consider the case of inserting items into an `std::map`. The `insert` method returns an `std::pair` containing an iterator for the inserted element or the element that prevented the insertion, and a Boolean indicating whether the insertion was successful or not. The following code is very explicit and the use of `second` or `first->second` makes the code harder to read because you need to constantly figure out what they represent:

```
std::map<int, std::string> m;

auto result = m.insert({ 1, "one" });
std::cout << "inserted = " << result.second << '\n'
          << "value = " << result.first->second << '\n';
```

The preceding code can be made more readable with the use of `std::tie`, which unpacks tuples into individual objects (and works with `std::pair` because `std::tuple` has a converting assignment from `std::pair`):

```
std::map<int, std::string> m;
std::map<int, std::string>::iterator it;
bool inserted;

std::tie(it, inserted) = m.insert({ 1, "one" });
std::cout << "inserted = " << inserted << '\n'
          << "value = " << it->second << '\n';

std::tie(it, inserted) = m.insert({ 1, "two" });
std::cout << "inserted = " << inserted << '\n'
          << "value = " << it->second << '\n';
```

The code is not necessarily simpler because it requires defining the objects that the pair is unpacked to in advance. Similarly, the more elements the tuple has, the more objects you need to define, but using named objects makes the code easier to read.

C++17 structured bindings elevates unpacking tuple elements into named objects to the rank of a language feature; it does not require the use of `std::tie()`, and objects are initialized when declared:

```
std::map<int, std::string> m;
{
  auto [it, inserted] = m.insert({ 1, "one" });
  std::cout << "inserted = " << inserted << '\n'
            << "value = " << it->second << '\n';
}

{
  auto [it, inserted] = m.insert({ 1, "two" });
  std::cout << "inserted = " << inserted << '\n'
            << "value = " << it->second << '\n';
}
```

The use of multiple blocks in the preceding example is necessary because variables cannot be redeclared in the same block, and structured bindings imply a declaration using the `auto` specifier. Therefore, if you need to make multiple calls, as in the preceding example, and use structured bindings, you must either use different variable names or multiple blocks. An alternative to that is to avoid structured bindings and use `std::tie()`, because it can be called multiple times with the same variables, so you only need to declare them once.

In C++17, it is also possible to declare variables in `if` and `switch` statements in the form `if(init; condition)` and `switch(init; condition)`, respectively. This could be combined with structured bindings to produce simpler code. Let's look at an example:

```
if(auto [it, inserted] = m.insert({ 1, "two" }); inserted)
{ std::cout << it->second << '\n'; }
```

In the preceding snippet, we attempted to insert a new value into a map. The result of the call is unpacked into two variables, `it` and `inserted`, defined in the scope of the `if` statement in the initialization part. Then, the condition of the `if` statement is evaluated from the value of the `inserted` variable.

There's more...

Although we focused on binding names to the elements of tuples, structured bindings can be used in a broader scope because they also support binding to array elements or data members of a class. If you want to bind to the elements of an array, you must provide a name for every element of the array; otherwise, the declaration is ill-formed. The following is an example of binding to array elements:

```
int arr[] = { 1,2 };
auto [a, b] = arr;
auto& [x, y] = arr;

arr[0] += 10;
arr[1] += 10;

std::cout << arr[0] << ' ' << arr[1] << '\n'; // 11 12
std::cout << a << ' ' << b << '\n';           // 1 2
std::cout << x << ' ' << y << '\n';           // 11 12
```

In this example, `arr` is an array with two elements. We first bind `a` and `b` to its elements, and then we bind the `x` and `y` references to its elements. Changes that are made to the elements of the array are not visible through the variables `a` and `b` but are visible through the `x` and `y` references, as shown in the comments that print these values to the console. This happens because when we do the first binding, a copy of the array is created and `a` and `b` are bound to the elements of the copy.

As we already mentioned, it's also possible to bind to data members of a class. The following restrictions apply:

- Binding is possible only for non-static members of the class.
- The class cannot have anonymous union members.
- The number of identifiers must match the number of non-static members of the class.

The binding of identifiers occurs in the order of the declaration of the data members, which can include bitfields. An example is shown here:

```
struct foo
{
   int         id;
   std::string name;
};
```

```
foo f{ 42, "john" };
auto [i, n] = f;
auto& [ri, rn] = f;

f.id = 43;

std::cout << f.id << ' ' << f.name << '\n';    // 43 john
std::cout << i << ' ' << n << '\n';             // 42 john
std::cout << ri << ' ' << rn << '\n';           // 43 john
```

Again, changes to the `foo` object are not visible to the variables `i` and `n` but are to `ri` and `rn`. This is because each identifier in the structure binding becomes the name of an lvalue that refers to a data member of the class (just like with an array, it refers to an element of the array). However, the reference type of an identifier is the corresponding data member (or array element).

The new C++20 standard has introduced a series of improvements to structure bindings, including the following:

- Possibility to include the `static` or `thread_local` storage-class specifiers in the declaration of the structure bindings.
- Allow the use of the `[[maybe_unused]]` attribute for the declaration of a structured binding. Some compilers, such as Clang and GCC, already supported this feature.
- Allow us to capture structure binding identifiers in lambdas. All identifiers, including those bound to bitfields, can be captured by value. On the other hand, all identifiers except for those bound to bitfields can also be captured by reference.

These changes enable us to write the following:

```
foo f{ 42, "john" };
auto [i, n] = f;
auto l1 = [i] {std::cout << i; };
auto l2 = [=] {std::cout << i; };
auto l3 = [&i] {std::cout << i; };
auto l4 = [&] {std::cout << i; };
```

These examples show the various ways structured bindings can be captured in lambdas in C++20.

See also

- *Using auto whenever possible* to understand how automatic type deduction works in C++
- *Using lambdas with standard algorithms* in *Chapter 3, Exploring Functions* to learn how lambdas can be used with standard library general-purpose algorithms
- *Providing metadata to the compiler with attributes* in *Chapter 4, Preprocessing and Compilation*, to learn about providing hints to the compiler with the use of standard attributes

Simplifying code with class template argument deduction

Templates are ubiquitous in C++, but having to specify template arguments all the time can be annoying. There are cases when the compiler can actually infer the template arguments from the context. This feature, available in C++17, is called *class template argument deduction* and enables the compiler to deduce the missing template arguments from the type of the initializer. In this recipe, we will learn how to take advantage of this feature.

How to do it...

In C++17, you can skip specifying template arguments and let the compiler deduce them in the following cases:

- When you declare a variable or a variable template and initialize it:

```
std::pair   p{ 42, "demo" };  // deduces std::pair<int, char
const*>
std::vector v{ 1, 2 };         // deduces std::vector<int>
std::less   l;                 // deduces std::less<void>
```

- When you create an object using a new expression:

```
template <class T>
struct foo
{
   foo(T v) :data(v) {}
private:
   T data;
};
```

```
auto f = new foo(42);
```

- When you perform function-like cast expressions:

```
std::mutex mx;

// deduces std::lock_guard<std::mutex>
auto lock = std::lock_guard(mx);

std::vector<int> v;
// deduces std::back_insert_iterator<std::vector<int>>
std::fill_n(std::back_insert_iterator(v), 5, 42);
```

How it works...

Prior to C++17, you had to specify all the template arguments when initializing variables, because all of them must be known in order to instantiate the class template, such as in the following example:

```
std::pair<int, char const*> p{ 42, "demo" };
std::vector<int>            v{ 1, 2 };
foo<int>                    f{ 42 };
```

The problem of explicitly specifying template arguments could have been avoided with a function template, such as `std::make_pair()`, which benefits from function template argument deduction, and allows us to write code such as the following:

```
auto p = std::make_pair(42, "demo");
```

In the case of the `foo` class template shown here, we can write the following `make_foo()` function template to enable the same behavior:

```
template <typename T>
constexpr foo<T> make_foo(T&& value)
{
   return foo{ value };
}

auto f = make_foo(42);
```

In C++17, this is no longer necessary in the cases listed in the *How it works...* section. Let's take the following declaration as an example:

```
std::pair p{ 42, "demo" };
```

In this context, `std::pair` is not a type, but acts as a placeholder for a type that activates class template argument deduction. When the compiler encounters it during the declaration of a variable with initialization or a function-style cast, it builds a set of deduction guides. These deduction guides are fictional constructors of a hypothetical class type. As a user, you can complement this set with user-defined deduction rules. This set is used to perform template argument deduction and overload resolution.

In the case of `std::pair`, the compiler will build a set of deduction guides that includes the following fictional function templates (but not only these):

```
template <class T1, class T2>
std::pair<T1, T2> F();

template <class T1, class T2>
std::pair<T1, T2> F(T1 const& x, T2 const& y);

template <class T1, class T2, class U1, class U2>
std::pair<T1, T2> F(U1&& x, U2&& y);
```

These compiler-generated deduction guides are created from the constructors of the class template, and if none are present, then a deduction guide is created for a hypothetical default constructor. In addition, in all cases, a deduction guide for a hypothetical copy constructor is always created.

The user-defined deduction guides are function signatures with trailing return type and without the `auto` keyword (since they represent hypothetical constructors that don't have a return value). They must be defined in the namespace of the class template they apply to.

To understand how this works, let's consider the same example with the `std::pair` object:

```
std::pair p{ 42, "demo" };
```

The type that the compiler is deducing is `std::pair<int, char const*>`. If we want to instruct the compiler to deduce `std::string` instead of `char const*`, then we need several user-defined deduction rules, as shown here:

```
namespace std {
```

```
    template <class T>
    pair(T&&, char const*)->pair<T, std::string>;

    template <class T>
    pair(char const*, T&&)->pair<std::string, T>;

    pair(char const*, char const*)->pair<std::string, std::string>;
}
```

These will enable us to perform the following declarations, where the type of the string `"demo"` is always deduced to be `std::string`:

```
std::pair  p1{ 42, "demo" };    // std::pair<int, std::string>
std::pair  p2{ "demo", 42 };    // std::pair<std::string, int>
std::pair  p3{ "42", "demo" }; // std::pair<std::string, std::string>
```

As you can see from this example, deduction guides do not have to be function templates.

It is important to note that class template argument deduction does not occur if the template argument list is present, regardless of the number of specified arguments. Examples of this are shown here:

```
std::pair<>     p1 { 42, "demo" };
std::pair<int> p2 { 42, "demo" };
```

Because both these declarations specify a template argument list, they are invalid and produce compiler errors.

See also

- *Understanding uniform initialization* to see how brace-initialization works

2

Working with Numbers and Strings

Numbers and strings are the fundamental types of any programming language; all other types are based on or composed of these ones. Developers are confronted all the time with tasks such as converting between numbers and strings, parsing and formatting strings, and generating random numbers. This chapter is focused on providing useful recipes for these common tasks using modern C++ language and library features.

The recipes included in this chapter are as follows:

- Converting between numeric and string types
- Limits and other properties of numeric types
- Generating pseudo-random numbers
- Initializing all the bits of the internal state of a pseudo-random number generator
- Creating cooked user-defined literals
- Creating raw, user-defined literals
- Using raw string literals to avoid escaping characters
- Creating a library of string helpers
- Verifying the format of a string using regular expressions
- Parsing the content of a string using regular expressions
- Replacing the content of a string using regular expressions

- Using `std::string_view` instead of constant string references
- Formatting text with `std::format`
- Using `std::format` with user-defined types

Let's start this chapter by looking at a very common problem developers face on a daily basis, which is converting between numeric and string types.

Converting between numeric and string types

Converting between number and string types is a ubiquitous operation. Prior to C++11, there was little support for converting numbers to strings and back, so developers had to resort mostly to type-unsafe functions, and they usually wrote their own utility functions in order to avoid writing the same code over and over again. With C++11, the standard library provides utility functions for converting between numbers and strings. In this recipe, you will learn how to convert between numbers and strings and the other way around using modern C++ standard functions.

Getting ready

All the utility functions mentioned in this recipe are available in the `<string>` header.

How to do it...

Use the following standard conversion functions when you need to convert between numbers and strings:

- To convert from an integer or floating-point type to a string type, use `std::to_string()` or `std::to_wstring()`, as shown in the following code snippet:

```
auto si = std::to_string(42);      // si="42"
auto sl = std::to_string(42L);     // sl="42"
auto su = std::to_string(42u);     // su="42"
auto sd = std::to_wstring(42.0);   // sd=L"42.000000"
auto sld = std::to_wstring(42.0L); // sld=L"42.000000"
```

- To convert from a string type to an integer type, use `std::stoi()`, `std::stol()`, `std::stoll()`, `std::stoul()`, or `std::stoull()`, as shown in the following code snippet:

```
auto i1 = std::stoi("42");                    // i1 = 42
auto i2 = std::stoi("101010", nullptr, 2); // i2 = 42
auto i3 = std::stoi("052", nullptr, 8);     // i3 = 42
auto i4 = std::stoi("0x2A", nullptr, 16);  // i4 = 42
```

- To convert from a string type to a floating-point type, use `std::stof()`, `std::stod()`, or `std::stold()`, as shown in the following code snippet:

```
// d1 = 123.45000000000000
auto d1 = std::stod("123.45");
// d2 = 123.45000000000000
auto d2 = std::stod("1.2345e+2");
// d3 = 123.44999980926514
auto d3 = std::stod("0xF.6E6666p3");
```

How it works...

To convert an integral or floating-point type to a string type, you can use either the `std::to_string()` function (which converts to a `std::string`) or the `std::to_wstring()` function (which converts to a `std::wstring`). These functions are available in the `<string>` header and have overloads for signed and unsigned integer and real types. They produce the same result as `std::sprintf()` and `std::swprintf()` would produce when called with the appropriate format specifier for each type. The following code snippet lists all the overloads of these two functions:

```
std::string to_string(int value);
std::string to_string(long value);
std::string to_string(long long value);
std::string to_string(unsigned value);
std::string to_string(unsigned long value);
std::string to_string(unsigned long long value);
std::string to_string(float value);
std::string to_string(double value);
std::string to_string(long double value);
std::wstring to_wstring(int value);
std::wstring to_wstring(long value);
std::wstring to_wstring(long long value);
std::wstring to_wstring(unsigned value);
std::wstring to_wstring(unsigned long value);
std::wstring to_wstring(unsigned long long value);
```

```
std::wstring to_wstring(float value);
std::wstring to_wstring(double value);
std::wstring to_wstring(long double value);
```

When it comes to the opposite conversion, there is an entire set of functions that have a name with the format **ston** (**string to number**), where **n** stands for **i** (`integer`), **l** (`long`), **ll** (`long long`), **ul** (`unsigned long`), or **ull** (`unsigned long long`). The following list shows all these functions, each of them with two overloads—one that takes an `std::string` and one that takes an `std::wstring` as the first parameter:

```
int stoi(const std::string& str, std::size_t* pos = 0,
         int base = 10);
int stoi(const std::wstring& str, std::size_t* pos = 0,
         int base = 10);
long stol(const std::string& str, std::size_t* pos = 0,
         int base = 10);
long stol(const std::wstring& str, std::size_t* pos = 0,
         int base = 10);
long long stoll(const std::string& str, std::size_t* pos = 0,
                int base = 10);
long long stoll(const std::wstring& str, std::size_t* pos = 0,
                int base = 10);
unsigned long stoul(const std::string& str, std::size_t* pos = 0,
                    int base = 10);
unsigned long stoul(const std::wstring& str, std::size_t* pos = 0,
                    int base = 10);
unsigned long long stoull(const std::string& str,
                          std::size_t* pos = 0, int base = 10);
unsigned long long stoull(const std::wstring& str,
                          std::size_t* pos = 0, int base = 10);
float       stof(const std::string& str, std::size_t* pos = 0);
float       stof(const std::wstring& str, std::size_t* pos = 0);
double      stod(const std::string& str, std::size_t* pos = 0);
double      stod(const std::wstring& str, std::size_t* pos = 0);
long double stold(const std::string& str, std::size_t* pos = 0);
long double stold(const std::wstring& str, std::size_t* pos = 0);
```

The way the string to integral type functions work is by discarding all white spaces before a non-whitespace character, then taking as many characters as possible to form a signed or unsigned number (depending on the case), and then converting that to the requested integral type (`stoi()` will return an `integer`, `stoul()` will return an `unsigned long`, and so on). In all the following examples, the result is the integer `42`, except for the last example, where the result is `-42`:

```
auto i1 = std::stoi("42");                  // i1 = 42
auto i2 = std::stoi("   42");               // i2 = 42
auto i3 = std::stoi("   42fortytwo");  // i3 = 42
auto i4 = std::stoi("+42");                 // i4 = 42
auto i5 = std::stoi("-42");                 // i5 = -42
```

A valid integral number may consist of the following parts:

- A sign, plus (+) or minus (-) (optional)
- Prefix `0` to indicate an octal base (optional)
- Prefix `0x` or `0X` to indicate a hexadecimal base (optional)
- A sequence of digits

The optional prefix `0` (for octal) is applied only when the specified base is `8` or `0`. Similarly, the optional prefix `0x` or `0X` (for hexadecimal) is applied only when the specified base is `16` or `0`.

The functions that convert a string to an integer have three parameters:

- The input string.
- A pointer that, when not null, will receive the number of characters that were processed. This can include any leading whitespaces that were discarded, the sign, and the base prefix, so it should not be confused with the number of digits the integral value has.
- A number indicating the base; by default, this is `10`.

The valid digits in the input string depend on the base. For base `2`, the only valid digits are `0` and `1`; for base `5`, they are `01234`. For base `11`, the valid digits are `0-9` and the characters `A` and `a`. This continues until we reach base `36`, which has the valid characters `0-9`, `A-Z`, and `a-z`.

The following are additional examples of strings with numbers in various bases converted to decimal integers. Again, in all cases, the result is either `42` or `-42`:

```
auto i6 = std::stoi("052", nullptr, 8);
auto i7 = std::stoi("052", nullptr, 0);
auto i8 = std::stoi("0x2A", nullptr, 16);
auto i9 = std::stoi("0x2A", nullptr, 0);
auto i10 = std::stoi("101010", nullptr, 2);
auto i11 = std::stoi("22", nullptr, 20);
auto i12 = std::stoi("-22", nullptr, 20);
```

```
auto pos = size_t{ 0 };
auto i13 = std::stoi("42", &pos);      // pos = 2
auto i14 = std::stoi("-42", &pos);     // pos = 3
auto i15 = std::stoi("  +42dec", &pos);// pos = 5
```

An important thing to note is that these conversion functions throw an exception if the conversion fails. There are two exceptions that can be thrown:

- `std::invalid_argument`: If the conversion cannot be performed:

```
try
{
  auto i16 = std::stoi("");
}
catch (std::exception const & e)
{
  // prints "invalid stoi argument"
  std::cout << e.what() << '\n';
}
```

- `std::out_of_range`: If the converted value is outside the range of the result type (or if the underlying function sets `errno` to `ERANGE`):

```
try
{
  // OK
  auto i17 = std::stoll("12345678901234");
  // throws std::out_of_range
  auto i18 = std::stoi("12345678901234");
}
catch (std::exception const & e)
{
  // prints "stoi argument out of range"
  std::cout << e.what() << '\n';
}
```

The other set of functions that convert a string to a floating-point type is very similar, except that they don't have a parameter for the numeric base. A valid floating-point value can have different representations in the input string:

- Decimal floating-point expression (optional sign, sequence of decimal digits with optional point, optional `e` or `E`, followed by exponent with optional sign).

- Binary floating-point expression (optional sign, `0x` or `0X` prefix, sequence of hexadecimal digits with optional point, optional `p` or `P`, followed by exponent with optional sign).
- Infinity expression (optional sign followed by case-insensitive `INF` or `INFINITY`).
- A non-number expression (optional sign followed by case-insensitive `NAN` and possibly other alphanumeric characters).

The following are various examples of converting strings to doubles:

```
auto d1 = std::stod("123.45");          // d1 =  123.45000000000000
auto d2 = std::stod("+123.45");         // d2 =  123.45000000000000
auto d3 = std::stod("-123.45");         // d3 = -123.45000000000000
auto d4 = std::stod("  123.45");        // d4 =  123.45000000000000
auto d5 = std::stod("  -123.45abc");    // d5 = -123.45000000000000
auto d6 = std::stod("1.2345e+2");       // d6 =  123.45000000000000
auto d7 = std::stod("0xF.6E6666p3");    // d7 =  123.44999980926514

auto d8 = std::stod("INF");             // d8 = inf
auto d9 = std::stod("-infinity");       // d9 = -inf
auto d10 = std::stod("NAN");            // d10 = nan
auto d11 = std::stod("-nanabc");        // d11 = -nan
```

The floating-point base 2 scientific notation, seen earlier in the form `0xF.6E6666p3`, is not the topic of this recipe. However, for a clear understanding, a short description is provided; but it is recommended that you look at additional references for details (such as `https://en.cppreference.com/w/cpp/language/floating_literal`). A floating-point constant in the base 2 scientific notation is composed of several parts:

- The hexadecimal prefix `0x`.
- An integer part, which in this example was `F`, which in decimal is 15.
- A fractional part, which in this example was `6E6666`, or `011011100110011001100110` in binary. To convert that into decimal, we need to add inverse powers of two: `1/4 + 1/8 + 1/32 + 1/64 + 1/128 + ....`
- A suffix, representing a power of 2; in this example, `p3` means 2 at the power of 3.

The value of the decimal equivalent is determined by multiplying the significant (composed of the integer and fractional parts) and the base at the power of the exponent.

For the given hexadecimal base 2 floating-point literal, the significant is `15.4312499...` (please note that digits after the seventh one are not shown), the base is 2, and the exponent is 3. Therefore, the result is `15.4212499... * 8`, which is `123.44999980926514`.

See also

- *Limits and other properties of numeric types* to learn about the minimum and maximum values, as well as the other properties of numerical types

Limits and other properties of numeric types

Sometimes, it is necessary to know and use the minimum and maximum values that can be represented with a numeric type, such as `char`, `int`, or `double`. Many developers use standard C macros for this, such as `CHAR_MIN`/`CHAR_MAX`, `INT_MIN`/`INT_MAX`, and `DBL_MIN`/`DBL_MAX`. C++ provides a class template called `numeric_limits` with specializations for every numeric type that enables you to query the minimum and maximum value of a type. However, `numeric_limits` is not limited to that functionality, and offers additional constants for type property querying, such as whether a type is signed or not, how many bits it needs for representing its values, whether it can represent infinity for floating-point types, and many others. Prior to C++11, the use of `numeric_limits<T>` was limited because it could not be used in places where constants were needed (examples include the size of arrays and switch cases). Due to that, developers preferred to use C macros throughout their code. In C++11, that is no longer the case, as all the static members of `numeric_limits<T>` are now `constexpr`, which means they can be used everywhere a constant expression is expected.

Getting ready

The `numeric_limits<T>` class template is available in the namespace `std` in the `<limits>` header.

How to do it...

Use `std::numeric_limits<T>` to query various properties of a numeric type `T`:

- Use the `min()` and `max()` static methods to get the smallest and largest finite numbers of a type. The following are examples of how these could be used:

```
template<typename T, typename Iter>
T minimum(Iter const start, Iter const end) // finds the
                                            // minimum value
                                            // in a range
{
  T minval = std::numeric_limits<T>::max();
  for (auto i = start; i < end; ++i)
  {
    if (*i < minval)
      minval = *i;
  }
  return minval;
}

int range[std::numeric_limits<char>::max() + 1] = { 0 };

switch(get_value())
{
  case std::numeric_limits<int>::min():
  // do something
  break;
}
```

- Use other static methods and static constants to retrieve other properties of a numeric type. In the following example, the variable `bits` is an `std::bitset` object that contains a sequence of bits that are necessary to represent the numerical value represented by the variable `n` (which is an integer):

```
auto n = 42;
std::bitset<std::numeric_limits<decltype(n)>::digits>
   bits { static_cast<unsigned long long>(n) };
```

In C++11, there is no limitation to where `std::numeric_limits<T>` can be used; therefore, preferably, use it over C macros in your modern C++ code.

How it works...

The `std::numeric_limits<T>` class template enables developers to query properties of numeric types. Actual values are available through specializations, and the standard library provides specializations for all the built-in numeric types (`char`, `short`, `int`, `long`, `float`, `double`, and so on). In addition, third parties may provide additional implementations for other types. An example could be a numeric library that implements a `bigint` integer type and a `decimal` type and provides specializations of `numeric_limits` for these types (such as `numeric_limits<bigint>` and `numeric_limits<decimal>`).

The following specializations of numeric types are available in the `<limits>` header. Note that specializations for `char16_t` and `char32_t` are new in C++11; the others were available previously. Apart from the specializations listed ahead, the library also includes specializations for every `cv-qualified` version of these numeric types, and they are identical to the unqualified specialization. For example, consider the type `int`; there are four actual specializations (and they are identical): `numeric_limits<int>`, `numeric_limits<const int>`, `numeric_limits<volatile int>`, and `numeric_limits<const volatile int>`:

```
template<> class numeric_limits<bool>;
template<> class numeric_limits<char>;
template<> class numeric_limits<signed char>;
template<> class numeric_limits<unsigned char>;
template<> class numeric_limits<wchar_t>;
template<> class numeric_limits<char16_t>;
template<> class numeric_limits<char32_t>;
template<> class numeric_limits<short>;
template<> class numeric_limits<unsigned short>;
template<> class numeric_limits<int>;
template<> class numeric_limits<unsigned int>;
template<> class numeric_limits<long>;
template<> class numeric_limits<unsigned long>;
template<> class numeric_limits<long long>;
template<> class numeric_limits<unsigned long long>;
template<> class numeric_limits<float>;
template<> class numeric_limits<double>;
template<> class numeric_limits<long double>;
```

As mentioned earlier, in C++11, all static members of `std::numeric_limits` are `constexpr`, which means they can be used in all the places where constant expressions are needed. These have several major advantages over C++ macros:

- They are easier to remember, as the only thing you need to know is the name of the type, which you should know anyway, and not countless names of macros.
- They support types that are not available in C, such as `char16_t` and `char32_t`.
- They are the only possible solutions for templates where you don't know the type.
- Minimum and maximum are only two of the various properties of types it provides; therefore, its actual use is beyond the numeric limits shown. As a side note, for this reason, the class should have been perhaps called `numeric_properties`, instead of `numeric_limits`.

The following function template, `print_type_properties()`, prints the minimum and maximum finite values of the type, as well as other information:

```
template <typename T>
void print_type_properties()
{
  std::cout
    << "min="
    << std::numeric_limits<T>::min()        << '\n'
    << "max="
    << std::numeric_limits<T>::max()        << '\n'
    << "bits="
    << std::numeric_limits<T>::digits       << '\n'
    << "decdigits="
    << std::numeric_limits<T>::digits10     << '\n'
    << "integral="
    << std::numeric_limits<T>::is_integer   << '\n'
    << "signed="
    << std::numeric_limits<T>::is_signed    << '\n'
    << "exact="
    << std::numeric_limits<T>::is_exact     << '\n'
    << "infinity="
    << std::numeric_limits<T>::has_infinity << '\n';
}
```

If we call the `print_type_properties()` function for `unsigned short`, `int`, and `double`, we will get the following output:

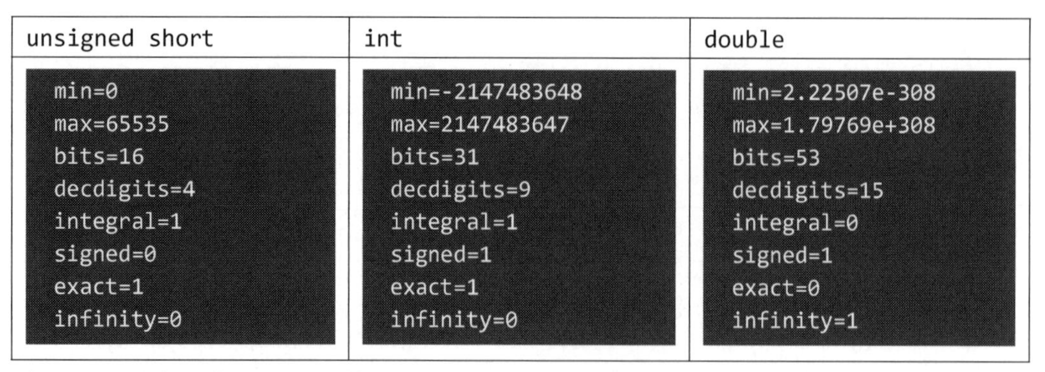

unsigned short	int	double
min=0	min=-2147483648	min=2.22507e-308
max=65535	max=2147483647	max=1.79769e+308
bits=16	bits=31	bits=53
decdigits=4	decdigits=9	decdigits=15
integral=1	integral=1	integral=0
signed=0	signed=1	signed=1
exact=1	exact=1	exact=0
infinity=0	infinity=0	infinity=1

Please note that there is a difference between the `digits` and `digits10` constants:

- `digits` represents the number of bits (excluding the sign bit if present) and padding bits (if any) for integral types and the number of bits of the mantissa for floating-point types.
- `digits10` is the number of decimal digits that can be represented by a type without a change. To understand this better, let's consider the case of `unsigned short`. This is a 16-bit integral type. It can represent numbers between 0 and 65,536. It can represent numbers up to five decimal digits, 10,000 to 65,536, but it cannot represent all five decimal digit numbers, as numbers from 65,537 to 99,999 require more bits. Therefore, the largest numbers that it can represent without requiring more bits have four decimal digits (numbers from 1,000 to 9,999). This is the value indicated by `digits10`. For integral types, it has a direct relationship to constant `digits`; for an integral type, `T`, the value of `digits10` is `std::numeric_limits<T>::digits * std::log10(2)`.

It's worth mentioning that the standard library types that are aliases of arithmetic types (such as `std::size_t`) may also be inspected with `std::numeric_limits`. On the other hand, other standard types that are not arithmetic types, such as `std::complex<T>` or `std::nullptr_t`, do not have `std::numeric_limits` specializations.

See also

- *Converting between numeric and string types* to learn how to convert between numbers and strings

Generating pseudo-random numbers

Generating random numbers is necessary for a large variety of applications, from games to cryptography, from sampling to forecasting. However, the term *random numbers* is not actually correct, as the generation of numbers through mathematical formulas is deterministic and does not produce true random numbers, but numbers that look random and are called *pseudo-random*. True randomness can only be achieved through hardware devices, based on physical processes, and even that can be challenged as we may consider even the universe to be actually deterministic. Modern C++ provides support for generating pseudo-random numbers through a pseudo-random number library containing number generators and distributions. Theoretically, it can also produce true random numbers, but in practice, those could actually be only pseudo-random.

Getting ready

In this recipe, we'll discuss the standard support for generating pseudo-random numbers. Understanding the difference between random and pseudo-random numbers is key. True random numbers are numbers that cannot be predicted better than by random chance, and are produced with the help of hardware random number generators. Pseudo-random numbers are numbers produced with the help of algorithms that generate sequences with properties that approximate the ones of true random numbers.

Furthermore, being familiar with various statistical distributions is a plus. It is mandatory, though, that you know what a uniform distribution is, because all engines in the library produce numbers that are uniformly distributed. Without going into any details, we will just mention that uniform distribution is a probability distribution that is concerned with events that are equally likely to occur (within certain bounds).

How to do it...

To generate pseudo-random numbers in your application, you should perform the following steps:

1. Include the header `<random>`:

   ```
   #include <random>
   ```

2. Use an `std::random_device` generator for seeding a pseudo-random engine:

   ```
   std::random_device rd{};
   ```

3. Use one of the available engines for generating numbers and initialize it with a random seed:

```
auto mtgen = std::mt19937{ rd() };
```

4. Use one of the available distributions for converting the output of the engine to one of the desired statistical distributions:

```
auto ud = std::uniform_int_distribution<>{ 1, 6 };
```

5. Generate the pseudo-random numbers:

```
for(auto i = 0; i < 20; ++i)
  auto number = ud(mtgen);
```

How it works...

The pseudo-random number library contains two types of components:

- *Engines*, which are generators of random numbers; these can produce either pseudo-random numbers with a uniform distribution or, if available, actual random numbers.
- *Distributions* that convert the output of an engine to a statistical distribution.

All engines (except for `random_device`) produce integer numbers in a uniform distribution, and all engines implement the following methods:

- `min()`: This is a static method that returns the minimum value that can be produced by the generator.
- `max()`: This is a static method that returns the maximum value that can be produced by the generator.
- `seed()`: This initializes the algorithm with a start value (except for `random_device`, which cannot be seeded).
- `operator()`: This generates a new number uniformly distributed between `min()` and `max()`.
- `discard()`: This generates and discards a given number of pseudo-random numbers.

The following engines are available:

- `linear_congruential_engine`: This is a linear congruential generator that produces numbers using the following formula:

  $x(i) = (A * x(i - 1) + C) \bmod M$

- `mersenne_twister_engine`: This is a Mersenne twister generator that keeps a value on $W * (N - 1) * R$ bits. Each time a number needs to be generated, it extracts W bits. When all the bits have been used, it twists the large value by shifting and mixing the bits so that it has a new set of bits to extract from.
- `subtract_with_carry_engine`: This is a generator that implements a *subtract with carry* algorithm based on the following formula:

  $x(i) = (x(i - R) - x(i - S) - cy(i - 1)) \bmod M$

  In the preceding formula, cy is defined as:

  $$cy(i) = \begin{cases} 0;\ x(i-S) - x(i-R) - cy(i-1) \geq 0 \\ 1;\ x(i-S) - x(i-R) - cy(i-1) < 0 \end{cases}$$

In addition, the library provides engine adapters that are also engines wrapping another engine and producing numbers based on the output of the base engine. Engine adapters implement the same methods mentioned earlier for the base engines. The following engine adapters are available:

- `discard_block_engine`: A generator that, from every block of P numbers generated by the base engine, keeps only R numbers, discarding the rest.
- `independent_bits_engine`: A generator that produces numbers with a different number of bits than the base engine.
- `shuffle_order_engine`: A generator that keeps a shuffled table of K numbers produced by the base engine and returns numbers from this table, replacing them with numbers generated by the base engine.

Choosing a pseudo-random number generator should be done based on the specific requirements of your application. The linear congruential engine is medium fast but has very small storage requirements for its internal state. The subtract with carry engine is very fast, including on machines that don't have a processor with advanced arithmetic instructions set. However, it requires larger storage for its internal state and the sequence of generated numbers has fewer desirable characteristics. The Mersenne twister is the slowest of these engines and has the greatest storage durations, but produces the longest non-repeating sequences of pseudo-numbers.

All these engines and engine adaptors produce pseudo-random numbers. The library, however, provides another engine called `random_device` that is supposed to produce non-deterministic numbers, but this is not an actual constraint as physical sources of random entropy might not be available. Therefore, implementations of `random_device` could actually be based on a pseudo-random engine. The `random_device` class cannot be seeded like the other engines and has an additional method called `entropy()` that returns the random device entropy, which is 0 for a deterministic generator and nonzero for a non-deterministic generator.

However, this is not a reliable method for determining whether the device is actually deterministic or non-deterministic. For instance, both GNU `libstdc++` and LLVM `libc++` implement a non-deterministic device, but return `0` for entropy. On the other hand, `VC++` and `boost.random` return `32` and `10`, respectively, for entropy.

All these generators produce integers in a uniform distribution. This is, however, only one of the many possible statistical distributions where random numbers are needed in most applications. To be able to produce numbers (either integer or real) in other distributions, the library provides several classes called *distributions*. These convert the output of an engine according to the statistical distribution it implements. The following distributions are available:

Type	**Class name**	**Numbers**	**Statistical distribution**
Uniform	`uniform_int_distribution`	Integer	Uniform
	`uniform_real_distribution`	Real	Uniform
Bernoulli	`bernoulli_distribution`	Boolean	Bernoulli
	`binomial_distribution`	Integer	Binomial
	`negative_binomial_distribution`	Integer	Negative binomial
	`geometric_distribution`	Integer	Geometric
Poisson	`poisson_distribution`	Integer	Poisson
	`exponential_distribution`	Real	Exponential
	`gamma_distribution`	Real	Gamma
	`weibull_distribution`	Real	Weibull
	`extreme_value_distribution`	Real	Extreme value
Normal	`normal_distribution`	Real	Standard normal (Gaussian)
	`lognormal_distribution`	Real	Lognormal
	`chi_squared_distribution`	Real	Chi-squared
	`cauchy_distribution`	Real	Cauchy
	`fisher_f_distribution`	Real	Fisher's F-distribution
	`student_t_distribution`	Real	Student's t-distribution

Sampling	discrete_distribution	Integer	Discrete
	piecewise_constant_distribution	Real	Values distributed on constant subintervals
	piecewise_linear_distribution	Real	Values distributed on defined subintervals

Each of the engines provided by the library has advantages and disadvantages, as it was mentioned earlier. The Mersenne twister, although the slowest and one that has the largest internal state, when initialized appropriately, can produce the longest non-repeating sequence of numbers. In the following examples, we will use `std::mt19937`, a 32-bit Mersenne twister with 19,937 bits of internal state.

The simplest way to generate random numbers looks like this:

```
auto mtgen = std::mt19937 {};
for (auto i = 0; i < 10; ++i)
  std::cout << mtgen() << '\n';
```

In this example, `mtgen` is `std::mt19937` for the Mersenne twister. To generate numbers, you only need to use the call operator that advances the internal state and returns the next pseudo-random number. However, this code is flawed, as the engine is not seeded. As a result, it always produces the same sequence of numbers, which is probably not what you want in most cases.

There are different approaches for initializing the engine. One approach, common with the C `random` library, is to use the current time. In modern C++, it should look like this:

```
auto seed = std::chrono::high_resolution_clock::now()
            .time_since_epoch()
            .count();
auto mtgen = std::mt19937{ static_cast<unsigned int>(seed) };
```

In this example, `seed` is a number representing the number of ticks since the clock's epoch until the present moment. This number is then used to seed the engine. The problem with this approach is that the value of that `seed` is actually deterministic, and in some classes of applications, it could be prone to attacks. A more reliable approach is to seed the generator with actual random numbers.

The `std::random_device` class is an engine that is supposed to return true random numbers, though implementations could actually be based on a pseudo-random generator:

```
std::random_device rd;
auto mtgen = std::mt19937 {rd()};
```

Numbers produced by all engines follow a uniform distribution. To convert the result to another statistical distribution, we have to use a distribution class. To show how generated numbers are distributed according to the selected distribution, we will use the following function. This function generates a specified number of pseudo-random numbers and counts their repetition in a map. The values from the map are then used to produce a bar-like diagram showing how often each number occurred:

```
void generate_and_print(std::function<int(void)> gen,
                        int const iterations = 10000)
{
  // map to store the numbers and their repetition
  auto data = std::map<int, int>{};

  // generate random numbers
  for (auto n = 0; n < iterations; ++n)
    ++data[gen()];

  // find the element with the most repetitions
  auto max = std::max_element(
               std::begin(data), std::end(data),
               [](auto kvp1, auto kvp2) {
    return kvp1.second < kvp2.second; });

  // print the bars
  for (auto i = max->second / 200; i > 0; --i)
  {
    for (auto kvp : data)
    {
      std::cout
        << std::fixed << std::setprecision(1) << std::setw(3)
        << (kvp.second / 200 >= i ? (char)219 : ' ');
    }

    std::cout << '\n';
  }
```

```
  // print the numbers
  for (auto kvp : data)
  {
    std::cout
      << std::fixed << std::setprecision(1) << std::setw(3)
      << kvp.first;
  }

  std::cout << '\n';
}
```

The following code generates random numbers using the `std::mt19937` engine with a uniform distribution in the range `[1, 6]`; this is basically what you get when you throw a dice:

```
std::random_device rd{};
auto mtgen = std::mt19937{ rd() };
auto ud = std::uniform_int_distribution<>{ 1, 6 };
generate_and_print([&mtgen, &ud]() {return ud(mtgen); });
```

The output of the program looks like this:

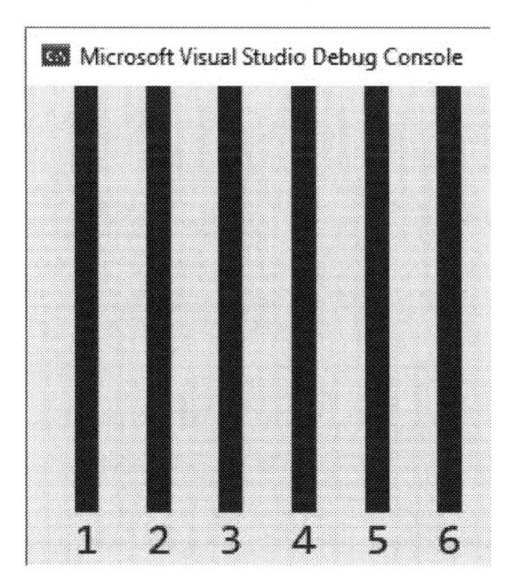

Figure 2.1: Uniform distribution of the range [1,6]

In the next and final example, we're changing the distribution to a normal distribution with a mean of `5` and a standard deviation of `2`. This distribution produces real numbers; therefore, in order to use the previous `generate_and_print()` function, the numbers must be rounded to integers:

```
std::random_device rd{};
auto mtgen = std::mt19937{ rd() };
```

```
auto nd = std::normal_distribution<>{ 5, 2 };

generate_and_print(
  [&mtgen, &nd]() {
    return static_cast<int>(std::round(nd(mtgen))); });
```

The following will be the output of the preceding code:

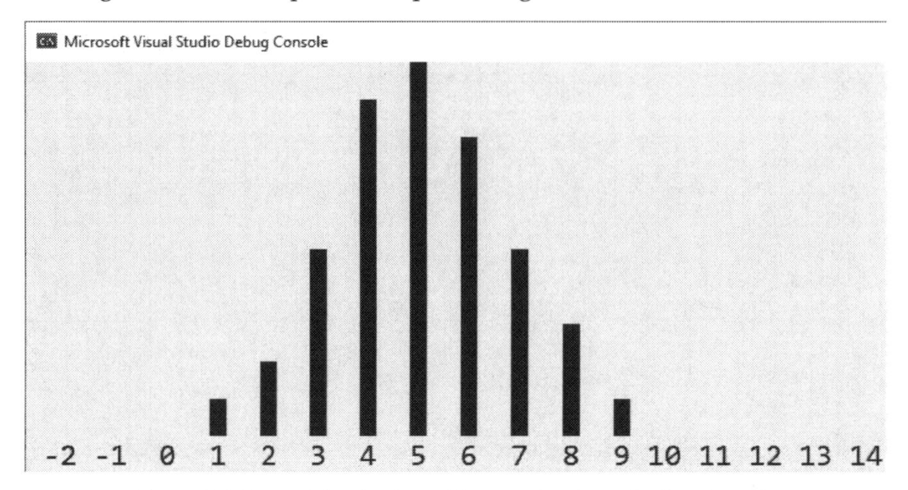

Figure 2.2: Normal distribution with mean 5 and standard variance 2

Here, we can see that, based on the graphical representation, the distribution has changed from a uniform one to a normal one with the mean at value 5.

See also

- *Initializing all bits of internal state of a pseudo-random number generator* to learn how to properly initialize random number engines

Initializing all bits of internal state of a pseudo-random number generator

In the previous recipe, we looked at the pseudo-random number library, along with its components, and how it can be used to produce numbers in different statistical distributions. One important factor that was overlooked in that recipe is the proper initialization of the pseudo-random number generators.

With careful analysis (that is beyond the purpose of this recipe or this book), it can be shown that the Mersenne twister engine has a bias toward producing some values repeatedly and omitting others, thus generating numbers not in a uniform distribution, but rather in a binomial or Poisson distribution. In this recipe, you will learn how to initialize a generator in order to produce pseudo-random numbers with a true uniform distribution.

Getting ready

You should read the previous recipe, *Generating pseudo-random numbers*, to get an overview of what the pseudo-random number library offers.

How to do it...

To properly initialize a pseudo-random number generator to produce a uniformly distributed sequence of pseudo-random numbers, perform the following steps:

1. Use an `std::random_device` to produce random numbers to be used as seeding values:

   ```
   std::random_device rd;
   ```

2. Generate random data for all internal bits of the engine:

   ```
   std::array<int, std::mt19937::state_size> seed_data {};
   std::generate(std::begin(seed_data), std::end(seed_data),
                 std::ref(rd));
   ```

3. Create an `std::seed_seq` object from the previously generated pseudo-random data:

   ```
   std::seed_seq seq(std::begin(seed_data), std::end(seed_data));
   ```

4. Create an engine object and initialize all the bits representing the internal state of the engine; for example, an `mt19937` has 19,937 bits of internal states:

   ```
   auto eng = std::mt19937{ seq };
   ```

5. Use the appropriate distribution based on the requirements of the application:

   ```
   auto dist = std::uniform_real_distribution<>{ 0, 1 };
   ```

How it works...

In all the examples shown in the previous recipe, we used the `std::mt19937` engine to produce pseudo-random numbers. Though the Mersenne twister is slower than the other engines, it can produce the longest sequences of non-repeating numbers with the best spectral characteristics. However, initializing the engine in the manner shown in the previous recipe will not have this effect. The problem is that the internal state of `mt19937` has 624 32-bit integers, and in the examples from the previous recipe, we have only initialized one of them.

When working with the pseudo-random number library, remember the following rule of thumb (shown in the information box):

In order to produce the best results, engines must have all their internal state properly initialized before generating numbers.

The pseudo-random number library provides a class for this particular purpose, called `std::seed_seq`. This is a generator that can be seeded with any number of 32-bit integers and produces the requested number of integers evenly distributed in the 32-bit space.

In the preceding code from the *How to do it...* section, we defined an array called `seed_data` with a number of 32-bit integers equal to the internal state of the `mt19937` generator; that is, 624 integers. Then, we initialized the array with random numbers produced by `std::random_device`. The array was later used to seed `std::seed_seq`, which, in turn, was used to seed the `mt19937` generator.

See also

- *Generating pseudo-random numbers* to familiarize yourself with the capabilities of the standard numerics library for generating pseudo-random numbers

Creating cooked user-defined literals

Literals are constants of built-in types (numerical, Boolean, character, character string, and pointer) that cannot be altered in a program. The language defines a series of prefixes and suffixes to specify literals (and the prefix/suffix is actually part of the literal). C++11 allows us to create user-defined literals by defining functions called *literal operators*, which introduce suffixes for specifying literals. These work only with numerical character and character string types.

This opens the possibility of defining both standard literals in future versions and allows developers to create their own literals. In this recipe, we will learn how to create our own cooked literals.

Getting ready

User-defined literals can have two forms: *raw* and *cooked*. Raw literals are not processed by the compiler, whereas cooked literals are values processed by the compiler (examples can include handling escape sequences in a character string or identifying numerical values such as integer 2898 from literal 0xBAD). Raw literals are only available for integral and floating-point types, whereas cooked literals are also available for character and character string literals.

How to do it...

To create cooked user-defined literals, you should follow these steps:

1. Define your literals in a separate namespace to avoid name clashes.
2. Always prefix the user-defined suffix with an underscore (_).
3. Define a literal operator of one of the following forms for cooked literals:

```
T operator "" _suffix(unsigned long long int);
T operator "" _suffix(long double);
T operator "" _suffix(char);
T operator "" _suffix(wchar_t);
T operator "" _suffix(char16_t);
T operator "" _suffix(char32_t);
T operator "" _suffix(char const *, std::size_t);
T operator "" _suffix(wchar_t const *, std::size_t);
T operator "" _suffix(char16_t const *, std::size_t);
T operator "" _suffix(char32_t const *, std::size_t);
```

The following example creates a user-defined literal for specifying kilobytes:

```
namespace compunits
{
  constexpr size_t operator "" _KB(unsigned long long const size)
  {
    return static_cast<size_t>(size * 1024);
  }
}
```

```
auto size{ 4_KB };          // size_t size = 4096;

using byte = unsigned char;
auto buffer = std::array<byte, 1_KB>{};
```

How it works...

When the compiler encounters a user-defined literal with a user-defined suffix, `S` (it always has a leading underscore for third-party suffixes, as suffixes without a leading underscore are reserved for the standard library), it does an unqualified name lookup in order to identify a function with the name `operator "" S`. If it finds one, then it calls it according to the type of the literal and the type of the literal operator. Otherwise, the compiler will yield an error.

In the example shown in the *How to do it...* section, the literal operator is called `operator "" _KB` and has an argument of type `unsigned long long int`. This is the only integral type possible for literal operators for handling integral types. Similarly, for floating-point user-defined literals, the parameter type must be `long double` since for numeric types, the literal operators must be able to handle the largest possible values. This literal operator returns a `constexpr` value so that it can be used where compile-time values are expected, such as specifying the size of an array, as shown in the preceding example.

When the compiler identifies a user-defined literal and has to call the appropriate user-defined literal operator, it will pick the overload from the overload set according to the following rules:

- **For integral literals**: It calls in the following order: the operator that takes an `unsigned long long`, the raw literal operator that takes a `const char*`, or the literal operator template.
- **For floating-point literals**: It calls in the following order: the operator that takes a `long double`, the raw literal operator that takes a `const char*`, or the literal operator template.
- **For character literals**: It calls the appropriate operator, depending on the character type (`char`, `wchar_t`, `char16_t`, and `char32_t`).
- **For string literals**: It calls the appropriate operator, depending on the string type, that takes a pointer to the string of characters and the size.

In the following example, we're defining a system of units and quantities. We want to operate with kilograms, pieces, liters, and other types of units. This could be useful in a system that can process orders and you need to specify the amount and unit for each article.

The following are defined in the namespace `units`:

- A scoped enumeration for the possible types of units (kilogram, meter, liter, and pieces):

```
enum class unit { kilogram, liter, meter, piece, };
```

- A class template to specify quantities of a particular unit (such as 3.5 kilograms or 42 pieces):

```
template <unit U>
class quantity
{
  const double amount;
public:
  constexpr explicit quantity(double const a) : amount(a)
  {}

  explicit operator double() const { return amount; }
};
```

- The `operator+` and `operator-` functions for the `quantity` class template in order to be able to add and subtract quantities:

```
template <unit U>
constexpr quantity<U> operator+(quantity<U> const &q1,
                                quantity<U> const &q2)
{
  return quantity<U>(static_cast<double>(q1) +
                     static_cast<double>(q2));
}

template <unit U>
constexpr quantity<U> operator-(quantity<U> const &q1,
                                quantity<U> const &q2)
{
  return quantity<U>(static_cast<double>(q1) -
                     static_cast<double>(q2));
}
```

- Literal operators to create `quantity` literals, defined in an inner namespace called `unit_literals`. The purpose of this is to avoid possible name clashes with literals from other namespaces.

If such collisions do happen, developers could select the ones that they should use using the appropriate namespace in the scope where the literals need to be defined:

```
namespace unit_literals
{
  constexpr quantity<unit::kilogram> operator "" _kg(
      long double const amount)
  {
    return quantity<unit::kilogram>
      { static_cast<double>(amount) };
  }

  constexpr quantity<unit::kilogram> operator "" _kg(
      unsigned long long const amount)
  {
    return quantity<unit::kilogram>
      { static_cast<double>(amount) };
  }

  constexpr quantity<unit::liter> operator "" _l(
      long double const amount)
  {
    return quantity<unit::liter>
      { static_cast<double>(amount) };
  }

  constexpr quantity<unit::meter> operator "" _m(
      long double const amount)
  {
    return quantity<unit::meter>
      { static_cast<double>(amount) };
  }

  constexpr quantity<unit::piece> operator "" _pcs(
      unsigned long long const amount)
  {
    return quantity<unit::piece>
      { static_cast<double>(amount) };
  }
}
```

By looking carefully, you can note that the literal operators defined earlier are not the same:

- `_kg` is defined for both integral and floating-point literals; that enables us to create both integral and floating-point values such as `1_kg` and `1.0_kg`.
- `_l` and `_m` are defined only for floating-point literals; this means we can only define quantity literals for these units with floating points, such as `4.5_l` and `10.0_m`.
- `_pcs` is only defined for integral literals; this means we can only define quantities of an integer number of pieces, such as `42_pcs`.

Having these literal operators available, we can operate with various quantities. The following examples show both valid and invalid operations:

```
using namespace units;
using namespace unit_literals;

auto q1{ 1_kg };    // OK
auto q2{ 4.5_kg };  // OK
auto q3{ q1 + q2 }; // OK
auto q4{ q2 - q1 }; // OK

// error, cannot add meters and pieces
auto q5{ 1.0_m + 1_pcs };
// error, cannot have an integer number of liters
auto q6{ 1_l };
// error, can only have an integer number of pieces
auto q7{ 2.0_pcs}
```

`q1` is a quantity of 1 kg; this is an integer value. Since an overloaded `operator "" _kg(unsigned long long const)` exists, the literal can be correctly created from the integer 1. Similarly, `q2` is a quantity of 4.5 kilograms; this is a real value. Since an overloaded `operator "" _kg(long double)` exists, the literal can be created from the double floating-point value 4.5.

On the other hand, `q6` is a quantity of 1 liter. Since there is no overloaded `operator "" _l(unsigned long long)`, the literal cannot be created. It would require an overload that takes an `unsigned long long`, but such an overload does not exist. Similarly, `q7` is a quantity of 2.0 pieces, but piece literals can only be created from integer values and, therefore, this generates another compiler error.

There's more...

Though user-defined literals are available from C++11, standard literal operators have been available only from C++14. Further standard user-defined literals have been added to the next versions of the standard. The following is a list of these standard literal operators:

- `operator""s` for defining `std::basic_string` literals and `operator""sv` (in C++17) for defining `std::basic_string_view` literals:

```
using namespace std::string_literals;

auto s1{  "text"s }; // std::string
auto s2{ L"text"s }; // std::wstring
auto s3{ u"text"s }; // std::u16string
auto s4{ U"text"s }; // std::u32string
using namespace std::string_view_literals;
auto s5{ "text"sv }; // std::string_view
```

- `operator""h`, `operator""min`, `operator""s`, `operator""ms`, `operator""us`, and `operator""ns` for creating an `std::chrono::duration` value:

```
using namespace std::chrono_literals;

// std::chrono::duration<long long>
auto timer {2h + 42min + 15s};
```

- `operator""y` for creating an `std::chrono::year` literal and `operator""d` for creating an `std::chrono::day` literal that represents a day of a month, both added to C++20:

```
using namespace std::chrono_literals;

auto year { 2020y }; // std::chrono::year
auto day { 15d };    // std::chrono::day
```

- `operator""if`, `operator""i`, and `operator""il` for creating an `std::complex` value:

```
using namespace std::complex_literals;

auto c{ 12.0 + 4.5i }; // std::complex<double>
```

The standard user-defined literals are available in multiple namespaces. For instance, the `""s` and `""sv` literals for strings are defined in the namespace `std::literals::string_literals`.

However, both `literals` and `string_literals` are inlined namespaces. Therefore, you can access the literals with `using namespace std::literals`, `using namespace std::string_literals`, or `using namespace std::literals::string_literals`. In the previous examples, the second form was preferred.

See also

- *Using raw string literals to avoid escaping characters* to learn how to define string literals without the need to escape special characters
- *Creating raw user-defined literals* to understand how to provide a custom interpretation of an input sequence so that it changes the normal behavior of the compiler
- *Using inline namespaces for symbol versioning* in *Chapter 1*, *Learning Modern Core Language Features*, to learn how to version your source code using inline namespaces and conditional compilation

Creating raw user-defined literals

In the previous recipe, we looked at the way C++11 allows library implementers and developers to create user-defined literals and the user-defined literals available in the C++14 standard. However, user-defined literals have two forms: a cooked form, where the literal value is processed by the compiler before being supplied to the literal operator, and a raw form, in which the literal is not processed by the compiler before being supplied to the literal operator. The latter is only available for integral and floating-point types. Raw literals are useful for altering the compiler's normal behavior. For instance, a sequence such as 3.1415926 is interpreted by the compiler as a floating-point value, but with the use of a raw user-defined literal, it could be interpreted as a user-defined decimal value. In this recipe, we will look at creating raw user-defined literals.

Getting ready

Before continuing with this recipe, it is strongly recommended that you go through the previous one, *Creating cooked user-defined literals*, as general details about user-defined literals will not be reiterated here.

To exemplify the way raw user-defined literals can be created, we will define binary literals. These binary literals can be of 8-bit, 16-bit, and 32-bit (unsigned) types. These types will be called `byte8`, `byte16`, and `byte32`, and the literals we will create will be called `_b8`, `_b16`, and `_b32`.

How to do it...

To create raw user-defined literals, you should follow these steps:

1. Define your literals in a separate namespace to avoid name clashes.
2. Always prefix the used-defined suffix with an underscore (_).
3. Define a literal operator or literal operator template of the following form:

```
T operator "" _suffix(const char*);

template<char...> T operator "" _suffix();
```

The following example shows a possible implementation of 8-bit, 16-bit, and 32-bit binary literals:

```
namespace binary
{
  using byte8  = unsigned char;
  using byte16 = unsigned short;
  using byte32 = unsigned int;

  namespace binary_literals
  {
    namespace binary_literals_internals
    {
      template <typename CharT, char... bits>
      struct binary_struct;

      template <typename CharT, char... bits>
      struct binary_struct<CharT, '0', bits...>
      {
        static constexpr CharT value{
          binary_struct<CharT, bits...>::value };
      };

      template <typename CharT, char... bits>
      struct binary_struct<CharT, '1', bits...>
      {
        static constexpr CharT value{
          static_cast<CharT>(1 << sizeof...(bits)) |
          binary_struct<CharT, bits...>::value };
      };
```

```
      template <typename CharT>
      struct binary_struct<CharT>
      {
        static constexpr CharT value{ 0 };
      };
    }

    template<char... bits>
    constexpr byte8 operator""_b8()
    {
      static_assert(
        sizeof...(bits) <= 8,
        "binary literal b8 must be up to 8 digits long");

      return binary_literals_internals::
                binary_struct<byte8, bits...>::value;
    }

    template<char... bits>
    constexpr byte16 operator""_b16()
    {
      static_assert(
        sizeof...(bits) <= 16,
        "binary literal b16 must be up to 16 digits long");

      return binary_literals_internals::
                binary_struct<byte16, bits...>::value;
    }

    template<char... bits>
    constexpr byte32 operator""_b32()
    {
      static_assert(
        sizeof...(bits) <= 32,
        "binary literal b32 must be up to 32 digits long");

      return binary_literals_internals::
                binary_struct<byte32, bits...>::value;
    }

  }
}
```

How it works...

First of all, we define everything inside a namespace called `binary` and start with introducing several type aliases: `byte8`, `byte16`, and `byte32`. These represent integral types of 8 bits, 16 bits, and 32 bits, as the names imply.

The implementation in the previous section enables us to define binary literals of the form `1010_b8` (a `byte8` value of decimal 10) or `000010101100_b16` (a `byte16` value of decimal 2130496). However, we want to make sure that we do not exceed the number of digits for each type. In other words, values such as `111100001_b8` should be illegal and the compiler should yield an error.

The literal operator templates are defined in a nested namespace called `binary_literal_internals`. This is a good practice in order to avoid name collisions with other literal operators from other namespaces. Should something like that happen, you can choose to use the appropriate namespace in the right scope (such as one namespace in a function or block and another namespace in another function or block).

The three literal operator templates are very similar. The only things that are different are their names (`_b8`, `_16`, and `_b32`), return type (`byte8`, `byte16`, and `byte32`), and the condition in the static assert that checks the number of digits.

We will explore the details of variadic templates and template recursion in a later recipe; however, for a better understanding, this is how this particular implementation works: `bits` is a template parameter pack that is not a single value, but all the values the template could be instantiated with. For example, if we consider the literal `1010_b8`, then the literal operator template would be instantiated as `operator"" _b8<'1', '0', '1', '0'>()`. Before proceeding with computing the binary value, we check the number of digits in the literal. For `_b8`, this must not exceed eight (including any trailing zeros). Similarly, it should be up to 16 digits for `_b16` and 32 for `_b32`. For this, we use the `sizeof...` operator, which returns the number of elements in a parameter pack (in this case, `bits`).

If the number of digits is correct, we can proceed to expand the parameter pack and recursively compute the decimal value represented by the binary literal. This is done with the help of an additional class template and its specializations. These templates are defined in yet another nested namespace, called `binary_literals_internals`. This is also a good practice because it hides (without proper qualification) the implementation details from the client (unless an explicit `using namespace` directive makes them available to the current namespace).

Even though this looks like recursion, it is not a true runtime recursion. This is because after the compiler expands and generates the code from templates, what we end up with is basically calls to overloaded functions with a different number of parameters. This is explained later in the *Writing a function template with a variable number of arguments* recipe.

The `binary_struct` class template has a template type of `CharT` for the return type of the function (we need this because our literal operator templates should return either `byte8`, `byte16`, or `byte32`) and a parameter pack:

```
template <typename CharT, char... bits>
struct binary_struct;
```

Several specializations of this class template are available with parameter pack decomposition. When the first digit of the pack is `'0'`, the computed value remains the same, and we continue expanding the rest of the pack. If the first digit of the pack is `'1'`, then the new value is 1, shifted to the left with the number of digits in the remainder of the pack bit, or the value of the rest of the pack:

```
template <typename CharT, char... bits>
struct binary_struct<CharT, '0', bits...>
{
  static constexpr CharT value{
    binary_struct<CharT, bits...>::value };
};

template <typename CharT, char... bits>
struct binary_struct<CharT, '1', bits...>
{
  static constexpr CharT value{
    static_cast<CharT>(1 << sizeof...(bits)) |
    binary_struct<CharT, bits...>::value };
};
```

The last specialization covers the case where the pack is empty; in this case, we return 0:

```
template <typename CharT>
struct binary_struct<CharT>
{
  static constexpr CharT value{ 0 };
};
```

After defining these helper classes, we could implement the `byte8`, `byte16`, and `byte32` binary literals as intended. Note that we need to bring the content of the namespace `binary_literals` into the current namespace in order to use the literal operator templates:

```
using namespace binary;
using namespace binary_literals;
auto b1 = 1010_b8;
auto b2 = 101010101010_b16;
auto b3 = 101010101010101010101010_b32;
```

The following definitions trigger compiler errors:

```
// binary literal b8 must be up to 8 digits long
auto b4 = 0011111111_b8;
// binary literal b16 must be up to 16 digits long
auto b5 = 001111111111111111_b16;
// binary literal b32 must be up to 32 digits long
auto b6 = 0011111111111111111111111111111111_b32;
```

The reason for this is that the condition in `static_assert` is not met. The length of the sequence of characters preceding the literal operator is greater than expected, in all cases.

See also

- *Using raw string literals to avoid escaping characters* to learn how to define string literals without the need to escape special characters
- *Creating cooked user-defined literals* to learn how to create literals of user-defined types
- *Writing a function template with a variable number of arguments* in *Chapter 3* to see how variadic templates enable us to write functions that can take any number of arguments
- *Creating type aliases and alias templates* in *Chapter 1* to learn about aliases for types

Using raw string literals to avoid escaping characters

Strings may contain special characters, such as non-printable characters (newline, horizontal and vertical tab, and so on), string and character delimiters (double and single quotes), or arbitrary octal, hexadecimal, or Unicode values. These special characters are introduced with an escape sequence that starts with a backslash, followed by either the character (examples include `'` and `"`), its designated letter (examples include `n` for a new line, `t` for a horizontal tab), or its value (examples include octal 050, hexadecimal XF7, or Unicode U16F0). As a result, the backslash character itself has to be escaped with another backslash character. This leads to more complicated literal strings that can be hard to read.

To avoid escaping characters, C++11 introduced raw string literals that do not process escape sequences. In this recipe, you will learn how to use the various forms of raw string literals.

Getting ready

In this recipe, and throughout the rest of this book, I will use the `s` suffix to define `basic_string` literals. This was covered earlier in this chapter in the *Creating cooked user-defined literals* recipe.

How to do it...

To avoid escaping characters, define the string literals with one of the following forms:

- `R"( literal )"` as the default form:

  ```
  auto filename {R"(C:\Users\Marius\Documents\)"s};
  auto pattern {R"((\w+)=(\d+)$)"s};

  auto sqlselect {
    R"(SELECT *
    FROM Books
    WHERE Publisher='Packtpub'
    ORDER BY PubDate DESC)"s};
  ```

- `R"delimiter( literal )delimiter"`, where `delimiter` is any sequence of characters excluding parentheses, backslash, and spaces, and `literal` is any sequence of characters with the limitation that it cannot include the closing sequence `)delimiter"`. Here is an example with `!!` as delimiter:

```
auto text{ R"!!(This text contains both "( and )".)!!"s };
std::cout << text << '\n';
```

How it works...

When string literals are used, escapes are not processed, and the actual content of the string is written between the delimiter (in other words, what you see is what you get). The following example shows what appears as the same raw literal string; however, the second one still contains escaped characters. Since these are not processed in the case of string literals, they will be printed as they are in the output:

```
auto filename1 {R"(C:\Users\Marius\Documents\)"s};
auto filename2 {R"(C:\\Users\\Marius\\Documents\\)"s};

// prints C:\Users\Marius\Documents\
std::cout << filename1 << '\n';

// prints C:\\Users\\Marius\\Documents\\
std::cout << filename2 << '\n';
```

If the text has to contain the `)"` sequence, then a different delimiter must be used, in the `R"delimiter( literal )delimiter"` form. According to the standard, the possible characters in a delimiter can be as follows:

> *"Any member of the basic source character set except: space, the left parenthesis (the right parenthesis), the backslash \, and the control characters representing horizontal tab, vertical tab, form feed, and newline."*

Raw string literals can be prefixed by one of `L`, `u8`, `u`, and `U` to indicate a wide, UTF-8, UTF-16, or UTF-32 string literal, respectively. The following are examples of such string literals:

```
auto t1{ LR"(text)"  };  // const wchar_t*
auto t2{ u8R"(text)" };  // const char*
auto t3{ uR"(text)"  };  // const char16_t*
auto t4{ UR"(text)"  };  // const char32_t*

auto t5{ LR"(text)"s  }; // wstring
```

```
auto t6{ u8R"(text)"s }; // string
auto t7{ uR"(text)"s  }; // u16string
auto t8{ UR"(text)"s  }; // u32string
```

Note that the presence of the suffix `""s` at the end of the string makes the compiler deduce the type as various string classes and not character arrays.

See also

- *Creating cooked user-defined literals* to learn how to create literals of user-defined types

Creating a library of string helpers

The string types from the standard library are a general-purpose implementation that lacks many helpful methods, such as changing the case, trimming, splitting, and others that may address different developer needs. Third-party libraries that provide rich sets of string functionalities exist. However, in this recipe, we will look at implementing several simple, yet helpful, methods you may often need in practice. The purpose is rather to see how string methods and standard general algorithms can be used for manipulating strings, but also to have a reference to reusable code that can be used in your applications.

In this recipe, we will implement a small library of string utilities that will provide functions for the following:

- Changing a string into lowercase or uppercase
- Reversing a string
- Trimming white spaces from the beginning and/or the end of the string
- Trimming a specific set of characters from the beginning and/or the end of the string
- Removing occurrences of a character anywhere in the string
- Tokenizing a string using a specific delimiter

Before we start with the implementation, let's look at some prerequisites.

Getting ready

The string library we will be implementing should work with all the standard string types; that is, `std::string`, `std::wstring`, `std::u16string`, and `std::u32string`.

To avoid specifying long names such as std::basic_string<CharT, std::char_traits<CharT>, std::allocator<CharT>>, we will use the following alias templates for strings and string streams:

```
template <typename CharT>
using tstring =
  std::basic_string<CharT, std::char_traits<CharT>,
                    std::allocator<CharT>>;

template <typename CharT>
using tstringstream =
  std::basic_stringstream<CharT, std::char_traits<CharT>,
                          std::allocator<CharT>>;
```

To implement these string helper functions, we need to include the header <string> for strings and <algorithm> for the general standard algorithms we will use.

In all the examples in this recipe, we will use the standard user-defined literal operators for strings from C++14, for which we need to explicitly use the std::string_literals namespace.

How to do it...

1. To convert a string to lowercase or uppercase, apply the tolower() or toupper() functions to the characters of a string using the general-purpose algorithm std::transform():

```
template<typename CharT>
inline tstring<CharT> to_upper(tstring<CharT> text)
{
  std::transform(std::begin(text), std::end(text),
                 std::begin(text), toupper);
  return text;
}

template<typename CharT>
inline tstring<CharT> to_lower(tstring<CharT> text)
{
  std::transform(std::begin(text), std::end(text),
                 std::begin(text), tolower);
  return text;
}
```

2. To reverse a string, use the general-purpose algorithm `std::reverse()`:

```
template<typename CharT>
inline tstring<CharT> reverse(tstring<CharT> text)
{
  std::reverse(std::begin(text), std::end(text));
  return text;
}
```

3. To trim a string, at the beginning, end, or both, use the `std::basic_string` methods `find_first_not_of()` and `find_last_not_of()`:

```
template<typename CharT>
inline tstring<CharT> trim(tstring<CharT> const & text)
{
  auto first{ text.find_first_not_of(' ') };
  auto last{ text.find_last_not_of(' ') };
  return text.substr(first, (last - first + 1));
}

template<typename CharT>
inline tstring<CharT> trimleft(tstring<CharT> const & text)
{
  auto first{ text.find_first_not_of(' ') };
  return text.substr(first, text.size() - first);
}

template<typename CharT>
inline tstring<CharT> trimright(tstring<CharT> const & text)
{
  auto last{ text.find_last_not_of(' ') };
  return text.substr(0, last + 1);
}
```

4. To trim characters in a given set from a string, use overloads of the `std::basic_string` methods `find_first_not_of()` and `find_last_not_of()`, which take
a string parameter that defines the set of characters to look for:

```
template<typename CharT>
inline tstring<CharT> trim(tstring<CharT> const & text,
                           tstring<CharT> const & chars)
{
  auto first{ text.find_first_not_of(chars) };
  auto last{ text.find_last_not_of(chars) };
```

```
   return text.substr(first, (last - first + 1));
}

template<typename CharT>
inline tstring<CharT> trimleft(tstring<CharT> const & text,
                               tstring<CharT> const & chars)
{
   auto first{ text.find_first_not_of(chars) };
   return text.substr(first, text.size() - first);
}

template<typename CharT>
inline tstring<CharT> trimright(tstring<CharT> const &text,
                                tstring<CharT> const &chars)
{
   auto last{ text.find_last_not_of(chars) };
   return text.substr(0, last + 1);
}
```

5. To remove characters from a string, use `std::remove_if()` and `std::basic_string::erase()`:

```
template<typename CharT>
inline tstring<CharT> remove(tstring<CharT> text,
                             CharT const ch)
{
   auto start = std::remove_if(
                  std::begin(text), std::end(text),
                  [=](CharT const c) {return c == ch; });
   text.erase(start, std::end(text));
   return text;
}
```

6. To split a string based on a specified delimiter, use `std::getline()` to read from an `std::basic_stringstream` initialized with the content of the string. The tokens extracted from the stream are pushed into a vector of strings:

```
template<typename CharT>
inline std::vector<tstring<CharT>> split
   (tstring<CharT> text, CharT const delimiter)
{
   auto sstr = tstringstream<CharT>{ text };
   auto tokens = std::vector<tstring<CharT>>{};
   auto token = tstring<CharT>{};
```

```
    while (std::getline(sstr, token, delimiter))
    {
      if (!token.empty()) tokens.push_back(token);
    }
    return tokens;
  }
```

How it works...

To implement the utility functions from the library, we have two options:

- Functions would modify a string passed by a reference
- Functions would not alter the original string but return a new string

The second option has the advantage that it preserves the original string, which may be helpful in many cases. Otherwise, in those cases, you would first have to make a copy of the string and alter the copy. The implementation provided in this recipe takes the second approach.

The first functions we implemented in the *How to do it...* section were `to_upper()` and `to_lower()`. These functions change the content of a string either to uppercase or lowercase. The simplest way to implement this is using the `std::transform()` standard algorithm. This is a general-purpose algorithm that applies a function to every element of a range (defined by a begin and end iterator) and stores the result in another range for which only the begin iterator needs to be specified. The output range can be the same as the input range, which is exactly what we did to transform the string. The applied function is `toupper()` or `tolower()`:

```
auto ut{ string_library::to_upper("this is not UPPERCASE"s) };
// ut = "THIS IS NOT UPPERCASE"

auto lt{ string_library::to_lower("THIS IS NOT lowercase"s) };
// lt = "this is not lowercase"
```

The next function we considered was `reverse()`, which, as the name implies, reverses the content of a string. For this, we used the `std::reverse()` standard algorithm. This general-purpose algorithm reverses the elements of a range defined by a begin and end iterator:

```
auto rt{string_library::reverse("cookbook"s)}; // rt = "koobkooc"
```

When it comes to trimming, a string can be trimmed at the beginning, end, or both sides. Because of that, we implemented three different functions: `trim()` for trimming at both ends, `trimleft()` for trimming at the beginning of a string, and `trimright()` for trimming at the end of a string. The first version of the function trims only spaces. In order to find the right part to trim, we use the `find_first_not_of()` and `find_last_not_of()` methods of `std::basic_string`. These return the first and last characters in the string that are not of the specified character. Subsequently, a call to the `substr()` method of `std::basic_string` returns a new string. The `substr()` method takes an index in the string and a number of elements to copy to the new string:

```
auto text1{"   this is an example   "s};
// t1 = "this is an example"
auto t1{ string_library::trim(text1) };
// t2 = "this is an example   "
auto t2{ string_library::trimleft(text1) };
// t3 = "   this is an example"
auto t3{ string_library::trimright(text1) };
```

Sometimes, it can be useful to trim other characters and then spaces from a string. In order to do that, we provided overloads for the trimming functions that specify a set of characters to be removed. That set is also specified as a string. The implementation is very similar to the previous one because both `find_first_not_of()` and `find_last_not_of()` have overloads that take a string containing the characters to be excluded from the search:

```
auto chars1{" !%\n\r"s};
auto text3{"!!  this % needs a lot\rof trimming  !\n"s};

auto t7{ string_library::trim(text3, chars1) };
// t7 = "this % needs a lot\rof trimming"

auto t8{ string_library::trimleft(text3, chars1) };
// t8 = "this % needs a lot\rof trimming  !\n"

auto t9{ string_library::trimright(text3, chars1) };
// t9 = "!!  this % needs a lot\rof trimming"
```

If removing characters from any part of the string is necessary, the trimming methods are not helpful because they only treat a contiguous sequence of characters at the start and end of a string. For that, however, we implemented a simple `remove()` method. This uses the `std:remove_if()` standard algorithm.

Both `std::remove()` and `std::remove_if()` work in a way that may not be very intuitive at first. They remove elements that satisfy the criteria from a range defined by a first and last iterator by rearranging the content of the range (using move assignment). The elements that need to be removed are placed at the end of the range, and the function returns an iterator to the first element in the range that represents the removed elements. This iterator basically defines the new end of the range that was modified. If no element was removed, the returned iterator is the end iterator of the original range. The value of this returned iterator is then used to call the `std::basic_string::erase()` method, which actually erases the content of the string defined by two iterators. The two iterators in our case are the iterator returned by `std::remove_if()` and the end of the string:

```
auto text4{"must remove all * from text**"s};

auto t10{ string_library::remove(text4, '*') };
// t10 = "must remove all  from text"

auto t11{ string_library::remove(text4, '!') };
// t11 = "must remove all * from text**"
```

The last method we implemented, `split()`, splits the content of a string based on a specified delimiter. There are various ways to implement this. In this implementation, we used `std::getline()`. This function reads characters from an input stream until a specified delimiter is found and places the characters in a string. Before starting to read from the input buffer, it calls `erase()` on the output string to clear its content. Calling this method in a loop produces tokens that are placed in a vector. In our implementation, empty tokens were skipped from the result set:

```
auto text5{"this text will be split   "s};

auto tokens1{ string_library::split(text5, ' ') };
// tokens1 = {"this", "text", "will", "be", "split"}

auto tokens2{ string_library::split(""s, ' ') };
// tokens2 = {}
```

Two examples of text splitting are shown here. In the first example, the text from the `text5` variable is split into words and, as mentioned earlier, empty tokens are ignored. In the second example, splitting an empty string produces an empty vector of `token`.

See also

- *Creating cooked user-defined literals* to learn how to create literals of user-defined types
- *Creating type aliases and alias templates* in *Chapter 1, Learning Modern Core Language Features*, to learn about aliases for types

Verifying the format of a string using regular expressions

Regular expressions are a language intended for performing pattern matching and replacements in texts. C++11 provides support for regular expressions within the standard library through a set of classes, algorithms, and iterators available in the header `<regex>`. In this recipe, we will learn how regular expressions can be used to verify that a string matches a pattern (examples can include verifying an email or IP address formats).

Getting ready

Throughout this recipe, we will explain, whenever necessary, the details of the regular expressions that we use. However, you should have at least some basic knowledge of regular expressions in order to use the C++ standard library for regular expressions. A description of regular expressions syntax and standards is beyond the purpose of this book; if you are not familiar with regular expressions, it is recommended that you read more about them before continuing with the recipes that focus on regular expressions. Good online resources for learning, building, and debugging regular expressions can be found at `https://regexr.com` and `https://regex101.com`.

How to do it...

In order to verify that a string matches a regular expression, perform the following steps:

1. Include the headers `<regex>` and `<string>` and the namespace `std::string_literals` for C++14 standard user-defined literals for strings:

```
#include <regex>
#include <string>
using namespace std::string_literals;
```

2. Use raw string literals to specify the regular expression to avoid escaping backslashes (which can occur frequently). The following regular expression validates most email formats:

```
auto pattern {R"(^[A-Z0-9._%+-]+@[A-Z0-9.-]+\.[A-Z]{2,}$)"s};
```

3. Create an `std::regex`/`std::wregex` object (depending on the character set that is used) to encapsulate the regular expression:

```
auto rx = std::regex{pattern};
```

4. To ignore casing or specify other parsing options, use an overloaded constructor that has an extra parameter for regular expression flags:

```
auto rx = std::regex{pattern, std::regex_constants::icase};
```

5. Use `std::regex_match()` to match the regular expression with an entire string:

```
auto valid = std::regex_match("marius@domain.com"s, rx);
```

How it works...

Considering the problem of verifying the format of email addresses, even though this may look like a trivial problem, in practice, it is hard to find a simple regular expression that covers all the possible cases for valid email formats. In this recipe, we will not try to find that ultimate regular expression, but rather apply a regular expression that is good enough for most cases. The regular expression we will use for this purpose is this:

```
^[A-Z0-9._%+-]+@[A-Z0-9.-]+\.[A-Z]{2,}$
```

The following table explains the structure of the regular expression:

Part	Description
`^`	Start of string.
`[A-Z0-9._%+-]+`	At least one character in the range `A-Z`, `0-9`, or one of `-`, `%`, `+`, or `-` that represents the local part of the email address.
`@`	The character `@`.
`[A-Z0-9.-]+`	At least one character in the range `A-Z`, `0-9`, or one of `-`, `%`, `+`, or `-` that represents the hostname of the domain part.
`\.`	A dot that separates the domain hostname and label.
`[A-Z]{2,}`	The DNS label of a domain that can have between 2 and 63 characters.
`$`	End of the string.

Bear in mind that, in practice, a domain name is composed of a hostname followed by a dot-separated list of DNS labels. Examples include `localhost`, `gmail.com` and `yahoo.co.uk`. This regular expression we are using does not match domains without DNS labels, such as `localhost` (an email, such as `root@localhost`, is a valid email). The domain name can also be an IP address specified in brackets, such as `[192.168.100.11]` (as in `john.doe@[192.168.100.11]`). Email addresses containing such domains will not match the regular expression defined previously. Even though these rather rare formats will not be matched, the regular expression can cover most email formats.

The regular expression for the example in this chapter is provided for didactical purposes only, and is not intended to be used as it is in production code. As explained earlier, this sample does not cover all possible email formats.

We began by including the necessary headers; that is, `<regex>` for regular expressions and `<string>` for strings. The `is_valid_email()` function, shown in the following code (which basically contains the samples from the *How to do it...* section), takes a string representing an email address and returns a Boolean indicating whether the email has a valid format or not.

We first construct an `std::regex` object to encapsulate the regular expression indicated with the raw string literal. Using raw string literals is helpful because it avoids escaping backslashes, which are used for escape characters in regular expressions too. The function then calls `std::regex_match()`, passing the input text and the regular expression:

```
bool is_valid_email_format(std::string const & email)
{
  auto pattern {R"(^[A-Z0-9._%+-]+@[A-Z0-9.-]+\.[A-Z]{2,}$)"s};

  auto rx = std::regex{pattern, std::regex_constants::icase};

  return std::regex_match(email, rx);
}
```

The `std::regex_match()` method tries to match the regular expression against the entire string. If successful, it returns `true`; otherwise, it returns `false`:

```
auto ltest = [](std::string const & email)
{
  std::cout << std::setw(30) << std::left
            << email << " : "
```

```
        << (is_valid_email_format(email) ?
            "valid format" : "invalid format")
        << '\n';
};

ltest("JOHN.DOE@DOMAIN.COM"s);          // valid format
ltest("JOHNDOE@DOMAIL.CO.UK"s);         // valid format
ltest("JOHNDOE@DOMAIL.INFO"s);          // valid format
ltest("J.O.H.N_D.O.E@DOMAIN.INFO"s);    // valid format
ltest("ROOT@LOCALHOST"s);               // invalid format
ltest("john.doe@domain.com"s);          // invalid format
```

In this simple test, the only emails that do not match the regular expression are `ROOT@LOCALHOST` and `john.doe@domain.com`. The first contains a domain name without a dot-prefixed DNS label, and that case is not covered in the regular expression. The second contains only lowercase letters, and in the regular expression, the valid set of characters for both the local part and the domain name was uppercase letters, A to Z.

Instead of complicating the regular expression with additional valid characters (such as `[A-Za-z0-9._%+-]`), we can specify that the match can ignore this case. This can be done with an additional parameter to the constructor of the `std::basic_regex` class. The available constants for this purpose are defined in the `regex_constants` namespace. The following slight change to `is_valid_email_format()` will make it ignore the case and allow emails with both lowercase and uppercase letters to correctly match the regular expression:

```
bool is_valid_email_format(std::string const & email)
{
  auto rx = std::regex{
    R"(^[A-Z0-9._%+-]+@[A-Z0-9.-]+\.[A-Z]{2,}$)"s,
    std::regex_constants::icase};

  return std::regex_match(email, rx);
}
```

This `is_valid_email_format()` function is pretty simple, and if the regular expression was provided as a parameter, along with the text to match, it could be used for matching anything. However, it would be nice to be able to handle not only multi-byte strings (`std::string`), but also wide strings (`std::wstring`), with a single function. This can be achieved by creating a function template where the character type is provided as a template parameter:

```
template <typename CharT>
```

```
using tstring = std::basic_string<CharT, std::char_traits<CharT>,
                                  std::allocator<CharT>>;

template <typename CharT>
bool is_valid_format(tstring<CharT> const & pattern,
                     tstring<CharT> const & text)
{
  auto rx = std::basic_regex<CharT>{
    pattern, std::regex_constants::icase };

  return std::regex_match(text, rx);
}
```

We start by creating an alias template for `std::basic_string` in order to simplify its use. The new `is_valid_format()` function is a function template very similar to our implementation of `is_valid_email()`. However, we now use `std::basic_regex<CharT>` instead of the typedef `std::regex`, which is `std::basic_regex<char>`, and the pattern is provided as the first argument. We now implement a new function called `is_valid_email_format_w()` for wide strings that relies on this function template. The function template, however, can be reused for implementing other validations, such as if a license plate has a particular format:

```
bool is_valid_email_format_w(std::wstring const & text)
{
  return is_valid_format(
    LR"(^[A-Z0-9._%+-]+@[A-Z0-9.-]+\.[A-Z]{2,}$)"s,
    text);
}

auto ltest2 = [](auto const & email)
{
  std::wcout << std::setw(30) << std::left
     << email << L" : "
     << (is_valid_email_format_w(email) ? L"valid" : L"invalid")
     << '\n';
};

ltest2(L"JOHN.DOE@DOMAIN.COM"s);        // valid
ltest2(L"JOHNDOE@DOMAIL.CO.UK"s);       // valid
ltest2(L"JOHNDOE@DOMAIL.INFO"s);        // valid
ltest2(L"J.O.H.N_D.O.E@DOMAIN.INFO"s); // valid
ltest2(L"ROOT@LOCALHOST"s);             // invalid
ltest2(L"john.doe@domain.com"s);        // valid
```

Of all the examples shown here, the only one that does not match is ROOT@LOCALHOST, as expected.

The std::regex_match() method has, in fact, several overloads, and some of them have a parameter that is a reference to an std::match_results object to store the result of the match. If there is no match, then std::match_results is empty and its size is 0. Otherwise, if there is a match, the std::match_results object is not empty and its size is 1, plus the number of matched subexpressions.

The following version of the function uses the mentioned overloads and returns the matched subexpressions in an std::smatch object. Note that the regular expression is changed as three caption groups are defined—one for the local part, one for the hostname part of the domain, and one for the DNS label. If the match is successful, then the std::smatch object will contain four submatch objects: the first to match the entire string, the second for the first capture group (the local part), the third for the second capture group (the hostname), and the fourth for the third and last capture group (the DNS label). The result is returned in a tuple, where the first item actually indicates success or failure:

```
std::tuple<bool, std::string, std::string, std::string>
is_valid_email_format_with_result(std::string const & email)
{
  auto rx = std::regex{
    R"(^([A-Z0-9._%+-]+)@([A-Z0-9.-]+)\.([A-Z]{2,})$)"s,
    std::regex_constants::icase };
  auto result = std::smatch{};
  auto success = std::regex_match(email, result, rx);

  return std::make_tuple(
    success,
    success ? result[1].str() : ""s,
    success ? result[2].str() : ""s,
    success ? result[3].str() : ""s);
}
```

Following the preceding code, we use C++17 structured bindings to unpack the content of the tuple into named variables:

```
auto ltest3 = [](std::string const & email)
{
  auto [valid, localpart, hostname, dnslabel] =
    is_valid_email_format_with_result(email);

  std::cout << std::setw(30) << std::left
```

```
        << email << " : "
        << std::setw(10) << (valid ? "valid" : "invalid")
        << "local=" << localpart
        << ";domain=" << hostname
        << ";dns=" << dnslabel
        << '\n';
};

ltest3("JOHN.DOE@DOMAIN.COM"s);
ltest3("JOHNDOE@DOMAIL.CO.UK"s);
ltest3("JOHNDOE@DOMAIL.INFO"s);
ltest3("J.O.H.N_D.O.E@DOMAIN.INFO"s);
ltest3("ROOT@LOCALHOST"s);
ltest3("john.doe@domain.com"s);
```

The output of the program will be as follows:

```
Microsoft Visual Studio Debug Console
JOHN.DOE@DOMAIN.COM              : valid
   local=JOHN.DOE;domain=DOMAIN;dns=COM
JOHNDOE@DOMAIL.CO.UK             : valid
   local=JOHNDOE;domain=DOMAIL.CO;dns=UK
JOHNDOE@DOMAIL.INFO              : valid
   local=JOHNDOE;domain=DOMAIL;dns=INFO
J.O.H.N_D.O.E@DOMAIN.INFO        : valid
   local=J.O.H.N_D.O.E;domain=DOMAIN;dns=INFO
ROOT@LOCALHOST                   : invalid
   local=;domain=;dns=
john.doe@domain.com              : valid
   local=john.doe;domain=domain;dns=com
```

Figure 2.3: Output of tests

There's more...

There are multiple versions of regular expressions, and the C++ standard library supports six of them: ECMAScript, basic POSIX, extended POSIX, awk, grep, and egrep (grep with the option `-E`). The default grammar used is ECMAScript, and in order to use another, you have to explicitly specify the grammar when defining the regular expression. In addition to specifying the grammar, you can also specify parsing options, such as matching by ignoring the case.

The standard library provides more classes and algorithms than what we have seen so far. The main classes available in the library are as follows (all of them are class templates and, for convenience, typedefs are provided for different character types):

- The class template `std::basic_regex` defines the regular expression object:

```
typedef basic_regex<char>    regex;
typedef basic_regex<wchar_t> wregex;
```

- The class template `std::sub_match` represents a sequence of characters that matches a capture group; this class is actually derived from `std::pair`, and its `first` and `second` members represent iterators to the first and the one-past-end characters in the match sequence. If there is no match sequence, the two iterators are equal:

```
typedef sub_match<const char *>               csub_match;
typedef sub_match<const wchar_t *>            wcsub_match;
typedef sub_match<string::const_iterator>     ssub_match;
typedef sub_match<wstring::const_iterator>    wssub_match;
```

- The class template `std::match_results` is a collection of matches; the first element is always a full match in the target, while the other elements are matches of subexpressions:

```
typedef match_results<const char *>              cmatch;
typedef match_results<const wchar_t *>           wcmatch;
typedef match_results<string::const_iterator>    smatch;
typedef match_results<wstring::const_iterator>   wsmatch;
```

The algorithms available in the regular expressions standard library are as follows:

- **`std::regex_match()`**: This tries to match a regular expression (represented by an `std::basic_regex` instance) to an entire string.
- **`std::regex_search()`**: This tries to match a regular expression (represented by an `std::basic_regex` instance) to a part of a string (including the entire string).
- **`std::regex_replace()`**: This replaces matches from a regular expression according to a specified format.

The iterators available in the regular expressions standard library are as follows:

- `std::regex_interator`: A constant forward iterator used to iterate through the occurrences of a pattern in a string. It has a pointer to an `std::basic_regex` that must live until the iterator is destroyed. Upon creation and when incremented, the iterator calls `std::regex_search()` and stores a copy of the `std::match_results` object returned by the algorithm.

- `std::regex_token_iterator`: A constant forward iterator used to iterate through the submatches of every match of a regular expression in a string. Internally, it uses a `std::regex_iterator` to step through the submatches. Since it stores a pointer to an `std::basic_regex` instance, the regular expression object must live until the iterator is destroyed.

It should be mentioned that the standard regex library has poorer performance compared to other implementations (such as Boost.Regex) and does not support Unicode. Moreover, it could be argued that the API itself is cumbersome to use.

See also

- *Parsing the content of a string using regular expressions* to learn how to perform multiple matches of a pattern in a text
- *Replacing the content of a string using regular expressions* to see how to perform text replacements with the help of regular expressions
- *Using structured bindings to handle multi-return values* in *Chapter 1, Learning Modern Core Language Features*, to learn how to bind variables to subobjects or elements from the initializing expressions

Parsing the content of a string using regular expressions

In the previous recipe, we looked at how to use `std::regex_match()` to verify that the content of a string matches a particular format. The library provides another algorithm called `std::regex_search()` that matches a regular expression against any part of a string, and not only the entire string, as `regex_match()` does. This function, however, does not allow us to search through all the occurrences of a regular expression in an input string. For this purpose, we need to use one of the iterator classes available in the library.

In this recipe, you will learn how to parse the content of a string using regular expressions. For this purpose, we will consider the problem of parsing a text file containing name-value pairs. Each such pair is defined on a different line and has the format `name = value`, but lines starting with a # represent comments and must be ignored. The following is an example:

```
#remove # to uncomment a line
timeout=120
server = 127.0.0.1

#retrycount=3
```

Before looking at the implementation details, let's consider some prerequisites.

Getting ready

For general information about regular expression support in C++11, refer to the *Verifying the format of a string using regular expressions* recipe, earlier in this chapter. Basic knowledge of regular expressions is required to proceed with this recipe.

In the following examples, `text` is a variable that's defined as follows:

```
auto text {
  R"(
    #remove # to uncomment a line
    timeout=120
    server = 127.0.0.1

    #retrycount=3
  )"s};
```

The sole purpose of this is to simplify our snippets, although in a real-world example, you will probably be reading the text from a file or other source.

How to do it...

In order to search for occurrences of a regular expression through a string, you should do the following:

1. Include the headers `<regex>` and `<string>` and the namespace `std::string_literals` for C++14 standard user-defined literals for strings:

   ```
   #include <regex>
   #include <string>
   using namespace std::string_literals;
   ```

2. Use raw string literals to specify a regular expression in order to avoid escaping backslashes (which can occur frequently). The following regular expression validates the file format proposed earlier:

   ```
   auto pattern {R"(^(?!#)(\w+)\s*=\s*([\w\d]+[\w\d._,\-:]*)$)"s};
   ```

3. Create an `std::regex`/`std::wregex` object (depending on the character set that is used) to encapsulate the regular expression:

   ```
   auto rx = std::regex{pattern};
   ```

4. To search for the first occurrence of a regular expression in a given text, use the general-purpose algorithm `std::regex_search()` (example 1):

```
auto match = std::smatch{};
if (std::regex_search(text, match, rx))
{
  std::cout << match[1] << '=' << match[2] << '\n';
}
```

5. To find all the occurrences of a regular expression in a given text, use the iterator `std::regex_iterator` (example 2):

```
auto end = std::sregex_iterator{};
for (auto it=std::sregex_iterator{ std::begin(text),
                                   std::end(text), rx };
     it != end; ++it)
{
  std::cout << '\'' << (*it)[1] << "'='"
            << (*it)[2] << '\'' << '\n';
}
```

6. To iterate through all the subexpressions of a match, use the iterator `std::regex_token_iterator` (example 3):

```
auto end = std::sregex_token_iterator{};
for (auto it = std::sregex_token_iterator{
                 std::begin(text), std::end(text), rx };
     it != end; ++it)
{
  std::cout << *it << '\n';
}
```

How it works...

A simple regular expression that can parse the input file shown earlier may look like this:

```
^(?!#)(\w+)\s*=\s*([\w\d]+[\w\d._,\-:]*)$
```

This regular expression is supposed to ignore all lines that start with a `#`; for those that do not start with `#`, match a name followed by the equals sign and then a value that can be composed of alphanumeric characters and several other characters (underscore, dot, comma, and so on). The exact meaning of this regular expression is explained as follows:

Part	Description
`^`	Start of line.
`(?!#)`	A negative lookahead that makes sure that it is not possible to match the # character.
`(\w)+`	A capturing group representing an identifier of at least a one-word character.
`\s*`	Any whitespaces.
`=`	Equals sign.
`\s*`	Any whitespaces.
`([\w\d]+[\w\d._,\-:]*)`	A capturing group representing a value that starts with an alphanumeric character, but can also contain a dot, comma, backslash, hyphen, colon, or an underscore.
`$`	End of line.

We can use `std::regex_search()` to search for a match anywhere in the input text. This algorithm has several overloads, but in general, they work in the same way. You must specify the range of characters to work through, an output `std::match_results` object that will contain the result of the match, and an `std::basic_regex` object representing the regular expression and matching flags (which define the way the search is done). The function returns `true` if a match was found or `false` otherwise.

In the first example from the previous section (see the fourth list item), `match` is an instance of `std::smatch` that is a typedef of `std::match_results` with `string::const_iterator` as the template type. If a match was found, this object will contain the matching information in a sequence of values for all matched subexpressions. The submatch at index 0 is always the entire match. The submatch at index 1 is the first subexpression that was matched, the submatch at index 2 is the second subexpression that was matched, and so on. Since we have two capturing groups (which are subexpressions) in our regular expression, the `std::match_results` will have three submatches in the event of success. The identifier representing the name is at index 1, and the value after the equals sign is at index 2. Therefore, this code only prints the following:

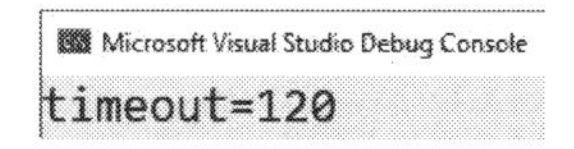

Figure 2.4: Output of first example

The `std::regex_search()` algorithm is not able to iterate through all the possible matches in a piece of text. To do that, we need to use an iterator. `std::regex_iterator` is intended for this purpose. It allows not only iterating through all the matches, but also accessing all the submatches of a match.

The iterator actually calls `std::regex_search()` upon construction and on each increment, and it remembers the resulting `std::match_results` from the call. The default constructor creates an iterator that represents the end of the sequence and can be used to test when the loop through the matches should stop.

In the second example from the previous section (see the fifth list item), we first create an end-of-sequence iterator, and then we start iterating through all the possible matches. When constructed, it will call `std::regex_match()`, and if a match is found, we can access its results through the current iterator. This will continue until no match is found (the end of the sequence). This code will print the following output:

```
Microsoft Visual Studio Debug Console
'timeout'='120'
'server'='127.0.0.1'
```

Figure 2.5: Output of second example

An alternative to `std::regex_iterator` is `std::regex_token_iterator`. This works similar to the way `std::regex_iterator` works and, in fact, it contains such an iterator internally, except that it enables us to access a particular subexpression from a match. This is shown in the third example in the *How to do it...* section (see the sixth list item). We start by creating an end-of-sequence iterator and then loop through the matches until the end-of-sequence is reached. In the constructor we used, we did not specify the index of the subexpression to access through the iterator; therefore, the default value of 0 is used. This means this program will print all the matches:

```
Microsoft Visual Studio Debug Console
timeout=120
server = 127.0.0.1
```

Figure 2.6: Output of third example

If we wanted to access only the first subexpression (this means the names in our case), all we had to do was specify the index of the subexpression in the constructor of the token iterator, as shown here:

```
auto end = std::sregex_token_iterator{};
for (auto it = std::sregex_token_iterator{ std::begin(text),
               std::end(text), rx, 1 };
     it != end; ++it)
{
  std::cout << *it << '\n';
}
```

This time, the output that we get contains only the names. This is shown in the following image:

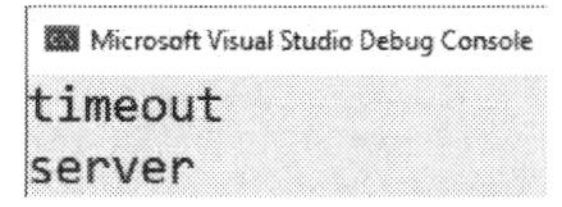

Figure 2.7: Output containing only the names

An interesting thing about the token iterator is that it can return the unmatched parts of the string if the index of the subexpressions is `-1`, in which case it returns an `std::match_results` object that corresponds to the sequence of characters between the last match and the end of the sequence:

```
auto end = std::sregex_token_iterator{};
for (auto it = std::sregex_token_iterator{ std::begin(text),
               std::end(text), rx, -1 };
     it != end; ++it)
{
  std::cout << *it << '\n';
}
```

This program will output the following:

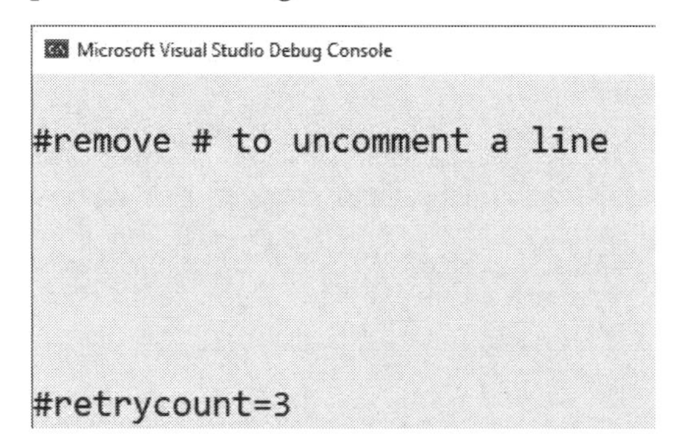

Figure 2.8: Output including empty lines

Please note that the empty lines in the output correspond to empty tokens.

See also

- *Verifying the format of a string using regular expressions* to familiarize yourself with the C++ library support for working with regular expressions
- *Replacing the content of a string using regular expressions* to learn how to perform multiple matches of a pattern in a text

Replacing the content of a string using regular expressions

In the previous two recipes, we looked at how to match a regular expression on a string or a part of a string and iterate through matches and submatches. The regular expression library also supports text replacement based on regular expressions. In this recipe, we will learn how to use `std::regex_replace()` to perform such text transformations.

Getting ready

For general information about regular expressions support in C++11, refer to the *Verifying the format of a string using regular expressions* recipe, earlier in this chapter.

How to do it...

In order to perform text transformations using regular expressions, you should perform the following:

- Include `<regex>` and `<string>` and the namespace `std::string_literals` for C++14 standard user-defined literals for strings:

  ```
  #include <regex>
  #include <string>
  using namespace std::string_literals;
  ```

- Use the `std::regex_replace()` algorithm with a replacement string as the third argument. Consider this example: replace all words composed of exactly three characters that are either `a`, `b`, or `c` with three hyphens:

  ```
  auto text{"abc aa bca ca bbbb"s};
  auto rx = std::regex{ R"(\b[a|b|c]{3}\b)"s };
  auto newtext = std::regex_replace(text, rx, "---"s);
  ```

- Use the `std::regex_replace()` algorithm with match identifiers prefixed with a `$` for the third argument. For example, replace names in the format "lastname, firstname" with names in the format "firstname lastname", as follows:

  ```
  auto text{ "bancila, marius"s };
  auto rx = std::regex{ R"((\w+),\s*(\w+))"s };
  auto newtext = std::regex_replace(text, rx, "$2 $1"s);
  ```

How it works...

The `std::regex_replace()` algorithm has several overloads with different types of parameters, but the meaning of the parameters is as follows:

- The input string on which the replacement is performed.
- An `std::basic_regex` object that encapsulates the regular expression used to identify the parts of the strings to be replaced.
- The string format used for replacement.
- Optional matching flags.

The return value is, depending on the overload used, either a string or a copy of the output iterator provided as an argument. The string format used for replacement can either be a simple string or a match identifier, indicated with a `$` prefix:

- `$&` indicates the entire match.
- `$1`, `$2`, `$3`, and so on indicate the first, second, and third submatches, and so on.
- `` $` `` indicates the part of the string before the first match.
- `$'` indicates the part of the string after the last match.

In the first example shown in the *How to do it...* section, the initial text contains two words made of exactly three `a`, `b`, and `c` characters, `abc` and `bca`. The regular expression indicates an expression of exactly three characters between word boundaries. This means a subtext, such as `bbbb`, will not match the expression. The result of the replacement is that the string text will be `--- aa --- ca bbbb`.

Additional flags for the match can be specified for the `std::regex_replace()` algorithm. By default, the matching flag is `std::regex_constants::match_default`, which basically specifies ECMAScript as the grammar used for constructing the regular expression. If we want, for instance, to replace only the first occurrence, then we can specify `std::regex_constants::format_first_only`. In the following example, the result is `--- aa bca ca bbbb` as the replacement stops after the first match is found:

```
auto text{ "abc aa bca ca bbbb"s };
auto rx = std::regex{ R"(\b[a|b|c]{3}\b)"s };
auto newtext = std::regex_replace(text, rx, "---"s,
                   std::regex_constants::format_first_only);
```

The replacement string, however, can contain special indicators for the whole match, a particular submatch, or the parts that were not matched, as explained earlier. In the second example shown in the *How to do it...* section, the regular expression identifies a word of at least one character, followed by a comma and possible white spaces, and then another word of at least one character. The first word is supposed to be the last name, while the second word is supposed to be the first name. The replacement string is in the `$2 $1` format. This is an instruction that's used to replace the matched expression (in this example, the entire original string) with another string formed of the second submatch, followed by a space and then the first submatch.

In this case, the entire string was a match. In the following example, there will be multiple matches inside the string, and they will all be replaced with the indicated string. In this example, we are replacing the indefinite article *a* when preceding a word that starts with a vowel (this, of course, does not cover words that start with a vowel sound) with the indefinite article *an*:

```
auto text{"this is a example with a error"s};
auto rx = std::regex{R"(\ba ((a|e|i|u|o)\w+))"s};
auto newtext = std::regex_replace(text, rx, "an $1");
```

The regular expression identifies the letter *a* as a single word (`\b` indicates a word boundary, so `\ba` means a word with a single letter, *a*), followed by a space and a word of at least two characters starting with a vowel. When such a match is identified, it is replaced with a string formed of the fixed string *an*, followed by a space and the first subexpression of the match, which is the word itself. In this example, the `newtext` string will be `this is an example with an error`.

Apart from the identifiers of the subexpressions (`$1`, `$2`, and so on), there are other identifiers for the entire match (`$&`), the part of the string before the first match (`` $` ``), and the part of the string after the last match (`$'`). In the last example, we change the format of a date from `dd.mm.yyyy` to `yyyy.mm.dd`, but also show the matched parts:

```
auto text{"today is 1.06.2016!!"s};
auto rx =
   std::regex{R"((\d{1,2})(\.|-|/)(\d{1,2})(\.|-|/)(\d{4}))"s};
// today is 2016.06.1!!
auto newtext1 = std::regex_replace(text, rx, R"($5$4$3$2$1)");
// today is [today is ][1.06.2016][!!]!!
auto newtext2 = std::regex_replace(text, rx, R"([$`][$&][$'])");
```

The regular expression matches a one- or two-digit number followed by a dot, hyphen, or slash; followed by another one- or two-digit number; then a dot, hyphen, or slash; and lastly a four-digit number.

For `newtext1`, the replacement string is `$5$4$3$2$1`; this means year, followed by the second separator, then month, the first separator, and finally day. Therefore, for the input string `today is 1.06.2016!`, the result is `today is 2016.06.1!!`.

For `newtext2`, the replacement string is `` [$`][$&][$'] ``; this means the part before the first match, followed by the entire match, and finally the part after the last match, are in square brackets. However, the result is not `[!!][1.06.2016][today is ]` as you perhaps might expect at first glance, but `today is [today is ][1.06.2016][!!]!!`. The reason for this is that what is replaced is the matched expression, and, in this case, that is only the date (`1.06.2016`). This substring is replaced with another string formed of all the parts of the initial string.

See also

- *Verifying the format of a string using regular expressions* to familiarize yourself with the C++ library support for working with regular expressions
- *Parsing the content of a string using regular expressions* to learn how to perform multiple matches of a pattern in a text

Using string_view instead of constant string references

When working with strings, temporary objects are created all the time, even if you might not be really aware of it. Many times, these temporary objects are irrelevant and only serve the purpose of copying data from one place to another (for example, from a function to its caller). This represents a performance issue because they require memory allocation and data copying, which should be avoided. For this purpose, the C++17 standard provides a new string class template called `std::basic_string_view` that represents a non-owning constant reference to a string (that is, a sequence of characters). In this recipe, you will learn when and how you should use this class.

Getting ready

The `string_view` class is available in the namespace `std` in the `string_view` header.

How to do it...

You should use `std::string_view` to pass a parameter to a function (or return a value from a function), instead of `std::string const &`, unless your code needs to call other functions that take `std::string` parameters (in which case, conversions would be necessary):

```
std::string_view get_filename(std::string_view str)
{
  auto const pos1 {str.find_last_of('')};
  auto const pos2 {str.find_last_of('.')};
  return str.substr(pos1 + 1, pos2 - pos1 - 1);
}

char const file1[] {R"(c:\test\example1.doc)"};
auto name1 = get_filename(file1);

std::string file2 {R"(c:\test\example2)"};
auto name2 = get_filename(file2);

auto name3 = get_filename(std::string_view{file1, 16});
```

How it works...

Before we look at how the new string type works, let's consider the following example of a function that is supposed to extract the name of a file without its extension. This is basically how you would write the function from the previous section before C++17:

```
std::string get_filename(std::string const & str)
{
  auto const pos1 {str.find_last_of('\\')};
  auto const pos2 {str.find_last_of('.')};
  return str.substr(pos1 + 1, pos2 - pos1 - 1);
}

auto name1 = get_filename(R"(c:\test\example1.doc)"); // example1
auto name2 = get_filename(R"(c:\test\example2)");     // example2
if(get_filename(R"(c:\test\_sample_.tmp)").front() == '_') {}
```

Note that in this example, the file separator is \ (backslash), as in Windows. For Linux-based systems, it has to be changed to / (slash).

The `get_filename()` function is relatively simple. It takes a constant reference to an `std::string` and identifies a substring bounded by the last file separator and the last dot, which basically represents a filename without an extension (and without folder names).

The problem with this code, however, is that it creates one, two, or possibly even more temporaries, depending on the compiler optimizations. The function parameter is a constant `std::string` reference, but the function is called with a string literal, which means `std::string` needs to be constructed from the literal. These temporaries need to allocate and copy data, which is both time- and resource-consuming. In the last example, all we want to do is check whether the first character of the filename is an underscore, but we create at least two temporary string objects for that purpose.

The `std::basic_string_view` class template is intended to solve this problem. This class template is very similar to `std::basic_string`, with the two having almost the same interface. The reason for this is that `std::basic_string_view` is intended to be used instead of a constant reference to an `std::basic_string` without further code changes. Just like with `std::basic_string`, there are specializations for all types of standard characters:

```
typedef basic_string_view<char>     string_view;
typedef basic_string_view<wchar_t>  wstring_view;
typedef basic_string_view<char16_t> u16string_view;
typedef basic_string_view<char32_t> u32string_view;
```

The `std::basic_string_view` class template defines a reference to a constant contiguous sequence of characters. As the name implies, it represents a view and cannot be used to modify the reference sequence of characters. An `std::basic_string_view` object has a relatively small size because all that it needs is a pointer to the first character in the sequence and the length. It can be constructed not only from an `std::basic_string` object but also from a pointer and a length, or from a null-terminated sequence of characters (in which case, it will require an initial traversal of the string in order to find the length). Therefore, the `std::basic_string_view` class template can also be used as a common interface for multiple types of strings (as long as data only needs to be read). On the other hand, converting from an `std::basic_string_view` to an `std::basic_string` is not possible.

You must explicitly construct an `std::basic_string` object from a `std::basic_string_view`, as shown in the following example:

```
std::string_view sv{ "demo" };
std::string s{ sv };
```

Passing `std::basic_string_view` to functions and returning `std::basic_string_view` still creates temporaries of this type, but these are small-sized objects on the stack (a pointer and a size could be 16 bytes for 64-bit platforms); therefore, they should incur fewer performance costs than allocating heap space and copying data.

Note that all major compilers provide an implementation of `std::basic_string`, which includes a small string optimization. Although the implementation details are different, they typically rely on having a statically allocated buffer of a number of characters (16 for VC++ and GCC 5 or newer) that does not involve heap operations, which are only required when the size of the string exceeds that number of characters.

In addition to the methods that are identical to those available in `std::basic_string`, the `std::basic_string_view` has two more:

- `remove_prefix()`: Shrinks the view by incrementing the start with *N* characters and decrementing the length with *N* characters.
- `remove_suffix()`: Shrinks the view by decrementing the length with *N* characters.

The two member functions are used in the following example to trim an `std::string_view` from spaces, both at the beginning and the end. The implementation of the function first looks for the first element that is not a space and then for the last element that is not a space. Then, it removes from the end everything after the last non-space character, and from the beginning everything until the first non-space character. The function returns the new view, trimmed at both ends:

```
std::string_view trim_view(std::string_view str)
{
  auto const pos1{ str.find_first_not_of(" ") };
  auto const pos2{ str.find_last_not_of(" ") };
  str.remove_suffix(str.length() - pos2 - 1);
  str.remove_prefix(pos1);

  return str;
}
```

```
auto sv1{ trim_view("sample") };
auto sv2{ trim_view("  sample") };
auto sv3{ trim_view("sample  ") };
auto sv4{ trim_view("  sample  ") };

std::string s1{ sv1 };
std::string s2{ sv2 };
std::string s3{ sv3 };
std::string s4{ sv4 };
```

When using `std::basic_string_view`, you must be aware of two things: you cannot change the underlying data referred to by a view and you must manage the lifetime of the data, as the view is a non-owning reference.

See also

- *Creating a library of string helpers* to see how to create useful text utilities that are not directly available in the standard library

Formatting text with std::format

The C++ language has two ways of formatting text: the `printf` family of functions and the I/O streams library. The `printf` functions are inherited from C and provide a separation of the formatting text and the arguments. The streams library provides safety and extensibility and is usually recommended over `printf` functions, but is, in general, slower. The C++20 standard proposes a new formatting library alternative for output formatting, which is similar in form to `printf` but safe and extensible and is intended to complement the existing streams library. In this recipe, we will learn how to use the new functionalities instead of the `printf` functions or the streams library.

Getting ready

The new formatting library is available in the header `<format>`. You must include this header for the following samples to work.

How to do it...

The `std::format()` function formats its arguments according to the provided formatting string. You can use it as follows:

- Provide empty replacement fields, represented by `{}`, in the format string for each argument:

  ```
  auto text = std::format("{} is {}", "John", 42);
  ```

- Specify the 0-based index of each argument in the argument list inside the replacement field, such as `{0}`, `{1}`, and so on. The order of the arguments is not important, but the index must be valid:

  ```
  auto text = std::format("{0} is {1}", "John", 42);
  ```

- Control the output text with format specifiers provided in the replacement field after a colon (`:`). For basic and string types, this is a standard format specification. For chrono types, this is a chrono format specification:

  ```
  auto text = std::format("{0} hex is {0:08X}", 42);

  auto now = std::chrono::system_clock::now();
  auto time = std::chrono::system_clock::to_time_t(now);
  auto text = std::format("Today is {:%Y-%m-%d}",
  *std::localtime(&time));
  ```

You can also write the arguments in an out format using an iterator with either `std::format_to()` or `std::format_to_n()`, as follows:

- Write to a buffer, such as an `std::string` or `std::vector<char>`, using `std::format_n()` and using the `std::back_inserter()` helper function:

  ```
  std::vector<char> buf;
  std::format_to(std::back_inserter(buf), "{} is {}", "John", 42);
  ```

- Use `std::formatted_size()` to retrieve the number of characters necessary to store the formatted representation of the arguments:

  ```
  auto size = std::formatted_size("{} is {}", "John", 42);
  std::vector<char> buf(size);
  std::format_to(buf.data(), "{} is {}", "John", 42);
  ```

- To limit the number of characters written to the output buffer, you can use `std::format_to_n()`, which is similar to `std::format_to()` but writes, at most, `n` characters:

```
char buf[100];
auto result = std::format_to_n(buf, sizeof(buf), "{} is {}",
"John", 42);
```

How it works...

The `std::format()` function has multiple overloads. You can specify the format string either as a string view or a wide string view, with the function returning either an `std::string` or an `std::wstring`. You can also specify, as the first argument, an `std::locale`, which is used for locale-specific formatting. The function overloads are all variadic function templates, which means you can specify any number of arguments after the format.

The format string consists of ordinary characters, replacement fields, and escape sequences. The escape sequences are `{{` and `}}` and are replaced with `{` and `}` in the output. A replacement field is provided within curly brackets `{}`. It can optionally contain a non-negative number, representing the 0-based index of the argument to be formatted, and a colon (`:`), followed by a format specifier. If the format specifier is invalid, an exception of the type `std::format_error` is thrown.

In a similar manner, `std::format_to()` has multiple overloads, just like `std::format()`. The difference between these two is that `std::format_to()` always takes an iterator to the output buffer as the first argument and returns an iterator past the end of the output range (and not a string as `std::format()` does). On the other hand, `std::format_to_n()` has one more parameter than `std::format_to()`. Its second parameter is a number representing the maximum number of characters to be written to the buffer.

The following listing shows the signature of the simplest overload of each of these three function templates:

```
template<class... Args>
std::string format(std::string_view fmt, const Args&... args);

template<class OutputIt, class... Args>
OutputIt format_to(OutputIt out,
```

```
                   std::string_view fmt, const Args&... args);

template<class OutputIt, class... Args>
std::format_to_n_result<OutputIt>
format_to_n(OutputIt out, std::iter_difference_t<OutputIt> n,
            std::string_view fmt, const Args&... args);
```

When you provide the format string, you can supply argument identifiers (their 0-based index) or omit them. However, it is illegal to use both. If the indexes are omitted in the replacement fields, the arguments are processed in the provided order, and the number of replacement fields must not be greater than the number of supplied arguments. If indexes are provided, they must be valid for the format string to be valid.

When a format specification is used, then:

- For basic types and string types, it is considered to be a standard format specification.
- For chrono types, it is considered to be a chrono format specification.
- For user-defined types, it is defined by a user-defined specialization of the `std::formatter` class for the desired type.

The standard format specification is based on the format specification in Python and has the following syntax:

```
fill-and-align(optional) sign(optional) #(optional) 0(optional)
width(optional) precision(optional) L(optional) type(optional)
```

These syntax parts are briefly described here.

`fill-and-align` is an optional fill character, followed by one of the align options:

- <: Forces the field to be left-aligned with the available space.
- >: Forces the field to be right-aligned with the available space.
- ^: Forces the field to be centered with the available space. To do so, it will insert n/2 characters to the left and n/2 characters to the right:

```
auto t1 = std::format("{:5}", 42);     // "   42"
auto t2 = std::format("{:5}", 'x');    // "x    "
auto t3 = std::format("{:*<5}", 'x'); // "x****"
auto t4 = std::format("{:*>5}", 'x'); // "****x"
auto t5 = std::format("{:*^5}", 'x'); // "**x**"
auto t6 = std::format("{:5}", true);  // "true "
```

`sign`, `#`, and `0` are only valid when a number (either an integer or a floating-point) is used. The sign can be one of:

- +: Specifies that the sign must be used for both negative and positive numbers.
- -: Specifies that the sign must be used only for negative numbers (which is the implicit behavior).
- A space: Specifies that the sign must be used for negative numbers and that a leading space must be used for non-negative numbers:

```
auto t7 = std::format("{0:},{0:+},{0:-},{0: }", 42);
// "42,+42,42, 42"
auto t8 = std::format("{0:},{0:+},{0:-},{0: }", -42);
// "-42,-42,-42,-42"
```

The symbol `#` causes the alternate form to be used. This can be one of the following:

- For integral types, when binary, octal, or hexadecimal representation is specified, the alternate form adds the prefix `0b`, `0`, or `0x` to the output.
- For floating-point types, the alternate form causes a decimal-point character to always be present in the formatted value, even if no digits follow it. In addition, when `g` or `G` are used, the trailing zeros are not removed from the output.

The digit `0` specifies that leading zeros should be outputted to the field width, except when the value of a floating-point type is infinity or `NaN`. When present alongside an align option, the specifier `0` is ignored:

```
auto t9  = std::format("{:+05d}", 42); // "+0042"
auto t10 = std::format("{:#05x}", 42); // "0x02a"
auto t11 = std::format("{:<05}", -42); // "-42  "
```

`width` specifies the minimum field width and can be either a positive decimal number or a nested replacement field. The `precision` field indicates the precision for floating-point types or, for string types, how many characters will be used from the string. It is specified with a dot (`.`), followed by a non-negative decimal number or a nested replacement field.

Locale-specific formatting is specified with the uppercase `L` and causes the locale-specific form to be used. This option is only available for arithmetic types.

The optional `type` determines how the data will be presented in the output. The available string presentation types are shown in the following table:

Type	Presentation type	Description
Strings	none, `s`	Copies the string to the output.
Integral types	`B`	Binary format with 0b as a prefix.
	`B`	Binary format with 0B as a prefix.
	`C`	Character format. Copies the value to the output as it was a character type.
	none or `d`	Decimal format.
	`O`	Octal format with 0 as a prefix (unless the value is 0).
	`X`	Hexadecimal format with 0x as a prefix.
	`X`	Hexadecimal format with 0X as a prefix.
`char` and `wchar_t`	none or `c`	Copies the character to the output.
	`b, B, c, d, o, x, X`	Integer presentation types.
`bool`	none or `s`	Copies true or false as a textual representation (or their local-specific form) to the output.
	`b, B, c, d, o, x, X`	Integer presentation types.
Floating-point	`A`	Hexadecimal representation. Same as if calling `std::to_chars(first, last, value, std::chars_format::hex, precision)` or `std::to_chars(first, last, value, std::chars_format::hex)`, depending on whether precision is specified or not.
	`A`	Same as `a` except that it uses uppercase letters for digits above 9 and uses P to indicate the exponent.
	`E`	Scientific representation. Produces the output as if calling `std::to_chars(first, last, value, std::chars_format::scientific, precision)`.
	`E`	Similar to `e` except that it uses `E` to indicate the exponent.
	`f, F`	Fixed representation. Produces the output as if by calling `std::to_chars(first, last, value, std::chars_format::fixed, precision)`. When no precision is specified, the default is 6.
	`G`	General floating-point representation. Produces the output as if by calling `std::to_chars(first, last, value, std::chars_format::general, precision)`. When no precision is specified, the default is 6.

	G	Same as g except that it uses E to indicate the exponent.
Pointer	none or p	Pointer representation. Produces the output as if by calling `std::to_chars(first, last, reinterpret_cast<std::uintptr_t>(value), 16)` with the prefix `0x` added to the output. This is available only when `std::uintptr_t` is defined; otherwise, the output is implementation-defined.

The chrono format specification has the following form:

```
fill-and-align(optional) width(optional) precision(optional) chrono-spec(optional)
```

The `fill-and-align`, `width`, and `precision` fields have the same meaning as in the standard format specification, described previously. The precision is only valid for `std::chrono::duration` types when the representation type is a floating-point type. Using it in other cases throws an `std::format_error` exception.

The chrono specification can be empty, in which case the argument is formatted as if by streaming it to an `std::stringstream` and copying the result string. Alternatively, it can consist of a series of conversion specifiers and ordinary characters. Some of these format specifiers are presented in the following table:

Conversion specifier	**Description**
`%%`	Writes a literal `%` character.
`%n`	Writes a newline character.
`%t`	Writes a horizontal tab character.
`%Y`	Writes the year as a decimal number. If the result is less than four digits, it is left-padded with `0` to four digits.
`%m`	Writes the month as a decimal number (January is `01`). If the result is a single digit, it is prefixed with `0`.
`%d`	Writes the day of month as a decimal number. If the result is a single decimal digit, it is prefixed with `0`.
`%w`	Writes the weekday as a decimal number (`0-6`), where Sunday is `0`.
`%D`	Equivalent to `%m/%d/%y`.
`%F`	Equivalent to `%Y-%m-%d`.
`%H`	Writes the hour (24-hour clock) as a decimal number. If the result is a single digit, it is prefixed with `0`.
`%I`	Writes the hour (12-hour clock) as a decimal number. If the result is a single digit, it is prefixed with `0`.

`%M`	Writes the minute as a decimal number. If the result is a single digit, it is prefixed with `0`.
`%S`	Writes the second as a decimal number. If the number of seconds is less than 10, the result is prefixed with `0`.
`%R`	Equivalent to `%H:%M`.
`%T`	Equivalent to `%H:%M:%S`.
`%X`	Writes the locale's time representation.

The complete list of format specifiers for the chrono library can be consulted at `https://en.cppreference.com/w/cpp/chrono/system_clock/formatter`.

See also

- *Using std::format with user-defined types* to learn how to create custom formatting specialization for user-defined types
- *Converting between numeric and string types* to learn how to convert between numbers and strings

Using std::format with user-defined types

The C++20 formatting library is a modern alternative to using `printf`-like functions or the I/O streams library, which it actually complements. Although the standard provides default formatting for basic types, such as integral and floating-point types, `bool`, character types, strings, and chrono types, the user can create custom specialization for user-defined types. In this recipe, we will learn how to do that.

Getting ready

You should read the previous recipe, *Formatting text with std::format*, to familiarize yourself with the formatting library.

In the examples that we'll be showing here, we will use the following class:

```
struct employee
{
   int         id;
   std::string firstName;
   std::string lastName;
};
```

In the next section, we'll introduce the necessary steps to implement to enable text formatting using `std::format()` for user-defined types.

How to do it...

To enable formatting using the new formatting library for user-defined types, you must do the following:

- Define a specialization of the `std::formatter<T, CharT>` class in the `std` namespace.
- Implement the `parse()` method to parse the portion of the format string corresponding to the current argument. If the class inherits from another formatter, then this method can be omitted.
- Implement the `format()` method to format the argument and write the output via `format_context`.

For the `employee` class listed here, a formatter that formats `employee` to the form `[42] John Doe` (that is `[id] firstName lastName`) can be implemented as follows:

```
template <>
struct std::formatter<employee>
{
   constexpr auto parse(format_parse_context& ctx)
   {
      return ctx.begin();
   }

   auto format(employee const & value, format_context& ctx) {
      return std::format_to(ctx.out(),
                            "[{}] {} {}",
                            e.id, e.firstName, e.lastName);
   }
};
```

How it works...

The formatting library uses the `std::formatter<T, CharT>` class template to define formatting rules for a given type. Built-in types, string types, and chrono types have formatters provided by the library. These are implemented as specializations of the `std::formatter<T, CharT>` class template.

This class has two methods:

- `parse()`, which takes a single argument of the type `std::basic_format_parse_context<CharT>` and parses the format's specification for the type `T`, provided by the parse context. The result of the parsing is supposed to be stored in member fields of the class. If the parsing succeeds, this function should return a value of the type `std::basic_format_parse_context<CharT>::iterator`, which represents the end of the format specification. If the parsing fails, the function should throw an exception of the type `std::format_error` to provide details about the error.
- `format()`, which takes two arguments, the first being the object of the type `T` to format and the second being a formatting context object of the type `std::basic_format_context<OutputIt, CharT>`. This function should write the output to `ctx.out()` according to the desired specifiers (which could be something implicit or the result of parsing the format specification). The function must return a value of the type `std::basic_format_context<OutputIt, CharT>::iterator`, representing the end of the output.

In the implementation shown here, the `parse()` function does not do anything other than return an iterator representing the beginning of the format specification. The formatting is always done by printing the employee identifier between square brackets, followed by the first name and the last name, such as in `[42] John Doe`. An attempt to use a format specifier would result in a runtime exception:

```
employee e{ 42, "John", "Doe" };
auto s1 = std::format("{}", e);   // [42] John Doe
auto s2 = std::format("{:L}", e); // error
```

If you want your user-defined types to support format specifiers, then you must properly implement the `parse()` method. To show how this can be done, we will support the `L` specifier for the `employee` class. When this specifier is used, the `employee` is formatted with the identifier in square brackets, followed by the last name, a comma, and then the first name, such as in `[42] Doe, John`:

```
template<>
struct std::formatter<employee>
{
   bool lexicographic_order = false;

   template <typename ParseContext>
   constexpr auto parse(ParseContext& ctx)
   {
      auto iter = ctx.begin();
```

```
        auto get_char = [&]() { return iter != ctx.end() ? *iter : 0; };

        if (get_char() == ':') ++iter;
        char c = get_char();

        switch (c)
        {
        case '}': return ++iter;
        case 'L': lexicographic_order = true; return ++iter;
        case '{': return ++iter;
        default: throw std::format_error("invalid format");
        }
    }

    template <typename FormatContext>
    auto format(employee const& e, FormatContext& ctx)
    {
        if(lexicographic_order)
            return std::format_to(ctx.out(), "[{}] {}, {}",
                                  e.id, e.lastName, e.firstName);

        return std::format_to(ctx.out(), "[{}] {} {}",
                              e.id, e.firstName, e.lastName);
    }
};
```

With this defined, the preceding sample code would work. However, using other format specifiers, such as `A`, for example, would still throw an exception:

```
auto s1 = std::format("{}", e);    // [42] John Doe
auto s2 = std::format("{:L}", e); // [42] Doe, John
auto s3 = std::format("{:A}", e); // error (invalid format)
```

If you do not need to parse the format specifier in order to support various options, you could entirely omit the `parse()` method. However, in order to do so, your `std::formatter` specialization must derive from another `std::formatter` class. An implementation is shown here:

```
template<>
struct fmt::formatter<employee> : fmt::formatter<char const*>
{
    template <typename FormatContext>
```

```
    auto format(employee const& e, FormatContext& ctx)
    {
       return std::format_to(ctx.out(), "[{}] {} {}",
                             e.id, e.firstName, e.lastName);
    }
};
```

This specialization for the `employee` class is equivalent to the first implementation shown earlier in the *How to do it...* section.

See also

- *Formatting text with std::format* to get a good introduction to the new C++20 text formatting library

3

Exploring Functions

Functions are a fundamental concept in programming; regardless of the topic we discuss, we end up writing functions. Trying to cover functions in a single chapter is not only hard but also not very rational. Being a fundamental element of the language, functions are encountered in every recipe of this book. This chapter, however, covers modern language features related to functions and callable objects, with a focus on lambda expressions, concepts from functional languages such as higher-order functions, and type-safe functions with a variable number of arguments.

The recipes included in this chapter are as follows:

- Defaulted and deleted functions
- Using lambdas with standard algorithms
- Using generic and template lambdas
- Writing a recursive lambda
- Writing a function template with a variable number of arguments
- Using fold expressions to simplify variadic function templates
- Implementing the higher-order functions `map` and `fold`
- Composing functions into a higher-order function
- Uniformly invoking anything callable

We will start this chapter by learning about a feature that makes it easier for us to provide special class member functions or prevent any function (member or non-member) from being invoked.

Defaulted and deleted functions

In C++, classes have special members (constructors, destructors, and assignment operators) that may be either implemented by default by the compiler or supplied by the developer. However, the rules for what can be default implemented are a bit complicated and can lead to problems. On the other hand, developers sometimes want to prevent objects from being copied, moved, or constructed in a particular way. This is possible by implementing different tricks using these special members. The C++11 standard has simplified many of these by allowing functions to be deleted or defaulted in the manner we will see in the next section.

Getting started

For this recipe, you need to be familiar with the following concepts:

- Special member functions (default constructor, destructor, copy constructor, move constructor, copy assignment operator, move assignment operator)
- The copyable concept (a class features a copy constructor and copy assignment operator making it possible to create copies)
- The moveable concept (a class features a move constructor and a move assignment operator making it possible to move objects)

With this in mind, let's learn how to define default and deleted special functions.

How to do it...

Use the following syntax to specify how functions should be handled:

- To default a function, use `=default` instead of the function body. Only special class member functions that have defaults can be defaulted:

  ```
  struct foo
  {
    foo() = default;
  };
  ```

- To delete a function, use `=delete` instead of the function body. Any function, including non-member functions, can be deleted:

  ```
  struct foo
  {
    foo(foo const &) = delete;
  };
  ```

```
void func(int) = delete;
```

Use defaulted and deleted functions to achieve various design goals, such as the following examples:

- To implement a class that is not copyable, and implicitly not movable, declare the copy constructor and the copy assignment operator as deleted:

```
class foo_not_copyable
{
public:
  foo_not_copyable() = default;

  foo_not_copyable(foo_not_copyable const &) = delete;
  foo_not_copyable& operator=(foo_not_copyable const&) = delete;
};
```

- To implement a class that is not copyable, but is movable, declare the copy operations as deleted and explicitly implement the move operations (and provide any additional constructors that are needed):

```
class data_wrapper
{
  Data* data;
public:
  data_wrapper(Data* d = nullptr) : data(d) {}
  ~data_wrapper() { delete data; }

  data_wrapper(data_wrapper const&) = delete;
  data_wrapper& operator=(data_wrapper const &) = delete;

  data_wrapper(data_wrapper&& other) :data(std::move(other.
data))
  {
    other.data = nullptr;
  }

  data_wrapper& operator=(data_wrapper&& other)
  {
    if (this != std::addressof(other))
    {
      delete data;
      data = std::move(other.data);
      other.data = nullptr;
    }
```

```
        return *this;
    }
};
```

- To ensure a function is called only with objects of a specific type, and perhaps prevent type promotion, provide deleted overloads for the function (the following example with free functions can also be applied to any class member functions):

```
template <typename T>
void run(T val) = delete;

void run(long val) {} // can only be called with long integers
```

How it works...

A class has several special members that can be implemented, by default, by the compiler. These are the default constructor, copy constructor, move constructor, copy assignment, move assignment, and destructor (for a discussion on move semantics, refer to the *Implementing move semantics* recipe in *Chapter 9, Robustness and Performance*). If you don't implement them, then the compiler does it so that instances of a class can be created, moved, copied, and destructed. However, if you explicitly provide one or more of these special methods, then the compiler will not generate the others according to the following rules:

- If a user-defined constructor exists, the default constructor is not generated by default.
- If a user-defined virtual destructor exists, the default constructor is not generated by default.
- If a user-defined move constructor or move assignment operator exists, then the copy constructor and copy assignment operator are not generated by default.
- If a user-defined copy constructor, move constructor, copy assignment operator, move assignment operator, or destructor exists, then the move constructor and move assignment operator are not generated by default.
- If a user-defined copy constructor or destructor exists, then the copy assignment operator is generated by default.
- If a user-defined copy assignment operator or destructor exists, then the copy constructor is generated by default.

Note that the last two rules in the preceding list are deprecated rules and may no longer be supported by your compiler.

Sometimes, developers need to provide empty implementations of these special members or hide them in order to prevent the instances of the class from being constructed in a specific manner. A typical example is a class that is not supposed to be copyable. The classical pattern for this is to provide a default constructor and hide the copy constructor and copy assignment operators. While this works, the explicitly defined default constructor ensures the class is no longer considered trivial and, therefore, a POD type. The modern alternative to this is using a deleted function, as shown in the preceding section.

When the compiler encounters `=default` in the definition of a function, it will provide the default implementation. The rules for special member functions mentioned earlier still apply. Functions can be declared `=default` outside the body of a class if and only if they are inlined:

```
class foo
{
public:
  foo() = default;

  inline foo& operator=(foo const &);
};

inline foo& foo::operator=(foo const &) = default;
```

The defaulted implementations have several benefits, including the following:

- Can be more efficient than the explicit ones.
- Non-defaulted implementations, even if they are empty, are considered non-trivial, and that affects the semantics of the type, which becomes non-trivial (and, therefore, non-POD).
- Helps the user not write explicit default implementations. For instance, if a user-defined move constructor is present, then the copy constructor and the copy assignment operator are not provided by default by the compiler. However, you can still default explicitly and ask the compiler to provide them so that you don't have to do it manually.

When the compiler encounters the `=delete` in the definition of a function, it will prevent the calling of the function. However, the function is still considered during overload resolution, and only if the deleted function is the best match does the compiler generate an error. For example, by giving the previously defined overloads for the `run()` function, only calls with long integers are possible. Calls with arguments of any other type, including `int`, for which an automatic type promotion to `long` exists, will determine a deleted overload to be considered the best match and therefore the compiler will generate an error:

```
run(42);  // error, matches a deleted overload
run(42L); // OK, long integer arguments are allowed
```

Note that previously declared functions cannot be deleted as the `=delete` definition must be the first declaration in a translation unit:

```
void forward_declared_function();
// ...
void forward_declared_function() = delete; // error
```

The rule of thumb, also known as *The Rule of Five*, for class special member functions is that if you explicitly define any copy constructor, move constructor, copy assignment operator, move assignment operator, or destructor, then you must either explicitly define or default all of them.

The user-defined destructor, copy-constructor, and copy assignment operator are necessary because objects are constructed from copies in various situations (like passing parameters to functions). If they are not user-defined, they are provided by the compiler, but their default implementation may be wrong. If the class manages resources, then the default implementation does a shallow copy, meaning that it copies the value of the handle of the resource (such as a pointer to an object) and not the resource itself. In such cases, a user-defined implementation must do a deep copy that copies the resource, not the handle to it. The presence of the move constructor and move assignment operator are desirable in this case because they represent a performance improvement. Lacking these two is not an error but a missed optimization opportunity.

See also

- *Uniformly invoking anything callable* to learn how to use `std::invoke()` to invoke any callable object with the provided arguments

Using lambdas with standard algorithms

One of the most important modern features of C++ is lambda expressions, also referred to as lambda functions or simply lambdas. Lambda expressions enable us to define anonymous function objects that can capture variables in the scope and be invoked or passed as arguments to functions. Lambdas are useful for many purposes, and in this recipe, we will learn how to use them with standard algorithms.

Getting ready

In this recipe, we'll discuss standard algorithms that take an argument that's a function or predicate that's applied to the elements it iterates through. You need to know what unary and binary functions are and what predicates and comparison functions are. You also need to be familiar with function objects because lambda expressions are syntactic sugar for function objects.

How to do it...

You should prefer to use lambda expressions to pass callbacks to standard algorithms instead of functions or function objects:

- Define anonymous lambda expressions in the place of the call if you only need to use the lambda in a single place:

```
auto numbers =
  std::vector<int>{ 0, 2, -3, 5, -1, 6, 8, -4, 9 };
auto positives = std::count_if(
  std::begin(numbers), std::end(numbers),
  [](int const n) {return n > 0; });
```

- Define a named lambda, that is, one assigned to a variable (usually with the `auto` specifier for the type), if you need to call the lambda in multiple places:

```
auto ispositive = [](int const n) {return n > 0; };
auto positives = std::count_if(
  std::begin(numbers), std::end(numbers), ispositive);
```

- Use generic lambda expressions if you need lambdas that only differ in terms of their argument types (available since C++14):

```
auto positives = std::count_if(
  std::begin(numbers), std::end(numbers),
  [](auto const n) {return n > 0; });
```

How it works...

The non-generic lambda expression shown in the second bullet takes a constant integer and returns `true` if it is greater than `0`, or `false` otherwise. The compiler defines an unnamed function object with the call operator, which has the signature of the lambda expression:

```
struct __lambda_name__
{
  bool operator()(int const n) const { return n > 0; }
};
```

The way the unnamed function object is defined by the compiler depends on the way we define the lambda expression that can capture variables, use the `mutable` specifier or exception specifications, or have a trailing return type. The `__lambda_name__` function object shown earlier is actually a simplification of what the compiler generates because it also defines a default copy and move constructor, a default destructor, and a deleted assignment operator.

It must be well understood that the lambda expression is actually a class. In order to call it, the compiler needs to instantiate an object of the class. The object instantiated from a lambda expression is called a *lambda closure*.

In the following example, we want to count the number of elements in a range that are greater than or equal to 5 and less than or equal to 10. The lambda expression, in this case, will look like this:

```
auto numbers = std::vector<int>{ 0, 2, -3, 5, -1, 6, 8, -4, 9 };
auto minimum { 5 };
auto maximum { 10 };
auto inrange = std::count_if(
    std::begin(numbers), std::end(numbers),
    [minimum, maximum](int const n) {
      return minimum <= n && n <= maximum;});
```

This lambda captures two variables, `minimum` and `maximum`, by copy (that is, value). The resulting unnamed function object created by the compiler looks very much like the one we defined earlier. With the default and deleted special members mentioned earlier, the class looks like this:

```
class __lambda_name_2__
{
  int minimum_;
  int maximum_;
public:
  explicit __lambda_name_2__(int const minimum, int const maximum) :
  minimum_( minimum), maximum_( maximum)
  {}

  __lambda_name_2__(const __lambda_name_2__&) = default;
  __lambda_name_2__(__lambda_name_2__&&) = default;
  __lambda_name_2__& operator=(const __lambda_name_2__&)
    = delete;
  ~__lambda_name_2__() = default;

  bool operator() (int const n) const
  {
    return minimum_ <= n && n <= maximum_;
  }
};
```

The lambda expression can capture variables by copy (or value) or by reference, and different combinations of the two are possible. However, it is not possible to capture a variable multiple times and it is only possible to have `&` or `=` at the beginning of the capture list.

A lambda can only capture variables from an enclosing function scope. It cannot capture variables with static storage duration (that is, variables declared in a namespace scope or with the `static` or `external` specifier).

The following table shows various combinations for lambda captures semantics:

Lambda	Description
`[](){}`	Does not capture anything.
`[&](){}`	Captures everything by reference.
`[=](){}`	Captures everything by copy. Implicit capturing of the pointer `this` is deprecated in C++20.
`[&x](){}`	Capture only `x` by reference.
`[x](){}`	Capture only `x` by copy.
`[&x...](){}`	Capture pack extension `x` by reference.
`[x...](){}`	Capture pack extension `x` by copy.
`[&, x](){}`	Captures everything by reference except for `x` that is captured by copy.
`[=, &x](){}`	Captures everything by copy except for `x` that is captured by reference.
`[&, this](){}`	Captures everything by reference except for pointer `this` that is captured by copy (`this` is always captured by copy).
`[x, x](){}`	Error, `x` is captured twice.
`[&, &x](){}`	Error, everything is captured by reference, and we cannot specify again to capture `x` by reference.
`[=, =x](){}`	Error, everything is captured by copy, and we cannot specify again to capture `x` by copy.
`[&this](){}`	Error, the pointer `this` is always captured by copy.
`[&, =](){}`	Error, cannot capture everything both by copy and by reference.
`[x=expr](){}`	`x` is a data member of the lambda's closure initialized from the expression `expr`.
`[&x=expr](){}`	`x` is a reference data member of the lambda's closure initialized from the expression `expr`.

The general form of a lambda expression, as of C++17, looks like this:

```
[capture-list](params) mutable constexpr exception attr -> ret
{ body }
```

All parts shown in this syntax are actually optional except for the capture list, which can, however, be empty, and the body, which can also be empty. The parameter list can actually be omitted if no parameters are needed. The return type does not need to be specified as the compiler can infer it from the type of the returned expression. The `mutable` specifier (which tells the compiler the lambda can actually modify variables captured by copy), the `constexpr` specifier (which tells the compiler to generate a `constexpr` call operator), and the exception specifiers and attributes are all optional.

The simplest possible lambda expression is `[]{}`, though it is often written as `[](){}`.

The latter two examples in the preceding table are forms of generalized lambda captures. These were introduced in C++14 to allow us to capture variables with move-only semantics, but they can also be used to define new arbitrary objects in the lambda. The following example shows how variables can be captured by `move` with generalized lambda captures:

```
auto ptr = std::make_unique<int>(42);
auto l = [lptr = std::move(ptr)](){return ++*lptr;};
```

Lambdas that are written in class methods and need to capture class data members can do so in several ways:

- Capturing individual data members with the form `[x=expr]`:

```
struct foo
{
  int         id;
  std::string name;

  auto run()
  {
    return [i=id, n=name] { std::cout << i << ' ' << n << '\n';
};
  }
};
```

- Capturing the entire object with the form `[=]` (please notice that the implicit capture of pointer `this` via `[=]` is deprecated in C++20):

```
struct foo
{
  int         id;
  std::string name;

  auto run()
  {
    return [=] { std::cout << id << ' ' << name << '\n'; };
  }
};
```

- Capturing the entire object by capturing the `this` pointer. This is necessary if you need to invoke other methods of the class. This can be captured either as `[this]` when the pointer is captured by value, or `[*this]` when the object itself is captured by value. This can make a big difference if the object may go out of scope after the capture occurs but before the lambda is invoked:

```
struct foo
{
  int         id;
  std::string name;

  auto run()
  {
    return[this]{ std::cout << id << ' ' << name << '\n'; };
  }
};

auto l = foo{ 42, "john" }.run();
l(); // does not print 42 john
```

In this latter case seen here, the correct capture should be `[*this]` so that object is copied by value. In this case, invoking the lambda will print *42 john*, even though the temporary has gone out of scope.

The C++20 standard introduces several changes to capturing the pointer `this`:

- It deprecates the implicit capturing of `this` when you use `[=]`. This will produce a deprecation warning to be issued by the compiler.
- It introduces explicit capturing of the `this` pointer by value when you want to capture everything with `[=, this]`. You can still only capture the pointer `this` with a `[this]` capture.

There are cases where lambda expressions only differ in terms of their arguments. In this case, the lambdas can be written in a generic way, just like templates, but using the `auto` specifier for the type parameters (no template syntax is involved). This is addressed in the next recipe, as noted in the upcoming *See also* section.

See also

- *Using generic and template lambdas* to learn how to use `auto` for lambda parameters and how to define template lambdas in C++20
- *Writing a recursive lambda* to understand the technique we can use to make a lambda call itself recursively

Using generic and template lambdas

In the preceding recipe, we saw how to write lambda expressions and use them with standard algorithms. In C++, lambdas are basically syntactic sugar for unnamed function objects, which are classes that implement the call operator. However, just like any other function, this can be implemented generically with templates. C++14 takes advantage of this and introduces generic lambdas that do not need to specify actual types for their parameters and use the `auto` specifier instead. Though not referred to with this name, generic lambdas are basically lambda templates. They are useful in cases where we want to use the same lambda but with different types of parameter. Moreover, the C++20 standard takes this a step further and supports explicitly defining template lambdas. This helps with some scenarios where generic lambdas are cumbersome.

Getting started

It is recommended that you read the preceding recipe, *Using lambdas with standard algorithms*, before you continue with this one to familiarize yourself with the fundamentals of lambdas in C++.

How to do it...

In C++14, we can write generic lambdas:

- By using the `auto` specifier instead of actual types for lambda expression parameters
- When we need to use multiple lambdas that only differ by their parameter types

The following example shows a generic lambda used with the `std::accumulate()` algorithm, first with a vector of integers and then with a vector of strings:

```
auto numbers =
  std::vector<int>{0, 2, -3, 5, -1, 6, 8, -4, 9};

using namespace std::string_literals;
auto texts =
  std::vector<std::string>{"hello"s, " "s, "world"s, "!"s};

auto lsum = [](auto const s, auto const n) {return s + n;};
```

```
auto sum = std::accumulate(
  std::begin(numbers), std::end(numbers), 0, lsum);
  // sum = 22

auto text = std::accumulate(
  std::begin(texts), std::end(texts), ""s, lsum);
  // sum = "hello world!"s
```

In C++20, we can write template lambdas:

- By using a template parameter list in angle brackets (such as `<template T>`) after the capture clause
- When you want to:
    - Restrict the use of a generic lambda with only some types, such as a container, or types that satisfy a concept.
    - Make sure that two or more arguments of a generic lambda actually do have the same type.
    - Retrieve the type of a generic parameter so that, for example, we can create instances of it, invoke static methods, or use its iterator types.
    - Perform perfect forwarding in a generic lambda.

The following example shows a template lambda that can be invoked only using an `std::vector`:

```
std::vector<int> vi { 1, 1, 2, 3, 5, 8 };

auto tl = []<typename T>(std::vector<T> const& vec)
{
   std::cout << std::size(vec) << '\n';
};

tl(vi); // OK, prints 6
tl(42); // error
```

How it works...

In the first example from the previous section, we defined a named lambda expression; that is, a lambda expression that has its closure assigned to a variable. This variable is then passed as an argument to the `std::accumulate()` function.

This general algorithm takes the begin and the end iterators, which define a range, an initial value to accumulate over, and a function that is supposed to accumulate each value in the range to the total. This function takes a first parameter representing the currently accumulated value and a second parameter representing the current value to accumulate to the total, and it returns the new accumulated value. Note that I did not use the term `add` because this can be used for other things than just adding. It can also be used for calculating a product, concatenating, or other operations that aggregate values together.

The two calls to `std::accumulate()` in this example are almost the same; only the types of the arguments are different:

- In the first call, we pass iterators to a range of integers (from a `vector<int>`), 0 for the initial sum, and a lambda that adds two integers and returns their sum. This produces a sum of all integers in the range; for this example, it is `22`.
- In the second call, we pass iterators to a range of strings (from a `vector<string>`), an empty string for the initial value, and a lambda that concatenates two strings by adding them together and returning the result. This produces a string that contains all the strings in the range put together one after another; for this example, the result is `hello world!`.

Though generic lambdas can be defined anonymously in the place where they are called, it does not really make sense because the very purpose of a generic lambda (which is basically, as we mentioned earlier, a lambda expression template) is to be reused, as shown in the example from the *How to do it...* section.

When defining this lambda expression, when used with multiple calls to `std::accumulate()`, instead of specifying concrete types for the lambda parameters (such as `int` or `std::string`), we used the `auto` specifier and let the compiler deduce the type. When encountering a lambda expression that has the `auto` specifier for a parameter type, the compiler generates an unnamed function object that has a call operator template. For the generic lambda expression in this example, the function object would look like this:

```
struct __lambda_name__
{
  template<typename T1, typename T2>
  auto operator()(T1 const s, T2 const n) const { return s + n; }

  __lambda_name__(const __lambda_name__&) = default;
  __lambda_name__(__lambda_name__&&) = default;
  __lambda_name__& operator=(const __lambda_name__&) = delete;
  ~__lambda_name__() = default;
};
```

The call operator is a template with a type parameter for each parameter in the lambda that was specified with `auto`. The return type of the call operator is also `auto`, which means the compiler will deduce it from the type of the returned value. This operator template will be instantiated with the actual types the compiler will identify in the context where the generic lambda is used.

The C++20 template lambdas are an improvement of the C++14 generic lambdas, making some scenarios easier. A typical one was shown in the second example of the previous section, where the use of lambda was restricted with arguments of the type `std::vector`. Another example is when you want to make sure that two parameters of the lambda have the same type. Prior to C++20, this was difficult to do, but with template lambdas, it is very easy, as shown in the following example:

```
auto tl = []<typename T>(T x, T y)
{
  std::cout << x << ' ' << y << '\n';
};

tl(10, 20);   // OK
tl(10, "20"); // error
```

Another scenario for template lambdas is when you need to know the type of a parameter so that you can create instances of that type or invoke static members of it. With generic lambdas, the solution is as follows:

```
struct foo
{
   static void f() { std::cout << "foo\n"; }
};

auto tl = [](auto x)
{
  using T = std::decay_t<decltype(x)>;
  T other;
  T::f();
};

tl(foo{});
```

This solution requires the use of `std::decay_t` and `decltype`. However, in C++20, the same lambda can be written as follows:

```
auto tl = []<typename T>(T x)
{
  T other;
  T::f();
};
```

A similar situation occurs when we need to do perfect forwarding in a generic lambda, which requires the use of `decltype` to determine the types of the arguments:

```
template <typename ...T>
void foo(T&& ... args)
{ /* ... */ }

auto tl = [](auto&& ...args)
{
  return foo(std::forward<decltype(args)>(args)...);
};

tl(1, 42.99, "lambda");
```

With template lambda, we can rewrite it in a simpler way as follows:

```
auto tl = []<typename ...T>(T && ...args)
{
  return foo(std::forward<T>(args)...);
};
```

As seen in these examples, template lambdas are an improvement of generic lambdas, making it easier to handle the scenarios mentioned in this recipe.

See also

- *Using lambdas with standard algorithms* to explore the basics of lambda expressions and how you can utilize them with the standard algorithms
- *Using auto whenever possible* in *Chapter 1*, *Learning Modern Core Language Features*, to understand how automatic type deduction works in C++

Writing a recursive lambda

Lambdas are basically unnamed function objects, which means that it should be possible to call them recursively. Indeed, they can be called recursively; however, the mechanism for doing so is not obvious as it requires assigning the lambda to a function wrapper and capturing the wrapper by reference. Though it can be argued that a recursive lambda does not really make sense and that a function is probably a better design choice, in this recipe, we will look at how to write a recursive lambda.

Getting ready

To demonstrate how to write a recursive lambda, we will consider the well-known example of the Fibonacci function. This is usually implemented recursively in C++, as follows:

```
constexpr int fib(int const n)
{
  return n <= 2 ? 1 : fib(n - 1) + fib(n - 2);
}
```

Having this implementation as a starting point, let's see how we can rewrite it using a recursive lambda.

How to do it...

In order to write a recursive lambda function, you must do the following:

- Define the lambda in a function scope
- Assign the lambda to an `std::function` wrapper
- Capture the `std::function` object by reference in the lambda in order to call it recursively

The following are examples of recursive lambdas:

- A recursive Fibonacci lambda expression in the scope of a function that is invoked from the scope where it is defined:

```
void sample()
{
  std::function<int(int const)> lfib =
    [&lfib](int const n)
    {
      return n <= 2 ? 1 : lfib(n - 1) + lfib(n - 2);
    };
```

```
    auto f10 = lfib(10);
}
```

- A recursive Fibonacci lambda expression returned by a function, which can be invoked from any scope:

```
std::function<int(int const)> fib_create()
{
  std::function<int(int const)> f = [](int const n)
  {
    std::function<int(int const)> lfib = [&lfib](int n)
    {
      return n <= 2 ? 1 : lfib(n - 1) + lfib(n - 2);
    };
    return lfib(n);
  };
  return f;
}

void sample()
{
  auto lfib = fib_create();
  auto f10 = lfib(10);
}
```

How it works...

The first thing you need to consider when writing a recursive lambda is that a lambda expression is a function object and that, in order to call it recursively from the lambda's body, the lambda must capture its closure (that is, the instantiation of the lambda). In other words, the lambda must capture itself, and this has several implications:

- First of all, the lambda must have a name; an unnamed lambda cannot be captured so that it can be called again.
- Secondly, the lambda can only be defined in a function scope. The reason for this is that a lambda can only capture variables from a function scope; it cannot capture any variable that has a static storage duration. Objects defined in a namespace scope or with the static or external specifiers have static storage duration. If the lambda was defined in a namespace scope, its closure would have static storage duration and therefore the lambda would not capture it.

- The third implication is that the type of the lambda closure cannot remain unspecified; that is, it cannot be declared with the `auto` specifier. It is not possible for a variable declared with the `auto` type specifier to appear in its own initializer. This is because the type of the variable is not known when the initializer is being processed. Therefore, you must specify the type of the lambda closure. The way we can do this is by using the general-purpose function wrapper `std::function`.
- Last, but not least, the lambda closure must be captured by reference. If we capture by copy (or value), then a copy of the function wrapper is made, but the wrapper is uninitialized when the capturing is done. We end up with an object that we are not able to call. Even though the compiler will not complain about capturing by value, when the closure is invoked, an `std::bad_function_call` is thrown.

In the first example from the *How to do it...* section, the recursive lambda is defined inside another function called `sample()`. The signature and the body of the lambda expression are the same as those of the regular recursive function `fib ()`, which was defined in the introductory section. The lambda closure is assigned to a function wrapper called `lfib` that is then captured by reference by the lambda and called recursively from its body. Since the closure is captured by reference, it will be initialized at the time it has to be called from the lambda's body.

In the second example, we defined a function that returns the closure of a lambda expression that, in turn, defines and invokes a recursive lambda with the argument it was, in turn, invoked with. This is a pattern that must be implemented when a recursive lambda needs to be returned from a function. This is necessary because the lambda closure must still be available at the time the recursive lambda is called. If it is destroyed before that, we are left with a dangling reference, and calling it will cause the program to terminate abnormally. This erroneous situation is exemplified in the following example:

```
// this implementation of fib_create is faulty
std::function<int(int const)> fib_create()
{
  std::function<int(int const)> lfib = [&lfib](int const n)
  {
    return n <= 2 ? 1 : lfib(n - 1) + lfib(n - 2);
  };

  return lfib;
}
```

```
void sample()
{
  auto lfib = fib_create();
  auto f10 = lfib(10);        // crash
}
```

The solution for this is to create two nested lambda expressions, as shown in the *How to do it...* section. The `fib_create()` method returns a function wrapper that, when invoked, creates the recursive lambda that captures itself. This is slightly and subtly, yet fundamentally, different from the implementation shown in the preceding sample. The outer `f` lambda does not capture anything, especially by reference; therefore, we don't have this issue with dangling references. However, when invoked, it creates a closure of the nested lambda, which is the actual lambda we are interested in calling, and returns the result of applying that recursive `lfib` lambda to its parameter.

See also

- *Using generic and template lambdas* to learn how to use `auto` for lambda parameters and how to define template lambdas in C++20

Writing a function template with a variable number of arguments

It is sometimes useful to write functions with a variable number of arguments or classes with a variable number of members. Typical examples include functions such as `printf`, which takes a format and a variable number of arguments, or classes such as `tuple`. Before C++11, the former was possible only with the use of variadic macros (which enable writing only type-unsafe functions) and the latter was not possible at all. C++11 introduced variadic templates, which are templates with a variable number of arguments that make it possible to write both type-safe function templates with a variable number of arguments, and also class templates with a variable number of members. In this recipe, we will look at writing function templates.

Getting ready

Functions with a variable number of arguments are called *variadic functions*. Function templates with a variable number of arguments are called *variadic function templates*. Knowledge of C++ variadic macros (`va_start`, `va_end`, `va_arg` and `va_copy`, `va_list`) is not necessary for learning how to write variadic function templates, but it represents a good starting point.

We have already used variadic templates in our previous recipes, but this one will provide detailed explanations.

How to do it...

In order to write variadic function templates, you must perform the following steps:

1. Define an overload with a fixed number of arguments to end compile-time recursion if the semantics of the variadic function template require it (refer to `[1]` in the following code).
2. Define a template parameter pack that is a template parameter that can hold any number of arguments, including zero; these arguments can be either types, non-types, or templates (refer to `[2]`).
3. Define a function parameter pack to hold any number of function arguments, including zero; the size of the template parameter pack and the corresponding function parameter pack is the same. This size can be determined with the `sizeof...` operator (refer to `[3]` and refer to the end of the *How it works...*
   section for information on this operator).
4. Expand the parameter pack in order to replace it with the actual arguments being supplied (refer to `[4]`).

The following example, which illustrates all the preceding points, is a variadic function template that adds a variable number of arguments using `operator+`:

```
template <typename T>                  // [1] overload with fixed
T add(T value)                         //     number of arguments
{
  return value;
}

template <typename T, typename... Ts> // [2] typename... Ts
T add(T head, Ts... rest)              // [3] Ts... rest
{
  return head + add(rest...);          // [4] rest...
}
```

How it works...

At first glance, the preceding implementation looks like recursion, because the function `add()` calls itself, and in a way it is, but it is a compile-time recursion that does not incur any sort of runtime recursion and overhead. The compiler actually generates several functions with a different number of arguments, based on the variadic function template's usage, so only function overloading is involved and not any sort of recursion. However, implementation is done as if parameters would be processed in a recursive manner with an end condition.

In the preceding code, we can identify the following key parts:

- `Typename... Ts` is a template parameter pack that indicates a variable number of template type arguments.
- `Ts... rest` is a function parameter pack that indicates a variable number of function arguments.
- `rest...` is an expansion of the function parameter pack.

The position of the ellipsis is not syntactically relevant. `typename... Ts`, `typename ... Ts`, and `typename ...Ts` are all equivalent.

In the `add(T head, Ts... rest)` parameter, `head` is the first element of the list of arguments, while `...rest` is a pack with the rest of the parameters in the list (this can be zero or more). In the body of the function, `rest...` is an expansion of the function parameter pack. This means the compiler replaces the parameter pack with its elements in their order. In the `add()` function, we basically add the first argument to the sum of the remaining arguments, which gives the impression of recursive processing. This recursion ends when there is a single argument left, in which case the first `add()` overload (with a single argument) is called and returns the value of its argument.

This implementation of the function template `add()` enables us to write code, as shown here:

```
auto s1 = add(1, 2, 3, 4, 5);
// s1 = 15
auto s2 = add("hello"s, " "s, "world"s, "!"s);
// s2 = "hello world!"
```

When the compiler encounters `add(1, 2, 3, 4, 5)`, it generates the following functions (`arg1`, `arg2`, and so on are not the actual names the compiler generates), which show that this is actually only calls to overloaded functions and not recursion:

```
int add(int head, int arg1, int arg2, int arg3, int arg4)
{return head + add(arg1, arg2, arg3, arg4);}
int add(int head, int arg1, int arg2, int arg3)
{return head + add(arg1, arg2, arg3);}
int add(int head, int arg1, int arg2)
{return head + add(arg1, arg2);}
int add(int head, int arg1)
{return head + add(arg1);}
int add(int value)
{return value;}
```

With GCC and Clang, you can use the `__PRETTY_FUNCTION__` macro to print the name and the signature of the function.

By adding an `std::cout << __PRETTY_FUNCTION__ << std::endl` at the beginning of the two functions we wrote, we get the following when running the code:

```
T add(T, Ts ...) [with T = int; Ts = {int, int, int, int}]
T add(T, Ts ...) [with T = int; Ts = {int, int, int}]
T add(T, Ts ...) [with T = int; Ts = {int, int}]
T add(T, Ts ...) [with T = int; Ts = {int}]
T add(T) [with T = int]
```

Since this is a function template, it can be used with any type that supports `operator+`. The other example, `add("hello"s, " "s, "world"s, "!"s)`, produces the *hello world!* string. However, the `std::basic_string` type has different overloads for `operator+`, including one that can concatenate a string into a character, so we should be able to also write the following:

```
auto s3 = add("hello"s, ' ', "world"s, '!');
// s3 = "hello world!"
```

However, that will generate compiler errors, as follows (note that I actually replaced `std::basic_string<char, std::char_traits<char>, std::allocator<char> >` with the string *hello world!* for simplicity):

```
In instantiation of 'T add(T, Ts ...) [with T = char; Ts = {string, char}]':
16:29:   required from 'T add(T, Ts ...) [with T = string; Ts = {char, string, char}]'
22:46:   required from here
16:29: error: cannot convert 'string' to 'char' in return
 In function 'T add(T, Ts ...) [with T = char; Ts = {string, char}]':
17:1: warning: control reaches end of non-void function [-Wreturn-type]
```

What happens is that the compiler generates the code shown here, where the return type is the same as the type of the first argument. However, the first argument is either an `std::string` or a `char` (again, `std::basic_string<char, std::char_traits<char>, std::allocator<char> >` was replaced with `string` for simplicity). In cases where `char` is the type of the first argument, the type of the return value `head+add (...)`, which is an `std::string`, does not match the function return type and does not have an implicit conversion to it:

```
string add(string head, char arg1, string arg2, char arg3)
{return head + add(arg1, arg2, arg3);}
char add(char head, string arg1, char arg2)
{return head + add(arg1, arg2);}
string add(string head, char arg1)
{return head + add(arg1);}
char add(char value)
{return value;}
```

We can fix this by modifying the variadic function template so that it has `auto` for the return type instead of `T`. In this case, the return type is always inferred from the return expression, and in our example, it will be `std::string` in all cases:

```
template <typename T, typename... Ts>
auto add(T head, Ts... rest)
{
  return head + add(rest...);
}
```

It should be further added that a parameter pack can appear in a brace-initialization and that its size can be determined using the `sizeof...` operator. Also, variadic function templates do not necessarily imply compile-time recursion, as we have shown in this recipe. All these are shown in the following example:

```
template<typename... T>
auto make_even_tuple(T... a)
{
  static_assert(sizeof...(a) % 2 == 0,
                "expected an even number of arguments");
  std::tuple<T...> t { a... };

  return t;
}

auto t1 = make_even_tuple(1, 2, 3, 4); // OK

// error: expected an even number of arguments
auto t2 = make_even_tuple(1, 2, 3);
```

In the preceding snippet, we have defined a function that creates a tuple with an even number of members. We first use `sizeof...(a)` to make sure that we have an even number of arguments and assert by generating a compiler error otherwise. The `sizeof...` operator can be used with both template parameter packs and function parameter packs. `sizeof...(a)` and `sizeof...(T)` would produce the same value. Then, we create and return a tuple. The template parameter pack `T` is expanded (with `T...`) into the type arguments of the `std::tuple` class template, and the function parameter pack `a` is expanded (with `a...`) into the values for the tuple members using brace initialization.

See also

- *Using fold expressions to simplify variadic function templates* to learn how to write simpler and clearer code when creating function templates with a variable number of arguments
- *Creating raw user-defined literals* in *Chapter 2, Working with Numbers and Strings*, to understand how to provide a custom interpretation of an input sequence so that it changes the normal behavior of the compiler

Using fold expressions to simplify variadic function templates

In this chapter, we are discussing folding several times; this is an operation that applies a binary function to a range of values to produce a single value. We have seen this when we discussed variadic function templates, and will see it again with higher-order functions. It turns out there is a significant number of cases where the expansion of a parameter pack in variadic function templates is basically a folding operation. To simplify writing such variadic function templates, C++17 introduced fold expressions, which fold an expansion of a parameter pack over a binary operator. In this recipe, we will learn how to use fold expressions to simplify writing variadic function templates.

Getting ready

The examples in this recipe are based on the variadic function template `add ()`, which we wrote in the previous recipe, *Writing a function template with a variable number of arguments*. That implementation is a left-folding operation. For simplicity, we'll present the function again:

```
template <typename T>
T add(T value)
{
  return value;
}

template <typename T, typename... Ts>
T add(T head, Ts... rest)
{
  return head + add(rest...);
}
```

In the next section, we will learn how this particular implementation can be simplified, as well as other examples of using fold expressions.

How to do it...

To fold a parameter pack over a binary operator, use one of the following forms:

- Left folding with a unary form `(... op pack)`:

  ```
  template <typename... Ts>
  auto add(Ts... args)
  {
    return (... + args);
  }
  ```

- Left folding with a binary form `(init op ... op pack)`:

  ```
  template <typename... Ts>
  auto add_to_one(Ts... args)
  {
    return (1 + ... + args);
  }
  ```

- Right folding with a unary form `(pack op ...)`:

  ```
  template <typename... Ts>
  auto add(Ts... args)
  {
    return (args + ...);
  }
  ```

- Right folding with a binary form `(pack op ... op init)`:

  ```
  template <typename... Ts>
  auto add_to_one(Ts... args)
  {
    return (args + ... + 1);
  }
  ```

The parentheses shown here are part of the fold expression and cannot be omitted.

How it works...

When the compiler encounters a fold expression, it expands it in one of the following expressions:

Expression	Expansion
`(... op pack)`	`((pack$1 op pack$2) op ...) op pack$n`
`(init op ... op pack)`	`(((init op pack$1) op pack$2) op ...) op pack$n`
`(pack op ...)`	`pack$1 op (... op (pack$n-1 op pack$n))`
`(pack op ... op init)`	`pack$1 op (... op (pack$n-1 op (pack$n op init)))`

When the binary form is used, the operator on both the left-hand and right-hand sides of the ellipses must be the same, and the initialization value must not contain an unexpanded parameter pack.

The following binary operators are supported with fold expressions:

<table>
<tr><td>+</td><td>-</td><td>*</td><td>/</td><td>%</td><td>^</td><td>&</td><td>|</td><td>=</td><td><</td><td>></td><td><<</td></tr>
<tr><td>>></td><td>+=</td><td>-=</td><td>*=</td><td>/=</td><td>%=</td><td>^=</td><td>&=</td><td>|=</td><td><<=</td><td>>>=</td><td>==</td></tr>
<tr><td>!=</td><td><=</td><td>>=</td><td>&&</td><td>||</td><td>,</td><td>.*</td><td>->*.</td><td></td><td></td><td></td><td></td></tr>
</table>

When using the unary form, only operators such as `*`, `+`, `&`, `|`, `&&`, `||`, and `,` (comma) are allowed with an empty parameter pack. In this case, the value of the empty pack is as follows:

<table>
<tr><td>+</td><td>0</td></tr>
<tr><td>*</td><td>1</td></tr>
<tr><td>&</td><td>-1</td></tr>
<tr><td>|</td><td>0</td></tr>
<tr><td>&&</td><td>true</td></tr>
<tr><td>||</td><td>false</td></tr>
<tr><td>,</td><td>void()</td></tr>
</table>

Now that we have the function templates we implemented earlier (let's consider the left-folding version), we can write the following code:

```
auto sum = add(1, 2, 3, 4, 5);         // sum = 15
auto sum1 = add_to_one(1, 2, 3, 4, 5); // sum = 16
```

Considering the `add(1, 2, 3, 4, 5)` call, it will produce the following function:

```
int add(int arg1, int arg2, int arg3, int arg4, int arg5)
{
  return ((((arg1 + arg2) + arg3) + arg4) + arg5);
}
```

It's worth mentioning that due to the aggressive ways modern compilers do optimizations, this function can be inlined and, eventually, we may end up with an expression such as `auto sum = 1 + 2 + 3 + 4 + 5`.

There's more...

Fold expressions work with all overloads for the supported binary operators, but do not work with arbitrary binary functions. It is possible to implement a workaround for that by providing a wrapper type that will hold a value and an overloaded operator for that wrapper type:

```
template <typename T>
struct wrapper
{
  T const & value;
};

template <typename T>
constexpr auto operator<(wrapper<T> const & lhs,
                         wrapper<T> const & rhs)
{
  return wrapper<T> {
    lhs.value < rhs.value ? lhs.value : rhs.value};
}
```

In the preceding code, `wrapper` is a simple class template that holds a constant reference to a value of type `T`. An overloaded `operator<` is provided for this class template; this overload does not return a Boolean to indicate that the first argument is less than the second, but actually an instance of the `wrapper` class type to hold the minimum value of the two arguments. The variadic function template `min ()`, shown here, uses this overloaded `operator<` to fold the pack of arguments expanded to instances of the `wrapper` class template:

```
template <typename... Ts>
constexpr auto min(Ts&&... args)
{
  return (wrapper<Ts>{args} < ...).value;
}

auto m = min(3, 1, 2); // m = 1
```

This `min()` function is expanded by the compiler to something that could look like the following:

```
template<>
inline constexpr int min<int, int, int>(int && __args0,
                                        int && __args1,
                                        int && __args2)
{
  return
    operator<(wrapper_min<int>{__args0},
      operator<(wrapper_min<int>{__args1},
                wrapper_min<int>{__args2})).value;
}
```

What we can see here is cascading calls to the binary `operator <` that return a `Wrapper<int>` value. Without this, an implementation of the `min()` function using fold expressions would not be possible. The following implementation does not work:

```
template <typename... Ts>
constexpr auto minimum(Ts&&... args)
{
  return (args < ...);
}
```

The compiler would transform this, based on the call `min(3, 1, 2)`, to something such as the following:

```
template<>
inline constexpr bool minimum<int, int, int>(int && __args0,
                                             int && __args1,
                                             int && __args2)
{
  return __args0 < (static_cast<int>(__args1 < __args2));
}
```

The result is a function that returns a Boolean, and not the actual integer value, which is the minimum between the supplied arguments.

See also

- *Implementing higher-order functions map and fold* to learn about higher-order functions in functional programming and how to implement the widely used `map` and `fold` (or `reduce`) functions

Implementing the higher-order functions map and fold

Throughout the preceding recipes in this book, we have used the general-purpose algorithms `std::transform()` and `std::accumulate()` in several examples, such as for implementing string utilities to create uppercase or lowercase copies of a string or for summing the values of a range. These are basically implementations of higher-order functions, `map` and `fold`. A higher-order function is a function that takes one or more other functions as arguments and applies them to a range (a list, vector, map, tree, and so on), thus producing either a new range or a value. In this recipe, we will learn how to implement the `map` and `fold` functions so that they work with C++ standard containers.

Getting ready

Map is a higher-order function that applies a function to the elements of a range and returns a new range in the same order.

Fold is a higher-order function that applies a combining function to the elements of the range to produce a single result. Since the order of the processing can be important, there are usually two versions of this function. One is `foldleft`, which processes elements from left to right, while the other is `foldright`, which combines the elements from right to left.

Most descriptions of the function map indicate that it is applied to a list, but this is a general term that can indicate different sequential types, such as list, vector, and array, and also dictionaries (that is, maps), queues, and so on. For this reason, I prefer to use the term range when describing these higher-order functions.

As an example, the mapping operation could transform a range of strings into a range of integers representing the length of each string. The fold operation could then add these lengths to determine the combined length of all the strings.

How to do it...

To implement the `map` function, you should:

- Use `std::transform` on containers that support iterating and assignment to the elements, such as `std::vector` or `std::list`:

```
template <typename F, typename R>
R mapf(F&& func, R range)
{
  std::transform(
    std::begin(range), std::end(range), std::begin(range),
    std::forward<F>(func));
  return range;
}
```

- Use other means such as explicit iteration and insertion for containers that do not support assignment to the elements, such as `std::map`:

```
template<typename F, typename T, typename U>
std::map<T, U> mapf(F&& func, std::map<T, U> const & m)
{
  std::map<T, U> r;
  for (auto const kvp : m)
    r.insert(func(kvp));
  return r;
}

template<typename F, typename T>
std::queue<T> mapf(F&& func, std::queue<T> q)
{
  std::queue<T> r;
  while (!q.empty())
  {
    r.push(func(q.front()));
    q.pop();
  }
  return r;
}
```

To implement the `fold` function, you should:

- Use `std::accumulate()` on containers that support iterating:

```
template <typename F, typename R, typename T>
constexpr T foldl(F&& func, R&& range, T init)
{
  return std::accumulate(
    std::begin(range), std::end(range),
    std::move(init),
    std::forward<F>(func));
}
```

```
template <typename F, typename R, typename T>
constexpr T foldr(F&& func, R&& range, T init)
{
  return std::accumulate(
    std::rbegin(range), std::rend(range),
    std::move(init),
    std::forward<F>(func));
}
```

- Use other means to explicitly process containers that do not support iterating, such as `std::queue`:

```
template <typename F, typename T>
constexpr T foldl(F&& func, std::queue<T> q, T init)
{
  while (!q.empty())
  {
    init = func(init, q.front());
    q.pop();
  }
  return init;
}
```

How it works...

In the preceding examples, we implemented the map in a functional way, without side effects. This means it preserves the original range and returns a new one. The arguments of the function are the function to apply and the range. In order to avoid confusion with the `std::map` container, we have called this function `mapf`. There are several overloads for `mapf`, as shown earlier:

- The first overload is for containers that support iterating and assignment to its elements; this includes `std::vector`, `std::list`, and `std::array`, but also C-like arrays. The function takes an `rvalue` reference to a function and a range for which `std::begin()` and `std::end()` are defined. The range is passed by value so that modifying the local copy does not affect the original range. The range is transformed by applying the given function to each element using the standard algorithm `std::transform()`; the transformed range is then returned.
- The second overload is specialized for `std::map`, which does not support direct assignment to its elements (`std::pair<T, U>`). Therefore, this overload creates a new map, then iterates through its elements using a range-based for loop, and inserts the result of applying the input function to each element of the original map into the new map.

- The third overload is specialized for `std::queue`, which is a container that does not support iterating. It can be argued that a queue is not a typical structure to map over, but for the sake of demonstrating different possible implementations, we are considering it. In order to iterate over the elements of a queue, the queue must be altered—you need to pop elements from the front until the list is empty. This is what the third overload does—it processes each element of the input queue (passed by value) and pushes the result of applying the given function to the front element of the remaining queue.

Now that we have these overloads implemented, we can apply them to a lot of containers, as shown in the following examples:

- Retain absolute values from a vector. In this example, the vector contains both negative and positive values. After applying the mapping, the result is a new vector with only positive values:

  ```
  auto vnums =
    std::vector<int>{0, 2, -3, 5, -1, 6, 8, -4, 9};
  auto r = funclib::mapf([](int const i) {
    return std::abs(i); }, vnums);
  // r = {0, 2, 3, 5, 1, 6, 8, 4, 9}
  ```

- Square the numerical values of a list. In this example, the list contains integral values. After applying the mapping, the result is a list containing the squares of the initial values:

  ```
  auto lnums = std::list<int>{1, 2, 3, 4, 5};
  auto l = funclib::mapf([](int const i) {
    return i*i; }, lnums);
  // l = {1, 4, 9, 16, 25}
  ```

- Rounded amounts of floating points. For this example, we need to use `std::round()`; however, this has overloads for all floating-point types, which makes it impossible for the compiler to pick the right one. As a result, we either have to write a lambda that takes an argument of a specific floating-point type and returns the value of `std::round()` applied to that value, or create a function object template that wraps `std::round()` and enables its call operator only for floating point types. This technique is used in the following example:

  ```
  template<class T = double>
  struct fround
  {
    typename std::enable_if_t<
      std::is_floating_point_v<T>, T>
  ```

```
    operator()(const T& value) const
    {
      return std::round(value);
    }
  };

  auto amounts =
    std::array<double, 5> {10.42, 2.50, 100.0, 23.75, 12.99};
  auto a = funclib::mapf(fround<>(), amounts);
  // a = {10.0, 3.0, 100.0, 24.0, 13.0}
```

- Uppercase the string keys of a map of words (where the key is the word and the value is the number of appearances in the text). Note that creating an uppercase copy of a string is itself a mapping operation. Therefore, in this example, we use `mapf` to apply `toupper()` to the elements of the string representing the key in order to produce an uppercase copy:

```
  auto words = std::map<std::string, int>{
    {"one", 1}, {"two", 2}, {"three", 3}
  };
  auto m = funclib::mapf(
    [](std::pair<std::string, int> const kvp) {
      return std::make_pair(
        funclib::mapf(toupper, kvp.first),
        kvp.second);
    },
    words);
  // m = {{"ONE", 1}, {"TWO", 2}, {"THREE", 3}}
```

- Normalize values from a queue of priorities; initially, the values are from 1 to 100, but we want to normalize them into two values, 1=high and 2=normal. All the initial priorities that have a value up to 30 get high priority; the others get normal priority:

```
  auto priorities = std::queue<int>();
  priorities.push(10);
  priorities.push(20);
  priorities.push(30);
  priorities.push(40);
  priorities.push(50);
  auto p = funclib::mapf(
    [](int const i) { return i > 30 ? 2 : 1; },
    priorities);
  // p = {1, 1, 1, 2, 2}
```

To implement `fold`, we actually have to consider the two possible types of folding; that is, from left to right and from right to left. Therefore, we have provided two functions called `foldl` (for left folding) and `foldr` (for right folding). The implementations shown in the previous section are very similar: they both take a function, a range, and an initial value and call `std::algorithm()` to fold the values of the range into a single value. However, `foldl` uses direct iterators, whereas `foldr` uses reverse iterators to traverse and process the range. The second overload is a specialization for the type `std::queue`, which does not have iterators.

Based on these implementations for folding, we can implement the following examples:

- Adding the values of a vector of integers. In this case, both left and right folding will produce the same result. In the following examples, we pass either a lambda that takes a sum and a number and returns a new sum or the function object `std::plus<>` from the standard library, which applies `operator+` to two operands of the same type (basically similar to the closure of the lambda):

```
auto vnums =
  std::vector<int>{0, 2, -3, 5, -1, 6, 8, -4, 9};

auto s1 = funclib::foldl(
  [](const int s, const int n) {return s + n; },
  vnums, 0);                    // s1 = 22

auto s2 = funclib::foldl(
  std::plus<>(), vnums, 0); // s2 = 22

auto s3 = funclib::foldr(
  [](const int s, const int n) {return s + n; },
  vnums, 0);                    // s3 = 22

auto s4 = funclib::foldr(
  std::plus<>(), vnums, 0); // s4 = 22
```

- Concatenating strings from a vector into a single string:

```
auto texts =
  std::vector<std::string>{"hello"s, " "s, "world"s, "!"s};

auto txt1 = funclib::foldl(
  [](std::string const & s, std::string const & n) {
  return s + n;},
  texts, ""s);    // txt1 = "hello world!"
```

```
auto txt2 = funclib::foldr(
  [](std::string const & s, std::string const & n) {
  return s + n; },
  texts, ""s);    // txt2 = "!world hello"
```

- Concatenating an array of characters into a string:

```
char chars[] = {'c','i','v','i','c'};

auto str1 = funclib::foldl(std::plus<>(), chars, ""s);
// str1 = "civic"

auto str2 = funclib::foldr(std::plus<>(), chars, ""s);
// str2 = "civic"
```

- Counting the number of words in text based on their already computed appearances, available in a `map<string, int>`:

```
auto words = std::map<std::string, int>{
  {"one", 1}, {"two", 2}, {"three", 3} };

auto count = funclib::foldl(
  [](int const s, std::pair<std::string, int> const kvp) {
    return s + kvp.second; },
  words, 0); // count = 6
```

There's more...

These functions can be pipelined; that is, they can call one function with the result of another. The following example maps a range of integers into a range of positive integers by applying the `std::abs()` function to its elements. The result is then mapped into another range of squares. These are then summed together by applying a left fold on the range:

```
auto vnums = std::vector<int>{ 0, 2, -3, 5, -1, 6, 8, -4, 9 };

auto s = funclib::foldl(
  std::plus<>(),
  funclib::mapf(
    [](int const i) {return i*i; },
    funclib::mapf(
      [](int const i) {return std::abs(i); },
      vnums)),
  0); // s = 236
```

As an exercise, we could implement the `fold` function as a variadic function template, in the manner seen earlier. The function that performs the actual folding is provided as an argument:

```
template <typename F, typename T1, typename T2>
auto foldl(F&&f, T1 arg1, T2 arg2)
{
  return f(arg1, arg2);
}

template <typename F, typename T, typename... Ts>
auto foldl(F&& f, T head, Ts... rest)
{
  return f(head, foldl(std::forward<F>(f), rest...));
}
```

When we compare this with the `add()` function template that we wrote in the *Writing a function template with a variable number of arguments* recipe, we can notice several differences:

- The first argument is a function, which is perfectly forwarded when calling `foldl` recursively.
- The end case is a function that requires two arguments because the function we use for folding is a binary one (taking two arguments).
- The return type of the two functions we wrote is declared as `auto` because it must match the return type of the supplied binary function `f`, which is not known until we call `foldl`.

The `foldl()` function can be used as follows:

```
auto s1 = foldl(std::plus<>(), 1, 2, 3, 4, 5);
// s1 = 15
auto s2 = foldl(std::plus<>(), "hello"s, ' ', "world"s, '!');
// s2 = "hello world!"
auto s3 = foldl(std::plus<>(), 1); // error, too few arguments
```

Notice that the last call produces a compiler error because the variadic function template `foldl()` requires at least two arguments to be passed, in order to invoke the supplied binary function.

See also

- *Creating a library of string helpers* in *Chapter 2, Working with Numbers and Strings*, to see how to create useful text utilities that are not directly available in the standard library
- *Writing a function template with a variable number of arguments* to see how variadic templates enable us to write functions that can take any number of arguments
- *Composing functions into a higher-order function* to learn the functional programming technique for creating a new function from one or more other functions

Composing functions into a higher-order function

In the previous recipe, we implemented two higher-order functions, `map` and `fold`, and saw various examples of using them. At the end of the recipe, we saw how they can be pipelined to produce a final value after several transformations of the original data. Pipelining is a form of composition, which means creating one new function from two or more given functions. In the mentioned example, we didn't actually compose functions; we only called a function with the result produced by another, but in this recipe, we will learn how to actually compose functions together into a new function. For simplicity, we will only consider unary functions (functions that take only one argument).

Getting ready

Before you go forward, it is recommended that you read the previous recipe, *Implementing higher-order functions map and fold*. It is not mandatory for understanding this recipe, but we will refer to the `map` and `fold` functions we implemented there.

How to do it...

To compose unary functions into a higher-order function, you should:

- For composing two functions, provide a function that takes two functions, `f` and `g`, as arguments and returns a new function (a lambda) that returns `f(g(x))`, where `x` is the argument of the composed function:

```
template <typename F, typename G>
auto compose(F&& f, G&& g)
{
  return [=](auto x) { return f(g(x)); };
}

auto v = compose(
  [](int const n) {return std::to_string(n); },
  [](int const n) {return n * n; })(-3); // v = "9"
```

- For composing a variable number of functions, provide a variadic template overload of the function described previously:

```
template <typename F, typename... R>
auto compose(F&& f, R&&... r)
{
  return [=](auto x) { return f(compose(r...)(x)); };
}

auto n = compose(
  [](int const n) {return std::to_string(n); },
  [](int const n) {return n * n; },
  [](int const n) {return n + n; },
  [](int const n) {return std::abs(n); })(-3); // n = "36"
```

How it works...

Composing two unary functions into a new one is relatively trivial. Create a template function, which we called `compose()` in the earlier examples, with two arguments—`f` and `g`—that represent functions, and return a function that takes one argument, `x`, and returns `f(g(x))`. It is important that the type of the value returned by the `g` function is the same as the type of the argument of the `f` function. The returned value of the compose function is a closure; that is, it's an instantiation of a lambda.

In practice, it is useful to be able to combine more than just two functions. This can be achieved by writing a variadic template version of the `compose()` function. Variadic templates are explained in more detail in the *Writing a function template with a variable number of arguments* recipe.

Variadic templates imply compile-time recursion by expanding the parameter pack. This implementation is very similar to the first version of `compose()`, except for the following:

- It takes a variable number of functions as arguments.
- The returned closure calls `compose()` recursively with the expanded parameter pack; recursion ends when only two functions are left, in which case the previously implemented overload is called.

Even if the code looks like recursion is happening, this is not true recursion. It could be called compile-time recursion, but with every expansion, we get a call to another method with the same name but a different number of arguments, which does not represent recursion.

Now that we have these variadic template overloads implemented, we can rewrite the last example from the previous recipe, *Implementing higher-order functions map and fold*. Refer to the following snippet:

```
auto s = compose(
  [](std::vector<int> const & v) {
    return foldl(std::plus<>(), v, 0); },
  [](std::vector<int> const & v) {
    return mapf([](int const i) {return i + i; }, v); },
  [](std::vector<int> const & v) {
    return mapf([](int const i) {return std::abs(i); }, v); })(vnums);
```

Having an initial vector of integers, we map it to a new vector with only positive values by applying `std::abs()` to each element. The result is then mapped to a new vector by doubling the value of each element. Finally, the values in the resulting vector are folded together by adding them to the initial value, `0`.

There's more...

Composition is usually represented by a dot (`.`) or asterisk (`*`), such as `f . g` or `f * g`. We can actually do something similar in C++ by overloading `operator*` (it would make little sense to try to overload the operator dot). Similar to the `compose()` function, `operator*` should work with any number of arguments; therefore, we will have two overloads, just like in the case of `compose()`:

- The first overload takes two arguments and calls `compose()` to return a new function.

- The second overload is a variadic template function that, again, calls `operator*` by expanding the parameter pack.

Based on these considerations, we can implement `operator*` as follows:

```
template <typename F, typename G>
auto operator*(F&& f, G&& g)
{
  return compose(std::forward<F>(f), std::forward<G>(g));
}

template <typename F, typename... R>
auto operator*(F&& f, R&&... r)
{
  return operator*(std::forward<F>(f), r...);
}
```

We can now simplify the actual composition of functions by applying `operator*` instead of the more verbose call to `compose()`:

```
auto n =
  ([](int const n) {return std::to_string(n); } *
   [](int const n) {return n * n; } *
   [](int const n) {return n + n; } *
   [](int const n) {return std::abs(n); })(-3); // n = "36"

auto c =
  [](std::vector<int> const & v) {
    return foldl(std::plus<>(), v, 0); } *
  [](std::vector<int> const & v) {
    return mapf([](int const i) {return i + i; }, v); } *
  [](std::vector<int> const & v) {
    return mapf([](int const i) {return std::abs(i); }, v); };

auto vnums = std::vector<int>{ 0, 2, -3, 5, -1, 6, 8, -4, 9 };
auto s = c(vnums); // s = 76
```

Although it may not be intuitive at first glance, the functions are applied in reverse order rather than the one shown in the text. For instance, in the first example, the absolute value of the argument is retained. Then, the result is doubled, and the result of that operation is then multiplied with itself. Finally, the result is converted to a string. For the supplied argument, `-3`, the final result is the string `"36"`.

See also

- *Writing a function template with a variable number of arguments* to see how variadic templates enable us to write functions that can take any number of arguments

Uniformly invoking anything callable

Developers, and especially those who implement libraries, sometimes need to invoke a callable object in a uniform manner. This can be a function, a pointer to a function, a pointer to a member function, or a function object. Examples of such cases include `std::bind`, `std::function`, `std::mem_fn`, and `std::thread::thread`. C++17 defines a standard function called `std::invoke()` that can invoke any callable object with the provided arguments. This is not intended to replace direct calls to functions or function objects, but it is useful in template metaprogramming for implementing various library functions.

Getting ready

For this recipe, you should be familiar with how to define and use function pointers.

To exemplify how `std::invoke()` can be used in different contexts, we will use the following function and class:

```
int add(int const a, int const b)
{
  return a + b;
}

struct foo
{
  int x = 0;

  void increment_by(int const n) { x += n; }
};
```

In the next section, we'll explore the possible use cases for the `std::invoke()` function.

How to do it...

The `std::invoke()` function is a variadic function template that takes the callable object as the first argument and a variable list of arguments that are passed to the call. `std::invoke()` can be used to call the following:

- Free functions:

```
auto a1 = std::invoke(add, 1, 2);   // a1 = 3
```

- Free functions through pointer to function:

```
auto a2 = std::invoke(&add, 1, 2);  // a2 = 3
int(*fadd)(int const, int const) = &add;
auto a3 = std::invoke(fadd, 1, 2);  // a3 = 3
```

- Member functions through pointer to member function:

```
foo f;
std::invoke(&foo::increment_by, f, 10);
```

- Data members:

```
foo f;
auto x1 = std::invoke(&foo::x, f);  // x1 = 0
```

- Function objects:

```
foo f;
auto x3 = std::invoke(std::plus<>(),
  std::invoke(&foo::x, f), 3); // x3 = 3
```

- Lambda expressions:

```
auto l = [](auto a, auto b) {return a + b; };
auto a = std::invoke(l, 1, 2); // a = 3
```

In practice, `std:invoke()` should be used in template metaprogramming for invoking a function with an arbitrary number of arguments. To exemplify such a case, we'll present a possible implementation for our `std::apply()` function, and also a part of the standard library, as of C++17, that calls a function by unpacking the members of a tuple into the arguments of the function:

```
namespace details
{
  template <class F, class T, std::size_t... I>
  auto apply(F&& f, T&& t, std::index_sequence<I...>)
  {
    return std::invoke(
      std::forward<F>(f),
      std::get<I>(std::forward<T>(t))...);
  }
}

template <class F, class T>
auto apply(F&& f, T&& t)
{
  return details::apply(
    std::forward<F>(f),
    std::forward<T>(t),
    std::make_index_sequence<
      std::tuple_size_v<std::decay_t<T>>> {});
}
```

How it works...

Before we see how `std::invoke()` works, let's have a quick look at how different callable objects can be invoked. Given a function, obviously, the ubiquitous way of invoking it is by directly passing it the necessary parameters. However, we can also invoke the function using function pointers. The trouble with function pointers is that defining the type of the pointer can be cumbersome. Using `auto` can simplify things (as shown in the following code), but in practice, you usually need to define the type of the pointer to function first, and then define an object and initialize it with the correct function address. Here are several examples:

```
// direct call
auto a1 = add(1, 2);    // a1 = 3

// call through function pointer
int(*fadd)(int const, int const) = &add;
auto a2 = fadd(1, 2);   // a2 = 3

auto fadd2 = &add;
auto a3 = fadd2(1, 2);  // a3 = 3
```

Calling through a function pointer becomes more cumbersome when you need to invoke a class function through an object that is an instance of the class. The syntax for defining the pointer to a member function and invoking it is not simple:

```
foo f;
f.increment_by(3);
auto x1 = f.x;    // x1 = 3

void(foo::*finc)(int const) = &foo::increment_by;
(f.*finc)(3);
auto x2 = f.x;    // x2 = 6

auto finc2 = &foo::increment_by;
(f.*finc2)(3);
auto x3 = f.x;    // x3 = 9
```

Regardless of how cumbersome this kind of call may look, the actual problem is writing library components (functions or classes) that are able to call any of these types of callable objects, in a uniform manner. This is what benefits, in practice, from a standard function, such as `std::invoke()`.

The implementation details of `std::invoke()` are complex, but the way it works can be explained in simple terms. Supposing the call has the form `invoke(f, arg1, arg2, ..., argN)`, then consider the following:

- If `f` is a pointer to a member function of a `T` class, then the call is equivalent to either:
    - `(arg1.*f)(arg2, ..., argN)`, if `arg1` is an instance of `T`
    - `(arg1.get().*f)(arg2, ..., argN)`, if `arg1` is a specialization of `reference_wrapper`
    - `((*arg1).*f)(arg2, ..., argN)`, if it is otherwise
- If `f` is a pointer to a data member of a `T` class and there is a single argument, in other words, the call has the form `invoke(f, arg1)`, then the call is equivalent to either:
    - `arg1.*f` if `arg1` is an instance class `T`
    - `arg1.get().*f` if `arg1` is a specialization of `reference_wrapper`
    - `(*arg1).*f`, if it is otherwise
- If `f` is a function object, then the call is equivalent to `f(arg1, arg2, ..., argN)`

The standard library also provides a series of related type traits: `std::is_invocable` and `std::is_nothrow_invocable` on one hand, and `std::is_invocable_r` and `std::is_nothrow_invocable_r` on the other hand. The first set determines whether a function can be invocable with the supplied arguments, while the second determines whether it can be invocable with the supplied arguments and produce a result that can be implicitly converted to a specified type. The *nothrow* versions of these type traits verify that the call can be done without any exception being thrown.

See also

- *Writing a function template with a variable number of arguments* to see how variadic templates enable us to write functions that can take any number of arguments

4
Preprocessing and Compilation

In C++, compilation is the process by which source code is transformed to machine code and organized in object files that are then linked together to produce an executable. The compiler actually works on a single file at a time, produced by the preprocessor (the part of the compiler that handles preprocessing directives) from a single source file and all the header files that it includes. This is, however, an oversimplification of what happens when we compile the code. This chapter addresses topics related to preprocessing and compilation, with a focus on various methods to perform conditional compilation, but also touching other modern topics such as using attributes to provide implementation-defined language extensions.

The recipes included in this chapter are as follows:

- Conditionally compiling your source code
- Using the indirection pattern for preprocessor stringification and concatenation
- Performing compile-time assertion checks with `static_assert`
- Conditionally compiling classes and functions with `enable_if`
- Selecting branches at compile time with *constexpr if*
- Providing metadata to the compiler with attributes

The recipe that we will start this chapter with addresses a very common problem faced by developers, which is compiling only parts of a code base depending on various conditions.

Conditionally compiling your source code

Conditional compilation is a simple mechanism that enables developers to maintain a single code base, but only consider some parts of the code for compilation to produce different executables, usually in order to run on different platforms or hardware, or depend on different libraries or library versions. Common examples include using or ignoring code based on the compiler, platform (x86, x64, ARM, and so on), configuration (debug or release), or any user-defined specific conditions. In this recipe, we'll take a look at how conditional compilation works.

Getting ready

Conditional compilation is a technique used extensively for many purposes. In this recipe, we will look at several examples and explain how they work. This technique is not in any way limited to these examples. For the scope of this recipe, we will only consider the three major compilers: GCC, Clang, and VC++.

How to do it...

To conditionally compile portions of code, use the `#if`, `#ifdef`, and `#ifndef` directives (with the `#elif`, `#else`, and `#endif` directives). The general form for conditional compilation is as follows:

```
#if condition1
  text1
#elif condition2
  text2
#elif condition3
  text3
#else
  text4
#endif
```

To define macros for conditional compilation, you can use either of the following:

- A `#define` directive in your source code:

  ```
  #define VERBOSE_PRINTS
  #define VERBOSITY_LEVEL 5
  ```

- Compiler command-line options that are specific to each compiler. Examples for the most widely used compilers are as follows:
    - For Visual C++, use `/Dname` or `/Dname=value` (where `/Dname` is equivalent to `/Dname=1`), for example, `cl /DVERBOSITY_LEVEL=5`.
    - For GCC and Clang, use `-D name` or `-D name=value` (where `-D name` is equivalent to `-D name=1`), for example, `gcc -D VERBOSITY_LEVEL=5`.

The following are typical examples of conditional compilation:

- Header guards to avoid duplicate definitions:

```
#if !defined(UNIQUE_NAME)
#define UNIQUE_NAME
class widget { };
#endif
```

- Compiler-specific code for cross-platform applications. The following is an example of printing a message to the console with the name of the compiler:

```
void show_compiler()
{
  #if defined _MSC_VER
    std::cout << "Visual C++\n";
  #elif defined __clang__
    std::cout << "Clang\n";
  #elif defined __GNUG__
    std::cout << "GCC\n";
  #else
    std::cout << "Unknown compiler\n";
  #endif
}
```

- Target-specific code for multiple architectures, for example, for conditionally compiling code for multiple compilers and architectures:

```
void show_architecture()
{
#if defined _MSC_VER

#if defined _M_X64
  std::cout << "AMD64\n";
#elif defined _M_IX86
  std::cout << "INTEL x86\n";
```

```
#elif defined _M_ARM
  std::cout << "ARM\n";
#else
  std::cout << "unknown\n";
#endif

#elif defined __clang__ || __GNUG__

#if defined __amd64__
  std::cout << "AMD64\n";
#elif defined __i386__
  std::cout << "INTEL x86\n";
#elif defined __arm__
  std::cout << "ARM\n";
#else
  std::cout << "unknown\n";
#endif

#else
#error Unknown compiler
#endif
}
```

- Configuration-specific code, for example, for conditionally compiling code for debug and release builds:

```
void show_configuration()
{
#ifdef _DEBUG
  std::cout << "debug\n";
#else
  std::cout << "release\n";
#endif
}
```

How it works...

When you use the preprocessing directives `#if`, `#ifndef`, `#ifdef`, `#elif`, `#else`, and `#endif`, the compiler will select, at most, one branch whose body will be included in the translation unit for compilation. The body of these directives can be any text, including other preprocessing directives. The following rules apply:

- `#if`, `#ifdef`, and `#ifndef` must be matched by a `#endif`.
- The `#if` directive may have multiple `#elif` directives, but only one `#else`, which must also be the last one before `#endif`.
- `#if`, `#ifdef`, `#ifndef`, `#elif`, `#else`, and `#endif` can be nested.
- The `#if` directive requires a constant expression, whereas `#ifdef` and `#ifndef` require an identifier.
- The operator `defined` can be used for preprocessor constant expressions, but only in `#if` and `#elif` directives.
- `defined(identifier)` is considered `true` if `identifier` is defined; otherwise, it is considered `false`.
- An identifier defined as an empty text is considered defined.
- `#ifdef identifier` is equivalent to `#if defined(identifier)`.
- `#ifndef identifier` is equivalent to `#if !defined(identifier)`.
- `defined(identifier)` and `defined identifier` are equivalent.

Header guards are one of the most common forms of conditional compilation. This technique is used to prevent the content of a header file from being compiled several times (although the header is still scanned every time in order to detect what should be included). Since headers are often included in multiple source files, having them compiled for every translation unit where they are included would produce multiple definitions for the same symbols, which is an error. Therefore, the code in headers is guarded for multiple compilations in the manner shown in the example given in the previous section. The way this works, considering the given example, is that if the macro `UNIQUE_NAME` (this is a generic name from the previous section) is not defined, then the code after the `#if` directive, until `#endif`, is included in the translation unit and compiled. When that happens, the macro `UNIQUE_NAME` is defined with the `#define` directive. The next time the header is included in a translation unit, the macro `UNIQUE_NAME` is defined and the code in the body of the `#if` directive is not included in the translation unit and, therefore, not compiled again.

Note that the name of the macro must be unique throughout the application; otherwise, only the code from the first header where the macro is used will be compiled. Code from other headers using the same name will be ignored. Typically, the name of the macro is based on the name of the header file where it is defined.

Another important example of conditional compilation is cross-platform code, which needs to account for different compilers and architectures, usually one of Intel x86, AMD64, or ARM. However, the compiler defines its own macros for the possible platforms. The samples from the *How to do it...* section show how to conditionally compile code for multiple compilers and architectures.

Note that in the aforementioned example, we only consider a few architectures. In practice, there are multiple macros that can be used to identify the same architecture. Ensure that you read the documentation of each compiler before using these types of macros in your code.

Configuration-specific code is also handled with macros and conditional compilation. Compilers such as GCC and Clang do not define any special macros for debug configurations (when the `-g` flag is used). Visual C++ does define `_DEBUG` for a debug configuration, which was shown in the last example in the *How to do it...* section. For the other compilers, you would have to explicitly define a macro to identify such a debug configuration.

See also

- *Using the indirection pattern for preprocessor stringification and concatenation* to learn how to transform identifiers to strings and concatenate identifiers together during preprocessing

Using the indirection pattern for preprocessor stringification and concatenation

The C++ preprocessor provides two operators for transforming identifiers to strings and concatenating identifiers together. The first one, operator `#`, is called the **stringizing operator**, while the second one, operator `##`, is called the **token-pasting**, **merging**, or **concatenating operator**. Although their use is limited to some particular cases, it is important to understand how they work.

Getting ready

For this recipe, you need to know how to define macros using the preprocessing directive `#define`.

How to do it...

To create a string from an identifier using the preprocessing operator #, use the following pattern:

1. Define a helper macro taking one argument that expands to #, followed by the argument:

```
#define MAKE_STR2(x) #x
```

2. Define the macro you want to use, taking one argument that expands to the helper macro:

```
#define MAKE_STR(x) MAKE_STR2(x)
```

To concatenate identifiers together using the preprocessing operator ##, use the following pattern:

1. Define a helper macro with one or more arguments that use the token-pasting operator ## to concatenate arguments:

```
#define MERGE2(x, y)    x##y
```

2. Define the macro you want to use by using the helper macro:

```
#define MERGE(x, y)     MERGE2(x, y)
```

How it works...

To understand how these work, let's consider the MAKE_STR and MAKE_STR2 macros defined earlier. When used with any text, they will produce a string containing that text. The following example shows how both these macros can be used to define strings containing the text "sample":

```
std::string s1 { MAKE_STR(sample) };  // s1 = "sample"
std::string s2 { MAKE_STR2(sample) }; // s2 = "sample"
```

On the other hand, when a macro is passed as an argument, the results are different. In the following example, NUMBER is a macro that expands to an integer, 42. When used as an argument to MAKE_STR, it indeed produces the string "42"; however, when used as an argument to MAKE_STR2, it produces the string "NUMBER":

```
#define NUMBER 42

std::string s3 { MAKE_STR(NUMBER) };    // s3 = "42"
std::string s4 { MAKE_STR2(NUMBER) };   // s4 = "NUMBER"
```

The C++ standard defines the following rules for argument substitution in function-like macros (paragraph 16.3.1):

> "*After the arguments for the invocation of a function-like macro have been identified, argument substitution takes place. A parameter in the replacement list, unless preceded by a # or ## preprocessing token or followed by a ## preprocessing token (see below), is replaced by the corresponding argument after all the macros contained therein have been expanded. Before being substituted, each argument's preprocessing tokens are completely macro replaced as if they formed the rest of the preprocessing file; no other preprocessing tokens are available.*"

What this says is that macro arguments are expanded before they are substituted into the macro body, except for the case when the operator # or ## is preceding or following a parameter in the macro body. As a result, the following happens:

- For `MAKE_STR2(NUMBER)`, the `NUMBER` parameter in the replacement list is preceded by `#` and, therefore, it is not expanded before substituting the argument in the macro body; therefore, after the substitution, we have `#NUMBER`, which becomes `"NUMBER"`.
- For `MAKE_STR(NUMBER)`, the replacement list is `MAKE_STR2(NUMBER)`, which has no `#` or `##`; therefore, the `NUMBER` parameter is replaced with its corresponding argument, `42`, before being substituted. The result is `MAKE_STR2(42)`, which is then scanned again, and, after expansion, it becomes `"42"`.

The same processing rules apply to macros using the token-pasting operator. Therefore, in order to make sure that your stringification and concatenation macros work for all cases, always apply the indirection pattern described in this recipe.

The token-pasting operator is typically used in macros that factor repetitive code to avoid writing the same thing explicitly over and over again. The following simple example shows a practical use of the token-pasting operator; given a set of classes, we want to provide factory methods that create an instance of each class:

```
#define DECL_MAKE(x)    DECL_MAKE2(x)
#define DECL_MAKE2(x)   x* make##_##x() { return new x(); }

struct bar {};
struct foo {};

DECL_MAKE(foo)
DECL_MAKE(bar)

auto f = make_foo(); // f is a foo*
auto b = make_bar(); // b is a bar*
```

Those familiar with the Windows platform have probably used the _T (or _TEXT) macro for declaring string literals that are either translated to Unicode or ANSI strings (both single- and multi-type character strings):

```
auto text{ _T("sample") }; // text is either "sample" or L"sample"
```

The Windows SDK defines the _T macro as follows. Note that when _UNICODE is defined, the token-pasting operator is defined to concatenate together the L prefix and the actual string being passed to the macro:

```
#ifdef _UNICODE
#define __T(x)    L ## x
#else
#define __T(x)    x
#endif

#define _T(x)     __T(x)
#define _TEXT(x) __T(x)
```

At first glance, it seems unnecessary to have one macro calling another macro, but this level of indirection is key for making the # and ## operators work with other macros, as we have seen in this recipe.

See also

- *Conditionally compiling your source code* to learn how to compile only parts of your code, depending on various conditions

Performing compile-time assertion checks with static_assert

In C++, it is possible to perform both runtime and compile-time assertion checks to ensure that specific conditions in your code are true. Runtime assertions have the disadvantage that they are verified late when the program is running, and only if the control flow reaches them. There is no alternative when the condition depends on runtime data; however, when that is not the case, compile-time assertion checks are to be preferred. With compile-time assertions, the compiler is able to notify you early in the development stage with an error that a particular condition has not been met. These, however, can only be used when the condition can be evaluated at compile time. In C++11, compile-time assertions are performed with `static_assert`.

Getting ready

The most common use of static assertion checks is with template metaprogramming, where they can be used for validating that preconditions on template types are met (examples can include whether a type is a POD type, copy-constructible, a reference type, and so on). Another typical example is to ensure that types (or objects) have an expected size.

How to do it...

Use `static_assert` declarations to ensure that conditions in different scopes are met:

- **namespace**: In this example, we validate that the size of the class `item` is always 16:

```
struct alignas(8) item
{
  int      id;
  bool     active;
  double   value;
};

static_assert(sizeof(item) == 16,
              "size of item must be 16 bytes");
```

- **class**: In this example, we validate that `pod_wrapper` can only be used with POD types:

```
template <typename T>
class pod_wrapper
{
  static_assert(std::is_standard_layout_v<T>,
                "POD type expected!");
  T value;
};

struct point
{
  int x;
  int y;
  };
pod_wrapper<int>         w1; // OK
pod_wrapper<point>       w2; // OK
pod_wrapper<std::string> w3; // error: POD type expected
```

- **block (function)**: In this example, we validate that a function template has only arguments of an integral type:

```
template<typename T>
auto mul(T const a, T const b)
{
  static_assert(std::is_integral_v<T>,
                "Integral type expected");
  return a * b;
}

auto v1 = mul(1, 2);       // OK
auto v2 = mul(12.0, 42.5); // error: Integral type expected
```

How it works...

`static_assert` is basically a declaration, but it does not introduce a new name. These declarations have the following form:

```
static_assert(condition, message);
```

The condition must be convertible to a Boolean value at compile time, and the message must be a string literal. As of C++17, the message is optional.

When the condition in a `static_assert` declaration evaluates to `true`, nothing happens. When the condition evaluates to `false`, the compiler generates an error that contains the specified message, if any.

See also

- *Conditionally compiling classes and functions with enable_if* to learn about SFINAE and how to use it to specify type constraints for templates
- *Specifying requirements on template arguments with concepts* in *Chapter 12, C++20 Core Features*, to learn the fundamentals of C++20 concepts and how to use them to specify constraints for template types
- *Selecting branches at compile time with constexpr if* to learn how to compile only parts of your code with *constexpr if* statements

Conditionally compiling classes and functions with enable_if

Template metaprogramming is a powerful feature of C++ that enables us to write generic classes and functions that work with any type. This is a problem sometimes because the language does not define any mechanism for specifying constraints on the types that can be substituted for the template parameters. However, we can still achieve this using metaprogramming tricks and by leveraging a rule called **substitution failure is not an error**, also known as **SFINAE**. This rule determines whether the compiler discards, from the overloaded set, a specialization when substituting the explicitly specified or deduced type for the template parameter when it fails, instead of generating an error. This recipe will focus on implementing type constraints for templates.

Getting ready

Developers have used a class template usually called `enable_if` for many years in conjunction with SFINAE to implement constraints on template types. The `enable_if` family of templates has become part of the C++11 standard and is implemented as follows:

```
template<bool Test, class T = void>
struct enable_if
{};

template<class T>
struct enable_if<true, T>
{
  typedef T type;
};
```

To be able to use `std::enable_if`, you must include the header `<type_traits>`.

How to do it...

`std::enable_if` can be used in multiple scopes to achieve different purposes; consider the following examples:

- On a class template parameter to enable a class template only for types that meet a specified condition:

```
template <typename T,
          typename = typename
          std::enable_if_t<std::is_standard_layout_v<T>, T>>
class pod_wrapper
{
  T value;
};

struct point
{
  int x;
  int y;
};

pod_wrapper<int>         w1; // OK
pod_wrapper<point>       w2; // OK
pod_wrapper<std::string> w3; // error: too few template arguments
```

- On a function template parameter, function parameter, or function return type to enable a function template only for types that meet a specified condition:

```
template<typename T,
         typename = typename std::enable_if_t<
             std::is_integral_v<T>, T>>
auto mul(T const a, T const b)
{
  return a * b;
}

auto v1 = mul(1, 2);     // OK
auto v2 = mul(1.0, 2.0);
// error: no matching overloaded function found
```

To simplify the cluttered code that we end up writing when we use `std::enable_if`, we can leverage alias templates and define two aliases, called `EnableIf` and `DisableIf`:

```
template <typename Test, typename T = void>
using EnableIf = typename std::enable_if_t<Test::value, T>;

template <typename Test, typename T = void>
using DisableIf = typename std::enable_if_t<!Test::value, T>;
```

Based on these alias templates, the following definitions are equivalent to the preceding ones:

```
template <typename T, typename = EnableIf<std::is_standard_layout<T>>>
class pod_wrapper
{
  T value;
};

template<typename T, typename = EnableIf<std::is_integral<T>>>
auto mul(T const a, T const b)
{
  return a * b;
}
```

How it works...

`std::enable_if` works because the compiler applies the SFINAE rule when performing overload resolution. Before we can explain how `std::enable_if` works, we should have a quick look at what SFINAE is.

When the compiler encounters a function call, it needs to build a set of possible overloads and select the best match for the call based on the arguments for the function call. When building this overload set, the compiler evaluates function templates too and has to perform a substitution for the specified or deduced types in the template arguments. According to SFINAE, when the substitution fails, instead of yielding an error, the compiler should just remove the function template from the overload set and continue.

The standard specifies a list of type and expression errors that are also SFINAE errors. These include an attempt to create an array of `void` or an array of size zero, an attempt to create a reference to `void`, an attempt to create a function type with a parameter of type `void`, and an attempt to perform an invalid conversion in a template argument expression or in an expression used in a function declaration. For the complete list of exceptions, consult the C++ standard or other resources.

Let's consider the following two overloads of a function called `func()`. The first overload is a function template that has a single argument of type `T::value_type`; this means it can only be instantiated with types that have an inner type called `value_type`. The second overload is a function that has a single argument of type `int`:

```
template <typename T>
void func(typename T::value_type const a)
{ std::cout << "func<>" << '\n'; }

void func(int const a)
{ std::cout << "func" << '\n'; }

template <typename T>
struct some_type
{
  using value_type = T;
};
```

If the compiler encounters a call such as `func(42)`, then it must find an overload that can take an `int` argument. When it builds the overload set and substitutes the template parameter with the provided template argument, the result, `void func(int::value_type const)`, is invalid, because `int` does not have a `value_type` member. Due to SFINAE, the compiler will not emit an error and stop, but will simply ignore the overload and continue. It then finds `void func(int const)`, and that will be the best (and only) match that it will call.

If the compiler encounters a call such as `func<some_type<int>>(42)`, then it builds an overload set containing `void func(some_type<int>::value_type const>` and `void func(int const)`, and the best match in this case is the first overload; no SFINAE is involved this time.

On the other hand, if the compiler encounters a call such as `func("string"s)`, then it again relies on SFINAE to ignore the function template, because `std::basic_string` does not have a `value_type` member either. This time, however, the overload set does not contain any match for the string argument; therefore, the program is ill-formed and the compiler emits an error and stops.

The class template `enable_if<bool, T>` does not have any members, but its partial specialization, `enable_if<true, T >`, does have an inner type called `type`, which is a synonym for `T`. When the compile-time expression supplied as the first argument to `enable_if` evaluates to `true`, the inner member `type` is available; otherwise, it is not.

Considering the last definition of the function `mul()` from the *How to do it...* section, when the compiler encounters a call such as `mul(1, 2)`, it tries to substitute `int` for the template parameter, `T`; since `int` is an integral type, `std::is_integral<T>` evaluates to `true` and, therefore, a specialization of `enable_if` that defines an inner type called `type` is instantiated. As a result, the alias template `EnableIf` becomes a synonym for this type, which is `void` (from the expression `typename T = void`). The result is a function template, `int mul<int, void>(int a, int b)`, that can be called with the supplied arguments.

On the other hand, when the compiler encounters a call such as `mul(1.0, 2.0)`, it tries to substitute `double` for the template parameter, `T`. However, this is not an integral type; as a result, the condition in `std::enable_if` evaluates to `false` and the class template does not define an inner member `type`. This results in a substitution error, but according to SFINAE, the compiler will not emit an error but move on. However, since no other overload is found, there will be no `mul()` function that can be called. Therefore, the program is considered ill-formed and the compiler stops with an error.

A similar situation is encountered with the class template `pod_wrapper`. It has two template type parameters: the first is the actual POD type that is being wrapped, while the second is the result of the substitution of `enable_if` and `is_pod`. If the type is a POD type (as in `pod_wrapper<int>`), then the inner member `type` from `enable_if` exists and it substitutes the second template type parameter. However, if the inner member `type` is not a POD type (as in `pod_wrapper<std::string>`), then the inner member `type` is not defined, and the substitution fails, producing an error such as *too few template arguments*.

There's more...

`static_assert` and `std::enable_if` can be used to achieve the same goals. In fact, in the previous recipe, *Performing compile-time assertion checks with static_assert*, we defined the same class template, `pod_wrapper`, and function template, `mul()`. For these examples, `static_assert` seems like a better solution because the compiler emits better error messages (provided that you specify relevant messages in the `static_assert` declaration). These two, however, work quite differently and are not intended as alternatives.

`static_assert` does not rely on SFINAE and is applied after overload resolution is performed. The result of a failed assert is a compiler error. On the other hand, `std::enable_if` is used to remove candidates from the overload set and does not trigger compiler errors (given that the exceptions the standard specifies for SFINAE do not occur). The actual error that can occur after SFINAE is an empty overload set that makes a program ill-formed. This is because a particular function call cannot be performed.

To understand the difference between `static_assert` and `std::enable_if` with SFINAE, let's consider a case where we want to have two function overloads: one that should be called for arguments of integral types and one for arguments of any type other than integral types. With `static_assert`, we can write the following (note that the dummy second type parameter on the second overload is necessary to define two different overloads; otherwise, we would just have two definitions of the same function):

```
template <typename T>
auto compute(T const a, T const b)
{
   static_assert(std::is_integral_v<T>,
                 "An integral type expected");
   return a + b;
}

template <typename T, typename = void>
auto compute(T const a, T const b)
{
   static_assert(!std::is_integral_v<T>,
                 "A non-integral type expected");
   return a * b;
}

auto v1 = compute(1, 2);
// error: ambiguous call to overloaded function

auto v2 = compute(1.0, 2.0);
// error: ambiguous call to overloaded function
```

Regardless of how we try to call this function, we end up with an error, because the compiler finds two overloads that it could potentially call. This is because `static_assert` is only considered after the overload resolution has been resolved, which, in this case, builds a set of two possible candidates.

The solution to this problem is `std::enable_if` and SFINAE. We use `std::enable_if` via the alias templates `EnableIf` and `DisableIf` defined previously on a template parameter (although we still use the dummy template parameter on the second overload to introduce two different definitions). The following example shows the two overloads rewritten. The first overload is enabled only for integral types, while the second is disabled for integral types:

```
template <typename T, typename = EnableIf<std::is_integral<T>>>
auto compute(T const a, T const b)
{
   return a * b;
}

template <typename T, typename = DisableIf<std::is_integral<T>>,
          typename = void>
```

```
auto compute(T const a, T const b)
{
  return a + b;
}
auto v1 = compute(1, 2);     // OK; v1 = 2
auto v2 = compute(1.0, 2.0); // OK; v2 = 3.0
```

With SFINAE at work, when the compiler builds the overload set for either `compute(1, 2)` or `compute(1.0, 2.0);`, it will simply discard the overload that produces a substitution failure and move on, where in each case we'll end up with an overload set containing a single candidate.

See also

- *Performing compile-time assertion checks with static_assert* to learn how to define assertions that are verified at compile time
- *Creating type aliases and alias templates* in *Chapter 1*, *Learning Modern Core Language Features*, to learn about aliases for types

Selecting branches at compile time with constexpr if

In the previous recipes, we saw how we can impose restrictions on types and functions using `static_assert` and `std::enable_if` and how these two are different. Template metaprogramming can become complicated and cluttered when we use SFINAE and `std::enable_if` to define function overloads or when we write variadic function templates. A new feature of C++17 is intended to simplify such code; it is called *constexpr if*, and it defines an `if` statement with a condition that is evaluated at compile time, resulting in the compiler selecting the body of a branch or another in the translation unit. Typical usage of *constexpr if* is for simplification of variadic templates and `std::enable_if`-based code.

Getting ready

In this recipe, we will refer to and simplify the code written in previous recipes. Before continuing with this recipe, you should take a moment to go back and review the code we have written in the previous recipes, as follows:

- The `compute()` overloads for integral and non-integral types from the *Conditionally compiling classes and functions with enable_if* recipe.

- User-defined 8-bit, 16-bit, and 32-bit binary literals from the *Creating raw user-defined literals* recipe of *Chapter 2, Working with Numbers and Strings*.

These implementations have several issues:

- They are hard to read. There is a lot of focus on the template declaration, yet the body of the functions are very simple, for instance. The biggest problem, though, is that it requires greater attention from developers because it is cluttered with complicated declarations, such as `typename = std::enable_if<std::is_integral<T>::value, T>::type`.
- There is too much code. The end purpose in the first example is to have a generic function that behaves differently for different types, yet we had to write two overloads for the function; moreover, to differentiate the two, we had to use an extra, unused, template parameter. In the second example, the purpose was to build an integer value out of characters `'0'` and `'1'`, yet we had to write one class template and three specializations to make it happen.
- It requires advanced template metaprogramming skills, which shouldn't be necessary for doing something this simple.

The syntax for *constexpr if* is very similar to regular `if` statements and requires the `constexpr` keyword before the condition. The general form is as follows:

```
if constexpr (init-statement condition) statement-true
else statement-false
```

In the following section, we'll explore several use cases for conditional compilation with *constexpr if*.

How to do it...

Use *constexpr if* statements to do the following:

- To avoid using `std::enable_if` and relying on SFINAE to impose restrictions on function template types and conditionally compile code:

```
template <typename T>
auto value_of(T value)
{
  if constexpr (std::is_pointer_v<T>)
     return *value;
  else
     return value;
}
```

- To simplify writing variadic templates and implement metaprogramming compile-time recursion:

```
namespace binary
{
  using byte8 = unsigned char;

  namespace binary_literals
  {
    namespace binary_literals_internals
    {
      template <typename CharT, char d, char... bits>
      constexpr CharT binary_eval()
      {
        if constexpr(sizeof...(bits) == 0)
          return static_cast<CharT>(d-'0');
        else if constexpr(d == '0')
          return binary_eval<CharT, bits...>();
        else if constexpr(d == '1')
          return static_cast<CharT>(
            (1 << sizeof...(bits)) |
            binary_eval<CharT, bits...>());
      }
    }

    template<char... bits>
    constexpr byte8 operator""_b8()
    {
      static_assert(
        sizeof...(bits) <= 8,
        "binary literal b8 must be up to 8 digits long");

      return binary_literals_internals::
                binary_eval<byte8, bits...>();
    }
  }
}
```

How it works...

The way *constexpr if* works is relatively simple: the condition in the `if` statement must be a compile-time expression that evaluates or is convertible to a Boolean. If the condition is `true`, the body of the `if` statement is selected, which means it ends up in the translation unit for compilation. If the condition is `false`, the `else` branch, if any is defined, is evaluated. Return statements in discarded *constexpr if* branches do not contribute to the function return type deduction.

In the first example from the *How to do it...* section, the `value_of()` function template has a clean signature. The body is also very simple; if the type that is substituted for the template parameter is a pointer type, the compiler will select the first branch (that is, `return *value;`) for code generation and discard the `else` branch. For non-pointer types, because the condition evaluates to `false`, the compiler will select the `else` branch (that is, `return value;`) for code generation and discard the rest. This function can be used as follows:

```
auto v1 = value_of(42);

auto p = std::make_unique<int>(42);
auto v2 = value_of(p.get());
```

However, without the help of *constexpr if*, we could only implement this using `std::enable_if`. The following implementation is a more cluttered alternative:

```
template <typename T,
          typename = typename std::enable_if_t<std::is_pointer_v<T>,
T>>
auto value_of(T value)
{
  return *value;
}

template <typename T,
          typename = typename std::enable_if_t<!std::is_pointer_v<T>,
T>>
T value_of(T value)
{
  return value;
}
```

As you can see, the *constexpr if* variant is not only shorter but more expressive and easier to read and understand.

In the second example from the *How to do it...* section, the internal helper function `binary_eval()` is a variadic template function without any parameters; it only has template parameters. The function evaluates the first argument and then does something with the rest of the arguments in a recursive manner (but remember this is not a runtime recursion). When there is a single character left and the size of the remaining pack is `0`, we return the decimal value represented by the character (`0` for `'0'` and `1` for `'1'`). If the current first element is a `'0'`, we return the value determined by evaluating the rest of the arguments pack, which involves a recursive call. If the current first element is a `'1'`, we return the value by shifting a `1` to the left on a number of positions given by the size of the remaining pack bit or the value determined. We do this by evaluating the rest of the arguments pack, which again involves a recursive call.

See also

- *Conditionally compiling classes and functions with enable_if* to learn about SFINAE and how to use it to specify type constraints for templates

Providing metadata to the compiler with attributes

C++ has been very deficient when it comes to features that enable reflection or introspection on types or data or standard mechanisms to define language extensions. Because of that, compilers have defined their own specific extensions for this purpose. Examples include the VC++ `__declspec()` specifier or the GCC `__attribute__((...))`. C++11, however, introduces the concept of attributes, which enable compilers to implement extensions in a standard way or even embedded domain-specific languages. The new C++ standards define several attributes all compilers should implement, and that will be the topic of this recipe.

How to do it...

Use standard attributes to provide hints for the compiler about various design goals such as in the scenarios listed here, but not only these:

- To ensure that the return value from a function cannot be ignored, declare the function with the `[[nodiscard]]` attribute. In C++20, you can specify a string literal, of the form `[[nodiscard(text)]]`, to explain why the result should not be discarded:

```
[[nodiscard]] int get_value1()
{
  return 42;
}

get_value1();
// warning: ignoring return value of function
//          declared with 'nodiscard' attribute get_value1();
```

- Alternatively, you can declare enumerations and classes used as the return type of a function with the `[[nodiscard]]` attribute; in this case, the return value of any function returning such a type cannot be ignored:

```
enum class[[nodiscard]] ReturnCodes{ OK, NoData, Error };

ReturnCodes get_value2()
{
  return ReturnCodes::OK;
}

struct[[nodiscard]] Item{};

Item get_value3()
{
  return Item{};
}

// warning: ignoring return value of function
//          declared with 'nodiscard' attribute
get_value2();
get_value3();
```

- To ensure that the usage of functions or types that are considered deprecated is flagged by the compiler with a warning, declare them with the `[[deprecated]]` attribute:

```
[[deprecated("Use func2()")]] void func()
{
}

// warning: 'func' is deprecated : Use func2()
func();

class [[deprecated]] foo
{
};

// warning: 'foo' is deprecated
foo f;
```

- To ensure that the compiler does not emit a warning for unused variables, use the `[[maybe_unused]]` attribute:

```
double run([[maybe_unused]] int a, double b)
{
  return 2 * b;
}

[[maybe_unused]] auto i = get_value1();
```

- To ensure that intentional fall-through case labels in a `switch` statement are not flagged by the compiler with a warning, use the `[[fallthrough]]` attribute:

```
void option1() {}
void option2() {}

int alternative = get_value1();
switch (alternative)
{
  case 1:
    option1();
    [[fallthrough]]; // this is intentional
  case 2:
    option2();
}
```

- To help the compiler optimize paths of execution that are more or less likely to execute, use the C++20 `[[likely]]` and `[[unlikely]]` attributes:

```
void execute_command(char cmd)
{
  switch(cmd)
  {
    [[likely]]
    case 'a': /* add */ break;

    [[unlikely]]
    case 'd': /* delete */ break;

    case 'p': /* print */  break;

    default:  /* do something else */ break;
  }
}
```

How it works...

Attributes are a very flexible feature of C++; they can be used almost everywhere, but the actual usage is specifically defined for each particular attribute. They can be used on types, functions, variables, names, code blocks, or entire translation units.

Attributes are specified between double square brackets (for example, `[[attr1]]`) and more than one attribute can be specified in a declaration (for example, `[[attr1, attr2, attr3]]`).

Attributes can have arguments, for example, `[[mode(greedy)]]`, and can be fully qualified, for example, `[[sys::hidden]]` or `[[using sys: visibility(hidden), debug]]`.

Attributes can appear either before or after the name of the entity on which they are applied, or both, in which case they are combined. The following are several examples that exemplify this:

```
// attr1 applies to a, attr2 applies to b
int a [[attr1]], b [[attr2]];

// attr1 applies to a and b
int [[attr1]] a, b;
```

```
// attr1 applies to a and b, attr2 applies to a
int [[attr1]] a [[attr2]], b;
```

Attributes cannot appear in a namespace declaration, but they can appear as a single line declaration anywhere in a namespace. In this case, it is specific to each attribute whether it applies to the following declaration, to the namespace, or to the translation unit:

```
namespace test
{
  [[debug]];
}
```

The standard does define several attributes all compilers must implement, and using them can help you write better code. We have seen some of them in the examples given in the previous section. These attributes have been defined in different versions of the standard:

- In C++11:
    - The `[[noreturn]]` attribute indicates that a function does not return.
    - The `[[carries_dependency]]` attribute indicates that the dependency chain in release-consume `std::memory_order` propagates in and out of the function, which allows the compiler to skip unnecessary memory fence instructions.
- In C++14:
    - The `[[deprecated]]` and `[[deprecated("reason")]]` attributes indicate that the entity declared with these attributes is considered deprecated and should not be used. These attributes can be used with classes, non-static data members, typedefs, functions, enumerations, and template specializations. The `"reason"` string is an optional parameter.
- In C++17:
    - The `[[fallthrough]]` attribute indicates that fall-through between labels in a `switch` statement is intentional. The attribute must appear on a line of its own immediately before a `case` label.
    - The `[[nodiscard]]` attribute indicates that a return value from a function cannot be ignored.
    - The `[[maybe_unused]]` attribute indicates that an entity may be unused, but the compiler should not emit a warning about that. This attribute can be applied to variables, classes, non-static data members, enumerations, enumerators, and typedefs.

- In C++20:
    - The `[[nodiscard(text)]]` attribute is an extension of the C++17 `[[nodiscard]]` attribute and provides a text that describes the reason a result should not be discarded.
    - The `[[likely]]` and `[[unlikely]]` attributes provide hints for the compiler that a path of execution is more or less likely to execute, therefore allowing it to optimize accordingly. They can be applied to statements (but not declarations) and labels, but only one of them, as they are mutually exclusive.
    - The `[[no_unique_address]]` attribute can be applied to non-static data members, excluding bitfields, and tells the compiler that the member does not have to have a unique address. When applied to a member that has an empty type, the compiler can optimize it to occupy no space, as in the case of it being an empty base. On the other hand, if the member's type is not empty, the compiler may reuse any ensuing padding to store other data members.

Attributes are often ignored or briefly mentioned in books and tutorials on modern C++ programming, and the reason for that is probably the fact that developers cannot actually write attributes, as this language feature is intended for compiler implementations. For some compilers, though, it may be possible to define user-provided attributes; one such compiler is GCC, which supports plugins that add extra features to the compiler, and they can be used for defining new attributes too.

See also

- *Using noexcept for functions that do not throw* in *Chapter 9, Robustness and Performance*, to learn how to inform the compiler that a function should not throw exceptions

5

Standard Library Containers, Algorithms, and Iterators

The C++ standard library has evolved a lot with C++11, C++14, C++17, and now C++20. However, at its core initially sat three main pillars: containers, algorithms, and iterators. They are all implemented as general-purpose classes or function templates. In this chapter, we'll look at how these can be employed together for achieving various goals.

We will cover the following recipes in this chapter:

- Using vector as a default container
- Using bitset for fixed-size sequences of bits
- Using `vector<bool>` for variable-size sequences of bits
- Using the bit manipulation utilities
- Finding elements in a range
- Sorting a range
- Initializing a range
- Using set operations on a range
- Using iterators to insert new elements into a container
- Writing your own random-access iterator
- Container access with non-member functions

We'll begin this chapter by exploring the functionalities of the de facto default container in C++, which is `std::vector`.

Using vector as a default container

The standard library provides various types of containers that store collections of objects; the library includes sequence containers (such as `vector`, `array`, and `list`), ordered and unordered associative containers (such as `set` and `map`), and container adapters that do not store data but provide an adapted interface toward a sequence container (such as `stack` and `queue`). All of them are implemented as class templates, which means they can be used with any type (providing it meets the container requirements). In general, you should always use the container that is the most appropriate for a particular problem, which not only provides good performance in terms of speed of inserts, deletes, access to elements, and memory usage but also makes the code easy to read and maintain. However, the default choice should be `vector`. In this recipe, we will see why `vector` should be the preferred choice for a container in many cases and what the most common operations with `vector` are.

Getting ready

For this recipe, you must be familiar with arrays, both statically and dynamically allocated. A couple examples are provided here:

```
double d[3];           // a statically allocated array of 3 doubles
int* arr = new int[5]; // a dynamically allocated array of 5 ints
```

The class template `vector` is available in the `std` namespace in the `<vector>` header.

How to do it...

To initialize an `std::vector` class template, you can use any of the following methods, but you are not restricted to only these:

- Initialize from an initialization list:

  ```
  std::vector<int> v1 { 1, 2, 3, 4, 5 };
  ```

- Initialize from an array:

  ```
  int arr[] = { 1, 2, 3, 4, 5 };
  std::vector<int> v21(arr, arr + 5); // v21 = { 1, 2, 3, 4, 5 }
  std::vector<int> v22(arr+1, arr+4); // v22 = { 2, 3, 4 }
  ```

- Initialize from another container:

```
std::list<int> l{ 1, 2, 3, 4, 5 };
std::vector<int> v3(l.begin(), l.end()); //{ 1, 2, 3, 4, 5 }
```

- Initialize from a count and a value:

```
std::vector<int> v4(5, 1); // {1, 1, 1, 1, 1}
```

To modify the content of `std::vector`, you can use any of the following methods (you're not restricted to just these):

- Add an element at the end of the vector with `push_back()`:

```
std::vector<int> v1{ 1, 2, 3, 4, 5 };
v1.push_back(6); // v1 = { 1, 2, 3, 4, 5, 6 }
```

- Remove an element from the end of the vector with `pop_back()`:

```
v1.pop_back();
```

- Insert anywhere in the vector with `insert()`:

```
int arr[] = { 1, 2, 3, 4, 5 };
std::vector<int> v21;
v21.insert(v21.begin(), arr, arr + 5); // v21 = { 1, 2, 3, 4, 5 }
std::vector<int> v22;
v22.insert(v22.begin(), arr, arr + 3); // v22 = { 1, 2, 3 }
```

- Add an element by creating it at the end of the vector with `emplace_back()`:

```
struct foo
{
  int a;
  double b;
  std::string c;

  foo(int a, double b, std::string const & c) :
    a(a), b(b), c(c) {}
};

std::vector<foo> v3;
v3.emplace_back(1, 1.0, "one"s);
// v3 = { foo{1, 1.0, "one"} }
```

- Insert an element by creating it anywhere in the vector with `emplace()`:

```
v3.emplace(v3.begin(), 2, 2.0, "two"s);
// v3 = { foo{2, 2.0, "two"}, foo{1, 1.0, "one"} }
```

To modify the whole content of the vector, you can use any of the following methods, although you're not restricted to just these:

- Assign from another vector with `operator=`; this replaces the content of the container:

  ```
  std::vector<int> v1{ 1, 2, 3, 4, 5 };
  std::vector<int> v2{ 10, 20, 30 };
  v2 = v1; // v2 = { 1, 2, 3, 4, 5 }
  ```

- Assign from another sequence defined by a begin and end iterator with the `assign()` method; this replaces the content of the container:

  ```
  int arr[] = { 1, 2, 3, 4, 5 };
  std::vector<int> v31;
  v31.assign(arr, arr + 5);     // v31 = { 1, 2, 3, 4, 5 }
  std::vector<int> v32;
  v32.assign(arr + 1, arr + 4); // v32 = { 2, 3, 4 }
  ```

- Swap the content of two vectors with the `swap()` method:

  ```
  std::vector<int> v4{ 1, 2, 3, 4, 5 };
  std::vector<int> v5{ 10, 20, 30 };
  v4.swap(v5); // v4 = { 10, 20, 30 }, v5 = { 1, 2, 3, 4, 5 }
  ```

- Remove all the elements with the `clear()` method:

  ```
  std::vector<int> v6{ 1, 2, 3, 4, 5 };
  v6.clear(); // v6 = { }
  ```

- Remove one or more elements with the `erase()` method (which requires either an iterator or a pair of iterators that define the range of elements from the vector to be removed):

  ```
  std::vector<int> v7{ 1, 2, 3, 4, 5 };
  v7.erase(v7.begin() + 2, v7.begin() + 4); // v7 = { 1, 2, 5 }
  ```

To get the address of the first element in a vector, usually to pass the content of a vector to a C-like API, use any of the following methods:

- Use the `data()` method, which returns a pointer to the first element, providing direct access to the underlying contiguous sequence of memory where the vector elements are stored; this is only available since C++11:

  ```
  void process(int const * const arr, size_t const size)
  { /* do something */ }

  std::vector<int> v{ 1, 2, 3, 4, 5 };
  process(v.data(), v.size());
  ```

- Get the address of the first element:

```
process(&v[0], v.size());
```

- Get the address of the element referred to by the `front()` method:

```
process(&v.front(), v.size());
```

- Get the address of the element pointed by the iterator returned from `begin()`:

```
process(&*v.begin(), v.size());
```

How it works...

The `std::vector` class is designed to be the C++ container most similar to and inter-operable with arrays. A vector is a variable-sized sequence of elements, guaranteed to be stored contiguously in memory, which makes the content of a vector easily passable to a C-like function that takes a pointer to an element of an array and, usually, a size. There are many benefits of using a vector instead of arrays, and these benefits include:

- No direct memory management is required from the developer as the container does this internally, allocating memory, reallocating it, and releasing it.

Note that a vector is intended for storing object instances. If you need to store pointers, do not store raw pointers but smart pointers. Otherwise, you need to handle the lifetime management of the pointed objects.

- The possibility of modifying the size of the vector.
- Simple assignment or concatenation of two vectors.
- Direct comparison of two vectors.

The `vector` class is a very efficient container, with all its implementations providing a lot of optimizations that most developers are not capable of doing with arrays. Random access to its elements and insertion and removal at the end of a vector is a constant `O(1)` operation (provided that reallocation is not necessary), while insertion and removal anywhere else is a linear `O(n)` operation.

Compared to other standard containers, the vector has various benefits:

- It is compatible with arrays and C-like APIs. If a function takes an array as a parameter, the content of other containers (except for `std::array`) needs to be copied to a `vector` before being passed as an argument to the function.

- It has the fastest access to elements of all containers (but the same as `std::array`).
- It has no per-element memory overhead for storing elements. This is because elements are stored in a contiguous space, like arrays are. Therefore, `vector` has a small memory footprint, unlike other containers, such as `list`, which require additional pointers to other elements, or associative containers, which require hash values.

`std::vector` is very similar in semantics to arrays but has a variable size. The size of a vector can increase and decrease. There are two properties that define the size of a vector:

- *Capacity* is the number of elements the vector can accommodate without performing additional memory allocations; this is indicated by the `capacity()` method.
- *Size* is the actual number of elements in the vector; this is indicated by the `size()` method.

Size is always smaller than or equal to capacity. When size is equal to capacity and a new element needs to be added, the capacity needs to be modified so that the vector has space for more elements. In this case, the vector allocates a new chunk of memory and moves the previous content to the new location before freeing the previously allocated memory. Though this sounds time-consuming—and it is—implementations increase the capacity exponentially by doubling it each time it needs to be changed. As a result, on average, each element of the vector only needs to be moved once (that is because all the elements of the vector are moved during an increase of capacity, but then an equal number of elements can be added without incurring more moves, given that insertions are performed at the end of the vector).

If you know beforehand how many elements will be inserted in the vector, you can first call the `reserve()` method to increase the capacity to at least the specified amount (this method does nothing if the specified size is smaller than the current capacity) and only then insert the elements.

On the other hand, if you need to free additional reserved memory, you can use the `shrink_to_fit()` method to request this, but it is an implementation decision as to whether to free any memory or not. An alternative to this non-binding method, available since C++11, is to do a swap with a temporary, empty vector:

```
std::vector<int> v{ 1, 2, 3, 4, 5 };
std::vector<int>().swap(v); // v.size = 0, v.capacity = 0
```

Calling the `clear()` method only removes all the elements from the vector but does not free any memory.

It should be noted that the `vector` class implements some operations that are specific to other types of containers:

- *stack*: With `push_back()` and `emplace_back()` to add at the end and `pop_back()` to remove from the end. Keep in mind that `pop_back()` does not return the last element that has been removed. You need to access that explicitly, if that is necessary, for instance, using the `back()` method before removing the element.
- *list*: With `insert()` and `emplace()` to add elements in the middle of the sequence and `erase()` to remove elements from anywhere in the sequence.

A good rule of thumb for C++ containers is to use `std::vector` as the default container unless you have good reasons to use another one.

See also

- *Using bitset for fixed-size sequences of bits* to learn about the standard container for handling bit sequences of fixed sizes.
- *Using vector<bool> for variable-size sequences of bits* to learn about the specialization of `std::vector` for the `bool` type, intended for handling bit sequences of variable sizes.

Using bitset for fixed-size sequences of bits

It is not uncommon for developers to operate with bit flags. This can be either because they work with operating system APIs (usually written in C) that take various types of arguments (such as options or styles) in the form of bit flags, or because they work with libraries that do similar things, or simply because some types of problems are naturally solved with bit flags. We can think of alternatives to working with bits and bit operations, such as defining arrays that have one element for every option/flag, or defining a structure with members and functions to model the bit flags, but these are often more complicated; and in the case where you need to pass a numerical value representing bit flags to a function, you still need to convert the array or the structure to a sequence of bits. For this reason, the C++ standard provides a container called `std::bitset` for fixed-size sequences of bits.

Getting ready

For this recipe, you must be familiar with bitwise operations (AND, OR, XOR, NOT, and shifting).

The `bitset` class is available in the `std` namespace in the `<bitset>` header. A bitset represents a fixed-size sequence of bits, with the size defined at compile time. For convenience, in this recipe, most examples will be with bitsets of 8 bits.

How to do it...

To construct an `std::bitset` object, use one of the available constructors:

- An empty bitset with all bits set to `0`:

  ```
  std::bitset<8> b1;              // [0,0,0,0,0,0,0,0]
  ```

- A bitset from a numerical value:

  ```
  std::bitset<8> b2{ 10 };        // [0,0,0,0,1,0,1,0]
  ```

- A bitset from a string of `'0'` and `'1'`:

  ```
  std::bitset<8> b3{ "1010"s }; // [0,0,0,0,1,0,1,0]
  ```

- A bitset from a string containing any two characters representing `'0'` and `'1'`; in this case, we must specify which character represents a `0` (the fourth parameter, `'o'`) and which character represents a `1` (the fifth parameter, `'x'`):

  ```
  std::bitset<8> b4
    { "ooooxoxo"s, 0, std::string::npos, 'o', 'x' };
    // [0,0,0,0,1,0,1,0]
  ```

To test individual bits in the set or the entire set for specific values, use any of the available methods:

- `count()` to get the number of bits set to `1`:

  ```
  std::bitset<8> bs{ 10 };
  std::cout << "has " << bs.count() << " 1s" << '\n';
  ```

- `any()` to check whether there is at least one bit set to `1`:

  ```
  if (bs.any()) std::cout << "has some 1s" << '\n';
  ```

- `all()` to check whether all the bits are set to `1`:

```
if (bs.all()) std::cout << "has only 1s" << '\n';
```

- `none()` to check whether all the bits are set to `0`:

```
if (bs.none()) std::cout << "has no 1s" << '\n';
```

- `test()` to check the value of an individual bit (whose position is the only argument to the function):

```
if (!bs.test(0)) std::cout << "even" << '\n';
```

- `operator[]` to access and test individual bits:

```
if(!bs[0]) std::cout << "even" << '\n';
```

To modify the content of a bitset, use any of the following methods:

- Member operators `|=`, `&=`, `^=`, and `~` to perform the binary operation OR, AND, XOR, and NOT, respectively. Alternatively, use the non-member operators `|`, `&`, and `^`:

```
std::bitset<8> b1{ 42 }; // [0,0,1,0,1,0,1,0]
std::bitset<8> b2{ 11 }; // [0,0,0,0,1,0,1,1]
auto b3 = b1 | b2;       // [0,0,1,0,1,0,1,1]
auto b4 = b1 & b2;       // [0,0,0,0,1,0,1,0]
auto b5 = b1 ^ b2;       // [1,1,0,1,1,1,1,0]
auto b6 = ~b1;           // [1,1,0,1,0,1,0,1]
```

- Member operators `<<=`, `<<`, `>>=`, and `>>` to perform shifting operations:

```
auto b7 = b1 << 2;       // [1,0,1,0,1,0,0,0]
auto b8 = b1 >> 2;       // [0,0,0,0,1,0,1,0]
```

- `flip()` to toggle the entire set or an individual bit from `0` to `1` or from `1` to `0`:

```
b1.flip();               // [1,1,0,1,0,1,0,1]
b1.flip(0);              // [1,1,0,1,0,1,0,0]
```

- `set()` to change the entire set or an individual bit to `true` or the specified value:

```
b1.set(0, true);         // [1,1,0,1,0,1,0,1]
b1.set(0, false);        // [1,1,0,1,0,1,0,0]
```

- `reset()` to change the entire set or an individual bit to `false`:

```
b1.reset(2);             // [1,1,0,1,0,0,0,0]
```

To convert a bitset to a numerical or string value, use the following methods:

- `to_ulong()` and `to_ullong()` to convert to `unsigned long` or `unsigned long long`. These operations throw an `std::overflow_error` exception if the value cannot be represented in the output type. Refer to the following examples:

```
std::bitset<8> bs{ 42 };
auto n1 = bs.to_ulong();  // n1 = 42UL
auto n2 = bs.to_ullong(); // n2 = 42ULL
```

- `to_string()` to convert to `std::basic_string`. By default, the result is a string containing `'0'` and `'1'`, but you can specify a different character for these two values:

```
auto s1 = bs.to_string();            // s1 = "00101010"
auto s2 = bs.to_string('o', 'x'); // s2 = "ooxoxoxo"
```

How it works...

If you've ever worked with C or C-like APIs, chances are you either wrote or at least have seen code that manipulates bits to define styles, options, or other kinds of values. This usually involves operations such as:

- Defining the bit flags; these can be enumerations, static constants in a class, or macros introduced with `#define` in the C style. Usually, there is a flag representing no value (style, option, and so on). Since these are supposed to be bit flags, their values are powers of 2.
- Adding and removing flags from the set (that is, a numerical value). Adding a bit flag is done with the bit-or operator (`value |= FLAG`) and removing a bit flag is done with the bit-and operator, with the negated flag (`value &= ~FLAG`).
- Testing whether a flag is added to the set (`value & FLAG == FLAG`).
- Calling functions with the flags as an argument.

The following shows a simple example of flags defining the border style of a control that can have a border on the left, right, top, or bottom side, or any combination of these, including no border:

```
#define BORDER_NONE   0x00
#define BORDER_LEFT   0x01
#define BORDER_TOP    0x02
#define BORDER_RIGHT  0x04
#define BORDER_BOTTOM 0x08
```

```
void apply_style(unsigned int const style)
{
  if (style & BORDER_BOTTOM) { /* do something */ }
}

// initialize with no flags
unsigned int style = BORDER_NONE;
// set a flag
style = BORDER_BOTTOM;
// add more flags
style |= BORDER_LEFT | BORDER_RIGHT | BORDER_TOP;
// remove some flags
style &= ~BORDER_LEFT;
style &= ~BORDER_RIGHT;
// test if a flag is set
if ((style & BORDER_BOTTOM) == BORDER_BOTTOM) {}
// pass the flags as argument to a function
apply_style(style);
```

The standard `std::bitset` class is intended as a C++ alternative to this C-like working style with sets of bits. It enables us to write more robust and safer code because it abstracts the bit operations with member functions, though we still need to identify what each bit in the set is representing:

- Adding and removing flags is done with the `set()` and `reset()` methods, which set the value of a bit indicated by its position to `1` or `0` (or `true` and `false`); alternatively, we can use the index operator for the same purpose.
- Testing if a bit is set with the `test()` method.
- Conversion from an integer or a string is done through the constructor, and conversion to an integer or string is done with member functions so that the values from the bitsets can be used where integers are expected (such as arguments to functions).

In addition to these operations, the `bitset` class has additional methods for performing bitwise operations on bits, shifting, testing, and others that have been shown in the previous section.

Conceptually, `std::bitset` is a representation of a numerical value that enables you to access and modify individual bits. Internally, however, a `bitset` has an array of integer values on which it performs bit operations. The size of a `bitset` is not limited to the size of a numerical type; it can be anything, except that it is a compile-time constant.

The example of the control border styles from the previous section can be written using `std::bitset` in the following manner:

```
struct border_flags
{
  static const int left = 0;
  static const int top = 1;
  static const int right = 2;
  static const int bottom = 3;
};

// initialize with no flags
std::bitset<4> style;
// set a flag
style.set(border_flags::bottom);
// set more flags
style
  .set(border_flags::left)
  .set(border_flags::top)
  .set(border_flags::right);
// remove some flags
style[border_flags::left] = 0;
style.reset(border_flags::right);
// test if a flag is set
if (style.test(border_flags::bottom)) {}
// pass the flags as argument to a function
apply_style(style.to_ulong());
```

Keep in mind this is only a possible implementation. For instance, the `border_flags` class could have been an enumeration. However, the resulting code is more expressive and easier to understand.

There's more...

A bitset can be created from an integer and can convert its value to an integer using the `to_ulong()` or `to_ullong()` methods. However, if the size of the bitset is larger than the size of these numerical types and any of the bits beyond the size of the requested numerical type is set to `1`, then these methods throw an `std::overflow_error` exception. This is because the value cannot be represented on `unsigned long` or `unsigned long long`. In order to extract all the bits, we need to do the following operations:

- Clear the bits beyond the size of `unsigned long` or `unsigned long long`.
- Convert the value to `unsigned long` or `unsigned long long`.
- Shift the bitset with the number of bits in `unsigned long` or `unsigned long long`.
- Do this until all the bits are retrieved.

These are implemented as follows:

```
template <size_t N>
std::vector<unsigned long> bitset_to_vectorulong(std::bitset<N> bs)
{
  auto result = std::vector<unsigned long> {};
  auto const size = 8 * sizeof(unsigned long);
  auto const mask = std::bitset<N>{ static_cast<unsigned long>(-1)};

  auto totalbits = 0;
  while (totalbits < N)
  {
    auto value = (bs & mask).to_ulong();
    result.push_back(value);
    bs >>= size;
    totalbits += size;
  }

  return result;
}

std::bitset<128> bs =
    (std::bitset<128>(0xFEDC) << 96) |
    (std::bitset<128>(0xBA98) << 64) |
    (std::bitset<128>(0x7654) << 32) |
    std::bitset<128>(0x3210);

std::cout << bs << '\n';

auto result = bitset_to_vectorulong(bs);
for (auto const v : result)
  std::cout << std::hex << v << '\n';
```

For cases where the size of the `bitset` cannot be known at compile time, the alternative is `std::vector<bool>`, which we will cover in the next recipe.

See also

- *Using vector<bool> for variable-size sequences of bits* to learn about the specialization of `std::vector` for the `bool` type, which is used for handling bit sequences of variable sizes.
- *Using the bit manipulation utilities* to explore the C++20 set of utility functions for bit manipulation from the numeric library.

Using vector<bool> for variable-size sequences of bits

In the previous recipe, we looked at using `std::bitset` for fixed-size sequences of bits. Sometimes, however, `std::bitset` is not a good choice because you do not know the number of bits at compile time, and just defining a set of a large enough number of bits is not a good idea. This is because you can get into a situation where the number is not actually large enough. The standard alternative for this is to use the `std::vector<bool>` container, which is a specialization of `std::vector` with space and speed optimizations since implementations do not actually store Boolean values, but individual bits for each element.

For this reason, however, `std::vector<bool>` does not meet the requirements of a standard container or sequential container, nor does `std::vector<bool>::iterator` meet the requirements of a forward iterator. As a result, this specialization cannot be used in generic code where a vector is expected. On the other hand, being a vector, it has a different interface from that of `std::bitset` and cannot be viewed as a binary representation of a number. There are no direct ways to construct `std::vector<bool>` from a number or string, nor to convert it to a number or string.

Getting ready...

This recipe assumes you are familiar with both `std::vector` and `std::bitset`. If you didn't read the previous recipes, *Using vector as a default container* and *Using bitset for fixed-size sequences of bits*, you should read them before continuing.

The `vector<bool>` class is available in the `std` namespace in the `<vector>` header.

How to do it...

To manipulate an `std::vector<bool>`, use the same methods you would use for an `std::vector<T>`, as shown in the following examples:

- Creating an empty vector:

```
std::vector<bool> bv; // []
```

- Adding bits to the vector:

```
bv.push_back(true);  // [1]
bv.push_back(true);  // [1, 1]
bv.push_back(false); // [1, 1, 0]
bv.push_back(false); // [1, 1, 0, 0]
bv.push_back(true);  // [1, 1, 0, 0, 1]
```

- Setting the values of individual bits:

```
bv[3] = true;        // [1, 1, 0, 1, 1]
```

- Using generic algorithms:

```
auto count_of_ones = std::count(bv.cbegin(), bv.cend(), true);
```

- Removing bits from the vector:

```
bv.erase(bv.begin() + 2); // [1, 1, 1, 1]
```

How it works...

`std::vector<bool>` is not a standard vector because it is designed to provide space optimization by storing a single bit for each element instead of a Boolean value. Therefore, its elements are not stored in a contiguous sequence and cannot be substituted for an array of Booleans. Due to this:

- The index operator cannot return a reference to a specific element because elements are not stored individually:

```
std::vector<bool> bv;
bv.resize(10);
auto& bit = bv[0];      // error
```

- Dereferencing an iterator cannot produce a reference to `bool` for the same reason as mentioned earlier:

```
auto& bit = *bv.begin(); // error
```

- There is no guarantee that individual bits can be manipulated independently at the same time from different threads.
- The vector cannot be used with algorithms that require forward iterators, such as `std::search()`.
- The vector cannot be used in some generic code where `std::vector<T>` is expected if such code requires any of the operations mentioned in this list.

An alternative to `std::vector<bool>` is `std::dequeu<bool>`, which is a standard container (a double-ended queue) that meets all container and iterator requirements and can be used with all standard algorithms. However, this will not have the space optimization that `std::vector<bool>` provides.

There's more...

The `std::vector<bool>` interface is very different from `std::bitset`. If you want to be able to write code in a similar manner, you can create a wrapper on `std::vector<bool>`, which looks like `std::bitset`, where possible. The following implementation provides members similar to what is available in `std::bitset`:

```
class bitvector
{
  std::vector<bool> bv;
public:
  bitvector(std::vector<bool> const & bv) : bv(bv) {}
  bool operator[](size_t const i) { return bv[i]; }

  inline bool any() const {
    for (auto b : bv) if (b) return true;
    return false;
  }

  inline bool all() const {
    for (auto b : bv) if (!b) return false;
    return true;
  }

  inline bool none() const { return !any(); }

  inline size_t count() const {
    return std::count(bv.cbegin(), bv.cend(), true);
  }
```

```
inline size_t size() const { return bv.size(); }

inline bitvector & add(bool const value) {
  bv.push_back(value);
  return *this;
}

inline bitvector & remove(size_t const index) {
  if (index >= bv.size())
    throw std::out_of_range("Index out of range");
  bv.erase(bv.begin() + index);
  return *this;
}

inline bitvector & set(bool const value = true) {
  for (size_t i = 0; i < bv.size(); ++i)
    bv[i] = value;
  return *this;
}

inline bitvector& set(size_t const index, bool const value = true) {
  if (index >= bv.size())
    throw std::out_of_range("Index out of range");
  bv[index] = value;
  return *this;
}

inline bitvector & reset() {
  for (size_t i = 0; i < bv.size(); ++i) bv[i] = false;
  return *this;
}

inline bitvector & reset(size_t const index) {
  if (index >= bv.size())
    throw std::out_of_range("Index out of range");
  bv[index] = false;
  return *this;
}

inline bitvector & flip() {
  bv.flip();
  return *this;
}
```

```
   std::vector<bool>& data() { return bv; }
};
```

This is only a basic implementation, and if you want to use such a wrapper, you should add additional methods, such as bit logic operations, shifting, maybe reading and writing from and to streams, and so on. However, with the preceding code, we can write the following examples:

```
bitvector bv;
bv.add(true).add(true).add(false); // [1, 1, 0]
bv.add(false);                     // [1, 1, 0, 0]
bv.add(true);                      // [1, 1, 0, 0, 1]

if (bv.any()) std::cout << "has some 1s" << '\n';
if (bv.all()) std::cout << "has only 1s" << '\n';
if (bv.none()) std::cout << "has no 1s" << '\n';
std::cout << "has " << bv.count() << " 1s" << '\n';

bv.set(2, true);                   // [1, 1, 1, 0, 1]
bv.set();                          // [1, 1, 1, 1, 1]

bv.reset(0);                       // [0, 1, 1, 1, 1]
bv.reset();                        // [0, 0, 0, 0, 0]

bv.flip();                         // [1, 1, 1, 1, 1]
```

These examples are very similar to the examples where an `std::bitset` was used. This `bitvector` class has a compatible API to `std::bitset` but is useful for handling bit sequences of variable sizes.

See also

- *Using vector as a default container* to learn how to use the `std::vector` standard container.
- *Using bitset for fixed-size sequences of bits* to learn about the standard container for handling bit sequences of fixed sizes.
- *Using the bit manipulation utilities* to explore the C++20 set of utility functions for bit manipulation from the numeric library.

Using the bit manipulation utilities

In the previous recipes, we have seen how to use `std::bitset` and `std::vector<bool>` to work with fixed and variable sequences of bits. There are, however, situations when we need to manipulate or process individual or multiple bits of an unsigned integral value. This includes operations such as counting or rotating bits. The C++20 standard provides a set of utility functions for bit manipulation as part of the numeric library. In this recipe, we will learn what they are and how to use these utilities.

Getting ready

The function templates discussed in this recipe are all available in the `std` namespace in the new C++20 header `<bit>`.

How to do it...

Use the following function templates to manipulate bits of unsigned integral types:

- If you need to perform a circular shift, use `std::rotl<T>()` for left rotation and `std::rotr<T>()` for right rotation:

```
unsigned char n = 0b00111100;

auto vl1 = std::rotl(n, 0); // 0b00111100
auto vl2 = std::rotl(n, 1); // 0b01111000
auto vl3 = std::rotl(n, 3); // 0b11100001
auto vl4 = std::rotl(n, 9); // 0b01111000
auto vl5 = std::rotl(n, -2);// 0b00001111

auto vr1 = std::rotr(n, 0);  // 0b00111100
auto vr2 = std::rotr(n, 1);  // 0b00011110
auto vr3 = std::rotr(n, 3);  // 0b10000111
auto vr4 = std::rotr(n, 9);  // 0b00011110
auto vr5 = std::rotr(n, -2); // 0b11110000
```

- If you need to count the number of consecutive `0` bits (that is, until a `1` is found), use `std::countl_zero<T>()` to count from left to right (that is, starting with the most significant bit) and `std::countr_zero<T>()` to count from right to left (that is, starting with the least significant bit):

```
std::cout << std::countl_zero(0b00000000) << '\n'; // 8
std::cout << std::countl_zero(0b11111111) << '\n'; // 0
```

```
std::cout << std::countl_zero(0b00111010) << '\n'; // 2

std::cout << std::countr_zero(0b00000000) << '\n'; // 8
std::cout << std::countr_zero(0b11111111) << '\n'; // 0
std::cout << std::countr_zero(0b00111010) << '\n'; // 1
```

- If you need to count the number of consecutive `1` bits (that is, until a `0` is found), use `std::countl_one<T>()` to count from left to right (that is, starting with the most significant bit) and `std::countr_one<T>()` to count from right to left (that is, starting with the least significant bit):

```
std::cout << std::countl_one(0b00000000) << '\n'; // 0
std::cout << std::countl_one(0b11111111) << '\n'; // 8
std::cout << std::countl_one(0b11000101) << '\n'; // 2

std::cout << std::countr_one(0b00000000) << '\n'; // 0
std::cout << std::countr_one(0b11111111) << '\n'; // 8
std::cout << std::countr_one(0b11000101) << '\n'; // 1
```

- If you need to count the number of `1` bits, use `std::popcount<T>()`. The number of `0` bits is the number of digits used to represent the value (this can be determined with `std::numeric_limits<T>::digits`), minus the count of `1` bits:

```
std::cout << std::popcount(0b00000000) << '\n'; // 0
std::cout << std::popcount(0b11111111) << '\n'; // 8
std::cout << std::popcount(0b10000001) << '\n'; // 2
```

- If you need to check whether a number is a power of two, use `std::has_single_bit<T>()`:

```
std::cout << std::boolalpha << std::has_single_bit(0) << '\n';
// false
std::cout << std::boolalpha << std::has_single_bit(1) << '\n';
// true
std::cout << std::boolalpha << std::has_single_bit(2) << '\n';
// true
std::cout << std::boolalpha << std::has_single_bit(3) << '\n';
// false
std::cout << std::boolalpha << std::has_single_bit(4) << '\n';
// true
```

- If you need to find the smallest power of two that is greater than or equal to a given number, use `std::bit_ceil<T>()`. On the other hand, if you need to find the largest power of two that is smaller than or equal to a given number, use `std::bit_floor<T>()`:

```
std::cout << std::bit_ceil(0)  << '\n'; // 0
std::cout << std::bit_ceil(3)  << '\n'; // 4
std::cout << std::bit_ceil(4)  << '\n'; // 4
std::cout << std::bit_ceil(31) << '\n'; // 32
std::cout << std::bit_ceil(42) << '\n'; // 64

std::cout << std::bit_floor(0)  << '\n'; // 0
std::cout << std::bit_floor(3)  << '\n'; // 2
std::cout << std::bit_floor(4)  << '\n'; // 4
std::cout << std::bit_floor(31) << '\n'; // 16
std::cout << std::bit_floor(42) << '\n'; // 32
```

- If you need to determine the smallest number of digits to represent a number, use `std::bit_width<T>()`:

```
std::cout << std::bit_width(0)    << '\n'; // 1
std::cout << std::bit_width(2)    << '\n'; // 3
std::cout << std::bit_width(15)   << '\n'; // 4
std::cout << std::bit_width(16)   << '\n'; // 5
std::cout << std::bit_width(1000) << '\n'; // 10
```

- If you need to reinterpret the object representation of a type `F` as that of a type `T`, then use `std::bit_cast<T, F>()`:

```
const double pi = 3.1415927;
const uint64_t bits = std::bit_cast<uint64_t>(pi);
const double pi2 = std::bit_cast<double>(bits);

std::cout
   << std::fixed << pi   << '\n'   // 3.1415923
   << std::hex   << bits << '\n'   // 400921fb5a7ed197
   << std::fixed << pi2  << '\n';  // 3.1415923
```

How it works...

All the function templates mentioned in the previous section, with the exception of `std::bit_cast<T, F>()` are only available for unsigned integral types. That includes the types `unsigned char`, `unsigned short`, `unsigned int`, `unsigned long`, and `unsigned long long`, as well as the extended unsigned integer types (such as `uint8_t`, `uint64_t`, `uint_least8_t`, `uintmax_t`, and so on). These functions are simple and should not require a detailed description.

The function that is different from the rest is `std::bit_cast<T, F>()`. Here, `F` is the type that is reinterpreted, and `T` is the type that we interpret to. This function template does not require `T` and `F` to be unsigned integral types, but both of them must be trivially copyable. Moreover, the `sizeof(T)` must be the same as the `sizeof(F)`.

The specification for this function does not mention the value of padding bits in the result. On the other hand, if the result value does not correspond to a valid value of the type `T`, then the behavior is undefined.

`std::bit_cast<T, F>()` can be `constexpr` if `T`, `F`, and the types of all their sub-objects is not a union type, a pointer type, a pointer to member type, a volatile-qualified type, and has no non-static data members of a reference type.

See also

- *Using bitset for fixed-size sequences of bits* to learn about the standard container for handling bit sequences of fixed sizes.
- *Using vector<bool> for variable-size sequences of bits* to learn about the specialization of `std::vector` for the `bool` type intended for handling bit sequences of variable sizes.

Finding elements in a range

One of the most common operations we do in any application is searching through data. Therefore, it is not surprising that the standard library provides many generic algorithms for searching through standard containers, or anything that can represent a range and is defined by a start and a past-the-end iterator. In this recipe, we will see what these standard algorithms are and how they can be used.

Getting ready

For all the examples in this recipe, we will use `std::vector`, but all the algorithms work with ranges defined by a begin and past-the-end, either input or forward iterators, depending on the algorithm (for more information about the various types of iterators, see the *Writing your own random access iterator* recipe, later in this chapter). All these algorithms are available in the `std` namespace in the `<algorithm>` header.

How to do it...

The following is a list of algorithms that can be used for finding elements in a range:

- Use `std::find()` to find a value in a range; this algorithm returns an iterator to the first element equal to the value:

```
std::vector<int> v{ 1, 1, 2, 3, 5, 8, 13 };

auto it = std::find(v.cbegin(), v.cend(), 3);
if (it != v.cend()) std::cout << *it << '\n';
```

- Use `std::find_if()` to find a value in a range that meets a criterion from a unary predicate; this algorithm returns an iterator to the first element for which the predicate returns `true`:

```
std::vector<int> v{ 1, 1, 2, 3, 5, 8, 13 };

auto it = std::find_if(v.cbegin(), v.cend(),
                       [](int const n) {return n > 10; });
if (it != v.cend()) std::cout << *it << '\n';
```

- Use `std::find_if_not()` to find a value in a range that does not meet a criterion from a unary predicate; this algorithm returns an iterator to the first element for which the predicate returns `false`:

```
std::vector<int> v{ 1, 1, 2, 3, 5, 8, 13 };

auto it = std::find_if_not(v.cbegin(), v.cend(),
                     [](int const n) {return n % 2 == 1; });
if (it != v.cend()) std::cout << *it << '\n';
```

- Use `std::find_first_of()` to search for the occurrence of any value from a range in another range; this algorithm returns an iterator to the first element that is found:

```
std::vector<int> v{ 1, 1, 2, 3, 5, 8, 13 };
std::vector<int> p{ 5, 7, 11 };

auto it = std::find_first_of(v.cbegin(), v.cend(),
                             p.cbegin(), p.cend());
if (it != v.cend())
  std::cout << "found " << *it
            << " at index " << std::distance(v.cbegin(), it)
            << '\n';
```

- Use `std::find_end()` to find the last occurrence of a subrange of elements in a range; this algorithm returns an iterator to the first element of the last subrange in the range:

```
std::vector<int> v1{ 1, 1, 0, 0, 1, 0, 1, 0, 1, 0, 1, 1 };
std::vector<int> v2{ 1, 0, 1 };

auto it = std::find_end(v1.cbegin(), v1.cend(),
                        v2.cbegin(), v2.cend());
if (it != v1.cend())
  std::cout << "found at index "
            << std::distance(v1.cbegin(), it) << '\n';
```

- Use `std::search()` to search for the first occurrence of a subrange in a range; this algorithm returns an iterator to the first element of the subrange in the range:

```
auto text = "The quick brown fox jumps over the lazy dog"s;
auto word = "over"s;

auto it = std::search(text.cbegin(), text.cend(),
                      word.cbegin(), word.cend());

if (it != text.cend())
  std::cout << "found " << word
            << " at index "
            << std::distance(text.cbegin(), it) << '\n';
```

- Use `std::search()` with a *searcher*, which is a class that implements a searching algorithm and meets some predefined criteria. This overload of `std::search()` was introduced in C++17, and available standard searchers implement the *Boyer-Moore* and *Boyer-Moore-Horspool* string searching algorithms:

```
auto text = "The quick brown fox jumps over the lazy dog"s;
auto word = "over"s;

auto it = std::search(
  text.cbegin(), text.cend(),
  std::make_boyer_moore_searcher(word.cbegin(), word.cend()));

if (it != text.cend())
  std::cout << "found " << word
            << " at index "
            << std::distance(text.cbegin(), it) << '\n';
```

- Use `std::search_n()` to search for *N* consecutive occurrences of a value in a range; this algorithm returns an iterator to the first element of the found sequence in the range:

```
std::vector<int> v{ 1, 1, 0, 0, 1, 0, 1, 0, 1, 0, 1, 1 };

auto it = std::search_n(v.cbegin(), v.cend(), 2, 0);
if (it != v.cend())
  std::cout << "found at index "
            << std::distance(v.cbegin(), it) << '\n';
```

- Use `std::adjacent_find()` to find two adjacent elements in a range that are equal or satisfy a binary predicate; this algorithm returns an iterator to the first element that is found:

```
std::vector<int> v{ 1, 1, 2, 3, 5, 8, 13 };

auto it = std::adjacent_find(v.cbegin(), v.cend());
if (it != v.cend())
  std::cout << "found at index "
            << std::distance(v.cbegin(), it) << '\n';

auto it = std::adjacent_find(
  v.cbegin(), v.cend(),
  [](int const a, int const b) {
    return IsPrime(a) && IsPrime(b); });

if (it != v.cend())
  std::cout << "found at index "
            << std::distance(v.cbegin(), it) << '\n';
```

- Use `std::binary_search()` to find whether an element exists in a sorted range; this algorithm returns a Boolean value to indicate whether the value was found or not:

```
std::vector<int> v{ 1, 1, 2, 3, 5, 8, 13 };

auto success = std::binary_search(v.cbegin(), v.cend(), 8);
if (success) std::cout << "found" << '\n';
```

- Use `std::lower_bound()` to find the first element in a range not less than a specified value; this algorithm returns an iterator to the element:

```
std::vector<int> v{ 1, 1, 2, 3, 5, 8, 13 };

auto it = std::lower_bound(v.cbegin(), v.cend(), 1);
```

```
if (it != v.cend())
  std::cout << "lower bound at "
            << std::distance(v.cbegin(), it) << '\n';
```

- Use `std::upper_bound()` to find the first element in a range greater than a specified value; this algorithm returns an iterator to the element:

```
std::vector<int> v{ 1, 1, 2, 3, 5, 8, 13 };

auto it = std::upper_bound(v.cbegin(), v.cend(), 1);
if (it != v.cend())
  std::cout << "upper bound at "
            << std::distance(v.cbegin(), it) << '\n';
```

- Use `std::equal_range()` to find a subrange in a range whose values are equal to a specified value. This algorithm returns a pair of iterators defining the first and the one-past-end iterators to the subrange; these two iterators are equivalent to those returned by `std::lower_bound()` and `std::upper_bound()`:

```
std::vector<int> v{ 1, 1, 2, 3, 5, 8, 13 };

auto bounds = std::equal_range(v.cbegin(), v.cend(), 1);
std::cout << "range between indexes "
          << std::distance(v.cbegin(), bounds.first)
          << " and "
          << std::distance(v.cbegin(), bounds.second)
          << '\n';
```

How it works...

The way these algorithms work is very similar: they all take, as arguments, iterators that define the searchable range and additional arguments that depend on each algorithm. The exceptions are `std::search()`, which returns a Boolean, and `std::equal_range()`, which returns a pair of iterators. They all return an iterator to the searched element or to a subrange. These iterators must be compared with the end iterator (that is, the past-last-element) of the range to check whether the search was successful or not. If the search did not find an element or a subrange, then the returned value is the end iterator.

All these algorithms have multiple overloads, but in the *How to do it...* section, we only looked at one particular overload to show how the algorithm can be used. For a complete reference of all overloads, you should see other sources.

In all the preceding examples, we used constant iterators, but all these algorithms work the same with mutable iterators and with reverse iterators. Because they take iterators as input arguments, they can work with standard containers, arrays, or anything that represents a sequence and has iterators available.

A special note on the `std::binary_search()` algorithm is necessary: the iterator parameters that define the range to search in should at least meet the requirements of the forward iterators. Regardless of the type of the supplied iterators, the number of comparisons is always logarithmic on the size of the range. However, the number of iterator increments is different if the iterators are random access, in which case the number of increments is also logarithmic, or are not random access, in which case it is linear and proportional to the size of the range.

All these algorithms, except for `std::find_if_not()`, were available before C++11. However, some overloads of them have been introduced in the newer standards. An example is `std::search()`, which has several overloads that were introduced in C++17. One of these overloads has the following form:

```
template<class ForwardIterator, class Searcher>
ForwardIterator search(ForwardIterator first, ForwardIterator last,
                       const Searcher& searcher );
```

This overload searches for the occurrence of a pattern defined by a searcher function object for which the standard provides several implementations:

- `default_searcher` basically delegates the searching to the standard `std::search()` algorithm.
- `boyer_moore_searcher` implements the Boyer-Moore algorithm for string searching.
- `boyer_moore_horspool_algorithm` implements the Boyer-Moore-Horspool algorithm for string searching.

Many standard containers have a member function `find()` for finding elements in the container. When such a method is available and suits your needs, it should be preferred to the general algorithms because these member functions are optimized based on the particularities of each container.

See also

- *Using vector as a default container* to see how to use the `std::vector` standard container.
- *Initializing a range* to explore the standard algorithms for filling a range with values.

- *Using set operations on a range* to learn about the standard algorithms used to perform union, intersection, or difference of sorted ranges.
- *Sorting a range* to learn about the standard algorithms for sorting ranges.

Sorting a range

In the previous recipe, we looked at the standard general algorithms for searching in a range. Another common operation we often need to do is sorting a range because many routines, including some of the algorithms for searching, require a sorted range. The standard library provides several general algorithms for sorting ranges, and in this recipe, we will see what these algorithms are and how they can be used.

Getting ready

The sorting general algorithms work with ranges defined by a start and end iterator and, therefore, can sort standard containers, arrays, or anything that represents a sequence and has random iterators available. However, all the examples in this recipe will use `std::vector`.

How to do it...

The following is a list of standard general algorithms for searching a range:

- Use `std::sort()` for sorting a range:

```
std::vector<int> v{3, 13, 5, 8, 1, 2, 1};

std::sort(v.begin(), v.end());
// v = {1, 1, 2, 3, 5, 8, 13}

std::sort(v.begin(), v.end(), std::greater<>());
// v = {13, 8, 5, 3, 2, 1, 1}
```

- Use `std::stable_sort()` for sorting a range but keeping the order of the equal elements:

```
struct Task
{
  int priority;
  std::string name;
};
```

```
bool operator<(Task const & lhs, Task const & rhs) {
  return lhs.priority < rhs.priority;
}

bool operator>(Task const & lhs, Task const & rhs) {
  return lhs.priority > rhs.priority;
}

std::vector<Task> v{
  { 10, "Task 1"s }, { 40, "Task 2"s }, { 25, "Task 3"s },
  { 10, "Task 4"s }, { 80, "Task 5"s }, { 10, "Task 6"s },
};

std::stable_sort(v.begin(), v.end());
// {{ 10, "Task 1" },{ 10, "Task 4" },{ 10, "Task 6" },
//  { 25, "Task 3" },{ 40, "Task 2" },{ 80, "Task 5" }}

std::stable_sort(v.begin(), v.end(), std::greater<>());
// {{ 80, "Task 5" },{ 40, "Task 2" },{ 25, "Task 3" },
//  { 10, "Task 1" },{ 10, "Task 4" },{ 10, "Task 6" }}
```

- Use `std::partial_sort()` for sorting a part of a range (and leaving the rest in an unspecified order):

```
std::vector<int> v{ 3, 13, 5, 8, 1, 2, 1 };

std::partial_sort(v.begin(), v.begin() + 4, v.end());
// v = {1, 1, 2, 3, ?, ?, ?}

std::partial_sort(v.begin(), v.begin() + 4, v.end(),
                  std::greater<>());
// v = {13, 8, 5, 3, ?, ?, ?}
```

- Use `std::partial_sort_copy()` for sorting a part of a range by copying the sorted elements to a second range and leaving the original range unchanged:

```
std::vector<int> v{ 3, 13, 5, 8, 1, 2, 1 };
std::vector<int> vc(v.size());

std::partial_sort_copy(v.begin(), v.end(),
                       vc.begin(), vc.end());
// v = {3, 13, 5, 8, 1, 2, 1}
// vc = {1, 1, 2, 3, 5, 8, 13}
```

```
std::partial_sort_copy(v.begin(), v.end(),
                       vc.begin(), vc.end(),
                       std::greater<>());
// vc = {13, 8, 5, 3, 2, 1, 1}
```

- Use `std::nth_element()` for sorting a range so that the *N*th element is the one that would be in that position if the range was completely sorted, and the elements before it are all smaller and the ones after it are all greater, without any guarantee that they are also ordered:

```
std::vector<int> v{ 3, 13, 5, 8, 1, 2, 1 };

std::nth_element(v.begin(), v.begin() + 3, v.end());
// v = {1, 1, 2, 3, 5, 8, 13}

std::nth_element(v.begin(), v.begin() + 3, v.end(),
                 std::greater<>());
// v = {13, 8, 5, 3, 2, 1, 1}
```

- Use `std::is_sorted()` to check whether a range is sorted:

```
std::vector<int> v { 1, 1, 2, 3, 5, 8, 13 };

auto sorted = std::is_sorted(v.cbegin(), v.cend());
sorted = std::is_sorted(v.cbegin(), v.cend(),
                        std::greater<>());
```

- Use `std::is_sorted_until()` to find a sorted subrange from the beginning of a range:

```
std::vector<int> v{ 3, 13, 5, 8, 1, 2, 1 };

auto it = std::is_sorted_until(v.cbegin(), v.cend());
auto length = std::distance(v.cbegin(), it);
```

How it works...

All the preceding general algorithms take random iterators as arguments to define the range to be sorted. Some of them also take an output range. They all have overloads: one that requires a comparison function for sorting the elements and one that does not and uses `operator<` for comparing the elements.

These algorithms work in the following way:

- `std::sort()` modifies the input range so that its elements are sorted according to the default or the specified comparison function; the actual algorithm for sorting is an implementation detail.
- `std::stable_sort()` is similar to `std::sort()`, but it guarantees to preserve the original order of elements that are equal.
- `std::partial_sort()` takes three iterator arguments indicating the first, middle, and last element in a range, where middle can be any element, not just the one at the natural middle position. The result is a partially sorted range so that that first *middle* – *first* smallest elements from the original range, that is, [*first*, *last*), are found in the [*first*, *middle*) subrange and the rest of the elements are in an unspecified order, in the [*middle*, *last*) subrange.
- `std::partial_sort_copy()` is not a variant of `std::partial_copy()`, as the name may suggest, but of `std::sort()`. It sorts a range without altering it by copying its elements to an output range. The arguments of the algorithm are the first and last iterators of the input and output ranges. If the output range has a size *M* that is greater than or equal to the size *N* of the input range, the input range is entirely sorted and copied to the output range; the first *N* elements of the output range are overwritten, and the last *M* - *N* elements are left untouched. If the output range is smaller than the input range, then only the first *M* sorted elements from the input range are copied to the output range (which is entirely overwritten in this case).
- `std::nth_element()` is basically an implementation of a selection algorithm, which is an algorithm for finding the *N*th smallest element of a range. This algorithm takes three iterator arguments representing the first, *N*th, and last element, and partially sorts the range so that, after sorting, the *N*th element is the one that would be in that position if the range had been entirely sorted. In the modified range, all the *N* – 1 elements before the *N*th one are smaller than it, and all the elements after the *N*th element are greater than it. However, there is no guarantee on the order of these other elements.
- `std::is_sorted()` checks whether the specified range is sorted according to the specified or default comparison function and returns a Boolean value to indicate that.
- `std::is_sorted_until()` finds a sorted subrange of the specified range, starting from the beginning, using either a provided comparison function or the default `operator<`. The returned value is an iterator representing the upper bound of the sorted subrange, which is also the iterator of the one-past-last sorted element.

Some standard containers, `std::list` and `std::forward_list`, provide a member function, `sort()`, which is optimized for those containers. These member functions should be preferred over the general standard algorithm, `std::sort()`.

See also

- *Using vector as a default container* to learn how to use the `std::vector` standard container.
- *Initializing a range* to explore the standard algorithms for filling a range with values.
- *Using set operations on a range* to learn about the standard algorithms used to perform union, intersection, or difference of sorted ranges.
- *Finding elements in a range* to learn about the standard algorithms for searching through sequences of values.

Initializing a range

In the previous recipes, we explored the general standard algorithms for searching in a range and sorting a range. The algorithms library provides many other general algorithms, and among them are several that are intended for filling a range with values. In this recipe, you will learn what these algorithms are and how they should be used.

Getting ready

All the examples in this recipe use `std::vector`. However, like all the general algorithms, the ones we will see in this recipe take iterators to define the bounds of a range and can therefore be used with any standard container, arrays, or custom types representing a sequence that have forward iterators defined.

Except for `std::iota()`, which is available in the `<numeric>` header, all the other algorithms are found in the `<algorithm>` header.

How to do it...

To assign values to a range, use any of the following standard algorithms:

- `std::fill()` to assign a value to all the elements of a range; the range is defined by a first and last forward iterator:

  ```
  std::vector<int> v(5);
  std::fill(v.begin(), v.end(), 42);
  // v = {42, 42, 42, 42, 42}
  ```

- `std::fill_n()` to assign values to a number of elements of a range; the range is defined by a first forward iterator and a counter that indicates how many elements should be assigned the specified value:

  ```
  std::vector<int> v(10);
  std::fill_n(v.begin(), 5, 42);
  // v = {42, 42, 42, 42, 42, 0, 0, 0, 0, 0}
  ```

- `std::generate()` to assign the value returned by a function to the elements of a range; the range is defined by a first and last forward iterator, and the function is invoked once for each element in the range:

  ```
  std::random_device rd{};
  std::mt19937 mt{ rd() };
  std::uniform_int_distribution<> ud{1, 10};
  std::vector<int> v(5);
  std::generate(v.begin(), v.end(),
                [&ud, &mt] {return ud(mt); });
  ```

- `std::generate_n()` to assign the value returned by a function to a number of elements of a range; the range is defined by a first forward iterator and a counter that indicates how many elements should be assigned the value from the function that is invoked once for each element:

  ```
  std::vector<int> v(5);
  auto i = 1;
  std::generate_n(v.begin(), v.size(), [&i] { return i*i++; });
  // v = {1, 4, 9, 16, 25}
  ```

- `std::iota()` to assign sequentially increasing values to the elements of a range; the range is defined by a first and last forward iterator, and the values are incremented using the prefix `operator++` from an initial specified value:

  ```
  std::vector<int> v(5);
  std::iota(v.begin(), v.end(), 1);
  // v = {1, 2, 3, 4, 5}
  ```

How it works...

`std::fill()` and `std::fill_n()` work similarly but differ in the way the range is specified: for the former by a first and last iterator, for the latter by a first iterator and a count. The second algorithm returns an iterator, representing either the one-past-last assigned element if the counter is greater than zero, or an iterator to the first element of the range otherwise.

`std::generate()` and `std::generate_n()` are also similar, differing only in the way the range is specified. The first takes two iterators, defining the range's lower and upper bounds, while the second takes an iterator to the first element and a count. Like `std::fill_n()`, `std::generate_n()` also returns an iterator, representing either the one-past-last assigned element if the count is greater than zero, or an iterator to the first element of the range otherwise. These algorithms call a specified function for each element in the range and assign the returned value to the element. The generating function does not take any argument, so the value of the argument cannot be passed to the function. This is because it's intended as a function to initialize the elements of a range. If you need to use the value of the elements to generate new values, you should use `std::transform()`.

`std::iota()` takes its name from the ι (iota) function from the APL programming language, and though it was a part of the initial STL, it was only included in the standard library in C++11. This function takes a first and last iterator to a range, as well as an initial value that is assigned to the first element of the range. These are then used to generate sequentially increasing values using the prefix `operator++` for the rest of the elements in the range.

See also

- *Sorting a range* to learn about the standard algorithms for sorting ranges.
- *Using set operations on a range* to learn about the standard algorithms used to perform union, intersection, or difference of sorted ranges.
- *Finding elements in a range* to learn about the standard algorithms for searching through sequences of values.
- *Generating pseudo-random numbers* in *Chapter 2, Working with Numbers and Strings*, to understand the proper ways for generating pseudo-random numbers in C++.
- *Initializing all bits of internal state of a pseudo-random number generator* in *Chapter 2, Working with Numbers and Strings*, to learn how to properly initialize random number engines.

Using set operations on a range

The standard library provides several algorithms for set operations that enable us to do unions, intersections, or differences of sorted ranges. In this recipe, we will see what these algorithms are and how they work.

Getting ready

The algorithms for set operations work with iterators, which means they can be used for standard containers, arrays, or any custom type representing a sequence that has input iterators available. All the examples in this recipe will use `std::vector`.

For all the examples in the next section, we will use the following ranges:

```
std::vector<int> v1{ 1, 2, 3, 4, 4, 5 };
std::vector<int> v2{ 2, 3, 3, 4, 6, 8 };
std::vector<int> v3;
```

In the following section, we will explore the use of the standard algorithm for set operations.

How to do it...

Use the following general algorithms for set operations:

- `std::set_union()` to compute the union of two ranges into a third range:

  ```
  std::set_union(v1.cbegin(), v1.cend(),
                 v2.cbegin(), v2.cend(),
                 std::back_inserter(v3));
  // v3 = {1, 2, 3, 3, 4, 4, 5, 6, 8}
  ```

- `std::merge()` to merge the content of two ranges into a third one; this is similar to `std::set_union()` except that it copies the entire content of the input ranges into the output one, not just their union:

  ```
  std::merge(v1.cbegin(), v1.cend(),
             v2.cbegin(), v2.cend(),
             std::back_inserter(v3));
  // v3 = {1, 2, 2, 3, 3, 3, 4, 4, 4, 5, 6, 8}
  ```

- `std::set_intersection()` to compute the intersection of the two ranges into a third range:

```
std::set_intersection(v1.cbegin(), v1.cend(),
                      v2.cbegin(), v2.cend(),
                      std::back_inserter(v3));
// v3 = {2, 3, 4}
```

- `std::set_difference()` to compute the difference of two ranges into a third range; the output range will contain elements from the first range, which are not present in the second range:

```
std::set_difference(v1.cbegin(), v1.cend(),
                    v2.cbegin(), v2.cend(),
                    std::back_inserter(v3));
// v3 = {1, 4, 5}
```

- `std::set_symmetric_difference()` to compute a dual difference of the two ranges into a third range; the output range will contain elements that are present in any of the input ranges, but only in one:

```
std::set_symmetric_difference(v1.cbegin(), v1.cend(),
                              v2.cbegin(), v2.cend(),
                              std::back_inserter(v3));
// v3 = {1, 3, 4, 5, 6, 8}
```

- `std::includes()` to check if one range is a subset of another range (that is, all its elements are also present in the other range):

```
std::vector<int> v1{ 1, 2, 3, 4, 4, 5 };
std::vector<int> v2{ 2, 3, 3, 4, 6, 8 };
std::vector<int> v3{ 1, 2, 4 };
std::vector<int> v4{ };

auto i1 = std::includes(v1.cbegin(), v1.cend(),
                        v2.cbegin(), v2.cend()); // i1 = false
auto i2 = std::includes(v1.cbegin(), v1.cend(),
                        v3.cbegin(), v3.cend()); // i2 = true
auto i3 = std::includes(v1.cbegin(), v1.cend(),
                        v4.cbegin(), v4.cend()); // i3 = true
```

How it works...

All the set operations that produce a new range from two input ranges have the same interface and work in a similar way:

- They take two input ranges, each defined by a first and last input iterator.
- They take an output iterator to an output range where elements will be inserted.
- They have an overload that takes an extra argument representing a comparison binary function object that must return `true` if the first argument is less than the second. When a comparison function object is not specified, `operator<` is used.
- They return an iterator past the end of the constructed output range.
- The input ranges must be sorted using either `operator<` or the provided comparison function, depending on the overload that is used.
- The output range must not overlap any of the two input ranges.

We will demonstrate the way they work with additional examples using vectors of a POD type called `Task` that we also used in a previous recipe:

```
struct Task
{
  int         priority;
  std::string name;
};

bool operator<(Task const & lhs, Task const & rhs) {
  return lhs.priority < rhs.priority;
}

bool operator>(Task const & lhs, Task const & rhs) {
  return lhs.priority > rhs.priority;
}

std::vector<Task> v1{
  { 10, "Task 1.1"s },
  { 20, "Task 1.2"s },
  { 20, "Task 1.3"s },
```

```
    { 20, "Task 1.4"s },
    { 30, "Task 1.5"s },
    { 50, "Task 1.6"s },
};

std::vector<Task> v2{
    { 20, "Task 2.1"s },
    { 30, "Task 2.2"s },
    { 30, "Task 2.3"s },
    { 30, "Task 2.4"s },
    { 40, "Task 2.5"s },
    { 50, "Task 2.6"s },
};
```

The particular way each algorithm produces the output range is described here:

- `std::set_union()` copies all the elements present in one or both of the input ranges to the output range, producing a new sorted range. If an element is found *M* times in the first range and *N* times in the second range, then all the *M* elements from the first range will be copied to the output range in their existing order, and then the *N* - *M* elements from the second range are copied to the output range if *N* > *M*, or `0` elements otherwise:

```
std::vector<Task> v3;
std::set_union(v1.cbegin(), v1.cend(),
               v2.cbegin(), v2.cend(),
               std::back_inserter(v3));
// v3 = {{10, "Task 1.1"},{20, "Task 1.2"},{20, "Task 1.3"},
//       {20, "Task 1.4"},{30, "Task 1.5"},{30, "Task 2.3"},
//       {30, "Task 2.4"},{40, "Task 2.5"},{50, "Task 1.6"}}
```

- `std::merge()` copies all the elements from both the input ranges into the output range, producing a new range sorted with respect to the comparison function:

```
std::vector<Task> v4;
std::merge(v1.cbegin(), v1.cend(),
           v2.cbegin(), v2.cend(),
           std::back_inserter(v4));
// v4 = {{10, "Task 1.1"},{20, "Task 1.2"},{20, "Task 1.3"},
//       {20, "Task 1.4"},{20, "Task 2.1"},{30, "Task 1.5"},
//       {30, "Task 2.2"},{30, "Task 2.3"},{30, "Task 2.4"},
//       {40, "Task 2.5"},{50, "Task 1.6"},{50, "Task 2.6"}}
```

- `std::set_intersection()` copies all the elements that are found in both the input ranges into the output range, producing a new range sorted with respect to the comparison function:

```
std::vector<Task> v5;
std::set_intersection(v1.cbegin(), v1.cend(),
                      v2.cbegin(), v2.cend(),
                      std::back_inserter(v5));
// v5 = {{20, "Task 1.2"},{30, "Task 1.5"},{50, "Task 1.6"}}
```

- `std::set_difference()` copies to the output range all the elements from the first input range that are not found in the second input range. For equivalent elements that are found in both ranges, the following rule applies: if an element is found *M* times in the first range and *N* times in the second range, and if $M > N$, then it is copied $M - N$ times; otherwise, it is not copied:

```
std::vector<Task> v6;
std::set_difference(v1.cbegin(), v1.cend(),
                    v2.cbegin(), v2.cend(),
                    std::back_inserter(v6));
// v6 = {{10, "Task 1.1"},{20, "Task 1.3"},{20, "Task 1.4"}}
```

- `std::set_symmetric_difference()` copies to the output range all the elements that are found in either of the two input ranges but not in both of them. If an element is found *M* times in the first range and *N* times in the second range, then if $M > N$, the last $M - N$ of those elements from the first range are copied into the output range; otherwise, the last $N - M$ of those elements from the second range will be copied into the output range:

```
std::vector<Task> v7;
std::set_symmetric_difference(v1.cbegin(), v1.cend(),
                              v2.cbegin(), v2.cend(),
                              std::back_inserter(v7));
// v7 = {{10, "Task 1.1"},{20, "Task 1.3"},{20, "Task 1.4"}
//       {30, "Task 2.3"},{30, "Task 2.4"},{40, "Task 2.5"}}
```

On the other hand, `std::includes()` does not produce an output range; it only checks whether the second range is included in the first range. It returns a Boolean value that is `true` if the second range is empty or all its elements are included in the first range, or `false` otherwise. It also has two overloads, one of which specifies a comparison binary function object.

See also

- *Using vector as a default container* to learn how to use the `std::vector` standard container.
- *Sorting a range* to learn about the standard algorithms for sorting ranges.
- *Using iterators to insert new elements in a container* to learn how to use iterators and iterator adapters to add elements to a range.
- *Finding elements in a range* to learn about the standard algorithms for searching through sequences of values.

Using iterators to insert new elements into a container

When you're working with containers, it is often useful to insert new elements at the beginning, end, or somewhere in the middle. There are algorithms, such as the ones we saw in the previous recipe, *Using set operations on a range*, that require an iterator to a range to insert into, but if you simply pass an iterator, such as the one returned by `begin()`, it will not insert but overwrite the elements of the container. Moreover, it's not possible to insert at the end by using the iterator returned by `end()`. In order to perform such operations, the standard library provides a set of iterators and iterator adapters that enable these scenarios..

Getting ready

The iterators and adapters discussed in this recipe are available in the `std` namespace in the `<iterator>` header. If you include headers such as `<algorithm>`, you do not have to explicitly include `<iterator>`.

How to do it...

Use the following iterator adapters to insert new elements into a container:

- `std::back_inserter()` to insert elements at the end, for containers that have a `push_back()` method:

```
std::vector<int> v{ 1,2,3,4,5 };
std::fill_n(std::back_inserter(v), 3, 0);
// v={1,2,3,4,5,0,0,0}
```

- `std::front_inserter()` to insert elements at the beginning, for containers that have a `push_front()` method:

  ```
  std::list<int> l{ 1,2,3,4,5 };
  std::fill_n(std::front_inserter(l), 3, 0);
  // l={0,0,0,1,2,3,4,5}
  ```

- `std::inserter()` to insert anywhere in a container, for containers that have an `insert()` method:

  ```
  std::vector<int> v{ 1,2,3,4,5 };
  std::fill_n(std::inserter(v, v.begin()), 3, 0);
  // v={0,0,0,1,2,3,4,5}

  std::list<int> l{ 1,2,3,4,5 };
  auto it = l.begin();
  std::advance(it, 3);
  std::fill_n(std::inserter(l, it), 3, 0);
  // l={1,2,3,0,0,0,4,5}
  ```

How it works...

`std::back_inserter()`, `std::front_inserter()`, and `std::inserter()` are all helper functions that create iterator adapters of the types `std::back_insert_iterator`, `std::front_insert_iterator`, and `std::insert_iterator`. These are all output iterators that append, prepend, or insert into the container for which they were constructed. Incrementing and dereferencing these iterators does not do anything. However, upon assignment, these iterators call the following methods from the container:

- `std::back_insterter_iterator` calls `push_back()`
- `std::front_inserter_iterator` calls `push_front()`
- `std::insert_iterator` calls `insert()`

The following is the oversimplified implementation of `std::back_inserter_iterator`:

```
template<class C>
class back_insert_iterator {
public:
  typedef back_insert_iterator<C> T;
  typedef typename C::value_type V;
```

```
    explicit back_insert_iterator( C& c ) :container( &c ) { }

    T& operator=( const V& val ) {
      container->push_back( val );
      return *this;
    }

    T& operator*() { return *this; }

    T& operator++() { return *this; }

    T& operator++( int ) { return *this; }
  protected:
    C* container;
  };
```

Because of the way the assignment operator works, these iterators can only be used with some standard containers:

- `std::back_insert_iterator` can be used with `std::vector`, `std::list`, `std::deque`, and `std::basic_string`.
- `std::front_insert_iterator` can be used with `std::list`, `std::forward_list`, and `std:deque`.
- `std::insert_iterator` can be used with all the standard containers.

The following example inserts three elements with the value `0` at the beginning of an `std::vector`:

```
std::vector<int> v{ 1,2,3,4,5 };
std::fill_n(std::inserter(v, v.begin()), 3, 0);
// v={0,0,0,1,2,3,4,5}
```

The `std::inserter()` adapter takes two arguments: the container and the iterator where an element is supposed to be inserted. Upon calling `insert()` on the container, the `std::insert_iterator` increments the iterator, so upon being assigned again, it can insert a new element into the next position. Take a look at the following snippet:

```
T& operator=(const V& v)
{
  iter = container->insert(iter, v);
  ++iter;
  return (*this);
}
```

This snippet shows (conceptually) how the assignment operator is implemented for this `std::inserter_iterator` adapter. You can see that it first calls the member function `insert()` of the container and then increments the returned iterator. Because all the standard containers have a method called `insert()` with this signature, this adapter can be used with all these containers.

There's more...

These iterator adapters are intended to be used with algorithms or functions that insert multiple elements into a range. They can be used, of course, to insert a single element, but that is rather an anti-pattern, since simply calling `push_back()`, `push_front()`, or `insert()` is much simpler and intuitive in this case. Consider the following snippets:

```
std::vector<int> v{ 1,2,3,4,5 };
*std::back_inserter(v) = 6; // v = {1,2,3,4,5,6}

std::back_insert_iterator<std::vector<int>> it(v);
*it = 7;                    // v = {1,2,3,4,5,6,7}
```

The examples shown here should be avoided. They do not provide any benefit; they only make the code cluttered.

See also

- *Using set operations on a range* to learn about the standard algorithms used to perform union, intersection, or difference of sorted ranges.

Writing your own random-access iterator

In the first chapter, we saw how we can enable range-based for loops for custom types by implementing iterators, as well as free `begin()` and `end()` functions to return iterators to the first and one-past-the-last element of the custom range. You might have noticed that the minimal iterator implementation that we provided in that recipe does not meet the requirements for a standard iterator. This is because it cannot be copy constructible or assigned and cannot be incremented. In this recipe, we will build upon that example and show you how to create a random-access iterator that meets all requirements.

Getting ready

For this recipe, you should know the types of iterators the standard defines and how they are different. A good overview of their requirements is available at `http://www.cplusplus.com/reference/iterator/`.

To exemplify how to write a random access iterator, we will consider a variant of the `dummy_array` class used in the *Enabling range-based for loops for custom types* recipe of *Chapter 1, Learning Modern Core Language Features*. This is a very simple array concept with no practical value other than serving as a code base for demonstrating iterators:

```
template <typename Type, size_t const SIZE>
class dummy_array
{
  Type data[SIZE] = {};
public:
  Type& operator[](size_t const index)
  {
    if (index < SIZE) return data[index];
    throw std::out_of_range("index out of range");
  }

  Type const & operator[](size_t const index) const
  {
    if (index < SIZE) return data[index];
    throw std::out_of_range("index out of range");
  }

  size_t size() const { return SIZE; }
};
```

All the code shown in the next section, the iterator classes, typedefs, and the `begin()` and `end()` functions, will be a part of this class.

How to do it...

To provide mutable and constant random-access iterators for the `dummy_array` class shown in the previous section, add the following members to the class:

- An iterator class template, which is parameterized with the type of elements and the size of the array. The class must have the following public typedefs that define standard synonyms:

```
template <typename T, size_t const Size>
class dummy_array_iterator
{
public:
  typedef dummy_array_iterator              self_type;
  typedef T                                 value_type;
  typedef T&                                reference;
  typedef T*                                pointer;
  typedef std::random_access_iterator_tag iterator_category;
  typedef ptrdiff_t                         difference_type;
};
```

- Private members for the iterator class—a pointer to the array data and a current index into the array:

```
private:
  pointer ptr = nullptr;
  size_t index = 0;
```

- Private method for the iterator class to check whether two iterator instances point to the same array data:

```
private:
  bool compatible(self_type const & other) const
  {
    return ptr == other.ptr;
  }
```

- An explicit constructor for the iterator class:

```
public:
  explicit dummy_array_iterator(pointer ptr,
                                size_t const index)
  : ptr(ptr), index(index) { }
```

- Iterator class members to meet common requirements for all iterators—copy-constructible, copy-assignable, destructible, prefix, and postfix incrementable. In this implementation, the post-increment operator is implemented in terms of the pre-increment operator to avoid code duplication:

```
dummy_array_iterator(dummy_array_iterator const & o)
    = default;
dummy_array_iterator& operator=(dummy_array_iterator const & o)
    = default;
~dummy_array_iterator() = default;
```

```
self_type & operator++ ()
{
  if (index >= Size)
    throw std::out_of_range("Iterator cannot be incremented
                             past the end of range.");
  ++index;
  return *this;
}

self_type operator++ (int)
{
  self_type tmp = *this;
  ++*this;
  return tmp;
}
```

- Iterator class members to meet input iterator requirements—test for equality/inequality, dereferenceable as `rvalues`:

```
bool operator== (self_type const & other) const
{
  assert(compatible(other));
  return index == other.index;
}

bool operator!= (self_type const & other) const
{
  return !(*this == other);
}

reference operator* () const
{
  if (ptr == nullptr)
    throw std::bad_function_call();
  return *(ptr + index);
}

reference operator-> () const
{
  if (ptr == nullptr)
    throw std::bad_function_call();
  return *(ptr + index);
}
```

- Iterator class members to meet forward iterator requirements—default constructible:

```
dummy_array_iterator() = default;
```

- Iterator class members to meet bidirectional iterator requirements—decrementable:

```
self_type & operator--()
{
  if (index <= 0)
    throw std::out_of_range("Iterator cannot be decremented
                             past the end of range.");
  --index;
  return *this;
}

self_type operator--(int)
{
  self_type tmp = *this;
  --*this;
  return tmp;
}
```

- Iterator class members to meet random access iterator requirements—arithmetic add and subtract, comparable for inequality with other iterators, compound assignments, and offset dereferenceable:

```
self_type operator+(difference_type offset) const
{
  self_type tmp = *this;
  return tmp += offset;
}

self_type operator-(difference_type offset) const
{
  self_type tmp = *this;
  return tmp -= offset;
}

difference_type operator-(self_type const & other) const
{
  assert(compatible(other));
  return (index - other.index);
}
```

```
bool operator<(self_type const & other) const
{
  assert(compatible(other));
  return index < other.index;
}

bool operator>(self_type const & other) const
{
  return other < *this;
}

bool operator<=(self_type const & other) const
{
  return !(other < *this);
}

bool operator>=(self_type const & other) const
{
  return !(*this < other);
}

self_type & operator+=(difference_type const offset)
{
  if (index + offset < 0 || index + offset > Size)
    throw std::out_of_range("Iterator cannot be incremented
                             past the end of range.");
  index += offset;
  return *this;
}

self_type & operator-=(difference_type const offset)
{
  return *this += -offset;
}

value_type & operator[](difference_type const offset)
{
```

```
    return (*(*this + offset));
  }

  value_type const & operator[](difference_type const offset)
  const
  {
    return (*(*this + offset));
  }
```

- Add typedefs to the `dummy_array` class for mutable and constant iterator synonyms:

```
public:
  typedef dummy_array_iterator<Type, SIZE>
      iterator;
  typedef dummy_array_iterator<Type const, SIZE>
      constant_iterator;
```

- Add the public `begin()` and `end()` functions to the `dummy_array` class to return the iterators to the first and one-past-last elements in the array:

```
iterator begin()
{
  return iterator(data, 0);
}

iterator end()
{
  return iterator(data, SIZE);
}

constant_iterator begin() const
{
  return constant_iterator(data, 0);
}

constant_iterator end() const
{
  return constant_iterator(data, SIZE);
}
```

How it works...

The standard library defines five categories of iterators:

- **Input iterators**: These are the simplest category and guarantee validity only for single-pass sequential algorithms. After being incremented, the previous copies may become invalid.
- **Output iterators**: These are basically input iterators that can be used to write to the pointed element.
- **Forward iterators**: These can read (and write) data to the pointed element. They satisfy the requirements for input iterators and, in addition, must be default constructible and must support multi-pass scenarios without invalidating the previous copies.
- **Bidirectional iterators**: These are forward iterators that, in addition, support decrementing so that they can move in both directions.
- **Random access iterators**: These support access to any element in the container in constant time. They implement all the requirements for bidirectional iterators, and, in addition, support arithmetic operations `+` and `-`, compound assignments `+=` and `-=`, comparisons with other iterators with `<`, `<=`, `>`, `>=`, and the offset dereference operator.

Forward, bidirectional, and random-access iterators that also implement the requirements of output iterators are called *mutable iterators*.

In the previous section, we saw how to implement random access iterators, with a step-by-step walkthrough of the requirements of each category of iterators (as each iterator category includes the requirements of the previous category and adds new requirements). The iterator class template is common for both constant and mutable iterators, and we have defined two synonyms for it called `iterator` and `constant_iterator`.

After implementing the inner iterator class template, we also defined the `begin()` and `end()` member functions, which return an iterator to the first and the one-past-last element in the array, respectively. These methods have overloads to return mutable or constant iterators, depending on whether the `dummy_array` class instance is mutable or constant.

With this implementation of the `dummy_array` class and its iterators, we can write the following samples:

```
dummy_array<int, 3> a;
a[0] = 10;
a[1] = 20;
```

```
a[2] = 30;

std::transform(a.begin(), a.end(), a.begin(),
               [](int const e) {return e * 2; });

for (auto&& e : a) std::cout << e << '\n';

auto lp = [](dummy_array<int, 3> const & ca)
{
  for (auto const & e : ca)
    std::cout << e << '\n';
};

lp(a);

dummy_array<std::unique_ptr<Tag>, 3> ta;
ta[0] = std::make_unique<Tag>(1, "Tag 1");
ta[1] = std::make_unique<Tag>(2, "Tag 2");
ta[2] = std::make_unique<Tag>(3, "Tag 3");

for (auto it = ta.begin(); it != ta.end(); ++it)
  std::cout << it->id << " " << it->name << '\n';
```

For more examples, check the source code that accompanies this book.

There's more...

Apart from `begin()` and `end()`, a container may have additional methods such as `cbegin()`/`cend()` (for constant iterators), `rbegin()`/`rend()` (for mutable reverse iterators), and `crbegin()`/ `crend()` (for constant reverse iterators). Implementing this is left as an exercise for you.

On the other hand, in modern C++, these functions that return the first and last iterators do not have to be member functions but can be provided as non-member functions. In fact, this is the topic of the next recipe, *Container access with non-member functions*.

See also

- *Enabling range-based for loops for custom types* in *Chapter 1, Learning Modern Core Language Features,* to learn to execute one or more statements for each element of a collection.

- *Creating type aliases and alias templates* in *Chapter 1, Learning Modern Core Language Features*, to learn about aliases for types.

Container access with non-member functions

Standard containers provide the begin() and end() member functions for retrieving iterators for the first and one-past-last elements of the container. There are actually four sets of these functions. Apart from begin()/end(), containers provide cbegin()/cend() to return constant iterators, rbegin()/rend() to return mutable reverse iterators, and crbegin()/crend() to return constant reverse iterators. In C++11/C++14, all these have non-member equivalents that work with standard containers, arrays, and any custom type that specializes them. In C++17, even more non-member functions have been added: std::data(), which returns a pointer to the block of memory containing the elements of the container; std::size(), which returns the size of a container or array; and std::empty(), which returns whether the given container is empty. These non-member functions are intended for generic code but can be used anywhere in your code. Moreover, in C++20, the std::ssize() non-member function was introduced, to return the size of a container or array as a signed integer.

Getting ready

In this recipe, we will use the dummy_array class and its iterators that we implemented in the previous recipe, *Writing your own random-access iterator*, as an example. You should read that recipe before continuing with this one.

Non-member begin()/end() functions and the other variants, as well as non-member data(), size(), and empty() functions are available in the std namespace in the <iterator> header, which is implicitly included with any of the following headers: <array>, <deque>, <forward_list>, <list>, <map>, <regex>, <set>, <string>, <unordered_map>, <unordered_set>, and <vector>.

In this recipe, we will refer to the std::begin()/std::end() functions, but everything discussed also applies to the other functions: std::cbegin()/std::cend(), std::rbegin()/std::rend(), and std::crbegin()/std::crend().

How to do it...

Use the non-member std::begin()/std::end() function and the other variants, as well as std::data(), std::size(), and std::empty() with:

- Standard containers:

```
std::vector<int> v1{ 1, 2, 3, 4, 5 };
auto sv1 = std::size(v1);  // sv1 = 5
auto ev1 = std::empty(v1); // ev1 = false
auto dv1 = std::data(v1);  // dv1 = v1.data()
for (auto i = std::begin(v1); i != std::end(v1); ++i)
  std::cout << *i << '\n';

std::vector<int> v2;
std::copy(std::cbegin(v1), std::cend(v1),
          std::back_inserter(v2));
```

- Arrays:

```
int a[5] = { 1, 2, 3, 4, 5 };
auto pos = std::find_if(std::crbegin(a), std::crend(a),
                        [](int const n) {return n % 2 == 0; });
auto sa = std::size(a);  // sa = 5
auto ea = std::empty(a); // ea = false
auto da = std::data(a);  // da = a
```

- Custom types that provide the corresponding member functions; that is, `begin()/end()`, `data()`, `empty()`, or `size()`:

```
dummy_array<std::string, 5> sa;
dummy_array<int, 5> sb;
sa[0] = "1"s;
sa[1] = "2"s;
sa[2] = "3"s;
sa[3] = "4"s;
sa[4] = "5"s;

std::transform(
  std::begin(sa), std::end(sa),
  std::begin(sb),
  [](std::string const & s) {return std::stoi(s); });
// sb = [1, 2, 3, 4, 5]

auto sa_size = std::size(sa); // sa_size = 5
```

- Generic code where the type of the container is not known:

```
template <typename F, typename C>
void process(F&& f, C const & c)
{
```

```
   std::for_each(std::begin(c), std::end(c),
                 std::forward<F>(f));
}

auto l = [](auto const e) {std::cout << e << '\n'; };

process(l, v1); // std::vector<int>
process(l, a);  // int[5]
process(l, sa); // dummy_array<std::string, 5>
```

How it works...

These non-member functions were introduced in different versions of the standard, but all of them were modified in C++17 to return `constexpr auto`:

- `std::begin()` and `std::end()` in C++11
- `std::cbegin()/std::cend()`, `std::rbegin()/std::rend()`, and `std::crbegin()/std::crend()` in C++14
- `std::data()`, `std::size()`, and `std::empty()` in C++17
- `std::ssize()` in C++20

The `begin()/end()` family of functions have overloads for container classes and arrays, and all they do is the following:

- Return the results of calling the container-corresponding member function for containers
- Return a pointer to the first or one-past-last element of the array for arrays

The actual typical implementation for `std::begin()/std::end()` is as follows:

```
template<class C>
constexpr auto inline begin(C& c) -> decltype(c.begin())
{
  return c.begin();
}

template<class C>
constexpr auto inline end(C& c) -> decltype(c.end())
{
  return c.end();
}
```

```
template<class T, std::size_t N>
constexpr T* inline begin(T (&array)[N])
{
  return array;
}

template<class T, std::size_t N>
constexpr T* inline begin(T (&array)[N])
{
  return array+N;
}
```

Custom specialization can be provided for containers that do not have corresponding `begin()/end()` members but can still be iterated. The standard library actually provides such specializations for `std::initializer_list` and `std::valarray`.

Specializations must be defined in the same namespace where the original class or function template has been defined. Therefore, if you want to specialize any of the `std::begin()/std::end()` pairs, you must do so in the `std` namespace.

The other non-member functions for container access that were introduced in C++17 also have several overloads:

- `std::data()` has several overloads; for a class `C` it returns `c.data()`, for arrays it returns the `array`, and for `std::initializer_list<T>` it returns the `il.begin()`:

  ```
  template <class C>
  constexpr auto data(C& c) -> decltype(c.data())
  {
    return c.data();
  }

  template <class C>
  constexpr auto data(const C& c) -> decltype(c.data())
  {
    return c.data();
  }

  template <class T, std::size_t N>
  constexpr T* data(T (&array)[N]) noexcept
  {
  ```

```
  return array;
}

template <class E>
constexpr const E* data(std::initializer_list<E> il) noexcept
{
  return il.begin();
}
```

- `std::size()` has two overloads; for a class `C` it returns `c.size()`, and for arrays it returns the size `N`:

```
template <class C>
constexpr auto size(const C& c) -> decltype(c.size())
{
  return c.size();
}

template <class T, std::size_t N>
constexpr std::size_t size(const T (&array)[N]) noexcept
{
  return N;
}
```

- `std::empty()` has several overloads; for a class `C` it returns `c.empty()`, for arrays it returns `false`, and for `std::initializer_list<T>` it returns `il.size() == 0`:

```
template <class C>
constexpr auto empty(const C& c) -> decltype(c.empty())
{
  return c.empty();
}

template <class T, std::size_t N>
constexpr bool empty(const T (&array)[N]) noexcept
{
  return false;
}
```

```
template <class E>
constexpr bool empty(std::initializer_list<E> il) noexcept
{
  return il.size() == 0;
}
```

In C++20, the `std::ssize()` non-member function was added as a companion to `std::size()` to return the number of elements in a given container or an array as a signed integer. `std::size()` returns an unsigned integer, but there are scenarios where a signed value is desired. For instance, the C++20 class `std::span`, which represents a view to a contiguous sequence of objects, has a `size()` member function that returns a signed integer, unlike standard library containers where the `size()` member function returns an unsigned integer.

The reason the function `size()` of `std::span` returns a signed integer is that the value -1 is supposed to represent a sentinel for types whose size was not known at compile time. Performing mixed signed and unsigned arithmetic can lead to errors in code that are hard to find. `std::ssize()` has two overloads: for a class `C` it returns `c.size()` statically cast to a signed integer (typically `std::ptrdiff_t`) and for arrays it returns `N`, the number of elements. Take a look at the following code snippets:

```
template <class C>
constexpr auto ssize(const C& c)
    -> std::common_type_t<std::ptrdiff_t,
                          std::make_signed_t<decltype(c.size())>>
{
    using R = std::common_type_t<std::ptrdiff_t,
                        std::make_signed_t<decltype(c.size())>>;
    return static_cast<R>(c.size());
}

template <class T, std::ptrdiff_t N>
constexpr std::ptrdiff_t ssize(const T (&array)[N]) noexcept
{
    return N;
}
```

The preceding snippets show possible implementations for the `std::ssize()` function for containers and arrays.

There's more...

These non-member functions are mainly intended for template code where the container is not known and can be a standard container, an array, or a custom type. Using the non-member version of these functions enables us to write simpler and less code that works with all these types of containers.

However, the use of these functions is not and should not be limited to generic code. Though it is rather a matter of personal preference, it can be a good habit to be consistent and use them everywhere in your code. All these methods have lightweight implementations that will most likely be inlined by the compiler, which means that there will be no overhead at all for using the corresponding member functions.

See also

- *Writing your own random-access iterator* to understand what you need to do to write a custom, random-access iterator

6

General-Purpose Utilities

The standard library contains many general-purpose utilities and libraries beyond the containers, algorithms, and iterators discussed in the previous chapter. This chapter is focused on three areas: the `chrono` library for working with dates, times, calendars, and time zones; type traits, which provide meta-information about other types; and the new C++17 types `std::any`, `std::optional`, and `std::variant` and the C++20 type `std::span`.

The recipes included in this chapter are as follows:

- Expressing time intervals with `chrono::duration`
- Working with calendars
- Converting times between time zones
- Measuring function execution time with a standard clock
- Generating hash values for custom types
- Using `std::any` to store any value
- Using `std::optional` to store optional values
- Using `std::variant` as a type-safe union
- Visiting an `std::variant`
- Using `std::span` for contiguous sequences of objects
- Registering a function to be called when a program exits normally
- Using type traits to query properties of types
- Writing your own type traits
- Using `std::conditional` to choose between types

The first part of the chapter focuses on the chrono library, which provides time and date utilities.

Expressing time intervals with chrono::duration

Working with times and dates is a common operation, regardless of the programming language. C++11 provides a flexible date and time library as part of the standard library that enables us to define time points and time intervals. This library, called chrono, is a general-purpose utility library designed to work with a timer and clocks that can be different on different systems and, therefore, be precision-neutral. The library is available in the <chrono> header in the std::chrono namespace and defines and implements several components, as follows:

- *Durations*, which represent time intervals
- *Time points*, which present a duration of time since the epoch of a clock
- *Clocks*, which define an epoch (that is, start of time) and a tick

In this recipe, we will learn how to work with durations.

Getting ready

This recipe is not intended as a complete reference to the duration class. It is recommended that you consult additional resources for that purpose (the library reference documentation is available at http://en.cppreference.com/w/cpp/chrono).

In the chrono library, a time interval is represented by the std::chrono::duration class.

How to do it...

To work with time intervals, use the following:

- std::chrono::duration typedefs for hours, minutes, seconds, milliseconds, microseconds, and nanoseconds:

```
std::chrono::hours        half_day(12);
std::chrono::minutes      half_hour(30);
std::chrono::seconds      half_minute(30);
std::chrono::milliseconds half_second(500);
```

```
std::chrono::microseconds half_millisecond(500);
std::chrono::nanoseconds  half_microsecond(500);
```

- Use the standard user-defined literal operators from C++14, available in the namespace `std::chrono_literals`, for creating durations of hours, minutes, seconds, milliseconds, microseconds, and nanoseconds:

```
using namespace std::chrono_literals;

auto half_day         = 12h;
auto half_hour        = 30min;
auto half_minute      = 30s;
auto half_second      = 500ms;
auto half_millisecond = 500us;
auto half_microsecond = 500ns;
```

- Use direct conversion from a lower precision duration to a higher precision duration:

```
std::chrono::hours half_day_in_h(12);
std::chrono::minutes half_day_in_min(half_day_in_h);
std::cout << half_day_in_h.count() << "h" << '\n';    //12h
std::cout << half_day_in_min.count() << "min" << '\n';//720min
```

- Use `std::chrono::duration_cast` to convert from a higher precision to a lower precision duration:

```
using namespace std::chrono_literals;

auto total_seconds = 12345s;
auto hours =
  std::chrono::duration_cast<std::chrono::hours>
    (total_seconds);
auto minutes =
  std::chrono::duration_cast<std::chrono::minutes>
    (total_seconds % 1h);
auto seconds =
  std::chrono::duration_cast<std::chrono::seconds>
    (total_seconds % 1min);

std::cout << hours.count() << ':'
          << minutes.count() << ':'
          << seconds.count() << '\n'; // 3:25:45
```

- Use the conversion functions `floor()`, `round()`, and `ceil()` available in C++17 when rounding is necessary:

```
using namespace std::chrono_literals;

auto total_seconds = 12345s;
auto m1 = std::chrono::floor<std::chrono::minutes>(
  total_seconds); // 205 min
auto m2 = std::chrono::round<std::chrono::minutes>(
  total_seconds); // 206 min
auto m3 = std::chrono::ceil<std::chrono::minutes>(
  total_seconds); // 206 min
auto sa = std::chrono::abs(total_seconds);
```

- Use arithmetic operations, compound assignments, and comparison operations to modify and compare time intervals:

```
using namespace std::chrono_literals;

auto d1 = 1h + 23min + 45s; // d1 = 5025s
auto d2 = 3h + 12min + 50s; // d2 = 11570s
if (d1 < d2) { /* do something */ }
```

How it works...

The `std::chrono::duration` class defines a number of ticks (the increment between two moments in time) over a unit of time. The default unit is the second, and for expressing other units, such as minutes or milliseconds, we need to use a ratio. For units greater than the second, the ratio is greater than one, such as `ratio<60>` for minutes. For units smaller than the second, the ratio is smaller than one, such as `ratio<1, 1000>` for milliseconds. The number of ticks can be retrieved with the `count()` member function.

The standard library defines several type synonyms for durations of nanoseconds, microseconds, milliseconds, seconds, minutes, and hours that we used in the first example in the previous section. The following code shows how these durations are defined in the `chrono` namespace:

```
namespace std {
  namespace chrono {
    typedef duration<long long, ratio<1, 1000000000>> nanoseconds;
```

```
        typedef duration<long long, ratio<1, 1000000>> microseconds;
        typedef duration<long long, ratio<1, 1000>> milliseconds;
        typedef duration<long long> seconds;
        typedef duration<int, ratio<60> > minutes;
        typedef duration<int, ratio<3600> > hours;
    }
}
```

However, with this flexible definition, we can express time intervals such as *1.2 sixths of a minute* (which means 12 seconds), where 1.2 is the number of ticks of the duration and `ratio<10>` (as in 60/6) is the time unit:

```
std::chrono::duration<double, std::ratio<10>> d(1.2); // 12 sec
```

In C++14, several standard user-defined literal operators have been added to the namespace `std::chrono_literals`. This makes it easier to define durations, but you must include the namespace in the scope where you want to use the literal operators.

You should only include namespaces for user-defined literal operators in the scope where you want to use them, and not in larger scopes, in order to avoid conflict with other operators with the same name from different libraries and namespaces.

All arithmetic operations are available for the `duration` class. It is possible to add and subtract durations, multiply or divide them by a value, or apply the `modulo` operation. However, it is important to note that when two durations of different time units are added or subtracted, the result is a duration of the greatest common divisor of the two time units. This means that if you add a duration representing seconds and a duration representing minutes, the result is a duration representing seconds.

Conversion from a duration with a less precise time unit to a duration with a more precise time unit is done implicitly. On the other hand, conversion from a more precise to a less precise time unit requires an explicit cast. This is done with the non-member function `std::chrono::duration_cast()`. In the *How to do it...* section, you saw an example for determining the number of hours, minutes, and seconds of a given duration expressed in seconds.

C++17 has added several more non-member conversion functions that perform duration casting with rounding: `floor()` to round down, `ceil()` to round up, and `round()` to round to the nearest. Also, C++17 added a non-member function called `abs()` to retain the absolute value of a duration.

There's more...

`chrono` is a general-purpose library that, before C++20, lacked many useful features, such as expressing a date with the year, month, and day parts, working with time zones and calendars, and others. The C++20 standard added support for calendars and time zones, which we will see in the following recipes. Third-party libraries can implement these features and a recommended one is Howard Hinnant's `date` library, available under the MIT license at `https://github.com/HowardHinnant/date`. This library was the foundation for the C++20 `chrono` additions.

See also

- *Measuring function execution time with a standard clock* to see how you can determine the execution time of a function.
- *Working with calendars* to discover the C++20 additions to the `chrono` library for working with dates and calendars.
- *Converting times between time zones* to learn how you can convert time points between different time zones in C++20.

Working with calendars

The `chrono` library, available in C++11, offered support for clocks, time points, and durations but did not make it easy for expressing times and dates, especially with respect to calendars and time zones. The new C++20 standard corrects this by extending the existing `chrono` library with:

- More clocks, such as a UTC clock, an International Atomic Time clock, a GPS clock, a file time clock, and a pseudo-clock representing local time.
- Time of day, representing the time elapsed since midnight split into hours, minutes, and seconds.
- Calendars, which enable us to express dates with year, month, and day parts.
- Time zones, which enable us to express time points with respect to a time zone and make it possible to convert times between different time zones.
- I/O support for parsing chrono objects from a stream.

In this recipe, we will learn about working with calendar objects.

Getting ready

All the new chrono functionalities are available in the same `std::chrono` and `std::chrono_literals` namespaces in the `<chrono>` header.

How to do it...

You can use the C++20 chrono calendar functionalities to:

- Represent Gregorian calendar dates with year, month, and day, as instances of the `year_month_day` type. Use the standard user-defined literals, constants, and the overloaded operator `/` to construct such objects:

```
// format: year / month /day
year_month_day d1 = 2020y / 1 / 15;
year_month_day d2 = 2020y / January / 15;
// format: day / month / year
year_month_day d3 = 15d / 1 / 2020;
year_month_day d4 = 15d / January / 2020;
// format: month / day / year
year_month_day d5 = 1 / 15d / 2020;
year_month_day d6 = January / 15 / 2020;
```

- Represent the *n*th weekday of a specific year and month as instances of the `year_month_weekday` type:

```
// format: year / month / weekday
year_month_weekday d1 = 2020y / January / Monday[1];
// format: weekday / month / year
year_month_weekday d2 = Monday[1] / January / 2020;
// format: month / weekday / year
year_month_weekday d3 = January / Monday[1] / 2020;
```

- Determine the current date, as well as compute other dates from it, such as the dates for tomorrow and yesterday:

```
auto today = floor<days>(std::chrono::system_clock::now());
auto tomorrow = today + days{ 1 };
auto yesterday = today - days{ 1 };
```

- Determine the first and last day of a specific month and year:

```
year_month_day today = floor<days>(
  std::chrono::system_clock::now());
year_month_day first_day_this_month = today.year() / today.
month() / 1;
```

```
year_month_day last_day_this_month = today.year() / today.
month() / last;
year_month_day last_day_feb_2020 = 2020y / February / last;

year_month_day_last ymdl {today.year(),
                          month_day_last{ month{ 2 } }};
year_month_day last_day_feb { ymdl };
```

- Compute the number of days between two dates:

```
inline int number_of_days(date::sys_days const& first,
                          date::sys_days const& last)
{
  return (last - first).count();
}

auto days = number_of_days(2020_y / apr / 1, 2020_y / dec / 25);
```

- Check whether a date is valid:

```
auto day = 2020_y / January / 33;
auto is_valid = day.ok();
```

- Represent the time of day with hour, minutes, and seconds using the `time_of_day<Duration>` class template:

```
time_of_day<std::chrono::seconds> td(13h + 12min + 11s);
std::cout << td << '\n';  // 13:12:11
```

- Create time points with date and time parts:

```
auto tp = sys_days{ 2020_y / April / 1 } + 12h + 30min + 45s;
std::cout << tp << '\n';  // 2020-04-01 12:30:45
```

- Determine the current time of day and express it with various precisions:

```
auto tp = std::chrono::system_clock::now();
auto dp = floor<days>(tp);

time_of_day<std::chrono::milliseconds> time{
std::chrono::duration_cast<std::chrono::milliseconds>(tp - dp)
};
std::cout << time << '\n';  // 13:12:11.625

time_of_day<std::chrono::minutes> time{
  std::chrono::duration_cast<std::chrono::minutes>(tp - dp) };
std::cout << time << '\n';  // 13:12
```

How it works...

The year_month_day and year_month_weekday types we have seen in the examples here are only some of the many new types added to the chrono library for calendar support. The following table lists all these types in the std::chrono namespace and what they represent:

Type	Represents
day	A day of a month
month	A month of a year
year	A year in the Gregorian calendar
weekday	A day of the week in the Gregorian calendar
weekday_indexed	The *n*th weekday of a month, where *n* is in the range [1, 5] (1 is the 1st weekday of the month and 5 is the 5th—if it exists—weekday of the month)
weekday_last	The last weekday of a month
month_day	A specific day of a specific month
month_day_last	The last day of a specific month
month_weekday	The *n*th weekday of a specific month
month_weekday_last	The last weekday of a specific month
year_month	A specific month of a specific year
year_month_day	A specific year, month, and day
year_month_day_last	The last day of a specific year and month
year_month_weekday	The *n*th weekday of a specific year and month
year_month_weekday_last	The last weekday of a specific year and month

All the types listed in this table have:

- A default constructor that leaves the member fields uninitialized
- Member functions to access the parts of the entity
- A member function called ok() that checks if the stored value is valid
- Non-member comparison operators to compare values of the type
- An overloaded operator<< to output a value of the type to a stream
- An overloaded function template called from_stream() that parses a value from a stream according to the provided format
- A specialization of the std::formatter<T, CharT> class template for the text formatting library

In addition, the `operator/` is overloaded for many of these types to enable us to easily create Gregorian calendar dates. When you create a date (with year, month, and day), you can choose between three different formats:

- **year/month/day** (used in countries such as China, Japan, Korea, Canada, but others too, sometimes together with the day/month/year format)
- **month/day/year** (used in the USA)
- **day/month/year** (used in most parts of the world)

In these cases, **day** can be either:

- An actual day of the month (values from 1 to 31)
- `std:chrono::last` to indicate the last day of the month
- `weekday[n]`, to indicate the *n*th weekday of the month (where *n* can take values from 1 to 5)
- `weekday[std::chrono::last]`, to indicate the last week day of the month

In order to disambiguate between integers that represent the day, month, and year, the library provides two user-defined literals: `""y` to construct a literal of the type `std::chrono::year`, and `""d` to construct a literal of the type `std::chrono::day`.

In addition, there are constants that represent:

- An `std::chrono::month`, named `January`, `February`, up to `December`.
- An `std::chrono::weekday`, named `Sunday`, `Monday`, `Tuesday`, `Wednesday`, `Thursday`, `Friday`, or `Saturday`.

You can use all these to construct dates such as `2020y/April/1`, `25d/December/2020`, or `Sunday[last]/May/2020`.

The `year_month_day` type provides implicit conversion to and from `std::chrono::sys_days`. This type is an `std::chrono::time_point` with the precision of a day (24 hours). There is a companion type called `std::chrono::sys_seconds`, which is a `time_point` with the precision of one second. Explicit conversion between `time_point` and `sys_days` / `sys_seconds` can be performed using `std::chrono::time_point_cast()` or `std::chrono::floor()`.

To represent a moment of time during a day, we can use the `std::chrono::time_of_day` type. This class represents the time elapsed since midnight, broken down into hours, minutes, seconds, and sub-seconds. There are specializations of this class template for different precisions (`std::chrono::hours`, `std::chrono::minutes`, and `std::chrono::seconds`). This type is mostly intended as a formatting tool. It has two members called `make12()` and `make24()` that change the time format used to output to either a 12-hour or a 24-hour format.

There's more...

The date and time facilities described here are all based on the `std::chrono::system_clock`. Since C++20, this clock is defined to measure the Unix time, which is the time since 00:00:00 UTC on 1 January 1970. This means the implicit time zone is UTC. However, in most cases, you might be interested in the local time of a specific time zone. To help with that, the `chrono` library added support for time zones, which is what we will learn about in the next recipe.

See also

- *Expressing time intervals with chrono::duration* to familiarize yourself with the fundamentals of the C++11 `chrono` library and to work with durations, time points, and points.
- *Converting times between time zones* to learn how you can convert time points between different time zones in C++20.

Converting times between time zones

In the previous recipe, we talked about C++20 support for working with calendars and expressing dates in the Gregorian calendar with the `year_month_day` type and others from the `chrono` library.

We also saw how to represent times of day with the `time_of_day` type. However, in all these examples, we worked with the time points using the system clock, which measures Unix time and therefore uses UTC as the default time zone. However, we are usually interested in the local time and, sometimes, in the time in some other time zone. This is possible with the facilities added to the `chrono` library to support time zones. In this recipe, you will learn about the most important functionalities of chrono's time zones.

Getting ready

Before continuing with this recipe, it is recommended that you read the previous one, *Working with calendars*, if you have not done so already.

How to do it...

You can do the following using the C++20 `chrono` library:

- Use the `std::chrono::current_zone()` to retrieve the local time zone from the time zone database.
- Use `std::chrono::locate_zone()` to retrieve a particular time zone, using its name, from the time zone database.
- Represent a time point in a particular time zone using the `std::chrono::zoned_time` class template.
- Retrieve and display the current local time:

```
auto time = zoned_time{ current_zone(), system_clock::now() };
std::cout << time << '\n'; // 2020-01-16 22:10:30.9274320 EET
```

- Retrieve and display the current time in another time zone. In the following example, we use the time in Italy:

```
auto time = zoned_time{ locate_zone("Europe/Rome"),
                        system_clock::now() };
std::cout << time << '\n'; // 2020-01-16 21:10:30.9291091 CET
```

- Display the current local time with proper locale formatting. In this example, the current time is Romanian time, and the locale being used is for Romania:

```
auto time = zoned_time{ current_zone(), system_clock::now() };
std::cout << date::format(std::locale{"ro_RO"}, "%c", time)
          << '\n'; // 16.01.2020 22:12:57
```

- Represent a time point in a particular time zone and display it. In the following example this is the New York's time:

```
auto time = local_days{ 2020_y / June / 1 } + 12h + 30min + 45s
+ 256ms;
auto ny_time = zoned_time<std::chrono::milliseconds>{
                  locate_zone("America/New_York"), time};
std::cout << ny_time << '\n';
// 2020-06-01 12:30:45.256 EDT
```

- Convert a time point in a particular time zone into a time point in another time zone. In the following example, we convert the time from New York into the time in Los Angeles:

```
auto la_time = zoned_time<std::chrono::milliseconds>(
                  locate_zone("America/Los_Angeles"),
                  ny_time);
std::cout << la_time << '\n'; // 2020-06-01 09:30:45.256 PDT
```

How it works…

The system maintains a copy of the IANA Time Zone Database (which is available online at `https://www.iana.org/time-zones`). As a user, you cannot create or alter the database, but only retrieve a read-only copy of it with functions such as `std::chrono::tzdb()` or `std::chrono::get_tzdb_list()`. Information about a time zone is stored in an `std::chrono::time_zone` object. Instances of this class cannot be created directly; they are only created by the library when initializing the time zone database. However, it is possible to obtain constant access to these instances, using two functions:

- `std::chrono::current_zone()` retrieves the `time_zone` object representing the local time zone.
- `std::chrono::locate_zone()`retrieves the `time_zone` object representing the specified time zone.

Examples of time zone names include Europe/Berlin, Asia/Dubai, and America/Los_Angeles. When the name of the location contains multiple words, spaces are replaced by an underscore (_), such as in the preceding example where Los Angeles is written as Los_Angeles. A list of all the time zones from the IANA TZ database can be found at `https://en.wikipedia.org/wiki/List_of_tz_database_time_zones`.

There are two set of types in the C++20 `chrono` library to represent time points:

- `sys_days` and `sys_seconds` (having day and second precision) represent a time point in the system's time zone, which is UTC. These are type aliases for `std::chrono::sys_time`, which, in turn, is an alias for `std::chrono::time_point`, which is using the `std::chrono::system_clock`.
- `local_days` and `local_seconds` (having also day and second precision) represent a time point with respect to a time zone that has not yet been specified. These are type aliases for `std::chrono::local_time`, which is, in turn, a type alias for an `std::chrono::time_point` using the `std::chrono::local_t` pseudo-clock. The sole purpose of this clock is to indicate a not-yet-specified time zone.

The `std::chrono::zoned_time` class template represents a pairing of a time zone with a time point. It can be created from either a `sys_time`, a `local_time`, or another `zoned_time` object. Examples for all these cases are shown here:

```
auto zst = zoned_time<std::chrono::seconds>(
  current_zone(),
  sys_days{ 2020_y / May / 10 } +14h + 20min + 30s);
std::cout << zst << '\n'; // 2020-05-10 17:20:30 EEST
```

```
auto zlt = zoned_time<std::chrono::seconds>(
  current_zone(),
  local_days{ 2020_y / May / 10 } +14h + 20min + 30s);
std::cout << zlt << '\n'; // 2020-05-10 14:20:30 EEST

auto zpt = zoned_time<std::chrono::seconds>(
  locate_zone("Europe/Paris"),
  zlt);
std::cout << zpt << '\n'; //2020-05-10 13:20:30 CEST
```

In this sample code, the times in the comments are based on the Romanian time zone. Notice that in the first example, the time is expressed with `sys_days`, which uses the UTC time zone. Since Romanian time is UTC+3 on 10 May 2020 (because of Daylight Saving Time), the local time is 17:20:30. In the second example, the time is specified with `local_days`, which is time zone-agnostic. For this reason, when pairing with the current time zone, the time is actually 14:20:30. In the third and last example, the local Romanian time is converted to the time in Paris, which is 13:20:30 (because on that day, the time in Paris is UTC+2).

See also

- *Expressing time intervals with chrono::duration* to familiarize yourself with the fundamentals of the C++11 `chrono` library and to work with durations, time points, and points.
- *Working with calendars* to discover the C++20 additions to the `chrono` library for working with dates and calendars.

Measuring function execution time with a standard clock

In the previous recipe, we saw how to work with time intervals using the `chrono` standard library. However, we also often need to handle time points. The `chrono` library provides such a component, representing a duration of time since the epoch of a clock (that is, the beginning of time as defined by a clock). In this recipe, we will learn how to use the `chrono` library and time points to measure the execution of a function.

Getting ready

This recipe is tightly related to the preceding one, *Expressing time intervals with chrono::duration*. If you did not go through that recipe previously, you should do that before continuing with this one.

For the examples in this recipe, we will consider the following function, which does nothing, but takes some time to execute:

```
void func(int const count = 100000000)
{
  for (int i = 0; i < count; ++i);
}
```

It should go without saying that this function is only meant for testing purposes and does nothing valuable. In practice, you will use the counting utility provided here to test your own functions.

How to do it...

To measure the execution of a function, you must perform the following steps:

1. Retrieve the current moment of time using a standard clock:
   ```
   auto start = std::chrono::high_resolution_clock::now();
   ```
2. Call the function you want to measure:
   ```
   func();
   ```
3. Retrieve the current moment of time again; the difference between the two is the execution time of the function:
   ```
   auto diff = std::chrono::high_resolution_clock::now() - start;
   ```
4. Convert the difference (which is expressed in nanoseconds) to the actual resolution you are interested in:
   ```
   std::cout
     << std::chrono::duration<double, std::milli>(diff).count()
     << "ms" << '\n';
   std::cout
     << std::chrono::duration<double, std::nano>(diff).count()
     << "ns" << '\n';
   ```

To implement this pattern in a reusable component, perform the following steps:

1. Create a class template parameterized with the resolution and the clock.
2. Create a static variadic function template that takes a function and its arguments.
3. Implement the pattern shown previously, invoking the function with its arguments.
4. Return a duration, not the number of ticks.

This is exemplified in the following snippet:

```
template <typename Time = std::chrono::microseconds,
          typename Clock = std::chrono::high_resolution_clock>
struct perf_timer
{
  template <typename F, typename... Args>
  static Time duration(F&& f, Args... args)
  {
    auto start = Clock::now();

    std::invoke(std::forward<F>(f), std::forward<Args>(args)...);

    auto end = Clock::now();

    return std::chrono::duration_cast<Time>(end - start);
  }
};
```

How it works...

A clock is a component that defines two things:

- A beginning of time called an *epoch*; there is no constraint regarding what the epoch is, but typical implementations use January 1, 1970.
- A *tick rate* that defines the increment between two time points (such as a millisecond or nanosecond).

A time point is a duration of time since the epoch of a clock. There are several time points that are of particular importance:

- The current time, returned by the clock's static member `now()`.
- The epoch, or the beginning of time; this is the time point created by the default constructor of `time_point` for a particular clock.
- The minimum time that can be represented by a clock, returned by the static member `min()` of `time_point`.
- The maximum time that can be represented with a clock, returned by the static member `max()` of a `time point`.

The standard defines several clocks:

- `system_clock`: This uses the real-time clock of the current system to represent time points.
- `high_resolution_clock`: This represents a clock that uses the shortest possible tick period on the current system.
- `steady_clock`: This indicates a clock that is never adjusted. This means that, unlike the other clocks, as the time advances, the difference between two time points is always positive.
- `utc_clock`: This is a C++20 clock for Coordinated Universal Time.
- `tai_clock`: This is a C++20 clock for International Atomic Clock.
- `gps_clock`: This is a C++20 clock for GPS time.
- `file_clock`: This is a C++20 clock used for expressing file times.

The following example prints the precision of the first three clocks in this list (the ones available in C++11), regardless of whether it is steady (or monotone) or not:

```
template <typename T>
void print_clock()
{
  std::cout << "precision: "
            << (1000000.0 * double(T::period::num)) / (T::period::den)
            << '\n';
  std::cout << "steady: " << T::is_steady << '\n';
}

print_clock<std::chrono::system_clock>();
print_clock<std::chrono::high_resolution_clock>();
print_clock<std::chrono::steady_clock>();
```

A possible output is the following:

```
precision: 0.1
steady: 0
precision: 0.001
steady: 1
precision: 0.001
steady: 1
```

This means that the `system_clock` has a resolution of 0.1 milliseconds and is not a monotone clock. On the other hand, the other two clocks, `high_resolution_clock` and `steady_clock`, both have a resolution of 1 nanosecond and are monotone clocks.

The steadiness of a clock is important when measuring the execution time of a function, because if the clock is adjusted while the function runs, the result will not yield the actual execution time, and values can even be negative. You should rely on a steady clock to measure the function execution time. The typical choice for that is the `high_resolution_clock`, and that was the clock we used in the examples in the *How to do it...* section.

When we measure the execution time, we need to retrieve the current time before making the call and after the call returns. For that, we use the clock's `now()` static method. The result is a `time_point`; when we subtract two time points, the result is a `duration`, defined by the duration of the clock.

In order to create a reusable component that can be used to measure the execution time of any function, we have defined a class template called `perf_timer`. This class template is parameterized with the resolution we are interested in, which, by default, is microseconds, and the clock we want to use, which, by default, is `high_resolution_clock`. The class template has a single static member called `duration()`—a variadic function template—that takes a function to execute and its variable number of arguments. The implementation is relatively simple: we retrieve the current time, invoke the function using `std::invoke` (so that it handles the different mechanisms for invoking anything callable), and then retrieve the current time again. The return value is a `duration` (with the defined resolution). The following snippet shows an example of this:

```
auto t = perf_timer<>::duration(func, 100000000);

std::cout << std::chrono::duration<double, std::milli>(t).count()
          << "ms" << '\n';
std::cout << std::chrono::duration<double, std::nano>(t).count()
          << "ns" << '\n';
```

It is important to note that we are not returning a number of ticks from the `duration()` function, but an actual `duration` value. The reason is that by returning a number of ticks, we lose the resolution and won't know what they actually represent. It is better to call `count()` only when the actual count of ticks is necessary. This is exemplified here:

```
auto t1 = perf_timer<std::chrono::nanoseconds>::duration(func, 100000000);
auto t2 = perf_timer<std::chrono::microseconds>::duration(func, 100000000);
auto t3 = perf_timer<std::chrono::milliseconds>::duration(func, 100000000);

std::cout
  << std::chrono::duration<double, std::micro>(t1 + t2 + t3).count()
  << "us" << '\n';
```

In this example, we measure the execution of three different functions, using three different resolutions (nanoseconds, microseconds, and milliseconds). The values `t1`, `t2`, and `t3` represent durations. These make it possible to easily add them together and convert the result to microseconds.

See also

- *Expressing time intervals with chrono::duration* to familiarize yourself with the fundamentals of the C++11 `chrono` library and how to work with durations, time points, and points,
- *Uniformly invoking anything callable* in *Chapter 3, Exploring Functions*, to learn how to use `std::invoke()` to call functions and any callable object,

Generating hash values for custom types

The standard library provides several unordered associative containers: `std::unordered_set`, `std::unordered_multiset`, `std::unordered_map`, and `std::unordered_map`. These containers do not store their elements in a particular order; instead, they are grouped in buckets. The bucket an element belongs to depends on the hash value of the element. These standard containers use, by default, the `std::hash` class template to compute the hash value. The specialization for all basic types and also some library types is available. However, for custom types, you must specialize the class template yourself. This recipe will show you how to do that and also explain how a good hash value can be computed. A good hash value can be computed fast and is uniformly dispersed across the value domain, therefore minimizing the chances of duplicate values (collisions) existing.

Getting ready

For the examples in this recipe, we will use the following class:

```
struct Item
{
  int id;
  std::string name;
  double value;

  Item(int const id, std::string const & name, double const value)
    :id(id), name(name), value(value)
  {}

  bool operator==(Item const & other) const
  {
    return id == other.id && name == other.name &&
           value == other.value;
  }
};
```

This recipe covers hashing functionalities from the standard library. You should be familiar with the concepts of hashes and hash functions.

How to do it...

In order to use your custom types with the unordered associative containers, you must perform the following steps:

1. Specialize the `std::hash` class template for your custom type; the specialization must be done in the `std` namespace.
2. Define synonyms for the argument and result type.
3. Implement the call operator so that it takes a constant reference to your type and returns a hash value.

To compute a good hash value, you should do the following:

1. Start with an initial value, which should be a prime number (for example, 17).
2. For each field that is used to determine whether two instances of the class are equal, adjust the hash value according to the following formula:
   ```
   hashValue = hashValue * prime + hashFunc(field);
   ```

3. You can use the same prime number for all fields with the preceding formula, but it is recommended to have a different value than the initial value (for instance, 31).
4. Use a specialization of `std::hash` to determine the hash value for class data members.

Based on the steps described here, the `std::hash` specialization for the class `Item` looks like this:

```
namespace std
{
  template<>
  struct hash<Item>
  {
    typedef Item argument_type;
    typedef size_t result_type;

    result_type operator()(argument_type const & item) const
    {
      result_type hashValue = 17;
      hashValue = 31 * hashValue +
                  std::hash<int>{}(item.id);
      hashValue = 31 * hashValue +
                  std::hash<std::string>{}(item.name);
      hashValue = 31 * hashValue +
                  std::hash<double>{}(item.value);

      return hashValue;
    }
  };
}
```

This specialization makes it possible to use the `Item` class with unordered associative containers, such as `std::unordered_set`. An example is provided here:

```
std::unordered_set<Item> set2
{
  { 1, "one"s, 1.0 },
  { 2, "two"s, 2.0 },
  { 3, "three"s, 3.0 },
};
```

How it works...

The class template `std::hash` is a function object template whose call operator defines a hash function with the following properties:

- Takes an argument of the template parameter type and returns a `size_t` value.
- Does not throw any exceptions.
- For two arguments that are equal, it returns the same hash value.
- For two arguments that are not equal, the probability of returning the same value is very small (should be close to `1.0/std::numeric_limits<size_t>::max()`).

The standard provides specialization for all basic types, such as `bool`, `char`, `int`, `long`, `float`, `double` (along with all the possible `unsigned` and `long` variations), and the pointer type, but also library types including the `basic_string` and `basic_string_view` types, `unique_ptr` and `shared_ptr`, `bitset` and `vector<bool>`, `optional` and `variant` (in C++17), and several other types. However, for custom types, you have to provide your own specialization. This specialization must be in the namespace `std` (because that is the namespace where the class template `hash` is defined) and must meet the requirements enumerated earlier.

The standard does not specify how hash values should be computed. You can use any function you want as long as it returns the same value for equal objects, and also has a very small chance of returning the same value for non-equal objects. The algorithm described in this recipe was presented in the book *Effective Java 2nd Edition* by Joshua Bloch.

When computing the hash value, consider only the fields that participate in determining whether two instances of the class are equal (in other words, fields that are used in `operator==`). However, you must use all these fields that are used with `operator==`. In our example, all three fields of the class `Item` are used to determine the equality of two objects; therefore, we must use them all to compute the hash. The initial hash value should be nonzero, and in our example, we picked the prime number 17. The important thing is that these values should not be zero; otherwise, the initial fields (that is, the first in the order of processing) that produce the hash value zero will not alter the hash (which remains zero since `x * 0 + 0 = 0`). For every field used to compute the hash, we alter the current hash by multiplying its previous value with a prime number and adding the hash of the current field. For this purpose, we use specializations of the class template `std::hash`. The use of the prime number 31 is advantageous for performance optimizations because `31 * x` can be replaced by the compiler with `(x << 5) - x`, which is faster. Similarly, you can use 127, because `127 * x` is equal to `(x << 7) - x` or 8191, because `8191 * x` is equal to `(x << 13) - x`.

If your custom type contains an array and is used to determine the equality of two objects and, therefore, needs to be used to compute the hash, then treat the array as if its elements were data members of the class. In other words, apply the same algorithm described earlier to all elements of the array.

See also

- *Limits and other properties of numeric types* in *Chapter 2*, *Working with Numbers and Strings*, to learn about the minimum and maximum values, as well as the other properties of numerical types.

Using std::any to store any value

C++ does not have a hierarchical type system like other languages (such as C# or Java) and, therefore, it can't store multiple types of a value in a single variable like it is possible to with type `Object` in .NET and Java or natively in JavaScript. Developers have long used `void*` for that purpose, but this only helps us store pointers to anything and is not type-safe. Depending on the end goal, alternatives can include templates or overloaded functions. However, C++17 has introduced a standard type-safe container, called `std::any`, that can hold a single value of any type.

Getting ready

`std::any` has been designed based on `boost::any` and is available in the `<any>` header. If you are familiar with `boost::any` and have used it in your code, you can migrate it seamlessly to `std::any`.

How to do it...

Use the following operations to work with `std::any`:

- To store values, use the constructor or assign them directly to an `std::any` variable:

```
std::any value(42); // integer 42
value = 42.0;       // double 42.0
value = "42"s;      // std::string "42"
```

- To read values, use the non-member function `std::any_cast()`:

```
std::any value = 42.0;
```

```
try
{
  auto d = std::any_cast<double>(value);
  std::cout << d << '\n';
}
catch (std::bad_any_cast const & e)
{
  std::cout << e.what() << '\n';
}
```

- To check the type of the stored value, use the member function `type()`:

```
inline bool is_integer(std::any const & a)
{
  return a.type() == typeid(int);
}
```

- To check whether the container stores a value, use the `has_value()` member function:

```
auto ltest = [](std::any const & a) {
  if (a.has_value())
    std::cout << "has value" << '\n';
  else
    std::cout << "no value" << '\n';
  };

std::any value;
ltest(value); // no value
value = 42;
ltest(value); // has value
```

- To modify the stored value, use the member functions `emplace()`, `reset()`, or `swap()`:

```
std::any value = 42;
ltest(value); // has value
value.reset();
ltest(value); // no value
```

How it works...

`std::any` is a type-safe container that can hold values of any type that is (or rather whose decayed type is) copy constructible. Storing values in the container is very simple—you can either use one of the available constructors (the default constructor creates a container that stores no value) or the assignment operator. However, reading values is not directly possible, and you need to use the non-member function `std::any_cast()`, which casts the stored value to the specified type. This function throws `std::bad_any_cast` if the stored value has a different type than the one you are casting to. Casting between implicitly convertible types, such as `int` and `long`, is not possible either. `std::bad_any_cast` is derived from `std::bad_cast`; therefore, you can catch any of these two exception types.

It is possible to check the type of the stored value using the `type()` member function, which returns a `type_info` constant reference. If the container is empty, this function returns `typeid(void)`. To check whether the container stores a value, you can use the member function `has_value()`, which returns `true` if there is a value or `false` if the container is empty.

The following example shows how to check whether the container has any value, how to check the type of the stored value, and how to read the value from the container:

```
void log(std::any const & value)
{
  if (value.has_value())
  {
    auto const & tv = value.type();
    if (tv == typeid(int))
    {
      std::cout << std::any_cast<int>(value) << '\n';
    }
    else if (tv == typeid(std::string))
    {
      std::cout << std::any_cast<std::string>(value) << '\n';
    }
    else if (tv == typeid(
```

```
      std::chrono::time_point<std::chrono::system_clock>))
    {
      auto t = std::any_cast<std::chrono::time_point<
        std::chrono::system_clock>>(value);
      auto now = std::chrono::system_clock::to_time_t(t);
      std::cout << std::put_time(std::localtime(&now), "%F %T")
                << '\n';
    }
    else
    {
      std::cout << "unexpected value type" << '\n';
    }
  }
  else
  {
    std::cout << "(empty)" << '\n';
  }
}

log(std::any{});                        // (empty)
log(42);                                // 42
log("42"s);                             // 42
log(42.0);                              // unexpected value type
log(std::chrono::system_clock::now()); // 2016-10-30 22:42:57
```

If you want to store multiple values of any type, use a standard container such as `std::vector` to hold values of the type `std::any`. An example is presented here:

```
std::vector<std::any> values;
values.push_back(std::any{});
values.push_back(42);
values.push_back("42"s);
values.push_back(42.0);
values.push_back(std::chrono::system_clock::now());

for (auto const v : values)
  log(v);
```

In this snippet, the vector called `values` contains elements of the `std::any` type, which, in turn, contain an `int`, `std::string`, `double`, and `std::chrono::time_point` value.

See also

- *Using std::optional to store optional values* to learn about the C++17 class template `std::optional`, which manages a value that may or may not exist.
- *Using std::variant as a type-safe union* to learn how to use the C++17 `std::variant` class to represent type-safe unions.

Using std::optional to store optional values

Sometimes, it is useful to be able to store either a value or a null if a value is not available. A typical example for such a case is the return value of a function that may fail to produce a return value, but this failure is not an error. For instance, think of a function that finds and returns values from a dictionary by specifying a key. Not finding a value is a probable case and, therefore, the function would either return a Boolean (or an integer value, if more error codes are necessary) and have a reference argument to hold the return value or return a pointer (raw or smart pointer). In C++17, `std::optional` is a better alternative to these solutions. The class template `std::optional` is a template container for storing a value that may or may not exist. In this recipe, we will see how to use this container and its typical use cases.

Getting ready

The class template `std::optional<T>` was designed based on `boost::optional` and is available in the `<optional>` header. If you are familiar with `boost::optional` and have used it in your code, you can migrate it seamlessly to `std::optional`.

How to do it...

Use the following operations to work with `std::optional`:

- To store a value, use the constructor or assign the value directly to an `std::optional` object:

```
std::optional<int> v1;      // v1 is empty
std::optional<int> v2(42);  // v2 contains 42
v1 = 42;                    // v1 contains 42
std::optional<int> v3 = v2; // v3 contains 42
```

- To read the stored value, use `operator*` or `operator->`:

```
std::optional<int> v1{ 42 };
std::cout << *v1 << '\n';   // 42
std::optional<foo> v2{ foo{ 42, 10.5 } };
std::cout << v2->a << ", "
          << v2->b << '\n'; // 42, 10.5
```

- Alternatively, use the member functions `value()` and `value_or()` to read the stored value:

```
std::optional<std::string> v1{ "text"s };
std::cout << v1.value()
          << '\n'; // text

std::optional<std::string> v2;
std::cout << v2.value_or("default"s)
          << '\n'; // default
```

- To check whether the container stores a value, use a conversion operator to `bool` or the member function `has_value()`:

```
struct foo
{
  int    a;
  double b;
};

std::optional<int> v1{ 42 };
if (v1) std::cout << *v1 << '\n';

std::optional<foo> v2{ foo{ 42, 10.5 } };
if (v2.has_value())
  std::cout << v2->a << ", " << v2->b << '\n';
```

- To modify the stored value, use the member functions `emplace()`, `reset()`, or `swap()`:

```
std::optional<int> v{ 42 }; // v contains 42
v.reset();                  // v is empty
```

Use `std::optional` to model any of the following:

- Return values from functions that may fail to produce a value:

```
template <typename K, typename V>
std::optional<V> find(int const key,
```

```
                        std::map<K, V> const & m)
{
  auto pos = m.find(key);
  if (pos != m.end())
    return pos->second;
  return {};
}

std::map<int, std::string> m{
  { 1, "one"s },{ 2, "two"s },{ 3, "three"s } };

auto value = find(2, m);
if (value) std::cout << *value << '\n'; // two

value = find(4, m);
if (value) std::cout << *value << '\n';
```

- Parameters to functions that are optional:

```
std::string extract(std::string const & text,
                    std::optional<int> start,
                    std::optional<int> end)
{
  auto s = start.value_or(0);
  auto e = end.value_or(text.length());
  return text.substr(s, e - s);
}

auto v1 = extract("sample"s, {}, {});
std::cout << v1 << '\n'; // sample

auto v2 = extract("sample"s, 1, {});
std::cout << v2 << '\n'; // ample

auto v3 = extract("sample"s, 1, 4);
std::cout << v3 << '\n'; // amp
```

- Class data members that are optional:

```
struct book
{
  std::string                title;
  std::optional<std::string> subtitle;
  std::vector<std::string>   authors;
```

```
    std::string              publisher;
    std::string              isbn;
    std::optional<int>       pages;
    std::optional<int>       year;
  };
```

How it works...

The class template `std::optional` is a class template that represents a container for an optional value. If the container does have a value, that value is stored as part of the `optional` object; no heap allocations and pointers are involved. The `std::optional` class template is conceptually implemented like this:

```
template <typename T>
class optional
{
  bool _initialized;
  std::aligned_storage_t<sizeof(t), alignof(T)> _storage;
};
```

The `std::aligned_storage_t` alias template allows us to create uninitialized chunks of memory that can hold objects of a given type. The class template `std::optional` does not contain a value if it was default constructed, or if it was copy constructed or copy assigned from another empty optional object or from an `std::nullopt_t` value. This is a helper type, implemented as an empty class, that indicates an optional object with an uninitialized state.

The typical use for an `optional` type (called *nullable* in other programming languages) is the return type from a function that may fail. Possible solutions for this situation include the following:

- Return an `std::pair<T, bool>`, where `T` is the type of the return value; the second element of the pair is a Boolean flag that indicates whether the value of the first element is valid or not.
- Return a `bool`, take an extra parameter of the type `T&`, and assign a value to this parameter only if the function succeeds.
- Return a raw or smart pointer type, and use `nullptr` to indicate a failure.

The class template `std::optional` is a better approach because, on one hand, it does not involve output parameters to the function (which is unnatural for returning values) and does not require working with pointers, and, on the other hand, it better encapsulates the details of an `std::pair<T, bool>`. However, optional objects can also be used for class data members, and compilers are able to optimize the memory layout for efficient storage.

The class template `std::optional` cannot be used to return polymorphic types. If you write, for instance, a factory method that needs to return different types from a hierarchy of types, you cannot rely on `std::optional` and need to return a pointer, preferably an `std::unique_ptr` or `std::shared_ptr` (depending if ownership of the object needs to be shared or not).

When you use `std::optional` to pass optional arguments to a function, you need to understand that it may incur creating copies, which can be a performance issue if large objects are involved. Let's consider the following example of a function that has a constant reference to the `std::optional` parameter:

```
struct bar { /* details */ };

void process(std::optional<bar> const & arg)
{
  /* do something with arg */
}

std::optional<bar> b1{ bar{} };
bar b2{};

process(b1); // no copy
process(b2); // copy construction
```

The first call to `process()` does not involve any additional object construction because we pass an `std::optional<bar>` object. The second call, however, will involve the copy construction of a `bar` object, because `b2` is a `bar` and needs to be copied to an `std::optional<bar>`; a copy is made even if `bar` has move semantics implemented. If `bar` was a small object, this shouldn't be of great concern, but for large objects, it can prove to be a performance issue. The solution to avoid this depends on the context, and can involve creating a second overload that takes a constant reference to `bar`, or entirely avoiding using `std::optional`.

See also

- *Using std::any to store any value* to learn how to use the C++17 class `std::any`, which represents a type-safe container for single values of any type,
- *Using std::variant as a type-safe union* to learn how to use the C++17 `std::variant` class to represent type-safe unions.

Using std::variant as a type-safe union

In C++, union is a special class type that, at any point, holds a value of one of its data members. Unlike regular classes, unions cannot have base classes, nor can they be derived, and they cannot contain virtual functions (that would not make sense anyway). Unions are mostly used to define different representations of the same data. However, unions only work for types that are **Plain Old Data** (**POD**). If a union contains values of non-POD types, then these members require explicit construction with a placement `new` and explicit destruction, which is cumbersome and error-prone. In C++17, a type-safe union is available in the form of a standard library class template called `std::variant`. In this recipe, you will learn how to use it to model alternative values.

Getting ready

Although discriminated unions are not directly discussed in this recipe, being familiar with them will help us understand the design of, and the way, `variant` works better.

The class template `std::variant` was designed based on `boost::variant`, and is available in the `<variant>` header. If you are familiar with `boost::variant` and have used it in your code, you can migrate your code with little effort to use the standard `variant` class template.

How to do it...

Use the following operations to work with `std::variant`:

- To modify the stored value, use the member functions `emplace()` or `swap()`:

```
struct foo
{
  int value;
  explicit foo(int const i) : value(i) {}
};

std::variant<int, std::string, foo> v = 42; // holds int
v.emplace<foo>(42);                         // holds foo
```

- To read the stored values, use the non-member functions `std::get` or `std::get_if`:

```
std::variant<int, double, std::string> v = 42;
auto i1 = std::get<int>(v);
auto i2 = std::get<0>(v);

try
{
  auto f = std::get<double>(v);
}
catch (std::bad_variant_access const & e)
{
  std::cout << e.what() << '\n'; // Unexpected index
}
```

- To store a value, use the constructor or assign a value directly to a variant object:

```
std::variant<int, double, std::string> v;
v = 42;   // v contains int 42
v = 42.0; // v contains double 42.0
v = "42"; // v contains string "42"
```

- To check what is the stored alternative, use the member function `index()`:

```
std::variant<int, double, std::string> v = 42;
static_assert(std::variant_size_v<decltype(v)> == 3);
std::cout << "index = " << v.index() << '\n';
v = 42.0;
std::cout << "index = " << v.index() << '\n';
v = "42";
std::cout << "index = " << v.index() << '\n';
```

- To check whether a variant holds an alternative, use the non-member function `std::holds_alternative()`:

```
std::variant<int, double, std::string> v = 42;
std::cout << "int? " << std::boolalpha
          << std::holds_alternative<int>(v)
          << '\n'; // int? true

v = "42";
std::cout << "int? " << std::boolalpha
          << std::holds_alternative<int>(v)
          << '\n'; // int? false
```

- To define a variant whose first alternative is not default constructible, use `std::monostate` as the first alternative (in this example, `foo` is the same class we used earlier):

```
std::variant<std::monostate, foo, int> v;
v = 42;          // v contains int 42
std::cout << std::get<int>(v) << '\n';
v = foo{ 42 }; // v contains foo{42}
std::cout << std::get<foo>(v).value << '\n';
```

- To process the stored value of a variant and do something depending on the type of the alternative, use `std::visit()`:

```
std::variant<int, double, std::string> v = 42;
std::visit(
  [](auto&& arg) {std::cout << arg << '\n'; },
  v);
```

How it works...

`std::variant` is a class template that models a type-safe union, holding a value of one of its possible alternatives at any given time. In some rare cases, though, it is possible that a variant object does not store any value. `std::variant` has a member function called `valueless_by_exception()` that returns `true` if the variant does not hold a value, which is possible only in case of an exception during initialization; therefore, the name of the function.

The size of an `std::variant` object is as large as its largest alternative. A variant does not store additional data. The value stored by the variant is allocated within the memory representation of the object itself.

A variant can hold multiple alternatives of the same type, and also hold different constant- and volatile-qualified versions of the same time. On the other hand, it cannot hold an alternative of the type `void`, or alternatives of array and reference types. On the other hand, the first alternative must always be default constructible. The reason for this is that, just like discriminated unions, a variant is default initialized with the value of its first alternative. If the first alternative type is not default constructible, then the variant must use `std::monostate` as the first alternative. This is an empty type indented for making variants default constructible.

It is possible to query a `variant` at compile time for its size (that is, the number of alternatives it defines) and for the type of an alternative specified by its zero-based index. On the other hand, you can query the index of the currently held alternative at runtime using the member function `index()`.

There's more...

A typical way of manipulating the content of a variant is through visitation. This is basically the execution of an action based on the alternative hold by the variant. Since it is a larger topic, it is addressed separately in the next recipe.

See also

- *Using std::any to store any value* to learn how to use the C++17 class `std::any`, which represents a type-safe container for single values of any type,
- *Using std::optional to store optional values* to learn about the C++17 class template `std::optional`, which manages a value that may or may not exist.
- *Visiting a std::variant* to understand how to perform type matching and execute different actions based on the type of a variant's alternatives.

Visiting an std::variant

`std::variant` is a new standard container that was added to C++17 based on the `boost.variant` library. A variant is a type-safe union that holds the value of one of its alternative types. Although in the previous recipe we have seen various operations with variants, the variants we used were rather simple, with POD types mostly, which is not the actual purpose for which `std::variant` was created. Variants are intended to be used for holding alternatives of similar non-polymorphic and non-POD types. In this recipe, we will see a more real-world example of using variants and will learn how to visit variants.

Getting ready

For this recipe, you should be familiar with the `std::variant` type. It is recommended that you first read the previous recipe, *Using std::variant as a type-safe union.*

To explain how variant visitation can be done, we will consider a variant for representing a media DVD. Let's suppose we want to model a store or library that has DVDs that could contain either music, a movie, or software. However, these options are not modeled as a hierarchy with common data and virtual functions, but rather as non-related types that may have similar properties, such as a title. For simplicity, we'll consider the following properties:

- For a movie: Title and length (in minutes)
- For an album: Title, artist name, and a list of tracks (each track having a title and length in seconds)

- For software: Title and manufacturer

The following code shows a simple implementation of these types, without any functions, because that is not relevant to the visitation of a variant holding alternatives of these types:

```
enum class Genre { Drama, Action, SF, Comedy };

struct Movie
{
  std::string title;
  std::chrono::minutes length;
  std::vector<Genre> genre;
};

struct Track
{
  std::string title;
  std::chrono::seconds length;
};

struct Music
{
  std::string title;
  std::string artist;
  std::vector<Track> tracks;
};

struct Software
{
  std::string title;
  std::string vendor;
};

using dvd = std::variant<Movie, Music, Software>;
```

With these defined, let's start looking at how visiting variants should be performed.

How to do it...

To visit a variant, you must provide one or more actions for the possible alternatives of the variant. There are several types of visitors that are used for different purposes:

- A void visitor that does not return anything, but has side effects. The following example prints the title of each DVD to the console:

```
for (auto const & d : dvds)
{
  std::visit([](auto&& arg) {
               std::cout << arg.title << '\n'; },
             d);
}
```

- A visitor that returns a value; the value should have the same type, regardless of the current alternative of the variant, or can be itself a variant. In the following example, we visit a variant and return a new variant of the same type that has the `title` property from any of its alternatives transformed to uppercase letters:

```
for (auto const & d : dvds)
{
  dvd result = std::visit(
    [](auto&& arg) -> dvd
    {
      auto cpy { arg };
      cpy.title = to_upper(cpy.title);
      return cpy;
    },
  d);

  std::visit(
    [](auto&& arg) {
      std::cout << arg.title << '\n'; },
    result);
}
```

- A visitor that does type matching (which can either be a void or a value-returning visitor) implemented by providing a function object that has an overloaded call operator for each alternative type of the variant:

```
struct visitor_functor
{
  void operator()(Movie const & arg) const
  {
    std::cout << "Movie" << '\n';
    std::cout << " Title: " << arg.title << '\n';
    std::cout << " Length: " << arg.length.count()
              << "min" << '\n';
```

```
    }

    void operator()(Music const & arg) const
    {
      std::cout << "Music" << '\n';
      std::cout << " Title: " << arg.title << '\n';
      std::cout << " Artist: " << arg.artist << '\n';

      for (auto const & t : arg.tracks)
        std::cout << " Track: " << t.title
                  << ", " << t.length.count()
                  << "sec" << '\n';
    }

    void operator()(Software const & arg) const
    {
      std::cout << "Software" << '\n';
      std::cout << " Title: " << arg.title << '\n';
      std::cout << " Vendor: " << arg.vendor << '\n';
    }
  };

  for (auto const & d : dvds)
  {
    std::visit(visitor_functor(), d);
  }
```

- A visitor that does type matching that's implemented by providing a lambda expression that performs an action based on the type of the alternative:

```
  for (auto const & d : dvds)
  {
    std::visit([](auto&& arg) {
      using T = std::decay_t<decltype(arg)>;
      if constexpr (std::is_same_v<T, Movie>)
      {
        std::cout << "Movie" << '\n';
        std::cout << " Title: " << arg.title << '\n';
        std::cout << " Length: " << arg.length.count()
                  << "min" << '\n';
```

```
        }
        else if constexpr (std::is_same_v<T, Music>)
        {
          std::cout << "Music" << '\n';
          std::cout << " Title: " << arg.title << '\n';
          std::cout << " Artist: " << arg.artist << '\n';

          for (auto const & t : arg.tracks)
            std::cout << " Track: " << t.title
                      << ", " << t.length.count()
                      << "sec" << '\n';
        }
        else if constexpr (std::is_same_v<T, Software>)
        {
          std::cout << "Software" << '\n';
          std::cout << " Title: " << arg.title << '\n';
          std::cout << " Vendor: " << arg.vendor << '\n';
        }
      },
      d);
  }
```

How it works...

A visitor is a callable object (a function, a lambda expression, or a function object) that accepts every possible alternative from a variant. Visitation is done by invoking `std::visit()` with the visitor and one or more variant objects. The variants do not have to be of the same type, but the visitor must be able to accept every possible alternative from all the variants it is invoked for. In the examples earlier, we visited a single variant object, but visiting multiple variants does not imply anything more than passing them as arguments to `std::visit()`.

When you visit a variant, the callable object is invoked with the value currently stored in the variant. If the visitor does not accept an argument of the type stored in the variant, the program is ill-formed. If the visitor is a function object, then it must overload its call operator for all the possible alternative types of the variant. If the visitor is a lambda expression, it should be a generic lambda, which is basically a function object with a call operator template, instantiated by the compiler with the actual type that it is invoked with.

Examples of both approaches were shown in the previous section for a type-matching visitor. The function object in the first example is straightforward and should not require additional explanations. On the other hand, the generic lambda expression uses *constexpr if* to select a particular `if` branch based on the type of the argument at compile time. The result is that the compiler will create a function object with an operator call template and a body that contains *constexpr if* statements; when it instantiates that function template, it will produce an overload for each possible alternative type of the variant, and in each of these overloads, it will select only the *constexpr if* branch that matches the type of the call operator argument. The result is conceptually equivalent to the implementation of the `visitor_functor` class.

See also

- *Using std::any to store any value* to learn how to use the C++17 class `std::any`, which represents a type-safe container for single values of any type,
- *Using std::optional to store optional values* to learn about the C++17 class template `std::optional`, which manages a value that may or may not exist,
- *Using std::variant as a type-safe union* to see how to use the C++17 `std::variant` class to represent type-safe unions,

Using std::span for contiguous sequences of objects

In C++17, the `std::string_view` type was added to the standard library. This is an object that represents a view over a constant contiguous sequence of characters. The view is typically implemented with a pointer to the first element of the sequence and a length. Strings are one of the data types that are most used in any programming language, and having a non-owning view that does not allocate memory, avoids copies, and has some operations faster than `std::string`, which is an important benefit. However, a string is just a special vector of characters with operations specific for text. Therefore, it makes sense to have a type that is a view of a contiguous sequence of objects, regardless of their type. This is what the `std::span` class template in C++20 represents. We could say that `std::span` is to `std::vector` and array types what `std::string_view` is to `std::string`.

Getting ready

The `std::span` class template is available in the header `<span>`.

How to do it...

Prefer to use `std::span<T>` instead of a pointer and size pair as you typically would with C-like interfaces. In other words, replace functions like this:

```
void func(int* buffer, size_t length) { /* ... */ }
```

with this:

```
void func(std::span<int> buffer) { /* ... */ }
```

When working with `std::span`, you can do the following:

- Create a span with a compile-time length (called *static extent*) by specifying the number of elements in the span:

```
int arr[] = {1, 1, 2, 3, 5, 8, 13};
std::span<int, 7> s {arr};
```

- Create a span with a runtime length (called *dynamic extent*) by not specifying the number of elements in the span:

```
int arr[] = {1, 1, 2, 3, 5, 8, 13};
std::span<int> s {arr};
```

- You can use a span in a range-based for loop:

```
void func(std::span<int> buffer)
{
   for(auto const e : buffer)
      std::cout << e << ' ';
   std::cout << '\n';
}
```

- You can access the elements of a span using the methods `front()`, `back()`, `data()` and the `operator[]`:

```
int arr[] = {1, 1, 2, 3, 5, 8, 13};
std::span<int, 7> s {arr};
std::cout << s.front() << " == " << s[0] << '\n';    // 1 == 1
std::cout << s.back() << " == " << s[s.size() - 1] << '\n'; //
13 == 13
```

- You can obtain sub-spans of a span with the methods `first()`, `last()`, and `subspan()`:

```
std::span<int> first_3 = s.first(3);
func(first_3);  // 1 1 2.
```

```
std::span<int> last_3 = s.last(3);
func(last_3);   // 5 8 13
std::span<int> mid_3 = s.subspan(2, 3);
func(mid_3);    // 2 3 5
```

How it works...

The `std::span` class template is not a container of objects but a lightweight wrapper that defines a view of a contiguous sequence of objects. Initially, the span was called `array_view`, which some argue was a better name, both because it clearly indicates that the type is a non-owning view of a sequence and because it would be consistent with the name of `string_view`. However, the type was adopted in the standard library under the name span.

Although the standard does not specify the implementation details, the span is typically implemented by storing a pointer to the first element of the sequence and a length, representing the number of elements in the view. A span can, therefore, be used to define a non-owning view over (but not only) an `std::vector`, `std::array`, `T[]`, or `T*`. However, it cannot be used with lists or associative containers (for instance, `std::list`, `std::map`, or `std::set`) because these are not containers for a contiguous sequence of elements.

The span can have either a compile-time size or a runtime size. When the number of elements in the span is specified at compile-time, we have a span with a static extent (compile-time size). If the number of elements is not specified, but determined at runtime, we have a dynamic extent.

The `std::span` class has a simple interface, mainly consisting of the following members:

`begin()`, `end()`
 	
`cbegin()`, `cend()`
	Mutable and constant iterators to the first and the one-past last element of the sequence.

`rbegin()`, `rend()`
 	
`cbegin()`, `crend()`
	Mutable and constant reverse iterators to the beginning and end of the sequence.

`front()`, `back()`	Accesses the first and last element of the sequence.
`data()`	Returns a pointer to the beginning of the sequence of elements.
`operator[]`	Accesses an element of the sequence specified by its index.
`size()`	Retrieves the number of elements in the sequence.
`size_bytes()`	Retrieves the size of the sequence in bytes.
`empty()`	Checks if the sequence is empty.

`first()`	Retrieves a sub-span with the first *N* elements of the sequence.
`last()`	Retrieves a sub-span with the last *N* elements of the sequence.
`subspan()`	Retrieves a sub-span with *N* elements starting from a specified offset. If the count *N* is not specified, it returns a span with all the elements from offset until the end of the sequence.

A span is not intended to be used with general-purpose algorithms that work with a pair of iterators to the beginning and the end of a range (such as `sort`, `copy`, `find_if`, and so on), nor as a replacement for standard containers. Its main purpose is to build better interfaces than the C-like ones where a pointer and a size are passed to a function. The user may pass a wrong value for the size, which could end in accessing memory beyond the bounds of the sequence. The span provides safety and bounds checking. It is also a good alternative to passing to a const reference to a function to `std::vector<T>` (`std::vector<T> const &`). The span does not own its elements and is small enough to be passed by value (you should not pass spans by reference or constant reference).

Unlike `std::string_view`, which does not support changing the value of the elements in the sequence, the `std::span` defines a mutable view and supports modifying its elements. For this purpose, functions such as `front()`, `back()`, and `operator[]` return a reference.

See also

- *Using string_view instead of constant string references* in *Chapter 2, Working with Numbers and Strings*, to learn how to use `std::string_view` to improve performance in some scenarios when working with strings.

Registering a function to be called when a program exits normally

It is common that a program, upon exit, must clean up code to release resources, write something to a log, or do some other end operation. The standard library provides two utility functions that enable us to register functions to be called when a program terminates normally, either by returning from `main()` or through a call to `std::exit()` or `std::quick_exit()`. This is particularly useful for libraries that need to perform an action before the program is terminated, without relying on the user to explicitly call an end function. In this recipe, you will learn how to install exit handlers and how they work..

Getting ready

All the functions discussed in this recipe, `exit()`, `quick_exit()`, `atexit()`, and `at_quick_exit()`, are available in the namespace `std` in the header `<cstdlib>`.

How to do it...

To register functions to be called upon termination of a program, you should use the following:

- `std::atexit()` to register functions to be invoked when they return from `main()` or when a call to `std::exit()` is made:

```
void exit_handler_1()
{
  std::cout << "exit handler 1" << '\n';
}

void exit_handler_2()
{
  std::cout << "exit handler 2" << '\n';
}

std::atexit(exit_handler_1);
std::atexit(exit_handler_2);
std::atexit([]() {std::cout << "exit handler 3" << '\n'; });
```

- `std::at_quick_exit()` to register functions to be invoked when a call to `std::quick_exit()` is made:

```
void quick_exit_handler_1()
{
  std::cout << "quick exit handler 1" << '\n';
}

void quick_exit_handler_2()
{
  std::cout << "quick exit handler 2" << '\n';
}

std::at_quick_exit(quick_exit_handler_1);
std::at_quick_exit(quick_exit_handler_2);
std::at_quick_exit([]() {
  std::cout << "quick exit handler 3" << '\n'; });
```

How it works...

The exit handlers, regardless of the method they are registered with, are called only when the program terminates normally or quickly. If termination is done in an abnormal way, via a call to `std::terminate()` or `std::abort()`, none of them are called. If any of these handlers exits via an exception, then `std::terminate()` is called. Exit handlers must not have any parameters and must return `void`. Once registered, an exit handler cannot be unregistered.

A program can install multiple handlers. The standard guarantees that at least 32 handlers can be registered with each method, although actual implementations can support any higher number. Both `std::atexit()` and `std::at_quick_exit()` are thread-safe and, therefore, can be called simultaneously from different threads without incurring race conditions.

If multiple handlers are registered, then they are called in the reverse order of their registration. The following table shows the output of a program that registered the exit handlers, as shown in the previous section, when the program terminates via an `std::exit()` call and an `std::quick_exit()` call:

`std::exit(0);`	`std::quick_exit(0);`
exit handler 3 exit handler 2 exit handler 1	quick exit handler 3 quick exit handler 2 quick exit handler 1

On the other hand, on normal termination of the program, destruction of objects with local storage duration, destruction of objects with static storage duration, and calls to registered exit handlers are done concurrently. However, it is guaranteed that exit handlers registered before the construction of a static object are called after the destruction of that static object, and exit handlers registered after the construction of a static object are called before the destruction of that static object. To better exemplify this, let's consider the following class:

```
struct static_foo
{
  ~static_foo() { std::cout << "static foo destroyed!" << '\n'; }
  static static_foo* instance()
  {
    static static_foo obj;
    return &obj;
  }
};
```

In this context, we will refer to the following code snippet:

```
std::atexit(exit_handler_1);
static_foo::instance();
std::atexit(exit_handler_2);
std::atexit([]() {std::cout << "exit handler 3" << '\n'; });

std::exit(42);
```

When the preceding code snippet is executed, `exit_handler_1` is registered before the creation of the static object `static_foo`. On the other hand, `exit_handler_2` and the lambda expression are both registered, in that order, after the static object was constructed. As a result, the order of calls at normal termination is as follows:

1. Lambda expression
2. `exit_handler_2`
3. Destructor of `static_foo`
4. `exit_handler_1`

The output for the preceding program is listed here:

```
exit handler 3
exit handler 2
static foo destroyed!
exit handler 1
```

When `std::at_quick_exit()` is used, the registered functions are not called in the case of normal program termination. If a function needs to be called in that case, you must register it with `std::atexit()`.

See also

- *Using lambdas with standard algorithms* in *Chapter 3, Exploring Functions*, to explore the basics of lambda expressions and how you can utilize them with the standard algorithms.

Using type traits to query properties of types

Template metaprogramming is a powerful feature of the language that enables us to write and reuse generic code that works with all types. In practice, however, it is often necessary that generic code should work differently, or not at all, with different types, either through intent, or for semantic correctness, performance, or other reasons. For example, you may want a generic algorithm to be implemented differently for POD and non-POD types, or you want a function template to be instantiated only with integral types. C++11 provides a set of type traits to help with this.

Type traits are basically meta-types that provide information about other types. The type traits library contains a long list of traits for querying type properties (such as checking whether a type is an integral type or whether two types are the same), but also for performing type transformation (such as removing the `const` and `volatile` qualifiers or adding a pointer to a type). We have used type traits in several recipes earlier in this book; however, in this recipe, we will look into what the type traits are and how they work.

Getting ready

All type traits introduced in C++11 are available in the namespace `std` in the `<type_traits>` header.

Type traits can be used in many metaprogramming contexts, and throughout this book, we have seen them used in various situations. In this recipe, we will summarize some of these use cases and see how type traits work.

In this recipe, we will discuss full and partial template specialization. Familiarity with these concepts will help you better understand the way type traits work.

How to do it...

The following list shows various situations where type traits are used to achieve various design goals:

- With `enable_if`, to define preconditions for the types a function template can be instantiated with:

```
template <typename T,
          typename = typename std::enable_if_t<
                std::is_arithmetic_v<T> > >
T multiply(T const t1, T const t2)
```

```
{
  return t1 * t2;
}

auto v1 = multiply(42.0, 1.5);     // OK
auto v2 = multiply("42"s, "1.5"s); // error
```

- With static_assert, to ensure that invariants are met:

```
template <typename T>
struct pod_wrapper
{
  static_assert(std::is_standard_layout_v<T> &&
                std::is_trivial_v<T>,
                "Type is not a POD!");
  T value;
};

pod_wrapper<int> i{ 42 };            // OK
pod_wrapper<std::string> s{ "42"s }; // error
```

- With std::conditional, to select between types:

```
template <typename T>
struct const_wrapper
{
  typedef typename std::conditional_t<
            std::is_const_v<T>,
            T,
            typename std::add_const_t<T>> const_type;
        };

static_assert(
  std::is_const_v<const_wrapper<int>::const_type>);

static_assert(
  std::is_const_v<const_wrapper<int const>::const_type>);
```

- With constexpr if, to enable the compiler to generate different code based on the type the template is instantiated with:

```
template <typename T>
auto process(T arg)
{
  if constexpr (std::is_same_v<T, bool>)
```

```
    return !arg;
  else if constexpr (std::is_integral_v<T>)
    return -arg;
  else if constexpr (std::is_floating_point_v<T>)
    return std::abs(arg);
  else
    return arg;
}

auto v1 = process(false); // v1 = true
auto v2 = process(42);    // v2 = -42
auto v3 = process(-42.0); // v3 = 42.0
auto v4 = process("42"s); // v4 = "42"
```

How it works...

Type traits are classes that provide meta-information about types or can be used to modify types. There are actually two categories of type traits:

- Traits that provide information about types, their properties, or their relations (such as `is_integer`, `is_arithmetic`, `is_array`, `is_enum`, `is_class`, `is_const`, `is_trivial`, `is_standard_layout`, `is_constructible`, `is_same`, and so on). These traits provide a constant `bool` member called `value`.
- Traits that modify properties of types (such as `add_const`, `remove_const`, `add_pointer`, `remove_pointer`, `make_signed`, `make_unsigned`, and so on). These traits provide a member typedef called `type` that represents the transformed type.

Both of these categories of types have been shown in the *How to do it...* section; examples have been discussed and explained in detail in other recipes. For convenience, a short summary is provided here:

- In the first example, the function template `multiply()` is allowed to be instantiated only with arithmetic types (that is, integral or floating point); when instantiated with a different kind of type, `enable_if` does not define a typedef member called `type`, which produces a compilation error.
- In the second example, `pod_wrapper` is a class template that is supposed to be instantiated only with POD types. A `static_assert` declaration produces a compilation error if a non-POD type is used (it is either not trivial or not in the standard layout).
- In the third example, `const_wrapper` is a class template that provides a typedef member called `const_type` that represents a const-qualified type.

- In this example, we used `std::conditional` to select between two types at compile time: if the type parameter `T` is already a const type, then we just select `T`. Otherwise, we use the `add_const` type trait to qualify the type with the `const` specifier.
- If the fourth example, `process()` is a function template that contains a series of `if constexpr` branches. Based on the category of type, queried at compile time with various type traits (`is_same`, `is_integer`, `is_floating_point`), the compiler selects one branch only to be put into the generated code and discards the rest. Therefore, a call such as `process(42)` will produce the following instantiation of the function template:

```
int process(int arg)
{
  return -arg;
}
```

Type traits are implemented by providing a class template and a partial or full specialization for it. The following represent conceptual implementations for some type traits:

- The `is_void()` method indicates whether a type is `void`; this uses full specialization:

```
template <typename T>
struct is_void
{ static const bool value = false; };

template <>
struct is_void<void>
{ static const bool value = true; };
```

- The `is_pointer()` method indicates whether a type is a pointer to an object or a pointer to a function; this uses partial specialization:

```
template <typename T>
struct is_pointer
{ static const bool value = false; };

template <typename T>
struct is_pointer<T*>
{ static const bool value = true; };
```

Note that, in C++20, the concept of the POD type has been deprecated. This also includes the deprecation of the `std::is_pod` type trait. A POD type is a type that is both *trivial* (has special members that are compiler-provided or explicitly defaulted and occupy a contiguous memory area) and has a *standard layout* (a class that does not contain language features, such as virtual functions, which are incompatible with the C language, and all members have the same access control). Therefore, as of C++20, the more fine-grained concepts of trivial and standard layout types are preferred. This also implies that you should no longer use `std::is_pod`, but `std::is_trivial` and, respectively, `std::is_standard_layout`.

There's more...

Type traits are not limited to what the standard library provides. Using similar techniques, you can define your own type traits to achieve various goals. In the next recipe, *Writing your own type traits*, we will learn how to define and use our own type traits.

See also

- *Selecting branches at compile time with constexpr if* in *Chapter 4, Preprocessing and Compilation*, to learn how to compile only parts of your code with *constexpr if* statements.
- *Conditionally compiling classes and functions with enable_if* in *Chapter 4, Preprocessing and Compilation*, to learn about SFINAE and how to use it to specify type constraints for templates.
- *Performing compile-time assertion checks with static_assert* in *Chapter 4, Preprocessing and Compilation*, to see how to define assertions that are verified at compile time.
- *Writing your own type traits* to learn how to define your own type traits.
- *Using std::conditional to choose between types* to understand how to perform a compile-time selection of types on a compile-time Boolean expression.

Writing your own type traits

In the previous recipe, we learned what type traits are, what traits the standard provides, and how they can be used for various purposes. In this recipe, we'll go a step further and take a look at how to define our own custom traits.

Getting ready

In this recipe, we will learn how to solve the following problem: we have several classes that support serialization. Without getting into any details, let's suppose some provide a "plain" serialization to a string (regardless of what that can mean), whereas others do it based on a specified encoding. The end goal is to create a single, uniform API for serializing the objects of any of these types. For this, we will consider the following two classes: `foo`, which provides a simple serialization, and `bar`, which provides serialization with encoding:

```
struct foo
{
  std::string serialize()
  {
    return "plain"s;
  }
};

struct bar
{
  std::string serialize_with_encoding()
  {
    return "encoded"s;
  }
};
```

It is recommended that you read the *Using type traits to query properties of types* recipe first, before you continue with this one.

How to do it...

Implement the following class and function templates:

- A class template called `is_serializable_with_encoding` containing a `static const bool` variable set to `false`:

  ```
  template <typename T>
  struct is_serializable_with_encoding
  {
    static const bool value = false;
  };
  ```

- A full specialization of the `is_serializable_with_encoding` template for the class `bar` that has the `static const bool` variable set to `true`:

```
template <>
struct is_serializable_with_encoding<bar>
{
  static const bool value = true;
};
```

- A class template called `serializer`, containing a static template method called `serialize`, that takes an argument of the template type `T` and calls `serialize()` for that object:

```
template <bool b>
struct serializer
{
  template <typename T>
  static auto serialize(T& v)
  {
    return v.serialize();
  }
};
```

- A full specialization class template for `true`, whose `serialize()` static method calls `serialize_with_encoding()` for the argument:

```
template <>
struct serializer<true>
{
  template <typename T>
  static auto serialize(T& v)
  {
    return v.serialize_with_encoding();
  }
};
```

- A function template called `serialize()`, which uses the `serializer` class templates defined previously and the `is_serializable_with_encoding` type trait, to select which of the actual serialization methods (plain or with encoding) should be called:

```
template <typename T>
auto serialize(T& v)
{
  return serializer<is_serializable_with_encoding<T>::value>::
    serialize(v);
}
```

How it works...

`is_serializable_with_encoding` is a type trait that checks whether a type `T` is serializable with (a specified) encoding. It provides a static member of the type `bool` called `value` that is equal to `true` if `T` supports serialization with encoding, or `false` otherwise. It is implemented as a class template with a single type template parameter `T`; this class template is fully specialized for the types that support encoded serialization—in this particular example—for the class `bar`:

```
std::cout <<
  is_serializable_with_encoding<foo>::value << '\n';     // false
std::cout <<
  is_serializable_with_encoding<bar>::value << '\n';     // true
std::cout <<
  is_serializable_with_encoding<int>::value << '\n';     // false
std::cout <<
  is_serializable_with_encoding<string>::value << '\n'; // false
```

The `serialize()` method is a function template that represents a common API for serializing objects that support either type of serialization. It takes a single argument of the type template parameter `T` and uses a helper class template `serializer` to call either the `serialize()` or the `serialize_with_encoding()` method of its argument.

The `serializer` type is a class template with a single, non-type template parameter of the type `bool`. This class template contains a static function template called `serialize()`. This function template takes a single parameter of the type template parameter `T`, calls `serialize()` on the argument, and returns the value returned from that call. The `serializer` class template has a full specialization for the value `true` of its non-type template parameter. In this specialization, the function template `serialize()` has an unchanged signature, but calls `serialize_with_encoding()` instead of `serialize()`.

The selection between using the generic or the fully specialized class template is done in the `serialize()` function template using the `is_serializable_with_encoding` type trait. The static member `value` of the type trait is used as the argument for the non-type template parameter of `serializer`.

With all that defined, we can write the following code:

```
foo f;
bar b;

std::cout << serialize(f) << '\n'; // plain
std::cout << serialize(b) << '\n'; // encoded
```

In this snippet, calling `serialize()` with a `foo` argument will return the string *plain*, while calling `serialize()` with a `bar` argument will return the string *encoded*.

See also

- *Using type traits to query properties of types* to explore a C++ meta-programming technique that allows us to inspect and transform properties of types.
- *Using std::conditional to choose between types* to understand how to perform a compile-time selection of types on a compile-time Boolean expression.

Using std::conditional to choose between types

In the previous recipes, we looked at some of the features from the type support library, and type traits in particular. Related topics have been discussed in other parts of this book, such as using `std::enable_if` to hide function overloads, in *Chapter 4, Preprocessing and Compilation*, and `std::decay` to remove `const` and `volatile` qualifiers, when we discussed visiting variants, also in this chapter. Another type transformation feature worth discussing to a larger extent is `std::conditional`, which enables us to choose between two types at compile time, based on a compile-time Boolean expression. From this recipe, you will learn how it works and how to use it through several examples.

Getting ready

It is recommended that you first read the *Using type traits to query properties of types* recipe, earlier in this chapter.

How to do it...

The following is a list of examples that show you how to use `std::conditional` (and `std::conditional_t`) to choose between two types at compile time:

- In a type alias or typedef, to select between a 32-bit and 64-bit integer type, based on the platform (the pointer size is 4 bytes on 32-bit platforms and 8 bytes on 68-bit platforms):

```
using long_type = std::conditional_t<
    sizeof(void*) <= 4, long, long long>;
```

```
auto n = long_type{ 42 };
```

- In an alias template, to select between an 8-, 16-, 32-, or 64-bit integer type, based on the user specification (as a non-type template parameter):

```
template <int size>
using number_type =
  typename std::conditional_t<
    size<=1,
    std::int8_t,
    typename std::conditional_t<
      size<=2,
      std::int16_t,
      typename std::conditional_t<
        size<=4,
        std::int32_t,
        std::int64_t
      >
    >
  >;

auto n = number_type<2>{ 42 };

static_assert(sizeof(number_type<1>) == 1);
static_assert(sizeof(number_type<2>) == 2);
static_assert(sizeof(number_type<3>) == 4);
static_assert(sizeof(number_type<4>) == 4);
static_assert(sizeof(number_type<5>) == 8);
static_assert(sizeof(number_type<6>) == 8);
static_assert(sizeof(number_type<7>) == 8);
static_assert(sizeof(number_type<8>) == 8);
static_assert(sizeof(number_type<9>) == 8);
```

- In a type template parameter, to select between an integer and real uniform distribution, depending on whether the type template parameter is of an integral or floating-point type:

```
template <typename T,
          typename D = std::conditional_t<
                         std::is_integral_v<T>,
                         std::uniform_int_distribution<T>,
                         std::uniform_real_distribution<T>>,
          typename = typename std::enable_if_t<
```

```
                            std::is_arithmetic_v<T>>>
std::vector<T> GenerateRandom(T const min, T const max,
                              size_t const size)
{
  std::vector<T> v(size);

  std::random_device rd{};
  std::mt19937 mt{ rd() };

  D dist{ min, max };

  std::generate(std::begin(v), std::end(v),
    [&dist, &mt] {return dist(mt); });

  return v;
}

auto v1 = GenerateRandom(1, 10, 10);     // integers
auto v2 = GenerateRandom(1.0, 10.0, 10); // doubles
```

How it works...

`std::conditional` is a class template that defines a member called `type` as either one or the other of its two type template parameters. This selection is done based on a compile-time constant Boolean expression provided as an argument for a non-type template parameter. Its implementation looks like this:

```
template<bool Test, class T1, class T2>
struct conditional
{
  typedef T2 type;
};
template<class T1, class T2>
struct conditional<true, T1, T2>
{
  typedef T1 type;
};
```

Let's summarize the examples from the previous section:

- In the first example, if the platform is 32-bit, then the size of the pointer type is 4 bytes and, therefore, the compile-time expression `sizeof(void*) <= 4` is `true`; as a result, `std::conditional` defines its member type as `long`. If the platform is 64-bit, then the condition evaluates to `false`, because the size of the pointer type is 8 bytes, and therefore the member type is defined as `long long`.
- A similar situation is encountered in the second example, where `std::conditional` is used multiple times to emulate a series of `if...else` statements to select an appropriate type.
- In the third example, we used the alias template `std::conditional_t` to simplify the declaration of the function template `GenerateRandom`. Here, `std::conditional` is used to define the default value for a type template parameter representing a statistical distribution. Depending on whether the first type template parameter `T` is an integral or floating-point type, the default distribution type is chosen between `std::uniform_int_distribution<T>` and `std::uniform_real_distribution<T>`. Use of other types is disabled by employing `std::enable_if` with a third template parameter, as we have seen in other recipes already.

To help simplify the use of `std::conditional`, C++14 provides an alias template called `std::conditional_t`, which we have seen in the examples here, and that is defined as follows:

```
template<bool Test, class T1, class T2>
using conditional_t = typename conditional_t<Test,T1,T2>;
```

The use of this helper class (and the many others that are similar and from the standard library) is optional but helps with writing more concise code.

See also

- *Using type traits to query properties of types* to explore a C++ metaprogramming technique that allows us to inspect and transform properties of types.
- *Writing your own type traits* to learn how to define your own type traits.
- *Conditionally compiling classes and functions with enable_if* in *Chapter 4, Preprocessing and Compilation*, to learn about SFINAE and how to use it to specify type constraints for templates.

7
Working with Files and Streams

One of the most important parts of the C++ standard library is the **input/output** (**I/O**), stream-based library that enables developers to work with files, memory streams, or other types of I/O devices. The first part of this chapter provides solutions to some common stream operations, such as reading and writing data, localization settings, and manipulating the input and output of a stream. The second part of the chapter explores the new C++17 `filesystem` library that enables developers to perform operations with the filesystem and its objects, such as files and directories.

The recipes covered in this chapter are as follows:

- Reading and writing raw data from/to binary files
- Reading and writing objects from/to binary files
- Using localized settings for streams
- Using I/O manipulators to control the output of a stream
- Using monetary I/O manipulators
- Using time I/O manipulators
- Working with filesystem paths
- Creating, copying, and deleting files and directories
- Removing content from a file
- Checking the properties of an existing file or directory
- Enumerating the content of a directory
- Finding a file

We will start the chapter with a couple of recipes on how to serialize and deserialize data to/from files.

Reading and writing raw data from/to binary files

Some of the data programs you work with must be persisted to disk files in various ways, including storing data in a database or to flat files, either as text or binary data. This recipe, and the next one, are focused on persisting and loading both raw data and objects from and to binary files. In this context, raw data means unstructured data, and, in this recipe, we will consider writing and reading the content of a buffer (that is, a contiguous sequence of memory) that can either be an array, an `std::vector`, or an `std::array`.

Getting ready

For this recipe, you should be familiar with the standard stream I/O library, although some explanations, to the extent that is required to understand this recipe, are provided next. You should also be familiar with the differences between binary and text files.

In this recipe, we will use the `ofstream` and `ifstream` classes, which are available in the namespace `std` in the `<fstream>` header.

How to do it...

To write the content of a buffer (in our example, an `std::vector`) to a binary file, you should perform the following steps:

1. Open a file stream for writing in binary mode by creating an instance of the `std::ofstream` class:

   ```
   std::ofstream ofile("sample.bin", std::ios::binary);
   ```

2. Ensure that the file is actually open before writing data to the file:

   ```
   if(ofile.is_open())
   {
     // streamed file operations
   }
   ```

3. Write the data to the file by providing a pointer to the array of characters and the number of characters to write. In the following example, we write the content of a local vector; however, typically, this data comes from a different context:

   ```
   std::vector<unsigned char> output {0,1,2,3,4,5,6,7,8,9};
   ofile.write(reinterpret_cast<char*>(output.data()),
               output.size());
   ```

4. Optionally, you can flush the content of the stream's output buffer to the actual disk file by calling the `flush()` method. This determines the uncommitted changes in the stream to be synchronized with the external destination, which, in this case, is a disk file.
5. Close the stream by calling `close()`. This, in turn, calls `flush()`, making the preceding step unnecessary in most contexts:

   ```
   ofile.close();
   ```

To read the entire content of a binary file to a buffer, you should perform the following steps:

1. Open a file stream to read from a file in binary mode by creating an instance of the `std::ifstream` class:

   ```
   std::ifstream ifile("sample.bin", std::ios::binary);
   ```

2. Ensure that the file is actually open before reading data from it:

   ```
   if(ifile.is_open())
   {
     // streamed file operations
   }
   ```

3. Determine the length of the file by positioning the input position indicator to the end of the file, read its value, and then move the indicator to the beginning:

   ```
   ifile.seekg(0, std::ios_base::end);
   auto length = ifile.tellg();
   ifile.seekg(0, std::ios_base::beg);
   ```

4. Allocate memory to read the content of the file:

   ```
   std::vector<unsigned char> input;
   input.resize(static_cast<size_t>(length));
   ```

5. Read the content of the file to the allocated buffer by providing a pointer to the array of characters for receiving the data and the number of characters to read:

```
ifile.read(reinterpret_cast<char*>(input.data()), length);
```

6. Check that the read operation is completed successfully:

```
auto success = !ifile.fail() && length == ifile.gcount();
```

7. Finally, close the file stream:

```
ifile.close();
```

How it works...

The standard stream-based I/O library provides various classes that implement high-level input, output, or both input and output file stream, string stream and character array operations, manipulators that control how these streams behave, and several predefined stream objects (`cin`/`wcin`, `cout`/`wcout`, `cerr`/`wcerr`, and `clog`/`wclog`).

These streams are implemented as class templates, and, for files, the library provides several classes:

- `basic_filebuf` implements the I/O operations for a raw file and is similar in semantics to a C `FILE` stream.
- `basic_ifstream` implements the high-level file stream input operations defined by the `basic_istream` stream interface, internally using a `basic_filebuf` object.
- `basic_ofstream` implements the high-level file stream output operations defined by the `basic_ostream` stream interface, internally using a `basic_filebuf` object.
- `basic_fstream` implements the high-level file stream input and output operations defined by the `basic_iostream` stream interface, internally using a `basic_filebuf` object.

These classes are represented in the following class diagram to better understand their relationship:

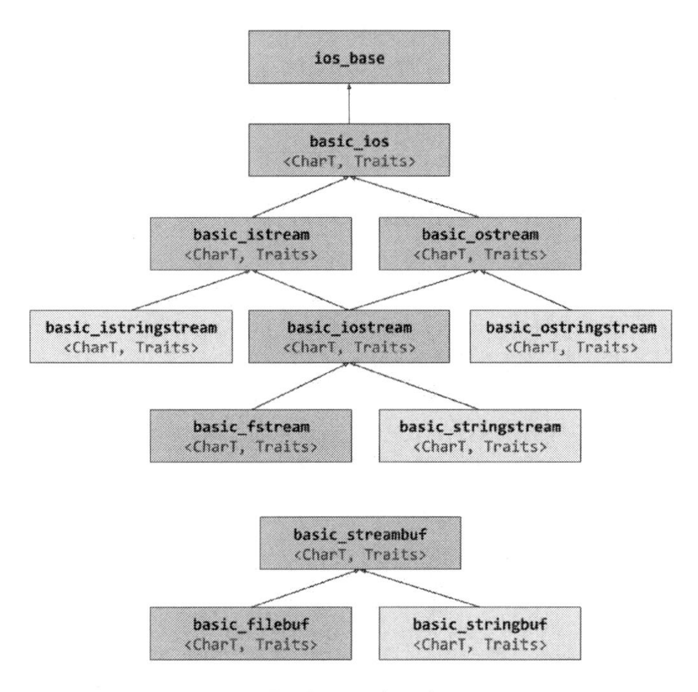

Figure 7.1: Stream class diagram

Notice that this diagram also features several classes designed to work with a string-based stream. These streams, however, will not be discussed here.

Several typedefs for the class templates mentioned earlier are also defined in the `<fstream>` header, in the `std` namespace. The `ofstream` and `ifstream` objects are the type synonyms used in the preceding examples:

```
typedef basic_ifstream<char>    ifstream;
typedef basic_ifstream<wchar_t> wifstream;
typedef basic_ofstream<char>    ofstream;
typedef basic_ofstream<wchar_t> wofstream;
typedef basic_fstream<char>     fstream;
typedef basic_fstream<wchar_t>  wfstream;
```

In the previous section, you saw how we can write and read raw data to and from a file stream. Now, we'll cover this process in more detail.

To write data to a file, we instantiated an object of the type `std::ofstream`. In the constructor, we passed the name of the file to be opened and the stream's open mode, for which we specified `std::ios::binary` to indicate binary mode. Opening the file like this discards the previous file content. If you want to append content to an existing file, you should also use the flag `std::ios::app` (that is, `std::ios::app | std::ios::binary`). This constructor internally calls `open()` on its underlying raw file object, that is, a `basic_filebuf` object. If this operation fails, a fail bit is set. To check whether the stream has been successfully associated with a file device, we used `is_open()` (this internally calls the method with the same name from the underlying `basic_filebuf`). Writing data to the file stream is done using the `write()` method, which takes a pointer to the string of characters to write and the number of characters to write. Since this method operates with strings of characters, a `reinterpret_cast` is necessary if data is of another type, such as `unsigned char` in our example. The write operation does not set a fail bit in the case of a failure, but it may throw an `std::ios_base::failure` exception. However, data is not written directly to the file device but stored in the `basic_filebuf` object. To write it to the file, the buffer needs to be flushed, which is done by calling `flush()`. This is done automatically when closing the file stream, as shown in the preceding example.

To read data from a file, we instantiated an object of type `std::ifstream`. In the constructor, we passed the same arguments that we used for opening the file to write the name of the file and the open mode, that is, `std::ios::binary`. The constructor internally calls `open()` on the underlying `std::basic_filebuf` object. To check whether the stream has been successfully associated with a file device, we use `is_open()` (this internally calls the method with the same name from the underlying `basic_filebuf`). In this example, we read the entire content of the file to a memory buffer, in particular, an `std::vector`. Before we can read the data, we must know the size of the file in order to allocate a buffer that is large enough to hold that data. To do this, we used `seekg()` to move the input position indicator to the end of the file.

Then, we called `tellg()` to return the current position, which, in this case, indicates the size of the file, in bytes, and then we moved the input position indicator to the beginning of the file to be able to start reading from the beginning. Calling `seekg()` to move the position indicator to the end can be avoided by opening the file with the position indicator moved directly to the end. This can be achieved by using the `std::ios::ate` opening flag in the constructor (or the `open()` method). After allocating enough memory for the content of the file, we copied the data from the file into memory using the `read()` method. This takes a pointer to the string of characters that receives the data read from the stream and the number of characters to be read. Since the stream operates on characters, a `reinterpret_cast` expression is necessary if the buffer contains other types of data, such as `unsigned char` in our example.

This operation throws an `std::basic_ios::failure` exception if an error occurs. To determine the number of characters that have been successfully read from the stream, we can use the `gcount()` method. Upon completing the read operation, we close the file stream.

The operations shown in these examples are the minimum ones required to write and read data to and from file streams. It is important, though, that you perform appropriate checks for the success of the operations and to catch any possible exceptions that could occur.

The example code discussed so far in this recipe can be reorganized in the form of two general functions for writing and reading data to and from a file:

```
bool write_data(char const * const filename,
                char const * const data,
                size_t const size)
{
  auto success = false;
  std::ofstream ofile(filename, std::ios::binary);

  if(ofile.is_open())
  {
    try
    {
      ofile.write(data, size);
      success = true;
    }
    catch(std::ios_base::failure &)
    {
      // handle the error
    }
    ofile.close();
  }

  return success;
}

size_t read_data(char const * const filename,
                 std::function<char*(size_t const)> allocator)
{
  size_t readbytes = 0;
  std::ifstream ifile(filename, std::ios::ate | std::ios::binary);
```

```
  if(ifile.is_open())
  {
    auto length = static_cast<size_t>(ifile.tellg());
    ifile.seekg(0, std::ios_base::beg);

    auto buffer = allocator(length);

    try
    {
      ifile.read(buffer, length);

      readbytes = static_cast<size_t>(ifile.gcount());
    }
    catch (std::ios_base::failure &)
    {
      // handle the error
    }

    ifile.close();
  }

  return readbytes;
}
```

`write_data()` is a function that takes the name of a file, a pointer to an array of characters, and the length of this array as arguments and writes the characters to the specified file. `read_data()` is a function that takes the name of a file and a function that allocates a buffer and reads the entire content of the file to the buffer that is returned by the allocated function. The following is an example of how these functions can be used:

```
std::vector<unsigned char> output {0, 1, 2, 3, 4, 5, 6, 7, 8, 9};
std::vector<unsigned char> input;

if(write_data("sample.bin",
              reinterpret_cast<char*>(output.data()),
              output.size()))
{
  if(read_data("sample.bin",
               [&input](size_t const length) {
    input.resize(length);
    return reinterpret_cast<char*>(input.data());}) > 0)
  {
```

```
    std::cout << (output == input ? "equal": "not equal")
              << '\n';
  }
}
```

Alternatively, we could use a dynamically allocated buffer, instead of the `std::vector`; the changes required for this are small in the overall example:

```
std::vector<unsigned char> output {0, 1, 2, 3, 4, 5, 6, 7, 8, 9};
unsigned char* input = nullptr;
size_t readb = 0;

if(write_data("sample.bin",
              reinterpret_cast<char*>(output.data()),
              output.size()))
{
  if((readb = read_data(
     "sample.bin",
     [&input](size_t const length) {
       input = new unsigned char[length];
       return reinterpret_cast<char*>(input); })) > 0)
  {
    auto cmp = memcmp(output.data(), input, output.size());
    std::cout << (cmp == 0 ? "equal": "not equal")
              << '\n';
  }
}

delete [] input;
```

However, this alternative is only provided to show that `read_data()` can be used with different kinds of input buffers. It is recommended that you avoid the explicit dynamic allocation of memory whenever possible.

There's more...

The way of reading data from a file to memory, as shown in this recipe, is only one of several. The following is a list of possible alternatives for reading data from a file stream:

- Initializing an `std::vector` directly using `std::istreambuf_iterator` iterators (similarly, this can be used with `std::string`):

```
std::vector<unsigned char> input;
std::ifstream ifile("sample.bin", std::ios::binary);
if(ifile.is_open())
{
  input = std::vector<unsigned char>(
    std::istreambuf_iterator<char>(ifile),
    std::istreambuf_iterator<char>());
  ifile.close();
}
```

- Assigning the content of an `std::vector` from `std::istreambuf_iterator` iterators:

```
std::vector<unsigned char> input;
std::ifstream ifile("sample.bin", std::ios::binary);
if(ifile.is_open())
{
  ifile.seekg(0, std::ios_base::end);
  auto length = ifile.tellg();
  ifile.seekg(0, std::ios_base::beg);

  input.reserve(static_cast<size_t>(length));
    input.assign(
    std::istreambuf_iterator<char>(ifile),
    std::istreambuf_iterator<char>());
  ifile.close();
}
```

- Copying the content of the file stream to a vector using `std::istreambuf_iterator` iterators and an `std::back_inserter` adapter to write to the end of the vector:

```
std::vector<unsigned char> input;
std::ifstream ifile("sample.bin", std::ios::binary);
if(ifile.is_open())
{
  ifile.seekg(0, std::ios_base::end);
  auto length = ifile.tellg();
  ifile.seekg(0, std::ios_base::beg);

  input.reserve(static_cast<size_t>(length));
  std::copy(std::istreambuf_iterator<char>(ifile),
```

```
            std::istreambuf_iterator<char>(),
            std::back_inserter(input));
  ifile.close();
}
```

Compared to these alternatives, however, the method described in the *How to do it...* section is the fastest one, even though the alternatives may look more appealing from an object-oriented perspective. It is beyond the scope of this recipe to compare the performance of these alternatives, but you can try it as an exercise.

See also

- *Reading and writing objects from/to binary files* to learn how to serialize and deserialize objects to and from binary files
- *Using I/O manipulators to control the output of a stream* to learn about the use of helper functions, called manipulators, that control input and output streams using the `<<` and `>>` stream operators

Reading and writing objects from/to binary files

In the previous recipe, we learned how to write and read raw data (that is, unstructured data) to and from a file. Many times, however, we must persist and load objects instead. Writing and reading in the manner shown in the previous recipe works for POD types only. For anything else, we must explicitly decide what is actually written or read, since writing or reading pointers, **virtual tables** (**vtables**), and any sort of metadata is not only irrelevant but also semantically wrong. These operations are commonly referred to as serialization and deserialization. In this recipe, we will learn how to serialize and deserialize both POD and non-POD types to and from binary files.

Getting ready

For the examples in this recipe, we will use the `foo` and `foopod` classes, as follows:

```
class foo
{
  int i;
  char c;
  std::string s;
```

```
public:
  foo(int const i = 0, char const c = 0, std::string const & s = {}):
    i(i), c(c), s(s)
  {}

  foo(foo const &) = default;
  foo& operator=(foo const &) = default;

  bool operator==(foo const & rhv) const
  {
    return i == rhv.i &&
           c == rhv.c &&
           s == rhv.s;
  }

  bool operator!=(foo const & rhv) const
  {
    return !(*this == rhv);
  }
};

struct foopod
{
  bool a;
  char b;
  int c[2];
};

bool operator==(foopod const & f1, foopod const & f2)
{
  return f1.a == f2.a && f1.b == f2.b &&
         f1.c[0] == f2.c[0] && f1.c[1] == f2.c[1];
}
```

It is recommended that you first read the previous recipe, *Reading and writing raw data from/to binary files*, before you continue. You should also know what POD (a type that is both trivial and has a standard layout) and non-POD types are and how operators can be overloaded. You can check the closing notes of the *Using type traits to query properties of types* recipe, in *Chapter 6, General-Purpose Utilities*, for further details on POD types.

How to do it...

To serialize/deserialize POD types that do not contain pointers, use `ofstream::write()` and `ifstream::read()`, as shown in the previous recipe:

- Serialize objects to a binary file using `ofstream` and the `write()` method:

```
std::vector<foopod> output {
  {true, '1', {1, 2}},
  {true, '2', {3, 4}},
  {false, '3', {4, 5}}
};

std::ofstream ofile("sample.bin", std::ios::binary);
if(ofile.is_open())
{
  for(auto const & value : output)
  {
    ofile.write(reinterpret_cast<const char*>(&value),
                sizeof(value));
  }

  ofile.close();
}
```

- Deserialize objects from a binary file using the `ifstream` and `read()` methods:

```
std::vector<foopod> input;
std::ifstream ifile("sample.bin", std::ios::binary);
if(ifile.is_open())
{
  while(true)
  {
    foopod value;
    ifile.read(reinterpret_cast<char*>(&value),
               sizeof(value));

    if(ifile.fail() || ifile.eof()) break;
    input.push_back(value);
  }

  ifile.close();
}
```

To serialize non-POD types (or POD types that contain pointers), you must explicitly write the value of the data members to a file, and to deserialize, you must explicitly read from the file to the data members in the same order. To demonstrate this, we will consider the `foo` class that we defined earlier:

- Add a member function called `write()` to serialize objects of this class. The method takes a reference to an `ofstream` and returns a `bool` indicating whether the operation was successful or not:

```
bool write(std::ofstream& ofile) const
{
  ofile.write(reinterpret_cast<const char*>(&i), sizeof(i));
  ofile.write(&c, sizeof(c));
  auto size = static_cast<int>(s.size());
  ofile.write(reinterpret_cast<char*>(&size), sizeof(size));
  ofile.write(s.data(), s.size());

  return !ofile.fail();
}
```

- Add a member function, called `read()`, to deserialize the objects of this class. This method takes a reference to an `ifstream` and returns a `bool` indicating whether the operation was successful or not:

```
bool read(std::ifstream& ifile)
{
  ifile.read(reinterpret_cast<char*>(&i), sizeof(i));
  ifile.read(&c, sizeof(c));
  auto size {0};
  ifile.read(reinterpret_cast<char*>(&size), sizeof(size));
  s.resize(size);
  ifile.read(reinterpret_cast<char*>(&s.front()), size);

  return !ifile.fail();
}
```

An alternative to the `write()` and `read()` member functions demonstrated earlier is to overload `operator<<` and `operator>>`. To do this, you should perform the following steps:

1. Add `friend` declarations for the non-member `operator<<` and `operator>>` to the class to be serialized/deserialized (in this case, the `foo` class):

```
friend std::ofstream& operator<<(std::ofstream& ofile,
                                 foo const& f);
```

```
friend std::ifstream& operator>>(std::ifstream& ifile,
                                 foo& f);
```

2. Overload `operator<<` for your class:

```
std::ofstream& operator<<(std::ofstream& ofile, foo const& f)
{
  ofile.write(reinterpret_cast<const char*>(&f.i),
              sizeof(f.i));
  ofile.write(&f.c, sizeof(f.c));
  auto size = static_cast<int>(f.s.size());
  ofile.write(reinterpret_cast<char*>(&size), sizeof(size));
  ofile.write(f.s.data(), f.s.size());

  return ofile;
}
```

3. Overload `operator>>` for your class:

```
std::ifstream& operator>>(std::ifstream& ifile, foo& f)
{
  ifile.read(reinterpret_cast<char*>(&f.i), sizeof(f.i));
  ifile.read(&f.c, sizeof(f.c));
  auto size {0};
  ifile.read(reinterpret_cast<char*>(&size), sizeof(size));
  f.s.resize(size);
  ifile.read(reinterpret_cast<char*>(&f.s.front()), size);

  return ifile;
}
```

How it works...

Regardless of whether we serialize the entire object (for POD types) or only parts of it, we use the same stream classes that we discussed in the previous recipe: `ofstream` for output file streams and `ifstream` for input file streams. Details about writing and reading data using these standard classes have been discussed in that recipe and will not be reiterated here.

When you serialize and deserialize objects to and from files, you should avoid writing the values of the pointers to a file. Additionally, you must not read pointer values from the file since these represent memory addresses and are meaningless across processes and even in the same process some moments later. Instead, you should write data referred by a pointer and read data into objects referred by a pointer.

This is a general principle, and, in practice, you may encounter situations where a source may have multiple pointers to the same object; in this case, you might want to write only one copy and also handle the reading in a corresponding manner.

If the objects you want to serialize are of the POD type, you can do it just like we did when we discussed raw data. In the example in this recipe, we serialized a sequence of objects of the `foopod` type. When we deserialize, we read from the file stream in a loop until the end of the file is read or a failure occurs. The way we read, in this case, may look counterintuitive, but doing it differently may lead to the duplication of the last read value:

- Reading is done in an infinite loop
- A read operation is performed in the loop
- A check for a failure or the end of file is performed, and if either of them has occurred, the infinite loop is exited
- The value is added to the input sequence and the looping continues

If reading is done using a loop with an exit condition that checks the end of the file bit, that is, `while(!ifile.eof())`, the last value will be added to the input sequence twice. The reason for this is that upon reading the last value, the end of the file has not yet been encountered (as that is a mark beyond the last byte of the file). The end of the file mark is only reached at the next read attempt, which, therefore, sets the `eofbit` of the stream. However, the input variable still has the last value since it hasn't been overwritten with anything, and this is added to the input vector for a second time.

If the objects you want to serialize and deserialize are of non-POD types, writing/reading these objects as raw data is not possible. For instance, such an object may have a virtual table. Writing the virtual table to a file does not cause problems, even though it does not have any value; however, reading from a file, and, therefore, overwriting the virtual table of an object will have catastrophic effects on the object and the program.

When serializing/deserializing non-POD types, there are various alternatives, and some of them have been discussed in the previous section. All of them provide explicit methods for writing and reading or overloading the standard << and >> operators. The second approach has an advantage in that it enables the use of your class in generic code, where objects are written and read to and from stream files using these operators.

When you plan to serialize and deserialize your objects, consider versioning your data from the very beginning to avoid problems if the structure of your data changes over time. How versioning should be done is beyond the scope of this recipe.

See also

- *Reading and writing raw data from/to binary files* to learn how to write and read unstructured data to binary files
- *Using I/O manipulators to control the output of a stream* to learn about the use of helper functions, called manipulators, that control input and output streams using the << and >> stream operators

Using localized settings for streams

How writing or reading to and from streams is performed may depend on the language and regional settings. Examples include writing and parsing numbers, time values, or monetary values, or comparing (collating) strings. The C++ I/O library provides a general-purpose mechanism for handling internationalization features through *locales* and *facets*. In this recipe, you will learn how to use locales to control the behavior of input/output streams.

Getting ready

All of the examples in this recipe use the `std::cout` predefined console stream object. However, the same applies to all I/O stream objects. Also, in these recipe examples, we will use the following objects and lambda function:

```
auto now = std::chrono::system_clock::now();
auto stime = std::chrono::system_clock::to_time_t(now);
auto ltime = std::localtime(&stime);

std::vector<std::string> names
  {"John", "adele", "Øivind", "François", "Robert", "Åke"};

auto sort_and_print = [](std::vector<std::string> v,
                         std::locale const & loc)
{
  std::sort(v.begin(), v.end(), loc);
  for (auto const & s : v) std::cout << s << ' ';
```

```
    std::cout << '\n';
};
```

The locale names used in this recipe (en_US.utf8, de_DE.utf8, and so on) are the ones that are used on UNIX systems. The following table lists their equivalents for Windows systems:

UNIX	Windows
en_US.utf8	English_US.1252
en_GB.utf8	English_UK.1252
de_DE.utf8	German_Germany.1252
sv_SE.utf8	Swedish_Sweden.1252

How to do it...

To control the localization settings of a stream, you must do the following:

- Use the `std::locale` class to represent the localization settings. There are various ways in which to construct locale objects, including the following:
    - Default construct it to use the global locale (by default, the `C` locale at the program startup)
    - From a local name, such as `C`, `POSIX`, `en_US.utf8`, and so on, if supported by the operating system
    - From another locale, except for a specified facet
    - From another locale, except for all of the facets from a specified category that are copied from another specified locale:

```
// default construct
auto loc_def = std::locale {};

// from a name
auto loc_us = std::locale {"en_US.utf8"};

// from another locale except for a facet
auto loc1 = std::locale {loc_def,
                         new std::collate<wchar_t>};

// from another local, except the facet in a category
auto loc2 = std::locale {loc_def, loc_us,
                         std::locale::collate};
```

- To get a copy of the default `C` locale, use the `std::locale::classic()` static method:

```
auto loc = std::locale::classic();
```

- To change the default locale that is copied every time a locale is default-constructed, use the `std::locale::global()` static method:

```
std::locale::global(std::locale("en_US.utf8"));
```

- Use the `imbue()` method to change the current locale of an I/O stream:

```
std::cout.imbue(std::locale("en_US.utf8"));
```

The following list shows examples of using various locales:

- Use a particular locale, indicated by its name. In this example, the locale is for German:

```
auto loc = std::locale("de_DE.utf8");
std::cout.imbue(loc);

std::cout << 1000.50 << '\n';
// 1.000,5
std::cout << std::showbase << std::put_money(1050)
          << '\n';
// 10,50 €
std::cout << std::put_time(ltime, "%c") << '\n';
// So 04 Dez 2016 17:54:06 JST
sort_and_print(names, loc);
// adele Åke François John Øivind Robert
```

- Use a locale that corresponds to the user settings (as defined in the system). This is done by constructing an `std::locale` object from an empty string:

```
auto loc = std::locale("");
std::cout.imbue(loc);

std::cout << 1000.50 << '\n';
// 1,000.5
std::cout << std::showbase << std::put_money(1050)
          << '\n';
// $10.50
std::cout << std::put_time(ltime, "%c") << '\n';
// Sun 04 Dec 2016 05:54:06 PM JST
sort_and_print(names, loc);
// adele Åke François John Øivind Robert
```

- Set and use the global locale:

```
std::locale::global(std::locale("sv_SE.utf8")); // set global
auto loc = std::locale{};                        // use global
std::cout.imbue(loc);

std::cout << 1000.50 << '\n';
// 1 000,5
std::cout << std::showbase << std::put_money(1050)
          << '\n';
// 10,50 kr
std::cout << std::put_time(ltime, "%c") << '\n';
// sön 4 dec 2016 18:02:29
sort_and_print(names, loc);
// adele François John Robert Åke Øivind
```

- Use the default C locale:

```
auto loc = std::locale::classic();
std::cout.imbue(loc);

std::cout << 1000.50 << '\n';
// 1000.5
std::cout << std::showbase << std::put_money(1050)
          << '\n';
// 1050
std::cout << std::put_time(ltime, "%c") << '\n';
// Sun Dec 4 17:55:14 2016
sort_and_print(names, loc);
// François John Robert adele Åke Øivind
```

How it works...

A locale object does not actually store localized settings. A *locale* is a heterogeneous container of facets. A *facet* is an object that defines the localization and internationalization settings. The standard defines a list of facets that each locale must contain. In addition to this, a locale can contain any other user-defined facets. The following is a list of all standard-defined facets:

std::collate<char>	std::collate<wchar_t>
std::ctype<char>	std::ctype<wchar_t>
std::codecvt<char,char,mbstate_t> std::codecvt<char16_t,char,mbstate_t>	std::codecvt<char32_t,char,mbstate_t> std::codecvt<wchar_t,char,mbstate_t>
std::moneypunct<char> std::moneypunct<char,true>	std::moneypunct<wchar_t> std::moneypunct<wchar_t,true>
std::money_get<char>	std::money_get<wchar_t>
std::money_put<char>	std::money_put<wchar_t>
std::numpunct<char>	std::numpunct<wchar_t>
std::num_get<char>	std::num_get<wchar_t>
std::num_put<char>	std::num_put<wchar_t>
std::time_get<char>	std::time_get<wchar_t>
std::time_put<char>	std::time_put<wchar_t>
std::messages<char>	std::messages<wchar_t>

It is beyond the scope of this recipe to go through this list and discuss all of these facets. However, we could mention that `std::money_get` is a facet that encapsulates the rules for parsing monetary values from character streams, while `std::money_put` is a facet that encapsulates the rules for formatting monetary values as strings. In a similar manner, `std::time_get` encapsulates rules for data and time parsing, while `std::time_put` encapsulates rules for data and time formatting. These will form the subject of the next couple of recipes.

A locale is an immutable object containing immutable facet objects. Locales are implemented as a reference-counted array of reference-counted pointers to facets. The array is indexed by `std::locale::id`, and all facets must be derived from the base class `std::locale::facet` and must have a public static member of the `std::locale::id` type, called `id`.

It is only possible to create a locale object using one of the overloaded constructors or with the `combine()` method, which, as the name implies, combines the current locale with a new compile-time identifiable facet and returns a new locale object. On the other hand, it is possible to determine whether a locale contains a particular facet using the `std::has_facet()` function template, or to obtain a reference to a facet implemented by a particular locale using the `std::use_facet()` function template.

In the preceding examples, we sorted a vector of strings and passed a locale object as the third argument to the `std::sort()` general algorithm. This third argument is supposed to be a comparison function object. Passing a locale object works because `std::locale` has an `operator()` that lexicographically compares two strings using its collate facet. This is actually the only localization functionality that is directly provided by `std::locale`; however, what this does is invoke the collate facet's `compare()` method that performs the string comparison based on the facet's rules.

Every program has a global locale created when the program starts. The content of this global locale is copied into every default-constructed locale. The global locale can be replaced using the static method `std::locale::global()`. By default, the global locale is the `C` locale, which is a locale equivalent to ANSI C's locale with the same name. This locale was created to handle simple English texts, and it is the default one in C++ that provides compatibility with C. A reference to this locale can be obtained with the static method `std::locale::classic()`.

By default, all streams use the classic locale to write or parse text. However, it is possible to change the locale used by a stream using the stream's `imbue()` method. This is a member of the `std::ios_base` class that is the base for all I/O streams. A companion member is the `getloc()` method, which returns a copy of the current stream's locale.

In the preceding examples, we changed the locale for the `std::cout` stream object. In practice, you may want to set the same locale for all stream objects associated with the standard C streams: `cin`, `cout`, `cerr`, and `clog` (or `wcin`, `wcout`, `wcerr`, and `wclog`).

See also

- *Using I/O manipulators to control the output of a stream* to learn about the use of helper functions, called manipulators, that control input and output streams using the << and >> stream operators
- *Using monetary I/O manipulators* to learn how to use standard manipulators to write and read monetary values
- *Using time I/O manipulators* to learn how to use standard manipulators to write and read date and time values

Using I/O manipulators to control the output of a stream

Apart from the stream-based I/O library, the standard library provides a series of helper functions, called manipulators, that control the input and output streams using `operator<<` and `operator>>`. In this recipe, we will look at some of these manipulators and demonstrate their use through some examples that format the output to the console. We will continue covering more manipulators in the upcoming recipes.

Getting ready

The I/O manipulators are available in the `std` namespace in the headers `<ios>`, `<istream>`, `<ostream>`, and `<iomanip>`. In this recipe, we will only discuss some of the manipulators from `<ios>` and `<iomanip>`.

How to do it...

The following manipulators can be used to control the output or input of a stream:

- `boolalpha` and `noboolalpha` enable and disable the textual representation of Booleans:

```
std::cout << std::boolalpha << true << '\n';    // true
std::cout << false << '\n';                      // false
std::cout << std::noboolalpha << false << '\n'; // 0
```

- `left`, `right`, and `internal` affect the alignment of the fill characters; `left` and `right` affect all text, but `internal` affects only the integer, floating point, and monetary output:

```
std::cout << std::right << std::setw(10) << "right\n";
std::cout << std::setw(10) << "text\n";
std::cout << std::left << std::setw(10) << "left\n";
```

- `fixed`, `scientific`, `hexfloat`, and `defaultfloat` change the formatting used for floating-point types (for both the input and output streams). The latter two have only been available since C++11:

```
std::cout << std::fixed << 0.25 << '\n';
// 0.250000
std::cout << std::scientific << 0.25 << '\n';
// 2.500000e-01
std::cout << std::hexfloat << 0.25 << '\n';
// 0x1p-2
std::cout << std::defaultfloat << 0.25 << '\n';
// 0.25
```

- `dec`, `hex`, and `oct` control the base that is used for the integer types (in both the input and output streams):

```
std::cout << std::oct << 42 << '\n'; // 52
std::cout << std::hex << 42 << '\n'; // 2a
std::cout << std::dec << 42 << '\n'; // 42
```

- `setw` changes the width of the next input or output field. The default width is 0.
- `setfill` changes the fill character for the output stream; this is the character that is used to fill the next fields until the specified width is reached. The default fill character is whitespace:

```
std::cout << std::right
          << std::setfill('.') << std::setw(10)
          << "right" << '\n';
// .....right
```

- `setprecision` changes the decimal precision (how many digits are generated) for the floating-point types in both the input and output streams. The default precision is 6:

```
std::cout << std::fixed << std::setprecision(2) << 12.345
          << '\n';
// 12.35
```

How it works...

All of the I/O manipulators listed earlier, with the exception of `setw`, which only refers to the next output field, affect the stream. Additionally, all consecutive writing or reading operations use the last specified format until another manipulator is used again.

Some of these manipulators are called without arguments. Examples include `boolalpha`/`noboolalpha` or `dec`/`hex`/`oct`. These manipulators are functions that take a single argument, that is, a reference to a string, and return a reference to the same stream:

```
std::ios_base& hex(std::ios_base& str);
```

Expressions, such as `std::cout << std::hex`, are possible because both `basic_ostream::operator<<` and `basic_istream::operator>>` have special overloads that take a pointer to these functions.

Other manipulators, including some that are not mentioned here, are invoked with arguments. These manipulators are functions that take one or more arguments and return an object of an unspecified type:

```
template<class CharT>
/*unspecified*/ setfill(CharT c);
```

To better demonstrate the use of these manipulators, we will consider two examples that format output to the console.

In the first example, we will list the table of contents of a book with the following requirements:

- The chapter number is right-aligned and shown with Roman numerals.
- The chapter title is left-aligned and the remaining space until the page number is filled with dots.
- The page number of the chapter is right-aligned.

For this example, we will use the following classes and helper function:

```
struct Chapter
{
  int Number;
  std::string Title;
  int Page;
};

struct BookPart
{
  std::string Title;
  std::vector<Chapter> Chapters;
};
```

```
struct Book
{
  std::string Title;
  std::vector<BookPart> Parts;
};

std::string to_roman(unsigned int value)
{
  struct roman_t { unsigned int value; char const* numeral; };
  const static roman_t rarr[13] =
  {
    {1000, "M"}, {900, "CM"}, {500, "D"}, {400, "CD"},
    {100, "C"}, { 90, "XC"}, { 50, "L"}, { 40, "XL"},
    { 10, "X"}, { 9, "IX"}, { 5, "V"}, { 4, "IV"},
    { 1, "I"}
  };

  std::string result;
  for (auto const & number : rarr)
  {
    while (value >= number.value)
    {
      result += number.numeral;
      value -= number.value;
    }
  }

  return result;
}
```

The `print_toc()` function, as shown in the following code snippet, takes a `Book` as its argument and prints its content to the console according to the specified requirements. For this purpose, we use the following:

- `std::left` and `std::right` specify the text alignment
- `std::setw` specifies the width of each output field
- `std::fill` specifies the fill character (a blank space for the chapter number and a dot for the chapter title)

The implementation of the `print_toc()` function is listed here:

```
void print_toc(Book const & book)
{
  std::cout << book.Title << '\n';
  for(auto const & part : book.Parts)
  {
    std::cout << std::left << std::setw(15) << std::setfill(' ')
              << part.Title << '\n';
    std::cout << std::left << std::setw(15) << std::setfill('-')
              << '-' << '\n';

    for(auto const & chapter : part.Chapters)
    {
      std::cout << std::right << std::setw(4) << std::setfill(' ')
                << to_roman(chapter.Number) << ' ';
      std::cout << std::left << std::setw(35) << std::setfill('.')
                << chapter.Title;
      std::cout << std::right << std::setw(3) << std::setfill('.')
                << chapter.Page << '\n';
    }
  }
}
```

The following example uses this method with a `Book` object describing the table of contents from the book *The Fellowship of the Ring*:

```
auto book = Book
{
  "THE FELLOWSHIP OF THE RING"s,
  {
    {
      "BOOK ONE"s,
      {
        {1, "A Long-expected Party"s, 21},
        {2, "The Shadow of the Past"s, 42},
        {3, "Three Is Company"s, 65},
        {4, "A Short Cut to Mushrooms"s, 86},
        {5, "A Conspiracy Unmasked"s, 98},
```

```
            {6, "The Old Forest"s, 109},
            {7, "In the House of Tom Bombadil"s, 123},
            {8, "Fog on the Barrow-downs"s, 135},
            {9, "At the Sign of The Prancing Pony"s, 149},
            {10, "Strider"s, 163},
            {11, "A Knife in the Dark"s, 176},
            {12, "Flight to the Ford"s, 197},
         },
      },
      {
         "BOOK TWO"s,
         {
            {1, "Many Meetings"s, 219},
            {2, "The Council of Elrond"s, 239},
            {3, "The Ring Goes South"s, 272},
            {4, "A Journey in the Dark"s, 295},
            {5, "The Bridge of Khazad-dum"s, 321},
            {6, "Lothlorien"s, 333},
            {7, "The Mirror of Galadriel"s, 353},
            {8, "Farewell to Lorien"s, 367},
            {9, "The Great River"s, 380},
            {10, "The Breaking of the Fellowship"s, 390},
         },
      },
   }
};

print_toc(book);
```

In this case, the output is as follows:

```
THE FELLOWSHIP OF THE RING
BOOK ONE
---------------
   I A Long-expected Party..............21
  II The Shadow of the Past.............42
 III Three Is Company...................65
  IV A Short Cut to Mushrooms...........86
   V A Conspiracy Unmasked..............98
  VI The Old Forest....................109
 VII In the House of Tom Bombadil.......123
VIII Fog on the Barrow-downs...........135
```

```
   IX At the Sign of The Prancing Pony...149
    X Strider...........................163
   XI A Knife in the Dark...............176
  XII Flight to the Ford................197
BOOK TWO
--------------
    I Many Meetings.....................219
   II The Council of Elrond.............239
  III The Ring Goes South...............272
   IV A Journey in the Dark.............295
    V The Bridge of Khazad-dum..........321
   VI Lothlorien........................333
  VII The Mirror of Galadriel...........353
 VIII Farewell to Lorien................367
   IX The Great River...................380
    X The Breaking of the Fellowship.....390
```

For the second example, our goal is to output a table that lists the largest companies in the world by revenue. The table will have columns for the company name, the industry, the revenue (in USD billions), the increase/decrease in revenue growth, the revenue growth, the number of employees, and the country of origin. For this example, we will use the following class:

```
struct Company
{
  std::string Name;
  std::string Industry;
  double      Revenue;
  bool        RevenueIncrease;
  double      Growth;
  int         Employees;
  std::string Country;
};
```

The `print_companies()` function in the following code snippet uses several additional manipulators to the ones shown in the previous example:

- `std::boolalpha` displays Boolean values as `true` and `false` instead of `1` and `0`.
- `std::fixed` indicates a fixed floating-point representation, and then `std::defaultfloat` reverts to the default floating-point representation.

- `std::setprecision` specifies the number of decimal digits to be displayed in the output. Together with `std::fixed`, this is used to indicate a fixed representation with a decimal digit for the `Growth` field.

The implementation of the `print_companies()` function is listed here:

```
void print_companies(std::vector<Company> const & companies)
{
  for(auto const & company : companies)
  {
    std::cout << std::left << std::setw(26) << std::setfill(' ')
              << company.Name;
    std::cout << std::left << std::setw(18) << std::setfill(' ')
              << company.Industry;
    std::cout << std::left << std::setw(5) << std::setfill(' ')
              << company.Revenue;
    std::cout << std::left << std::setw(5) << std::setfill(' ')
              << std::boolalpha << company.RevenueIncrease
              << std::noboolalpha;
    std::cout << std::right << std::setw(5) << std::setfill(' ')
              << std::fixed << std::setprecision(1) << company.Growth
              << std::defaultfloat << std::setprecision(6) << ' ';
    std::cout << std::right << std::setw(8) << std::setfill(' ')
              << company.Employees << ' ';
    std::cout << std::left << std::setw(2) << std::setfill(' ')
              << company.Country
              << '\n';
  }
}
```

The following is an example of calling this method. The source of the data shown here is Wikipedia (`https://en.wikipedia.org/wiki/List_of_largest_companies_by_revenue`, as of 2016):

```
std::vector<Company> companies
{
  {"Walmart"s, "Retail"s, 482, false, 0.71,
    2300000, "US"s},
  {"State Grid"s, "Electric utility"s, 330, false, 2.91,
    927839, "China"s},
  {"Saudi Aramco"s, "Oil and gas"s, 311, true, 40.11,
    65266, "SA"s},
  {"China National Petroleum"s, "Oil and gas"s, 299,
```

```
    false, 30.21, 1589508, "China"s},
  {"Sinopec Group"s, "Oil and gas"s, 294, false, 34.11,
    810538, "China"s},
};

print_companies(companies);
```

In this case, the output has a table-based format, as follows:

```
Walmart                     Retail             482  false  0.7  2300000 US
State Grid                  Electric utility   330  false  2.9   927839 China
Saudi Aramco                Oil and gas        311  true  40.1    65266 SA
China National Petroleum    Oil and gas        299  false 30.2  1589508 China
Sinopec Group               Oil and gas        294  false 34.1   810538 China
```

As an exercise, you can try adding a table heading or even a grid line to precede these lines for a better tabulation of the data.

See also

- *Reading and writing raw data from/to binary files* to learn how to write and read unstructured data to binary files
- *Using monetary I/O manipulators* to learn how to use standard manipulators to write and read monetary values
- *Using time I/O manipulators* to learn how to use standard manipulators to write and read date and time values

Using monetary I/O manipulators

In the previous recipe, we looked at some of the manipulators that can be used to control input and output streams. The manipulators that we discussed were related to numeric values and text values. In this recipe, we will look at how to use standard manipulators to write and read monetary values.

Getting ready

You should now be familiar with locales and how to set them for a stream. This topic was discussed in the *Using localized settings for streams* recipe. It is recommended that you read that recipe before continuing.

The manipulators discussed in this recipe are available in the `std` namespace, in the `<iomanip>` header.

How to do it...

To write a monetary value to an output stream, you should do the following:

- Set the desired locale for controlling the monetary format:

```
std::cout.imbue(std::locale("en_GB.utf8"));
```

- Use either a `long double` or a `std::basic_string` value for the amount:

```
long double mon = 12345.67;
std::string smon = "12345.67";
```

- Use a `std::put_money` manipulator with a single argument, the monetary value, to display the value using the currency symbol (if any is available):

```
std::cout << std::showbase << std::put_money(mon)
          << '\n'; // £123.46
std::cout << std::showbase << std::put_money(smon)
          << '\n'; // £123.46
```

- Use `std::put_money` with two arguments, the monetary value and a Boolean flag set to `true`, to indicate the use of an international currency string:

```
std::cout << std::showbase << std::put_money(mon, true)
          << '\n'; // GBP 123.46
std::cout << std::showbase << std::put_money(smon, true)
          << '\n'; // GBP 123.46
```

To read a monetary value from an input stream, you should do the following:

- Set the desired locale for controlling the monetary format:

```
std::istringstream stext("$123.45 123.45 USD");
stext.imbue(std::locale("en_US.utf8"));
```

- Use either a `long double` or `std::basic_string` value to read the amount from the input stream:

```
long double v1;
std::string v2;
```

- Use `std::get_money()` with a single argument, the variable where the monetary value is to be written, if a currency symbol might be used in the input stream:

```
stext >> std::get_money(v1) >> std::get_money(v2);
// v1 = 12345, v2 = "12345"
```

- Use `std::get_money()` with two arguments, the variable where the monetary value is to be written and a Boolean flag set to `true`, to indicate the presence of an international currency string:

```
stext >> std::get_money(v1, true) >> std::get_money(v2, true);
// v1 = 0, v2 = "12345"
```

How it works...

The `put_money()` and `get_money()` manipulators are very similar. They are both function templates that take an argument representing either the monetary value to be written to the output stream or a variable to hold the monetary value read from an input stream, and a second, optional parameter, to indicate whether an international currency string is used. The default alternative is the currency symbol, if one is available. `put_money()` uses the `std::money_put()` facet settings to output a monetary value, and `get_money()` uses the `std::money_get()` facet to parse a monetary value. Both manipulator function templates return an object of an unspecified type. These functions do not throw exceptions:

```
template <class MoneyT>
/*unspecified*/ put_money(const MoneyT& mon, bool intl = false);

template <class MoneyT>
/*unspecified*/ get_money(MoneyT& mon, bool intl = false);
```

Both of these manipulator functions require the monetary value to be either a `long double` or a `std::basic_string`.

However, it is important to note that monetary values are stored as integral numbers of the smallest denomination of the currency defined by the locale in use. Considering US dollars as that currency, $100.00 is stored as 10000.0, and 1 cent, that is, $0.01, is stored as 1.0.

When writing a monetary value to an output stream, it is important to use the `std::showbase` manipulator if you want to display the currency symbol or the international currency string. This is normally used to indicate the prefix of a numeric base (such as `0x` for hexadecimal); however, for monetary values, it is used to indicate whether the currency symbol/string should be displayed or not. The following snippet provides an example:

```
// print 123.46
std::cout << std::put_money(12345.67) << '\n';
// print £123.46
std::cout << std::showbase << std::put_money(12345.67) << '\n';
```

In the preceding snippet, the first line will just print the numerical value representing a currency amount, 123.46, while the second line will print the same numerical value but preceded by the currency symbol.

See also

- *Using I/O manipulators to control the output of a stream* to learn about the use of helper functions, called manipulators, that control input and output streams using the `<<` and `>>` stream operators
- *Using time I/O manipulators* to learn how to use standard manipulators to write and read date and time values

Using time I/O manipulators

Similar to the monetary I/O manipulators that we discussed in the previous recipe, the C++11 standard provides manipulators that control the writing and reading of time values to and from streams, where time values are represented in the form of an `std::tm` object that holds a calendar date and time. In this recipe, you will learn how to use these time manipulators.

Getting ready

Time values used by the time I/O manipulators are expressed in `std::tm` values. You should be familiar with this structure from the `<ctime>` header.

You should also be familiar with locales and how to set them for a stream. This topic was discussed in the *Using localized settings for streams* recipe. It is recommended that you read that recipe before continuing.

The manipulators discussed in this recipe are available in the `std` namespace, in the `<iomanip>` header.

How to do it...

To write a time value to an output stream, you should perform the following steps:

1. Obtain a calendar date and time value corresponding to a given time. There are various ways in which to do this. The following shows several examples of how to convert the current time to a local time that is expressed as a calendar date and time:

   ```
   auto now = std::chrono::system_clock::now();
   auto stime = std::chrono::system_clock::to_time_t(now);
   auto ltime = std::localtime(&stime);

   auto ttime = std::time(nullptr);
   auto ltime = std::localtime(&ttime);
   ```

2. Use `std::put_time()` to supply a pointer to the `std::tm` object, representing the calendar date and time, and a pointer to a null-terminated character string, representing the format. The C++11 standard provides a long list of formats that can be used; this list can be consulted at `http://en.cppreference.com/w/cpp/io/manip/put_time`.

3. To write a standard date and time string according to the settings of a specific locale, first set the locale for the stream by calling `imbue()` and then use the `std::put_time()` manipulator:

   ```
   std::cout.imbue(std::locale("en_GB.utf8"));
   std::cout << std::put_time(ltime, "%c") << '\n';
   // Sun 04 Dec 2016 05:26:47 JST
   ```

The following list shows some examples of supported time formats:

- ISO 8601 date format `"%F"` or `"%Y-%m-%d"`:

  ```
  std::cout << std::put_time(ltime, "%F") << '\n';
  // 2016-12-04
  ```

- ISO 8601 time format `"%T"`:

  ```
  std::cout << std::put_time(ltime, "%T") << '\n';
  // 05:26:47
  ```

- ISO 8601 combined date and time in UTC format `"%FT%T%z"`:

  ```
  std::cout << std::put_time(ltime, "%FT%T%z") << '\n';
  // 2016-12-04T05:26:47+0900
  ```

- ISO 8601 week format `"%Y-W%V"`:

  ```
  std::cout << std::put_time(ltime, "%Y-W%V") << '\n';
  // 2016-W48
  ```

- ISO 8601 date with week number format "%Y-W%V-%u":

```
std::cout << std::put_time(ltime, "%Y-W%V-%u") << '\n';
// 2016-W48-7
```

- ISO 8601 ordinal date format "%Y-%j":

```
std::cout << std::put_time(ltime, "%Y-%j") << '\n';
// 2016-339
```

To read a time value from an input stream, you should perform the following steps:

1. Declare an object of the `std::tm` type to hold the time value read from the stream:

```
auto time = std::tm {};
```

2. Use `std::get_time()` to supply a pointer to the `std::tm` object, which will hold the time value, and a pointer to a null-terminated character string, which represents the format. The list of possible formats can be consulted at `http://en.cppreference.com/w/cpp/io/manip/get_time`. The following example parses an ISO 8601 combined date and time value:

```
std::istringstream stext("2016-12-04T05:26:47+0900");
stext >> std::get_time(&time, "%Y-%m-%dT%H:%M:%S");
if (!stext.fail()) { /* do something */ }
```

3. To read a standard date and time string according to the settings of a specific locale, first set the locale for the stream by calling `imbue()` and then use the `std::get_time()` manipulator:

```
std::istringstream stext("Sun 04 Dec 2016 05:35:30 JST");
stext.imbue(std::locale("en_GB.utf8"));
stext >> std::get_time(&time, "%c");
if (stext.fail()) { /* do something else */ }
```

How it works...

The two manipulators for time values, `put_time()` and `get_time()`, are very similar: they are both function templates with two arguments. The first argument is a pointer to an `std::tm` object representing the calendar date and time that holds the value to be written to the stream or the value that is read from the stream. The second argument is a pointer to a null-terminated character string representing the format of the time text. `put_time()` uses the `std::time_put()` facet to output a date and time value, and `get_time()` uses the `std::time_get()` facet to parse a date and time value. Both manipulator function templates return an object of an unspecified type. These functions do not throw exceptions:

```
template<class CharT>
/*unspecified*/ put_time(const std::tm* tmb, const CharT* fmt);

template<class CharT>
/*unspecified*/ get_time(std::tm* tmb, const CharT* fmt);
```

The string that results from using `put_time()` to write a date and time value to an output stream is the same as the one that results from a call to `std::strftime()` or `std::wcsftime()`.

The standard defines a long list of available conversion specifiers that compose the format string. These specifiers are prefixed with a `%`, and, in some cases, are followed by an `E` or a `0`. Some of them are also equivalent; for instance, `%F` is equivalent to `%Y-%m-%d` (this is the ISO 8601 date format), and `%T` is equivalent to `%H:%M:%S` (this is the ISO 8601 time format). The examples in this recipe mention only a few of the conversion specifiers, referring to ISO 8601 date and time formats. For the complete list of conversion specifiers, refer to the C++ standard or follow the links that were mentioned earlier.

It is important to note that not all of the conversion specifiers supported by `put_time()` are also supported by `get_time()`. Examples include the `z` (offset from UTC in the ISO 8601 format) and `Z` (time zone name or abbreviation) specifiers, which can only be used with `put_time()`. This is demonstrated in the following snippet:

```
std::istringstream stext("2016-12-04T05:26:47+0900");
auto time = std::tm {};

stext >> std::get_time(&time, "%Y-%m-%dT%H:%M:%S%z"); // fails
stext >> std::get_time(&time, "%Y-%m-%dT%H:%M:%S");   // OK
```

The text represented by some conversion specifiers is locale-dependent. All specifiers prefixed with `E` or `0` are locale-dependent. To set a particular locale for the stream, use the `imbue()` method, as demonstrated in the examples in the *How to do it...* section.

See also

- *Using I/O manipulators to control the output of a stream* to learn about the use of helper functions, called manipulators, that control input and output streams using the << and >> stream operators
- *Using monetary I/O manipulators* to learn how to use standard manipulators to write and read monetary values

Working with filesystem paths

An important addition to the C++17 standard is the filesystem library that enables us to work with paths, files, and directories in hierarchical filesystems (such as Windows or POSIX filesystems). This standard library has been developed based on the boost.filesystem library. In the next few recipes, we will explore those features of the library that enable us to perform operations with files and directories, such as creating, moving, or deleting them, but also querying properties and searching. It is important, however, to first look at how this library handles paths.

Getting ready

For this recipe, we will consider most of the examples using Windows paths. In the accompanying code, all examples have both Windows and POSIX alternatives.

The filesystem library is available in the std::filesystem namespace, in the <filesystem> header. To simplify the code, we will use the following namespace alias in all of the examples:

```
namespace fs = std::filesystem;
```

A path to a filesystem component (file, directory, hard link, or soft link) is represented by the path class.

How to do it...

The following is a list of the most common operations on paths:

- Create a path using the constructor, the assignment operator, or the assign() method:

  ```
  // Windows
  auto path = fs::path{"C:\\Users\\Marius\\Documents"};
  ```

```
// POSIX
auto path = fs::path{ "/home/marius/docs" };
```

- Append elements to a path by including a directory separator using the member `operator /=`, the non-member `operator /`, or the `append()` method:

```
path /= "Book";
path = path / "Modern" / "Cpp";
path.append("Programming");
// Windows: C:\Users\Marius\Documents\Book\Modern\Cpp\
Programming
// POSIX:   /home/marius/docs/Book/Modern/Cpp/Programming
```

- Concatenate elements to a path without including a directory separator by using the member `operator +=`, the non-member `operator +`, or the `concat()` method:

```
auto path = fs::path{ "C:\\Users\\Marius\\Documents" };
path += "\\Book";
path.concat("\\Modern");
// path = C:\Users\Marius\Documents\Book\Modern
```

- Decompose the elements of a path into its parts, such as the root, root directory, parent path, filename, extension, and so on, using member functions such as `root_name()`, `root_dir()`, `filename()`, `stem()`, `extension()`, and so on (all of them are shown in the following example):

```
auto path =
  fs::path{"C:\\Users\\Marius\\Documents\\sample.file.txt"};

std::cout
  << "root: "        << path.root_name() << '\n'
  << "root dir: "    << path.root_directory() << '\n'
  << "root path: "   << path.root_path() << '\n'
  << "rel path: "    << path.relative_path() << '\n'
  << "parent path: " << path.parent_path() << '\n'
  << "filename: "    << path.filename() << '\n'
  << "stem: "        << path.stem() << '\n'
  << "extension: "   << path.extension() << '\n';
```

- Query whether parts of a part are available using member functions such as `has_root_name()`, `has_root_directory()`, `has_filename()`, `has_stem()`, and `has_extension()` (all of them are shown in the following example):

```
auto path =
  fs::path{"C:\\Users\\Marius\\Documents\\sample.file.txt"};
```

```
std::cout
  << "has root: "        << path.has_root_name() << '\n'
  << "has root dir: "    << path.has_root_directory() << '\n'
  << "has root path: "   << path.has_root_path() << '\n'
  << "has rel path: "    << path.has_relative_path() << '\n'
  << "has parent path: " << path.has_parent_path() << '\n'
  << "has filename: "    << path.has_filename() << '\n'
  << "has stem: "        << path.has_stem() << '\n'
  << "has extension: "   << path.has_extension() << '\n';
```

- Check whether a path is relative or absolute:

```
auto path2 = fs::path{ "marius\\temp" };
std::cout
  << "absolute: " << path1.is_absolute() << '\n'
  << "absolute: " << path2.is_absolute() << '\n';
```

- Modify individual parts of the path, such as the filename with `replace_filename()` and `remove_filename()`, and the extension with `replace_extension()`:

```
auto path =
  fs::path{"C:\\Users\\Marius\\Documents\\sample.file.txt"};

path.replace_filename("output");
path.replace_extension(".log");
// path = C:\Users\Marius\Documents\output.log

path.remove_filename();
// path = C:\Users\Marius\Documents
```

- Convert the directory separator to the system-preferred separator:

```
// Windows
auto path = fs::path{"Users/Marius/Documents"};
path.make_preferred();
// path = Users\Marius\Documents

// POSIX
auto path = fs::path{ "\\home\\marius\\docs" };
path.make_preferred();
// path = /home/marius/docs
```

How it works...

The `std::filesystem::path` class models paths to filesystem components. However, it only handles the syntax and does not validate the existence of a component (such as a file or a directory) represented by the path.

The library defines a portable, generic syntax for paths that can accommodate various filesystems, such as POSIX or Windows, including the Microsoft Windows **Universal Naming Convention** (**UNC**) format. Both of them differ in several key aspects:

- POSIX systems have a single tree, no root name, a single root directory called `/`, and a single current directory. Additionally, they use `/` as the directory separator. Paths are represented as null-terminated strings of `char` encoded as UTF-8.
- Windows systems have multiple trees, each with a root name (such as `C:`), a root directory (such as `\`), and a current directory (such as `C:\Windows\System32`). Paths are represented as null-terminated strings of wide characters encoded as UTF-16.

A pathname, as defined in the `filesystem` library, has the following syntax:

- An optional root name (`C:` or `//localhost`)
- An optional root directory
- Zero or more filenames (which may refer to a file, a directory, a hard link, or a symbolic link) or directory separators

There are two special filenames that are recognized: the single dot (`.`), which represents the current directory, and the double dot (`..`), which represents the parent directory. The directory separator can be repeated, in which case it is treated as a single separator (in other words, `/home////docs` is the same as `/home/marius/docs`). A path that has no redundant current directory name (`.`), no redundant parent directory name (`..`), and no redundant directory separators is said to be in a normal form.

The path operations presented in the previous section are the most common operations with paths. However, their implementation defines additional querying and modifying methods, iterators, non-member comparison operators, and more. The following sample iterates through the parts of a path and prints them to the console:

```
auto path =
  fs::path{ "C:\\Users\\Marius\\Documents\\sample.file.txt" };
```

```
for (auto const & part : path)
{
  std::cout << part << '\n';
}
```

The following listing represents its result:

```
C:

Users
Marius
Documents
sample.file.txt
```

In this example, `sample.file.txt` is the filename. This is basically the part from the last directory separator to the end of the path. This is what the member function `filename()` would be returning for the given path. The extension for this file is `.txt`, which is the string returned by the `extension()` member function. To retrieve the filename without an extension, another member function called `stem()` is available. Here, the string returned by this method is `sample.file`. For all of these methods, but also all of the other decomposition methods, there is a corresponding querying method with the same name and prefix `has_`, such as `has_filename()`, `has_stem()`, and `has_extension()`. All of these methods return a `bool` value to indicate whether the path has the corresponding part.

See also

- *Creating, copying, and deleting files and directories* to learn how to perform these basic operations with files and directories independently of the filesystem in use
- *Checking the properties of an existing file or directory* to learn how to query the properties of files and directories, such as the type, permissions, file times, and more

Creating, copying, and deleting files and directories

Operations with files, such as copying, moving, and deleting, or with directories, such as creating, renaming, and deleting, are all supported by the `filesystem` library. Files and directories are identified using a path (which can be absolute, canonical, or relative), a topic that was covered in the previous recipes. In this recipe, we will look at what the standard functions for the previously mentioned operations are and how they work.

Getting ready

Before going forward, you should read the *Working with filesystem paths* recipe. The introductory notes from that recipe also apply here. However, all of the examples in this recipe are platform-independent.

For all of the following examples, we will use the following variables, and assume the current path is `C:\Users\Marius\Documents` on Windows and `/home/marius/docs` for a POSIX system:

```
auto err = std::error_code{};
auto basepath = fs::current_path();
auto path = basepath / "temp";
auto filepath = path / "sample.txt";
```

We will also assume the presence of a file called `sample.txt` in the `temp` subdirectory of the current path (such as `C:\Users\Marius\Documents\temp\sample.txt` or `/home/marius/docs/temp/sample.txt`).

How to do it...

Use the following library functions to perform operations with directories:

- To create a new directory, use `create_directory()`. This method does nothing if the directory already exists; however, it does not create directories recursively:

  ```
  auto success = fs::create_directory(path, err);
  ```

- To create new directories recursively, use `create_directories()`:

```
auto temp = path / "tmp1" / "tmp2" / "tmp3";
auto success = fs::create_directories(temp, err);
```

- To move an existing directory, use `rename()`:

```
auto temp = path / "tmp1" / "tmp2" / "tmp3";
auto newtemp = path / "tmp1" / "tmp3";

fs::rename(temp, newtemp, err);
if (err) std::cout << err.message() << '\n';
```

- To rename an existing directory, also use `rename()`:

```
auto temp = path / "tmp1" / "tmp3";
auto newtemp = path / "tmp1" / "tmp4";

fs::rename(temp, newtemp, err);
if (err) std::cout << err.message() << '\n';
```

- To copy an existing directory, use `copy()`. To recursively copy the entire content of a directory, use the `copy_options::recursive` flag:

```
fs::copy(path, basepath / "temp2",
         fs::copy_options::recursive, err);
if (err) std::cout << err.message() << '\n';
```

- To create a symbolic link to a directory, use `create_directory_symlink()`:

```
auto linkdir = basepath / "templink";
fs::create_directory_symlink(path, linkdir, err);
if (err) std::cout << err.message() << '\n';
```

- To remove an empty directory, use `remove()`:

```
auto temp = path / "tmp1" / "tmp4";
auto success = fs::remove(temp, err);
```

- To remove the entire content of a directory recursively, and the directory itself, use `remove_all()`:

```
auto success = fs::remove_all(path, err) !=
               static_cast<std::uintmax_t>(-1);
```

Use the following library functions to perform operations with files:

- To copy a file, use `copy()` or `copy_file()`. The next section explains the difference between the two:

```
auto success = fs::copy_file(filepath, path / "sample.bak",
err);
if (!success) std::cout << err.message() << '\n';

fs::copy(filepath, path / "sample.cpy", err);
if (err) std::cout << err.message() << '\n';
```

- To rename a file, use `rename()`:

```
auto newpath = path / "sample.log";
fs::rename(filepath, newpath, err);
if (err) std::cout << err.message() << '\n';
```

- To move a file, use `rename()`:

```
auto newpath = path / "sample.log";
fs::rename(newpath, path / "tmp1" / "sample.log", err);
if (err) std::cout << err.message() << '\n';
```

- To create a symbolic link to a file, use `create_symlink()`:

```
auto linkpath = path / "sample.txt.link";
fs::create_symlink(filepath, linkpath, err);
if (err) std::cout << err.message() << '\n';
```

- To delete a file, use `remove()`:

```
auto success = fs::remove(path / "sample.cpy", err);
if (!success) std::cout << err.message() << '\n';
```

How it works...

All of the functions mentioned in this recipe, and other similar functions that are not discussed here, have multiple overloads that can be grouped into two categories:

- Overloads that take, as the last argument, a reference to an `std::error_code`: these overloads do not throw an exception (they are defined with the `noexcept` specification). Instead, they set the value of the `error_code` object to the operating system error code if an operating system error has occurred. If no such error has occurred, then the `clear()` method on the `error_code` object is called to reset any possible previously set code.

- Overloads that do not take the last argument of the `std::error_code` type: these overloads throw exceptions if errors occur. If an operating system error occurs, they throw an `std::filesystem::filesystem_error` exception. On the other hand, if memory allocation fails, these functions throw an `std::bad_alloc` exception.

All the examples in the previous section used the overload that does not throw exceptions but, instead, sets a code when an error occurs. Some functions return a `bool` to indicate a success or a failure. You can check whether the `error_code` object holds the code of an error by either checking whether the value of the error code, returned by the method `value()`, is different from zero, or by using the conversion `operator bool`, which returns `true` for the same case and `false` otherwise. To retrieve the explanatory string for the error code, use the `message()` method.

Some `filesystem` library functions are common for both files and directories. This is the case for `rename()`, `remove()`, and `copy()`. The working details of each of these functions can be complex, especially in the case of `copy()`, and are beyond the scope of this recipe. You should refer to the reference documentation if you need to perform anything other than the simple operations covered here.

When it comes to copying files, there are two functions that can be used: `copy()` and `copy_file()`. These have equivalent overloads with identical signatures and, apparently, work the same way. However, there is an important difference (other than the fact that `copy()` also works for directories): `copy_file()` follows symbolic links. To avoid doing that and, instead, copy the actual symbolic link, you must use either `copy_symlink()` or `copy()` with the `copy_options::copy_symlinks` flag. Both the `copy()` and `copy_file()` functions have an overload that takes an argument of the `std::filesystem::copy_options` type, which defines how the operation should be performed. `copy_options` is a scoped `enum` with the following definition:

```
enum class copy_options
{
  none = 0,
  skip_existing = 1,
  overwrite_existing = 2,
  update_existing = 4,
  recursive = 8,
  copy_symlinks = 16,
  skip_symlinks = 32,
  directories_only = 64,
  create_symlinks = 128,
  create_hard_links = 256
};
```

The following table defines how each of these flags affects a copy operation, either with `copy()` or `copy_file()`. The table is taken from the 27.10.10.4 paragraph of the C++17 standard:

Option group controlling `copy_file` function effects for existing target files	
`none`	(Default) Error; file already exists
`skip_existing`	Do not overwrite existing file; do not report an error
`overwrite_existing`	Overwrite the existing file
`update_existing`	Overwrite the existing file if it is older than the replacement file
Option group controlling `copy` function effects for subdirectories	
`none`	(Default) Do not copy subdirectories
`recursive`	Recursively copy subdirectories and their contents
Option group controlling `copy` function effects for symbolic links	
`none`	(Default) Follow symbolic links
`copy_symlinks`	Copy symbolic links as symbolic links rather than copying the files that they point to
`skip_symlinks`	Ignore symbolic links
Option group controlling `copy` function effects for choosing the form of copying	
`none`	(Default) Copy contents
`directories_only`	Copy the directory structure only, do not copy non-directory files
`create_symlinks`	Make symbolic links instead of copies of files; the source path will be an absolute path unless the destination path is in the current directory
`create_hard_links`	Make hard links instead of copies of files

Another aspect that should be mentioned is related to symbolic links: `create_directory_symlink()` creates a symbolic link to a directory, whereas `create_symlink()` creates symbolic links to either files or directories. On POSIX systems, the two are identical when it comes to directories. On other systems (such as Windows), symbolic links to directories are created differently than symbolic links to files. Therefore, it is recommended that you use `create_directory_symlink()` for directories in order to write code that works correctly on all systems.

When you perform operations with files and directories, such as the ones described in this recipe, and you use the overloads that may throw exceptions, ensure that you `try-catch` the calls. Regardless of the type of overload used, you should check the success of the operation and take appropriate action in the case of a failure.

See also

- *Working with filesystem paths* to learn about the C++17 standard support for filesystem paths
- *Removing content from a file* to explore the possible ways of removing parts of the content of a file
- *Checking the properties of an existing file or directory* to learn how to query the properties of files and directories, such as the type, permissions, file times, and more

Removing content from a file

Operations such as copying, renaming, moving, or deleting files are directly provided by the `filesystem` library. However, when it comes to removing content from a file, you must perform explicit actions.

Regardless of whether you need to do this for text or binary files, you must implement the following pattern:

1. Create a temporary file.
2. Copy only the content that you want from the original file to the temporary file.
3. Delete the original file.
4. Rename/move the temporary file to the name/location of the original file.

In this recipe, we will learn how to implement this pattern for a text file.

Getting ready

For the purpose of this recipe, we will consider removing empty lines, or lines that start with a semicolon (`;`), from a text file. For this example, we will have an initial file, called `sample.dat`, that contains the names of Shakespeare's plays but also empty lines and lines that start with a semicolon. The following is a partial listing of this file (from the beginning):

```
;Shakespeare's plays, listed by genre

;TRAGEDIES
Troilus and Cressida
Coriolanus
Titus Andronicus
```

```
Romeo and Juliet
Timon of Athens
Julius Caesar
```

The code samples listed in the next section use the following variables:

```
auto path = fs::current_path();
auto filepath = path / "sample.dat";
auto temppath = path / "sample.tmp";
auto err = std::error_code{};
```

We will learn how to put this pattern into code in the following section.

How to do it...

Perform the following operations to remove content from a file:

1. Open the file for reading:

   ```
   std::ifstream in(filepath);
   if (!in.is_open())
   {
     std::cout << "File could not be opened!" << '\n';
     return;
   }
   ```

2. Open another temporary file for writing; if the file already exists, truncate its content:

   ```
   std::ofstream out(temppath, std::ios::trunc);
   if (!out.is_open())
   {
     std::cout << "Temporary file could not be created!"
               << '\n';
     return;
   }
   ```

3. Read, line by line, from the input file and copy the selected content to the output file:

   ```
   auto line = std::string{};
   while (std::getline(in, line))
   {
     if (!line.empty() && line.at(0) != ';')
     {
   ```

```
    out << line << 'n';
  }
}
```

4. Close both the input and output files:

```
in.close();
out.close();
```

5. Delete the original file:

```
auto success = fs::remove(filepath, err);
if(!success || err)
{
  std::cout << err.message() << '\n';
  return;
}
```

6. Rename/move the temporary file to the name/location of the original file:

```
fs::rename(temppath, filepath, err);
if (err)
{
  std::cout << err.message() << '\n';
}
```

How it works...

The pattern described here is the same for binary files too; however, for our convenience, we are only discussing an example with text files. The temporary file in this example is in the same directory as the original file. Alternatively, this can be located in a separate directory, such as a user temporary directory. To get a path to a temporary directory, you can use `std::filesystem::temp_directory_path()`. On Windows systems, this function returns the same directory as `GetTempPath()`. On POSIX systems, it returns the path specified in one of the environment variables `TMPDIR`, `TMP`, `TEMP`, or `TEMPDIR`; or, if none of them are available, it returns the path `/tmp`.

How content from the original file is copied to the temporary file varies from one case to another, depending on what needs to be copied. In the preceding example, we have copied entire lines, unless they are empty or start with a semicolon. For this purpose, we read the content of the original file, line by line, using `std::getline()` until there are no more lines to read. After all the necessary content has been copied, the files should be closed, so they can be moved or deleted.

To complete the operation, there are three options:

- Delete the original file and rename the temporary file to the same name as the original one, if they are in the same directory, or move the temporary file to the original file location, if they are in different directories. This is the approach taken in this recipe. For this, we used the `remove()` function to delete the original file and `rename()` to rename the temporary file to the original filename.
- Copy the content of the temporary file to the original file (for this, you can use either the `copy()` or `copy_file()` functions) and then delete the temporary file (use `remove()` for this).
- Rename the original file (for instance, changing the extension or the name) and then use the original filename to rename/move the temporary file.

If you take the first approach mentioned here, then you must make sure that the temporary file that is later replacing the original file has the same file permissions as the original file; otherwise, depending on the context of your solution, it can lead to problems.

See also

- *Creating, copying, and deleting files and directories* to learn how to perform these basic operations with files and directories independently of the filesystem in use

Checking the properties of an existing file or directory

The `filesystem` library provides functions and types that enable developers to check for the existence of a filesystem object, such as a file or directory, its properties, such as the type (the file, directory, symbolic link, and more), the last write time, permissions, and more. In this recipe, we will look at what these types and functions are and how they can be used.

Getting ready

For the following code samples, we will use the namespace alias `fs` for the `std::filesystem` namespace. The `filesystem` library is available in the header with the same name, `<filesystem>`. Also, we will use the variables shown here, `path` for the path of a file and `err` for receiving potential operating system error codes from the filesystem APIs:

```
auto path = fs::current_path() / "main.cpp";
auto err = std::error_code{};
```

Also, the function `to_time_t` shown here, will be referred in this recipe:

```
template <typename TP>
std::time_t to_time_t(TP tp)
{
   using namespace std::chrono;
   auto sctp = time_point_cast<system_clock::duration>(
     tp - TP::clock::now() + system_clock::now());
   return system_clock::to_time_t(sctp);
}
```

Before continuing with this recipe, you should read the *Working with filesystem paths* recipe.

How to do it...

Use the following library functions to retrieve information about filesystem objects:

- To check whether a path refers to an existing filesystem object, use `exists()`:

  ```
  auto exists = fs::exists(path, err);
  std::cout << "file exists: " << std::boolalpha
            << exists << '\n';
  ```

- To check whether two different paths refer to the same filesystem object, use `equivalent()`:

  ```
  auto same = fs::equivalent(path,
                 fs::current_path() / "." / "main.cpp");
  std::cout << "equivalent: " << same << '\n';
  ```

- To retrieve the size of a file in bytes, use `file_size()`:

  ```
  auto size = fs::file_size(path, err);
  std::cout << "file size: " << size << '\n';
  ```

- To retrieve the count of hard links to a filesystem object, use `hard_link_count()`:

  ```
  auto links = fs::hard_link_count(path, err);
  if(links != static_cast<uintmax_t>(-1))
    std::cout << "hard links: " << links << '\n';
  else
    std::cout << "hard links: error" << '\n';
  ```

- To retrieve or set the last modification time for a filesystem object, use `last_write_time()`:

```
auto lwt = fs::last_write_time(path, err);
auto time = to_time_t(lwt);
auto localtime = std::localtime(&time);
std::cout << "last write time: "
          << std::put_time(localtime, "%c") << '\n';
```

- To retrieve the file attributes, such as the type and permissions (as if returned by the POSIX `stat` function), use the `status()` function. This function follows symbolic links. To retrieve the file attributes of a symbolic link without following it, use `symlink_status()`:

```
auto print_perm = [](fs::perms p)
{
  std::cout
    << ((p & fs::perms::owner_read) != fs::perms::none ?
       "r" : "-")
    << ((p & fs::perms::owner_write) != fs::perms::none ?
       "w" : "-")
    << ((p & fs::perms::owner_exec) != fs::perms::none ?
       "x" : "-")
    << ((p & fs::perms::group_read) != fs::perms::none ?
       "r" : "-")
    << ((p & fs::perms::group_write) != fs::perms::none ?
       "w" : "-")
    << ((p & fs::perms::group_exec) != fs::perms::none ?
       "x" : "-")
    << ((p & fs::perms::others_read) != fs::perms::none ?
       "r" : "-")
    << ((p & fs::perms::others_write) != fs::perms::none ?
       "w" : "-")
    << ((p & fs::perms::others_exec) != fs::perms::none ?
       "x" : "-")
    << '\n';
};

auto status = fs::status(path, err);
std::cout << "type: " << static_cast<int>(status.type()) << '\n';
std::cout << "permissions: ";
print_perm(status.permissions());
```

- To check whether a path refers to a particular type of filesystem object, such as a file, directory, symbolic link, and so on, use the functions `is_regular_file()`, `is_directory()`, `is_symlink()`, and so on:

```
std::cout << "regular file? " <<
         fs::is_regular_file(path, err) << '\n';
std::cout << "directory? " <<
         fs::is_directory(path, err) << '\n';
std::cout << "char file? " <<
         fs::is_character_file(path, err) << '\n';
std::cout << "symlink? " <<
         fs::is_symlink(path, err) << '\n';
```

How it works...

These functions, used to retrieve information about the filesystem files and directories, are, in general, simple and straightforward. However, some considerations are necessary:

- Checking whether a filesystem object exists can be done using `exists()`, either by passing the path or an `std::filesystem::file_status` object that was previously retrieved using the `status()` function.
- The `equivalent()` function determines whether two filesystem objects have the same status, as retrieved by the function `status()`. If neither path exists, or if both exist but neither is a file, directory, or symbolic link, then the function returns an error. Hard links to the same file object are equivalent. A symbolic link and its target are also equivalent.
- The `file_size()` function can only be used to determine the size of regular files and symbolic links that target a regular file. For any other types of file objects, such as directories, this function fails. This function returns the size of the file in bytes, or `-1` if an error has occurred. If you want to determine whether a file is empty, you can use the `is_empty()` function. This works for all types of filesystem objects, including directories.
- The `last_write_time()` function has two sets of overloads: one that is used to retrieve the last modification time of the filesystem object, and one that is used to set the last modification time. Time is indicated by a `std::filesystem::file_time_type` object, which is basically a type alias for `std::chrono::time_point`. The following example changes the last write time for a file to 30 minutes earlier than its previous value:

```
using namespace std::chrono_literals;
auto lwt = fs::last_write_time(path, err);
fs::last_write_time(path, lwt - 30min);
```

- The `status()` function determines the type and permissions of a filesystem object. However, if the file is a symbolic link, the information returned is about the target of the symbolic link. To retrieve information about the symbolic link itself, the `symlink_status()` function must be used. Permissions are defined as an enumeration, `std::filesystem::perms`. Not all the enumerators of this scoped `enum` represent permissions; some of them represent controlling bits, such as `add_perms`, to indicate that permissions should be added, or `remove_perms`, to indicate that permissions should be removed. The `permissions()` function can be used to modify the permissions of a file or a directory. The following example adds all permissions to the owner and user group of a file:

```
fs::permissions(
  path,
  fs::perms::add_perms |
  fs::perms::owner_all | fs::perms::group_all,
  err);
```

- To determine the type of a filesystem object, such as a file, directory, or symbolic link, there are two options available: retrieve the file status and then check the type property, or use one of the available filesystem functions, such as `is_regular_file()`, `is_symlink()`, or `is_directory()`. The following examples that check whether a path refers to a regular file are equivalent:

```
auto s = fs::status(path, err);
auto isfile = s.type() == std::filesystem::file_type::regular;

auto isfile = fs::is_regular_file(path, err);
```

All of the functions discussed in this recipe have an overload that throws exceptions if an error occurs, and an overload that does not throw but returns an error code via a function parameter. All of the examples in this recipe used this approach. More information about these sets of overloads can be found in the *Creating, copying, and deleting files and directories* recipe.

See also

- *Working with filesystem paths* to learn about the C++17-standard support for filesystem paths
- *Creating, copying, and deleting files and directories* to learn how to perform these basic operations with files and directories independently of the filesystem in use
- *Enumerating the content of a directory* to learn how to iterate through the files and subdirectories of a directory

Enumerating the content of a directory

So far in this chapter, we have looked at many of the functionalities provided by the `filesystem` library, such as working with paths, performing operations with files and directories (creating, moving, renaming, deleting, and so on), and querying or modifying properties. Another useful functionality when working with the filesystem is to iterate through the content of a directory. The `filesystem` library provides two directory iterators, one called `directory_iterator`, which iterates the content of a directory, and one called `recursive_directory_iterator`, which recursively iterates the content of a directory and its subdirectories. In this recipe, we will learn how to use them.

Getting ready

For this recipe, we will consider a directory with the following structure:

```
test/
├──data/
│ ├──input.dat
│ └──output.dat
├──file_1.txt
├──file_2.txt
└──file_3.log
```

In this recipe, we will work with filesystem paths and check the properties of a filesystem object. Therefore, it is recommended that you first read the *Working with filesystem paths* and *Checking the properties of an existing file or directory* recipes.

How to do it...

Use the following patterns to enumerate the content of a directory:

- To iterate only the content of a directory without recursively visiting its subdirectories, use `directory_iterator`:

```
void visit_directory(fs::path const & dir)
{
  if (fs::exists(dir) && fs::is_directory(dir))
  {
    for (auto const & entry : fs::directory_iterator(dir))
    {
      auto filename = entry.path().filename();
```

```
        if (fs::is_directory(entry.status()))
          std::cout << "[+]" << filename << '\n';
        else if (fs::is_symlink(entry.status()))
          std::cout << "[>]" << filename << '\n';
        else if (fs::is_regular_file(entry.status()))
          std::cout << " " << filename << '\n';
        else
          std::cout << "[?]" << filename << '\n';
      }
    }
  }
```

- To iterate all the content of a directory, including its subdirectories, use `recursive_directory_iterator` when the order of processing the entries does not matter:

```
void visit_directory_rec(fs::path const & dir)
{
  if (fs::exists(dir) && fs::is_directory(dir))
  {
    for (auto const & entry :
         fs::recursive_directory_iterator(dir))
    {
      auto filename = entry.path().filename();
      if (fs::is_directory(entry.status()))
        std::cout << "[+]" << filename << '\n';
      else if (fs::is_symlink(entry.status()))
        std::cout << "[>]" << filename << '\n';
      else if (fs::is_regular_file(entry.status()))
        std::cout << " " << filename << '\n';
      else
        std::cout << "[?]" << filename << '\n';
    }
  }
}
```

- To iterate all the content of a directory, including its subdirectories, in a structured manner, such as traversing a tree, use a function similar to the one in the first example, which uses `directory_iterator` to iterate the content of a directory. However, instead, call it recursively for each subdirectory:

```
void visit_directory(
  fs::path const & dir,
  bool const recursive = false,
  unsigned int const level = 0)
{
  if (fs::exists(dir) && fs::is_directory(dir))
  {
    auto lead = std::string(level*3, ' ');
    for (auto const & entry : fs::directory_iterator(dir))
    {
      auto filename = entry.path().filename();
      if (fs::is_directory(entry.status()))
      {
        std::cout << lead << "[+]" << filename << '\n';
        if(recursive)
          visit_directory(entry, recursive, level+1);
      }
      else if (fs::is_symlink(entry.status()))
        std::cout << lead << "[>]" << filename << '\n';
      else if (fs::is_regular_file(entry.status()))
        std::cout << lead << "   " << filename << '\n';
      else
        std::cout << lead << "[?]" << filename << '\n';
    }
  }
}
```

How it works...

Both `directory_iterator` and `recursive_directory_iterator` are input iterators that iterate over the entries of a directory. The difference is that the first one does not visit the subdirectories recursively, while the second one, as its name implies, does. They both share a similar behavior:

- The order of iteration is unspecified.
- Each directory entry is visited only once.
- The special paths dot (`.`) and dot-dot (`..`) are skipped.

- A default-constructed iterator is the end iterator and two end iterators are always equal.
- When iterated past the last directory entries, it becomes equal to the end iterator.
- The standard does not specify what happens if a directory entry is added or deleted to the iterated directory after the iterator has been created.
- The standard defines the non-member functions `begin()` and `end()` for both `directory_iterator` and `recursive_directory_iterator`, which enables us to use these iterators in range-based `for` loops, as shown in the examples earlier.

Both iterators have overloaded constructors. Some overloads of the `recursive_directory_iterator` constructor take an argument of the `std::filesystem::directory_options` type, which specifies additional options for the iteration:

- `none`: This is the default that does not specify anything.
- `follow_directory_symlink`: This specifies that the iteration should follow symbolic links instead of serving the link itself.
- `Skip_permission_denied`: This specifies that you should ignore and skip the directories that could trigger an access denied error.

The elements that both directory iterators point to are of the `directory_entry` type. The `path()` member function returns the path of the filesystem object represented by this object. The status of the filesystem object can be retrieved with the member functions `status()` and `symlink_status()` for symbolic links.

The preceding examples follow a common pattern:

- Verify that the path to iterate actually exists.
- Use a range-based `for` loop to iterate all the entries of a directory.
- Use one of the two directory iterators available in the `filesystem` library, depending on the way the iteration is supposed to be done.
- Process each entry according to the requirements.

In our examples, we simply printed the names of the directory entries to the console. It is important to note, as we specified earlier, that the content of the directory is iterated in an unspecified order. If you want to process the content in a structured manner, such as showing subdirectories and their entries indented (for this particular case) or in a tree (in other types of applications), then using `recursive_directory_iterator` is not appropriate. Instead, you should use `directory_iterator` in a function that is called recursively from the iteration, for each subdirectory, as shown in the last example from the previous section.

Considering the directory structure presented at the beginning of this recipe (relative to the current path), we get the following output when using the recursive iterator, as follows:

```
visit_directory_rec(fs::current_path() / "test");
```

```
[+]data
   input.dat
   output.dat
   file_1.txt
   file_2.txt
   file_3.log
```

On the other hand, when using the recursive function from the third example, as shown in the following listing, the output is displayed ordered on sublevels, as intended:

```
visit_directory(fs::current_path() / "test", true);
```

```
[+]data
      input.dat
      output.dat
   file_1.txt
   file_2.txt
   file_3.log
```

Remember that the `visit_directory_rec()` function is a non-recursive function that uses the `recursive_directory_iterator` iterator, while the `visit_directory()` function is a recursive function that uses the `directory_iterator`. This example should help you to understand the difference between the two iterators.

There's more...

In the previous recipe, *Checking the properties of an existing file or directory*, we discussed, among other things, the `file_size()` function that returns the size of a file in bytes. However, this function fails if the specified path is a directory. To determine the size of a directory, we need to iterate recursively through the content of a directory, retrieve the size of the regular files or symbolic links, and add them together. However, we must make sure that we check the value returned by `file_size()`, that is, `-1` cast to an `std::uintmax_t`, in the case of an error. This value, indicating a failure, should not be added to the total size of a directory.

Consider the following function to exemplify this case:

```
std::uintmax_t dir_size(fs::path const & path)
{
  auto size = static_cast<uintmax_t>(-1);
  if (fs::exists(path) && fs::is_directory(path))
  {
    for (auto const & entry : fs::recursive_directory_iterator(path))
    {
      if (fs::is_regular_file(entry.status()) ||
      fs::is_symlink(entry.status()))
      {
        auto err = std::error_code{};
        auto filesize = fs::file_size(entry);
        if (filesize != static_cast<uintmax_t>(-1))
          size += filesize;
      }
    }
  }

  return size;
}
```

The preceding `dir_size()` function returns the size of all the files in a directory (recursively), or `-1`, as an `uintmax_t`, in the case of an error.

See also

- *Checking the properties of an existing file or directory* to learn how to query the properties of files and directories, such as the type, permissions, file times, and more
- *Finding a file* to learn how to search for files based on their name, extension, or other properties

Finding a file

In the previous recipe, we learned how we can use `directory_iterator` and `recursive_directory_iterator` to enumerate the content of a directory. Displaying the content of a directory, as we did in the previous recipe, is only one of the scenarios in which this is needed. The other major scenario is when searching for particular entries in a directory, such as files with a particular name, extension, and so on. In this recipe, we will demonstrate how we can use the directory iterators and the iterating patterns shown earlier to find files that match a given criterion.

Getting ready

You should read the previous recipe, *Enumerating the content of a directory*, for details about directory iterators. In this recipe, we will also use the same test directory structure that was presented in the previous recipe.

How to do it...

To find files that match particular criteria, use the following pattern:

1. Use `recursive_directory_iterator` to iterate through all the entries of a directory and recursively through its subdirectories.
2. Consider regular files (and any other types of files you may need to process).
3. Use a function object (such as a lambda expression) to filter only the files that match your criteria.
4. Add the selected entries to a range (such as a vector).

This pattern is exemplified in the `find_files()` function shown here:

```
std::vector<fs::path> find_files(
    fs::path const & dir,
    std::function<bool(fs::path const&)> filter)
{
  auto result = std::vector<fs::path>{};

  if (fs::exists(dir))
  {
    for (auto const & entry :
      fs::recursive_directory_iterator(
        dir,
        fs::directory_options::follow_directory_symlink))
    {
```

```
        if (fs::is_regular_file(entry) &&
            filter(entry))
        {
          result.push_back(entry);
        }
      }
    }

    return result;
}
```

How it works...

When we want to find files in a directory, the structure of the directory and the order its entries, including subdirectories, are visited in is probably not important. Therefore, we can use the `recursive_directory_iterator` to iterate through the entries.

The function `find_files()` takes two arguments: a path and a function wrapper that is used to select the entries that should be returned. The return type is a vector of `filesystem::path`, though. Alternatively, it could also be a vector of `filesystem::directory_entry`. The recursive directory iterator used in this example does not follow symbolic links, returning the link itself and not the target. This behavior can be changed using a constructor overload that has an argument of the type `filesystem::directory_options` and by passing `follow_directory_symlink`.

In the preceding example, we only consider the regular files and ignore the other types of filesystem objects. The predicate is applied to the directory entry, and, if it returns `true`, the entry is added to the result.

The following example uses the `find_files()` function to find all of the files in the test directory that start with the prefix `file_`:

```
auto results = find_files(
          fs::current_path() / "test",
          [](fs::path const & p) {
  auto filename = p.wstring();
  return filename.find(L"file_") != std::wstring::npos;
});

for (auto const & path : results)
{
  std::cout << path << '\n';
}
```

The output of executing this program, with paths relative to the current path, is as follows:

```
test\file_1.txt
test\file_2.txt
test\file_3.log
```

A second example shows how to find files that have a particular extension, in this case, the extension `.dat`:

```
auto results = find_files(
        fs::current_path() / "test",
        [](fs::path const & p) {
          return p.extension() == L".dat";});

for (auto const & path : results)
{
  std::cout << path << '\n';
}
```

The output, again relative to the current path, is shown here:

```
test\data\input.dat
test\data\output.dat
```

These two examples are very similar. The only thing that is different is the code in the lambda function, which checks the path received as an argument.

See also

- *Checking the properties of an existing file or directory* to learn how to query the properties of files and directories, such as the type, permissions, file times, and more
- *Enumerating the content of a directory* to learn how to iterate through the files and subdirectories of a directory

8

Leveraging Threading and Concurrency

Most computers contain multiple processors or at least multiple cores, and leveraging this computational power is the key for many categories of applications. Unfortunately, many developers still have a mindset of sequential code execution, even though operations that do not depend on each other could be executed concurrently. This chapter presents standard library support for threads, asynchronous tasks, and related components, as well as some practical examples at the end.

Most modern processors (except those dedicated to types of applications that do not require great computing power, such as Internet of Things applications) have two, four, or more cores that enable you to concurrently execute multiple threads of execution. Applications must be explicitly written to leverage the multiple processing units that exist; you can write such applications by executing functions on multiple threads at the same time. The C++ standard library provides support for working with threads, synchronization of shared data, thread communication, and asynchronous tasks. In this chapter, we'll explore the most important topics related to threads and tasks.

This chapter includes the following recipes:

- Working with threads
- Synchronizing access to shared data with mutexes and locks
- Avoiding using recursive mutexes
- Handling exceptions from thread functions

- Sending notifications between threads
- Using promises and futures to return values from threads
- Executing functions asynchronously
- Using atomic types
- Implementing parallel map and fold with threads
- Implementing parallel map and fold with tasks
- Implementing parallel map and fold with standard parallel algorithms
- Using joinable threads and cancellation mechanisms
- Using thread synchronization mechanisms

In the first part of this chapter, we will look at the various threading objects and mechanisms that have built-in support in the library, such as threads, locking objects, condition variables, exception handling, and others.

Working with threads

A thread is a sequence of instructions that can be managed independently by a scheduler, such as the operating system. Threads could be software or hardware. Software threads are threads of execution that are managed by the operating system. They can run on single processing units, usually by time slicing. This is a mechanism where each thread gets a time slot of execution (in the range of milliseconds) on the processing unit before the operating system schedules another software thread to run on the same processing unit. Hardware threads are threads of execution at the physical level. They are, basically, a CPU or a CPU core. They can run simultaneously, that is, in parallel, on systems with multiprocessors or multicores. Many software threads can run concurrently on a hardware thread, usually by using time slicing. The C++ library provides support for working with software threads. In this recipe, you will learn how to create and perform other operations with threads.

Getting ready

A thread of execution is represented by the `thread` class, available in the `std` namespace in the `<thread>` header. Additional thread utilities are available in the same header but in the `std::this_thread` namespace.

In the following examples, the `print_time()` function is used. This function prints the local time to the console. Its implementation is as follows:

```
inline void print_time()
{
  auto now = std::chrono::system_clock::now();
  auto stime = std::chrono::system_clock::to_time_t(now);
  auto ltime = std::localtime(&stime);

  std::cout << std::put_time(ltime, "%c") << '\n';
}
```

In the next section, we will see how to perform common operations with threads.

How to do it...

Use the following solutions to manage threads:

1. To create an `std::thread` object without starting the execution of a new thread, use its default constructor:

```
std::thread t;
```

2. Start the execution of a function on another thread by constructing an `std::thread` object and passing the function as an argument:

```
void func1()
{
  std::cout << "thread func without params" << '\n';
}

std::thread t(func1);
std::thread t([]() {
  std::cout << "thread func without params"
            << '\n'; });
```

3. Start the execution of a function with arguments on another thread by constructing an `std::thread` object, and then passing the function as an argument to the constructor, followed by its arguments:

```
void func2(int const i, double const d, std::string const s)
{
  std::cout << i << ", " << d << ", " << s << '\n';
}

std::thread t(func2, 42, 42.0, "42");
```

4. To wait for a thread to finish its execution, use the `join()` method on the `thread` object:

   ```
   t.join();
   ```

5. To allow a thread to continue its execution independently of the current `thread` object, use the `detach()` method. This means the thread will continue its execution until it finishes without being managed by the `std::thread` object, which will no longer own any thread:

   ```
   t.detach();
   ```

6. To pass arguments by reference to a function, thread wrap them in either `std::ref` or `std::cref` (if the reference is constant):

   ```
   void func3(int & i)
   {
     i *= 2;
   }

   int n = 42;

   std::thread t(func3, std::ref(n));
   t.join();
   std::cout << n << '\n'; // 84
   ```

7. To stop the execution of a thread for a specified duration, use the `std::this_thread::sleep_for()` function:

   ```
   void func4()
   {
     using namespace std::chrono;
     print_time();
     std::this_thread::sleep_for(2s);
     print_time();
   }

   std::thread t(func4);
   t.join();
   ```

8. To stop the execution of a thread until a specified moment in time, use the `std::this_thread::sleep_until()` function:

```
void func5()
{
  using namespace std::chrono;
  print_time();
  std::this_thread::sleep_until(
  std::chrono::system_clock::now() + 2s);
  print_time();
}

std::thread t(func5);
t.join();
```

9. To suspend the execution of the current thread and provide an opportunity to another thread to perform the execution, use `std::this_thread::yield()`:

```
void func6(std::chrono::seconds timeout)
{
  auto now = std::chrono::system_clock::now();
  auto then = now + timeout;
  do
  {
    std::this_thread::yield();
  } while (std::chrono::system_clock::now() < then);
}

std::thread t(func6, std::chrono::seconds(2));
t.join();
print_time();
```

How it works...

The `std::thread` class, which represents a single thread of execution, has several constructors:

- A default constructor that only creates the thread object but does not start the execution of a new thread.
- A move constructor that creates a new thread object to represent a thread of execution previously represented by the object it was constructed from. After the construction of the new object, the other object is no longer associated with the execution thread.

- A constructor with a variable number of arguments: the first being a function that represents the top-level thread function and the others being arguments to be passed to the thread function. Arguments need to be passed to the thread function by value. If the thread function takes parameters by reference or by constant reference, they must be wrapped in either an `std::ref` or `std::cref` object. These are helper function templates that generate objects of the type `std::reference_wrapper`, which wraps a reference in a copyable and assignable object.

The thread function, in this case, cannot return a value. It is not illegal for the function to actually have a return type other than `void`, but it ignores any value that is directly returned by the function. If it has to return a value, it can do so using a shared variable or a function argument. In the *Using promises and futures to return values from threads* recipe, later in this chapter, we will see how a thread function returns a value to another thread using a *promise*.

If the function terminates with an exception, the exception cannot be caught with a `try...catch` statement in the context where a thread was started and the program terminated abnormally with a call to `std::terminate()`. All exceptions must be caught within the executing thread, but they can be transported across threads via an `std::exception_ptr` object. We'll discuss this topic in a following recipe, called *Handling exceptions from thread functions*.

After a thread has started its execution, it is both joinable and detachable. Joining a thread implies blocking the execution of the current thread until the joined thread ends its execution. Detaching a thread means decoupling the thread object from the thread of execution it represents, allowing both the current thread and the detached thread to be executed at the same time. Joining a thread is done with `join()` and detaching a thread is done with `detach()`. Once you call either of these two methods, the thread is said to be non-joinable and the thread object can be safely destroyed. When a thread is detached, the shared data it may need to access must be available throughout its execution. The `joinable()` method indicates whether a thread can be joined or not.

Each thread has an identifier that can be retrieved. For the current thread, call the `std::this_thread::get_id()` function. For another thread of execution represented by a `thread` object, call its `get_id()` method.

There are several additional utility functions available in the `std::this_thread` namespace:

- The `yield()` method hints the scheduler to activate another thread. This is useful when implementing a busy-waiting routine, as in the last example from the previous section.

- The `sleep_for()` method blocks the execution of the current thread for at least the specified period of time (the actual time the thread is put to sleep may be longer than the requested period due to scheduling).
- The `sleep_until()` method blocks the execution of the current thread until at least the specified time point (the actual duration of the sleep may be longer than requested due to scheduling).

The `std::thread` class requires the `join()` method be called explicitly to wait for the thread to finish. This can lead to programming errors. The C++20 standard provides a new thread class, called `std::jthread`, that solves this inconvenience. This will be the topic of the recipe *Using joinable threads and cancellation mechanisms*, later in this chapter.

See also

- *Synchronizing access to shared data with mutexes and locks*, to see what mechanisms are available for synchronizing thread access to shared data and how they work.
- *Avoiding using recursive mutexes*, to learn why recursive mutexes should be avoided, and also how to transform a thread-safe type using a recursive mutex into a thread-safe type using a non-recursive mutex.
- *Handling exceptions from thread functions*, to understand how to handle exceptions thrown in a worker thread from the main thread or the thread where it was joined.
- *Sending notifications between threads*, to see how to use condition variables to send notifications between producer and consumer threads.
- *Using promises and futures to return values from threads*, to learn how to use an `std::promise` object to return a value or an exception from a thread.

Synchronizing access to shared data with mutexes and locks

Threads allow you to execute multiple functions at the same time, but it is often necessary that these functions access shared resources. Access to shared resources must be synchronized so that only one thread can read or write from or to the shared resource at a time. An example of this was shown in the previous recipe, where multiple threads had the ability to add objects to a shared container at the same time. In this recipe, we will see what mechanisms the C++ standard defines for synchronizing thread access to shared data and how they work.

Getting ready

The `mutex` and `lock` classes discussed in this recipe are available in the `std` namespace in the `<mutex>` header.

How to do it...

Use the following pattern for synchronizing access with a single shared resource:

1. Define a `mutex` in the appropriate context (class or global scope):

```
std::mutex g_mutex;
```

2. Acquire a `lock` on this `mutex` before accessing the shared resource in each thread:

```
void thread_func()
{
  using namespace std::chrono_literals;
  {
    std::lock_guard<std::mutex> lock(g_mutex);
    std::cout << "running thread "
              << std::this_thread::get_id() << '\n';
  }

  std::this_thread::yield();
  std::this_thread::sleep_for(2s);

  {
    std::lock_guard<std::mutex> lock(g_mutex);
    std::cout << "done in thread "
              << std::this_thread::get_id() << '\n';
  }
}
```

Use the following pattern for synchronizing access to multiple shared resources at the same time to avoid deadlocks:

1. Define a mutex for each shared resource in the appropriate context (global or class scope):

```
template <typename T>
struct container
{
  std::mutex     mutex;
```

```
  std::vector<T> data;
};
```

2. Lock the mutexes at the same time using a deadlock avoidance algorithm with `std::lock()`:

```
template <typename T>
void move_between(container<T> & c1, container<T> & c2,
                  T const value)
{
  std::lock(c1.mutex, c2.mutex);
  // continued at 3.
}
```

3. After locking them, adopt the ownership of each mutex into an `std::lock_guard` class to ensure they are safely released at the end of the function (or scope):

```
// continued from 2.
std::lock_guard<std::mutex> l1(c1.mutex, std::adopt_lock);
std::lock_guard<std::mutex> l2(c2.mutex, std::adopt_lock);

c1.data.erase(
  std::remove(c1.data.begin(), c1.data.end(), value),
  c1.data.end());
c2.data.push_back(value);
```

How it works...

A mutex is a synchronization primitive that allows us to protect simultaneous access to shared resources from multiple threads. The C++ standard library provides several implementations:

- `std::mutex` is the most commonly used mutex type; it is illustrated in the preceding code snippet. It provides methods to acquire and release the mutex. `lock()` tries to acquire the mutex and blocks it if it is not available, `try_lock()` tries to acquire the mutex and returns it without blocking if the mutex is not available, and `unlock()` releases the mutex.
- `std::timed_mutex` is similar to `std::mutex` but provides two more methods to acquire the mutex using a timeout: `try_lock_for()` tries to acquire the mutex and returns it if the mutex is not made available during the specified duration, and `try_lock_until()` tries to acquire the mutex and returns it if the mutex is not made available until a specified time point.

- `std::recursive_mutex` is similar to `std::mutex`, but the mutex can be acquired multiple times from the same thread without being blocked.
- `std::recursive_timed_mutex` is a combination of a recursive mutex and a timed mutex.
- `std::shared_timed_mutex`, since C++14, is to be used in scenarios when multiple readers can access the same resource at the same time without causing data races, while only one writer it allowed to do so. It implements locking with two levels of access – *shared* (several threads can share the ownership of the same mutex) and *exclusive* (only one thread can own the mutex) – and provides timeout facilities.
- `std::shared_mutex`, since C++17, similar to the `shared_timed_mutex` but without the timeout facilities.

The first thread that locks an available mutex takes ownership of it and continues with the execution. All consecutive attempts to lock the mutex from any thread fail, including the thread that already owns the mutex, and the `lock()` method blocks the thread until the mutex is released with a call to `unlock()`. If a thread needs to be able to lock a mutex multiple times without blocking it and therefore enter a deadlock, a `recursive_mutex` class template should be used.

The typical use of a mutex to protect access to a shared resource comprises locking the mutex, using the shared resource, and then unlocking the mutex:

```
g_mutex.lock();

// use the shared resource such as std::cout
std::cout << "accessing shared resource" << '\n';

g_mutex.unlock();
```

This method of using the mutex is, however, prone to error. This is because each call to `lock()` must be paired with a call to `unlock()` on all execution paths; that is, both normal return paths and exception return paths. In order to safely acquire and release a mutex, regardless of the way the execution of a function goes, the C++ standard defines several locking classes:

- `std::lock_guard` is the locking mechanism seen earlier; it represents a mutex wrapper implemented in an RAII manner. It attempts to acquire the mutex at the time of its construction and release it upon destruction. This is available in C++11. The following is a typical implementation of `lock_guard`:

  ```
  template <class M>
  class lock_guard
  ```

```
{
public:
  typedef M mutex_type;

  explicit lock_guard(M& Mtx) : mtx(Mtx)
  {
    mtx.lock();
  }

  lock_guard(M& Mtx, std::adopt_lock_t) : mtx(Mtx)
  { }

  ~lock_guard() noexcept
  {
    mtx.unlock();
  }

  lock_guard(const lock_guard&) = delete;
  lock_guard& operator=(const lock_guard&) = delete;
private:
  M& mtx;
};
```

- `std::unique_lock` is a mutex ownership wrapper that provides support for deferred locking, time locking, recursive locking, transfer of ownership, and using it with condition variables. This is available in C++11.
- `std::shared_lock` is a mutex-shared ownership wrapper that provides support for deferred locking, time locking, and transfer of ownership. This is available in C++14.
- `std::scoped_lock` is a wrapper for multiple mutexes implemented in an RAII manner. Upon construction, it attempts to acquire ownership of the mutexes in a deadlock avoidance manner as if it is using `std::lock()`, and upon destruction, it releases the mutexes in reverse order of the way they were acquired. This is available in C++17.

In the first example in the *How to do it...* section, we used `std::mutex` and `std::lock_guard` to protect access to the `std::cout` stream object, which is shared between all the threads in a program. The following example shows how the `thread_func()` function can be executed concurrently on several threads:

```
std::vector<std::thread> threads;
for (int i = 0; i < 5; ++i)
```

```
    threads.emplace_back(thread_func);

  for (auto & t : threads)
    t.join();
```

A possible output for this program is as follows:

```
running thread 140296854550272
running thread 140296846157568
running thread 140296837764864
running thread 140296829372160
running thread 140296820979456
done in thread 140296854550272
done in thread 140296846157568
done in thread 140296837764864
done in thread 140296820979456
done in thread 140296829372160
```

When a thread needs to take ownership of multiple mutexes that are meant to protect multiple shared resources, acquiring them one by one may lead to deadlocks. Let's consider the following example (where `container` is the class shown in the *How to do it...* section):

```
template <typename T>
void move_between(container<T> & c1, container<T> & c2, T const value)
{
  std::lock_guard<std::mutex> l1(c1.mutex);
  std::lock_guard<std::mutex> l2(c2.mutex);

  c1.data.erase(
    std::remove(c1.data.begin(), c1.data.end(), value),
    c1.data.end());
  c2.data.push_back(value);
}

container<int> c1;
c1.data.push_back(1);
c1.data.push_back(2);
c1.data.push_back(3);

container<int> c2;
c2.data.push_back(4);
c2.data.push_back(5);
```

```
c2.data.push_back(6);

std::thread t1(move_between<int>, std::ref(c1), std::ref(c2), 3);
std::thread t2(move_between<int>, std::ref(c2), std::ref(c1), 6);

t1.join();
t2.join();
```

In this example, the `container` class holds data that may be accessed simultaneously from different threads; therefore, it needs to be protected by acquiring a mutex. The `move_between()` function is a thread-safe function that removes an element from a container and adds it to a second container. To do so, it acquires the mutexes of the two containers sequentially, then erases the element from the first container and adds it to the end of the second container.

This function is, however, prone to deadlocks because a race condition might be triggered while acquiring the locks. Suppose we have a scenario where two different threads execute this function, but with different arguments:

- The first thread starts executing with the arguments `c1` and `c2` in this order.
- The first thread is suspended after it acquires the lock for the `c1` container. The second thread starts executing with the arguments `c2` and `c1` in this order.
- The second thread is suspended after it acquires the lock for the `c2` container.
- The first thread continues the execution and tries to acquire the mutex for `c2`, but the mutex is unavailable. Therefore, a deadlock occurs (this can be simulated by putting the thread to sleep for a short while after it acquires the first mutex).

To avoid possible deadlocks such as these, mutexes should be acquired in a deadlock avoidance manner, and the standard library provides a utility function called `std::lock()` that does that. The `move_between()` function needs to change by replacing the two locks with the following code (as shown in the *How to do it...* section):

```
std::lock(c1.mutex, c2.mutex);

std::lock_guard<std::mutex> l1(c1.mutex, std::adopt_lock);
std::lock_guard<std::mutex> l2(c2.mutex, std::adopt_lock);
```

The ownership of the mutexes must still be transferred to a lock guard object so they are properly released after the execution of the function ends (or depending on the case, when a particular scope ends).

In C++17, a new mutex wrapper is available, `std::scoped_lock`, that can be used to simplify code, such as the one in the preceding example. This type of lock can acquire the ownership of multiple mutexes in a deadlock-free manner. These mutexes are released when the scoped lock is destroyed. The preceding code is equivalent to the following single line of code:

```
std::scoped_lock lock(c1.mutex, c2.mutex);
```

The `scoped_lock` class provides a simplified mechanism for owning one or more mutexes for the duration of a scoped block, and also helps with writing simple and more robust code.

See also

- *Working with threads*, to learn about the `std::thread` class and the basic operations for working with threads in C++.
- *Using joinable threads and cancellation mechanisms*, to learn about the C++20 `std::jthread` class, which manages a thread of execution and automatically joins during its destruction, as well as the improved mechanisms for stopping the execution of threads.
- *Avoiding using recursive mutexes*, to learn why recursive mutexes should be avoided and how to transform a thread-safe type using a recursive mutex into a thread-safe type using a non-recursive mutex.

Avoiding using recursive mutexes

The standard library provides several mutex types for protecting access to shared resources. `std::recursive_mutex` and `std::recursive_timed_mutex` are two implementations that allow you to use multiple locking in the same thread. A typical use for a recursive mutex is to protect access to a shared resource from a recursive function. An `std::recursive_mutex` class may be locked multiple times from a thread, either with a call to `lock()` or `try_lock()`. When a thread locks an available recursive mutex, it acquires its ownership; as a result of this, consecutive attempts to lock the mutex from the same thread do not block the execution of the thread, creating a deadlock. The recursive mutex is, however, released only when an equal number of calls to `unlock()` are made. Recursive mutexes may also have a greater overhead than non-recursive mutexes. For these reasons, when possible, they should be avoided. This recipe presents a use case for transforming a thread-safe type using a recursive mutex into a thread-safe type using a non-recursive mutex.

Getting ready

You need to be familiar with the various mutexes and locks available in the standard library. I recommend that you read the previous recipe, *Synchronizing access to shared data with mutex and locks*, to get an overview of them.

For this recipe, we will consider the following class:

```
class foo_rec
{
  std::recursive_mutex m;
  int data;

public:
  foo_rec(int const d = 0) : data(d) {}

  void update(int const d)
  {
    std::lock_guard<std::recursive_mutex> lock(m);
    data = d;
  }

  int update_with_return(int const d)
  {
    std::lock_guard<std::recursive_mutex> lock(m);
    auto temp = data;
    update(d);
    return temp;
  }
};
```

The purpose of this recipe is to transform the `foo_rec` class so we can avoid using `std::recursive_mutex`.

How to do it...

To transform the preceding implementation into a thread-safe type using a non-recursive mutex, do this:

1. Replace `std::recursive_mutex` with `std::mutex`:

   ```
   class foo
   {
     std::mutex m;
   ```

```
    int         data;
    // continued at 2.
};
```

2. Define private non-thread-safe versions of the public methods or helper functions to be used in thread-safe public methods:

```
void internal_update(int const d) { data = d; }
// continued at 3.
```

3. Rewrite the public methods to use the newly defined non-thread-safe private methods:

```
public:
  foo(int const d = 0) : data(d) {}
  void update(int const d)
  {
    std::lock_guard<std::mutex> lock(m);
    internal_update(d);
  }

  int update_with_return(int const d)
  {
    std::lock_guard<std::mutex> lock(m);
    auto temp = data;
    internal_update(d);
    return temp;
  }
```

How it works...

The `foo_rec` class we just discussed uses a recursive mutex to protect access to shared data; in this case, it is an integer member variable that is accessed from two thread-safe public functions:

- `update()` sets a new value in the private variable.
- `update_and_return()` sets a new value in the private variable and returns the previous value to the called function. This function calls `update()` to set the new value.

The implementation of `foo_rec` was probably intended to avoid duplication of code, yet this particular approach is rather a design error that can be improved, as shown in the *How to do it...* section. Rather than reusing public thread-safe functions, we can provide private non-thread-safe functions that could then be called from the public interface.

The same solution can be applied to other similar problems: define a non-thread-safe version of the code and then provide perhaps lightweight, thread-safe wrappers.

See also

- *Working with threads*, to learn about the `std::thread` class and the basic operations for working with threads in C++.
- *Synchronizing access to shared data with mutexes and locks*, to see what mechanisms are available for synchronizing thread access to shared data and how they work.

Handling exceptions from thread functions

In the previous recipe, we introduced the thread support library and saw how to do some basic operations with threads. In that recipe, we briefly discussed exception handling in thread functions and mentioned that exceptions cannot leave the top-level thread function. This is because they cause the program to abnormally terminate with a call to `std::terminate()`.

On the other hand, exceptions can be transported between threads within an `std::exception_ptr` wrapper. In this recipe, we will see how to handle exceptions from thread functions.

Getting ready

You are now familiar with the thread operations we discussed in the previous recipe, *Working with threads*. The `exception_ptr` class is available in the `std` namespace, which is in the `<exception>` header; `mutex` (which we discussed in more detail previously) is also available in the same namespace but in the `<mutex>` header.

How to do it...

To properly handle exceptions thrown in a worker thread from the main thread or the thread where it was joined, do the following (assuming multiple exceptions can be thrown from multiple threads):

1. Use a global container to hold instances of `std::exception_ptr`:

   ```
   std::vector<std::exception_ptr> g_exceptions;
   ```

2. Use a global `mutex` to synchronize access to the shared container:

```
std::mutex g_mutex;
```

3. Use a `try...catch` block for the code that is being executed in the top-level thread function. Use `std::current_exception()` to capture the current exception and wrap a copy or its reference into an `std::exception_ptr` pointer, which is added to the shared container for exceptions:

```
void func1()
{
  throw std::runtime_error("exception 1");
}

void func2()
{
  throw std::runtime_error("exception 2");
}

void thread_func1()
{
  try
  {
    func1();
  }
  catch (...)
  {
    std::lock_guard<std::mutex> lock(g_mutex);
    g_exceptions.push_back(std::current_exception());
  }
}

void thread_func2()
{
  try
  {
    func2();
  }
  catch (...)
  {
    std::lock_guard<std::mutex> lock(g_mutex);
    g_exceptions.push_back(std::current_exception());
  }
}
```

4. Clear the container from the main thread before you start the threads:

```
g_exceptions.clear();
```

5. In the main thread, after the execution of all the threads has finished, inspect the caught exceptions and handle each of them appropriately:

```
std::thread t1(thread_func1);
std::thread t2(thread_func2);
t1.join();
t2.join();

for (auto const & e : g_exceptions)
{
  try
  {
    if(e != nullptr)
      std::rethrow_exception(e);
  }
  catch(std::exception const & ex)
  {
    std::cout << ex.what() << '\n';
  }
}
```

How it works...

For the example in the preceding section, we assumed that multiple threads could throw exceptions and therefore need a container to hold them all. If there is a single exception from a single thread at a time, then you do not need a shared container and a mutex to synchronize access to it. You can use a single global object of the type `std::exception_ptr` to hold the exception that's transported between threads.

`std::current_exception()` is a function that is typically used in a `catch` clause to capture the current exception and create an instance of `std::exception_ptr`. This is done to hold a copy or reference (depending on the implementation) to the original exception, which remains valid as long as there is an `std::exception_ptr` pointer available that refers to it. If this function is called when no exception is being handled, then it creates an empty `std::exception_ptr`.

The `std::exception_ptr` pointer is a wrapper for an exception captured with `std::current_exception()`. If default constructed, it does not hold any exception. Two objects of this type are equal if they are both empty or point to the same exception object. The `std::exception_ptr` objects can be passed to other threads, where they can be rethrown and caught in a `try...catch` block.

`std::rethrow_exception()` is a function that takes `std::exception_ptr` as an argument and throws the exception object referred to by its argument.

`std::current_exception()`, `std::rethrow_exception()`, and `std::exception_ptr` are all available in C++11.

In the example from the previous section, each thread function uses a `try...catch` statement for the entire code it executes so that no exception may leave the function uncaught. When an exception is handled, a lock on the global `mutex` object is acquired and the `std::exception_ptr` object holding the current exception is added to the shared container. With this approach, the thread function stops at the first exception; however, in other circumstances, you may need to execute multiple operations, even if the previous one throws an exception. In this case, you will have multiple `try...catch` statements and perhaps transport only some of the exceptions outside the thread.

In the main thread, after all the threads have finished executing, the container is iterated, and each non-empty exception is rethrown and caught with a `try...catch` block and handled appropriately.

See also

- *Working with threads*, to learn about the `std::thread` class and the basic operations for working with threads in C++.
- *Synchronizing access to shared data with mutexes and locks*, to see what mechanisms are available for synchronizing thread access to shared data and how they work.

Sending notifications between threads

Mutexes are synchronization primitives that can be used to protect access to shared data. However, the standard library provides a synchronization primitive, called a *condition variable*, that enables a thread to signal to others that a certain condition has occurred. The thread or the threads that are waiting on the condition variable are blocked until the condition variable is signaled or until a timeout or a spurious wakeup occurs. In this recipe, we will see how to use condition variables to send notifications between thread-producing data and thread-consuming data.

Getting ready

For this recipe, you need to be familiar with threads, mutexes, and locks. Condition variables are available in the `std` namespace in the `<condition_variable>` header.

How to do it...

Use the following pattern for synchronizing threads with notifications on condition variables:

1. Define a condition variable (in the appropriate context):

```
std::condition_variable cv;
```

2. Define a mutex for threads to lock on. A second mutex should be used for synchronizing access to the standard console from different threads:

```
std::mutex cv_mutex; // data mutex
std::mutex io_mutex; // I/O mutex
```

3. Define the shared data used between the threads:

```
int data = 0;
```

4. In the producing thread, lock the mutex before you modify the data:

```
std::thread p([&](){
  // simulate long running operation
  {
    using namespace std::chrono_literals;
    std::this_thread::sleep_for(2s);
  }

  // produce
  {
    std::unique_lock lock(cv_mutex);
    data = 42;
  }

  // print message
  {
    std::lock_guard l(io_mutex);
    std::cout << "produced " << data << '\n';
  }

  // continued at 5.
});
```

5. In the producing thread, signal the condition variable with a call to `notify_one()` or `notify_all()` (do this after the mutex used to protect the shared data is unlocked):

```
// continued from 4.
cv.notify_one();
```

6. In the consuming thread, acquire a unique lock on the mutex and use it to wait on the condition variable. Beware that spurious wakeups may occur, which is a subject we'll discuss in detail in the following section:

```
std::thread c([&](){
  // wait for notification
  {
    std::unique_lock lock(cv_mutex);
    cv.wait(lock);
  }

  // continued at 7.
});
```

7. In the consuming thread, use the shared data after the condition is notified:

```
// continued from 6.
{
  std::lock_guard lock(io_mutex);
  std::cout << "consumed " << data << '\n';
}
```

How it works...

The preceding example represents two threads that share common data (in this case, an integer variable). One thread produces data after a lengthy computation (simulated with a sleep), while the other consumes it only after it is produced. To do so, they use a synchronization mechanism that uses a mutex and a condition variable that blocks the consuming thread until a notification arises from the producer thread, indicating that data has been made available. The key in this communication channel is the condition variable that the consuming thread waits on until the producing thread notifies it. Both threads start about the same time. The producer thread begins a long computation that is supposed to produce data for the consuming thread. At the same time, the consuming thread cannot actually proceed until the data is made available; it must remain blocked until it is notified that the data has been produced. Once notified, it can continue its execution. The entire mechanism works as follows:

- There must be at least one thread waiting on the condition variable to be notified.
- There must be at least one thread that is signaling the condition variable.
- The waiting threads must first acquire a lock on a mutex (`std::unique_lock<std::mutex>`) and pass it to the `wait()`, `wait_for()`, or `wait_until()` method of the condition variable. All the waiting methods atomically release the mutex and block the thread until the condition variable is signaled. At this point, the thread is unblocked and the mutex is atomically acquired again.
- The thread that signals the condition variable can do so with either `notify_one()`, where one blocked thread is unblocked, or `notify_all()`, where all the blocked threads waiting for the condition variable are unblocked.

Condition variables cannot be made completely predictable on multiprocessor systems. Therefore, *spurious wakeups* may occur, and a thread is unlocked even if nobody signals the condition variable. So, it is necessary to check whether the condition is true after the thread has been unblocked. However, spurious wakeups may occur multiple times and, therefore, it is necessary to check the condition variable in a loop.

The C++ standard provides two implementations of condition variables:

- `std::condition_variable`, used in this recipe, defines a condition variable associated with `std::unique_lock`.
- `std::condition_variable_any` represents a more general implementation that works with any lock that meets the requirements of a basic lock (implements the `lock()` and `unlock()` methods). A possible use of this implementation is providing interruptible waits, as explained by Anthony Williams in *C++ concurrency in action* (2012):

> *"A custom lock operation would both lock the associated mutex as expected and also perform the necessary job of notifying this condition variable when the interrupting signal is received."*

All the waiting methods of the condition variable have two overloads:

- The first overload takes `std::unique_lock<std::mutex>` (based on the type; that is, duration or time point) and causes the thread to remain blocked until the condition variable is signaled. This overload atomically releases the mutex and blocks the current thread, and then adds it to the list of threads waiting on the condition variable. The thread is unblocked when the condition is notified with either `notify_one()` or `notify_all()`, a spurious wakeup occurs, or a timeout occurs (depending on the function overload). When this happens, the mutex is atomically acquired again.
- The second overload takes a predicate in addition to the arguments of the other overloads. This predicate can be used to avoid spurious wakeups while waiting for a condition to become `true`. This overload is equivalent to the following:

```
while(!pred())
  wait(lock);
```

The following code illustrates a similar but more complex example than the one presented in the previous section. The producing thread generates data in a loop (in this example, it is a finite loop), and the consuming thread waits for new data to be made available and consumes it (prints it to the console). The producing thread terminates when it finishes producing data, and the consuming thread terminates when there is no more data to consume. Data is added to `queue<int>`, and a Boolean variable is used to indicate to the consuming thread that the process of producing data is finished. The following snippet shows the implementation of the `producer` thread:

```
std::mutex g_lockprint;
std::mutex g_lockqueue;
std::condition_variable g_queuecheck;
std::queue<int> g_buffer;
bool g_done;

void producer(
  int const id,
  std::mt19937& generator,
  std::uniform_int_distribution<int>& dsleep,
  std::uniform_int_distribution<int>& dcode)
{
  for (int i = 0; i < 5; ++i)
  {
    // simulate work
```

```
    std::this_thread::sleep_for(
      std::chrono::seconds(dsleep(generator)));

    // generate data
    {
      std::unique_lock<std::mutex> locker(g_lockqueue);
      int value = id * 100 + dcode(generator);
      g_buffer.push(value);

      {
        std::unique_lock<std::mutex> locker(g_lockprint);
        std::cout << "[produced(" << id << ")]: " << value
                  << '\n';
      }
    }

    // notify consumers
    g_queuecheck.notify_one();
  }
}
```

On the other hand, the consumer thread's implementation is listed here:

```
void consumer()
{
  // loop until end is signaled
  while (!g_done)
  {
    std::unique_lock<std::mutex> locker(g_lockqueue);

    g_queuecheck.wait_for(
      locker,
      std::chrono::seconds(1),
      [&]() {return !g_buffer.empty(); });

    // if there are values in the queue process them
    while (!g_done && !g_buffer.empty())
    {
      std::unique_lock<std::mutex> locker(g_lockprint);
      std::cout
            << "[consumed]: " << g_buffer.front()
            << '\n';
```

```
        g_buffer.pop();
      }
    }
  }
```

The consumer thread does the following:

- Loops until it is signaled that the process of producing data is finished.
- Acquires a unique lock on the `mutex` object associated with the condition variable.
- Uses the `wait_for()` overload, which takes a predicate, checking that the buffer is not empty when a wakeup occurs (to avoid spurious wakeups). This method uses a timeout of 1 second and returns after the timeout has occurred, even if the condition is signaled.
- Consumes all of the data from the queue after it is signaled through the condition variable.

To test this, we can start several producing threads and one consuming thread. Producer threads generate random data and, therefore, share the pseudo-random generator engines and distributions. All of this is shown in the following code sample:

```
auto seed_data = std::array<int, std::mt19937::state_size> {};
std::random_device rd {};
std::generate(std::begin(seed_data), std::end(seed_data),
              std::ref(rd));
std::seed_seq seq(std::begin(seed_data), std::end(seed_data));
auto generator = std::mt19937{ seq };
auto dsleep = std::uniform_int_distribution<>{ 1, 5 };
auto dcode = std::uniform_int_distribution<>{ 1, 99 };

std::cout << "start producing and consuming..." << '\n';

std::thread consumerthread(consumer);
std::vector<std::thread> threads;
for (int i = 0; i < 5; ++i)
{
  threads.emplace_back(producer,
                       i + 1,
                       std::ref(generator),
                       std::ref(dsleep),
                       std::ref(dcode));
```

```
}

// work for the workers to finish
for (auto& t : threads)
  t.join();

// notify the logger to finish and wait for it
g_done = true;
consumerthread.join();

std::cout << "done producing and consuming" << '\n';
```

A possible output of this program is as follows (the actual output would be different for each execution):

```
start producing and consuming...
[produced(5)]: 550
[consumed]: 550
[produced(5)]: 529
[consumed]: 529
[produced(5)]: 537
[consumed]: 537
[produced(1)]: 122
[produced(2)]: 224
[produced(3)]: 326
[produced(4)]: 458
[consumed]: 122
[consumed]: 224
[consumed]: 326
[consumed]: 458
...
done producing and consuming
```

The standard also features a helper function called `notify_all_at_thread_exit()`, which provides a way for a thread to notify other threads through a `condition_variable` object that it's completely finished execution, including destroying all `thread_local` objects. This function has two parameters: a `condition_variable` and an `std::unique_lock<std::mutex>` associated with the condition variable (that it takes ownership of). The typical use case for this function is running a detached thread that calls this function just before finishing.

See also

- *Working with threads*, to learn about the `std::thread` class and the basic operations for working with threads in C++.
- *Synchronizing access to shared data with mutexes and locks*, to see what mechanisms are available for synchronizing thread access to shared data and how they work.

Using promises and futures to return values from threads

In the first recipe of this chapter, we discussed how to work with threads. You also learned that thread functions cannot return values and that threads should use other means, such as shared data, to do so; however, for this, synchronization is required. An alternative to communicating a return value or an exception with either the main or another thread is using `std::promise`. This recipe will explain how this mechanism works.

Getting ready

The `promise` and `future` classes used in this recipe are available in the `std` namespace in the `<future>` header.

How to do it...

To communicate a value from one thread to another through promises and futures, do this:

1. Make a promise available to the thread function through a parameter; for example:

   ```
   void produce_value(std::promise<int>& p)
   {
     // simulate long running operation
     {
       using namespace std::chrono_literals;
       std::this_thread::sleep_for(2s);
     }

     // continued at 2.
   }
   ```

2. Call `set_value()` on the premise to set the result to represent a value or `set_exception()` to set the result to indicate an exception:

```
// continued from 1.
p.set_value(42);
```

3. Make the future associated with the premise available to the other thread function through a parameter; for example:

```
void consume_value(std::future<int>& f)
{
  // continued at 4.
}
```

4. Call `get()` on the `future` object to get the result set to the promise:

```
// continued from 3.
auto value = f.get();
```

5. In the calling thread, use `get_future()` on the promise to get the `future` associated with the promise:

```
std::promise<int> p;
std::thread t1(produce_value, std::ref(p));

std::future<int> f = p.get_future();
std::thread t2(consume_value, std::ref(f));

t1.join();
t2.join();
```

How it works...

The promise-future pair is basically a communication channel that enables a thread to communicate a value or exception with another thread through a shared state. `promise` is an asynchronous provider of the result and has an associated `future` that represents an asynchronous return object. To establish this channel, you must first create a promise. This, in turn, creates a shared state that can be later read through the future associated with the promise.

To set a result to a promise, you can use any of the following methods:

- The `set_value()` or `set_value_at_thread_exit()` method is used to set a return value; the latter function stores the value in the shared state but only makes it available through the associated future if the thread exits.

- The `set_exception()` or `set_exception_at_thread_exit()` method is used to set an exception as a return value. The exception is wrapped in an `std::exception_ptr` object. The latter function stores the exception in the shared state but only makes it available when the thread exits.

To retrieve the `future` object associated with `promise`, use the `get_future()` method. To get the value from the `future` value, use the `get()` method. This blocks the calling thread until the value from the shared state is made available. The future class has several methods for blocking the thread until the result from the shared state is made available:

- `wait()` only returns when the result is available.
- `wait_for()` returns either when the result is available or when the specified timeout expires.
- `wait_until()` returns either when the result is available or when the specified time point is reached.

If an exception is set to the `promise` value, calling the `get()` method on the `future` object will throw this exception. The example from the previous section has been rewritten as follows to throw an exception instead of setting a result:

```
void produce_value(std::promise<int>& p)
{
  // simulate long running operation
  {
    using namespace std::chrono_literals;
    std::this_thread::sleep_for(2s);
  }

  try
  {
    throw std::runtime_error("an error has occurred!");
  }
  catch(...)
  {
    p.set_exception(std::current_exception());
  }
}

void consume_value(std::future<int>& f)
{
  std::lock_guard<std::mutex> lock(g_mutex);
  try
```

```
    {
      std::cout << f.get() << '\n';
    }
    catch(std::exception const & e)
    {
      std::cout << e.what() << '\n';
    }
  }
```

You can see here that, in the `consume_value()` function, the call to `get()` is put in a `try...catch` block. If an exception is caught - and in this particular implementation, it is - its message is printed to the console.

There's more...

Establishing a promise-future channel in this manner is a rather explicit operation that can be avoided by using the `std::async()` function; this is a higher-level utility that runs a function asynchronously, creates an internal promise and a shared state, and returns a future associated with the shared state. We will see how `std::async()` works in the next recipe, *Executing functions asynchronously*.

See also

- *Working with threads*, to learn about the `std::thread` class and the basic operations for working with threads in C++.
- *Handling exceptions from thread functions*, to understand how to handle exceptions thrown in a worker thread from the main thread or the thread where it was joined.

Executing functions asynchronously

Threads enable us to run multiple functions at the same time; this helps us take advantage of the hardware facilities in multiprocessor or multicore systems. However, threads require explicit, lower-level operations. An alternative to threads is tasks, which are units of work that run in a particular thread. The C++ standard does not provide a complete task library, but it enables developers to execute functions asynchronously on different threads and communicate results back through a promise-future channel, as seen in the previous recipe. In this recipe, we will see how to do this using `std::async()` and `std::future`.

Getting ready

For the examples in this recipe, we will use the following functions:

```
void do_something()
{
  // simulate long running operation
  {
    using namespace std::chrono_literals;
    std::this_thread::sleep_for(2s);
  }

  std::lock_guard<std::mutex> lock(g_mutex);
  std::cout << "operation 1 done" << '\n';
}

void do_something_else()
{
  // simulate long running operation
  {
    using namespace std::chrono_literals;
    std::this_thread::sleep_for(1s);
  }

  std::lock_guard<std::mutex> lock(g_mutex);
  std::cout << "operation 2 done" << '\n';
}

int compute_something()
{
  // simulate long running operation
  {
    using namespace std::chrono_literals;
    std::this_thread::sleep_for(2s);
  }

  return 42;
}

int compute_something_else()
{
  // simulate long running operation
```

```
    {
      using namespace std::chrono_literals;
      std::this_thread::sleep_for(1s);
    }

    return 24;
}
```

In this recipe, we will use futures; therefore, you are advised to read the previous recipe to get a quick overview of how they work. Both `async()` and `future` are available in the `std` namespace in the `<future>` header.

How to do it...

To execute a function asynchronously on another thread when the current thread is continuing with the execution without expecting a result, do the following:

1. Use `std::async()` to start a new thread to execute the specified function. Create an asynchronous provider and return a `future` associated with it. Use the `std::launch::async` policy for the first argument to the function in order to make sure the function will run asynchronously:

   ```
   auto f = std::async(std::launch::async, do_something);
   ```

2. Continue with the execution of the current thread:

   ```
   do_something_else();
   ```

3. Call the `wait()` method on the `future` object returned by `std::async()` when you need to make sure the asynchronous operation is completed:

   ```
   f.wait();
   ```

To execute a function asynchronously on a worker thread while the current thread continues its execution, until the result from the asynchronous function is needed in the current thread, do the following:

1. Use `std::async()` to start a new thread to execute the specified function, create an asynchronous provider, and return a `future` associated with it. Use the `std::launch::async` policy of the first argument to the function to make sure the function does run asynchronously:

   ```
   auto f = std::async(std::launch::async, compute_something);
   ```

2. Continue the execution of the current thread:

```
auto value = compute_something_else();
```

3. Call the get() method on the future object returned by std::async() when you need the result from the function to be executed asynchronously:

```
value += f.get();
```

How it works...

std::async() is a variadic function template that has two overloads: one that specifies a launch policy as the first argument and another that does not. The other arguments to std::async() are the function to execute and its arguments, if any. The launch policy is defined by a scoped enumeration called std::launch, available in the <future> header:

```
enum class launch : /* unspecified */
{
  async = /* unspecified */,
  deferred = /* unspecified */,
  /* implementation-defined */
};
```

The two available launch policies specify the following:

- With async, a new thread is launched to execute the task asynchronously.
- With deferred, the task is executed on the calling thread the first time its result is requested.

When both flags are specified (std::launch::async | std::launch::deferred), it is an implementation decision regarding whether to run the task asynchronously on a new thread or synchronously on the current thread. This is the behavior of the std::async() overload; it does not specify a launch policy. This behavior is not deterministic.

Do not use the non-deterministic overload of std::async() to run tasks asynchronously. For this purpose, always use the overload that requires a launch policy, and always use only std::launch::async.

Both overloads of `std::async()` return a `future` object that refers to the shared state created internally by `std::async()` for the promise-future channel it establishes. When you need the result of the asynchronous operation, call the `get()` method on the future. This blocks the current thread until either the result value or an exception is made available. If the future does not transport any value or if you are not actually interested in that value, but you want to make sure the asynchronous operation would be completed at some point, use the `wait()` method; it blocks the current thread until the shared state is made available through the future.

The future class has two more waiting methods: `wait_for()` specifies a duration after which the call ends and returns even if the shared state is not yet available through the future, while `wait_until()` specifies a time point after which the call returns, even if the shared state is not yet available. These methods could be used to create a polling routine and display a status message to the user, as shown in the following example:

```
auto f = std::async(std::launch::async, do_something);

while(true)
{
  using namespace std::chrono_literals;
  auto status = f.wait_for(500ms);

  if(status == std::future_status::ready)
    break;

  std::cout << "waiting..." << '\n';
}

std::cout << "done!" << '\n';
```

The result of running this program is as follows:

```
waiting...
waiting...
waiting...
operation 1 done
done!
```

See also

- *Using promises and futures to return values from threads*, to learn how to use an `std::promise` object to return a value or an exception from a thread.

Using atomic types

The thread support library offers functionalities for managing threads and synchronizing access to shared data with mutexes and locks, and, as of C++20, with latches, barriers, and semaphores. The standard library provides support for the complementary, lower-level atomic operations on data, which are indivisible operations that can be executed concurrently from different threads on shared data, without the risk of producing race conditions and without the use of locks. The support it provides includes atomic types, atomic operations, and memory synchronization ordering. In this recipe, we will see how to use some of these types and functions.

Getting ready

All the atomic types and operations are defined in the `std` namespace in the `<atomic>` header.

How to do it...

The following are a series of typical operations that use atomic types:

- Use the `std::atomic` class template to create atomic objects that support atomic operations, such as loading, storing, or performing arithmetic or bitwise operations:

```
std::atomic<int> counter {0};

std::vector<std::thread> threads;
for(int i = 0; i < 10; ++i)
{
  threads.emplace_back([&counter](){
    for(int i = 0; i < 10; ++i)
      ++counter;
    });
}
```

```
for(auto & t : threads) t.join();

std::cout << counter << '\n'; // prints 100
```

- In C++20, use the `std::atomic_ref` class template to apply atomic operations to a referenced object, which can be a reference or pointer to an integral type, a floating-point type, or a user-defined type:

```
void do_count(int& c)
{
  std::atomic_ref<int> counter{ c };

  std::vector<std::thread> threads;
  for (int i = 0; i < 10; ++i)
  {
    threads.emplace_back([&counter]() {
      for (int i = 0; i < 10; ++i)
        ++counter;
      });
  }

  for (auto& t : threads) t.join();
}

int main()
{
  int c = 0;
  do_count(c);
  std::cout << c << '\n'; // prints 100
}
```

- Use the `std::atomic_flag` class for an atomic Boolean type:

```
std::atomic_flag lock = ATOMIC_FLAG_INIT;
int counter = 0;
std::vector<std::thread> threads;

for(int i = 0; i < 10; ++i)
{
  threads.emplace_back([&](){
    while(lock.test_and_set(std::memory_order_acquire));
      ++counter;
      lock.clear(std::memory_order_release);
  });
```

```
}

for(auto & t : threads) t.join();

std::cout << counter << '\n'; // prints 10
```

- Use the atomic type's members - `load()`, `store()`, and `exchange()` - or non-member functions - `atomic_load()`/`atomic_load_explicit()`, `atomic_store()`/`atomic_store_explicit()`, and `atomic_exchange()`/`atomic_exchange_explicit()` - to atomically read, set, or exchange the value of an atomic object.
- Use its member functions `fetch_add()` and `fetch_sub()` or non-member functions `atomic_fetch_add()`/`atomic_fetch_add_explicit()` and `atomic_fetch_sub()`/`atomic_fetch_sub_explicit()` to atomically add or subtract a value to/from an atomic object and return its value before the operation:

```
std::atomic<int> sum {0};
std::vector<int> numbers = generate_random();
size_t size = numbers.size();
std::vector<std::thread> threads;

for(int i = 0; i < 10; ++i)
{
  threads.emplace_back([&sum, &numbers](size_t const start,
                                        size_t const end) {
  for(size_t i = start; i < end; ++i)
  {
    std::atomic_fetch_add_explicit(
      &sum, numbers[i],
      std::memory_order_acquire);

    // same as
    // sum.fetch_add(numbers[i], std::memory_order_acquire);
  }},
  i*(size/10),
  (i+1)*(size/10));
}

for(auto & t : threads) t.join();
```

- Use its member functions `fetch_and()`, `fetch_or()`, and `fetch_xor()` or non-member functions `atomic_fetch_and()`/`atomic_fetch_and_explicit()`, `atomic_fetch_or()`/ `atomic_fetch_or_explicit()`, and `atomic_fetch_xor()`/ `atomic_fetch_xor_explicit()` to perform AND, OR, and XOR atomic operations, respectively, with the specified argument and return the value of the atomic object before the operation.
- Use the `std::atomic_flag` member functions `test_and_set()` and `clear()` or non-member functions `atomic_flag_test_and_set()`/`atomic_flag_test_and_set_explicit()` and `atomic_flag_clear()`/`atomic_flag_clear_explicit()` to set or reset an atomic flag. In addition, in C++20, you can use the member function `test()` and the non-member function `atomic_flag_test()`/`atomic_flag_test_explicit()` to atomically return the value of the flag.
- In C++20, perform thread synchronization with member functions `wait()`, `notify_one()`, and `notify_all()`, available to `std::atomic`, `std::atomic_ref`, and `std::atomic_flag`, as well as the non-member functions `atomic_wait()`/ `atomic_wait_explicit()`, `atomic_notify_one()`, and `atomic_notify_all()`. These functions provide a more efficient mechanism for waiting for the value of an atomic object to change than polling.

How it works...

`std::atomic` is a class template that defines (including its specializations) an atomic type. The behavior of an object of an atomic type is well defined when one thread writes to the object and the other reads data, without using locks to protect access. The `std::atomic` class provides several specializations:

- Full specialization for `bool`, with a typedef called `atomic_bool`.
- Full specialization for all integral types, with typedefs called `atomic_int`, `atomic_long`, `atomic_char`, `atomic_wchar`, and many others.
- Partial specialization for pointer types.
- In C++20, full specializations for the floating-point types `float`, `double`, and `long double`.
- In C++20, partial specializations such as `std::atomic<std::shared_ptr<U>>` for `std::shared_ptr` and `std::atomic<std::weak_ptr<U>>` for `std::weak_ptr`.

The `atomic` class template has various member functions that perform atomic operations, such as the following:

- `load()` to atomically load and return the value of the object.

- `store()` to atomically store a non-atomic value in the object; this function does not return anything.
- `exchange()` to atomically store a non-atomic value in the object and return the previous value.
- `operator=`, which has the same effect as `store(arg)`.
- `fetch_add()` to atomically add a non-atomic argument to the atomic value and return the value stored previously.
- `fetch_sub()` to atomically subtract a non-atomic argument from the atomic value and return the value stored previously.
- `fetch_and()`, `fetch_or()`, and `fetch_xor()` to atomically perform a bitwise AND, OR, or XOR operation between the argument and the atomic value; store the new value in the atomic object; and return the previous value.
- Prefixing and postfixing `operator++` and `operator--` to atomically increment and decrement the value of the atomic object with 1. These operations are equivalent to using `fetch_add()` or `fetch_sub()`.
- `operator +=`, `-=`, `&=`, `|=`, and `^=` to add, subtract, or perform bitwise AND, OR, or XOR operations between the argument and the atomic value and store the new value in the atomic object. These operations are equivalent to using `fetch_add()`, `fetch_sub()`, `fetch_and()`, `fetch_or()`, and `fetch_xor()`.

Consider you have an atomic variable, such as `std::atomic<int> a`; the following is not an atomic operation:

```
a = a + 42;
```

This involves a series of operations, some of which are atomic:

- Atomically load the value of the atomic object
- Add 42 to the value that was loaded
- Atomically store the result in the atomic object `a`

On the other hand, the following operation, which uses the member operator `+=`, is atomic:

```
a += 42;
```

This operation has the same effect as either of the following:

```
a.fetch_add(42);               // using member function
std::atomic_fetch_add(&a, 42); // using non-member function
```

Though `std::atomic` has a full specialization for the `bool` type, called `std::atomic<bool>`, the standard defines yet another atomic type called `std::atomic_flag`, which is guaranteed to be lock-free. This atomic type, however, is very different than `std::atomic_bool`, and it has only the following member functions:

- `test_and_set()` atomically sets the value to `true` and returns the previous value.
- `clear()` atomically sets the value to `false`.
- In C++20, there's `test()`, which atomically returns the value of the flag.

Prior to C++20, the only way to initialize an `std::atomic_flag` to a definite value was by using the `ATOMIC_FLAG_INIT` macro. This initializes the atomic flag to the clear (`false`) value:

```
std::atomic_flag lock = ATOMIC_FLAG_INIT;
```

In C++20, this macro has been deprecated because the default constructor of `std::atomic_flag` initializes it to the clear state.

All member functions mentioned earlier, for both `std::atomic` and `std::atomic_flag`, have non-member equivalents that are prefixed with `atomic_` or `atomic_flag_`, depending on the type they refer to. For instance, the equivalent of `std::atomic::fetch_add()` is `std::atomic_fetch_add()`, and the first argument of these non-member functions is always a pointer to an `std::atomic` object. Internally, the non-member function calls the equivalent member function on the provided `std::atomic` argument. Similarly, the equivalent of `std::atomic_flag::test_and_set()` is `std::atomic_flag_test_and_set()`, and its first parameter is a pointer to an `std::atomic_flag` object.

All these member functions of `std::atomic` and `std::atomic_flag` have two sets of overloads; one of them has an extra argument representing a memory order. Similarly, all non-member functions – such as `std::atomic_load()`, `std::atomic_fetch_add()`, and `std::atomic_flag_test_and_set()` – have a companion with the suffix `_explicit` – `std::atomic_load_explicit()`, `std::atomic_fetch_add_explicit()`, and `std::atomic_flag_test_and_set_explicit()`; these functions have an extra argument that represents the memory order.

The memory order specifies how non-atomic memory accesses are to be ordered around atomic operations. By default, the memory order of all atomic types and operations is *sequential consistency*.

Additional ordering types are defined in the `std::memory_order` enumeration and can be passed as an argument to the member functions of `std::atomic` and `std::atomic_flag`, or the non-member functions with the suffix `_explicit()`.

Sequential consistency is a consistency model that requires that, in a multiprocessor system, all instructions are executed in some order and all writes become instantly visible throughout the system. This model was first proposed by Leslie Lamport in the 70s, and is described as follows:

"the results of any execution is the same as if the operations of all the processors were executed in some sequential order, and the operations of each individual processor appear in this sequence in the order specified by its program."

Various types of memory ordering functions are described in the following table, taken from the C++ reference website (`http://en.cppreference.com/w/cpp/atomic/memory_order`). The details of how each one of these works is beyond the scope of this book and can be looked up in the standard C++ reference (see the link we just came across):

Model	**Explanation**
`memory_order_relaxed`	This is a relaxed operation. There are no synchronization or ordering constraints; only atomicity is required from this operation.
`memory_order_consume`	A load operation with this memory order performs a consume operation on the affected memory location; no reads or writes in the current thread that are dependent on the value currently loaded can be reordered before this load operation. Writes to data-dependent variables in other threads that release the same atomic variable are visible in the current thread. On most platforms, this affects compiler optimizations only.
`memory_order_acquire`	A load operation with this memory order performs the acquire operation on the affected memory location; no reads or writes in the current thread can be reordered before this load. All writes in other threads that release the same atomic variable are visible in the current thread.

`memory_order_release`	A store operation with this memory order performs the release operation; no reads or writes in the current thread can be reordered after this store. All writes in the current thread are visible in other threads that acquire the same atomic variable, and writes that carry a dependency to the atomic variable become visible in other threads that consume the same atomic.
`memory_order_acq_rel`	A read-modify-write operation with this memory order is both an acquire operation and a release operation. No memory reads or writes in the current thread can be reordered before or after this store. All writes in other threads that release the same atomic variable are visible before the modification, and the modification is visible in other threads that acquire the same atomic variable.
`memory_order_seq_cst`	Any operation with this memory order is both an acquire operation and a release operation; a single total order exists in which all threads observe all modifications in the same order.

The first example in the *How to do it...* section shows several threads repeatedly modifying a shared resource - a counter - by incrementing it concurrently. This example can be refined further by implementing a class to represent an atomic counter with methods such as `increment()` and `decrement()`, which modify the value of the counter, and `get()`, which retrieves its current value:

```
template <typename T,
          typename I =
            typename std::enable_if<std::is_integral_v<T>>::type>
class atomic_counter
{
  std::atomic<T> counter {0};
public:
  T increment()
  {
    return counter.fetch_add(1);
  }

  T decrement()
  {
    return counter.fetch_sub(1);
  }

  T get()
  {
    return counter.load();
```

```
   }
};
```

With this class template, the first example can be rewritten in the following form with the same result:

```
atomic_counter<int> counter;

std::vector<std::thread> threads;
for(int i = 0; i < 10; ++i)
{
   threads.emplace_back([&counter](){
      for(int i = 0; i < 10; ++i)
         counter.increment();
      });
   }

for(auto & t : threads) t.join();

std::cout << counter.get() << '\n'; // prints 100
```

If you need to perform atomic operations to references, you cannot use `std::atomic`. However, in C++20, you can use the new `std::atomic_ref` type. This is a class template that applies atomic operations to the object it references. This object must outlive the `std::atomic_ref` object and, as long as any `std::atomic_ref` instance referencing this object exists, the object must be accessed only through the `std::atomic_ref` instances.

The `std::atomic_ref` type has the following specializations:

- The primary template that can be instantiated with any trivially-copyable type `T`, including `bool`.
- Partial specialization for all pointer types.
- Specializations for integral types (character types, signed and unsigned integer types, and any additional integral types needed by the typedefs in the `<cstdint>` header).
- Specializations for the floating-point types `float`, `double`, and `long double`.

When using `std::atomic_ref`, you must keep in mind that:

- It is not thread-safe to access any sub-object of the object referenced by an `std::atomic_ref`.
- It is possible to modify the referenced value through a const `std::atomic_ref` object.

Also, in C++20, there are new member and non-member functions that provide an efficient thread-synchronization mechanism:

- The member function `wait()` and non-member functions `atomic_wait()`/`atomic_wait_explicit()` and `atomic_flag_wait()`/`atomic_flag_wait_explicit()` perform atomic wait operations, blocking a thread until notified and the atomic value changes. Its behavior is similar to repeatedly comparing the provided argument with the value returned by `load()` and, if equal, blocks until notified by `notify_one()` or `notify_all()`, or the thread is unblocked spuriously. If the compared values are not equal, then the function returns without blocking.
- The member function `notify_one()` and non-member functions `atomic_notify_one()` and `atomic_flag_notify_one()` notify, atomically, at least one thread blocked in an atomic waiting operation. If there is no such thread blocked, the function does nothing.
- The member function `notify_all()` and the non-member functions `atomic_notify_all()` and `atomic_flag_notify_all()` unblock all the threads blocked in an atomic waiting operation, or do nothing if no such thread exists.

Finally, it should be mentioned that all the atomic objects from the atomic operations library – `std::atomic`, `std::atomic_ref`, and `std::atomic_flag` – are free of data races.

See also

- *Working with threads*, to learn about the `std::thread` class and the basic operations for working with threads in C++.
- *Synchronizing access to shared data with mutexes and locks*, to see what mechanisms are available for synchronizing thread access to shared data and how they work.
- *Executing functions asynchronously*, to learn how to use the `std::future` class and the `std::async()` function to execute functions asynchronously on different threads and communicate the result back.

Implementing parallel map and fold with threads

In *Chapter 3*, *Exploring Functions*, we discussed two higher-order functions: `map`, which applies a function to the elements of a range by either transforming the range or producing a new range, and `fold`, which combines the elements of a range into a single value. The various implementations we did were sequential. However, in the context of concurrency, threads, and asynchronous tasks, we can leverage the hardware and run parallel versions of these functions to speed up their execution for large ranges, or when the transformation and aggregation are time-consuming. In this recipe, we will see a possible solution for implementing `map` and `fold` using threads.

Getting ready

You need to be familiar with the concepts of the `map` and `fold` functions. It is recommended that you read the *Implementing higher-order functions map and fold* recipe from *Chapter 3*, *Exploring Functions*. In this recipe, we will use the various thread functionalities presented in the *Working with threads* recipe.

To measure the execution time of these functions and compare it with sequential alternatives, we will use the `perf_timer` class template, which we introduced in the *Measuring function execution time with a standard clock* recipe in *Chapter 6*, *General-Purpose Utilities*.

A parallel version of an algorithm can potentially speed up execution time, but this is not necessarily true in all circumstances. Context switching for threads and synchronized access to shared data can introduce a significant overhead. For some implementations and particular datasets, this overhead could make a parallel version actually take a longer time to execute than a sequential version.

To determine the number of threads required to split the work, we will use the following function:

```
unsigned get_no_of_threads()
{
  return std::thread::hardware_concurrency();
}
```

We'll explore a first possible implementation for a parallel version of the `map` and `fold` functions in the next section.

How to do it...

To implement a parallel version of the `map` function, do the following:

1. Define a function template that takes the `begin` and `end` iterators to a range and a function to apply to all the elements:

```
template <typename Iter, typename F>
void parallel_map(Iter begin, Iter end, F f)
{
}
```

2. Check the size of the range. If the number of elements is smaller than a predefined threshold (for this implementation, the threshold is 10,000), execute the mapping in a sequential manner:

```
auto size = std::distance(begin, end);
if(size <= 10000)
  std::transform(begin, end, begin, std::forward<F>(f));
```

3. For larger ranges, split the work on multiple threads and let each thread map be a part of the range. These parts should not overlap to avoid the need of synchronizing access to the shared data:

```
else
{
  auto no_of_threads = get_no_of_threads();
  auto part = size / no_of_threads;
  auto last = begin;
  // continued at 4. and 5.
}
```

4. Start the threads, and on each thread, run a sequential version of the mapping:

```
std::vector<std::thread> threads;
for(unsigned i = 0; i < no_of_threads; ++i)
{
  if(i == no_of_threads - 1) last = end;
  else std::advance(last, part);

  threads.emplace_back(
    [=,&f]{std::transform(begin, last,
```

```
                                   begin, std::forward<F>(f));});
      begin = last;
   }
```

5. Wait until all the threads have finished their execution:

```
   for(auto & t : threads) t.join();
```

The preceding steps, when put together, result in the following implementation:

```
template <typename Iter, typename F>
void parallel_map(Iter begin, Iter end, F f)
{
  auto size = std::distance(begin, end);
  if(size <= 10000)
    std::transform(begin, end, begin, std::forward<F>(f));
  else
  {
    auto no_of_threads = get_no_of_threads();
    auto part = size / no_of_threads;
    auto last = begin;

    std::vector<std::thread> threads;
    for(unsigned i = 0; i < no_of_threads; ++i)
    {
      if(i == no_of_threads - 1) last = end;
      else std::advance(last, part);

      threads.emplace_back(
        [=,&f]{std::transform(begin, last,
                              begin, std::forward<F>(f));});

      begin = last;
    }

    for(auto & t : threads) t.join();
  }
}
```

To implement a parallel version of the left `fold` function, do the following:

1. Define a function template that takes a `begin` and an `end` iterator to a range, an initial value, and a binary function to apply to the elements of the range:

```
template <typename Iter, typename R, typename F>
auto parallel_reduce(Iter begin, Iter end, R init, F op)
{
}
```

2. Check the size of the range. If the number of elements is smaller than a predefined threshold (for this implementation, it is 10,000), execute the folding in a sequential manner:

```
auto size = std::distance(begin, end);
if(size <= 10000)
  return std::accumulate(begin, end,
                         init, std::forward<F>(op));
```

3. For larger ranges, split the work into multiple threads and let each thread fold a part of the range. These parts should not overlap in order to avoid thread synchronization of shared data. The result can be returned through a reference passed to the thread function in order to avoid data synchronization:

```
else
{
  auto no_of_threads = get_no_of_threads();
  auto part = size / no_of_threads;
  auto last = begin;
  // continued with 4. and 5.
}
```

4. Start the threads, and on each thread, execute a sequential version of the folding:

```
std::vector<std::thread> threads;
std::vector<R> values(no_of_threads);
for(unsigned i = 0; i < no_of_threads; ++i)
{
  if(i == no_of_threads - 1) last = end;
  else std::advance(last, part);

  threads.emplace_back(
    [=,&op](R& result){
      result = std::accumulate(begin, last, R{},
                         std::forward<F>(op));},
    std::ref(values[i]));
  begin = last;
}
```

5. Wait until all the threads have finished execution and fold the partial results into the final result:

```
for(auto & t : threads) t.join();

return std::accumulate(std::begin(values), std::end(values),
                       init, std::forward<F>(op));
```

The steps we just put together result in the following implementation:

```
template <typename Iter, typename R, typename F>
auto parallel_reduce(Iter begin, Iter end, R init, F op)
{
  auto size = std::distance(begin, end);

  if(size <= 10000)
    return std::accumulate(begin, end, init, std::forward<F>(op));
  else
  {
    auto no_of_threads = get_no_of_threads();
    auto part = size / no_of_threads;
    auto last = begin;

    std::vector<std::thread> threads;
    std::vector<R> values(no_of_threads);
    for(unsigned i = 0; i < no_of_threads; ++i)
    {
      if(i == no_of_threads - 1) last = end;
      else std::advance(last, part);

      threads.emplace_back(
        [=,&op](R& result){
          result = std::accumulate(begin, last, R{},
                                   std::forward<F>(op));},
        std::ref(values[i]));

      begin = last;
    }

    for(auto & t : threads) t.join();
```

```
        return std::accumulate(std::begin(values), std::end(values),
                               init, std::forward<F>(op));
    }
}
```

How it works...

These parallel implementations of `map` and `fold` are similar in several aspects:

- They both fall back to a sequential version if the number of elements in the range is smaller than 10,000.
- They both start the same number of threads. These threads are determined using the static function `std::thread::hardware_concurrency()`, which returns the number of concurrent threads supported by the implementation. However, this value is rather a hint than an accurate value and should be used with that in mind.
- No shared data is used to avoid synchronization of access. Even though all the threads work on the elements from the same range, they all process parts of the range that do not overlap.
- Both these functions are implemented as function templates that take a begin and an end iterator to define the range to be processed. In order to split the range into multiple parts to be processed independently by different threads, use additional iterators in the middle of the range. For this, we use `std::advance()` to increment an iterator with a particular number of positions. This works well for vectors or arrays but is very inefficient for containers such as lists. Therefore, this implementation is suited only for ranges that have random access iterators.

The sequential versions of `map` and `fold` can be simply implemented in C++ with `std::transform()` and `std::accumulate()`. In fact, to verify the correctness of the parallel algorithms and check whether they provide any execution speedup, we can compare them with the execution of these general-purpose algorithms.

To put this to the test, we will use `map` and `fold` on a vector with sizes varying from 10,000 to 50 million elements. The range is first mapped (that is, transformed) by doubling the value of each element, and then the result is folded into a single value by adding together all the elements of the range. For simplicity, each element in the range is equal to its 1-based index (the first element is 1, the second element is 2, and so on). The following sample runs both the sequential and parallel versions of `map` and `fold` on vectors of different sizes and prints the execution time in a tabular format:

As an exercise, you can vary the number of elements, as well as the number of threads, and see how the parallel version performs compared to the sequential version.

```
std::vector<int> sizes
{
  10000, 100000, 500000,
  1000000, 2000000, 5000000,
  10000000, 25000000, 50000000
};

std::cout
  << std::right << std::setw(8) << std::setfill(' ') << "size"
  << std::right << std::setw(8) << "s map"
  << std::right << std::setw(8) << "p map"
  << std::right << std::setw(8) << "s fold"
  << std::right << std::setw(8) << "p fold"
  << '\n';

for (auto const size : sizes)
{
  std::vector<int> v(size);
  std::iota(std::begin(v), std::end(v), 1);

  auto v1 = v;
  auto s1 = 0LL;

  auto tsm = perf_timer<>::duration([&] {
    std::transform(std::begin(v1), std::end(v1), std::begin(v1),
                   [](int const i) {return i + i; }); });
  auto tsf = perf_timer<>::duration([&] {
    s1 = std::accumulate(std::begin(v1), std::end(v1), 0LL,
                         std::plus<>()); });

  auto v2 = v;
  auto s2 = 0LL;
  auto tpm = perf_timer<>::duration([&] {
    parallel_map(std::begin(v2), std::end(v2),
                 [](int const i) {return i + i; }); });
```

```
  auto tpf = perf_timer<>::duration([&] {
    s2 = parallel_reduce(std::begin(v2), std::end(v2), 0LL,
                         std::plus<>()); });

  assert(v1 == v2);
  assert(s1 == s2);

  std::cout
    << std::right << std::setw(8) << std::setfill(' ') << size
    << std::right << std::setw(8)
    << std::chrono::duration<double, std::micro>(tsm).count()
    << std::right << std::setw(8)
    << std::chrono::duration<double, std::micro>(tpm).count()
    << std::right << std::setw(8)
    << std::chrono::duration<double, std::micro>(tsf).count()
    << std::right << std::setw(8)
    << std::chrono::duration<double, std::micro>(tpf).count()
    << '\n';
}
```

A possible output of this program is shown in the following chart (executed on a machine running Windows 64-bit with an Intel Core i7 processor and 4 physical and 8 logical cores). The parallel version, especially the `fold` implementation, performs better than the sequential version. But this is true only when the length of the vector exceeds a certain size. In the following table, we can see that for up to 1 million elements, the sequential version is still faster. The parallel version executes faster when there are 2 million or more elements in the vector. Notice that the actual times vary slightly from one run to another, but they can be very different on different machines:

size	s map	p map	s fold	p fold
10000	11	10	7	10
100000	108	1573	72	710
500000	547	2006	361	862
1000000	1146	1163	749	862
2000000	2503	1527	1677	1289
5000000	5937	3000	4203	2314
10000000	11959	6269	8269	3868
25000000	29872	13823	20961	9156
50000000	60049	27457	41374	19075

To better visualize these results, we can represent the speedup of the parallel version in the form of a bar chart. In the following chart, the blue bars represent the speedup of a parallel `map` implementation, while the orange bars show the speedup of the parallel `fold` implementation. A positive value indicates that the parallel version is faster; a negative version indicates that the sequential version is faster:

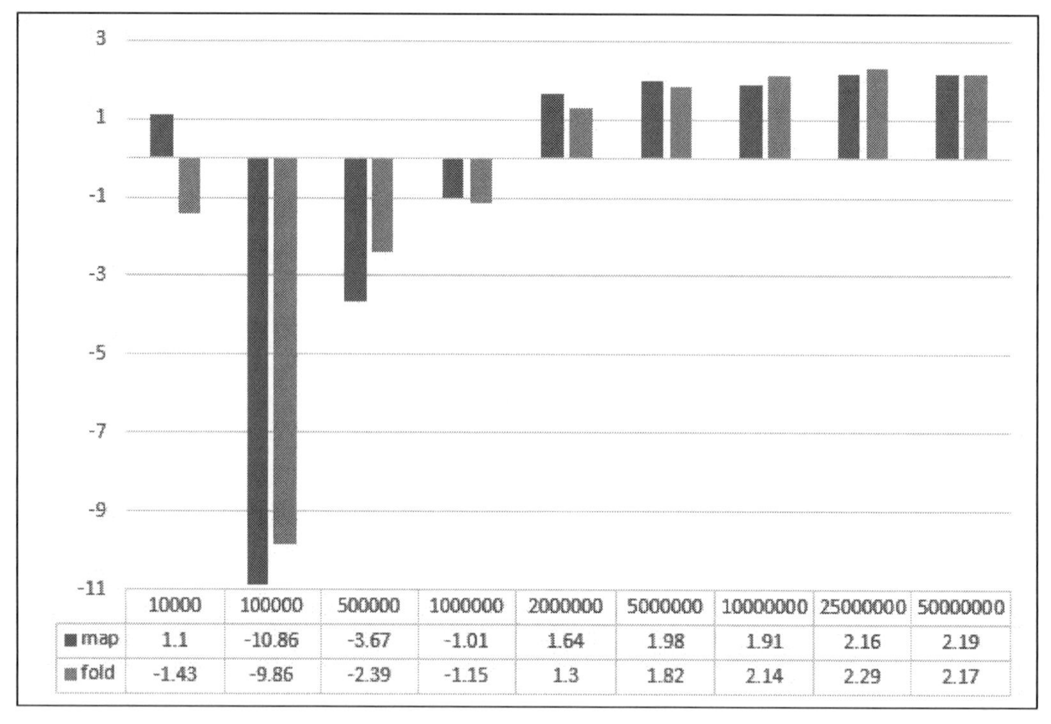

	10000	100000	500000	1000000	2000000	5000000	10000000	25000000	50000000
map	1.1	-10.86	-3.67	-1.01	1.64	1.98	1.91	2.16	2.19
fold	-1.43	-9.86	-2.39	-1.15	1.3	1.82	2.14	2.29	2.17

Figure 8.1: The speedup of the parallel implementation for map (in blue) and fold (in orange) for various processed elements

This chart makes it easier to see that only when the number of elements exceeds a certain threshold (which is about 2 million in my benchmarks) is the parallel implementation faster than the sequential version.

See also

- *Implementing higher-order functions map and fold*, in *Chapter 3, Exploring Functions*, to learn about higher-order functions in functional programming and see how to implement the widely used `map` and `fold` (or reduce) functions.
- *Implementing parallel map and fold with tasks*, to see how to implement the `map` and `fold` functions from functional programming using asynchronous functions.

- *Implementing parallel map and fold with standard parallel algorithms*, to see how to implement the `map` and `fold` functions from functional programming using parallel algorithms from C++17.
- *Working with threads*, to learn about the `std::thread` class and the basic operations for working with threads in C++.

Implementing parallel map and fold with tasks

Tasks are a higher-level alternative to threads for performing concurrent computations. `std::async()` enables us to execute functions asynchronously, without the need to handle lower-level threading details. In this recipe, we will take the same task of implementing a parallel version of the `map` and `fold` functions, as in the previous recipe, but we will use tasks and see how it compares with the thread version.

Getting ready

The solution presented in this recipe is similar in many aspects to the one that uses threads in the previous recipe, *Implementing parallel map and fold with threads*. Make sure you read that one before continuing with the current recipe.

How to do it...

To implement a parallel version of the `map` function, do the following:

1. Define a function template that takes a begin and end iterator to a range, and a function to apply to all the elements:

   ```
   template <typename Iter, typename F>
   void parallel_map(Iter begin, Iter end, F f)
   {
   }
   ```

2. Check the size of the range. For a number of elements smaller than the predefined threshold (for this implementation, the threshold is 10,000), execute the mapping in a sequential manner:

   ```
   auto size = std::distance(begin, end);
   if(size <= 10000)
     std::transform(begin, end, begin, std::forward<F>(f));
   ```

3. For larger ranges, split the work into multiple tasks and let each task map a part of the range. These parts should not overlap to avoid synchronizing thread access to shared data:

   ```
   else
   {
     auto no_of_tasks = get_no_of_threads();
     auto part = size / no_of_tasks;
     auto last = begin;
     // continued at 4. and 5.
   }
   ```

4. Start the asynchronous functions and run a sequential version of the mapping on each one of them:

   ```
   std::vector<std::future<void>> tasks;
   for(unsigned i = 0; i < no_of_tasks; ++i)
   {
     if(i == no_of_tasks - 1) last = end;
     else std::advance(last, part);

     tasks.emplace_back(std::async(
       std::launch::async,
         [=,&f]{std::transform(begin, last, begin,
                               std::forward<F>(f));}));
       begin = last;
   }
   ```

5. Wait until all the asynchronous functions have finished their execution:

   ```
   for(auto & t : tasks) t.wait();
   ```

These steps, when put together, result in the following implementation:

```
template <typename Iter, typename F>
void parallel_map(Iter begin, Iter end, F f)
{
  auto size = std::distance(begin, end);
  if(size <= 10000)
    std::transform(begin, end, begin, std::forward<F>(f));
  else
  {
    auto no_of_tasks = get_no_of_threads();
    auto part = size / no_of_tasks;
    auto last = begin;
```

```
    std::vector<std::future<void>> tasks;
    for(unsigned i = 0; i < no_of_tasks; ++i)
    {
      if(i == no_of_tasks - 1) last = end;
      else std::advance(last, part);

      tasks.emplace_back(std::async(
        std::launch::async,
          [=,&f]{std::transform(begin, last, begin,
                                std::forward<F>(f));}));

      begin = last;
    }

    for(auto & t : tasks) t.wait();
  }
}
```

To implement a parallel version of the left `fold` function, do the following:

1. Define a function template that takes a begin and end iterator to a range, an initial value, and a binary function to apply to the elements of the range:

   ```
   template <typename Iter, typename R, typename F>
   auto parallel_reduce(Iter begin, Iter end, R init, F op)
   {
   }
   ```

2. Check the size of the range. For a number of elements smaller than the predefined threshold (for this implementation, the threshold is 10,000), execute the folding in a sequential manner:

   ```
   auto size = std::distance(begin, end);
   if(size <= 10000)
     return std::accumulate(begin, end, init,
                            std::forward<F>(op));
   ```

3. For larger ranges, split the work into multiple tasks and let each task fold a part of the range. These parts should not overlap to avoid synchronizing thread access to the shared data. The result can be returned through a reference passed to the asynchronous function to avoid synchronization:

   ```
   else
   {
   ```

```
    auto no_of_tasks = get_no_of_threads();
    auto part = size / no_of_tasks;
    auto last = begin;
    // continued at 4. and 5.
  }
```

4. Start the asynchronous functions and execute a sequential version of folding on each one of them:

```
std::vector<std::future<R>> tasks;
for(unsigned i = 0; i < no_of_tasks; ++i)
{
  if(i == no_of_tasks - 1) last = end;
  else std::advance(last, part);

  tasks.emplace_back(
    std::async(
      std::launch::async,
      [=,&op]{return std::accumulate(
                        begin, last, R{},
                        std::forward<F>(op));}));
  begin = last;
}
```

5. Wait until all the asynchronous functions have finished execution and fold the partial results into the final result:

```
std::vector<R> values;
for(auto & t : tasks)
  values.push_back(t.get());

return std::accumulate(std::begin(values), std::end(values),
                       init, std::forward<F>(op));
```

These steps, when put together, result in the following implementation:

```
template <typename Iter, typename R, typename F>
auto parallel_reduce(Iter begin, Iter end, R init, F op)
{
  auto size = std::distance(begin, end);

  if(size <= 10000)
    return std::accumulate(begin, end, init, std::forward<F>(op));
```

```
    else
    {
      auto no_of_tasks = get_no_of_threads();
      auto part = size / no_of_tasks;
      auto last = begin;

      std::vector<std::future<R>> tasks;
      for(unsigned i = 0; i < no_of_tasks; ++i)
      {
        if(i == no_of_tasks - 1) last = end;
        else std::advance(last, part);

        tasks.emplace_back(
          std::async(
            std::launch::async,
            [=,&op]{return std::accumulate(
                              begin, last, R{},
                              std::forward<F>(op));}));

        begin = last;
      }

      std::vector<R> values;
      for(auto & t : tasks)
        values.push_back(t.get());

      return std::accumulate(std::begin(values), std::end(values),
                             init, std::forward<F>(op));
    }
  }
```

How it works...

The implementation just proposed is only slightly different than what we did in the previous recipe. Threads were replaced with asynchronous functions, starting with `std::async()`, and results were made available through the returned `std::future`. The number of asynchronous functions that are launched concurrently is equal to the number of threads the implementation can support. This is returned by the static method `std::thread::hardware_concurrency()`, but this value is only a hint and should not be considered very reliable.

There are mainly two reasons for taking this approach:

- Seeing how a function implemented for parallel execution with threads can be modified to use asynchronous functions and, therefore, avoid lower-level details of threading.
- Running a number of asynchronous functions equal to the number of supported threads can potentially run one function per thread; this could provide the fastest execution time for the parallel function because there is a minimum overhead of context switching and waiting time.

We can test the performance of the new `map` and `fold` implementations using the same method as in the previous recipe:

```
std::vector<int> sizes
{
  10000, 100000, 500000,
  1000000, 2000000, 5000000,
  10000000, 25000000, 50000000
};

std::cout
  << std::right << std::setw(8) << std::setfill(' ') << "size"
  << std::right << std::setw(8) << "s map"
  << std::right << std::setw(8) << "p map"
  << std::right << std::setw(8) << "s fold"
  << std::right << std::setw(8) << "p fold"
  << '\n';

for(auto const size : sizes)
{
  std::vector<int> v(size);
  std::iota(std::begin(v), std::end(v), 1);

  auto v1 = v;
  auto s1 = 0LL;

  auto tsm = perf_timer<>::duration([&] {
    std::transform(std::begin(v1), std::end(v1), std::begin(v1),
                   [](int const i) {return i + i; }); });
  auto tsf = perf_timer<>::duration([&] {
    s1 = std::accumulate(std::begin(v1), std::end(v1), 0LL,
                         std::plus<>()); });
```

```
    auto v2 = v;
    auto s2 = 0LL;
    auto tpm = perf_timer<>::duration([&] {
      parallel_map(std::begin(v2), std::end(v2),
                   [](int const i) {return i + i; }); });
    auto tpf = perf_timer<>::duration([&] {
      s2 = parallel_reduce(std::begin(v2), std::end(v2), 0LL,
                           std::plus<>()); });

    assert(v1 == v2);
    assert(s1 == s2);

    std::cout
      << std::right << std::setw(8) << std::setfill(' ') << size
      << std::right << std::setw(8)
      << std::chrono::duration<double, std::micro>(tsm).count()
      << std::right << std::setw(8)
      << std::chrono::duration<double, std::micro>(tpm).count()
      << std::right << std::setw(8)
      << std::chrono::duration<double, std::micro>(tsf).count()
      << std::right << std::setw(8)
      << std::chrono::duration<double, std::micro>(tpf).count()
      << '\n';
  }
```

A possible output of the preceding program, which can vary slightly from one execution to another and greatly from one machine to another, is as follows:

```
    size   s map   p map  s fold  p fold
   10000      11      11      11      11
  100000     117     260     113      94
  500000     576     303     571     201
 1000000    1180     573    1165     283
 2000000    2371     911    2330     519
 5000000    5942    2144    5841    1886
10000000   11954    4999   11643    2871
25000000   30525   11737   29053    9048
50000000   59665   22216   58689   12942
```

Similar to the illustration of the solution with threads, the speedup of the parallel `map` and `fold` implementations can be seen in the following chart.

Negative values indicate that the sequential version was faster:

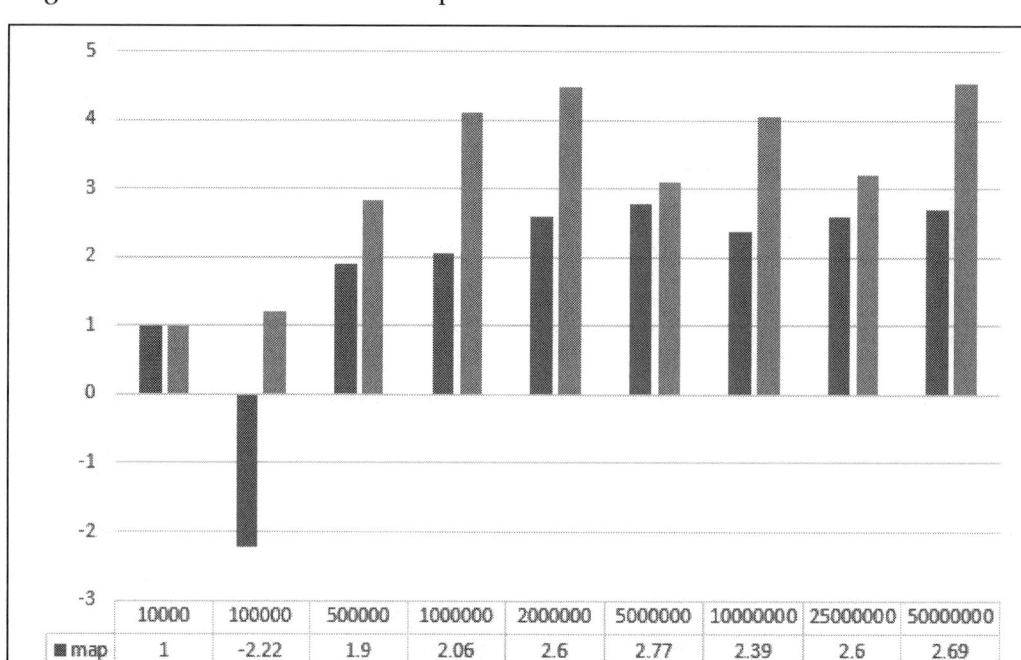

Figure 8.2: The speedup of the parallel implementation of map (in blue) and fold (in orange) using asynchronous functions, compared to the sequential implementation

If we compare this with the results from the parallel version using threads, we will find that these are faster execution times and that the speedup is significant, especially for the `fold` function. The following chart shows the speedup of the task's implementation over the thread's implementation. In this chart, a value smaller than 1 means that the thread's implementation was faster:

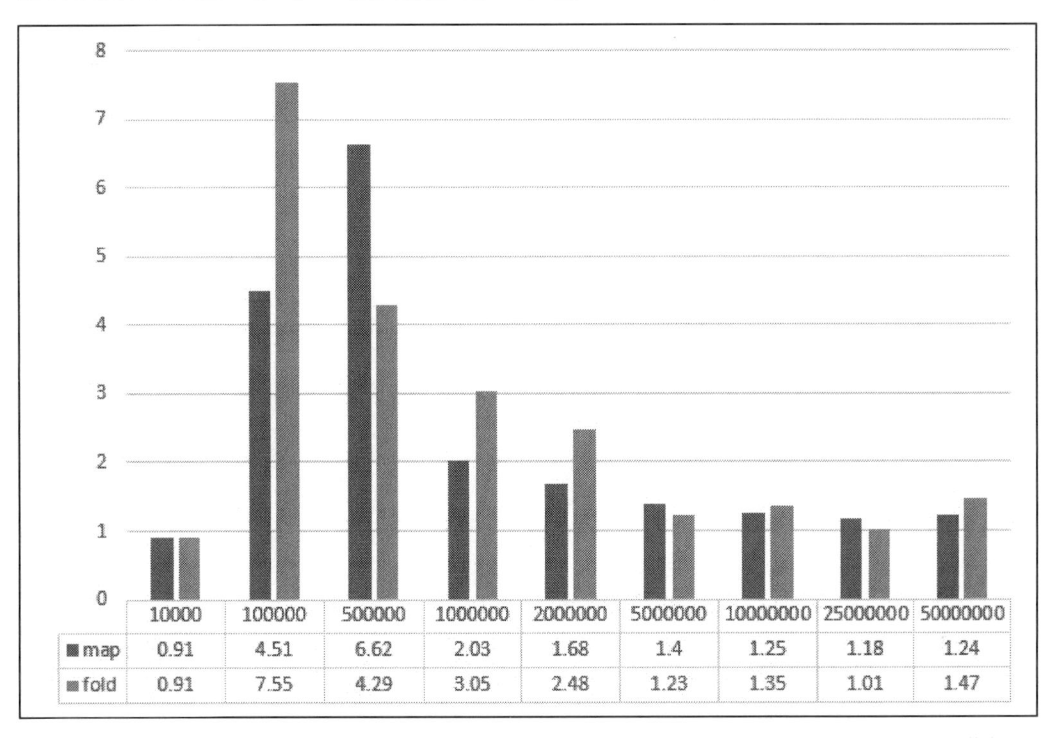

Figure 8.3: The speedup of the parallel implementation using asynchronous functions over the parallel implementation using threads for map (in blue) and fold (in orange)

There's more...

The implementation shown earlier is only one of the possible approaches we can take for parallelizing the `map` and `fold` functions. A possible alternative uses the following strategy:

- Divide the range to process into two equal parts.
- Recursively call the parallel function asynchronously to process the first part of the range.
- Recursively call the parallel function synchronously to process the second part of the range.
- After the synchronous recursive call is finished, wait for the asynchronous recursive call to end too before finishing the execution.

This divide-and-conquer algorithm can potentially create a lot of tasks. Depending on the size of the range, the number of asynchronous calls can greatly exceed the number of threads, and in this case, there will be lots of waiting time that will affect the overall execution time.

The `map` and `fold` functions can be implemented using a divide-and-conquer algorithm, as follows:

```
template <typename Iter, typename F>
void parallel_map(Iter begin, Iter end, F f)
{
  auto size = std::distance(begin, end);

  if(size <= 10000)
  {
    std::transform(begin, end, begin, std::forward<F>(f));
  }
  else
  {
    auto middle = begin;
    std::advance(middle, size / 2);

    auto result = std::async(
      std::launch::deferred,
      parallel_map<Iter, F>,
      begin, middle, std::forward<F>(f));
    parallel_map(middle, end, std::forward<F>(f));
    result.wait();
  }
}

template <typename Iter, typename R, typename F>
auto parallel_reduce(Iter begin, Iter end, R init, F op)
{
  auto size = std::distance(begin, end);

  if(size <= 10000)
    return std::accumulate(begin, end, init, std::forward<F>(op));
```

```
    else
    {
      auto middle = begin;
      std::advance(middle, size / 2);
      auto result1 = std::async(
        std::launch::async,
        parallel_reduce<Iter, R, F>,
        begin, middle, R{}, std::forward<F>(op));
      auto result2 = parallel_reduce(middle, end, init,
                                     std::forward<F>(op));
      return result1.get() + result2;
    }
  }
```

The execution times for this implementation are listed here, next to the ones for the previous implementations:

```
    size   s map p1 map  p2 map  s fold p1 fold p2 fold
   10000      11     11      10       7      10      10
  100000     111    275     120      72      96     426
  500000     551    230     596     365     210    1802
 1000000    1142    381    1209     753     303    2378
 2000000    2411    981    2488    1679     503    4190
 5000000    5962   2191    6237    4177    1969    7974
10000000   11961   4517   12581    8384    2966   15174
```

When we compare these execution times, we can see that this version (indicated by `p2` in the preceding output) is similar to the sequential version for both `map` and `fold` and much worse than the first parallel version shown earlier (indicated by `p1`).

See also

- *Implementing parallel map and fold with threads*, to see how to implement the `map` and `fold` functions from functional programming using raw threads.
- *Implementing parallel map and fold with standard parallel algorithms*, to see how to implement the `map` and `fold` functions from functional programming using parallel algorithms from C++17.
- *Executing functions asynchronously*, to learn how to use the `std::future` class and the `std::async()` function to execute functions asynchronously on different threads and communicate the result back.

Implementing parallel map and fold with standard parallel algorithms

In the previous two recipes, we implemented parallel versions of the map and fold functions (which are called `std::transform()` and `std::accumulate()` in the standard library) using threads and tasks. However, these implementations required manual handling of parallelization details, such as splitting data into chunks to be processed in parallel and creating threads or tasks, synchronizing their execution, and merging the results.

In C++17, many of the standard generic algorithms have been parallelized. In fact, the same algorithm can execute sequentially or in parallel, depending on a provided execution policy. In this recipe, we will learn how to implement `map` and `fold` in parallel with standard algorithms.

Getting ready

Before you continue with this recipe, it is recommended that you read the previous two to make sure you understand the differences between various parallel implementations.

How to do it...

To use the standard algorithms with parallel execution, you should do the following:

- Find a good candidate for an algorithm to parallelize. Not every algorithm runs faster in parallel. Make sure you correctly identify the parts of the program that can be improved with parallelization. Use profilers for this purpose and, in general, look at operations that have *O(n)* or worse complexity.
- Include the header `<execution>` for the execution policies.
- Provide the parallel execution policy (`std::execution::par`) as the first argument to the overloaded algorithm.

A parallel implementation of the map function using the parallel overload of `std::transform()` is as follows:

```
template <typename Iter, typename F>
void parallel_map(Iter begin, Iter end, F f)
{
   std::transform(std::execution::par,
```

```
                begin, end,
                begin,
                std::forward<F>(f));
}
```

A parallel implementation of the fold function using the parallel overload of `std::reduce()` is as follows:

```
template <typename Iter, typename R, typename F>
auto parallel_reduce(Iter begin, Iter end, R init, F op)
{
   return std::reduce(std::execution::par,
                      begin, end,
                      init,
                      std::forward<F>(op));
}
```

How it works...

In C++17, 69 of the standard generic algorithms have been overloaded to support parallel execution. These overloads take an execution policy as the first parameter. The available execution policies, from header `<execution>`, are as follows:

Policy	Since	Description	Global object
`std::execution::sequenced_policy`	C++17	Indicates that the algorithm may not execute in parallel.	`std::execution::seq`
`std::execution::parallel_policy`	C++17	Indicates that the algorithm's execution may be parallelized.	`std::execution::par`
`std::execution::parallel_unsequenced_policy`	C++17	Indicates that the algorithm's execution may be parallelized and vectorized.	`std::execution::par_unseq`
`std::execution::unsequenced_policy`	C++20	Indicates that the algorithm's execution may be vectorized.	`std::execution::unseq`

Apart from the existing algorithms that have been overloaded, seven new algorithms have been added:

Algorithm	Description
`std::for_each_n`	Applies a given function to the first N elements of the specified range, according to the specified execution policy.
`std::exclusive_scan`	Computes the partial sum of a range of elements but excludes the ith element from the ith sum. If the binary operation is associative, the result is the same as when using `std::partial_sum()`.
`std::inclusive_scan`	Computes the partial sum of a range of elements but includes the ith element in the ith sum.
`std::transform_exclusive_scan`	Applies a function and then calculates exclusive scan.
`std::transform_inclusive_scan`	Applies a function and then calculates inclusive scan.
`std::reduce`	An out of order version of `std::accumulate()`.
`std::transform_reduce`	Applies a function then accumulates out of order (that is, reduces).

In the preceding examples, we used `std::transform()` and `std::reduce()` with an execution policy - in our case, `std::execution::par`. The algorithm `std::reduce()` is similar to `std::accumulate()` but it processes the elements out of order. `std::accumulate()` does not have an overload for specifying an execution policy, so it can only execute sequentially.

It is important to note that, just because an algorithm supports parallelization, it doesn't mean that it will run faster than the sequential version. Execution depends on the actual hardware, datasets, and algorithm particularities. In fact, some of these algorithms may never or hardly execute faster when parallelized than sequentially. For this reason, the Microsoft implementation of several algorithms that permute, copy, or move elements does not perform parallelization but falls back to sequential execution in all cases. These algorithms are `copy()`, `copy_n()`, `fill()`, `fill_n()`, `move()`, `reverse()`, `reverse_copy()`, `rotate()`, `rotate_copy()`, and `swap_ranges()`. Moreover, the standard does not guarantee a particular execution; specifying a policy is actually a request for an execution strategy but with no guarantees implied.

On the other hand, the standard library allows parallel algorithms to allocate memory. When this cannot be done, an algorithm throws `std::bad_alloc`. However, again, the Microsoft implementation differs and instead of throwing, it falls back to the sequential version of the algorithm.

Another important aspect that must be known is that the standard algorithms work with different kinds of iterators. Some require forward iterators, some input iterators. However, all the overloads that allow to specify an execution policy restrict the use of the algorithm with forward iterators.

Take a look at the following table:

	Sequential		**Parallel algorithms**		Parallel threads		Parallel tasks	
Size	map	reduce	**map**	**reduce**	map	reduce	map	reduce
1000000	0.505	0.246	0.386	0.121	1.59	0.124	0.211	0.139
2000000	1.931	0.873	0.495	0.298	0.674	0.172	0.344	0.167
3000000	1.729	1.116	0.625	0.433	1.599	0.916	0.829	0.536
4000000	2.601	1.629	1.501	0.833	1.164	0.679	0.872	0.725
5000000	3.425	2.074	1.098	0.933	1.548	1.105	1.18	0.968
10000000	5.844	3.883	2.34	1.844	2.624	2.272	2.778	1.699
20000000	11.382	7.089	4.178	2.737	5.38	2.662	4.868	2.686
50000000	27.613	18.092	10.897	6.656	11.395	7.233	10.683	7.266
100000000	58.794	34.605	22.974	14.23	33.055	15.568	22.039	13.606
200000000	112.375	69.136	45.359	27.793	52.637	26.452	49.786	32.857
500000000	288.385	173.327	115.188	64.106	144.339	73.713	144.517	79.945

Figure 8.4: A comparison of execution times for sequential and parallel implementations of the map and reduce functions

Here, you can see a comparison of execution times for sequential and parallel implementations of the `map` and `reduce` functions. Highlighted are the versions of the functions implemented in this recipe. These times may vary slightly from execution to execution. These values were obtained by running a 64-bit released version compiled with Visual C++ 2019 16.4.x on a machine with an Intel Xeon CPU with four cores. Although the parallel versions perform better than the sequential version for these data sets, which one is actually better varies with the size of the dataset. This is why profiling is key when you optimize by parallelizing work.

There's more...

In this example, we have seen separate implementations for map and fold (which is also called reduce). However, in C++17, there is a standard algorithm called `std::transform_reduce()`, which composes the two operations into a single function call. This algorithm has overloads for sequential execution, as well as policy-based execution for parallelism and vectorization. We can, therefore, utilize this algorithm instead of the handwritten implementation we did in these previous three recipes.

The following are the sequential and parallel versions of the algorithm used to compute the sum of the doubles of all the elements of a range:

```
std::vector<int> v(size);
std::iota(std::begin(v), std::end(v), 1);

// sequential
auto sums = std::transform_reduce(
    std::begin(v), std::end(v),
    0LL,
    std::plus<>(),
    [](int const i) {return i + i; } );

// parallel
auto sump = std::transform_reduce(
    std::execution::par,
    std::begin(v), std::end(v),
    0LL,
    std::plus<>(),
    [](int const i) {return i + i; });
```

If we compare the execution time of these two calls, seen in the following table in the last two columns, with the total time for separately calling `map` and `reduce`, as seen in the other implementations, you can see that `std::transform_reduce()`, especially the parallel version, executes better in most cases:

					sequential	**parallel**
Size	Sequential	Parallel	Threads	Tasks	**transform_reduce**	
1000000	0.751	0.507	1.838	0.489	0.413	0.267
2000000	2.804	0.793	1.018	0.678	0.825	0.582
3000000	2.845	1.058	3.431	1.901	1.325	0.571
4000000	4.23	2.334	2.522	2.322	1.95	0.773
5000000	5.499	2.031	3.758	3.116	2.244	0.926
10000000	9.727	4.184	7.168	6.176	4.418	2.592
20000000	18.471	6.915	10.704	10.24	8.572	3.28
50000000	45.705	17.553	25.861	25.215	21.11	10.963
100000000	93.399	37.204	64.191	49.251	41.824	16.409
200000000	181.511	73.152	105.541	115.5	84.688	35.357
500000000	461.712	179.294	291.765	304.407	312.672	686.231

Figure 8.5: A comparison of execution times for the transform/reduce pattern with a highlight of the times for the std::transform_reduce() standard algorithm from C++17

See also

- *Implementing higher-order functions map and fold*, in *Chapter 3*, *Exploring Functions*, to learn about higher-order functions in functional programming and see how to implement the widely used `map` and `fold` (or reduce) functions.
- *Implementing parallel map and fold with threads*, to see how to implement the `map` and `fold` functions from functional programming using raw threads.
- *Implementing parallel map and fold with tasks*, to see how to implement the `map` and `fold` functions from functional programming using asynchronous functions.

Using joinable threads and cancellation mechanisms

The C++11 class `std::thread` represents a single thread of execution and allows multiple functions to execute concurrently. However, it has a major inconvenience: you must explicitly invoke the `join()` method to wait for the thread to finish execution. This can lead to problems because if an `std::thread` object is destroyed while it is still joinable, and then `std::terminate()` is called. C++20 provides an improved thread class called `std::jthread` (from *joinable thread*) that automatically calls `join()` if the thread is still joinable when the object is destroyed. Moreover, this type supports cancellation through `std::stop_source`/`std::stop_token` and its destructor also requests the thread to stop before joining. In this recipe, you will learn how to use these new C++20 types.

Getting ready

Before you continue with this, you should read the first recipe of this chapter, *Working with threads*, to make sure you are familiar with `std::thread`. To use `std::jthread`, you need to include the same `<thread>` header. For `std::stop_source` and `std::stop_token`, you need to include the header `<stop_token>`.

How to do it...

The typical scenarios for using joinable threads and a cooperative cancellation mechanism are as follows:

- If you want to automatically join a thread object when it goes out of scope, use `std::jthread` instead of `std::thread`. You can still use all the methods that `std::thread` has, such as explicitly joining with `join()`:

```
void thread_func(int i)
{
    while(i-- > 0)
    {
        std::cout << i << '\n';
    }
}

int main()
{
    std::jthread t(thread_func, 10);
}
```

- If you need to be able to cancel the execution of a thread, you should do the following:
    - Make sure the first parameter of the thread function is an `std::stop_token` object.
    - In the thread function, periodically check if stopping was requested using the `stop_requested()` method of the `std::stop_token` object and stop when signaled.
    - Use `std::jthread` for executing the function on a separate thread.
    - From the calling thread, use the `request_stop()` method of the `std::jthread` object to request the thread function to stop and return.

```
void thread_func(std::stop_token st, int& i)
{
    while(!st.stop_requested() && i < 100)
    {
        using namespace std::chrono_literals;
        std::this_thread::sleep_for(200ms);
        i++;
    }
}

int main()
{
    int a = 0;

    std::jthread t(thread_func, std::ref(a));

    using namespace std::chrono_literals;
```

```
    std::this_thread::sleep_for(1s);

    t.request_stop();

    std::cout << a << '\n';        // prints 4
}
```

- If you need to cancel the work of multiple threads, then you can do the following:
    - All thread functions must take an `std::stop_token` object as the first argument.
    - All thread functions should periodically check if a stop was requested by calling the `stop_requested()` method of `std::stop_token` and, if a stop was requested, abort the execution.
    - Use `std::jthread` to execute functions on different threads.
    - In the calling thread, create an `std::stop_source` object.
    - Get an `std::stop_token` object by calling the `get_token()` method of the `std::stop_source` object and pass it as the first argument for the thread function when creating `std::jthread` objects.
    - When you want to stop the execution of the thread functions, call the `request_stop()` method of the `std::stop_source` object.

```
void thread_func(std::stop_token st, int& i)
{
    while(!st.stop_requested() && i < 100)
    {
        using namespace std::chrono_literals;
        std::this_thread::sleep_for(200ms);
        i++;
    }
}

int main()
{
    int a = 0;
    int b = 10;

    std::stop_source st;

    std::jthread t1(thread_func, st.get_token(),
                    std::ref(a));
```

```
    std::jthread t2(thread_func, st.get_token(),
                    std::ref(b));

    using namespace std::chrono_literals;
    std::this_thread::sleep_for(1s);

    st.request_stop();

    std::cout << a << ' ' << b << '\n';        // prints 4
                                                // and 14
}
```

- If you need to execute a piece of code when a stop source is requesting cancellation, you can use an `std::stop_callback` created with the `std::stop_token` object, which signals the stop request and a callback function that is invoked when the stop is requested (through the `std::stop_source` object associated with `std::stop_token`):

```
void thread_func(std::stop_token st, int& i)
{
    while(!st.stop_requested() && i < 100)
    {
        using namespace std::chrono_literals;
        std::this_thread::sleep_for(200ms);
        i++;
    }
}

int main()
{
    int a = 0;

    std::stop_source src;
    std::stop_token token = src.get_token();
    std::stop_callback cb(token,
                          []{std::cout << "the end\n";});

    std::jthread t(thread_func, token, std::ref(a));

    using namespace std::chrono_literals;
    std::this_thread::sleep_for(1s);
```

```
    src.request_stop();

    std::cout << a << '\n';        // prints "the end" and 4
}
```

How it works...

`std::jthread` is very similar to `std::thread`. It is, in fact, the attempt to fix what was wrong with threads in C++11. Its public interface is very similar to `std::thread`. All the methods `std::thread` has are also present in `std:jthread`. However, it differs in the following key aspects:

- Internally, it maintains, at least logically, a shared stop-state, which allows for the request of the thread function to stop execution.
- It has several methods for handling cooperative cancellation: `get_stop_source()`, which returns an `std::stop_source` object associated with the shared stop state of the thread, `get_stop_token()`, which returns an `std::stop_token` associated with the shared stop state of the thread, and `request_stop()`, which requests the cancellation of the execution of the thread function via the shared stop state.
- The behavior of its destructor that, when the thread is joinable, calls `request_stop()` and then `join()` to first signal the request to stop execution and then wait until the thread has finished its execution.

You can create `std::jthread` objects just as you would create `std::thread` objects. However, the callable function that you pass to an `std::jthread` can have a first argument of the type `std::stop_token`. This is necessary when you want to be able to cooperatively cancel the thread's execution. Typical scenarios include graphical user interfaces where user interaction may cancel work in progress, but many other situations can be envisioned. The invocation of such a function thread happens as follows:

- If the first argument for the thread function, supplied when constructing `std::jthread`, is an `std::stop_token`, it is forwarded to the callable function.
- If the first argument, if any, for the callable function is not an `std::stop_token` object, then the `std::stop_token` object associated with the `std::jthread` object's internal shared stop-state is passed to the function. This token is obtained with a call to `get_stop_token()`.

The function thread must periodically check the status of the `std::stop_token` object. The `stop_requested()` method checks if a stop was requested. The request to stop comes from an `std::stop_source` object.

If multiple stop tokens are associated with the same stop source, a stop request is visible to all the stop tokens. If a stop is requested, it cannot be withdrawn, and successive stop requests have no meaning. To request a stop, you should call the `request_stop()` method. You can check if an `std::stop_source` is associated with a stop-state and can be requested to stop by calling the `stop_possible()` method.

If you need to invoke a callback function when a stop source is requested to stop, then you can use the `std::stop_callback` class. This associates an `std::stop_token` object with a callback function when the stop source of the stop token is requested to stop the callback is invoked. Callback functions are invoked as follows:

- In the same thread that invoked `request_stop()`.
- In the thread constructing the `std::stop_callback` object, if the stop has already been requested before the stop callback object has been constructed.

You can create any number of `std::stop_callback` objects for the same stop token. However, the order the callbacks are invoked in is unspecified. The only guarantee is that they will be executed synchronously, provided that the stop has been requested after the `std::stop_callback` objects have been created.

It is also important to note that, if any callback function returns via an exception, then `std::terminate()` will be invoked.

See also

- *Working with threads*, to learn about the `std::thread` class and the basic operations for working with threads in C++.
- *Sending notifications between threads*, to see how to use condition variables to send notifications between producer and consumer threads.

Using thread synchronization mechanisms

The thread support library from C++11 includes mutexes and condition variables that enable thread-synchronization to shared resources. A mutex allows only one thread of multiple processes to execute, while other threads that want to access a shared resource are put to sleep. Mutexes can be expensive to use in some scenarios. For this reason, the C++20 standard features several new simpler synchronization mechanisms: latches, barriers, and semaphores. Although these do not provide new use cases, they are simpler to use and can be more performant because they may internally rely on lock-free mechanisms.

At the time of writing this book, no compiler supports the C++20 thread synchronization mechanisms. Although based on the standard specifications, the sample code in this recipe could not be tested with any compiler, and we cannot guarantee their correctness.

Getting ready

The new C++20 synchronization mechanisms are defined in new headers. You have to include `<latch>` for `std::latch`, `<barrier>`, or `std::barrier`, and `<semaphore>` for `std::counting_semaphore` and `std::binary_semaphore`.

How to do it...

Use the C++20 synchronization mechanisms as follows:

- Use `std::latch` when you need threads to wait until a counter, decreased by other threads, reaches zero. The latch must be initialized with a non-zero count and multiple threads can decrease it, while others wait to the count to reach zero. When that happens, all waiting threads are awakened and the latch can no longer be used. In the following example, four threads are creating data (stored in a vector of integers) and the main thread waits for the completion of them all by utilizing an `std::latch`, decremented by each thread after completing its work:

```
int const jobs = 4;
std::latch work_done(jobs);
std::vector<int> data(jobs);
std::vector<std::jthread> threads;
for(int i = 1; i <= jobs; ++i)
{
   threads.push_back(std::jthread([&data, i, &work_done]{
      using namespace std::chrono_literals;
      std::this_thread::sleep_for(1s); // simulate work

      data[i] = create(i);     // create data

      work_done.count_down(); // decrement counter
   }));
}
work_done.wait();              // wait for all jobs to finish
process(data);                 // process data from all jobs
```

- Use `std::barrier` when you need to perform loop synchronization between parallel tasks. You construct a barrier with a count and, optionally, a completion function. Threads arrive at the barrier, decrease the internal counter, and block. When the counter reaches zero, the completion function is invoked, all blocked threads are awakened, and a new cycle begins. In the following example, four threads are creating data that they store in a vector of integers. When all the threads have completed a cycle, the data is processed in the main thread, by a completion function. Each thread blocks after completing a cycle until they are awakened through the use of an `std::barrier` object, which also stores the completion function. This process is repeated 10 times:

```
int const jobs = 4;
std::vector<int> data(jobs);
int cycle = 1;
std::stop_source st;

std::barrier<std::function<void()>>
   work_done(
      jobs,                        // counter
      [&data, &cycle, &st]() {     // completion function
         process(data);            // process data from all jobs
         cycle++;
         if (cycle == 10)
            st.request_stop();     // stop after ten cycles
      });

std::vector<std::jthread> threads;
for (int i = 1; i <= jobs; ++i)
{
   threads.push_back(std::jthread(
      [&cycle, &work_done](std::stop_token st, int const i)
      {
         while (!st.stop_requested())
         {
            // simulate work
            using namespace std::chrono_literals;
            std::this_thread::sleep_for(200ms);
            // create data
            data[i] = create(i, cycle);
```

```
            // decrement counter
            work_done.arrive_and_wait();          }
      }));
   }

   for (auto& t : threads) t.join();
```

- Use `std::counting_semaphore<N>` or `std::binary_semaphore` when you want to restrict a number of N threads (a single thread, in the case of `binary_semaphore`) to access a shared resource, or when you want to pass notifications between different threads. In the following example, four threads are creating data that is added to the end of a vector of integers. To avoid race conditions, a `binary_semaphore` object is used to restrict the access of a single thread to the vector:

```
int const jobs = 4;
std::vector<int> data;

std::binary_semaphore bs;

for (int i = 1; i <= jobs; ++i)
{
   threads.push_back(std::jthread([&data, i, &bs] {
      for (int k = 1; k < 5; ++k)
      {
         // simulate work
         using namespace std::chrono_literals;
         std::this_thread::sleep_for(200ms);
         // create data
         int value = create(i, k);

         // acquire the semaphore
         bs.acquire();
         // write to the shared resource
         data.push_back(value);
         // release the semaphore
         bs.release();      }
   }));
}

process(data); // process data from all jobs
```

How it works...

The `std::latch` class implements a counter that can be used to synchronize threads. It is a race-free class that works as follows:

- The counter is initialized when the latch is created and can only be decreased.
- A thread may decrease the value of the latch and can do so multiple times.
- A thread may block by waiting until the latch counter reaches zero.
- When the counter reaches zero, the latch becomes permanently signaled and all the threads that are blocked on the latch are awakened.

The `std::latch` class has the following methods:

Methods	Descriptions
`count_down()`	Decrements the internal counter by N (which is 1 by default) without blocking the caller. This operation is performed atomically. N must be a positive value not greater than the value of the internal counter; otherwise, the behavior is undefined.
`try_wait()`	Indicates whether the internal counter reaches zero, in which case it returns `true`. There is a very low probability that, although the counter has reached zero, the function may still return `false`.
`wait()`	Blocks the calling thread until the internal counter reaches zero. If the internal counter is already zero, the function returns immediately without blocking.
`arrive_and_wait()`	This function is equivalent to calling `count_down()`, followed by `wait()`. It decrements the internal counter with N (which is 1 by default), and then blocks the calling thread until the internal counter reaches zero.

In the first example in the previous section, we have an `std::latch`, called `work_done`, initialized with the number of threads (or jobs) that perform work. Each thread produces data that is then written in a shared resource, a vector of integers. Although this is shared, there is no race condition because each thread writes to a different place; therefore, there is no need for a synchronization mechanism. After completing its work, each thread decrements the counter of the latch. The main thread waits until the counter of the latch reaches zero, after which it processes the data from the threads.

Because the internal counter of `std::latch` cannot be incremented or reset, this synchronization mechanism can be used only once. A similar but reusable synchronization mechanism is `std::barrier`. A barrier allows threads to block until an operation is completed and is useful for managing repeated tasks performed by multiple threads.

A barrier works as follows:

- A barrier contains a counter that is initialized during its creation and can be decreased by threads arriving at the barrier. When the counter reaches zero, it is reset to its initial value and the barrier can be reused.
- A barrier also contains a completion function that is called when the counter reaches zero. If a default completion function is used, it is invoked as part of the call to `arrive_and_wait()` or `arrive_and_drop()`. Otherwise, the completion function is invoked on one of the threads that participates in the completion phase.
- The process through which a barrier goes from start to reset is called the **completion phase**. This starts with a so-called **synchronization point** and ends with the **completion step**.
- The first N threads that arrive at the synchronization point after the construction of the barrier are said to be the **set of participating threads**. Only these threads are allowed to arrive at the barrier during each of the following cycles.
- A thread that arrives at the synchronization point may decide to participate in the completion phase by calling `arrive_and_wait()`. However, a thread may remove itself from the participation set by calling `arrive_and_drop()`. In this case, another thread must take its place in the participation set.
- When all the threads in the participation set have arrived at the synchronization point, the completion phase is executed. There are three steps that occur: first, the completion function is invoked. Second, all the threads that are blocked are awakened. Third, and last, the barrier count is reset and a new cycle begins.

The `std::barrier` class has the following methods:

Methods	**Descriptions**
`arrive_and_wait()`	Arrives at the barrier's synchronization point and blocks. The calling thread must be in the participating set; otherwise, the behavior is undefined. This function only returns after the completion phase ends.
`arrive_and_drop()`	Arrives at the barrier's synchronization point and removes the thread from the participation set. It is an implementation detail whether the function blocks or not until the end of the completion phase. The calling thread must be in the participation set; otherwise, the behavior is undefined.

We saw an example with `std::barrier` in the second snippet from the *How to do it...* section. In this example, an `std::barrier` is created and initialized with a counter, which represents the number of threads, and a completion function. This function processes the data produced by all the threads, then increments a loop counter, and requests threads to stop after 10 loops. This basically means that the barrier will perform 10 cycles before the threads will finish their work. Each thread loops until a stop is requested, and, in each iteration, they produce some data, written to the shared vector of integers. At the end of the loop, each thread arrives at the barrier synchronization point, decrements the counter, and waits for it to reach zero and the completion function to execute. This is done with a call to the `arrive_and_wait()` method of the `std::barrier` class.

The last synchronization mechanism available in the thread support library in C++20 is represented by semaphores. A semaphore contains an internal counter that can be both decreased and increased by multiple threads. When the counter reaches zero, further attempts to decrease it will block the thread, until another thread increases the counter.

There are two semaphore classes: `std::counting_semaphore<N>` and `std::binary_semaphore`. The latter is actually just an alias for `std::counting_semaphore<1>`.

A `counting_semaphore` allows N threads to access a shared resource, unlike a mutex, which only allows one. `binary_semaphore`, is, in this matter, similar to the mutex, because only one thread can access the shared resource. On the other hand, a mutex is bound to a thread: the thread that locked the mutex must unlock it. However, this is not the case for semaphores. A semaphore can be released by threads that did not acquire it, and a thread that acquired a semaphore does not have to also release it.

The `std::counting_semaphore` class has the following methods:

Methods	**Descriptions**
`acquire()`	Decrements the internal counter by 1 if it is greater than 0. Otherwise, it blocks until the counter becomes greater than 0.
`try_acquire()`	Tries to decrement the counter by 1 if it is greater than 0. It returns `true` if it succeeds, or `false` otherwise. This method does not block.
`try_acquire_for()`	Tries to decrease the counter by 1 if it is greater than 0. Otherwise, it blocks either until the counter becomes greater than 0 or a specified timeout occurs. The function returns `true` if it succeeded in decreasing the counter.

`try_acquire_until()`	Tries to decrease the counter by 1 if it is greater than 0. Otherwise, it blocks either until the counter becomes greater than 0 or a specified time point has been passed. The function returns `true` if it succeeded in decreasing the counter.
`release()`	Increments the internal counter by the specified value (which is 1 by default). Any thread that was blocked waiting for the counter to become greater than zero is awakened.

All the increment and decrement operations performed on the counter by the methods listed here are executed atomically.

The last example in the *How to do it...* section shows how a `binary_semaphore` can be used. A number of threads (four, in this example) produce work in a loop and write to a shared resource. Unlike the previous examples, they simply add to the end of a vector of integers. Therefore, the access to this vector must be synchronized between the threads, and this is where the binary semaphore is used. In each loop, the thread function creates a new value (which may take some time). This value is then appended to the end of the vector. However, the thread must call the `acquire()` method of the semaphore to make sure it is the only thread that can continue execution and access the shared resource. After the write operation completes, the thread calls the `release()` method of the semaphore in order to increment the internal counter and allow another thread to access the shared resource.

Semaphores can be used for multiple purposes: to block access to shared resources (similar to mutexes), to signal or pass notifications between threads (similar to condition variables), or to implement barriers, often with better performance than similar mechanisms.

See also

- *Working with threads*, to learn about the `std::thread` class and the basic operations for working with threads in C++.
- *Synchronizing access to shared data with mutexes and locks*, to see what mechanisms are available for synchronizing thread access to shared data and how they work.
- *Sending notifications between threads*, to see how to use condition variables to send notifications between producer and consumer threads.

9

Robustness and Performance

C++ is often the first choice when it comes to selecting an object-oriented programming language with performance and flexibility as key goals. Modern C++ provides language and library features, such as rvalue references, move semantics, and smart pointers.

When combined with good practices for exception handling, constant correctness, type-safe conversions, resource allocation, and releasing, C++ enables developers to write better, more robust, and performant code. This chapter's recipes address all of these essential topics.

This chapter includes the following recipes:

- Using exceptions for error handling
- Using `noexcept` for functions that do not throw exceptions
- Ensuring constant correctness for a program
- Creating compile-time constant expressions
- Creating immediate functions
- Performing correct type casts
- Using `unique_ptr` to uniquely own a memory resource
- Using `shared_ptr` to share a memory resource
- Implementing move semantics
- Consistent comparison with the operator `<=>`

We will start this chapter with a couple of recipes that deal with exceptions.

Using exceptions for error handling

Exceptions are responses to exceptional circumstances that can appear when a program is running. They enable the transfer of the control flow to another part of the program. Exceptions are a mechanism for simpler and more robust error handling, as opposed to returning error codes, which could greatly complicate and clutter the code. In this recipe, we will look at some key aspects related to throwing and handling exceptions.

Getting ready

This recipe requires you to have basic knowledge of the mechanisms of throwing exceptions (using the `throw` statement) and catching exceptions (using `try...catch` blocks). This recipe is focused on good practices around exceptions and not on the details of the exception mechanism in the C++ language.

How to do it...

Use the following practices to deal with exceptions:

- Throw exceptions by value:

```
void throwing_func()
{
  throw std::runtime_error("timed out");
}

void another_throwing_func()
{
  throw std::system_error(
    std::make_error_code(std::errc::timed_out));
}
```

- Catch exceptions by reference, or in most cases, by constant reference:

```
try
{
  throwing_func();
}
catch (std::exception const & e)
{
  std::cout << e.what() << '\n';
}
```

- Order `catch` statements from the most derived class to the base class of the hierarchy when catching multiple exceptions from a class hierarchy:

```
auto exprint = [](std::exception const & e)
{
  std::cout << e.what() << '\n';
};

try
{
  another_throwing_func();
}
catch (std::system_error const & e)
{
  exprint(e);
}
catch (std::runtime_error const & e)
{
  exprint(e);
}
catch (std::exception const & e)
{
  exprint(e);
}
```

- Use `catch(...)` to catch all exceptions, regardless of their type:

```
try
{
  throwing_func();
}
catch (std::exception const & e)
{
  std::cout << e.what() << '\n';
}
catch (...)
{
  std::cout << "unknown exception" << '\n';
}
```

- Use `throw;` to rethrow the current exception. This can be used to create a single exception handling function for multiple exceptions.

Throw the exception object (for example, `throw e;`) when you want to hide the original location of the exception:

```
void handle_exception()
{
  try
  {
    throw; // throw current exception
  }
  catch (const std::logic_error & e)
  { /* ... */ }
  catch (const std::runtime_error & e)
  { /* ... */ }
  catch (const std::exception & e)
  { /* ... */ }
}

try
{
  throwing_func();
}
catch (...)
{
  handle_exception();
}
```

How it works...

Most functions have to indicate the success or failure of their execution. This can be achieved in different ways. Here are several possibilities:

- Return an error code (with a special value for success) to indicate the specific reason for failure:

```
int f1(int& result)
{
  if (...) return 1;
  // do something
  if (...) return 2;
  // do something more
  result = 42;
  return 0;
}
```

```
enum class error_codes {success, error_1, error_2};

error_codes f2(int& result)
{
  if (...) return error_codes::error_1;
  // do something
  if (...) return error_codes::error_2;
  // do something more
  result = 42;
  return error_codes::success;
}
```

- A variation of this is to return a Boolean value to only indicate success or failure:

```
bool g(int& result)
{
  if (...) return false;
  // do something
  if (...) return false;
  // do something more
  result = 42;
  return true;
}
```

- Another alternative is to return invalid objects, null pointers, or empty `std::optional<T>` objects:

```
std::optional<int> h()
{
  if (...) return {};
  // do something
  if (...) return {};
  // do something more
  return 42;
}
```

In any case, the return value from the functions should be checked. This can lead to complex, cluttered, and hard to read and maintain real-world code. Moreover, the process of checking the return value of a function is always executed, regardless of whether the function was successful or failed. On the other hand, exceptions are thrown and handled only when a function fails, which should happen more rarely than successful executions. This can actually lead to faster code than code that returns and tests error codes.

Exceptions and error codes are not mutually exclusive. Exceptions should be used only for transferring the control flow in exceptional situations, not for controlling the data flow in a program.

Class constructors are special functions that do not return any value. They are supposed to construct an object, but in the case of failure, they will not be able to indicate this with a return value. Exceptions should be a mechanism that constructors use to indicate failure. Together with the **resource acquisition is initialization** (**RAII**) idiom, this ensures the safe acquisition and release of resources in all situations. On the other hand, exceptions are not allowed to leave a destructor. When this happens, the program abnormally terminates with a call to `std::terminate()`. This is the case for destructors called during stack unwinding, due to the occurrence of another exception. When an exception occurs, the stack is unwound from the point where the exception was thrown to the block where the exception is handled. This process involves the destruction of all local objects in all those stack frames.

If the destructor of an object that is being destroyed during this process throws an exception, another stack unwinding process should begin, which conflicts with the one already under way. Because of this, the program terminates abnormally.

The rule of thumb for dealing with exceptions in constructors and destructors is as follows:

1. Use exceptions to indicate the errors that occur in constructors.
2. Do not throw or let exceptions leave destructors.

It is possible to throw any type of exception. However, in most cases, you should throw temporaries and catch exceptions by constant reference. The following are some guidelines for exception throwing:

- Prefer throwing either standard exceptions or your own exceptions derived from `std::exception` or another standard exception. The reason for this is that the standard library provides exception classes that are intended to be the first choice for representing exceptions. You should use the ones that are available already and when these are not good enough, build your own based on the standard ones. The main benefits of this are consistency and helping users catch exceptions via the base `std::exception` class.

- Avoid throwing exceptions of built-in types, such as integers. The reason for this is that numbers carry little information to the user, who must know what it represents, while an object can provide contextual information. For instance, the statement `throw 42;` tells nothing to the user, but `throw access_denied_exception{};` carries much more implicit information from the class name alone, and with the help of data members it carries anything useful or necessary about the exceptional situation.
- When using a library or framework that provides its own exception hierarchy, prefer throwing exceptions from this hierarchy or your own exceptions derived from it, at least in the parts of the code that are tightly related to it. The main reason for this is to keep the code that utilizes the library APIs consistent.

There's more...

As mentioned in the preceding section, when you need to create your own exception types, derive them from one of the standard exceptions that are available, unless you are using a library or framework with its own exception hierarchy. The C++ standard defines several categories of exceptions that need to be considered for this purpose:

- The `std::logic_error` represents an exception that indicates an error in the program logic, such as an invalid argument, an index beyond the bounds of a range, and so on. There are various standard derived classes, such as `std::invalid_argument`, `std::out_of_range`, and `std::length_error`.
- The `std::runtime_error` represents an exception that indicates an error beyond the scope of the program or that cannot be predicted due to various factors, including external ones, such as overflows and underflows or operating system errors. The C++ standard also provides several derived classes from `std::runtime_error`, including `std::overflow_error`, `std::underflow_error`, `std::system_error`, and `std::format_error` in C++20.
- Exceptions prefixed with `bad_`, such as `std::bad_alloc`, `std::bad_cast`, and `std::bad_function_call`, represent various errors in a program, such as failure to allocate memory, failure to dynamically cast or make a function call, and so on.

The base class for all these exceptions is `std::exception`. It has a non-throwing virtual method called `what()` that returns a pointer to an array of characters representing the description of the error.

When you need to derive custom exceptions from a standard exception, use the appropriate category, such as logical or runtime error. If none of these categories is suitable, then you can derive directly from `std::exception`. The following is a list of possible solutions you can use to derive from a standard exception:

- If you need to derive from `std::exception`, then override the virtual method `what()` to provide a description of the error:

```
class simple_error : public std::exception
{
public:
  virtual const char* what() const noexcept override
  {
    return "simple exception";
  }
};
```

- If you derive from `std::logic_error` or `std::runtime_error` and you only need to provide a static description that does not depend on runtime data, then pass the description text to the base class constructor:

```
class another_logic_error : public std::logic_error
{
public:
  another_logic_error():
    std::logic_error("simple logic exception")
  {}
};
```

- If you derive from `std::logic_error` or `std::runtime_error` but the description message depends on runtime data, provide a constructor with parameters and use them to build the description message. You can either pass the description message to the base class constructor or return it from the overridden `what()` method:

```
class advanced_error : public std::runtime_error
{
  int error_code;
  std::string make_message(int const e)
  {
    std::stringstream ss;
    ss << "error with code " << e;
```

```
      return ss.str();
    }
  public:
    advanced_error(int const e) :
      std::runtime_error(make_message(e).c_str()),error_code(e)
    {
    }

    int error() const noexcept
    {
      return error_code;
    }
  };
```

For a complete list of the standard exception classes, you can visit the `https://en.cppreference.com/w/cpp/error/exception` page.

See also

- *Handling exceptions from thread functions*, in *Chapter 8, Leveraging Threading and Concurrency*, to understand how to handle exceptions thrown in a worker thread from the main thread or the thread where it was joined.
- *Using noexcept for functions that do not throw exceptions*, to see how to inform the compiler that a function should not throw exceptions.

Using noexcept for functions that do not throw exceptions

Exception specification is a language feature that can enable performance improvements, but on the other hand, when done incorrectly, it can abnormally terminate the program. The exception specification from C++03, which allowed you to indicate what types of exceptions a function could throw, has been deprecated and replaced with the new C++11 `noexcept` specification. This specification only allows you to indicate that a function does not throw exceptions, but not the actual exceptions types that it throws. This recipe provides information about the modern exception specifications in C++, as well as guidelines on when to use them.

How to do it...

Use the following constructs to specify or query exception specifications:

- Use `nothrow` in a function declaration to indicate that the function is not throwing any exception:

```
void func_no_throw() noexcept
{
}
```

- Use `nothrow(expr)` in a function declaration, such as template metaprogramming, to indicate that the function may or may not throw an exception based on a condition that evaluates to `bool`:

```
template <typename T>
T generic_func_1()
  noexcept(std::is_nothrow_constructible_v<T>)
{
  return T{};
}
```

- Use the `noexcept` operator at compile time to check whether an expression is declared to not throw any exception:

```
template <typename T>
T generic_func_2() noexcept(noexcept(T{}))
{
  return T{};
}

template <typename F, typename A>
auto func(F&& f, A&& arg) noexcept
{
  static_assert(!noexcept(f(arg)), "F is throwing!");
  return f(arg);
}

std::cout << noexcept(func_no_throw) << '\n';
```

How it works...

As of C++17, exception specification is part of the function type, but not part of the function signature; it may appear as part of any function declarator. Because exception specification is not part of the function signature, two function signatures cannot differ only in the exception specification. Prior to C++17, exception specification was not part of the function type and could only appear as part of lambda declarators or top-level function declarators; they could not appear even in `typedef` or type alias declarations. Further discussions on exception specification refer solely to the C++17 standard.

There are several ways in which the process of throwing an exception can be specified:

- If no exception specification is present, then the function could potentially throw exceptions.
- `noexcept(false)` is equivalent to no exception specification.
- `noexcept(true)` and `noexcept` indicate that a function does not throw any exception.
- `throw()` was equivalent to `noexcept(true)` but was deprecated until C++20, when it was removed altogether.

Using exception specifications must be done with care because, if an exception (either thrown directly or from another function that is called) leaves a function marked as non-throwing, the program is terminated immediately and abnormally with a call to `std::terminate()`.

Pointers to the functions that do not throw exceptions can be implicitly converted to pointers to functions that may throw exceptions, but not vice versa. On the other hand, if a virtual function has a non-throwing exception specification, this indicates that all the declarations of all the overrides must preserve this specification unless an overridden function is declared as deleted.

At compile time, it is possible to check whether a function is declared to be non-throwing or not using the operator `noexcept`. This operator takes an expression and returns `true` if the expression is declared as either non-throwing or `false`. It does not evaluate the expression it checks.

The noexcept operator, along with the noexcept specifier, is particularly useful in template metaprogramming to indicate whether a function may throw exceptions for some types. It is also used with static_assert declarations to check whether an expression breaks the non-throwing guarantee of a function, as seen in the examples in the *How to do it...* section.

The following code provides more examples of how the noexcept operator works:

```
int double_it(int const i) noexcept
{
  return i + i;
}

int half_it(int const i)
{
  throw std::runtime_error("not implemented!");
}

struct foo
{
  foo() {}
};

std::cout << std::boolalpha
  << noexcept(func_no_throw()) <<  '\n'                 // true
  << noexcept(generic_func_1<int>()) <<  '\n'           // true
  << noexcept(generic_func_1<std::string>()) <<  '\n'// true
  << noexcept(generic_func_2<int>()) << '\n'            // true
  << noexcept(generic_func_2<std::string>()) <<  '\n'// true
  << noexcept(generic_func_2<foo>()) <<  '\n'           // false
  << noexcept(double_it(42)) <<  '\n'                   // true
  << noexcept(half_it(42)) <<  '\n'                     // false
  << noexcept(func(double_it, 42)) <<  '\n'             // true
  << noexcept(func(half_it, 42)) << '\n';               // true
```

It is important to note that the noexcept specifier does not provide compile-time checking for exceptions. It only represents a way for users to inform the compiler that a function is not expected to throw exceptions. The compiler can use this to enable certain optimizations. An example is the std::vector, which moves elements if their move constructor is noexcept and copies them otherwise.

There's more...

As mentioned earlier, a function declared with the `noexcept` specifier that exits due to an exception causes the program to terminate abnormally. Therefore, the `noexcept` specifier should be used with caution. Its presence can enable code optimizations, which help increase performance while preserving the strong exception guarantee. An example of this is library containers.

The strong exception guarantee specifies that either an operation is completed successfully, or that it is completed with an exception that leaves the program in the same state it was before the operation started. This ensures commit-or-rollback semantics.

Many standard containers provide some of their operations with a strong exception guarantee. An example is vector's `push_back()` method. This method could be optimized by using the move constructor or move assignment operator instead of the copy constructor or copy assignment operator of the vector's element type. However, in order to preserve its strong exception guarantee, this can only be done if the move constructor or assignment operator does not throw exceptions. If either does, then the copy constructor or the assignment operator must be used instead.

The `std::move_if_noexcept()` utility function does this if the move constructor of its type argument is marked with `noexcept`. The ability to indicate that move constructors or move assignment operators do not throw exceptions is probably the most important scenario where `noexcept` is used.

Consider the following rules for the exception specification:

- If a function could potentially throw an exception, then do not use any exception specifier.
- Mark only those functions with `noexcept` that are guaranteed not to throw an exception.
- Mark only those functions with `noexcept(expression)` that could potentially throw exceptions based on a condition.

These rules are important because, as already noted previously, throwing an exception from a `noexcept` function will immediately terminate the program with a call to `std::terminate()`.

See also

- *Using exceptions for error handling*, to explore the best practices for using exceptions in the C++ language.

Ensuring constant correctness for a program

Although there is no formal definition, constant correctness means objects that are not supposed to be modified (are immutable) remain unmodified indeed. As a developer, you can enforce this by using the `const` keyword for declaring parameters, variables, and member functions. In this recipe, we will explore the benefits of constant correctness and how to achieve it.

How to do it...

To ensure constant correctness for a program, you should always declare the following as constants:

- Parameters to functions that are not supposed to be modified within the function:

```
struct session {};

session connect(std::string const & uri,
                int const timeout = 2000)
{
  /* do something */
  return session { /* ... */ };
}
```

- Class data members that do not change:

```
class user_settings
{
public:
  int const min_update_interval = 15;
  /* other members */
};
```

- Class member functions that do not modify the object state, as seen from the outside:

```
class user_settings
{
  bool show_online;
public:
  bool can_show_online() const {return show_online;}
  /* other members */
};
```

- Function locals whose value do not change throughout their lifetime:

```
user_settings get_user_settings()
{
  return user_settings {};
}

void update()
{
  user_settings const us = get_user_settings();
  if(us.can_show_online()) { /* do something */ }
  /* do more */
}
```

How it works...

Declaring objects and member functions as constant has several important benefits:

- You prevent both accidental and intentional changes of the object, which, in some cases, can result in incorrect program behavior.
- You enable the compiler to perform better optimizations.
- You document the semantics of the code for other users.

Constant correctness is not a matter of personal style but a core principle that should guide C++ development.

Unfortunately, the importance of constant correctness has not been, and is still not, stressed enough in books, C++ communities, and working environments. But the rule of thumb is that everything that is not supposed to change should be declared as constant. This should be done all the time and not only at later stages of development, when you might need to clean up and refactor the code.

When you declare a parameter or variable as constant, you can either put the `const` keyword before the type (`const T c`) or after the type (`T const c`). These two are equivalent, but regardless of which of the two styles you use, reading of the declaration must be done from the right-hand side. `const T c` is read as *c is a T that is constant* and `T const c` as *c is a constant T*. This gets a little bit more complicated with pointers. The following table presents various pointer declarations and their meanings:

Expression	Description
`T* p`	`p` is a non-constant pointer to a non-constant `T`.
`const T* p`	`p` is a non-constant pointer to a `T` that is constant.
`T const * p`	`p` is a non-constant pointer to a constant `T` (same as the prior point).
`const T * const p`	`p` is a constant pointer to a `T` that is constant.
`T const * const p`	`p` is a constant pointer to a constant `T` (same as the prior point).
`T** p`	`p` is a non-constant pointer to a non-constant pointer to a non-constant `T`.
`const T** p`	`p` is a non-constant pointer to a non-constant pointer to a constant `T`.
`T const ** p`	Same as `T const ** p`.
`const T* const * p`	`p` is a non-constant pointer to a constant pointer, which is a constant `T`.
`T const * const * p`	Same as `T const * const * p`.

Placing the `const` keyword after the type is more natural because it is consistent with the reading direction, from right to left. For this reason, all the examples in this book use this style.

When it comes to references, the situation is similar: `const T & c` and `T const & c` are equivalent, which means *c is a reference to a constant T*. However, `T const & const c`, which would mean that *c is a constant reference to a constant T* does not make sense because references—aliases of a variable—are implicitly constant in the sense that they cannot be modified to represent an alias to another variable.

A non-constant pointer to a non-constant object, that is, `T*`, can be implicitly converted to a non-constant pointer to a constant object, `T const *`. However, `T**` cannot be implicitly converted to `T const **` (which is the same with `const T**`). This is because this could lead to constant objects being modified through a pointer to a non-constant object, as shown in the following example:

```
int const c = 42;
int* x;
int const ** p = &x; // this is an actual error
*p = &c;
*x = 0;              // this modifies c
```

If an object is constant, only the constant functions of its class can be invoked. However, declaring a member function as constant does not mean that the function can only be called on constant objects; it could also mean that the function does not modify the state of the object, as seen from the outside. This is a key aspect, but it is usually misunderstood. A class has an internal state that it can expose to its clients through its public interface.

However, not all the internal states might be exposed, and what is visible from the public interface might not have a direct representation in the internal state. (If you model order lines and have the item quantity and item selling price fields in the internal representation, then you might have a public method that exposes the order line amount by multiplying the quantity by the price.) Therefore, the state of an object, as visible from its public interface, is a logical state. Defining a method as constant is a statement that ensures the function does not alter the logical state. However, the compiler prevents you from modifying data members using such methods. To avoid this problem, data members that are supposed to be modified from constant methods should be declared `mutable`.

In the following example, `computation` is a class with the `compute()` method, which performs a long-running computation operation. Because it does not affect the logical state of the object, this function is declared constant. However, to avoid computing the result of the same input again, the computed values are stored in a cache. To be able to modify the cache from the constant function, it is declared `mutable`:

```
class computation
{
  double compute_value(double const input) const
  {
    /* long running operation */
    return input;
  }
```

```
    mutable std::map<double, double> cache;
public:
    double compute(double const input) const
    {
        auto it = cache.find(input);
        if(it != cache.end()) return it->second;

        auto result = compute_value(input);
        cache[input] = result;

        return result;
    }
};
```

A similar situation is represented by the following class, which implements a thread-safe container. Access to shared internal data is protected with `mutex`. The class provides methods such as adding and removing values, and also methods such as `contains()`, which indicate whether an item exists in the container. Because this member function is not intended to modify the logical state of the object, it is declared constant. However, access to the shared internal state must be protected with the mutex. In order to lock and unlock the mutex, both mutable operations (that modify the state of the object) and the mutex must be declared `mutable`:

```
template <typename T>
class container
{
    std::vector<T>     data;
    mutable std::mutex mt;
public:
    void add(T const & value)
    {
        std::lock_guard<std::mutex> lock(mt);
        data.push_back(value);
    }

    bool contains(T const & value) const
    {
        std::lock_guard<std::mutex> lock(mt);
        return std::find(std::begin(data), std::end(data), value)
               != std::end(data);
    }
};
```

The `mutable` specifier allows us to modify the class member on which it was used, even if the containing object is declared `const`. This is the case of the `mt` member of the `std::mutex` type, which is modified even within the `contains()` method, which is declared `const`.

Sometimes, a method or an operator is overloaded to have both constant and non-constant versions. This is often the case with the subscript operator or methods that provide direct access to the internal state. The reason for this is that the method is supposed to be available for both constant and non-constant objects. The behavior should be different, though: for non-constant objects, the method should allow the client to modify the data it provides access to, but for constant objects, it should not. Therefore, the non-constant subscript operator returns a reference to a non-constant object, and the constant subscript operator returns a reference to a constant object:

```
class contact {};

class addressbook
{
  std::vector<contact> contacts;
public:
  contact& operator[](size_t const index);
  contact const & operator[](size_t const index) const;
};
```

It should be noted that, if a member function is constant, even if an object is constant, the data that's returned by this member function may not be constant.

There's more...

The `const` qualifier of an object can be removed with a `const_cast` conversion, but this should only be used when you know that the object was not declared constant. You can read more about this in the *Performing correct type casts* recipe.

See also

- *Creating compile-time constant expressions*, to learn about the `constexpr` specifier and how to define variables and functions that can be evaluated at compile time.

- *Creating immediate functions*, to learn about the C++20 `consteval` specifier, which is used to define functions that are guaranteed to be evaluated at compile time.
- *Performing correct type casts*, to learn about the best practices for performing correct casts in the C++ language.

Creating compile-time constant expressions

The possibility to evaluate expressions at compile time improves runtime execution because there is less code to run and the compiler can perform additional optimizations. Compile-time constants can be not only literals (such as a number or string), but also the result of a function's execution. If all the input values of a function (regardless of whether they are arguments, locals, or globals) are known at compile time, the compiler can execute the function and have the result available at compile time. This is what generalized the constant expressions that were introduced in C++11, which were relaxed in C++14 and further more in C++20. The keyword `constexpr` (short for *constant expression*) can be used to declare compile-time constant objects and functions. We have seen this in several examples in the previous chapters. Now, it's time to learn how it actually works.

Getting ready

The way generalized constant expressions work has been relaxed in C++14 and C++20, but this introduced some breaking changes to C++11. For instance, in C++11, a `constexpr` function was implicitly `const`, but this is no longer the case in C++14. In this recipe, we will discuss generalized constant expressions, as defined in C++20.

How to do it...

Use the `constexpr` keyword when you want to:

- Define non-member functions that can be evaluated at compile time:

```
constexpr unsigned int factorial(unsigned int const n)
{
  return n > 1 ? n * factorial(n-1) : 1;
}
```

- Define constructors that can be executed at compile time to initialize `constexpr` objects and member functions to be invoked during this period:

```
class point3d
{
  double const x_;
  double const y_;
  double const z_;
public:
  constexpr point3d(double const x = 0,
                    double const y = 0,
                    double const z = 0)
    :x_{x}, y_{y}, z_{z}
  {}

  constexpr double get_x() const {return x_;}
  constexpr double get_y() const {return y_;}
  constexpr double get_z() const {return z_;}
};
```

- Define variables that can have their values evaluated at compile time:

```
constexpr unsigned int size = factorial(6);
char buffer[size] {0};
constexpr point3d p {0, 1, 2};
constexpr auto x = p.get_x();
```

How it works...

The `const` keyword is used for declaring variables as constant at runtime; this means that, once initialized, they cannot be changed. However, evaluating the constant expression may still imply runtime computation. The `constexpr` keyword is used for declaring variables that are constant at compile time or functions that can be executed at compile time. `constexpr` functions and objects can replace macros and hardcoded literals without any performance penalties.

Declaring a function as `constexpr` does not mean that it is always evaluated at compile time. It only enables the use of the function in expressions that are evaluated during compile time. This only happens if all the input values of the function can be evaluated at compile time. However, the function may also be invoked at runtime. The following code shows two invocations of the same function, first at compile time, and then at runtime:

```
constexpr unsigned int size = factorial(6);
// compile time evaluation

int n;
std::cin >> n;
auto result = factorial(n);
// runtime evaluation
```

There are some restrictions in regard to where `constexpr` can be used. These restrictions have evolved over time, with changes in C++14 and C++20. To keep the list in a reasonable form, only the requirements that need to be satisfied in C++20 are shown here:

- A variable that is `constexpr` must satisfy the following requirements:
    - Its type is a literal type.
    - It is initialized upon declaration.
    - The expression used for initializing the variable is a constant expression.
    - It must have constant destruction. This means that it must not be of a class type or an array of a class type; otherwise, the class type must have a `constexpr` destructor.
- A function that is `constexpr` must satisfy the following requirements:
    - It is not a coroutine.
    - The return type and the type of all its parameters are all literal types.

    - There is at least one set of arguments for which the invocation of the function would produce a constant expression.
    - The function body must not contain `goto` statements, labels (other than `case` and `default` in a switch), and local variables that are either of non-literal types, or of static or thread storage duration.
- A constructor that is `constexpr` must satisfy the following requirements, in addition to the preceding ones required for functions:
    - There is no virtual base class for the class.
    - All the constructors that initialize non-static data members, including base classes, must also be `constexpr`.
- A destructor that is `constexpr`, available only since C++20, must satisfy the following requirements, in addition to the preceding ones required for functions:
    - There is no virtual base class for the class.
    - All the destructors that destroy non-static data members, including base classes, must also be `constexpr`.

For a complete list of requirements in different versions of the standard, you should read the online documentation available at `https://en.cppreference.com/w/cpp/language/constexpr`.

A function that is `constexpr` is not implicitly `const` (as of C++14), so you need to explicitly use the `const` specifier if the function does not alter the logical state of the object. However, a function that is `constexpr` is implicitly `inline`. On the other hand, an object that is declared `constexpr` is implicitly `const`. The following two declarations are equivalent:

```
constexpr const unsigned int size = factorial(6);
constexpr unsigned int size = factorial(6);
```

There are situations when you may need to use both `constexpr` and `const` in a declaration, as they would refer to different parts of the declaration. In the following example, `p` is a `constexpr` pointer to a constant integer:

```
static constexpr int c = 42;
constexpr int const * p = &c;
```

Reference variables can also be constexpr if, and only if, they alias an object with static storage duration or a function. The following snippet provides an example:

```
static constexpr int const & r = c;
```

In this example, r is a constexpr reference that defines an alias for the compile-time constant variable c, defined in the previous snippet.

There's more...

In C++20, a new specifier was added to the language. This specifier is called constinit and is used for ensuring that variables with static or thread storage duration have static initialization. In C++, initialization of variables can be either static or dynamic. Static initialization can be either zero initialization (when the initial value of an object is set to zero) or constant initialization (when the initial value is set to a compile-time expression). The following snippet shows examples of zero and constant initialization:

```
struct foo
{
  int a;
  int b;
};

struct bar
{
  int   value;
  int*  ptr;
  constexpr bar() :value{ 0 }, ptr{ nullptr }{}
};

std::string text {};  // zero-initialized to unspecified value
double arr[10];       // zero-initialized to ten 0.0
int* ptr;             // zero-initialized to nullptr
foo f = foo();        // zero-initialized to a=0, b=0

foo const fc{ 1, 2 }; // const-initialized at runtime
constexpr bar b;      // const-initialized at compile-time
```

A variable that has static storage could have either static or dynamic initialization. In the latter case, hard to find bugs may appear. Imagine two static objects that are initialized in different translation units.

When the initialization of one of the two objects depends on the other object, then the order they are initialized in is important. This is because the object that is depending on the object must be initialized first. However, the order of the initialization of the translation units is not deterministic, so there is no guarantee on the order of these objects' initialization. However, variables with static storage duration that have static initialization are initialized at compile time. This implies that these objects can be safely used when performing dynamic initialization of translation units.

This is what the new specifier, `constinit`, is intended for. It ensures that a variable with static or thread-local storage has static initialization, and, therefore, its initialization is performed at compile time:

```
int f() { return 42; }
constexpr int g(bool const c) { return c ? 0 : f(); }

constinit int c = g(true);  // OK
constinit int d = g(false); /* error: variable does not have
                                      a constant initializer */
```

It can also be used in a non-initializing declaration to indicate that a variable with thread storage duration is already initialized, as shown in the following example:

```
extern thread_local constinit int data;
int get_data() { return data; }
```

The `constexpr`, `constinit`, and `consteval` specifiers cannot be used in the same declaration.

We will learn about `consteval` in the next recipe, *Creating immediate functions*.

See also

- *Creating immediate functions*, to learn about the C++20 `consteval` specifier, which is used to define functions that are guaranteed to be evaluated at compile time.
- *Ensuring constant correctness for a program*, to explore the benefits of constant correctness and how to achieve it.

Creating immediate functions

Constexpr functions enable the evaluation of functions at compile time, provided that all their inputs, if any, are also available at compile time. However, this is not a guarantee and constexpr functions may also execute at runtime, as we have seen in the previous recipe, *Creating compile-time constant expressions*. In C++20, a new category of functions has been introduced: *immediate functions*. These are functions that are guaranteed to always be evaluated at compile time; otherwise, they produce errors. Immediate functions are useful as replacements for macros and may be important in the possible future development of the language with reflection and meta-classes.

How to do it...

Use the `consteval` keyword when you want to:

- Define non-member functions or function templates that must be evaluated at compile time:

```
consteval unsigned int factorial(unsigned int const n)
{
  return n > 1 ? n * factorial(n-1) : 1;
}
```

- Define constructors that must be executed at compile time to initialize `constexpr` objects and member functions to be invoked only at compile time:

```
class point3d
{
  double x_;
  double y_;
  double z_;
public:
  consteval point3d(double const x = 0,
                    double const y = 0,
                    double const z = 0)
    :x_{x}, y_{y}, z_{z}
  {}

  consteval double get_x() const {return x_;}
  consteval double get_y() const {return y_;}
  consteval double get_z() const {return z_;}
};
```

How it works...

The `consteval` specifier was introduced in C++20. It can only be applied to functions and function templates and defines them as immediate functions. This means that any function invocation must be evaluated at compile time and therefore produce a compile-time constant expression. If the function cannot be evaluated at compile time, the program is ill-formed and the compiler issues an error.

The following rules apply to immediate functions:

- Destructors, allocation, and deallocation functions cannot be immediate functions.
- If any declaration of a function contains the `consteval` specifier, then all the declarations of that function must also include it.
- The `consteval` specifier cannot be used together with `constexpr` or `constinit`.
- An immediate function is an inline `constexpr` function. Therefore, immediate functions and function templates must satisfy the requirements applicable to `constexpr` functions.

Here is how we can use the `factorial()` function and the `point3d` class defined in the previous section:

```
constexpr unsigned int f = factorial(6);
std::cout << f << '\n';

constexpr point3d p {0, 1, 2};
std::cout << p.get_x() << ' ' << p.get_y() << ' ' << p.get_z() << '\n';
```

However, the following sample produces compiler errors because the immediate function `factorial()` and the constructor of `point3d` cannot be evaluated at compile time:

```
unsigned int n;
std::cin >> n;
const unsigned int f2 = factorial(n); // error

double x = 0, y = 1, z = 2;
constexpr point3d p2 {x, y, z};       // error
```

It is not possible to take the address on an immediate function unless it is also in a constant expression:

```
using pfact = unsigned int(unsigned int);
pfact* pf = factorial;
constexpr unsigned int f3 = pf(42);   // error

consteval auto addr_factorial()
{
  return &factorial;
}

consteval unsigned int invoke_factorial(unsigned int const n)
{
  return addr_factorial()(n);
}

constexpr auto ptr = addr_factorial();  // ERROR: cannot take the pointer
                                        // of an immediate function
constexpr unsigned int f2 = invoke_factorial(5); // OK
```

Because immediate functions are not visible at runtime, their symbols are not emitted for them and debuggers will not be able to show them.

See also

- *Ensuring constant correctness for a program,* to explore the benefits of constant correctness and how to achieve it.
- *Creating compile-time constant expressions,* to learn about the `constexpr` specifier and how to define variables and functions that can be evaluated at compile time.

Performing correct type casts

It is often the case that data has to be converted from one type into another type. Some conversions are necessary at compile time (such as `double` to `int`); others are necessary at runtime (such as upcasting and downcasting pointers to the classes in a hierarchy). The language supports compatibility with the C casting style in either the `(type)expression` or `type(expression)` form. However, this type of casting breaks the type safety of C++.

Therefore, the language also provides several conversions: `static_cast`, `dynamic_cast`, `const_cast`, and `reinterpret_cast`. They are used to better indicate intent and write safer code. In this recipe, we'll look at how these casts can be used.

How to do it...

Use the following casts to perform type conversions:

- Use `static_cast` to perform type casting of non-polymorphic types, including casting of integers to enumerations, from floating point to integral values, or from a pointer type to another pointer type, such as from a base class to a derived class (downcasting) or from a derived class to a base class (upcasting), but without any runtime checks:

```
enum options {one = 1, two, three};

int value = 1;
options op = static_cast<options>(value);

int x = 42, y = 13;
double d = static_cast<double>(x) / y;

int n = static_cast<int>(d);
```

- Use `dynamic_cast` to perform type casting of pointers or references of polymorphic types from a base class to a derived class or the other way around. These checks are performed at runtime and may require that **run-time type information** (**RTTI**) is enabled:

```
struct base
{
  virtual void run() {}
  virtual ~base() {}
};

struct derived : public base
{
};

derived d;
base b;

base* pb = dynamic_cast<base*>(&d);         // OK
derived* pd = dynamic_cast<derived*>(&b);   // fail
```

```
try
{
  base& rb = dynamic_cast<base&>(d);       // OK
  derived& rd = dynamic_cast<derived&>(b); // fail
}
catch (std::bad_cast const & e)
{
  std::cout << e.what() << '\n';
}
```

- Use `const_cast` to perform conversion between types with different `const` and `volatile` specifiers, such as removing `const` from an object that was not declared as `const`:

```
void old_api(char* str, unsigned int size)
{
  // do something without changing the string
}

std::string str{"sample"};
old_api(const_cast<char*>(str.c_str()),
        static_cast<unsigned int>(str.size()));
```

- Use `reinterpret_cast` to perform a bit reinterpretation, such as conversion between integers and pointer types, from pointer types to integer, or from a pointer type to any other pointer type, without involving any runtime checks:

```
class widget
{
public:
  typedef size_t data_type;

  void set_data(data_type d) { data = d; }
  data_type get_data() const { return data; }
private:
  data_type data;
};

widget w;
user_data* ud = new user_data();
// write
w.set_data(reinterpret_cast<widget::data_type>(ud));
// read
user_data* ud2 = reinterpret_cast<user_data*>(w.get_data());
```

How it works...

The explicit type conversion, sometimes referred to as *C-style casting* or *static casting*, is a legacy of the compatibility of C++ with the C language and enables you to perform various conversions including the following:

- Between arithmetical types
- Between pointer types
- Between integral and pointer types
- Between const or volatile qualified and unqualified types

This type of casting does not work well with polymorphic types or in templates. Because of this, C++ provides the four casts we saw in the examples earlier. Using these casts leads to several important benefits:

- They express user intent better, both to the compiler and others that read the code.
- They enable safer conversion between various types (except for `reinterpret_cast`).
- They can be easily searched in the source code.

`static_cast` is not a direct equivalent of explicit type conversion, or static casting, even though the name might suggest that. This cast is performed at compile time and can be used to perform implicit conversions, the reverse of implicit conversions, and conversion from pointers to types from a hierarchy of classes. It cannot be used to trigger a conversion between unrelated pointer types, though. For this reason, in the following example, converting from `int*` to `double*` using `static_cast` produces a compiler error:

```
int* pi = new int{ 42 };
double* pd = static_cast<double*>(pi);   // compiler error
```

However, converting from `base*` to `derived*` (where `base` and `derived` are the classes shown in the *How to do it...* section) does not produce a compiler error but a runtime error when trying to use the newly obtained pointer:

```
base b;
derived* pd = static_cast<derived*>(&b); // compilers OK, runtime error
base* pb1 = static_cast<base*>(pd);      // OK
```

On the other hand, `static_cast` cannot be used to remove `const` and `volatile` qualifiers. The following snippet exemplifies this:

```
int const c = 42;
int* pc = static_cast<int*>(&c);          // compiler error
```

Safely typecasting expressions up, down, or sideways along an inheritance hierarchy can be performed with `dynamic_cast`. This cast is performed at runtime and requires that RTTI is enabled. Because of this, it incurs a runtime overhead. Dynamic casting can only be used for pointers and references. When `dynamic_cast` is used to convert an expression into a pointer type and the operation fails, the result is a null pointer. When it is used to convert an expression into a reference type and the operation fails, an `std::bad_cast` exception is thrown. Therefore, always put a `dynamic_cast` conversion to a reference type within a `try...catch` block.

RTTI is a mechanism that exposes information about object data types at runtime. This is available only for polymorphic types (types that have at least one virtual method, including a virtual destructor, which all base classes should have). RTTI is usually an optional compiler feature (or might not be supported at all), which means using this functionality may require using a compiler switch.

Though dynamic casting is performed at runtime, if you attempt to convert it between non-polymorphic types, you'll get a compiler error:

```
struct struct1 {};
struct struct2 {};

struct1 s1;
struct2* ps2 = dynamic_cast<struct2*>(&s1); // compiler error
```

`reinterpret_cast` is more like a compiler directive. It does not translate into any CPU instructions; it only instructs the compiler to interpret the binary representation of an expression as it was of another, specified type. This is a type-unsafe conversion and should be used with care. It can be used to convert expressions between integral types and pointers, pointer types, and function pointer types. Because no checks are done, `reinterpret_cast` can be successfully used to convert expressions between unrelated types, such as from `int*` to `double*`, which produces undefined behavior:

```
int* pi = new int{ 42 };
double* pd = reinterpret_cast<double*>(pi);
```

A typical use of reinterpret_cast is to convert expressions between types in code that uses operating system or vendor-specific APIs. Many APIs store user data in the form of a pointer or an integral type. Therefore, if you need to pass the address of a user-defined type to such APIs, you need to convert values of unrelated pointer types or a pointer type value into an integral type value. A similar example was provided in the previous section, where widget was a class that stored user-defined data in a data member and provided methods for accessing it: set_data() and get_data(). If you need to store a pointer to an object in widget, then use reinterpret_cast, as shown in this example.

const_cast is similar to reinterpret_cast in the sense that it is a compiler directive and does not translate into CPU instructions. It is used to cast away const or volatile qualifiers, an operation that none of the other three conversions discussed here can do.

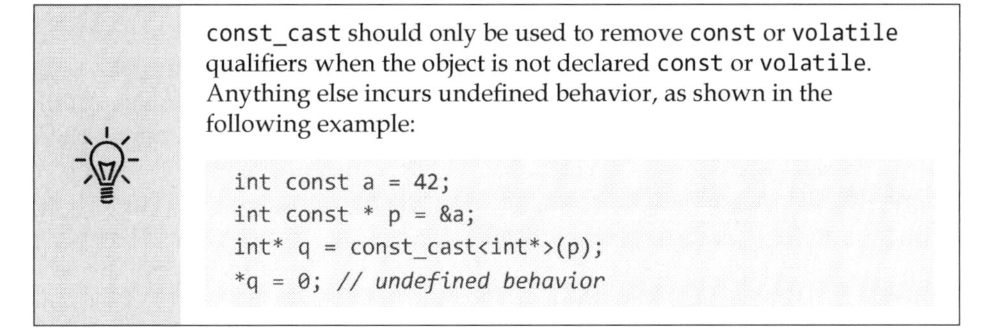

const_cast should only be used to remove const or volatile qualifiers when the object is not declared const or volatile. Anything else incurs undefined behavior, as shown in the following example:

```
int const a = 42;
int const * p = &a;
int* q = const_cast<int*>(p);
*q = 0; // undefined behavior
```

In this example, the variable p points to an object (the variable a) that was declared constant. By removing the const qualifier, the attempt to modify the pointed object introduces undefined behavior.

There's more...

When using explicit type conversion in the form (type)expression, be aware that it will select the first choice from the following list, which satisfies specific casts requirements:

1. `const_cast<type>(expression)`
2. `static_cast<type>(expression)`
3. `static_cast<type>(expression) + const_cast<type>(expression)`
4. `reinterpret_cast<type>(expression)`
5. `reinterpret_cast<type>(expression) + const_cast<type>(expression)`

Moreover, unlike the specific C++ casts, static cast can be used to convert between incomplete class types. If both `type` and `expression` are pointers to incomplete types, then it is not specified whether `static_cast` or `reinterpret_cast` is selected.

See also

- *Ensuring constant correctness for a program*, to explore the benefits of constant correctness and how to achieve it.

Using unique_ptr to uniquely own a memory resource

Manual handling of heap memory allocation and releasing it is one of the most controversial features of C++. All allocations must be properly paired with a corresponding delete operation in the correct scope. If the memory allocation is done in a function and needs to be released before the function returns, for instance, then this has to happen on all the return paths, including the abnormal situation where a function returns because of an exception. C++11 features, such as rvalues and move semantics, have enabled the development of smart pointers; these pointers can manage a memory resource and automatically release it when the smart pointer is destroyed. In this recipe, we will look at `std::unique_ptr`, a smart pointer that owns and manages another object or an array of objects allocated on the heap, and performs the disposal operation when the smart pointer goes out of scope.

Getting ready

In the following examples, we will use the ensuing class:

```
class foo
{
  int a;
  double b;
  std::string c;
public:
  foo(int const a = 0, double const b = 0, std::string const & c = "")
    :a(a), b(b), c(c)
  {}

  void print() const
  {
    std::cout << '(' << a << ',' << b << ',' << std::quoted(c) << ')'
```

```
                << '\n';
    }
};
```

For this recipe, you need to be familiar with move semantics and the `std::move()` conversion function. The `unique_ptr` class is available in the `std` namespace in the `<memory>` header.

How to do it...

The following is a list of typical operations you need to be aware of when working with `std::unique_ptr`:

- Use the available overloaded constructors to create an `std::unique_ptr` that manages objects or an array of objects through a pointer. The default constructor creates a pointer that does not manage any object:

```
std::unique_ptr<int>   pnull;
std::unique_ptr<int>   pi(new int(42));
std::unique_ptr<int[]> pa(new int[3]{ 1,2,3 });
std::unique_ptr<foo>   pf(new foo(42, 42.0, "42"));
```

- Alternatively, use the `std::make_unique()` function template, available in C++14, to create `std::unique_ptr` objects:

```
std::unique_ptr<int>   pi = std::make_unique<int>(42);
std::unique_ptr<int[]> pa = std::make_unique<int[]>(3);
std::unique_ptr<foo>   pf = std::make_unique<foo>(42, 42.0, "42");
```

- Use the `std::make_unique_for_overwrite()` function template, available in C++20, to create an `std::unique_ptr` to objects or an array of objects that are default initialized. These objects should later be overwritten with a determined value:

```
std::unique_ptr<int>   pi = std::make_unique_for_
overwrite<int>();
std::unique_ptr<foo[]> pa = std::make_unique_for_
overwrite<foo[]>();
```

- Use the overloaded constructor, which takes a custom deleter if the default `delete` operator is not appropriate for destroying the managed object or array:

```
struct foo_deleter
{
  void operator()(foo* pf) const
```

```
    {
      std::cout << "deleting foo..." << '\n';
      delete pf;
    }
};

std::unique_ptr<foo, foo_deleter> pf(
    new foo(42, 42.0, "42"),
    foo_deleter());
```

- Use `std::move()` to transfer the ownership of an object from one `std::unique_ptr` to another:

```
auto pi = std::make_unique<int>(42);
auto qi = std::move(pi);
assert(pi.get() == nullptr);
assert(qi.get() != nullptr);
```

- To access the raw pointer to the managed object, use `get()` if you want to retain ownership of the object or `release()` if you want to release the ownership as well:

```
void func(int* ptr)
{
  if (ptr != nullptr)
    std::cout << *ptr << '\n';
  else
    std::cout << "null" << '\n';
}

std::unique_ptr<int> pi;
func(pi.get()); // prints null

pi = std::make_unique<int>(42);
func(pi.get()); // prints 42
```

- Dereference the pointer to the managed object using `operator*` and `operator->`:

```
auto pi = std::make_unique<int>(42);
*pi = 21;

auto pf = std::make_unique<foo>();
pf->print();
```

- If an `std::unique_ptr` manages an array of objects, `operator[]` can be used to access individual elements of the array:

```
std::unique_ptr<int[]> pa = std::make_unique<int[]>(3);
for (int i = 0; i < 3; ++i)
  pa[i] = i + 1;
```

- To check whether `std::unique_ptr` can manage an object or not, use the explicit operator `bool` or check whether `get() != nullptr` (which is what the operator `bool` does):

```
std::unique_ptr<int> pi(new int(42));
if (pi) std::cout << "not null" << '\n';
```

- `std::unique_ptr` objects can be stored in a container. Objects returned by `make_unique()` can be stored directly. An lvalue object could be statically converted to an rvalue object with `std::move()` if you want to give up the ownership of the managed object to the `std::unique_ptr` object in the container:

```
std::vector<std::unique_ptr<foo>> data;
for (int i = 0; i < 5; i++)
  data.push_back(
std::make_unique<foo>(i, i, std::to_string(i)));

auto pf = std::make_unique<foo>(42, 42.0, "42");
data.push_back(std::move(pf));
```

How it works...

`std::unique_ptr` is a smart pointer that manages an object or an array allocated on the heap through a raw pointer. It performs an appropriate disposal when the smart pointer goes out of scope, is assigned a new pointer with `operator=`, or it gives up ownership using the `release()` method. By default, the operator `delete` is used to dispose of the managed object. However, the user may supply a custom deleter when constructing the smart pointer. This deleter must be a function object, either an lvalue reference to a function object or a function, and this callable object must take a single argument of the type `unique_ptr<T, Deleter>::pointer`.

C++14 has added the `std::make_unique()` utility function template to create an `std::unique_ptr`. It avoids memory leaks in some particular contexts, but it has some limitations:

- It can only be used to allocate arrays; you cannot use it to initialize them, which is possible with an `std::unique_ptr` constructor.

The following two pieces of sample code are equivalent:

```
// allocate and initialize an array
std::unique_ptr<int[]> pa(new int[3]{ 1,2,3 });

// allocate and then initialize an array
std::unique_ptr<int[]> pa = std::make_unique<int[]>(3);
for (int i = 0; i < 3; ++i)
  pa[i] = i + 1;
```

- It cannot be used to create an `std::unique_ptr` object with a user-defined deleter.

As we just mentioned, the great advantage of `make_unique()` is that it helps us avoid memory leaks in some contexts where exceptions are being thrown. `make_unique()` itself can throw `std::bad_alloc` if the allocation fails or any exception is thrown by the constructor of the object it creates. Let's consider the following example:

```
void some_function(std::unique_ptr<foo> p)
{ /* do something */ }

some_function(std::unique_ptr<foo>(new foo()));
some_function(std::make_unique<foo>());
```

Regardless of what happens with the allocation and construction of `foo`, there will be no memory leaks, irrespective of whether you use `make_unique()` or the constructor of `std::unique_ptr`. However, this situation changes in a slightly different version of the code:

```
void some_other_function(std::unique_ptr<foo> p, int const v)
{
}

int function_that_throws()
{
  throw std::runtime_error("not implemented");
}

// possible memory leak
some_other_function(std::unique_ptr<foo>(new foo),
                    function_that_throws());

// no possible memory leak
some_other_function(std::make_unique<foo>(),
                    function_that_throws());
```

In this example, some_other_function() has an extra parameter: an integer value. The integer argument that's passed to this function is the returned value of another function. If this function call throws an exception, using the constructor of std::unique_ptr to create the smart pointer can produce a memory leak. The reason for this is that, upon calling some_other_function(), the compiler might first call foo, then function_that_throws(), and then the constructor of std::unique_ptr. If function_that_throws() throws an error, then the allocated foo will leak. If the calling order is function_that_throws() and then new foo() and the constructor of unique_ptr, a memory leak will not happen; this is because the stack starts unwinding before the foo object is allocated. However, by using the make_unique() function, this situation is avoided. This is because the only calls made are to make_unique() and function_that_throws(). If function_that_throws() is called first, then the foo object will not be allocated at all. If make_unique() is called first, the foo object is constructed and its ownership is passed to std::unique_ptr. If a later call to function_that_throws() does throw, then std::unique_ptr will be destroyed when the stack is unwound and the foo object will be destroyed from the smart pointer's destructor.

In C++20, a new function, called std::make_unique_for_overwrite(), has been added. This is similar to make_unique() except that it default initializes the object or the array of objects. This function can be used in generic code where it's unknown whether the type template parameter is trivially copyable or not. This function expresses the intent to create a pointer to an object that may not be initialized so that it should be overwritten later.

Constant std::unique_ptr objects cannot transfer the ownership of a managed object or array to another std::unique_ptr object. On the other hand, access to the raw pointer to the managed object can be obtained with either get() or release(). The first method only returns the underlying pointer, but the latter also releases the ownership of the managed object, hence the name. After a call to release(), the std::unique_ptr object will be empty and a call to get() will return nullptr.

An std::unique_ptr that manages the object of a Derived class can be implicitly converted to an std::unique_ptr that manages an object of the class Base if Derived is derived from Base. This implicit conversion is safe only if Base has a virtual destructor (as all base classes should have); otherwise, undefined behavior is employed:

```
struct Base
{
  virtual ~Base()
  {
    std::cout << "~Base()" << '\n';
  }
};
```

```
struct Derived : public Base
{
  virtual ~Derived()
  {
    std::cout << "~Derived()" << '\n';
  }
};

std::unique_ptr<Derived> pd = std::make_unique<Derived>();
std::unique_ptr<Base> pb = std::move(pd);
```

`std::unique_ptr` can be stored in containers, such as `std::vector`. Because only one `std::unique_ptr` object can own the managed object at any point, the smart pointer cannot be copied to the container; it has to be moved. This is possible with `std::move()`, which performs a `static_cast` to an rvalue reference type. This allows the ownership of the managed object to be transferred to the `std::unique_ptr` object that is created in the container.

See also

- *Using shared_ptr to share a memory resource*, to learn about the `std::shared_ptr` class, which represents a smart pointer that shares ownership of an object or array of objects allocated on the heap.

Using shared_ptr to share a memory resource

Managing dynamically allocated objects or arrays with `std::unique_ptr` is not possible when the object or array has to be shared. This is because an `std::unique_ptr` retains its sole ownership. The C++ standard provides another smart pointer, called `std::shared_ptr`; it is similar to `std::unique_ptr` in many ways, but the difference is that it can share the ownership of an object or array with other `std::shared_ptr`. In this recipe, we will see how `std::shared_ptr` works and how it differs from `std::uniqueu_ptr`. We will also look at `std::weak_ptr`, which is a non-resource-owning smart pointer that holds a reference to an object managed by an `std::shared_ptr`.

Getting ready

Make sure you read the previous recipe, *Using unique_ptr to uniquely own a memory resource*, to become familiar with how `unique_ptr` and `make_unique()` work. We will use the `foo`, `foo_deleter`, `Base`, and `Derived` classes defined in this recipe, and also make several references to it.

Both the `shared_ptr` and `weak_ptr` classes, as well as the `make_shared()` function template, are available in the `std` namespace in the `<memory>` header.

For simplicity and readability, we will not use the fully qualified names `std::unique_ptr`, `std::shared_ptr`, and `std::weak_ptr` in this recipe, but `unique_ptr`, `shared_ptr`, and `weak_ptr`.

How to do it...

The following is a list of the typical operations you need to be aware of when working with `shared_ptr` and `weak_ptr`:

- Use one of the available overloaded constructors to create a `shared_ptr` that manages an object through a pointer. The default constructor creates an empty `shared_ptr`, which does not manage any object:

```
std::shared_ptr<int> pnull1;
std::shared_ptr<int> pnull2(nullptr);
std::shared_ptr<int> pi1(new int(42));
std::shared_ptr<int> pi2 = pi1;
std::shared_ptr<foo> pf1(new foo());
std::shared_ptr<foo> pf2(new foo(42, 42.0, "42"));
```

- Alternatively, use the `std::make_shared()` function template, available since C++11, to create `shared_ptr` objects:

```
std::shared_ptr<int> pi  = std::make_shared<int>(42);
std::shared_ptr<foo> pf1 = std::make_shared<foo>();
std::shared_ptr<foo> pf2 = std::make_shared<foo>(42, 42.0,
"42");
```

- Use the `std::make_shared_for_overwrite()` function template, available in C++20, to create `shared_ptrs` to objects or arrays of objects that are default initialized. These objects should later be overwritten with a determined value:

```
std::shared_ptr<int> pi = std::make_shared_for_overwrite<int>();
std::shared_ptr<foo[]> pa = std::make_shared_for_
overwrite<foo[]>(3);
```

- Use the overloaded constructor, which takes a custom deleter if the default delete operation is not appropriate for destroying the managed object:

```
std::shared_ptr<foo> pf1(new foo(42, 42.0, "42"),
                         foo_deleter());
std::shared_ptr<foo> pf2(
        new foo(42, 42.0, "42"),
        [](foo* p) {
          std::cout << "deleting foo from lambda..." << '\n';
          delete p;});
```

- Always specify a deleter when managing an array of objects. The deleter can either be a partial specialization of `std::default_delete` for arrays or any function that takes a pointer to the template type:

```
std::shared_ptr<int> pa1(
  new int[3]{ 1, 2, 3 },
  std::default_delete<int[]>());

std::shared_ptr<int> pa2(
  new int[3]{ 1, 2, 3 },
  [](auto p) {delete[] p; });
```

- To access the raw pointer to the managed object, use the `get()` function:

```
void func(int* ptr)
{
  if (ptr != nullptr)
    std::cout << *ptr << '\n';
  else
    std::cout << "null" << '\n';
}

std::shared_ptr<int> pi;
func(pi.get());

pi = std::make_shared<int>(42);
func(pi.get());
```

- Dereference the pointer to the managed object using `operator*` and `operator->`:

```
std::shared_ptr<int> pi = std::make_shared<int>(42);
*pi = 21;

std::shared_ptr<foo> pf = std::make_shared<foo>(42, 42.0, "42");
pf->print();
```

- If a `shared_ptr` manages an array of objects, `operator[]` can be used to access the individual elements of the array. This is only available in C++17:

  ```
  std::shared_ptr<int[]> pa1(
    new int[3]{ 1, 2, 3 },
    std::default_delete<int[]>());

  for (int i = 0; i < 3; ++i)
    pa1[i] *= 2;
  ```

- To check whether a `shared_ptr` could manage an object or not, use the explicit operator `bool` or check whether `get() != nullptr` (which is what the operator `bool` does):

  ```
  std::shared_ptr<int> pnull;
  if (pnull) std::cout << "not null" << '\n';

  std::shared_ptr<int> pi(new int(42));
  if (pi) std::cout << "not null" << '\n';
  ```

- `shared_ptr` objects can be stored in containers, such as `std::vector`:

  ```
  std::vector<std::shared_ptr<foo>> data;
  for (int i = 0; i < 5; i++)
    data.push_back(
      std::make_shared<foo>(i, i, std::to_string(i)));

  auto pf = std::make_shared<foo>(42, 42.0, "42");
  data.push_back(std::move(pf));
  assert(!pf);
  ```

- Use `weak_ptr` to maintain a non-owning reference to a shared object, which can be later accessed through a `shared_ptr` constructed from the `weak_ptr` object:

  ```
  auto sp1 = std::make_shared<int>(42);
  assert(sp1.use_count() == 1);

  std::weak_ptr<int> wpi = sp1;
  assert(sp1.use_count() == 1);

  auto sp2 = wpi.lock();
  assert(sp1.use_count() == 2);
  assert(sp2.use_count() == 2);

  sp1.reset();
  ```

```
assert(sp1.use_count() == 0);
assert(sp2.use_count() == 1);
```

- Use the `std::enable_shared_from_this` class template as the base class for a type when you need to create `shared_ptr` objects for instances that are already managed by another `shared_ptr` object:

```
struct Apprentice;

struct Master : std::enable_shared_from_this<Master>
{
  ~Master() { std::cout << "~Master" << '\n'; }
  void take_apprentice(std::shared_ptr<Apprentice> a);
private:
  std::shared_ptr<Apprentice> apprentice;
};

struct Apprentice
{
  ~Apprentice() { std::cout << "~Apprentice" << '\n'; }
  void take_master(std::weak_ptr<Master> m);
private:
  std::weak_ptr<Master> master;
};

void Master::take_apprentice(std::shared_ptr<Apprentice> a)
{
  apprentice = a;
  apprentice->take_master(shared_from_this());
}

void Apprentice::take_master(std::weak_ptr<Master> m)
{
  master = m;
}

auto m = std::make_shared<Master>();
auto a = std::make_shared<Apprentice>();
m->take_apprentice(a);
```

How it works...

shared_ptr is very similar to unique_ptr in many aspects; however, it serves a different purpose: sharing the ownership of an object or array. Two or more shared_ptr smart pointers can manage the same dynamically allocated object or array, which is automatically destroyed when the last smart pointer goes out of scope, is assigned a new pointer with operator=, or is reset with the method reset(). By default, the object is destroyed with operator delete; however, the user could supply a custom deleter to the constructor, something that is not possible using std::make_shared(). If shared_ptr is used to manage an array of objects, a custom deleter must be supplied. In this case, you can use std::default_delete<T[]>, which is a partial specialization of the std::default_delete class template that uses operator delete[] to delete the dynamically allocated array.

The utility function std::make_shared() (available since C++11), unlike std::make_unique(), which has only been available since C++14, should be used to create smart pointers unless you need to provide a custom deleter. The primary reason for this is the same as for make_unique(): avoiding potential memory leaks in some contexts when an exception is thrown. For more information on this, read the explanation provided on std::make_unique() in the previous recipe.

In C++20, a new function, called std::make_shared_for_overwrite(), has been added. This is similar to make_shared() except that it default initializes the object or the array of objects. This function can be used in generic code where it's unknown whether the type template parameter is trivially copyable or not. This function expresses the intent to create a pointer to an object that may not be initialized so that it should be overwritten later.

Also, as in the case of unique_ptr, a shared_ptr that manages an object of a Derived class can be implicitly converted to a shared_ptr that manages an object of the Base class. This is possible if the Derived class is derived from Base. This implicit conversion is safe only if Base has a virtual destructor (as all the base classes should have when objects are supposed to be deleted polymorphically through a pointer or reference to the base class); otherwise, undefined behavior is employed. In C++17, several new non-member functions have been added: std::static_pointer_cast(), std::dynamic_pointer_cast(), std::const_pointer_cast(), and std::reinterpret_pointer_cast(). These apply static_cast, dynamic_cast, const_cast, and reinterpret_cast to the stored pointer, returning a new shared_ptr to the designated type.

In the following example, `Base` and `Derived` are the same classes we used in the previous recipe:

```
std::shared_ptr<Derived> pd = std::make_shared<Derived>();
std::shared_ptr<Base> pb = pd;

std::static_pointer_cast<Derived>(pb)->print();
```

There are situations when you need a smart pointer for a shared object but without it contributing to the shared ownership. Suppose you model a tree structure where a node has references to its children and they are represented by `shared_ptr` objects. On the other hand, say a node needs to keep a reference to its parent. If this reference were also `shared_ptr`, then it would create circular references and no object would ever be automatically destroyed.

`weak_ptr` is a smart pointer that's used to break such circular dependencies. It holds a non-owning reference to an object or array managed by a `shared_ptr`. `weak_ptr` can be created from a `shared_ptr` object. In order to access the managed object, you need to get a temporary `shared_ptr` object. To do so, we need to use the `lock()` method. This method atomically checks whether the referred object still exists and returns either an empty `shared_ptr`, if the object no longer exists, or a `shared_ptr` that owns the object, if it still exists. Because `weak_ptr` is a non-owning smart pointer, the referred object can be destroyed before `weak_ptr` goes out of scope or when all the owning `shared_ptr` objects have been destroyed, reset, or assigned to other pointers. The method `expired()` can be used to check whether the referenced object has been destroyed or is still available.

In the *How to do it...* section, the preceding example models a master-apprentice relationship. There is a `Master` class and an `Apprentice` class. The `Master` class has a reference to an `Apprentice` class and a method called `take_apprentice()` to set the `Apprentice` object. The `Apprentice` class has a reference to a `Master` class and the method `take_master()` to set the `Master` object. In order to avoid circular dependencies, one of these references must be represented by a `weak_ptr`. In the proposed example, the `Master` class had a `shared_ptr` to own the `Apprentice` object, and the `Apprentice` class had a `weak_ptr` to track a reference to the `Master` object. This example, however, is a bit more complex because here, the `Apprentice::take_master()` method is called from `Master::take_apprentice()` and needs a `weak_ptr<Master>`. In order to call it from within the `Master` class, we must be able to create a `shared_ptr<Master>` in the `Master` class, using the `this` pointer. The only way to do this in a safe manner is to use `std::enable_shared_from_this`.

`std::enable_shared_from_this` is a class template that must be used as a base class for all the classes where you need to create a `shared_ptr` for the current object (the `this` pointer) when this object is already managed by another `shared_ptr`. Its type template parameter must be the class that derives from it, as in the curiously recurring template pattern. It has two methods: `shared_from_this()`, which returns a `shared_ptr`, which shares the ownership of the `this` object, and `weak_from_this()`, which returns a `weak_ptr`, which shares a non-owning reference to the `this` object. The latter method is only available in C++17. These methods can be called only on an object that is managed by an existing `shared_ptr`; otherwise, they throw an `std::bad_weak_ptr` exception, as of C++17. Prior to C++17, the behavior was undefined.

Not using `std::enable_shared_from_this` and creating a `shared_ptr<T>(this)` directly would lead to having multiple `shared_ptr` objects managing the same object independently, without knowing each other. When this happens, the object ends up being destroyed multiple times by different `shared_ptr` objects.

See also

- *Using unique_ptr to uniquely own a memory resource*, to learn about the `std::unique_ptr` class, which represents a smart pointer that owns and manages another object or array of objects allocated on the heap.

Implementing move semantics

Move semantics is a key feature that drives the performance improvements of modern C++. They enable moving, rather than copying, resources or, in general, objects that are expensive to copy. However, it requires that classes implement a move constructor and assignment operator. These are provided by the compiler in some circumstances, but in practice, it is often the case that you have to explicitly write them. In this recipe, we will see how to implement the move constructor and the move assignment operator.

Getting ready

You are expected to have basic knowledge of rvalue references and the special class functions (constructors, assignment operators, and destructor). We will demonstrate how to implement a move constructor and assignment operator using the following `Buffer` class:

```
class Buffer
{
  unsigned char* ptr;
  size_t length;
public:
  Buffer(): ptr(nullptr), length(0)
  {}

  explicit Buffer(size_t const size):
    ptr(new unsigned char[size] {0}), length(size)
  {}

  ~Buffer()
  {
    delete[] ptr;
  }

  Buffer(Buffer const& other):
    ptr(new unsigned char[other.length]),
    length(other.length)
  {
    std::copy(other.ptr, other.ptr + other.length, ptr);
  }

  Buffer& operator=(Buffer const& other)
  {
    if (this != &other)
    {
      delete[] ptr;

      ptr = new unsigned char[other.length];
      length = other.length;

      std::copy(other.ptr, other.ptr + other.length, ptr);
    }

    return *this;
  }

  size_t size() const { return length;}
  unsigned char* data() const { return ptr; }
};
```

Let's move on to the next section, where you'll learn how to modify this class in order to benefit from move semantics.

How to do it...

To implement the move constructor for a class, do the following:

1. Write a constructor that takes an rvalue reference to the class type:

   ```
   Buffer(Buffer&& other)
   {
   }
   ```

2. Assign all the data members from the rvalue reference to the current object. This can be done either in the body of the constructor, as follows, or in the initialization list, which is the preferred way:

   ```
   ptr = other.ptr;
   length = other.length;
   ```

3. Assign the data members from the rvalue reference to default values:

   ```
   other.ptr = nullptr;
   other.length = 0;
   ```

Put all together, the move constructor for the `Buffer` class looks like this:

```
Buffer(Buffer&& other)
{
  ptr = other.ptr;
  length = other.length;

  other.ptr = nullptr;
  other.length = 0;
}
```

To implement the move assignment operator for a class, do the following:

1. Write an assignment operator that takes an rvalue reference to the class type and returns a reference to it:

   ```
   Buffer& operator=(Buffer&& other)
   {
   }
   ```

2. Check that the rvalue reference does not refer to the same object as `this`, and if they are different, perform *steps 3* to *5*:

   ```
   if (this != &other)
   {
   }
   ```

3. Dispose of all the resources (such as memory, handles, and so on) from the current object:

   ```
   delete[] ptr;
   ```

4. Assign all the data members from the rvalue reference to the current object:

   ```
   ptr = other.ptr;
   length = other.length;
   ```

5. Assign the data members from the rvalue reference to the default values:

   ```
   other.ptr = nullptr;
   other.length = 0;
   ```

6. Return a reference to the current object, regardless of whether *steps 3* to *5* were executed or not:

   ```
   return *this;
   ```

Put all together, the move assignment operator for the `Buffer` class looks like this:

```
Buffer& operator=(Buffer&& other)
{
  if (this != &other)
  {
    delete[] ptr;

    ptr = other.ptr;
    length = other.length;

    other.ptr = nullptr;
    other.length = 0;
  }

  return *this;
}
```

How it works...

The move constructor and move assignment operator are provided by default by the compiler unless a user-defined copy constructor, move constructor, copy assignment operator, move assignment operator, or destructor exists already. When provided by the compiler, they perform a movement in a member-wise manner. The move constructor invokes the move constructors of the class data members recursively; similarly, the move assignment operator invokes the move assignment operators of the class data members recursively.

Move, in this case, represents a performance benefit for objects that are too large to copy (such as a string or container) or for objects that are not supposed to be copied (such as the `unique_ptr` smart pointer). Not all classes are supposed to implement both copy and move semantics. Some classes should only be movable, while others both copyable and movable. On the other hand, it does not make much sense for a class to be copyable but not moveable, though this can be technically achieved.

Not all types benefit from move semantics. In the case of built-in types (such as `bool`, `int`, or `double`), arrays, or PODs, the move is actually a copy operation. On the other hand, move semantics provide a performance benefit in the context of rvalues, that is, temporary objects. An rvalue is an object that does not have a name; it lives temporarily during the evaluation of an expression and is destroyed at the next semicolon:

```
T a;
T b = a;
T c = a + b;
```

In the preceding example, `a`, `b`, and `c` are lvalues; they are objects that have a name that can be used to refer to the object at any point throughout its lifetime. On the other hand, when you evaluate the expression `a+b`, the compiler creates a temporary object (which, in this case, is assigned to `c`) and then destroyed (when a semicolon is encountered). These temporary objects are called rvalues because they usually appear on the right-hand side of an assignment expression. In C++11, we can refer to these objects through rvalue references, expressed with `&&`.

Move semantics are important in the context of rvalues. This is because they allow you to take ownership of the resources from the temporary object that is destroyed, without the client being able to use it after the move operation is completed. On the other hand, lvalues cannot be moved; they can only be copied. This is because they can be accessed after the move operation, and the client expects the object to be in the same state. For instance, in the preceding example, the expression `b = a` assigns `a` to `b`.

After this operation is complete, the object a, which is an lvalue, can still be used by the client and should be in the same state as it was before. On the other hand, the result of a+b is temporary, and its data can be safely moved to c.

The move constructor is different than a copy constructor because it takes an rvalue reference to the class type T(T&&), as opposed to an lvalue reference in the case of the copy constructor T(T const&). Similarly, move assignment takes an rvalue reference, namely T& operator=(T&&), as opposed to an lvalue reference for the copy assignment operator, namely T& operator=(T const &). This is true even though both return a reference to the T& class. The compiler selects the appropriate constructor or assignment operator based on the type of argument, rvalue, or lvalue.

When a move constructor/assignment operator exists, an rvalue is moved automatically. lvalues can also be moved, but this requires an explicit static cast to an rvalue reference. This can be done using the std::move() function, which basically performs a static_cast<T&&>:

```
std::vector<Buffer> c;
c.push_back(Buffer(100));  // move

Buffer b(200);
c.push_back(b);            // copy
c.push_back(std::move(b)); // move
```

After an object is moved, it must remain in a valid state. However, there is no requirement regarding what this state should be. For consistency, you should set all member fields to their default value (numerical types to 0, pointers to nullptr, Booleans to false, and so on).

The following example shows the different ways in which Buffer objects can be constructed and assigned:

```
Buffer b1;                   // default constructor
Buffer b2(100);              // explicit constructor
Buffer b3(b2);               // copy constructor
b1 = b3;                     // assignment operator
Buffer b4(std::move(b1)); // move constructor
b3 = std::move(b4);          // move assignment
```

The constructor or assignment operator involved in the creation or assignment of the objects b1, b2, b3, and b4 is mentioned in the comments on each line.

There's more...

As seen with the `Buffer` example, implementing both the move constructor and move assignment operator involves writing similar code (the entire code of the move constructor was also present in the move assignment operator). This can actually be avoided by calling the move assignment operator in the move constructor:

```
Buffer(Buffer&& other) : ptr(nullptr), length(0)
{
  *this = std::move(other);
}
```

There are two points that must be noticed in this example:

- Member initialization in the constructor's initialization list is necessary because these members could potentially be used in the move assignment operator later on (such as the `ptr` member in this example).
- Static casting of `other` to an rvalue reference. Without this explicit conversion, the copy assignment operator would be called. This is because even if an rvalue is passed to this constructor as an argument, when it is assigned a name, it is bound to an lvalue. Therefore, `other` is actually an lvalue, and it must be converted to an rvalue reference in order to invoke the move assignment operator.

See also

- *Defaulted and deleted functions*, in *Chapter 3, Exploring Functions*, to learn about the use of the `default` specifier on special member functions and how to define functions as deleted with the `delete` specifier.

Consistent comparison with the operator <=>

The C++ language defines six relational operators that perform comparison: `==`, `!=`, `<`, `<=`, `>`, and `>=`. Although `!=` can be implemented in terms of `==`, and `<=`, `>=`, and `>` in terms of `<`, you still have to implement both `==` and `!=` if you want your user-defined type to support equality comparison, and `<`, `<=`, `>`, and `>=` if you want it to support ordering.

That means 6 functions if you want objects of your type—let's call it `T`—to be comparable, 12 if you want them to be comparable with another type, `U`, 18 if you also want values of a `U` type to be comparable with your `T` type, and so on. The new C++20 standard reduces this number to either one or two, or multiple of these (depending on the comparison with other types) by introducing a new comparison operator, called *the three-way comparison*, which is designated with the symbol `<=>`, for which reason it is popularly known as the *spaceship operator*. This new operator helps us write less code, better describe the strength of relations, and avoid possible performance issues of manually implementing comparison operators in terms of others.

Getting ready

It is necessary to include the header `<compare>` when defining or implementing the three-way comparison operator. This new C++20 header is part of the standard general utility library and provides classes, functions, and concepts for implementing comparison.

How to do it...

To optimally implement comparison in C++20, do the following:

- If you only want your type to support equality comparison (both `==` and `!=`), implement only the `==` operator and return a `bool`. You can default the implementation so that the compiler performs a member-wise comparison:

```
class foo
{
  int value;
public:
  foo(int const v):value(v){}

  bool operator==(foo const&) const = default;
};
```

- If you want your type to support both equality and ordering and the default member-wise comparison will do, then only define the `<=>` operator, returning `auto`, and default its implementation:

```
class foo
{
  int value;
public:
```

```
    foo(int const v) :value(v) {}

    auto operator<=>(foo const&) const = default;
};
```

- If you want your type to support both equality and ordering and you need to perform custom comparison, then implement both the `==` operator (for equality) and the `<=>` operator (for ordering):

```
class foo
{
    int value;
public:
    foo(int const v) :value(v) {}

    bool operator==(foo const& other) const
    { return value == other.value; }

    auto operator<=>(foo const& other) const
    { return value <=> other.value; }
};
```

When implementing the three-way comparison operator, follow these guidelines:

- Only implement the three-way comparison operator but always use the two-way comparison operators `<`, `<=`, `>`, and `>=` when comparing values.
- Implement the three-way comparison operator as a member function, even if you want the first operand of a comparison to be of a type other than your class.
- Implement the three-way comparison operator as non-member functions only if you want implicit conversion on both arguments (that means comparing two objects, neither of which is of your class).

How it works...

The new three-way comparison operator is similar to the `memcmp()`/`strcmp()` C functions and the `std::string::compare()` method. These functions take two arguments and return an integer value that is smaller than zero if the first is less than the second, zero if they are equal, or greater than zero if the first argument is greater than the second. The three-way comparison operator does not return an integer but a value of a comparison category type.

This can be one of the following:

- `std::strong_ordering` represents the result of a three-way comparison that supports all six relational operators, does not allow incomparable values (which means that at least one of `a < b`, `a == b`, and `a > b` must be true), and implies substitutability. This is a property such that if `a == b` and `f` is a function that reads only comparison-salient state (accessible via the argument's public constant members), then `f(a) == f(b)`.
- `std::weak_ordering` supports all the six relational operators, does not support incomparable values (which means that none of `a < b`, `a == b`, and `a > b` could be true), but also does not imply substitutability. A typical example of a type that defines weak ordering is a case-insensitive string type.
- `std::partial_ordering` supports all six relational operators, but does not imply substitutability and has a value that might not be comparable (for instance, a floating point `NaN` cannot be compared to any other value).

The `std::strong_ordering` type is the strongest of all these category types. It is not implicitly convertible from any other category, but it implicitly converts to both `std::weak_ordering` and `std::partial_ordering`. `std::weak_ordering` is also implicitly convertible to `std::partial_ordering`. We've summarized all these properties in the following table:

Category	**Operators**	**Substitutability**	**Comparable values**	**Implicit conversion**
`std::strong_ordering`	`==, !=, <, <=, >, >=`	Yes	Yes	↓
`std::weak_ordering`	`==, !=, <, <=, >, >=`	No	Yes	↓
`std::partial_ordering`	`==, !=, <, <=, >, >=`	No	No	

These comparison categories have values that are implicitly comparable with literal zero (but not with an integer variable with a value of zero). Their values are listed in the following table:

Category	**Numeric values**			**Non-numeric values**
	-1	**0**	**1**	
`strong_ordering`	less	equal equivalent	greater	
`weak_ordering`	less	equivalent	greater	
`partial_ordering`	less	equivalent	greater	unordered

To better understand how this works, let's look at the following example:

```
class cost_unit_t
{
  // data members
public:
  std::strong_ordering operator<=>(cost_unit_t const & other) const
noexcept = default;
};

class project_t : public cost_unit_t
{
  int         id;
  int         type;
  std::string name;
public:
  bool operator==(project_t const& other) const noexcept
  {
    return (cost_unit_t&)(*this) == (cost_unit_t&)other &&
           name == other.name &&
           type == other.type &&
           id == other.id;
  }

  std::strong_ordering operator<=>(project_t const & other) const
noexcept
  {
    // compare the base class members
    if (auto cmp = (cost_unit_t&)(*this) <=> (cost_unit_t&)other;
        cmp != 0)
      return cmp;

    // compare this class members in custom order
    if (auto cmp = name.compare(other.name); cmp != 0)
      return cmp < 0 ? std::strong_ordering::less :
                       std::strong_ordering::greater;
    if (auto cmp = type <=> other.type; cmp != 0)
      return cmp;
    return id <=> other.id;
  }
};
```

Here, `cost_unit_t` is a base class that contains some (unspecified) data members and defines the `<=>` operator, although it defaults the implementation. This means that the compiler will also provide the `==` and `!=` operators, not just `<`, `<=`, `>`, and `>=`. This class is derived by `project_t`, which contains several data fields: an identifier for the project, a type, and a name. However, for this type, we cannot default the implementation of the operators, because we do not want to compare the fields member-wise, but in a custom order: first the name, then the type, and lastly the identifier. In this case, we implement both the `==` operator, which returns a `bool` and tests the member fields for equality, and the `<=>` operator, which returns `std::strong_ordering` and uses the `<=>` operator itself to compare the values of its two arguments.

The following code snippet shows a type called `employee_t` that models employees in a company. An employee can have a manager, and an employee that is a manager has people that it manages. Conceptually, such a type could look as follows:

```
struct employee_t
{
  bool is_managed_by(employee_t const&) const { /* ... */ }
  bool is_manager_of(employee_t const&) const { /* ... */ }
  bool is_same(employee_t const&) const       { /* ... */ }

  bool operator==(employee_t const & other) const
  {
    return is_same(other);
  }

  std::partial_ordering operator<=>(employee_t const& other) const
noexcept
  {
    if (is_same(other))
      return std::partial_ordering::equivalent;
    if (is_managed_by(other))
      return std::partial_ordering::less;
    if (is_manager_of(other))
      return std::partial_ordering::greater;
    return std::partial_ordering::unordered;
  }
};
```

The methods `is_same()`, `is_manager_of()`, and `is_managed_by()` return the relationship of two employees. However, it is possible there are employees with no relationship; for instance, employees in different teams, or the same team that are not in a manager-subordinate position. Here, we can implement equality and ordering. However, since we cannot compare all employees with each other, the `<=>` operator must return an `std::partial_ordering` value. The return value is `partial_ordering::equivalent` if the values represent the same employee, `partial_ordering::less` if the current employee is managed by the supplied one, `partial_ordering::greater` if the current employee is the manager of the supplied one, and `partial_ordering::unorder` in all other cases.

Let's see one more example to understand how the three-way comparison operator works. In the following sample, the `ipv4` class models an IP version 4 address. It supports comparison with both other objects of the `ipv4` type but also `unsigned long` values (because there is a `to_unlong()` method that converts the IP address into a 32-bit unsigned integral value):

```
struct ipv4
{
  explicit ipv4(unsigned char const a=0, unsigned char const b=0,
                unsigned char const c=0, unsigned char const d=0)
noexcept :
    data{ a,b,c,d }
  {}

  unsigned long to_ulong() const noexcept
  {
    return
      (static_cast<unsigned long>(data[0]) << 24) |
      (static_cast<unsigned long>(data[1]) << 16) |
      (static_cast<unsigned long>(data[2]) << 8) |
      static_cast<unsigned long>(data[3]);
  }

  auto operator<=>(ipv4 const&) const noexcept = default;

  bool operator==(unsigned long const other) const noexcept
  {
    return to_ulong() == other;
  }

  std::strong_ordering
  operator<=>(unsigned long const other) const noexcept
```

```
    {
        return to_ulong() <=> other;
    }

private:
    std::array<unsigned char, 4> data;
};
```

In this example, we overloaded the `<=>` operator and allowed it to be default implemented. But we also explicitly implemented overloads for `operator==` and `operator<=>`, which compare an `ipv4` object with an `unsigned long` value. Because of these operators, we can write any of the following:

```
ipv4 ip(127, 0, 0, 1);
if(ip == 0x7F000001) {}
if(ip != 0x7F000001) {}
if(0x7F000001 == ip) {}
if(0x7F000001 != ip) {}
if(ip < 0x7F000001)  {}
if(0x7F000001 < ip)  {}
```

There are two things to notice here: the first is that although we only overloaded the `==` operator, we can also use the `!=` operator, and second, although we overloaded the `==` operator and the `<=>` operator to compare `ipv4` values to `unsigned long` values, we can also compare `unsigned long` values to `ipv4` values. This is because the compiler performs symmetrical overload resolution. That means that for an expression `a@b` where `@` is a two-way relational operator, it performs name lookup for `a@b`, `a<=>b`, and `b<=>a`. The following table shows the list of all possible transformations of the relational operators:

`a == b`	`b == a`	
`a != b`	`!(a == b)`	`!(b == a)`
`a <=> b`	`0 <=> (b <=> a)`	
`a < b`	`(a <=> b) < 0`	`0 > (b <=> a)`
`a <= b`	`(a <=> b) <= 0`	`0 >= (b <=> a)`
`a > b`	`(a <=> b) > 0`	`0 < (b <=> a)`
`a >= b`	`(a <=> b) >= 0`	`0 <= (b <=> a)`

This greatly reduces the number of overloads you must explicitly provide for supporting comparison in different forms. The three-way comparison operator can be implemented either as a member or as a non-member function. In general, you should prefer the member implementation.

The non-member form should be used only when you want implicit conversion on both arguments. The following shows an example:

```
struct A { int i; };

struct B
{
  B(A a) : i(a.i) { }
  int i;
};

inline auto
operator<=>(B const& lhs, B const& rhs) noexcept
{
  return lhs.i <=> rhs.i;
}

assert(A{ 2 } < A{ 1 });
```

Although the `<=>` operator is defined for the type `B`, because it is a non-member and because `A` can be implicitly converted to `B`, we can perform comparison on objects of the `A` type.

See also

- *Simplifying code with class template argument deduction*, in *Chapter 1*, *Learning Modern Core Language Features*, to learn how to use class templates without explicitly specifying template arguments.
- *Ensuring constant correctness for a program*, to explore the benefits of constant correctness and how to achieve it.

10
Implementing Patterns and Idioms

Design patterns are general reusable solutions that can be applied to common problems that appear in software development. Idioms are patterns, algorithms, or ways to structure the code in one or more programming languages. A great number of books have been written on design patterns. This chapter is not intended to reiterate them, but rather to show how to implement several useful patterns and idioms, with a focus on readability, performance, and robustness, in terms of modern C++.

The recipes included in this chapter are as follows:

- Avoiding repetitive `if...else` statements in factory patterns
- Implementing the pimpl idiom
- Implementing the named parameter idiom
- Separating interfaces from implementations with the non-virtual interface idiom
- Handling friendship with the attorney-client idiom
- Static polymorphism with the curiously recurring template pattern
- Implementing a thread-safe singleton

The first recipe of this chapter presents a simple mechanism for avoiding repetitive if-else statements. Let's explore how this mechanism works.

Avoiding repetitive if...else statements in factory patterns

It is often the case that we end up writing repetitive `if...else` statements (or an equivalent `switch` statement) that do similar things, often with little variation and often done by copying and pasting with small changes. As the number of alternative conditions increases, the code becomes both hard to read and hard to maintain. Repetitive `if...else` statements can be replaced with various techniques, such as polymorphism. In this recipe, we will see how to avoid `if...else` statements in factory patterns (a factory is a function or object that is used to create other objects) using a map of functions.

Getting ready

In this recipe, we will consider the following problem: building a system that can handle image files in various formats, such as bitmap, PNG, JPG, and so on. Obviously, the details are beyond the scope of this recipe; the part we are concerned with is creating objects that handle various image formats. For this, we will consider the following hierarchy of classes:

```
class Image {};
class BitmapImage : public Image {};
class PngImage    : public Image {};
class JpgImage    : public Image {};
```

On the other hand, we'll define an interface for a factory class that can create instances of the aforementioned classes, as well as a typical implementation using `if...else` statements:

```
struct IImageFactory
{
  virtual std::unique_ptr<Image> Create(std::string_view type) = 0;
};

struct ImageFactory : public IImageFactory
{
  std::unique_ptr<Image>
  Create(std::string_view type) override
  {
    if (type == "bmp")
      return std::make_unique<BitmapImage>();
    else if (type == "png")
```

```
        return std::make_unique<PngImage>();
      else if (type == "jpg")
        return std::make_unique<JpgImage>();
      return nullptr;
    }
};
```

The goal of this recipe is to see how this implementation can be refactored to avoid repetitive `if...else` statements.

How to do it...

Perform the following steps to refactor the factory shown earlier to avoid using `if...else` statements:

1. Implement the factory interface:

   ```
   struct ImageFactory : public IImageFactory
   {
     std::unique_ptr<Image> Create(std::string_view type) override
     {
       // continued with 2. and 3.
     }
   };
   ```

2. Define a map where the key is the type of objects to create and the value is a function that creates objects:

   ```
   static std::map<
     std::string,
     std::function<std::unique_ptr<Image>()>> mapping
   {
     { "bmp", []() {return std::make_unique<BitmapImage>(); } },
     { "png", []() {return std::make_unique<PngImage>(); } },
     { "jpg", []() {return std::make_unique<JpgImage>(); } }
   };
   ```

3. To create an object, look up the object type in the map and, if it is found, use the associated function to create a new instance of the type:

   ```
   auto it = mapping.find(type.data());
   if (it != mapping.end())
     return it->second();
   return nullptr;
   ```

How it works...

The repetitive `if...else` statements in the first implementation are very similar – they check the value of the `type` parameter and create an instance of the appropriate `Image` class. If the argument to check was an integral type (for instance, an enumeration type), the sequence of `if...else` statements could have also been written in the form of a `switch` statement. That code can be used like this:

```
auto factory = ImageFactory{};
auto image = factory.Create("png");
```

Regardless of whether the implementation was using `if...else` statements or a `switch`, refactoring to avoid repetitive checks is relatively simple. In the refactored code, we used a map that has the key type `std::string` representing the type, that is, the name of the image format. The value is an `std::function<std::unique_ptr<Image>()>`. This is a wrapper for a function that takes no arguments and returns an `std::unique_ptr<Image>` (a `unique_ptr` of a derived class is implicitly converted to a `unique_ptr` of a base class).

Now that we have this map of functions that create objects, the actual implementation of the factory is much simpler; check the type of the object to be created in the map and, if present, use the associated value from the map as the actual function to create the object, or return `nullptr` if the object type is not present in the map.

This refactoring is transparent for the client code, as there are no changes in the way clients use the factory. On the other hand, this approach does require more memory to handle the static map, which, for some classes of applications, such as IoT, might be an important aspect. The example presented here is relatively simple, because the purpose is to demonstrate the concept. In real-world code, it might be necessary to create objects differently, such as using a different number of arguments and different types of arguments. However, this is not specific to the refactored implementation and the solution with the `if...else`/`switch` statement needs to account for that too. Therefore, in practice, the solution to this problem that worked with `if...else` statements should also work with the map.

There's more...

In the preceding implementation, the map is a local static to the virtual function, but it can also be a member of the class or even a global. The following implementation has the map defined as a static member of the class. The objects are not created based on the format name, but on the type information, as returned by the `typeid` operator:

```
struct IImageFactoryByType
{
  virtual std::unique_ptr<Image> Create(
    std::type_info const & type)  = 0;
};

struct ImageFactoryByType : public IImageFactoryByType
{
  std::unique_ptr<Image> Create(std::type_info const & type)
  override
  {
    auto it = mapping.find(&type);
    if (it != mapping.end())
      return it->second();
    return nullptr;
  }
private:
  static std::map<
    std::type_info const *,
    std::function<std::unique_ptr<Image>()>> mapping;
};

std::map<
  std::type_info const *,
  std::function<std::unique_ptr<Image>()>> ImageFactoryByType::mapping
{
  {&typeid(BitmapImage),[](){
      return std::make_unique<BitmapImage>();}},
  {&typeid(PngImage),   [](){
      return std::make_unique<PngImage>();}},
  {&typeid(JpgImage),   [](){
      return std::make_unique<JpgImage>();}}
};
```

In this case, the client code is slightly different, because instead of passing a name representing the type to create, such as PNG, we pass the value returned by the `typeid` operator, such as `typeid(PngImage)`:

```
auto factory = ImageFactoryByType{};
auto movie = factory.Create(typeid(PngImage));
```

This alternative is arguably more robust because the map keys are not strings that could be more prone to errors. This recipe proposes a pattern as the solution to a common problem, and not an actual implementation. As in the case of most patterns, there are different ways they can be implemented, and it is up to you to pick the one that is the most suitable for each context.

See also

- *Implementing the pimpl idiom*, to learn a technique that enables the separation of the implementation details from an interface.
- *Using unique_ptr to uniquely own a memory resource*, in *Chapter 9, Robustness and Performance*, to learn about the `std::unique_ptr` class, which represents a smart pointer that owns and manages another object or array of objects allocated on the heap.

Implementing the pimpl idiom

pimpl stands for **pointer to implementation** (but is also known as the **Cheshire cat idiom** or the **compiler firewall idiom**) and is an opaque pointer technique that enables the separation of the implementation details from an interface. This has the advantage that it enables changing the implementation without modifying the interface and, therefore, avoiding the need to recompile the code that is using the interface. This has the potential of making libraries using the pimpl idiom on their ABIs to be backward-compatible with older versions when only implementation details change. In this recipe, we will see how to implement the pimpl idiom using modern C++ features.

Getting ready

The reader is expected to be familiar with smart pointers and `std::string_view`, both of which were discussed in previous chapters of this book.

To demonstrate the pimpl idiom in a practical manner, we will consider the following class, which we will then refactor following the pimpl pattern:

```
class control
{
  std::string text;
  int width = 0;
  int height = 0;
  bool visible = true;
```

```
  void draw()
  {
    std::cout
      << "control " << '\n'
      << " visible: " << std::boolalpha << visible <<
         std::noboolalpha << '\n'
      << " size: " << width << ", " << height << '\n'
      << " text: " << text << '\n';
  }
public:
  void set_text(std::string_view t)
  {
    text = t.data();
    draw();
  }

  void resize(int const w, int const h)
  {
    width = w;
    height = h;
    draw();
  }

  void show()
  {
    visible = true;
    draw();
  }

  void hide()
  {
    visible = false;
    draw();
  }
};
```

This class represents a control that has properties such as text, size, and visibility. Every time these properties are changed, the control is redrawn. In this mocked implementation, drawing means printing the value of the properties to the console.

How to do it...

Take the following steps to implement the pimpl idiom, exemplified here by refactoring the `control` class shown earlier:

1. Put all private members, both data and functions, into a separate class. We will call this the **pimpl class** and the original class the **public class**.
2. In the header file of the public class, put a forward declaration to the pimpl class:

   ```
   // in control.h
   class control_pimpl;
   ```

3. In the public class definition, declare a pointer to the pimpl class using a `unique_ptr`. This should be the only private data member of the class:

   ```
   class control
   {
     std::unique_ptr<
       control_pimpl, void(*)(control_pimpl*)> pimpl;
     public:
       control();
       void set_text(std::string_view text);
       void resize(int const w, int const h);
       void show();
       void hide();
   };
   ```

4. Put the pimpl class definition in the source file of the public class. The pimpl class mirrors the public interface of the public class:

   ```
   // in control.cpp
   class control_pimpl
   {
     std::string text;
     int width = 0;
     int height = 0;
     bool visible = true;

     void draw()
     {
       std::cout
         << "control " << '\n'
         << " visible: " << std::boolalpha << visible
         << std::noboolalpha << '\n'
   ```

```
        << " size: " << width << ", " << height << '\n'
        << " text: " << text << '\n';
  }

public:
  void set_text(std::string_view t)
  {
    text = t.data();
    draw();
  }

  void resize(int const w, int const h)
  {
    width = w;
    height = h;
    draw();
  }

  void show()
  {
    visible = true;
    draw();
  }

  void hide()
  {
    visible = false;
    draw();
  }
};
```

5. The pimpl class is instantiated in the constructor of the public class:

```
control::control() :
  pimpl(new control_pimpl(),
        [](control_pimpl* pimpl) {delete pimpl; })
{}
```

6. Public class member functions call the corresponding member functions of the pimpl class:

```
void control::set_text(std::string_view text)
{
  pimpl->set_text(text);
```

```
}

void control::resize(int const w, int const h)
{
  pimpl->resize(w, h);
}

void control::show()
{
  pimpl->show();
}

void control::hide()
{
  pimpl->hide();
}
```

How it works...

The pimpl idiom enables hiding the internal implementation of a class from the clients of the library or module the class is part of. This provides several benefits:

- A clean interface for a class that its clients see.
- Changes in the internal implementation do not affect the public interface, which enables binary backward-compatibility for newer versions of a library (when the public interface remains unchanged).
- Clients of a class that use this idiom do not need to be recompiled when changes to the internal implementation occur. This leads to shorter build times.
- The header file does not need to include the headers for the types and functions used in the private implementation. This, again, leads to shorter build times.

The benefits mentioned above do not come for free; there are also several drawbacks that need to be mentioned:

- There is more code to write and maintain.
- The code can arguably be less readable, as there is a level of indirection and all the implementation details need to be looked up in the other files. In this recipe, the pimpl class definition was provided in the source file of the public class, but in practice, it could be in separate files.

- There is a slight runtime overhead because of the level of indirection from the public class to the pimpl class, but in practice, this is rarely significant.
- This approach does not work with protected members because these have to be available to the derived classes.
- This approach does not work with the private virtual functions, which have to appear in the class, either because they override functions from a base class or have to be available for overriding in a derived class.

As a rule of thumb, when implementing the pimpl idiom, always put all the private member data and functions, except for the virtual ones, in the pimpl class and leave the protected data members and functions and all the private virtual functions in the public class.

In the example in this recipe, the `control_pimpl` class is basically identical to the original control class. In practice, where classes are larger, have virtual functions and protected members, and both functions and data, the pimpl class is not a complete equivalent of how the class would have looked like if it was not pimpled. Also, in practice, the pimpl class may require a pointer to the public class in order to call members that were not moved into the pimpl class.

Concerning the implementation of the refactored `control` class, the pointer to the `control_pimpl` object is managed by a `unique_ptr`. In the declaration of this pointer, we have used a custom deleter:

```
std::unique_ptr<control_pimpl, void(*)(control_pimpl*)> pimpl;
```

The reason for this is that the control class has a destructor implicitly defined by the compiler, at a point where the `control_pimpl` type is still incomplete (that is, in the header). This would result in an error with `unique_ptr`, which cannot delete an incomplete type. This problem can be solved in two ways:

- Provide a user-defined destructor for the control class that is explicitly implemented (even if declared as `default`) after the complete definition of the `control_pimpl` class is available.
- Provide a custom deleter for the `unique_ptr`, as we did in this example.

There's more...

The original `control` class was both copyable and movable:

```
control c;
c.resize(100, 20);
```

```
c.set_text("sample");
c.hide();

control c2 = c;             // copy
c2.show();

control c3 = std::move(c2); // move
c3.hide();
```

The refactored `control` class is only movable, not copyable. The following code shows an implementation of the `control` class that is both copyable and movable:

```
class control_copyable
{
  std::unique_ptr<control_pimpl, void(*)(control_pimpl*)> pimpl;
public:
  control_copyable();
  control_copyable(control_copyable && op) noexcept;
  control_copyable& operator=(control_copyable && op) noexcept;
  control_copyable(const control_copyable& op);
  control_copyable& operator=(const control_copyable& op);

  void set_text(std::string_view text);
  void resize(int const w, int const h);
  void show();
  void hide();
};

control_copyable::control_copyable() :
  pimpl(new control_pimpl(),
        [](control_pimpl* pimpl) {delete pimpl; })
{}

control_copyable::control_copyable(control_copyable &&)
   noexcept = default;
control_copyable& control_copyable::operator=(control_copyable &&)
   noexcept = default;

control_copyable::control_copyable(const control_copyable& op)
   : pimpl(new control_pimpl(*op.pimpl),
           [](control_pimpl* pimpl) {delete pimpl; })
{}
```

```
control_copyable& control_copyable::operator=(
   const control_copyable& op)
{
  if (this != &op)
  {
    pimpl = std::unique_ptr<control_pimpl,void(*)(control_pimpl*)>(
                new control_pimpl(*op.pimpl),
                [](control_pimpl* pimpl) {delete pimpl; });
  }
  return *this;
}

// the other member functions
```

The class `control_copyable` is both copyable and movable, but to make it so, we provided the copy constructor and copy assignment operator and both the move constructor and move assignment operator. The latter ones can be defaulted, but the former ones were explicitly implemented to create a new `control_pimpl` object from the object that it is copied from.

See also

- *Using unique_ptr to uniquely own a memory resource*, in *Chapter 9, Robustness and Performance*, to learn about the `std::unique_ptr` class, which represents a smart pointer that owns and manages another object or array of objects allocated on the heap.

Implementing the named parameter idiom

C++ supports only positional parameters, which means arguments are passed to a function based on the parameter's position. Other languages also support named parameters - that is, they specify parameter names when making a call and invoking arguments. This is particularly useful with parameters that have default values. A function may have parameters with default values, although they always appear after all the non-defaulted parameters.

However, if you want to provide values for only some of the defaulted parameters, there is no way to do this without providing arguments for the parameters that are positioned before them in the function parameters list.

A technique called the **named parameter idiom** provides a method to emulate named parameters and help solve this problem. We will explore this technique in this recipe.

Getting ready

To exemplify the named parameter idiom, we will use the `control` class shown in the following code snippet:

```
class control
{
  int id_;
  std::string text_;
  int width_;
  int height_;
  bool visible_;
public:
  control(
    int const id,
    std::string_view text = "",
    int const width = 0,
    int const height = 0,
    bool const visible = false):
      id_(id), text_(text),
      width_(width), height_(height),
      visible_(visible)
  {}
};
```

The `control` class represents a visual control, such as a button or an input, and has properties such as numerical identifier, text, size, and visibility. These are provided to the constructor and, except for the ID, all the others have default values. In practice, such a class would have many more properties, such as text brush, background brush, border style, font size, font family, and many others.

How to do it...

To implement the named parameter idiom for a function (usually with many default parameters), do the following:

1. Create a class to wrap the parameters of the function:

   ```
   class control_properties
   ```

```
{
   int id_;
   std::string text_;
   int width_ = 0;
   int height_ = 0;
   bool visible_ = false;
};
```

2. The class or function that needs to access these properties could be declared as `friend` to avoid writing getters:

```
friend class control;
```

3. Every positional parameter of the original function that does not have a default value should become a positional parameter, without a default value in the constructor of the class:

```
public:
   control_properties(int const id) :id_(id)
   {}
```

4. For every positional parameter of the original function that has a default value, there should be a function (with the same name) that sets the value internally and returns a reference to the class:

```
public:
   control_properties& text(std::string_view t)
   { text_ = t.data(); return *this; }

   control_properties& width(int const w)
   { width_ = w; return *this; }

   control_properties& height(int const h)
   { height_ = h; return *this; }

   control_properties& visible(bool const v)
   { visible_ = v; return *this; }
```

5. The original function should be modified, or an overload should be provided, to take an argument of the new class from which the property values will be read:

```
control(control_properties const & cp):
   id_(cp.id_),
   text_(cp.text_),
```

```
   width_(cp.width_),
   height_(cp.height_),
   visible_(cp.visible_)
{}
```

If we put all that together, the result is the following:

```
class control;

class control_properties
{
  int id_;
  std::string text_;
  int width_ = 0;
  int height_ = 0;
  bool visible_ = false;

  friend class control;
public:
  control_properties(int const id) :id_(id)
  {}

  control_properties& text(std::string_view t)
  { text_ = t.data(); return *this; }

  control_properties& width(int const w)
  { width_ = w; return *this; }

  control_properties& height(int const h)
  { height_ = h; return *this; }

  control_properties& visible(bool const v)
  { visible_ = v; return *this; }
};

class control
{
  int         id_;
  std::string text_;
  int         width_;
  int         height_;
  bool        visible_;
```

```
public:
  control(control_properties const & cp):
    id_(cp.id_),
    text_(cp.text_),
    width_(cp.width_),
    height_(cp.height_),
    visible_(cp.visible_)
  {}
};
```

How it works...

The initial control class had a constructor with many parameters. In real-world code, you can find examples like this where the number of parameters is much higher. A possible solution, often found in practice, is to group common Boolean type properties in bit flags, which could be passed together as a single integral argument (an example could be the border style for a control that defines the position where the border should be visible: top, bottom, left, right, or any combination of these four). Creating a control object with the initial implementation is done like this:

```
control c(1044, "sample", 100, 20, true);
```

The named parameter idiom has the advantage that it allows you to specify values only for the parameters that you want, in any order, using a name, which is much more intuitive than a fixed, positional order.

Although there isn't a single strategy for implementing the idiom, the example in this recipe is rather typical. The properties of the control class, provided as parameters in the constructor, have been put into a separate class, called control_properties, that declares the class control as a friend class to allow it to access its private data members without providing getters. This has the side effect that it limits the use of control_properties outside the control class. The non-optional parameters of the constructor of the control class are also non-optional parameters of the control_properties constructor. For all the other parameters with default values, the control_properties class defines a function with a relevant name that simply sets the data member to the provided argument, and then returns a reference to control_properties. This enables the client to chain calls to these functions in any order.

The constructor of the control class has been replaced with a new one that has a single parameter, a constant reference to a control_properties object, whose data members are copied into the control object's data members.

Creating a `control` object with the named parameter idiom implemented in this manner is done as in the following snippet:

```
control c(control_properties(1044)
          .visible(true)
          .height(20)
          .width(100));
```

See also

- *Separating interfaces and implementations with the non-virtual interface idiom,* to explore an idiom that promotes the separation of concerns of interfaces and implementations by making (public) interfaces non-virtual and virtual functions private.
- *Handling friendship with the attorney-client idiom,* to learn about a simple mechanism to restrict friends' access to only designated, private parts of a class.

Separating interfaces and implementations with the non-virtual interface idiom

Virtual functions provide specialization points for a class by allowing derived classes to modify implementations from a base class. When a derived class object is handled through a pointer or a reference to a base class, calls to overridden virtual functions end up invoking the overridden implementation from the derived class. On the other hand, a customization is an implementation detail, and a good design separates interfaces from implementation.

The **non-virtual interface idiom**, proposed by Herb Sutter in an article about virtuality in the *C/C++ Users Journal*, promotes the separation of concerns of interfaces and implementations by making (public) interfaces non-virtual and virtual functions private.

Public virtual interfaces prevent a class from enforcing pre- and post-conditions on its interface. Users expecting an instance of a base class do not have the guarantee that the expected behavior of a public virtual method is delivered, since it can be overridden in a derived class. This idiom helps enforce the promised contract of an interface.

Getting ready

The reader should be familiar with aspects related to virtual functions, such as defining and overriding virtual functions, abstract classes, and pure specifiers.

How to do it...

Implementing this idiom requires following several simple design guidelines, formulated by Herb Sutter in the *C/C++ Users Journal*, 19(9), September 2001:

1. Make (public) interfaces non-virtual.
2. Make virtual functions private.
3. Make virtual functions protected only if the base implementation has to be called from a derived class.
4. Make the base class destructor either public and virtual or protected and nonvirtual.

The following example of a simple hierarchy of controls abides by all these four guidelines:

```
class control
{
private:
  virtual void paint() = 0;
protected:
  virtual void erase_background()
  {
    std::cout << "erasing control background..." << '\n';
  }
public:
  void draw()
  {
    erase_background();
    paint();
  }

  virtual ~control() {}
};

class button : public control
{
private:
```

```
    virtual void paint() override
    {
      std::cout << "painting button..." << '\n';
    }
  protected:
    virtual void erase_background() override
    {
      control::erase_background();
      std::cout << "erasing button background..." << '\n';
    }
  };

  class checkbox : public button
  {
  private:
    virtual void paint() override
    {
      std::cout << "painting checkbox..." << '\n';
    }
  protected:
    virtual void erase_background() override
    {
      button::erase_background();
      std::cout << "erasing checkbox background..." << '\n';
    }
  };
```

How it works...

The NVI idiom uses the **template method** design pattern, which allows derived classes to customize parts (that is, steps) of a base class functionality (that is, an algorithm). This is done by splitting the overall algorithm into smaller parts, each of them implemented by a virtual function. The base class may provide, or not, a default implementation, and the derived classes could override them while maintaining the overall structure and meaning of the algorithm.

The core principles of the NVI idiom is that virtual functions should not be public; they should be either private or protected, in case the base class implementation could be called from a derived class. The interface of a class, the public part accessible to its clients, should be comprised exclusively of nonvirtual functions. This provides several advantages:

- It separates the interface from the details of implementation that are no longer exposed to the client.
- It enables changing the details of the implementation without altering the public interface and without requiring changes to the client code, therefore making base classes more robust.
- It allows a class to have sole control of its interface. If the public interface contains virtual methods, a derived class can alter the promised functionality, and therefore, the class cannot ensure its preconditions and postconditions. When none of the virtual methods (except for the destructor) are accessible to its clients, the class can enforce pre- and post-conditions on its interface.

A special mention of the destructor of a class is required for this idiom. It is often stressed that base class destructors should be virtual so that objects can be deleted polymorphically (through a pointer or references to a base class). Destructing objects polymorphically when the destructor is not virtual incurs undefined behavior. However, not all base classes are intended to be deleted polymorphically. For those particular cases, the base class destructor should not be virtual. However, it should also not be public, but protected.

The example from the previous section defines a hierarchy of classes representing visual controls:

- `control` is the base class, but there are derived classes, such as `button` and `checkbox`, which are a type of button and, therefore, are derived from this class.
- The only functionality defined by the `control` class is drawing the controls. The `draw()` method is nonvirtual, but it calls two virtual methods, `erase_background()` and `paint()`, to implement the two phases of drawing the control.
- `erase_background()` is a protected virtual method because derived classes need to call it in their own implementation.
- `paint()` is a private pure virtual method. Derived classes must implement it, but are not supposed to call a base implementation.
- The destructor of the control class is public and virtual because objects are expected to be deleted polymorphically.

An example of using these classes is shown as follows. Instances of these classes are managed by smart pointers to the base class:

```
std::vector<std::unique_ptr<control>> controls;

controls.emplace_back(std::make_unique<button>());
controls.emplace_back(std::make_unique<checkbox>());

for (auto& c : controls)
  c->draw();
```

The output of this program is as follows:

```
erasing control background...
erasing button background...
painting button...
erasing control background...
erasing button background...
erasing checkbox background...
painting checkbox...
destroying button...
destroying control...
destroying checkbox...
destroying button...
destroying control...
```

The NVI idiom introduces a level of indirection when a public function calls a non-public virtual function that does the actual implementation. In the previous example, the `draw()` method called several other functions, but in many cases, it could be only one call:

```
class control
{
protected:
  virtual void initialize_impl()
  {
    std::cout << "initializing control..." << '\n';
  }
public:
  void initialize()
  {
```

```
    initialize_impl();
  }
};

class button : public control
{
protected:
  virtual void initialize_impl()
  {
    control::initialize_impl();
    std::cout << "initializing button..." << '\n';
  }
};
```

In this example, the class `control` has an additional method called `initialize()` (the previous content of the class was not shown to keep it simple) that calls a single non-public virtual method called `initialize_impl()`, implemented differently in each derived class. This does not incur much overhead - if any at all - since simple functions like this are most likely inlined by the compiler anyway.

See also

- *Use override and final for virtual methods*, in *Chapter 1*, *Learning Modern Core Language Features*, to learn how to specify that a virtual function overrides another virtual function, as well as how to specify that a virtual function cannot be overridden in a derived class.

Handling friendship with the attorney-client idiom

Granting functions and classes access to the non-public parts of a class with a friend declaration has been usually seen as a sign of bad design, as friendship breaks encapsulation and ties classes and functions. Friends, whether they are classes or functions, get access to all the private parts of a class, although they may only need to access parts of it.

The **attorney-client idiom** provides a simple mechanism to restrict friends access to only designated private parts of a class.

Getting ready

To demonstrate how to implement this idiom, we will consider the following classes: `Client`, which has some private member data and functions (the public interface is not important here), and `Friend`, which is supposed to access only parts of the private details, for instance, `data1` and `action1()`, but has access to everything:

```
class Client
{
  int data_1;
  int data_2;

  void action1() {}
  void action2() {}

  friend class Friend;
public:
  // public interface
};

class Friend
{
public:
  void access_client_data(Client& c)
  {
    c.action1();
    c.action2();
    auto d1 = c.data_1;
    auto d2 = c.data_1;
  }
};
```

To understand this idiom, you must be familiar with how friendship is declared in the C++ language and how it works.

How to do it...

Take the following steps to restrict a friend's access to the private parts of a class:

1. In the `Client` class, which provides access to its private parts to a friend, declare the friendships to an intermediate class, called the `Attorney` class:

```
class Client
```

```
{
  int data_1;
  int data_2;

  void action1() {}
  void action2() {}

  friend class Attorney;
public:
  // public interface
};
```

2. Create a class that contains only private (inline) functions that access the private parts of the client. This intermediate class allows the actual friend to access its private parts:

```
class Attorney
{
  static inline void run_action1(Client& c)
  {
    c.action1();
  }

  static inline int get_data1(Client& c)
  {
    return c.data_1;
  }

  friend class Friend;
};
```

3. In the `Friend` class, access the private parts of only the `Client` class indirectly through the `Attorney` class:

```
class Friend
{
public:
  void access_client_data(Client& c)
  {
    Attorney::run_action1(c);
    auto d1 = Attorney::get_data1(c);
  }
};
```

How it works...

The attorney-client idiom lays out a simple mechanism to restrict access to the private parts of the client by introducing a middleman, the attorney. Instead of providing friendship directly to those using its internal state, the client class offers friendship to an attorney, which, in turn, provides access to a restricted set of private data or functions of the client. It does so by defining private static functions. Usually, these are also inline functions, which avoids any runtime overhead due to the level of indirection the attorney class introduces. The client's friend gets access to its private parts by actually using the private parts of the attorney. This idiom is called **attorney-client** because it is similar to the way an attorney-client relationship works, with the attorney knowing all the secrets of the client, but exposing only some of them to other parties.

In practice, it might be necessary to create more than one attorney for a client class if different friend classes or functions must access different private parts.

On the other hand, friendship is not inheritable, which means that a class or function that is friend to class `B` is not friend with class `D`, which is derived from `B`. However, virtual functions overridden in `D` are still accessible polymorphically through a pointer or reference to `B` from a friend class. Such an example is shown as follows; calling the `run()` method from `F` prints `base` and `derived`:

```
class B
{
  virtual void execute() { std::cout << "base" << '\n'; }
  friend class BAttorney;
};

class D : public B
{
  virtual void execute() override
  { std::cout << "derived" << '\n'; }
};

class BAttorney
{
  static inline void execute(B& b)
  {
    b.execute();
  }
  friend class F;
};
```

```
class F
{
public:
  void run()
  {
    B;
    BAttorney::execute(b); // prints 'base'

    D;
    BAttorney::execute(d); // prints 'derived'
  }
};

F;
f.run();
```

There are always trade-offs to using a design pattern, and this one makes no exception. There are situations when using this pattern may lead to too much overhead on development, testing, and maintenance. However, the pattern could prove extremely valuable for some types of applications, such as extensible frameworks.

See also

- *Implementing the pimpl idiom*, to learn a technique that enables the separation of the implementation details from an interface.

Static polymorphism with the curiously recurring template pattern

Polymorphism provides us with the ability to have multiple forms for the same interface. Virtual functions allow derived classes to override implementations from a base class. They represent the most common elements of a form of polymorphism, called **runtime polymorphism**, because the decision to call a particular virtual function from the class hierarchy happens at runtime. It is also called **late binding**, because the binding between a function call and the invocation of the function happens late, during the execution of the program. The opposite of this is called **early binding**, **static polymorphism**, or **compile time polymorphism** because it occurs at compile time through functions and operators overloading.

On the other hand, a technique called the **curiously recurring template pattern** (or **CRTP**) allows simulating the virtual functions-based runtime polymorphism at compile time, by deriving classes from a base class template parameterized with the derived class. This technique is used extensively in some libraries, including Microsoft's **Active Template Library** (**ATL**) and **Windows Template Library** (**WTL**). In this recipe, we will explore this CRTP pattern and learn how to implement it and how it works.

Getting ready

To demonstrate how the CRTP works, we will revisit the example with the hierarchy of control classes we implemented in the *Separating interfaces from implementations with the non-virtual interface idiom* recipe. We will define a set of control classes that have functionalities such as drawing the control, which is (in our example) an operation done in two phases: erasing the background and then painting the control. For simplicity, in our implementation, these will be operations that will only print text to the console.

How to do it...

To implement the curiously recurring template pattern in order to achieve static polymorphism, do the following:

1. Provide a class template that will represent the base class for other classes that should be treated polymorphically at compile time. Polymorphic functions are invoked from this class:

```
template <class T>
class control
{
public:
  void draw()
  {
    static_cast<T*>(this)->erase_background();
    static_cast<T*>(this)->paint();
  }
};
```

2. Derived classes use the class template as their base class; the derived class is also the template argument for the base class. The derived class implements the functions that are invoked from the base class:

```
class button : public control<button>
{
public:
  void erase_background()
  {
    std::cout << "erasing button background..." << '\n';
  }

  void paint()
  {
    std::cout << "painting button..." << '\n';
  }
};

class checkbox : public control<checkbox>
{
public:
  void erase_background()
  {
    std::cout << "erasing checkbox background..."
              << '\n';
  }

  void paint()
  {
    std::cout << "painting checkbox..." << '\n';
  }
};
```

3. Function templates can handle derived classes polymorphically through a pointer or reference to the base class template:

```
template <class T>
void draw_control(control<T>& c)
{
  c.draw();
}

button b;
draw_control(b);

checkbox c;
draw_control(c);
```

How it works...

Virtual functions can represent a performance issue, especially when they are small and called multiple times in a loop. Modern hardware has made most of these situations rather irrelevant, but there are still some categories of applications where performance is critical and any performance gains are important. The curiously recurring template pattern enables the simulation of virtual calls at compile time using metaprogramming, which eventually translates to functions overloading.

This pattern may look rather strange at first glance, but it is perfectly legal. The idea is to derive a class from a base class that is a template class, and then pass the derived class itself for the type template parameter of the base class. The base class then makes calls to the derived class functions. In our example, `control<button>::draw()` is declared before the `button` class is known to the compiler. However, the `control` class is a class template, which means it is instantiated only when the compiler encounters code that uses it. At that point, the `button` class, in this example, is already defined and known to the compiler, so calls to `button::erase_background()` and `button::paint()` can be made.

To invoke the functions from the derived class, we must first obtain a pointer to the derived class. That is done with a `static_cast` conversion, as seen in `static_cast<T*>(this)->erase_background()`. If this has to be done many times, the code can be simplified by providing a private function to do that:

```
template <class T>
class control
{
  T* derived() { return static_cast<T*>(this); }
public:
  void draw()
  {
    derived()->erase_background();
    derived()->paint();
  }
};
```

There are some pitfalls when using the CRTP that you must be aware of:

- All the functions in the derived classes that are called from the base class template must be public; otherwise, the base class specialization must be declared a friend of the derived class:

  ```
  class button : public control<button>
  {
  private:
  ```

```
    friend class control<button>;
    void erase_background()
    {
      std::cout << "erasing button background..." << '\n';
    }

    void paint()
    {
      std::cout << "painting button..." << '\n';
    }
  };
```

- It is not possible to store, in a homogeneous container, such as a `vector` or `list`, objects of CRTP types because each base class is a unique type (such as `control<button>` and `control<checkbox>`). If this is actually necessary, then a workaround can be used to implement it. This will be discussed and exemplified in the next section.
- When using this technique, the size of a program may increase, because of the way templates are instantiated.

There's more...

When objects of types implementing the CRTP need to be stored homogeneously in a container, an additional idiom must be used. The base class template must be, itself, derived from another class with pure virtual functions (and a virtual public destructor). To exemplify this on the `control` class, the following changes are necessary:

```
class controlbase
{
public:
  virtual void draw() = 0;
  virtual ~controlbase() {}
};

template <class T>
class control : public controlbase
{
public:
  virtual void draw() override
  {
    static_cast<T*>(this)->erase_background();
```

```
    static_cast<T*>(this)->paint();
  }
};
```

No changes need to be made to the derived classes, such as `button` and `checkbox`. Then, we can store pointers to the abstract class in a container, such as `std::vector`, as shown here:

```
void draw_controls(std::vector<std::unique_ptr<controlbase>>& v)
{
  for (auto & c : v)
  {
    c->draw();
  }
}

std::vector<std::unique_ptr<controlbase>> v;
v.emplace_back(std::make_unique<button>());
v.emplace_back(std::make_unique<checkbox>());

draw_controls(v);
```

See also

- *Implementing the pimpl idiom*, to learn a technique that enables the separation of the implementation details from an interface.
- *Separating interfaces from implementations with the non-virtual interface idiom*, to explore an idiom that promotes the separation of concerns of interfaces and implementations by making (public) interfaces non-virtual and virtual functions private.

Implementing a thread-safe singleton

Singleton is probably one of the most well-known design patterns. It restricts the instantiation of a single object of a class, something that is necessary in some cases, although many times the use of a singleton is rather an anti-pattern that can be avoided with other design choices.

Since a singleton means a single instance of a class is available to an entire program, it is likely that such a unique instance might be accessible from different threads. Therefore, when you implement a singleton, you should also make it thread-safe.

Before C++11, doing that was not an easy job, and a double-checked locking technique was the typical approach. However, Scott Meyers and Andrei Alexandrescu showed, in a paper called *C++ and the Perils of Double-Checked Locking*, that using this pattern did not guarantee a thread-safe singleton implementation in portable C++. Fortunately, this changed in C++11, and this recipe shows how to write a thread-safe singleton in modern C++.

Getting ready

For this recipe, you need to know how static storage duration, internal linkage, and deleted and defaulted functions work. You should also read the previous recipe, *Static polymorphism with the curiously recurring template pattern*, first if you have not done that yet and are not familiar with that pattern as we will use it later in this recipe.

How to do it...

To implement a thread-safe singleton, you should do the following:

1. Define the `Singleton` class:

```
class Singleton
{
};
```

2. Make the default constructor private:

```
private:
  Singleton() {}
```

3. Make the copy constructor and copy assignment operator `public` and `delete`, respectively:

```
public:
  Singleton(Singleton const &) = delete;
  Singleton& operator=(Singleton const&) = delete;
```

4. The function that creates and returns the single instance should be static and should return a reference to the class type. It should declare a static object of the class type and return a reference to it:

```
public:
  static Singleton& instance()
  {
    static Singleton single;
```

```
    return single;
}
```

How it works...

Since singleton objects are not supposed to be created by the user directly, all constructors are either private or public and `deleted`. The default constructor is private and not deleted because an instance of the class must be actually created in the class code. A static function, called `instance()`, in this implementation, returns the single instance of the class.

Though most implementations return a pointer, it actually makes more sense to return a reference, as there is no circumstance under which this function would return a null pointer (no object).

The implementation of the `instance()` method may look simplistic and not thread-safe at first glance, especially if you are familiar with the **double-checked locking pattern** (**DCLP**). In C++11, this is actually no longer necessary due to a key detail of how objects with static storage durations are initialized. Initialization happens only once, even if several threads attempt to initialize the same static object at the same time. The responsibility of the DCLP has been moved from the user to the compiler, although the compiler may use another technique to guarantee the result.

The following quote from the C++ standard, paragraph 6.7.4, defines the rules for static objects initialization (the highlight is the part related to concurrent initialization):

> *"The zero-initialization (8.5) of all block-scope variables with static storage duration (3.7.1) or thread storage duration (3.7.2) is performed before any other initialization takes place. Constant initialization (3.6.2) of a block-scope entity with static storage duration, if applicable, is performed before its block is first entered. An implementation is permitted to perform early initialization of other block-scope variables with static or thread storage duration under the same conditions that an implementation is permitted to statically initialize a variable with static or thread storage duration in namespace scope (3.6.2). Otherwise, such a variable is initialized the first time control passes through its declaration; such a variable is considered initialized upon the completion of its initialization. If the initialization exits by throwing an exception, the initialization is not complete, so it will be tried again the next time control enters the declaration.* ***If control enters the declaration concurrently while the variable is being initialized, the concurrent execution shall wait for completion of the initialization.*** *If control re-enters the declaration recursively while the variable is being initialized, the behavior is undefined."*

The static local object has storage duration, but it is instantiated only when it is first used (at the first call to the method `instance()`). The object is deallocated when the program exists. As a side note, the only possible advantage of returning a pointer and not a reference is the ability to delete this single instance at some point, before the program exists, and then maybe recreate it. This, again, does not make too much sense, as it conflicts with the idea of a single, global instance of a class, accessible at any point from any place in the program.

There's more...

There might be situations in larger code bases where you need more than one singleton type. In order to avoid writing the same pattern several times, you can implement it in a generic way. For this, we need to employ the **curiously recurring template pattern** (or **CRTP**) seen in the previous recipe. The actual singleton is implemented as a class template. The `instance()` method creates and returns an object of the type template parameter, which will be the derived class:

```
template <class T>
class SingletonBase
{
protected:
  SingletonBase() {}
public:
  SingletonBase(SingletonBase const &) = delete;
  SingletonBase& operator=(SingletonBase const&) = delete;

  static T& instance()
  {
    static T single;
    return single;
  }
};

class Single : public SingletonBase<Single>
{
  Single() {}
  friend class SingletonBase<Single>;
public:
  void demo() { std::cout << "demo" << '\n'; }
};
```

The `Singleton` class from the previous section has become the `SingletonBase` class template. The default constructor is no longer private but protected because it must be accessible from the derived class. In this example, the class that needs to have a single object instantiated is called `Single`. Its constructors must be private, but the default constructor must also be available to the base class template; therefore, `SingletonBase<Single>` is a friend of the `Single` class.

See also

- *Static polymorphism with the curiously recurring template pattern*, to learn about the CRTP pattern, which allows simulating runtime polymorphism at compile time by deriving classes from a base class template parameterized with the derived class.
- *Defaulted and deleted functions*, in *Chapter 3, Exploring Functions*, to learn about the use of the default specifier on special member functions and how to define functions as deleted with the delete specifier.

11

Exploring Testing Frameworks

Testing the code is an important part of software development. Although there is no support for testing in the C++ standard, there is a large variety of frameworks for unit testing C++ code. The purpose of this chapter is to get you started with several modern and widely used testing frameworks that enable you to write portable testing code. The frameworks that will be covered in this chapter are **Boost.Test**, **Google Test**, and **Catch2**.

This chapter includes the following recipes:

- Getting started with Boost.Test
- Writing and invoking tests with Boost.Test
- Asserting with Boost.Test
- Using test fixtures with Boost.Test
- Controlling output with Boost.Test
- Getting started with Google Test
- Writing and invoking tests with Google Test
- Asserting with Google Test
- Using test fixtures with Google Test
- Controlling output with Google Test
- Getting started with Catch2

- Writing and invoking tests with Catch2
- Asserting with Catch2
- Controlling output with Catch2

These three frameworks were chosen due to their wide use, rich capabilities, the ease with which they can be used to write and execute tests, their extensibility, and their customization. The following table shows a short comparison of the features of these three libraries:

Feature	Boost.Test	Google Test	Catch2
Easy to install	Yes	Yes	Yes
Header-only	Yes	No	Yes
Compiled library	Yes	Yes	Yes
Easy to write tests	Yes	Yes	Yes
Automatic test registration	Yes	Yes	Yes
Supports test suites	Yes	Yes	No (indirectly with tags)
Supports fixtures	Yes (setup/ teardown)	Yes (setup/ teardown)	Yes (multiple ways)
Rich set of asserts	Yes	Yes	Yes
Non-fatal asserts	Yes	Yes	Yes
Multiple output formats	Yes (includes HRF, XML)	Yes (includes HRF, XML)	Yes (includes HRF, XML)
Filtering of test execution	Yes	Yes	Yes
License	Boost	Apache 2.0	Boost

All these features will be discussed in detail for each framework. This chapter has a symmetric structure, with 4-5 recipes dedicated to each testing framework. The first framework to look at is Boost.Test.

Getting started with Boost.Test

Boost.Test is one of the oldest and most popular C++ testing frameworks. It provides an easy-to-use set of APIs for writing tests and organizing them into test cases and test suites. It has good support for asserting, exception handling, fixtures, and other important features required for a testing framework.

Throughout the next few recipes, we will explore the most important features it has that enable you to write unit tests. In this recipe, we will see how to install the framework and create a simple test project.

Getting ready

The Boost.Test framework has a macro-based API. Although you only need to use the supplied macros for writing tests, a good understanding of macros is recommended if you want to use the framework well.

How to do it...

In order to set up your environment to use Boost.Test, do the following:

1. Download the latest version of the Boost library from `http://www.boost.org/`.
2. Unzip the content of the archive.
3. Build the library using the provided tools and scripts in order to use either the static or shared library variant. This step is not necessary if you only plan to use the header-only version of the library.

To create your first test program using the header-only variant of the Boost.Test library, do the following:

1. Create a new, empty C++ project.
2. Do the necessary setup specific to the development environment you are using to make the boost `main` folder available to the project for including header files.
3. Add a new source file to the project with the following content:

```
#define BOOST_TEST_MODULE My first test module
#include <boost/test/included/unit_test.hpp>

BOOST_AUTO_TEST_CASE(first_test_function)
{
  int a = 42;
  BOOST_TEST(a > 0);
}
```

4. Build and run the project.

How it works...

The Boost.Test library can be downloaded, along with other Boost libraries, from `http://www.boost.org/`. In this book, I used version 1.73, but the features discussed in these recipes will probably be available for many future versions. The `Test` library comes in three variants:

- **Single header**: This enables you to write test programs without building the library; you just need to include a single header. Its limitation is that you can only have a single translation unit for the module; however, you can still split the module into multiple header files so that you can separate different test suites into different files.
- **Static library**: This enables you to split a module across different translation units, but the library needs to be built first as a static library.
- **Shared library**: This enables the same scenario as that of the static library. However, it has the advantage that, for programs with many test modules, this library is linked only once, and not once for each module, resulting in a smaller binary size. However, in this case, the shared library must be available at runtime.

For simplicity, we will use the single-header variant in this book. In the case of static and shared library variants, you'd need to build the library. The downloaded archive contains scripts for building the library. However, the exact steps vary, depending on the platform and the compiler; they will not be covered here but are available online.

There are several terms and concepts that you need to understand in order to use the library:

- **Test module** is a program that performs tests. There are two types of modules: **single-file** (when you use the single-header variant) and **multifile** (when you use either the static or shared variant).
- **Test assertion** is a condition that is checked by a test module.
- **Test case** is a group of one or more test assertions that is independently executed and monitored by a test module so that, if it fails or leaks uncaught exceptions, the execution of other tests will not be stopped.
- **Test suite** is a collection of one or more test cases or test suites.
- **Test unit** is either a test case or test suite.
- **Test tree** is a hierarchical structure of test units. In this structure, test cases are leaves and test suites are non-leaves.
- **Test runner** is a component that, given a test tree, performs the necessary initialization, execution of tests, and results reporting.

- **Test report** is the report produced by the test runner from executing the tests.
- **Test log** is the recording of all the events that occur during the execution of the test module.
- **Test setup** is the part of the test module responsible for the initialization of the framework, construction of the test tree, and individual test case setups.
- **Test cleanup** is a part of the test module responsible for cleanup operations.
- **Test fixture** is a pair of setup and cleanup operations that are invoked for multiple test units in order to avoid repetitive code.

With these concepts defined, it is possible to explain the sample code listed earlier:

1. `#define BOOST_TEST_MODULE My first test module` defines a stub for module initialization and sets a name for the main test suite. This must be defined before you include any library header.
2. `#include <boost/test/included/unit_test.hpp>` includes the single-header library, which includes all the other necessary headers.
3. `BOOST_AUTO_TEST_CASE(first_test_function)` declares a test case without parameters (`first_test_function`) and automatically registers it to be included in the test tree as part of the enclosing test suite. In this example, the test suite is the main test suite defined by `BOOST_TEST_MODULE`.
4. `BOOST_TEST(true);` performs a test assertion.

The output of executing this test module is as follows:

```
Running 1 test case...
*** No errors detected
```

There's more...

If you don't want the library to generate the `main()` function but want to write it yourself, then you need to define a couple more macros – `BOOST_TEST_NO_MAIN` and `BOOST_TEST_ALTERNATIVE_INIT_API` – before you include any of the library headers. Then, in the `main()` function that you supply, invoke the default test runner called `unit_test_main()` by providing the default initialization function called `init_unit_test()` as an argument, as shown in the following code snippet:

```
#define BOOST_TEST_MODULE My first test module
#define BOOST_TEST_NO_MAIN
#define BOOST_TEST_ALTERNATIVE_INIT_API
#include <boost/test/included/unit_test.hpp>
```

```
BOOST_AUTO_TEST_CASE(first_test_function)
{
  int a = 42;
  BOOST_TEST(a > 0);
}

int main(int argc, char* argv[])
{
  return boost::unit_test::unit_test_main(init_unit_test, argc, argv);
}
```

It is also possible to customize the initialization function of the test runner. In this case, you must remove the definition of the `BOOST_TEST_MODULE` macro and instead write an initialization function that takes no arguments and returns a `bool` value:

```
#define BOOST_TEST_NO_MAIN
#define BOOST_TEST_ALTERNATIVE_INIT_API
#include <boost/test/included/unit_test.hpp>
#include <iostream>

BOOST_AUTO_TEST_CASE(first_test_function)
{
  int a = 42;
  BOOST_TEST(a > 0);
}

bool custom_init_unit_test()
{
  std::cout << "test runner custom init\n";
  return true;
}

int main(int argc, char* argv[])
{
  return boost::unit_test::unit_test_main(
    custom_init_unit_test, argc, argv);
}
```

It is possible to customize the initialization function without writing the `main()` function yourself. In this case, the `BOOST_TEST_NO_MAIN` macro should not be defined and the initialization function should be called `init_unit_test()`.

See also

- *Writing and invoking tests with Boost.Test*, to see how to create test suites and test cases using the single-header version of the Boost.Test library, as well as how to run tests.

Writing and invoking tests with Boost.Test

The library provides both an automatic and manual way of registering test cases and test suites to be executed by the test runner. Automatic registration is the simplest way because it enables you to construct a test tree just by declaring test units. In this recipe, we will see how to create test suites and test cases using the single-header version of the library, as well as how to run tests.

Getting ready

To exemplify the creation of test suites and test cases, we will use the following class, which represents a three-dimensional point. This implementation contains methods for accessing the properties of a point, comparison operators, a stream output operator, and a method for modifying the position of a point:

```
class point3d
{
  int x_;
  int y_;
  int z_;
public:
  point3d(int const x = 0,
          int const y = 0,
          int const z = 0):x_(x), y_(y), z_(z) {}

  int x() const { return x_; }
  point3d& x(int const x) { x_ = x; return *this; }

  int y() const { return y_; }
  point3d& y(int const y) { y_ = y; return *this; }

  int z() const { return z_; }
  point3d& z(int const z) { z_ = z; return *this; }
```

```
  bool operator==(point3d const & pt) const
  {
    return x_ == pt.x_ && y_ == pt.y_ && z_ == pt.z_;
  }

  bool operator!=(point3d const & pt) const
  {
    return !(*this == pt);
  }

  bool operator<(point3d const & pt) const
  {
    return x_ < pt.x_ || y_ < pt.y_ || z_ < pt.z_;
  }

  friend std::ostream& operator<<(std::ostream& stream,
                                  point3d const & pt)
  {
    stream << "(" << pt.x_ << "," << pt.y_ << "," << pt.z_ << ")";
    return stream;
  }

  void offset(int const offsetx, int const offsety,
              int const offsetz)
  {
    x_ += offsetx;
    y_ += offsety;
    z_ += offsetz;
  }

  static point3d origin() { return point3d{}; }
};
```

Before you go any further, notice that the test cases in this recipe contain erroneous tests on purpose so that they produce failures.

How to do it...

Use the following macros to create test units:

- To create a test suite, use `BOOST_AUTO_TEST_SUITE(name)` and `BOOST_AUTO_TEST_SUITE_END()`:

```
BOOST_AUTO_TEST_SUITE(test_construction)
// test cases
BOOST_AUTO_TEST_SUITE_END()
```

- To create a test case, use `BOOST_AUTO_TEST_CASE(name)`. Test cases are defined between `BOOST_AUTO_TEST_SUITE(name)` and `BOOST_AUTO_TEST_SUITE_END()`, as shown in the following code snippet:

```
BOOST_AUTO_TEST_CASE(test_constructor)
{
  auto p = point3d{ 1,2,3 };
  BOOST_TEST(p.x() == 1);
  BOOST_TEST(p.y() == 2);
  BOOST_TEST(p.z() == 4); // will fail
}

BOOST_AUTO_TEST_CASE(test_origin)
{
  auto p = point3d::origin();
  BOOST_TEST(p.x() == 0);
  BOOST_TEST(p.y() == 0);
  BOOST_TEST(p.z() == 0);
}
```

- To create a nested test suite, define a test suite inside another test suite:

```
BOOST_AUTO_TEST_SUITE(test_operations)
BOOST_AUTO_TEST_SUITE(test_methods)

BOOST_AUTO_TEST_CASE(test_offset)
```

```
{
   auto p = point3d{ 1,2,3 };
   p.offset(1, 1, 1);
   BOOST_TEST(p.x() == 2);
   BOOST_TEST(p.y() == 3);
   BOOST_TEST(p.z() == 3); // will fail
}

BOOST_AUTO_TEST_SUITE_END()
BOOST_AUTO_TEST_SUITE_END()
```

- To add decorators to a test unit, add an additional parameter to the test unit's macros. Decorators could include description, label, precondition, dependency, fixture, and so on. Refer to the following code snippet, which illustrates this:

```
BOOST_AUTO_TEST_SUITE(test_operations)
BOOST_AUTO_TEST_SUITE(test_operators)

BOOST_AUTO_TEST_CASE(
   test_equal,
   *boost::unit_test::description("test operator==")
   *boost::unit_test::label("opeq"))
{
   auto p1 = point3d{ 1,2,3 };
   auto p2 = point3d{ 1,2,3 };
   auto p3 = point3d{ 3,2,1 };
   BOOST_TEST(p1 == p2);
   BOOST_TEST(p1 == p3); // will fail
}

BOOST_AUTO_TEST_CASE(
   test_not_equal,
   *boost::unit_test::description("test operator!=")
   *boost::unit_test::label("opeq")
   *boost::unit_test::depends_on(
      "test_operations/test_operators/test_equal"))
{
   auto p1 = point3d{ 1,2,3 };
   auto p2 = point3d{ 3,2,1 };
   BOOST_TEST(p1 != p2);
}
```

```
BOOST_AUTO_TEST_CASE(test_less)
{
  auto p1 = point3d{ 1,2,3 };
  auto p2 = point3d{ 1,2,3 };
  auto p3 = point3d{ 3,2,1 };
  BOOST_TEST(!(p1 < p2));
  BOOST_TEST(p1 < p3);
}

BOOST_AUTO_TEST_SUITE_END()
BOOST_AUTO_TEST_SUITE_END()
```

To execute the tests, do the following (notice that the command line is Windows-specific, but it should be trivial to replace that with the one specific to Linux or macOS):

- To execute the entire test tree, run the program (the test module) without any parameters:

```
chapter11bt_02.exe

Running 6 test cases...
f:/chapter11bt_02/main.cpp(12): error: in "test_construction/test_
constructor": check p.z() == 4 has failed [3 != 4]
f:/chapter11bt_02/main.cpp(35): error: in "test_operations/test_
methods/test_offset": check p.z() == 3 has failed [4 != 3]
f:/chapter11bt_02/main.cpp(55): error: in "test_operations/test_
operators/test_equal": check p1 == p3 has failed [(1,2,3) !=
(3,2,1)]
*** 3 failures are detected in the test module "Testing point 3d"
```

- To execute a single test suite, run the program with the argument `run_test`, specifying the path of the test suite:

```
chapter11bt_02.exe --run_test=test_construction

Running 2 test cases...
f:/chapter11bt_02/main.cpp(12): error: in "test_construction/test_
constructor": check p.z() == 4 has failed [3 != 4]
*** 1 failure is detected in the test module "Testing point 3d"
```

- To execute a single test case, run the program with the argument `run_test`, specifying the path of the test case:

```
chapter11bt_02.exe --run_test=test_construction/test_origin
```

```
Running 1 test case...
*** No errors detected
```

- To execute a collection of test suites and test cases defined under the same label, run the program with the argument `run_test`, specifying the label name prefixed with `@`:

```
chapter11bt_02.exe --run_test=@opeq

Running 2 test cases...
f:/chapter11bt_02/main.cpp(56): error: in "test_operations/test_
operators/test_equal": check p1 == p3 has failed [(1,2,3) !=
(3,2,1)]
*** 1 failure is detected in the test module "Testing point 3d"
```

How it works...

A test tree is constructed from test suites and test cases. A test suite can contain one or more test cases and other nested test suites as well. Test suites are similar to namespaces in the sense that they can be stopped and restarted multiple times in the same file or in different files. Automatic registration of test suites is done with the macros `BOOST_AUTO_TEST_SUITE`, which requires a name, and `BOOST_AUTO_TEST_SUITE_END`. Automatic registration of test cases is done with `BOOST_AUTO_TEST_CASE`. Test units (whether they're cases or suites) become members of the closest test suite. Test units defined at the file scope level become members of the master test suite—the implicit test suite created with the `BOOST_TEST_MODULE` declaration.

Both test suites and test cases can be decorated with a series of attributes that affect how test units will be processed during the execution of the test module. The currently supported decorators are as follows:

- `depends_on`: This indicates a dependency between the current test unit and a designated test unit.
- `description`: This provides a semantic description of a test unit.
- `enabled` / `disabled`: These set the default run status of a test unit to either `true` or `false`.
- `enable_if`: This sets the default run status of a test unit to either `true` or `false`, depending on the evaluation of a compile-time expression.
- `expected_failures`: This indicates the expected failures for a test unit.
- `fixture`: This specifies a pair of functions (startup and cleanup) to be called before and after the execution of a test unit.

- `label`: With this, you can associate a test unit with a label. The same label can be used for multiple test units, and a test unit can have multiple labels.
- `precondition`: This associates a predicate with a test unit, which is used at runtime to determine the run status of the test unit.
- `timeout`: Specifies a timeout for a unit test, in wall-clock time. If the test lasts longer than the specified timeout, the test fails.
- `tolerance`: This decorator specifies the default comparison tolerance for the floating-point type FTP in the decorated test unit.

If the execution of a test case results in an unhandled exception, the framework will catch the exception and terminate the execution of the test case with a failure. However, the framework provides several macros to test whether a particular piece of code raises, or does not raise, exceptions. For more information, see the next recipe, *Asserting with Boost.Test*.

The test units that compose the module's test tree can be executed entirely or partially. In both cases, to execute the test units, execute the (binary) program, which represents the test module. To execute only some of the test units, use the `--run_test` command-line option (or `--t` if you want to use a shorter name). This option allows you to filter the test units and specify either a path or label. A path consists of a sequence of test suite and/or test case names, such as `test_construction` or `test_operations/test_methods/test_offset`. A label is a name defined with the `label` decorator and is prefixed with `@` for the `run_test` parameter. This parameter is repeatable, which means you can specify multiple filters on it.

See also

- *Getting started with Boost.Test*, to learn how to install the Boost.Test framework and how to create a simple test project.
- *Asserting with Boost.Test*, to explore the rich set of assertion macros from the Boost.Test library.

Asserting with Boost.Test

A test case contains one or more tests. The `Boost.Test` library provides a series of APIs in the form of macros to write tests. In the previous recipe, you learned a bit about the `BOOST_TEST` macro, which is the most important and widely used macro of the library. In this recipe, we will discuss how the `BOOST_TEST` macro can be used in further detail.

Getting ready

You should now be familiar with writing test suites and test cases, a topic we covered in the previous recipe.

How to do it...

The following list shows some of the most commonly used APIs for performing tests:

- BOOST_TEST, in its plain form, is used for most tests:

```
int a = 2, b = 4;
BOOST_TEST(a == b);

BOOST_TEST(4.201 == 4.200);

std::string s1{ "sample" };
std::string s2{ "text" };
BOOST_TEST(s1 == s2, "not equal");
```

- BOOST_TEST, along with the tolerance() manipulator, is used to indicate the tolerance of floating-point comparisons:

```
BOOST_TEST(4.201 == 4.200,
           boost::test_tools::tolerance(0.001));
```

- BOOST_TEST, along with the per_element() manipulator, is used to perform an element-wise comparison of containers (even of different types):

```
std::vector<int> v{ 1,2,3 };
std::list<short> l{ 1,2,3 };

BOOST_TEST(v == l, boost::test_tools::per_element());
```

- BOOST_TEST, along with the ternary operator and compound statements using the logical || or &&, requires an extra set of parentheses:

```
BOOST_TEST((a > 0 ? true : false));
BOOST_TEST((a > 2 && b < 5));
```

- BOOST_ERROR is used to unconditionally fail a test and produce a message in the report. This is equivalent to BOOST_TEST(false, message):

```
BOOST_ERROR("this test will fail");
```

- `BOOST_TEST_WARN` is used to produce a warning in the report in case a test is failing, without increasing the number of encountered errors and stopping the execution of the test case:

```
BOOST_TEST_WARN(a == 4, "something is not right");
```

- `BOOST_TEST_REQUIRE` is used to ensure that test case preconditions are met; the execution of the test case is stopped otherwise:

```
BOOST_TEST_REQUIRE(a == 4, "this is critical");
```

- `BOOST_FAIL` is used to unconditionally stop the execution of the test case, increase the number of encountered errors, and produce a message in the report. This is equivalent to `BOOST_TEST_REQUIRE(false, message)`:

```
BOOST_FAIL("must be implemented");
```

- `BOOST_IS_DEFINED` is used to check whether a particular preprocessor symbol is defined at runtime. It is used together with `BOOST_TEST` to perform validation and logging:

```
BOOST_TEST(BOOST_IS_DEFINED(UNICODE));
```

How it works...

The library defines a variety of macros and manipulators for performing test assertions. The most commonly used one is `BOOST_TEST`. This macro simply evaluates an expression; if it fails, it increases the error count but continues the execution of the test case. It has three variants actually:

- `BOOST_TEST_CHECK` is the same as `BOOST_TEST` and is used to perform checks, as described in the previous section.
- `BOOST_TEST_WARN` is used for assertions meant to provide information, but without increasing the error count and stopping the execution of the test case.
- `BOOST_TEST_REQUIRE` is intended to ensure that pre-conditions that are required for test cases to continue execution are met. Upon failure, this macro increases the error count and stops the execution of the test case.

The general form of the test macro is `BOOST_TEST(statement)`. This macro provides rich and flexible reporting capabilities. By default, it shows not only the statement, but also the value of the operands, to enable quick identification of the failure's cause.

However, the user could provide an alternative failure description; in this scenario, the message is logged in the test report:

```
BOOST_TEST(a == b);
// error: in "regular_tests": check a == b has failed [2 != 4]

BOOST_TEST(a == b, "not equal");
// error: in "regular_tests": not equal
```

This macro also allows you to control the comparison process with special support for the following:

- The first is a floating-point comparison, where tolerance can be defined to test equality.
- Secondly, it supports a container's comparison using several methods: default comparison (using the overloaded operator ==), per-element comparison, and lexicographic comparison (using the lexicographical order). Per-element comparison enables the comparison of different types of containers (such as vector and list) in the order given by the forward iterators of the container; it also takes into account the size of the container (meaning that it first tests the sizes and, only if they are equal, continues with the comparison of the elements).
- Lastly, it supports bitwise comparison of the operands. Upon failure, the framework reports the index of the bit where the comparison failed.

The `BOOST_TEST` macro does have some limitations. It cannot be used with compound statements that use a comma, because such statements would be intercepted and handled by the preprocessor or the ternary operator, and compound statements using the logical operators `||` and `&&`. The latter cases have a workaround: a second pair of parentheses, as in `BOOST_TEST((statement))`.

Several macros are available for testing whether a particular exception is raised during the evaluation of an expression. In the following list, `<level>` is either `CHECK`, `WARN`, or `REQUIRE`:

- `BOOST_<level>_NO_THROW(expr)` checks whether an exception is raised from the `expr` expression. Any exception raised during the evaluation of `expr` is caught by this assertion and is not propagated to the test body. If any exception occurs, the assertion fails.

- `BOOST_<level>_THROW(expr, exception_type)` checks whether an exception of `exception_type` is raised from the `expr` expression. If the expression `expr` does not raise any exception, then the assertion fails. Exceptions of types other than `exception_type` are not caught by this assertion and can be propagated to the test body. Uncaught exceptions in a test case are caught by the execution monitor, but they result in failed test cases.
- `BOOST_<level>_EXCEPTION(expr, exception_type, predicate)` checks whether an exception of `exception_type` is raised from the `expr` expression. If so, it passes the expression to the predicate for further examination. If no exception is raised or an exception of a type different than `exception_type` is raised, then the assertion behaves like `BOOST_<level>_THROW`.

This recipe discussed only the most common APIs for testing and their typical usage. However, the library provides many more APIs. For further reference, check the online documentation. For version 1.73, refer to `https://www.boost.org/doc/libs/1_73_0/libs/test/doc/html/index.html`.

See also

- *Writing and invoking tests with Boost.Test*, to see how to create test suites and test cases using the single-header version of the Boost.Test library, as well as how to run tests.

Using fixtures in Boost.Test

The larger a test module is and the more similar the test cases are, the more likely it is to have test cases that require the same setup, cleanup, and maybe the same data. A component that contains these is called a **test fixture** or **test context**. Fixtures are important to establish a well-defined environment for running tests so that the results are repeatable. Examples can include copying a specific set of files to some location before executing the tests and deleting them after, or loading data from a particular data source.

Boost.Test provides several ways to define test fixtures for a test case, test suite, or a module (globally). In this recipe, we will look at how fixtures work.

Getting ready

The examples in this recipe use the following classes and functions for specifying test unit fixtures:

```
struct standard_fixture
{
  standard_fixture()  {BOOST_TEST_MESSAGE("setup");}
  ~standard_fixture() {BOOST_TEST_MESSAGE("cleanup");}
  int n {42};
};

struct extended_fixture
{
  std::string name;
  int         data;

  extended_fixture(std::string const & n = "") : name(n), data(0)
  {
    BOOST_TEST_MESSAGE("setup "+ name);
  }

  ~extended_fixture()
  {
    BOOST_TEST_MESSAGE("cleanup "+ name);
  }
};

void fixture_setup()
{
  BOOST_TEST_MESSAGE("fixture setup");
}

void fixture_cleanup()
{
  BOOST_TEST_MESSAGE("fixture cleanup");
}
```

The first two are classes whose constructors represent the setup function and the destructors represent the teardown function. At the end of the sample, there is a pair of functions, `fixture_setup()` and `fixture_cleanup()`, that represent functions for a test's setup and cleanup.

How to do it...

Use the following methods to define test fixtures for one or multiple test units:

- To define a fixture for a particular test case, use the BOOST_FIXTURE_TEST_CASE macro:

```
BOOST_FIXTURE_TEST_CASE(test_case, extended_fixture)
{
  data++;
  BOOST_TEST(data == 1);
}
```

- To define a fixture for all the test cases in a test suite, use BOOST_FIXTURE_TEST_SUITE:

```
BOOST_FIXTURE_TEST_SUITE(suite1, extended_fixture)

BOOST_AUTO_TEST_CASE(case1)
{
  BOOST_TEST(data == 0);
}

BOOST_AUTO_TEST_CASE(case2)
{
  data++;
  BOOST_TEST(data == 1);
}

BOOST_AUTO_TEST_SUITE_END()
```

- To define a fixture for all the test units in a test suite, except for one or several test units, use BOOST_FIXTURE_TEST_SUITE. You can overwrite it to a particular test unit with BOOST_FIXTURE_TEST_CASE for a test case and BOOST_FIXTURE_TEST_SUITE for a nested test suite:

```
BOOST_FIXTURE_TEST_SUITE(suite2, extended_fixture)

BOOST_AUTO_TEST_CASE(case1)
{
  BOOST_TEST(data == 0);
}

BOOST_FIXTURE_TEST_CASE(case2, standard_fixture)
{
```

```
    BOOST_TEST(n == 42);
  }

  BOOST_AUTO_TEST_SUITE_END()
```

- To define more than a single fixture for a test case or test suite, use `boost::unit_test::fixture` with the `BOOST_AUTO_TEST_SUITE` and `BOOST_AUTO_TEST_CASE` macros:

```
BOOST_AUTO_TEST_CASE(test_case_multifix,
  * boost::unit_test::fixture<extended_fixture>
      (std::string("fix1"))
  * boost::unit_test::fixture<extended_fixture>
      (std::string("fix2"))
  * boost::unit_test::fixture<standard_fixture>())
{
  BOOST_TEST(true);
}
```

- To use free functions as setup and teardown operations in the case of a fixture, use `boost::unit_test::fixture`:

```
BOOST_AUTO_TEST_CASE(test_case_funcfix,
  * boost::unit_test::fixture(&fixture_setup,
                              &fixture_cleanup))
{
  BOOST_TEST(true);
}
```

- To define a fixture for the module, use `BOOST_GLOBAL_FIXTURE`:

```
BOOST_GLOBAL_FIXTURE(standard_fixture);
```

How it works...

The library supports several fixture models:

- A **class model**, where the constructor acts as the setup function and the destructor as the cleanup function. An extended model allows the constructor to have one parameter. In the preceding example, `standard_fixture` implemented the first model and `extended_fixture` implemented the second model.
- A **pair of free functions**: one that defines the setup and the other, which is optional, that implements the cleanup code. In the preceding example, we came across these when discussing `fixture_setup()` and `fixture_cleanup()`.

Fixtures implemented as classes can also have data members, and these members are made available to the test unit. If a fixture is defined for a test suite, it is available implicitly to all the test units that are grouped under this test suite. However, it is possible that test units contained in such a test suite could redefine the fixture. In this case, the fixture defined in the closest scope is the one available to the test unit.

It is possible to define multiple fixtures for a test unit. However, this is done with the `boost::unit_test::fixture()` decorator, not with macros. The test suite and test case are defined, in this case, with the `BOOST_TEST_SUITE`/`BOOST_AUTO_TEST_SUITE` and `BOOST_TEST_CASE`/`BOOST_AUTO_TEST_CASE` macros. Multiple `fixture()` decorators can be composed together with `operator *`, as seen in the previous section. A drawback of this approach is that if you use the fixture decorator with a class that contains member data, then these members will not be available for the test units.

A new fixture object is constructed for each test case when it is executed, and the object is destroyed at the end of the test case.

The fixture state is not shared among different test cases. Therefore, the constructor and destructor are called once for each test case. You must make sure these special functions do not contain code that is supposed to be executed only once per module. If this is the case, you should set a global fixture for the entire module.

A global fixture uses the generic test class model (the model with the default constructor); you can define any number of global fixtures (allowing you to organize setup and cleanup by category, if necessary). Global fixtures are defined with the `BOOST_GLOBAL_FIXTURE` macro, and they have to be defined at the test file scope (not inside any test unit).

See also

- *Writing and invoking tests with Boost.Test*, to see how to create test suites and test cases using the single-header version of the Boost.Test library, as well as how to run tests.

Controlling outputs with Boost.Test

The framework provides us with the ability to customize what is shown in the test log and test report and then format the results. Currently, there are two that are supported: a human-readable format and XML (also with a JUNIT format for the test log). However, it is possible to create and add your own format.

The configuration of what is shown in the output can be done both at runtime, through command-line switches, and at compile time, through various APIs. During the execution of the tests, the framework collects all the events in a log. At the end, it produces a report that represents a summary of the execution with different levels of details. In the case of a failure, the report contains detailed information about the location and the cause, including actual and expected values. This helps developers quickly identify the error. In this recipe, we will see how to control what is written in the log and the report and in which format; we do this using the command-line options at runtime.

Getting ready

For the examples presented in this recipe, we will use the following test module:

```
#define BOOST_TEST_MODULE Controlling output
#include <boost/test/included/unit_test.hpp>

BOOST_AUTO_TEST_CASE(test_case)
{
  BOOST_TEST(true);
}

BOOST_AUTO_TEST_SUITE(test_suite)

BOOST_AUTO_TEST_CASE(test_case)
{
  int a = 42;
  BOOST_TEST(a == 0);
}

BOOST_AUTO_TEST_SUITE_END()
```

The next section presents how to control the test log and the test report's output through command-line options.

How to do it...

To control the test log's output, do the following:

- Use either the `--log_format=<format>` or `-f <format>` command-line option to specify the log format. The possible formats are `HRF` (the default value), `XML`, and `JUNIT`.

- Use either the `--log_level=<level>` or `-l <level>` command-line option to specify the log level. The possible log levels include `error` (default for HRF and XML), `warning`, `all`, and `success` (the default for JUNIT).
- Use either the `--log_sink=<stream or file name>` or `-k <stream or file name>` command-line option to specify the location where the framework should write the test log. The possible options are `stdout` (default for HRM and XML), `stderr`, or an arbitrary filename (default for JUNIT).

To control the test report's output, do the following:

- Use either the `--report_format=<format>` or `-m <format>` command-line option to specify the report format. The possible formats are `HRF` (the default value) and `XML`.
- Use either the `--report_level=<format>` or `-r <format>` command-line option to specify the report level. The possible formats are `confirm` (the default value), `no` (for no report), `short`, and `detailed`.
- Use either the `--report_sink=<stream or file name>` or `-e <stream or file name>` command-line option to specify the location where the framework should write the report log. The possible options are `stderr` (the default value), `stdout`, or an arbitrary filename.

How it works...

When you run the test module from a console/Terminal, you see both the test log and test report, with the test report following the test log. For the test module shown earlier, the default output is as follows. The first three lines represent the test log, while the last line represents the test report:

```
Running 2 test cases...
f:/chapter11bt_05/main.cpp(14): error: in "test_suite/test_case":
check a == 0 has failed [42 != 0]

*** 1 failure is detected in the test module "Controlling output"
```

The content of both the test log and test report can be made available in several formats. The default is a **human-readable format** (or **HRF**); however, the framework also supports XML, and for the test log, the JUNIT format. This is a format intended for automated tools, such as continuous build or integration tools. Apart from these options, you can implement your own format for the test log by implementing your own class derived from `boost::unit_test::unit_test_log_formatter`.

The following example shows how to format the test log (the first example) and the test report (the second example) using XML (each highlighted in bold):

```
chapter11bt_05.exe -f XML
<TestLog><Error file="f:/chapter11bt_05/main.cpp"
line="14"><![CDATA[check a == 0 has failed [42 != 0]]]>
</Error></TestLog>
*** 1 failure is detected in the test module "Controlling output"

chapter11bt_05.exe -m XML
Running 2 test cases...
f:/chapter11bt_05/main.cpp(14): error: in "test_suite/test_case":
check a == 0 has failed [42 != 0]
<TestResult><TestSuite name="Controlling output" result="failed"
assertions_passed="1" assertions_failed="1" warnings_failed="0"
expected_failures="0" test_cases_passed="1"
test_cases_passed_with_warnings="0" test_cases_failed="1"
test_cases_skipped="0" test_cases_aborted="0"></TestSuite>
</TestResult>
```

The log or report level represents the verbosity of the output. The possible values of the verbosity level of a log are shown in the following table, ordered from the lowest to the highest level. A higher level in the table includes all the messages of the levels above it:

Level	**Messages that are reported**
`Nothing`	Nothing is logged.
`fatal_error`	System or user fatal errors and all the messages describing failed assertions at the `REQUIRE` level (such as `BOOST_TEST_REQUIRE` and `BOOST_REQUIRE_`).
`system_error`	System non-fatal errors.
`cpp_exception`	Uncaught C++ exceptions.
`Error`	Failed assertion at the `CHECK` level (`BOOST_TEST` and `BOOST_CHECK_`).
`Warning`	Failed assertion at the `WARN` level (`BOOST_TEST_WARN` and `BOOST_WARN_`).
`Message`	Messages generated by `BOOST_TEST_MESSAGE`.
`test_suite`	Notification at the start and finish states of each test unit.
`all / success`	All the messages, including passed assertions.

The available formats of the test report are described in the following table:

Level	Description
`no`	No report is produced.
`confirm`	**Passing test**: *** No errors detected. **Skipped test**: *** The <name> test suite was skipped; see the standard output for details. **Aborted test**: *** The <name> test suite was aborted; see the standard output for details. **Failed test without failed assertions**: *** Errors were detected in the <name> test suite; see the standard output for details. **Failed test**: *** N failures are detected in the <name> test suite. **Failed test with some failures expected**: *** N failures are detected (M failures are expected) in the <name> test suite.
`detailed`	Results are reported in a hierarchical fashion (each test unit is reported as part of the parent test unit), but only relevant information appears. Test cases that do not have failing assertions do not produce entries in the report. The test case/suite <name> has passed/was skipped/was aborted/has failed/ with: N assertions out of M passed N assertions out of M failed N warnings out of M failed X failures expected
`short`	Similar to detailed, but this reports information only to the master test suite.

The standard output stream (`stdout`) is the default location where the test log is written, and the standard error stream (`stderr`) is the default location of the test report. However, both the test log and test report can be redirected to another stream or file.

In addition to these options, it is possible to specify a separate file for reporting memory leaks using the `--report_memory_leaks_to=<file name>` command-line option. If this option is not present and memory leaks are detected, they are reported to the standard error stream.

There's more...

In addition to the options discussed in this recipe, the framework provides additional compile-time APIs for controlling the output. For a comprehensive description of these APIs, as well as the features described in this recipe, check the framework documentation at `https://www.boost.org/doc/libs/1_73_0/libs/test/doc/html/index.html`.

See also

- *Writing and invoking tests with Boost.Test*, to see how to create test suites and test cases using the single-header version of the Boost.Test library, as well as how to run tests.
- *Asserting with Boost.Test*, to explore the rich set of assertion macros from the Boost.Test library.

Getting started with Google Test

Google Test is one of the most widely used testing frameworks for C++. The **Chromium** projects and the **LLVM** compiler are among the projects that are using it for unit testing. Google Test enables developers to write unit tests on multiple platforms, using multiple compilers. Google Test is a portable, lightweight framework that has a simple yet comprehensive API for writing tests using asserts; here, tests are grouped into test suites and test suites into test programs.

The framework provides useful features, such as repeating a test a number of times and breaking a test to invoke the debugger at the first failure. Its assertions work regardless of whether exceptions are enabled or not. The next recipe will cover the most important features of the framework. This recipe will show you how to install the framework and set up your first testing project.

Getting ready

The Google Test framework, just like Boost.Test, has a macro-based API. Although you only need to use the supplied macros for writing tests, a good understanding of macros is recommended in order to use the framework well.

How to do it...

In order to set up your environment to use Google Test, do the following:

1. Clone or download the Git repository from `https://github.com/google/googletest`.
2. Once you've downloaded the repository, unzip the content of the archive.
3. Build the framework using the provided build scripts.

To create your first test program using Google Test, do the following:

1. Create a new empty C++ project.
2. Do the necessary setup specific to the development environment you are using to make the framework's headers folder (called include) available to the project for including header files.
3. Link the project to the `gtest` shared library.
4. Add a new source file to the project with the following content:

```
#include <gtest/gtest.h>

TEST(FirstTestSuite, FirstTest)
{
  int a = 42;
  ASSERT_TRUE(a > 0);
}

int main(int argc, char **argv)
{
  ::testing::InitGoogleTest(&argc, argv);
  return RUN_ALL_TESTS();
}
```

5. Build and run the project.

How it works...

The Google Test framework provides a simple and easy-to-use set of macros for creating tests and writing assertions. The structure of the test is also simplified compared to other testing frameworks, such as Boost.Test. Tests are grouped into test suites and test suites into test programs.

It is important to mention several aspects related to terminology. Traditionally, Google Test did not use the term **test suite**. A **test case** in Google Test was basically a test suite and equivalent to the test suites in Boost.Test. On the other hand, a test function was equivalent to a test case. Because this has led to confusion, Google Test has adhered to the common terminology, used by the **International Software Testing Qualifications Board** (**ISTQB**), of test cases and test suites and has started to replace this throughout its code and documentation. In this book, we will use these terms.

The framework provides a rich set of assertions, both fatal and non-fatal, great support for exception handling, and the ability to customize the way tests are executed and how the output should be generated. However, unlike with the Boost.Test library, the test suites in Google Test cannot contain other test suites, but only test functions.

Documentation for the framework is available on the project's page at GitHub. For this edition of this book, I used Google Test framework version 1.10, but the code presented here works with previous versions of the framework and is expected to also work with future versions of the framework. The sample code shown in the previous section contains the following parts:

1. `#include <gtest/gtest.h>` includes the main header of the framework.
2. `TEST(FirstTestSuite, FirstTest)` declares a test called `FirstTest` as part of a test suite called `FirstTestSuite`. These names must be valid C++ identifiers but are not allowed to contain underscores. The actual name of a test function is composed through concatenation with an underscore from the name of the test suite and the test name. For our example, the name is `FirstTestSuite_FirstTest`. Tests from different test suites may have the same individual name. A test function has no arguments and returns `void`. Multiple tests can be grouped with the same test suite.
3. `ASSERT_TRUE(a > 0);` is an assertion macro that yields a fatal error and returns from the current function in case the condition evaluates to `false`. The framework defines many more assertion macros, which we will see in the *Asserting with Google Test* recipe.
4. `::testing::InitGoogleTest(&argc, argv);` initializes the framework and must be called before `RUN_ALL_TESTS()`.

5. `return RUN_ALL_TESTS();` automatically detects and calls all the tests defined with either the `TEST()` or `TEST_F()` macro. The return value returned from the macro is used as the return value of the `main()` function. This is important, because the automated testing service determines the result of a test program according to the value returned from the `main()` function, not the output printed to the `stdout` or `stderr` streams. The `RUN_ALL_TESTS()` macro must be called only once; calling it multiple times is not supported because it conflicts with some advanced features of the framework.

Executing this test program will provide the following result:

```
[==========] Running 1 test from 1 test suite.
[----------] Global test environment set-up.
[----------] 1 test from FirstTestCase
[ RUN      ] FirstTestCase.FirstTestFunction
[       OK ] FirstTestCase.FirstTestFunction (1 ms)
[----------] 1 test from FirstTestCase (1 ms total)

[----------] Global test environment tear-down
[==========] 1 test from 1 test suite ran. (2 ms total)
[  PASSED  ] 1 test.
```

For many test programs, the content of the `main()` function is identical to the one shown in this recipe, in the example from the *How to do it...* section. To avoid writing such a `main()` function, the framework provides a basic implementation that you can use by linking your program with the `gtest_main` shared library.

There's more...

The Google Test framework can also be used with other testing frameworks. You can write tests using another testing framework, such as Boost.Test or CppUnit, and use the Google Test assertion macros. To do so, set the `throw_on_failure` flag, either from the code or command line, with the `--gtest_throw_on_failure` argument. Alternatively, use the `GTEST_THROW_ON_FAILURE` environment variable and initialize the framework, as shown in the following code snippet:

```
#include "gtest/gtest.h"

int main(int argc, char** argv)
{
  ::testing::GTEST_FLAG(throw_on_failure) = true;
  ::testing::InitGoogleTest(&argc, argv);
}
```

When you enable the `throw_on_failure` option, assertions that fail will print an error message and throw an exception, which will be caught by the host testing framework and treated as a failure. If exceptions are not enabled, then a failed Google Test assertion will tell your program to exit with a non-zero code, which again will be treated as a failure by the host testing framework.

See also

- *Writing and invoking tests with Google Test*, to see how to create tests and test suites using the Google Test library, as well as how to run tests.
- *Asserting with Google Test*, to explore the various assertion macros from the Google Test library.

Writing and invoking tests with Google Test

In the previous recipe, we had a glimpse of what it takes to write simple tests with the Google Test framework. Multiple tests can be grouped into a test suite and one or more test suites grouped into a test program. In this recipe, we will see how to create and run tests.

Getting ready

For the sample code in this recipe, we'll use the `point3d` class we discussed in the *Writing and invoking tests with Boost.Test* recipe.

How to do it...

Use the following macros to create tests:

- `TEST(TestSuiteName, TestName)` defines a test called `TestName` as part of a test suite called `TestSuiteName`:

```
TEST(TestConstruction, TestConstructor)
{
  auto p = point3d{ 1,2,3 };
  ASSERT_EQ(p.x(), 1);
  ASSERT_EQ(p.x(), 2);
  ASSERT_EQ(p.x(), 3);
}
```

```
TEST(TestConstruction, TestOrigin)
{
   auto p = point3d::origin();
   ASSERT_EQ(p.x(), 0);
   ASSERT_EQ(p.x(), 0);
   ASSERT_EQ(p.x(), 0);
}
```

- `TEST_F(TestSuiteWithFixture, TestName)` defines a test called `TestName` as part of a test suite, using a fixture called `TestSuiteWithFixture`. You'll find details about how this works in the *Using test fixtures with Google Test* recipe.

To execute the tests, do the following:

- Use the `RUN_ALL_TESTS()` macro to run all the tests defined in the test program. This must be called only once from the `main()` function after the framework has been initialized.
- Use the `--gtest_filter=<filter>` command-line option to filter the tests to run.
- Use the `--gtest_repeat=<count>` command-line option to repeat the selected tests the specified number of times.
- Use the `--gtest_break_on_failure` command-line option to attach the debugger to debug the test program when the first test fails.

How it works...

There are several macros available for defining tests (as part of a test case). The most common ones are `TEST` and `TEST_F`. The latter is used with fixtures, which will be discussed in detail in the *Using test fixtures with Google Test* recipe. Other macros for defining tests are `TYPED_TEST` for writing typed tests and `TYPED_TEST_P` for writing type-parameterized tests. However, these are more advanced topics and are beyond the scope of this book. The `TEST` and `TEST_F` macros take two arguments: the first is the name of the test suite and the second is the name of the test. These two arguments form the full name of a test, and they must be valid C++ identifiers; they should not contain underscores, though. Different test suites can contain tests with the same name (because the full name is still unique). Both macros automatically register the tests with the framework; therefore, no explicit input is required from the user to do this.

A test can either fail or succeed. A test fails if an assertion fails or an uncaught exception occurs. Except for these two instances, the test always succeeds.

To invoke the test, call `RUN_ALL_TESTS()`. However, you can do this only once in a test program and only after the framework has been initialized with a call to `::testing::InitGoogleTest()`. This macro runs all the tests in the test program. However, it is possible that you select only some tests to run. You can do this either by setting up an environment variable called `GTEST_FILTER` with the appropriate filter, or by passing the filter as a command-line argument with the `--gtest_filter` flag. If any of these two are present, the framework only runs the tests whose full name matches the filter. The filter may include wildcards: * to match any string and the ? symbol to match any character. Negative patterns (what should be omitted) are introduced with a hyphen (-). The following are examples of filters:

Filter	Description
`--gtest_filter=*`	Run all the tests
`--gtest_filter=TestConstruction.*`	Run all the tests from the test suite called `TestConstruction`
`--gtest_filter=TestOperations.*-TestOperations.TestLess`	Run all the tests from the test suite called `TestOperations`, except for a test called `TestLess`
`--gtest_filter=*Operations*:*Construction*`	Run all the tests whose full name contains either `Operations` or `Construction`

The following listing is the output of a test program containing the tests shown earlier when invoked with the command-line argument `--gtest_filter=TestConstruction.*-TestConstruction.TestConstructor`:

```
Note: Google Test filter = TestConstruction.*-TestConstruction.
TestConstructor
[==========] Running 1 test from 1 test suite.
[----------] Global test environment set-up.
[----------] 1 test from TestConstruction
[ RUN      ] TestConstruction.TestOrigin
[       OK ] TestConstruction.TestOrigin (0 ms)
[----------] 1 test from TestConstruction (0 ms total)

[----------] Global test environment tear-down
[==========] 1 test from 1 test suite ran. (2 ms total)
[  PASSED  ] 1 test.
```

It is possible for you to disable some of the tests by prefixing either the name of a test with `DISABLED_` or the name of a test suite with the same identifier, in which case all the tests in the test suite will be disabled. This is exemplified here:

```
TEST(TestConstruction, DISABLED_TestConversionConstructor)
{ /* ... */ }
TEST(DISABLED_TestComparisons, TestEquality)
{ /* ... */ }
TEST(DISABLED_TestComparisons, TestInequality)
{ /* ... */ }
```

None of these tests will be executed. However, you will receive a report in the output stating that you have a number of disabled tests.

Keep in mind that this feature is only meant for temporarily disabling tests. This is useful when you need to perform some code changes that make tests fail and you don't have time to fix them right away. Therefore, this feature should be used judiciously.

See also

- *Getting started with Google Test*, to learn how to install the Google Test framework and how to create a simple test project.
- *Asserting with Google Test*, to explore the various assertion macros from the Google Test library.
- *Using test fixtures with Google Test*, to learn how to define test fixtures when using the Google Test library.

Asserting with Google Test

The Google Test framework provides a rich set of both fatal and non-fatal assertion macros, which resemble function calls, to verify the tested code. When these assertions fail, the framework displays the source file, line number, and relevant error message (including custom error messages) to help developers quickly identify the failed code. We have already seen some simple examples on how to use the `ASSERT_TRUE` macro; in this recipe, we will look at other available macros.

How to do it...

Use the following macros to verify the tested code:

- Use `ASSERT_TRUE(condition)` or `EXPECT_TRUE(condition)` to check whether the condition is `true` and `ASSERT_FALSE(condition)` or `EXPECT_FALSE(condition)` to check whether the condition is `false`, as shown in the following code:

  ```
  EXPECT_TRUE(2 + 2 == 2 * 2);
  EXPECT_FALSE(1 == 2);

  ASSERT_TRUE(2 + 2 == 2 * 2);
  ASSERT_FALSE(1 == 2);
  ```

- Use `ASSERT_XX(val1, val2)` or `EXPECT_XX(val1, val2)` to compare two values, where `XX` is one of the following: `EQ(val1 == val2)`, `NE(val1 != val2)`, `LT(val1 < val2)`, `LE(val1 <= val2)`, `GT(val1 > val2)`, or `GE(val1 >= val2)`. This is illustrated in the following code:

  ```
  auto a = 42, b = 10;
  EXPECT_EQ(a, 42);
  EXPECT_NE(a, b);
  EXPECT_LT(b, a);
  EXPECT_LE(b, 11);
  EXPECT_GT(a, b);
  EXPECT_GE(b, 10);
  ```

- Use `ASSERT_STRXX(str1, str2)` or `EXPECT_STRXX(str1, str2)` to compare two null-terminated strings, where `XX` is one of the following: `EQ` (the strings have the same content), `NE` (the strings don't have the same content), `CASEEQ` (the strings have the same content with the case ignored), and `CASENE` (the strings don't have the same content with the case ignored). This is illustrated in the following code snippet:

  ```
  auto str = "sample";
  EXPECT_STREQ(str, "sample");
  EXPECT_STRNE(str, "simple");
  ASSERT_STRCASEEQ(str, "SAMPLE");
  ASSERT_STRCASENE(str, "SIMPLE");
  ```

- Use `ASSERT_FLOAT_EQ(val1, val2)` or `EXPECT_FLOAT_EQ(val1, val2)` to check whether two `float` values are almost equal and `ASSERT_DOUBLE_EQ(val1, val2)` or `EXPECT_DOUBLE_EQ(val1, val2)` to check whether two `double` values are almost equal; they should differ by at most 4 **ULP** (**units in the last place**). Use `ASSERT_NEAR(val1, val2, abserr)` to check whether the difference between the two values is not greater than the specified absolute value:

```
EXPECT_FLOAT_EQ(1.9999999f, 1.9999998f);
ASSERT_FLOAT_EQ(1.9999999f, 1.9999998f);
```

- Use `ASSERT_THROW(statement, exception_type)` or `EXPECT_THROW(statement, exception_type)` to check whether the statement throws an exception of the specified type, `ASSERT_ANY_THROW(statement)` or `EXPECT_ANY_THROW(statement)` to check whether the statement throws an exception of any type, and `ASSERT_NO_THROW(statement)` or `EXPECT_NO_THROW(statement)` to check whether the statement throws any exception:

```
void function_that_throws()
{
  throw std::runtime_error("error");
}

void function_no_throw()
{
}

TEST(TestAssertions, Exceptions)
{
  EXPECT_THROW(function_that_throws(),
               std::runtime_error);
  EXPECT_ANY_THROW(function_that_throws());
  EXPECT_NO_THROW(function_no_throw());

  ASSERT_THROW(function_that_throws(),
               std::runtime_error);
  ASSERT_ANY_THROW(function_that_throws());
  ASSERT_NO_THROW(function_no_throw());
}
```

- Use ASSERT_PRED1(pred, val) or EXPECT_PRED1(pred, val) to check whether pred(val) returns true, ASSERT_PRED2(pred, val1, val2) or EXPECT_PRED2(pred, val1, val2) to check whether pred(val1, val2) returns true, and so on; use this for n-ary predicate functions or functors:

```
bool is_positive(int const val)
{
  return val != 0;
}

bool is_double(int const val1, int const val2)
{
  return val2 + val2 == val1;
}

TEST(TestAssertions, Predicates)
{
  EXPECT_PRED1(is_positive, 42);
  EXPECT_PRED2(is_double, 42, 21);

  ASSERT_PRED1(is_positive, 42);
  ASSERT_PRED2(is_double, 42, 21);
}
```

- Use ASSERT_HRESULT_SUCCEEDED(expr) or EXPECT_HRESULT_SUCCEEDED(expr) to check whether expr is a success HRESULT and ASSERT_HRESULT_FAILED(expr) or EXPECT_HRESULT_FAILED(expr) to check whether expr is a failure HRESULT. These assertions are intended to be used on Windows.
- Use FAIL() to generate a fatal failure and ADD_FAILURE() or ADD_FAILURE_AT(filename, line) to generate non-fatal failures:

```
ADD_FAILURE();
ADD_FAILURE_AT(__FILE__, __LINE__);
```

How it works...

All these asserts are available in two versions:

- ASSERT_*: This generates fatal failures, preventing further execution of the current test function.
- EXPECT_*: This generates non-fatal failures, which means that the execution of the test function continues, even if the assertion fails.

Use the `EXPECT_*` assertion if not meeting the condition is not a critical error or if you want the test function to continue, in order to get as many error messages as possible. In other cases, use the `ASSERT_*` version of the test assertions.

You will find details about the assertions presented here in the framework's online documentation, which is available on GitHub at `https://github.com/google/googletest`; this is where the project is located. A special note on floating-point comparison is, however, necessary. Due to round-offs (fractional parts cannot be represented as a finite sum of the inverse powers of two), floating-point values do not match exactly. Therefore, a comparison should be done within a relative error bound. The macros `ASSERT_EQ`/`EXPECT_EQ` are not suitable for comparing floating points, and the framework provides another set of assertions. `ASSERT_FLOAT_EQ`/`ASSERT_DOUBLE_EQ` and `EXPECT_FLOAT_EQ`/`EXPECT_DOUBLE_EQ` perform a comparison with a default error of 4ULP.

ULP is a unit of measurement for the spacing between floating-point numbers, that is, the value the least significant digit represents if it is 1. For more information on this, read the *Comparing Floating Point Numbers, 2012 Edition* article by Bruce Dawson: `https://randomascii.wordpress.com/2012/02/25/comparing-floating-point-numbers-2012-edition/`.

See also

- *Writing and invoking tests with Google Test*, to see how to create tests and test suites using the Google Test library, as well as how to run tests.

Using test fixtures with Google Test

The framework provides support for using fixtures as reusable components for all the tests that are part of a test suite. It also provides support for setting up the global environment in which the tests will run. In this recipe, you will find stepwise instructions on how to define and use test fixtures, as well as set up the test environment.

Getting ready

You should now be familiar with writing and invoking tests using the Google Test framework, a topic that was covered earlier in this chapter, specifically in the *Writing and invoking tests with Google Test* recipe.

How to do it...

To create and use a test fixture, do the following:

1. Create a class derived from the `::testing::Test` class:

```
class TestFixture : public ::testing::Test
{
};
```

2. Use the constructor to initialize the fixture and the destructor to clean it up:

```
protected:
  TestFixture()
  {
    std::cout << "constructing fixture\n";
    data.resize(10);
    std::iota(std::begin(data), std::end(data), 1);
  }

  ~TestFixture()
  {
    std::cout << "destroying fixture\n";
  }
```

3. Alternatively, you can override the virtual methods `SetUp()` and `TearDown()` for the same purpose.
4. Add member data and functions to the class to make them available to the tests:

```
protected:
  std::vector<int> data;
```

5. Use the `TEST_F` macro to define tests using fixtures, and specify the fixture class name as the test suite name:

```
TEST_F(TestFixture, TestData)
{
  ASSERT_EQ(data.size(), 10);
  ASSERT_EQ(data[0], 1);
  ASSERT_EQ(data[data.size()-1], data.size());
}
```

To customize the setup of the environment for running tests, do the following:

1. Create a class derived from `::testing::Environment`:

```
class TestEnvironment : public ::testing::Environment
{
};
```

2. Override the virtual methods `SetUp()` and `TearDown()` to perform setup and cleanup operations:

```
public:
  virtual void SetUp() override
  {
    std::cout << "environment setup\n";
  }

  virtual void TearDown() override
  {
    std::cout << "environment cleanup\n";
  }

  int n{ 42 };
```

3. Register the environment with a call to `::testing::AddGlobalTestEnvironment()` before calling `RUN_ALL_TESTS()`:

```
int main(int argc, char **argv)
{
  ::testing::InitGoogleTest(&argc, argv);
  ::testing::AddGlobalTestEnvironment(new TestEnvironment{});
  return RUN_ALL_TESTS();
}
```

How it works...

Text fixtures enable users to share data configurations between multiple tests. Fixture objects are not shared between tests. A different fixture object is created for each test that is associated with the text function. The following operations are performed by the framework for each test coming from a fixture:

1. Create a new fixture object.
2. Call its `SetUp()` virtual method.
3. Run the test.
4. Call the fixture's `TearDown()` virtual method.
5. Destroy the fixture object.

You can set up and clean the fixture objects in two ways: by using the constructor and destructor, or by using the `SetUp()` and `TearDown()` virtual methods. For most cases, the former way is preferred. The use of virtual methods is suitable in several cases, though:

- When the teardown operation throws an exception, as exceptions are not allowed to leave destructors.
- If you are required to use assertion macros during cleanup and you use the `--gtest_throw_on_failure` flag, which determines the macros to be thrown upon a failure occurring.
- If you need to call virtual methods (which might be overridden in a derived class), as virtual calls should not be invoked from the constructor or destructor.

Tests that use fixtures must be defined using the `TEST_F` macro (where `_F` stands for fixture). Trying to declare them using the `TEST` macro will generate compiler errors.

The environments in which tests are run can also be customized. The mechanism is similar to test fixtures: you derive from the base `testing::Environment` class and override the `SetUp()` and `TearDown()` virtual functions. Instances of these derived environment classes must be registered with the framework with a call to `testing::AddGlobalTestEnvironment()`; however, this has to be done before you run the tests. You can register as many instances as you want, in which case the `SetUp()` method is called for the objects in the order they were registered and the `TearDown()` method is called in reverse order. You must pass dynamically instantiated objects to this function. The framework takes ownership of the objects and deletes them before the program terminates; therefore, do not delete them yourself.

Environment objects are not available to the tests, nor intended to provide data to the tests. Their purpose is to customize the global environment for running the tests.

See also

- *Writing and invoking tests with Google Test*, to see how to create tests and test suites using the Google Test library, as well as how to run tests.

Controlling output with Google Test

By default, the output of a Google Test program goes to the standard stream, printed in a human-readable form. The framework provides several options for customizing the output, including printing XML to a disk file in a JUNIT-based format. This recipe will explore the options available to control the output.

Getting ready

For the purpose of this recipe, let's consider the following test program:

```
#include <gtest/gtest.h>

TEST(Sample, Test)
{
  auto a = 42;
  ASSERT_EQ(a, 0);
}

int main(int argc, char **argv)
{
  ::testing::InitGoogleTest(&argc, argv);
  return RUN_ALL_TESTS();
}
```

Its output is as follows:

```
[==========] Running 1 test from 1 test suite.
[----------] Global test environment set-up.
[----------] 1 test from Sample
[ RUN      ] Sample.Test
f:\chapter11gt_05\main.cpp(6): error: Expected equality of these values:
  a
    Which is: 42
  0
[  FAILED  ] Sample.Test (1 ms)
[----------] 1 test from Sample (1 ms total)
[----------] Global test environment tear-down
[==========] 1 test from 1 test suite ran. (3 ms total)
[  PASSED  ] 0 tests.
[  FAILED  ] 1 test, listed below:
[  FAILED  ] Sample.Test

 1 FAILED TEST
```

We will use this simple testing program to demonstrate the various options we can use to control the program's output, which are exemplified in the following section.

How to do it...

To control the output of a test program, you can:

- Use the `--gtest_output` command-line option or the `GTEST_OUTPUT` environment variable with the `xml:filepath` string to specify the location of a file where the XML report is to be written:

```
chapter11gt_05.exe --gtest_output=xml:report.xml

<?xml version="1.0" encoding="UTF-8"?>
<testsuites tests="1" failures="1" disabled="0" errors="0"
            time="0.007" timestamp="2020-05-18T19:00:17"
            name="AllTests">
  <testsuite name="Sample" tests="1" failures="1" disabled="0"
             errors="0" time="0.002"
             timestamp="2020-05-18T19:00:17">
    <testcase name="Test" status="run" result="completed" time="0"
              timestamp="2020-05-18T19:00:17" classname="Sample">
      <failure message="f:\chapter11gt_05\main.cpp:6&#x0A;Expected
equality of these values:&#x0A;  a&#x0A;    Which is: 42&#x0A;  0"
type=""><![CDATA[f:\chapter11gt_05\main.cpp:6
Expected equality of these values:
  a
    Which is: 42
  0]]></failure>
    </testcase>
  </testsuite>
</testsuites>
```

- Use the `--gtest_color` command-line option or the `GTEST_COLOR` environment variable and specify either `auto`, `yes`, or `no` to indicate whether the report should be printed to a Terminal using colors or not:

```
chapter11gt_05.exe --gtest_color=no
```

- Use the `--gtest_print_time` command-line option or the `GTEST_PRINT_TIME` environment variable with the value `0` to suppress the printing time each test takes to execute:

```
chapter11gt_05.exe --gtest_print_time=0

[==========] Running 1 test from 1 test suite.
[----------] Global test environment set-up.
[----------] 1 test from Sample
[ RUN      ] Sample.Test
```

```
f:\chapter11gt_05\main.cpp(6): error: Expected equality of these
values:
  a
    Which is: 42
  0
[  FAILED  ] Sample.Test
[----------] Global test environment tear-down
[==========] 1 test from 1 test suite ran.
[  PASSED  ] 0 tests.
[  FAILED  ] 1 test, listed below:
[  FAILED  ] Sample.Test

 1 FAILED TEST
```

How it works...

Generating a report in an XML format does not affect the human-readable report printed to the Terminal. The output path can indicate either a file, a directory (in which case a file with the name of the executable is created - if it already exists from a previous run, it creates a file with a new name by suffixing it with a number), or nothing, in which case the report is written to a file called `test_detail.xml` in the current directory.

The XML report format is based on the JUnitReport Ant task and contains the following main elements:

- `<testsuites>`: This is the root element and it corresponds to the entire test program.
- `<testsuite>`: This corresponds to a test suite.
- `<testcase>`: This corresponds to a test function, as Google Test functions are equivalent to test cases in other frameworks.

By default, the framework reports the time it takes for each test to execute. This feature can be suppressed using the `--gtest_print_time` command-line option or the `GTEST_PRINT_TIME` environment variable, as shown earlier.

See also

- *Writing and invoking tests with Google Test*, to see how to create tests and test suites using the Google Test library, as well as how to run tests.
- *Using test fixtures with Google Test*, to learn how to define test fixtures when using the Google Test library.

Getting started with Catch2

Catch2 is a multiparadigm testing framework for C++ and Objective-C. The name Catch2 follows on from Catch, the first version of the framework, which stands for **C++ Automated Test Cases in Headers**. It enables developers to write tests using either the traditional style of test functions grouped in test cases or the **behavior-driven development** (**BDD**) style with *given-when-then* sections. Tests are self-registered and the framework provides several assertion macros; out of these, two are used the most: one fatal, namely `REQUIRE`, and one non-fatal, namely `CHECK`. They perform expression decomposition of both the left-hand and right-hand side values, which are logged in case of failure. Unlike its first version, Catch2 no longer supports C++03. For the remaining recipes of this chapter, we will learn how to write unit tests using Catch2.

Getting ready

The Catch2 test framework has a macro-based API. Although you only need to use the supplied macros for writing tests, a good understanding of macros is recommended if you want to use the framework well.

How to do it...

In order to set up your environment to use the Catch2 testing framework, do the following:

1. Clone or download the Git repository from `https://github.com/catchorg/Catch2`.
2. Once you've downloaded the repository, unzip the content of the archive.

To create your first test program using Catch2, do the following:

1. Create a new empty C++ project.
2. Do the necessary setup specific to the development environment you are using to make the framework's `single_header` folder available to the project for including header files.
3. Add a new source file to the project with the following content:

```
#define CATCH_CONFIG_MAIN
#include "catch2/catch.hpp"
```

```
TEST_CASE("first_test_case", "[learn][catch]")
{
  SECTION("first_test_function")
  {
    auto i{ 42 };
    REQUIRE(i == 42);
  }
}
```

4. Build and run the project.

How it works...

Catch2 enables developers to write test cases as self-registered functions; it can even provide a default implementation for the `main()` function so that you can focus on testing code and writing less setup code. Test cases are divided into sections that are run in isolation. The framework does not adhere to the style of the **setup-test-teardown** architecture. Instead, the test case sections (or rather the innermost ones, since sections can be nested) are the units of testing that are executed, along with their enclosing sections. This makes the need for fixtures obsolete because data and setup and teardown code can be reused on multiple levels.

Test cases and sections are identified using strings, not identifiers (as in most testing frameworks). Test cases can also be tagged so that tests can be executed or listed based on tags. Test results are printed in a textual human-readable form; however, they can also be exported to XML, using either a Catch2-specific schema or a JUNIT ANT schema for easy integration with continuous delivery systems. The execution of the tests can be parameterized to break upon failure (on Windows and Mac) so that you can attach a debugger and inspect the program.

The framework is easy to install and use. There are two alternatives: a single header file (available in the `single_header/catch2` folder) or a collection of header and source files (in the `include` folder). In both cases, the only header file you have to include in your test program is `catch.hpp`. However, if you do not use the single header version, you will have to build the library and link it to your project. In this book, we're using the single header implementation of the library.

The sample code shown in the previous section has the following parts:

1. `#define CATCH_CONFIG_MAIN` defines a macro that instructs the framework to provide a default implementation of the `main()` function.
2. `#include "catch2/catch.hpp"` includes the single header of the library.

3. `TEST_CASE("first_test_case", "[learn][catch]")` defines a test case called `first_test_case`, which has several associated tags: `learn` and `catch`. Tags are used to select either running or just listing test cases. Multiple test cases can be tagged with the same tags.
4. `SECTION("first_test_function")` defines a section, that is, a test function, called `first_test_function`, as part of the outer test case.
5. `REQUIRE(i == 42);` is an assertion that tells the test to fail if the condition is not satisfied.

The output of running this program is as follows:

```
=========================================================
All tests passed (1 assertion in 1 test cases)
```

There's more...

As mentioned previously, the framework enables us to write tests using the BDD style with *give-when-then* sections. This was made possible using several aliases: `SCENARIO` for `TEST_CASE` and `GIVE`, `WHEN`, `AND_WHEN`, `THEN`, and `AND_THEN` for `SECTION`. Using this style, we can rewrite the test shown earlier, as follows:

```
SCENARIO("first_scenario", "[learn][catch]")
{
  GIVEN("an integer")
  {
    auto i = 0;
    WHEN("assigned a value")
    {
      i = 42;
      THEN("the value can be read back")
      {
        REQUIRE(i == 42);
      }
    }
  }
}
```

When executed successfully, the program prints the following output:

```
=========================================================
All tests passed (1 assertion in 1 test cases)
```

However, upon failure (let's suppose we got the wrong condition: `i == 0`), the expression that failed, as well as the values on the left-hand and right-hand sides are printed in the output, as shown in the following snippet:

```
---------------------------------------------------------------
f:\chapter11ca_01\main.cpp(11)
...............................................................

f:\chapter11ca_01\main.cpp(13): FAILED:
  REQUIRE( i == 0 )
with expansion:
  42 == 0

===============================================================
test cases: 1 | 1 failed
assertions: 1 | 1 failed
```

The output presented here, as well as in other snippets throughout the following recipes, has been slightly trimmed or compressed from the actual console output to make it easier to list within the pages of this book.

See also

- *Writing and invoking tests with Catch2*, to see how to create tests with the Catch2 library, either using the traditional style based on test cases, or the BDD style with scenarios, as well as how to run tests.
- *Asserting with Catch2*, to explore the various assertion macros from the Catch2 library.

Writing and invoking tests with Catch2

The Catch2 framework enables you to write tests using either the traditional style of test cases and test functions or the BDD style with scenarios and *given-when-then* sections. Tests are defined as separate sections of a test case and can be nested as deep as you want. Whichever style you prefer, tests are defined with only two base macros. This recipe will show what these macros are and how they work.

How to do it...

To write tests using the traditional style, with test cases and test functions, do this:

- Use the `TEST_CASE` macro to define a test case with a name (as a string), and optionally, a list of its associated tags:

```
TEST_CASE("test construction", "[create]")
{
  // define sections here
}
```

- Use the `SECTION` macro to define a test function inside a test case, with the name as a string:

```
TEST_CASE("test construction", "[create]")
{
  SECTION("test constructor")
  {
    auto p = point3d{ 1,2,3 };
    REQUIRE(p.x() == 1);
    REQUIRE(p.y() == 2);
    REQUIRE(p.z() == 4);
  }
}
```

- Define nested sections if you want to reuse the setup and teardown code or organize your tests in a hierarchical structure:

```
TEST_CASE("test operations", "[modify]")
{
  SECTION("test methods")
  {
    SECTION("test offset")
    {
      auto p = point3d{ 1,2,3 };
      p.offset(1, 1, 1);
      REQUIRE(p.x() == 2);
      REQUIRE(p.y() == 3);
      REQUIRE(p.z() == 3);
    }
  }
}
```

To write tests using the BDD style, do this:

- Define scenarios using the `SCENARIO` macro, specifying a name for it:

```
SCENARIO("modify existing object")
{
  // define sections here
}
```

- Define nested sections inside the scenario using the `GIVEN`, `WHEN`, and `THEN` macros, specifying a name for each of them:

```
SCENARIO("modify existing object")
{
  GIVEN("a default constructed point")
  {
    auto p = point3d{};
    REQUIRE(p.x() == 0);
    REQUIRE(p.y() == 0);
    REQUIRE(p.z() == 0);

    WHEN("increased with 1 unit on all dimensions")
    {
      p.offset(1, 1, 1);

      THEN("all coordinates are equal to 1")
      {
        REQUIRE(p.x() == 1);
        REQUIRE(p.y() == 1);
        REQUIRE(p.z() == 1);
      }
    }
  }
}
```

To execute the tests, do the following:

- To execute all the tests from your program (except hidden ones), run the test program without any command-line arguments (from the ones described in the following code).

- To execute only a specific set of test cases, provide a filter as a command-line argument. This can contain test case names, wildcards, tag names, and tag expressions:

```
chapter11ca_02.exe "test construction"

test construction
   test constructor
-------------------------------------------------
f:\chapter11ca_02\main.cpp(7)
.................................................
f:\chapter11ca_02\main.cpp(12): FAILED:
  REQUIRE( p.z() == 4 )
with expansion:
  3 == 4

=================================================
test cases: 1 | 1 failed
assertions: 6 | 5 passed | 1 failed
```

- To execute only a particular section (or set of sections), use the command-line argument `--section` or `-c` with the section name (can be used multiple times for multiple sections):

```
chapter11ca_02.exe "test construction" --section "test origin"
Filters: test construction
=================================================
All tests passed (3 assertions in 1 test case)
```

- To specify the order in which test cases should be run, use the command-line argument `--order` with one of the following values: `decl` (for the order of declaration), `lex` (for a lexicographic ordering by the name), or `rand` (for a random order determined with `std::random_shuffle()`). Here's an illustration of this:

```
chapter11ca_02.exe --order lex
```

How it works...

Test cases are self-registered and do not require any additional work from the developer to set the test program, other than defining the test cases and test functions. Test functions are defined as sections of test cases (using the `SECTION` macro), and they can be nested.

There is no limit to the depth of section nesting. Test cases and test functions, which from here on will be referred to as sections, form a tree structure, with the test cases on the root nodes and the most inner sections as leaves. When the test program runs, it is the leaf sections that are executed. Each leaf section is executed in isolation of the other leaf sections. However, the execution path starts at the root test case and continues downward, toward the innermost section. All of the code that's encountered on the path is executed entirely for each run. This means that when multiple sections share common code (from a parent section or the test case), the same code is executed once for each section, without any data being shared between executions. This has the effect that it eliminates the need for a special fixture approach on the one hand. On the other hand, it enables multiple fixtures for each section (everything that is encountered up in the path), a feature that many testing frameworks lack.

The BDD style of writing test cases is powered by the same two macros, namely, `TEST_CASE` and `SECTION`, and the ability to test sections. In fact, the macro `SCENARIO` is a redefinition of `TEST_CASE`, and `GIVEN`, `WHEN`, `AND_WHEN`, `THEN`, and `AND_THEN` are redefinitions of `SECTION`:

```
#define SCENARIO( ... ) TEST_CASE( "Scenario: " __VA_ARGS__ )

#define GIVEN( desc )     INTERNAL_CATCH_DYNAMIC_SECTION( "    Given: "
<< desc )
#define AND_GIVEN( desc ) INTERNAL_CATCH_DYNAMIC_SECTION( "And given: "
<< desc )
#define WHEN( desc )      INTERNAL_CATCH_DYNAMIC_SECTION( "     When: "
<< desc )
#define AND_WHEN( desc )  INTERNAL_CATCH_DYNAMIC_SECTION( " And when: "
<< desc )
#define THEN( desc )      INTERNAL_CATCH_DYNAMIC_SECTION( "     Then: "
<< desc )
#define AND_THEN( desc )  INTERNAL_CATCH_DYNAMIC_SECTION( "      And: "
<< desc )
```

When you execute a test program, all defined tests are run. This, however, excludes hidden tests, which are specified either using a name that starts with `./` or a tag that starts with a period. It is possible to force the running of hidden tests too by providing the command-line argument `[.]` or `[hide]`.

It is possible to filter the test cases to execute. This can be done using either the name or the tags. The following table displays some of the possible options:

Argument	Description
"test construction"	The test case called `test construction`
test*	All test cases that start with `test`
~"test construction"	All test cases, except the one called `test construction`
~*equal*	All test cases, except those that contain the word `equal`
a* ~ab* abc	All tests that start with `a`, except those that start with `ab`, except `abc`, which is included
[modify]	All test cases tagged with `[modify]`
[modify],[compare][op]	All test cases that are tagged with either `[modify]` or both `[compare]` and `[op]`
-#sourcefile	All tests from the file `sourcefile.cpp`

The execution of particular test functions is also possible by specifying one or more section names with the command-line argument `--section` or `-c`. However, wildcards are not supported for this option. If you specify a section to run, be aware that the entire test path from the root test case to the selected section will be executed. Moreover, if you do not specify a test case or a set of test cases first, then all the test cases will be executed, though only the matching sections within them.

See also

- *Getting started with Catch2*, to learn how to install the Catch2 framework and how to create a simple test project.
- *Asserting with Catch2*, to explore the various assertion macros from the Catch2 library.

Asserting with Catch2

Unlike other testing frameworks, Catch2 does not provide a large set of assertion macros. It has two main macros: `REQUIRE`, which produces a fatal error, stopping the execution of the test case upon failure, and `CHECK`, which produces a non-fatal error upon failure, continuing the execution of the test case. Several additional macros are defined; in this recipe, we will see how to put them to work.

Getting ready

You should now be familiar with writing test cases and test functions using Catch2, a topic we covered in the previous recipe, *Writing and invoking tests with Catch2*.

How to do it...

The following list contains the available options for asserting with the Catch2 framework:

- Use `CHECK(expr)` to check whether `expr` evaluates to `true`, continuing the execution in case of failure, and `REQUIRE(expr)` to make sure that `expr` evaluates to `true`, stopping the execution of the test in case of failure:

```
int a = 42;
CHECK(a == 42);
REQUIRE(a == 42);
```

- Use `CHECK_FALSE(expr)` and `REQUIRE_FALSE(expr)` to make sure that `expr` evaluates to `false` and produces either a non-fatal or fatal error in case of failure:

```
int a = 42;
CHECK_FALSE(a > 100);
REQUIRE_FALSE(a > 100);
```

- Use the `Approx` class to compare floating-point values with a given approximation. The method `epsilon()` sets a maximum percentage (as a value between 0 and 1) by which the value can differ:

```
double a = 42.5;
CHECK(42.0 == Approx(a).epsilon(0.02));
REQUIRE(42.0 == Approx(a).epsilon(0.02));
```

- Use `CHECK_NOTHROW(expr)/REQUIRE_NOTHROW(expr)` to verify that expr does not throw any error, `CHECK_THROWS(expr)/REQUIRE_THROWS(expr)` to verify that `expr` does throw an error of any type, `CHECK_THROWS_AS(expr, exctype)/REQUIRE_THROWS_AS(expr, exctype)` to verify that `expr` throws an exception of the type `exctype`, or `CHECK_THROWS_WITH(expression, string or string matcher)/REQUIRE_THROWS_WITH(expression, string or string matcher)` to verify that `expr` throws an expression whose description matches the specified string:

```
void function_that_throws()
{
  throw std::runtime_error("error");
}

void function_no_throw()
{
}
```

```
SECTION("expressions")
{
  CHECK_NOTHROW(function_no_throw());
  REQUIRE_NOTHROW(function_no_throw());

  CHECK_THROWS(function_that_throws());
  REQUIRE_THROWS(function_that_throws());

  CHECK_THROWS_AS(function_that_throws(),
                  std::runtime_error);
  REQUIRE_THROWS_AS(function_that_throws(),
                    std::runtime_error);

  CHECK_THROWS_WITH(function_that_throws(),
                    "error");
  REQUIRE_THROWS_WITH(function_that_throws(),
          Catch::Matchers::Contains("error"));
}
```

- Use `CHECK_THAT(value, matcher expression)`/`REQUIRE_THAT(expr, matcher expression)` to check whether the given matcher expression evaluates to `true` for the specified value:

```
std::string text = "this is an example";
CHECK_THAT(
  text,
  Catch::Matchers::Contains("EXAMPLE", Catch::CaseSensitive::No));
REQUIRE_THAT(
  text,
  Catch::Matchers::StartsWith("this") &&
  Catch::Matchers::Contains("an"));
```

- Use `FAIL(message)` to report `message` and fail the test case, `WARN(message)` to log the message without stopping the execution of the test case, and `INFO(message)` to log the message to a buffer and only report it with the next assertion that would fail.

How it works...

The `REQUIRE/CATCH` family of macros decompose the expression into its left- and right-hand side terms and, upon failure, report the location of the failure (source file and line), the expression, and the values on the left- and right-hand sides:

```
f:\chapter11ca_03\main.cpp(19): FAILED:
  REQUIRE( a == 1 )
with expansion:
  42 == 1
```

However, these macros do not support complex expressions composed using logical operators, such as && and ||. The following example is an error:

```
REQUIRE(a < 10 || a %2 == 0);   // error
```

The solution for this is to create a variable to hold the result of the expression evaluation and use it in the assertion macros. In this case, however, the ability to print the expansion of the elements of the expression is lost:

```
auto expr = a < 10 || a % 2 == 0;
REQUIRE(expr);
```

An alternative is to use another set of parentheses. However, this too stops the decomposition from working:

```
REQUIRE((a < 10 || a %2 == 0)); // OK
```

Special handling is provided to floating-point values. The framework provides a class called `Approx`. It overloads the equality/inequality and comparison operators with values through which a `double` value can be constructed. The margin by which the two values can either differ or be considered equal can be specified as a percentage of the given value. This is set using the member function `epsilon()`. The value must be between 0 and 1 (for example, the value of 0.05 is 5 percent). The default value of epsilon is set to `std::numeric_limits<float>::epsilon()*100`.

Two sets of assertions, namely `CHECK_THAT`/`REQUIRE_THAT` and `CHECK_THROWS_WITH`/`REQUIRE_THROWS_WITH`, work with matchers. Matchers are extensible and composable components that perform value matching. The framework provides several matchers, including for:

- Strings: `StartsWith`, `EndsWith`, `Contains`, `Equals`, and `Matches`
- `std::vector`: `Contains`, `VectorContains`, `Equals`, `UnorderedEquals`, and `Approx`
- Floating-point values: `WithinAbsMatcher`, `WithinUlpMatcher`, and `WithinRelMatch`
- Exceptions: `ExceptionMessageMatcher`

The difference between `Contains()` and `VectorContains()` is that `Contains()` searches for a vector in another vector and `VectorContains()` searches for a single element inside a vector.

You can create your own matchers, either to extend the existing framework capabilities or to work with your own types. There are two things that are necessary:

1. A matcher class derived from `Catch::MatcherBase<T>`, where `T` is the type being compared. There are two virtual functions that must be overridden: `match()`, which takes a value to match and returns a Boolean indicating whether the match was successful, and `describe()`, which takes no arguments but returns a string describing the matcher.
2. A builder function that is called from the test code.

The following example defines a matcher for the `point3d` class, which we have seen throughout this chapter, to check whether a given 3D point lies on a line in the three-dimensional space:

```
class OnTheLine : public Catch::MatcherBase<point3d>
{
  point3d const p1;
  point3d const p2;
public:
  OnTheLine(point3d const & p1, point3d const & p2):
    p1(p1), p2(p2)
  {}

  virtual bool match(point3d const & p) const override
  {
    auto rx = p2.x() - p1.x() != 0 ?
             (p.x() - p1.x()) / (p2.x() - p1.x()) : 0;
    auto ry = p2.y() - p1.y() != 0 ?
             (p.y() - p1.y()) / (p2.y() - p1.y()) : 0;
    auto rz = p2.z() - p1.z() != 0 ?
             (p.z() - p1.z()) / (p2.z() - p1.z()) : 0;

    return
      Approx(rx).epsilon(0.01) == ry &&
      Approx(ry).epsilon(0.01) == rz;
  }
```

```
protected:
  virtual std::string describe() const
  {
    std::ostringstream ss;
    ss << "on the line between " << p1 << " and " << p2;
    return ss.str();
  }
};

inline OnTheLine IsOnTheLine(point3d const & p1,
                             point3d const & p2)
{
  return OnTheLine {p1, p2};
}
```

The following test case contains an example of how to use this custom matcher:

```
TEST_CASE("matchers")
{
  SECTION("point origin")
  {
    point3d p { 2,2,2 };
    REQUIRE_THAT(p, IsOnTheLine(point3d{ 0,0,0 },
                                point3d{ 3,3,3 }));
  }
}
```

This test ensures that the point `{2,2,2}` lies on the line defined by the points `{0,0,0}` and `{3,3,3}` by using the `IsOnTheLine()` custom matcher implemented previously.

See also

- *Writing and invoking tests with Catch2*, to see how to create tests with the Catch2 library, either using the traditional style based on test cases, or the BDD style with scenarios, as well as how to run tests.

Controlling output with Catch2

As with other testing frameworks discussed in this book, Catch2 reports the results of a test program's execution in a human-readable format to the `stdout` standard stream. Additional options are supported, such as reporting using XML format or writing to a file. In this recipe, we will look at the main options available for controlling the output when using Catch2.

Getting ready

To exemplify the way the test program's execution output could be modified, use the following test cases:

```
TEST_CASE("case1")
{
  SECTION("function1")
  {
    REQUIRE(true);
  }
}

TEST_CASE("case2")
{
  SECTION("function2")
  {
    REQUIRE(false);
  }
}
```

The output of running these two test cases is as follows:

```
-------------------------------------------------------------------------------
case2
  function2
-------------------------------------------------------------------------------
f:\chapter11ca_04\main.cpp(14)
...............................................................................
f:\chapter11ca_04\main.cpp(16): FAILED:
  REQUIRE( false )
===============================================================================
test cases: 2 | 1 passed | 1 failed
assertions: 2 | 1 passed | 1 failed
```

In the following section, we'll explore some of the various options for controlling the output of a Catch2 test program.

How to do it...

To control the output of a test program when using Catch2, you can:

- Use the command-line argument `-r` or `--reporter <reporter>` to specify the reporter used to format and structure the results. The default options supplied with the framework are `console`, `compact`, `xml`, and `junit`:

```
chapter11ca_04.exe -r junit

<?xml version="1.0" encoding="UTF-8"?>
<testsuites>
  <testsuite name="chapter11ca_04.exe" errors="0"
             failures="1"
             tests="2" hostname="tbd"
             time="0.002039"
             timestamp="2020-05-02T21:17:04Z">
    <testcase classname="case1" name="function1"
              time="0.00016"/>
    <testcase classname="case2"
              name="function2" time="0.00024">
      <failure message="false" type="REQUIRE">
        at f:\chapter11ca_04\main.cpp(16)
      </failure>
    </testcase>
    <system-out/>
    <system-err/>
  </testsuite>
</testsuites>
```

- Use the command-line argument `-s` or `--success` to display the results of successful test cases too:

```
chapter11ca_04.exe -s

-------------------------------------------------
case1
  function1
-------------------------------------------------
f:\chapter11ca_04\main.cpp(6)
.................................................
```

```
f:\chapter11ca_04\main.cpp(8):
PASSED:
  REQUIRE( true )
-------------------------------------------------
case2
  function2
-------------------------------------------------
f:\chapter11ca_04\main.cpp(14)
.................................................
f:\chapter11ca_04\main.cpp(16):
FAILED:
  REQUIRE( false )
=================================================
test cases: 2 | 1 passed | 1 failed
assertions: 2 | 1 passed | 1 failed
```

- Use the command-line argument `-o` or `--out <filename>` to send all of the output to a file instead of the standard stream:

```
chapter11ca_04.exe -o test_report.log
```

- Use the command-line argument `-d` or `--durations <yes/no>` to display the time that it takes each test case to execute:

```
chapter11ca_04.exe -d yes

0.000 s: scenario1
0.000 s: case1
-------------------------------------------------
case2
   scenario2
-------------------------------------------------
f:\chapter11ca_04\main.cpp(14)
.................................................
f:\chapter11ca_04\main.cpp(16):
FAILED:
  REQUIRE( false )

0.003 s: scenario2
0.000 s: case2
0.000 s: case2
=================================================
test cases: 2 | 1 passed | 1 failed
assertions: 2 | 1 passed | 1 failed
```

How it works...

Apart from the human-readable format used, by default, for reporting the results of the test program execution, the Catch2 framework supports two XML formats:

- A Catch2-specific XML format (specified with `-r xml`)
- A JUnit-like XML format, following the structure of the JUnit ANT task (specified with `-r junit`)

The former reporter streams the XML content as unit tests are executed and results are available. It can be used as input to an XSLT transformation to generate an HTML report for the instance. The latter reporter needs to gather all of the program execution data in order to structure the report before printing it. The JUnit XML format is useful for being consumed by third-party tools, such as a continuous integration server.

Several additional reporters are provided but in standalone headers. They need to be pulled into the project and explicitly included in the source code of the test program (all the headers of the additional reporters have the name format as `catch_reporter_*.hpp`). These additional available reporters are:

- **TeamCity** reporter (specified with `-r teamcity`), which writes TeamCity service messages to the standard output stream. It is suitable only for integration with TeamCity. It is a streamed reporter; data is written as it is available.
- **Automake** reporter (specified with `-r automake`), which writes the meta tags expected by automake via make check.
- **Test Anything Protocol** (or **TAP**, for short) reporter (specified with `-r tap`).
- **SonarQube** reporter (specified with `-r sonarqube`), which writes using the SonarQube generic test data XML format.

The following example shows how to include the TeamCity header file in order to produce the report using the TeamCity reporter:

```
#define CATCH_CONFIG_MAIN
#include "catch.hpp"
#include "catch_reporter_teamcity.hpp"
```

The default target of the test report is the standard stream `stdout` (even data written explicitly to `stderr` ends up being redirected to `stdout`). However, it is possible that the output is written to a file instead. These formatting options can be combined. Take a look at the following command:

```
chapter11ca_04.exe -r junit -o test_report.xml
```

This command specifies that the report should use the JUnit XML format and be saved to a file called `test_report.xml`.

See also

- *Getting started with Catch2*, to learn how to install the Catch2 framework and how to create a simple test project.
- *Writing and invoking tests with Catch2*, to see how to create tests with the Catch2 library, either using the traditional style based on test cases, or the BDD style with scenarios, as well as how to run tests.

12
C++20 Core Features

The new C++20 standard is a major step in the development of the C++ language. C++20 brings many new features both to the language and to the standard library. Some of these have been already discussed in previous chapters, such as the text formatting library, the calendar extensions to the chrono library, the changes to the thread support library, and many others. However, the features that impact the language the most are modules, concepts, coroutines, and the new ranges library. The specification of these features is very lengthy, which makes it difficult to cover them in great detail in this book. Therefore, in this chapter, we will look at the most important aspects and use cases of these features. This chapter is intended to help you start using these features.

This chapter includes the following recipes:

- Working with modules
- Understanding module partitions
- Specifying requirements on template arguments with concepts
- Using requires expressions and clauses
- Iterating over collections with the ranges library
- Creating your own range view
- Creating a coroutine task type for asynchronous computations
- Creating a coroutine generator type for sequences of values

Let's start this chapter by learning about modules, which are the most disruptive change that's happened to the C++ language in decades.

Working with modules

Modules are one of the most important changes in the C++20 standard. They represent a fundamental change to the C++ language and the way we write and consume code. Modules are made available in source files that are compiled separately from the translation units that consume them.

Modules provide multiple advantages, especially in comparison to the use of header files.

- They are only imported once and the order they're imported in does not matter.
- They do not require splitting interfaces and implementation in different source files, although this is still possible.
- Modules have the potential of reducing compilation time, in some cases significantly. The entities exported from a module are described in a binary file that the compiler can process faster than traditional precompiled headers.
- Moreover, this file can potentially be used to build integrations and interop with C++ code from other languages.

In this recipe, you will learn how to get started with modules.

Getting ready

At the time of writing this book, the major compilers (VC++, Clang, GCC) provide work in progress, experimental support for modules. Build systems, such as CMake, are lagging in terms of adoption for modules. Because different compilers have different ways and different compiler options for supporting modules, this book will not provide details for how to build these samples. The reader is invited to consult online documentation for specific compilers.

The source code accompanying this book includes scripts for building the source code presented in this recipe and the next one using the Visual C++ 2019 16.5 compiler.

There are several types of module files: *module interface units*, *module interface partitions*, and *module implementation partitions*. In this recipe, we'll refer solely to the first; the other two, we will learn about in the next recipe.

How to do it...

When you modularize your code, you can do the following:

- Import a module using the `import` directive, followed by the module name. The Standard Library, although not yet modularized, may be available as compiler-specific modules. The following snippet uses the `std.core` module from Visual C++, which contains most of the functionality of the Standard Library, including the streams library:

```
import std.core;

int main()
{
  std::cout << "Hello, World!\n";
}
```

- Export a module by creating a **module interface unit** (**MIU**) that can contain functions, types, constants, and even macros. Their declaration must be preceded by the keyword `export`. The module interface unit file must have the extension `.ixx` for VC++. Clang accepts different extensions, including `.cpp`, `.cppm`, and even `.ixx`. The following sample exports a class template called `point`, a function called `distance()` that computes the distance between two points, and a user-defined literal operator called `_ip` that creates objects of the type `point` from strings in the form `"0,0"` or `"12,-3"`:

```
// --- geometry.ixx/.cppm ---
export module geometry;

import std.core;

export template <class T,
   typename = typename std::enable_if_t<std::is_arithmetic_v<T>,
T>>
struct point
{
   T x;
   T y;
};
export using int_point = point<int>;
```

```
export constexpr int_point int_point_zero{ 0,0 };

export template <class T>
double distance(point<T> const& p1,
                point<T> const& p2)
{
   return std::sqrt((p2.x - p1.x) * (p2.x - p1.x) +
                    (p2.y - p1.y) * (p2.y - p1.y));
}

namespace geometry_literals
{
   export int_point operator ""_ip(const char* ptr,
                                   std::size_t size)
   {
      int x = 0, y = 0;
      while (*ptr != ',' && *ptr != ' ')
         x = x * 10 + (*ptr++ - '0');
      while (*ptr == ',' || *ptr == ' ') ptr++;
      while (*ptr != 0)
         y = y * 10 + (*ptr++ - '0');
      return { x, y };
   }
}

// --- main.cpp ---

import std.core;
import geometry;

int main()
{
   int_point p{ 3, 4 };
   std::cout << distance(int_point_zero, p) << '\n';

   {
      using namespace geometry_literals;
      std::cout << distance("0,0"_ip, "30,40"_ip) << '\n';
   }
}
```

- Use the `import` directive to also import the content of a header. The example presented here uses the same type and functions seen in the preceding example:

```
// --- geometry.h ---
#pragma once

#include <cmath>

template <class T,
   typename = typename std::enable_if_t<std::is_arithmetic_v<T>,
T>>
struct point
{
   T x;
   T y;
};

using int_point = point<int>;

constexpr int_point int_point_zero{ 0,0 };

template <class T>
double distance(point<T> const& p1,
                point<T> const& p2)
{
   return std::sqrt((p2.x - p1.x) * (p2.x - p1.x) +
                    (p2.y - p1.y) * (p2.y - p1.y));
}

namespace geometry_literals
{
   int_point operator ""_ip(const char* ptr,
                            std::size_t size)
   {
      int x = 0, y = 0;
      while (*ptr != ',' && *ptr != ' ')
         x = x * 10 + (*ptr++ - '0');
      while (*ptr == ',' || *ptr == ' ') ptr++;
      while (*ptr != 0)
         y = y * 10 + (*ptr++ - '0');
      return { x, y };
   }
```

```
}

// --- main.cpp ---
import std.core;
import "geometry.h";

int main()
{
   int_point p{ 3, 4 };
   std::cout << distance(int_point_zero, p) << '\n';

   {
      using namespace geometry_literals;
      std::cout << distance("0,0"_ip, "30,40"_ip) << '\n';
   }
}
```

How it works...

A module unit is composed of several parts, mandatory or optional:

- The *global module fragment*, introduced with a `module;` statement. This part is optional and, if present, may only contain preprocessor directives. Everything that is added here is said to belong to the *global module*, which is the collection of all the global module fragments and all translation units that are not modules.
- The *module declaration*, which is a required statement of the form `export module name;`.
- The *module preamble*, which is optional, and may only contain import declarations.
- The *module purview*, which is the content of the unit, starting with the module declaration and extending to the end of the module unit.

The following diagram shows a module unit containing all of the parts mentioned previously. On the left side, we have the source code of the module, and on the right side, the module parts are explained:

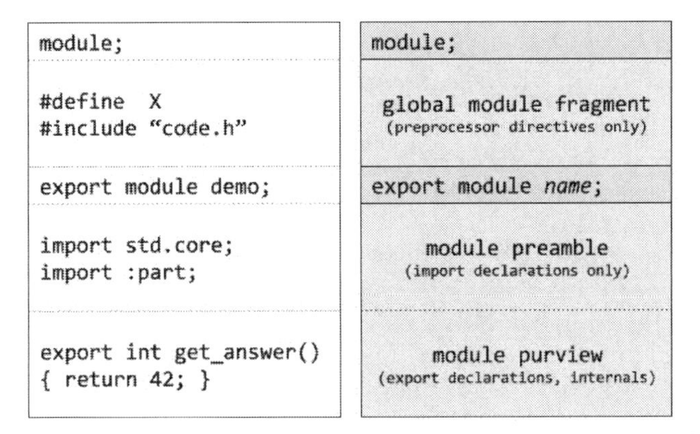

Figure 12.1: An example of a module (on the left side) with each part highlighted and explained (on the right side)

A module can export any entity, such as functions, classes, and constants. Every export must be preceded by the `export` keyword. This keyword is always the first keyword, preceding others such as `class`/`struct`, `template`, or `using`. Several examples have been provided in the **geometry** module shown in the previous section:

- E class template called `point`, which represents a point in the two-dimensional space
- A type alias for `point<int>` called `int_point`
- A compile-time constant called `int_point_zero`
- A function template, `distance()`, that computes the distance between two points
- A user-defined literal `_ip` that creates `int_point` objects from strings such as `"3,4"`

A translation unit that uses modules instead of headers does not require any other changes except for replacing `#include` preprocessor directives with `import` directives. Moreover, headers can also be imported as modules using the same `import` directive, as shown in an example earlier.

There is no relationship between modules and namespaces. These two are orthogonal concepts. The module's geometry exports the user-defined literal `""_ip` in the namespace `geometry_literals`, while all the other exports in the module are available in the global namespace.

There is also no relationship between the module names and the name of the unit file. The geometry module was defined in a file called `geometry.ixx/.cppm`, although any filename would have had the same result. It is recommended that you follow a consistent naming scheme and use the module name for the module filename too. On the other hand, the extension used for module units differs with each compiler, although this could be something that may change in the future when module support reaches maturity.

The Standard Library is not yet modularized, although this is likely to happen in a future version of the standard. However, compilers have already made it available in modules. The Clang compiler provides a different module for each header. On the other hand, the Visual C++ compiler provides the following modules for the Standard Library:

- `std.regex`: The content of the `<regex>` header
- `std.filesystem`: The content of the `<filesystem>` header
- `std.memory`: The content of the `<memory>` header
- `std.threading`: The content of the headers `<atomic>`, `<condition_variable>`, `<future>`, `<mutex>`, `<shared_mutex>`, and `<thread>`
- `std.core`: The rest of the C++ Standard Library

As you can see from these module names, such as `std.core` or `std.regex`, the name of the module can be a series of identifiers concatenated with a dot (`.`). The dot has no significance other than helping to split the name into parts representing a logical hierarchy, such as `company.project.module`. The use of a dot can arguably provide better readability compared to the use of an underscore (such as in `std_core` or `std_regex`), which is also legal, like anything else that may form an identifier.

See also

- *Understanding module partitions*, to learn about interface and implementation partitions.

Understanding module partitions

The source code of a module may become large and difficult to maintain. Moreover, a module may be composed of logically separate parts. To help with scenarios such as these, modules support composition from parts called *partitions*. A module unit that is a partition that exports entities is called a *module interface partition*.

However, there could also be internal partitions that do not export anything. Such a partition unit is called a *module implementation partition*. In this recipe, you will learn how to work with interface and implementation partitions.

Getting ready

You should read the previous recipe, *Working with modules*, before continuing with this one. You will need both the module fundamentals we discussed there and the code examples that we will continue with in this recipe.

How to do it...

You can split a module into several partitions as follows:

- Each partition unit must start with a statement of the form `export module modulename:partitionname;`. Only the global module fragment may precede this declaration:

```
// --- geometry-core.ixx/.cppm ---
export module geometry:core;

import std.core;

export template <class T,
   typename = typename std::enable_if_t<std::is_arithmetic_v<T>,
T>>
struct point
{
   T x;
   T y;
};
export using int_point = point<int>;

export constexpr int_point int_point_zero{ 0,0 };

export template <class T>
double distance(point<T> const& p1,
                point<T> const& p2)
{
   return std::sqrt((p2.x - p1.x) * (p2.x - p1.x) +
                    (p2.y - p1.y) * (p2.y - p1.y));
}
```

```
// --- geometry-literals.ixx/.cppm ---
export module geometry:literals;

import :core;

namespace geometry_literals
{
   export int_point operator ""_ip(const char* ptr,
                                   std::size_t size)
   {
      int x = 0, y = 0;
      while (*ptr != ',' && *ptr != ' ')
         x = x * 10 + (*ptr++ - '0');
      while (*ptr == ',' || *ptr == ' ') ptr++;
      while (*ptr != 0)
         y = y * 10 + (*ptr++ - '0');
      return { x, y };
   }
}
```

- In the primary module interface unit, import and then export the partitions with statements of the form `export import :partitionname`, such as in the following example:

```
// --- geometry.ixx/.cppm ---
export module geometry;

export import :core;
export import :literals;
```

- The code importing a module composed from multiple partitions only sees the module as a whole if it was built from a single module unit:

```
// --- main.cpp ---
import std.core;
import geometry;

int main()
{
   int_point p{ 3, 4 };
   std::cout << distance(int_point_zero, p) << '\n';
```

```
    {
      using namespace geometry_literals;
      std::cout << distance("0,0"_ip, "30,40"_ip) << '\n';
    }
  }
```

- It is possible to create internal partitions that do not export anything but contain code that can be used in the same module. Such a partition must start with a statement of the form `module modulename:partitionname;` (without the keyword `export`). Different compilers may also require a different extension for the file containing an internal partition. For VC++, the extension must be `.cpp`:

```
// --- geometry-details.cpp --
module geometry:details;

import std.core;

std::pair<int, int> split(const char* ptr,
                          std::size_t size)
{
  int x = 0, y = 0;
  while (*ptr != ',' && *ptr != ' ')
    x = x * 10 + (*ptr++ - '0');
  while (*ptr == ',' || *ptr == ' ') ptr++;
  while (*ptr != 0)
    y = y * 10 + (*ptr++ - '0');
  return { x, y };
}
// --- geometry-literals.ixx/.cppm ---
export module geometry:literals;

import :core;
import :details;

namespace geometry_literals
{
  export int_point operator ""_ip(const char* ptr,
                                  std::size_t size)
  {
    auto [x, y] = split(ptr, size);
    return {x, y};
  }
}
```

How it works...

The code shown earlier is a follow-up of the modules example presented in the previous recipe. The `geometry` module has been split into two different partitions called `core` and `literals`.

However, when you declare the partition, you must use the name in the form `modulename:partitionname`, such as in `geometry:core` and `geometry:literals`. This is not necessary when you import a partition elsewhere in the module. This can be seen both in the primary partition unit `geometry.ixx` and in the module interface partition `geometry-literals.ixx`. Here are the snippets again, for clarity:

```
// --- geometry-literals.ixx/.cppm ---
export module geometry:literals;

// import the core partition
import :core;


// --- geometry.ixx/.cppm ---
export module geometry;

// import the core partition and then export it
export import :core;

// import the literals partition and then export it
export import :literals;
```

Although module partitions are distinct files, they are not available as separate modules or submodules to translation units using a module. They are exported together as a single, aggregated module. If you compare the source code in the `main.cpp` file with the one from the previous recipe, you will see no difference.

As with module interface units, there are no rules for naming the files containing partitions. However, compilers may require different extensions or support some particular naming schemes. For instance, VC++ uses the scheme `<module-name>-<partition-name>.ixx`, which simplifies build commands.

Partitions, just like modules, may contain code that is not exported from the module. A partition may contain no exports at all, in which case it is an internal partition only. Such a partition is called a *module implementation partition*. It is defined without using the `export` keyword in the module's declaration.

An example of an internal partition is the `geometry:details` partition shown earlier. It provides a helper function, called `split()`, for parsing two integers separated with a comma from a string. This partition is then imported into the `geometry:literals` partitions, where the `split()` function is used to implement the user-defined literal `_ip`.

There's more...

Partitions are divisions of a module. However, they are not submodules. They do not logically exist outside of the module. There is no concept of a submodule in the C++ language. The code shown in this recipe using partitions could be written slightly differently using modules:

```
// --- geometry-core.ixx ---
export module geometry.core;

import std.core;

export template <class T,
   typename = typename std::enable_if_t<std::is_arithmetic_v<T>, T>>
struct point
{
   T x;
   T y;
};

export using int_point = point<int>;

export constexpr int_point int_point_zero{ 0,0 };

export template <class T>
double distance(point<T> const& p1,
                point<T> const& p2)
{
   return std::sqrt(
      (p2.x - p1.x) * (p2.x - p1.x) +
      (p2.y - p1.y) * (p2.y - p1.y));
}

// --- geometry-literals.ixx ---
export module geometry.literals;
```

```
import geometry.core;

namespace geometry_literals
{
   export int_point operator ""_ip(const char* ptr,
                                   std::size_t size)
   {
      int x = 0, y = 0;
      while (*ptr != ',' && *ptr != ' ')
         x = x * 10 + (*ptr++ - '0');
      while (*ptr == ',' || *ptr == ' ') ptr++;
      while (*ptr != 0)
         y = y * 10 + (*ptr++ - '0');
      return { x, y };
   }
}

// --- geometry.ixx ---
export module geometry;

export import geometry.core;
export import geometry.literals;
```

In this example, we have three modules: `geometry.core`, `geometry.literals`, and `geometry`. Here, `geometry` imports and then re-exports the entire content of the first two. Because of this, the code in `main.cpp` does not need to change. By solely importing the `geometry` module, we get access to the content of the `geometry.core` and `geometry.literals` modules.

However, if we do not define the `geometry` module any more, then we need to explicitly import the two modules, as shown in the following snippet:

```
import std.core;
import geometry.core;
import geometry.literals;

int main()
{
   int_point p{ 3, 4 };
   std::cout << distance(int_point_zero, p) << '\n';
```

```
    {
        using namespace geometry_literals;
        std::cout << distance("0,0"_ip, "30,40"_ip) << '\n';
    }
}
```

Choosing between using partitions or multiple modules for componentizing your source code should depend on the particularities of your project. If you use multiple smaller modules, you provide better granularity for imports. This can be important if you're developing a large library because users should only import things they use (and not a very large module when they only need some functionalities).

See also

- *Working with modules,* to explore the fundamentals of C++20 modules.

Specifying requirements on template arguments with concepts

Template metaprogramming is an important part of the C++ language, empowering the development of general-purpose libraries, including the standard library. However, template metaprogramming is not trivial. On the contrary, complex tasks could be tedious and difficult to get right without a lot of experience. In fact, the C++ Core Guidelines, an initiative created by Bjarne Stroustrup and Herb Sutter, have a rule called *Use template metaprogramming only when you really need to,* which reasons that:

> "*Template metaprogramming is hard to get right, slows down compilation, and is often very hard to maintain.*"

An important aspect concerning template metaprogramming has been the specification of constraints for type template parameters in order to impose restrictions on the types a template can be instantiated with. The C++20 concepts library is designed to solve this problem. A concept is a named set of constraints and a constraint is a requirement for a template argument. These are used to select the appropriate function overloads and template specializations.

In this recipe, we will see how we can use C++20 concepts to specify requirements on template arguments.

Getting ready

Before we begin learning about concepts, let's consider the following class template, called `NumericalValue`, which is supposed to hold a value of an integral or floating-point type. This C++11 implementation employs the use of `std::enable_if` to specify requirements for the `T` template argument:

```
template <typename T,
          typename = typename std::enable_if_t<std::is_arithmetic_v<T>,
T>>
struct NumericalValue
{
  T value;
};

template <typename T>
NumericalValue<T> wrap(T value) { return { value }; }

template <typename T>
T unwrap(NumericalValue<T> t)   { return t.value; }

auto nv = wrap(42);
std::cout << nv.value << '\n';   // prints 42

auto v = unwrap(nv);
std::cout << v << '\n';          // prints 42

using namespace std::string_literals;
auto ns = wrap("42"s);           // error
```

This snippet will be the basis for the examples shown in this recipe.

How to do it...

You can specify requirements for template arguments as follows:

- Create a concept using the `concept` keyword with the following form:

  ```
  template <class T>
  concept Numerical = std::is_arithmetic_v<T>;
  ```

- Alternatively, you can use one of the standard-defined concepts, available in the header `<concepts>` (or one of the other standard library headers):

```
template <class T>
concept Numerical = std::integral<T> || std::floating_point<T>;
```

- Use the concept name instead of the `class` or `typename` keywords in function templates, class templates, or variable templates:

```
template <Numerical T>
struct NumericalValue
{
  T value;
};

template <Numerical T>
NumericalValue<T> wrap(T value) { return { value }; }

template <Numerical T>
T unwrap(NumericalValue<T> t)   { return t.value; }
```

- Instantiate class templates and call function templates with no changes in syntax:

```
auto nv = wrap(42);
std::cout << nv.value << '\n';   // prints 42

auto v = unwrap(nv);
std::cout << v << '\n';          // prints 42

using namespace std::string_literals;
auto ns = wrap("42"s);           // error
```

How it works...

A concept is a set of one or more constraints that is always defined in a namespace scope. The definition of a concept is similar to a variable template. The following snippet shows a concept being used for a variable template:

```
template <class T>
concept Real = std::is_floating_point_v<T>;
```

```
template<Real T>
constexpr T pi = T(3.1415926535897932385L);

std::cout << pi<double> << '\n';
std::cout << pi<int>    << '\n'; // error
```

Concepts cannot be constrained themselves, nor can they refer to themselves recursively. In the examples shown so far, the `Numerical` and `Real` concepts are composed of a single, atomic constraint. However, concepts can be created from multiple constraints. A constraint created from two constraints using the `&&` logical operator is called a *conjunction*, while a constraint created from two constraints using the `||` logical operator is called a *disjunction*.

The `Numerical` concept defined in the *How to do it...* section was defined using the `std::is_arithmetic_v` type trait. However, we could have two concepts, `Real` and `Integral`, as follows:

```
template <class T>
concept Integral = std::is_integral_v<T>;

template <class T>
concept Real = std::is_floating_point_v<T>;
```

From these two, we can compose the `Numerical` concept, using the `&&` logical operator. The result is a disjunction:

```
template <class T>
concept Numerical = Integral<T> || Real<T>;
```

Semantically, there is no difference between these two versions of the `Numerical` concept, although they are defined in different ways.

To understand conjunctions, let's look at another example. Consider two base classes, `IComparableToInt` and `IConvertibleToInt`, that are supposed to be derived by classes that should support comparison or conversion to `int`. These could be defined as follows:

```
struct IComparableToInt
{
  virtual bool CompareTo(int const o) = 0;
};

struct IConvertibleToInt
{
```

```
  virtual int ConvertTo() = 0;
};
```

Some classes may implement both of them, others only one or the other. The `SmartNumericalValue<T>` class here implements both while `DullNumericalValue<T>` only implements the `IConvertibleToInt` class:

```
template <typename T>
struct SmartNumericalValue : public IComparableToInt, IConvertibleToInt
{
  T value;

  SmartNumericalValue(T v) :value(v) {}

  bool CompareTo(int const o) override
  { return static_cast<int>(value) == o; }

  int ConvertTo() override
  { return static_cast<int>(value); }
};

template <typename T>
struct DullNumericalValue : public IConvertibleToInt
{
  T value;

  DullNumericalValue(T v) :value(v) {}

  int ConvertTo() override
  { return static_cast<int>(value); }
};
```

What we want to do is write a function template that only accepts arguments that are both comparable and can be converted to `int`. The `IComparableAndConvertible` concept shown here is a conjunction of the `IntComparable` and `IntConvertible` concepts. They can be implemented as follows:

```
template <class T>
concept IntComparable = std::is_base_of_v<IComparableToInt, T>;

template <class T>
concept IntConvertible = std::is_base_of_v<IConvertibleToInt, T>;
```

```
template <class T>
concept IntComparableAndConvertible = IntComparable<T> &&
IntConvertible<T>;

template <IntComparableAndConvertible T>
void print(T o)
{
   std::cout << o.value << '\n';
}
```

Conjunctions and disjunctions are evaluated left to right and are short-circuited. This means that for a conjunction, the right constraint is evaluated only if the left one is satisfied, and for a disjunction, the right constraint is evaluated only if the left one is not satisfied.

The third category of constraints is *atomic constraints*. These are composed of an expression `E` and a mapping between the type parameters from `E` and the template arguments of the constrained entity, called *parameter mapping*. The atomic constraints are formed during *constraint normalization*, which is the process of transforming a constraint expression into a sequence of conjunctions and disjunctions of atomic constraints. An atomic constraint is checked by substituting the parameter mapping and the template arguments into the expression `E`. The result must be a valid prvalue constant expression of type `bool`; otherwise, the constraint is not satisfied.

The Standard Library defines a series of concepts that can be used to define compile-time requirements on template arguments. Although most of these concepts impose both syntactic and semantic requirements, the compiler can usually ensure only the former. When the semantic requirements are not met, the program is considered ill-formed and the compiler is not required to provide any diagnostics about the problem. The standard concepts are available in several places:

- In the concepts library, in the `<concepts>` header and the `std` namespace. This includes core language concepts (such as `same_as`, `integral`, `floating_point`, `copy_constructible`, and `move_constructible`), comparison concepts (such as `equality_comparable` and `totally_ordered`), object concepts (such as `copyable`, `moveable`, and `regular`), and callable concepts (such as `invocable` and `predicate`).

- In the algorithms library, in the `<iterator>` header and the `std` namespace. This includes algorithm requirements (such as `sortable`, `permutable`, and `mergeable`) and indirect callable concepts (such as `indirect_unary_predicate` and `indirect_binary_predicate`).
- In the ranges library, in the `<ranges>` header and the `std::ranges` namespace. This includes concepts specific for ranges, such as `range`, `view`, `input_range`, `output_range`, `forward_range`, and `random_access_range`.

There's more...

The concepts defined in this recipe used the already available type traits. However, there are many cases when requirements on template arguments cannot be described in this way. For this reason, concepts can be defined with a *requires expression*, which is a prvalue expression of type `bool` describing a template argument requirement. This will be the topic of the next recipe.

See also

- *Using requires expressions and clauses*, to learn about in-place constraints.

Using requires expressions and clauses

In the previous recipe, we introduced the topic of concepts and constraints, and learned about them with the help of several examples that were solely based on already existing type traits. Moreover, we also used the terser syntax for specifying concepts, with the concept name used instead of the `typename` or the `class` keyword in the template declaration. However, it is possible to define more complex concepts with the help of *requires expressions*. These are prvalues of the type `bool` that describe the constraints on some template arguments.

In this recipe, we will learn how to write requires expressions and an alternative way to specify constraints on template arguments.

Getting ready

The class template `NumericalValue<T>` and the function template `wrap()` defined in the previous recipe will be used in the code snippets presented in this recipe.

How to do it...

To specify requirements for template arguments, you can use requires expressions, introduced with the `requires` keyword, such as the following:

- Use a simple expression that the compiler validates for correctness. In the following snippet, the operator + must be overloaded for the `T` template argument:

```
template <typename T>
concept Addable = requires (T a, T b) {a + b;};

template <Addable T>
T add(T a, T b)
{
  return a + b;
}

add(1, 2);          // OK, integers
add("1"s, "2"s);  // OK, std::string user-defined literals

NumericalValue<int> a{1};
NumericalValue<int> b{2};
add(a, b); // error: no matching function for call to 'add'
           // 'NumericalValue<int>' does not satisfy 'Addable'
```

- Use a simple expression to require the existence of a particular function. In the following snippet, a function called `wrap()`, which is overloaded with a parameter of the `T` template argument, must exist:

```
template <typename T>
concept Wrapable = requires(T x) { wrap(x); };

template <Wrapable T>
void do_wrap(T x)
{
  [[maybe_unused]] auto v = wrap(x);
}

do_wrap(42);      // OK, can wrap an int
do_wrap(42.0);  // OK, can wrap a double
do_wrap("42"s); // error, cannot wrap a std::string
```

- Use a type requirement, specified with the keyword `typename`, followed by the name of a type, optionally qualified, to specify requirements such as member names, class template specializations, or alias template substitutions. In the following snippet, the `T` template argument must have two inner types called `value_type` and `iterator`. Additionally, two functions, `begin()` and `end()`, which take a `T` argument, must be available:

```
template <typename T>
concept Container = requires(T x)
{
  typename T::value_type;
  typename T::iterator;
  begin(x);
  end(x);
};

template <Container T>
void pass_container(T const & c)
{
  for(auto const & x : c)
    std::cout << x << '\n';
}

std::vector<int> v { 1, 2, 3};
std::array<int, 3> a {1, 2, 3};
int arr[] {1,2,3};

pass_container(v);   // OK
pass_container(a);   // OK
pass_container(arr); // error: 'int [3]' does not satisfy
                     // 'Container'
```

- Use a compound requirement to specify the requirements of an expression, as well as the result of the evaluation of the expression. In the following example, there must be a function called `wrap()` that can be called with an argument of the `T` template argument type, and the result of calling the function must be of the `NumericalValue<T>` type:

```
template <typename T>
concept NumericalWrapable =
requires(T x)
{
  {wrap(x)} -> std::same_as<NumericalValue<T>>;
};
```

```
template <NumericalWrapable T>
void do_wrap_numerical(T x)
{
  [[maybe_unused]] auto v = wrap(x);
}

template <typename T>
class any_wrapper
{
public:
  T value;
};

any_wrapper<std::string> wrap(std::string s)
{
  return any_wrapper<std::string>{s};
}

// OK, wrap(int) returns NumericalValue<int>
do_wrap_numerical(42);

// error, wrap(string) returns any_wrapper<string>
do_wrap_numerical("42"s);
```

Constraints on the template arguments can be also specified using a syntax involving the `requires` keyword. These are called *requires clauses* and can be used as follows:

- Use a requires clause after the template parameter list:

```
template <typename T> requires Addable<T>
T add(T a, T b)
{
  return a + b;
}
```

- Alternatively, use the requires clause after the last element of a function declarator:

```
template <typename T>
T add(T a, T b) requires Addable<T>
{
  return a + b;
}
```

- Combine a requires clause with a requires expression, instead of a named concept. In this case, the `requires` keyword appears twice, as shown in the following snippet:

```
template <typename T>
T add(T a, T b) requires requires (T a, T b) {a + b;}
{
  return a + b;
}
```

How it works...

The new `requires` keyword has multiple purposes. On one hand, it is used to introduce a requires clause that specifies constraints on template arguments. On the other hand, it is used to define a requires expression that is a prvalue of type `bool` used to define constraints on template arguments.

If you are not familiar with C++ value categories (*lvalue, rvalue, prvalue, xvalue, glvalue*), you are recommended to check `https://en.cppreference.com/w/cpp/language/value_category`. The term *prvalue,* meaning *pure rvalue,* specifies an rvalue that is not an xvalue (expiring value). An example is the result of calling a function whose return type is not a reference.

In a requires clause, the `requires` keyword must be followed by a constant expression of the type `bool`. The expression must be either a primary expression (such as `std::is_arithmetic_v<T>` or `std::integral<T>`), an expression in parentheses, or any sequence of such expressions joined with either the `&&` or the `||` operator.

A requires expression has the form `requires (parameters-list) { requirements }`. The parameters list is optional and can be entirely omitted (including the parentheses). The specified requirements may refer to:

- The template parameters that are in scope
- The local parameters introduced in `parameters-list`
- Any other declarations that are visible from the enclosing context

The requirements sequence of the requires expression can contain requirements of the following types:

- **Simple requirements**. These are arbitrary expressions that do not start with the `requires` keyword. The compiler only checks its language correctness.

- **Type requirements**. These are expressions that start with the keyword `typename` followed by a type name, which must be valid. This enables the compiler to validate that a certain nested name exists, or that a class template specialization or an alias template substitution exists.
- **Compound requirements**. They have the form `{expression} noexcept -> type-constraint`. The `noexcept` keyword is optional, in which case the expression must not be potentially throwing. The requirement for the return type, introduced with `->`, is also optional. However, if it is present, then `decltype(expression)` must satisfy the constraints imposed by `type-constraint`.
- **Nested requirements**. These are more complex expressions that specify constraints defined as a requires expression, which can, in turn, be another nested requirement. A requirement that starts with the keyword `requires` is considered a nested requirement.

Before they are evaluated, the body of every name concept and every `requires` expression is substituted until a sequence of conjunctions and disjunctions of atomic constraints is obtained. This process is called *normalization*. The actual details of normalization and the analysis the compiler is performing are beyond the scope of this book.

See also

- *Specifying requirements on template arguments with concepts*, to explore the fundamentals of C++20 concepts.

Iterating over collections with the ranges library

The C++ Standard Library provides three important pillars—containers, iterators, and algorithms—that enable us to work with collections. Because these algorithms are for general purpose and are designed to work with iterators, which define a range, they often require writing explicit and sometimes complex code to achieve simple tasks. The C++20 ranges library has been designed to solve this problem by providing components for handling ranges of elements. These components include range adapters (or views) and constrained algorithms that work with a range instead of iterators. In this recipe, we will look at some of these views and algorithms and see how they can simplify coding.

Getting ready

In the following snippets, we will refer to a function called `is_prime()`, which takes an integer and returns a Boolean indicating whether the number is prime or not. A simple implementation is shown here:

```
bool is_prime(int const number)
{
  if (number != 2)
  {
    if (number < 2 || number % 2 == 0) return false;
    auto root = std::sqrt(number);
    for (int i = 3; i <= root; i += 2)
      if (number % i == 0) return false;
  }
  return true;
}
```

For an efficient algorithm, which is beyond the scope of this recipe, I recommend the Miller-Rabin primality test.

The ranges library is available in the new `<ranges>` header, in the `std::ranges` namespace. For simplicity, the following namespace aliases will be used in this recipe:

```
namespace rv = std::ranges::views;
namespace rg = std::ranges;
```

We will explore various uses of the ranges library in the next section.

How to do it...

The ranges library can be used to iterate through ranges with operations such as the following:

- Generate a sequence of consecutive integers with the `iota_view` / `views::iota` view. The following snippet prints all integers from 1 to 9:

  ```
  for (auto i : rv::iota(1, 10))
    std::cout << i << ' ';
  ```

- Filter the elements of a range with `filter_view` / `views::filter`, by retaining only those that satisfy a predicate. The first snippet here prints all the prime numbers from 1 to 99. However, the second snippet retains and prints all the prime numbers from a vector of integers:

```
// prints 2 3 5 7 11 13 ... 79 83 89 97
for (auto i : rv::iota(1, 100) | rv::filter(is_prime))
  std::cout << i << ' ';

// prints 2 3 5 13
std::vector<int> nums{ 1, 1, 2, 3, 5, 8, 13, 21 };
for (auto i : nums | rv::filter(is_prime))
  std::cout << i << ' ';
```

- Transform the elements of a range with `transform_view` / `views::transform` by applying a unary function to each element. The following snippet prints the successor of all the prime numbers from 1 to 99:

```
// prints 3 4 6 8 12 14 ... 80 84 90 98
for (auto i : rv::iota(1, 100) |
              rv::filter(is_prime) |
              rv::transform([](int const n) {return n + 1; }))
  std::cout << i << ' ';
```

- Retain only the first *N* elements of a view with `take_view` / `views::take`. The following snippet prints only the 10 first prime numbers from 1 and 99:

```
// prints 2 3 5 7 11 13 17 19 23 29
for (auto i : rv::iota(1, 100) |
              rv::filter(is_prime) |
              rv::take(10))
  std::cout << i << ' ';
```

- Iterate a range in reverse order with `reverse_view` / `views::reverse`. The first snippet here prints the first 10 prime numbers from 99 to 1 (in descending order), while the second snippet prints the last 10 prime numbers from 1 to 99 (in ascending order):

```
// prints 97 89 83 79 73 71 67 61 59 53
for (auto i : rv::iota(1, 100) |
              rv::reverse |
              rv::filter(is_prime) |
              rv::take(10))
  std::cout << i << ' ';
```

```
// prints 53 59 61 67 71 73 79 83 89 97
for (auto i : rv::iota(1, 100) |
              rv::reverse |
              rv::filter(is_prime) |
              rv::take(10) |
              rv::reverse)
   std::cout << i << ' ';
```

- Skip the first *N* elements of a range with `drop_view` / `views::drop`. The snippet here prints, in ascending order, the prime numbers between 1 and 99, but skips the first and last 10 primes in the sequence:

```
// prints 31 37 41 43 47
for (auto i : rv::iota(1, 100) |
              rv::filter(is_prime) |
              rv::drop(10) |
              rv::reverse |
              rv::drop(10) |
              rv::reverse)
   std::cout << i << ' ';
```

The ranges library can also be used to call algorithms using a range instead of iterators. Most algorithms have overloads for this purpose. Examples are shown here:

- Determine the maximum element of a range:

```
std::vector<int> v{ 5, 2, 7, 1, 4, 2, 9, 5 };
auto m = rg::max(v); // 5
```

- Sort a range:

```
rg::sort(v); // 1 2 2 4 5 5 7 9
```

- Copy a range. The following snippet copies the elements of the range to the standard output stream:

```
rg::copy(v, std::ostream_iterator<int>(std::cout, " "));
```

- Reverse the elements of a range:

```
rg::reverse(v);
```

- Count the elements of a range (that verify a predicate):

```
auto primes = rg::count_if(v, is_prime);
```

How it works...

The C++20 ranges library provides various components for dealing with ranges of elements. These include:

- Range concepts, such as range and view.
- Range access functions, such as begin(), end(), size(), empty(), and data().
- Range factories that create sequences of elements, such as empty_view, single_view, and iota_view.
- Range adaptors, or views, that create a lazy evaluated view from a range, such as filter_view, transform_view, take_view, and drop_view.

A range is defined as a sequence of elements that can be iterated over with an iterator and an end sentinel. Ranges are of different types, depending on the capabilities of the iterators that define the range. The following concepts define types of ranges:

Concept	Iterator type	Capabilities
input_range	input_iterator	Can be iterated at least once for reading.
output_range	output_iterator	Can be iterated for writing.
forward_range	forward_iterator	Can be iterated multiple times.
bidirectional_range	bidirectional_iterator	Can be iterated also in reverse order.
random_access_range	random_access_iterator	Elements can be accessed randomly in constant time.
contiguous_range	contiguous_iterator	Elements are stored contiguously in memory.

Because a forward_iterator satisfies the requirements of an input_iterator, and a bidirectional_iterator satisfies those of a forward_iterator and so on (from top to bottom in the preceding table), so do the ranges. A forward_range satisfies the requirements of an input_range, and a bidirectional_range satisfies those of a forward_range, and so on. Apart from the range concepts listed in the preceding table, there are other range concepts. One worth mentioning is sized_range, which requires that a range must know its size in constant time.

The standard containers meet the requirements of different range concepts. The most important of them are listed in the following table:

	Input range	Forward range	Bidirectional range	Random access range	Contiguous range
`forward_list`	YES	YES			
`list`	YES	YES	YES		
`dequeue`	YES	YES	YES	YES	
`array`	YES	YES	YES	YES	YES
`vector`	YES	YES	YES	YES	YES
`set`	YES	YES	YES		
`map`	YES	YES	YES		
`multiset`	YES	YES	YES		
`multimap`	YES	YES	YES		
`unordered_set`	YES	YES			
`unordered_map`	YES	YES			
`unordered_multiset`	YES	YES			
`unordered_multimap`	YES	YES			

A central concept of the ranges library is the range *adaptor*, also called a *view*. A view is a non-owning wrapper of a range of elements that requires constant time to copy, move, or assign elements. Views are composable adaptations of ranges. However, these adaptations happen lazily, only when the view is iterated.

In the previous section, we have seen examples of using various views: filter, transform, take, drop, and reverse. There is a total of 16 views available in the library. All the views are available in the namespace `std::ranges` and have names such as `filter_view`, `transform_view`, `take_view`, `drop_view`, and `reverse_view`. However, for simplicity of use, these views can be used with expressions of the form `views::filter`, `views::take`, `views::reverse`, and so on. Notice that the types and values of these expressions are unspecified and are a compiler implementation detail.

To understand how the views work, let's take a look at the following example:

```
std::vector<int> nums{ 1, 1, 2, 3, 5, 8, 13, 21 };
auto v = nums | rv::filter(is_prime) | rv::take(3) | rv::reverse;
for (auto i : v) std::cout << i << ' ';
```

The object `v` in this snippet represents a view. It does not evaluate the range it adapts until we start iterating over the elements. This is done, in this example, with the `for` statement. The views are said to be lazy. The pipe operator (`|`) is overloaded to simplify the composition of views.

The composition of views is equivalent to the following:

```
auto v = rv::reverse(rv::take(rv::filter(nums, is_prime), 3));
```

In general, the following rules apply:

- If an adaptor `A` takes only one argument, a range `R`, then `A(R)` and `R|A` are equivalent.
- If an adaptor `A` takes multiple arguments, a range `R` and `args...`, then the following three are equivalent: `A(R, args...)`, `A(args...)(R)`, and `R|A(args...)`.

Apart from ranges and range adaptors (or views), overloads of the general-purpose algorithms are also available in C++20, in the same `std::ranges` namespace. These overloads are called *constrained algorithms*. A range can be provided either as a single argument (as seen in the examples in this recipe) or as an iterator-sentinel pair. Also, for these overloads, the return type has been changed to provide additional information that's computed during the execution of the algorithm.

There's more...

The standard ranges library has been designed based on the **range-v3** library, created by Eric Niebler and available on GitHub at `https://github.com/ericniebler/range-v3`. This library provides a larger set of range adaptors (views), as well as actions that provide mutating operations (such as sorting, erasing, shuffling, and so on). The transition from the range-v3 library to the C++20 ranges library can be very smooth. In fact, all the samples provided in this recipe work with both libraries. All you have to do is include the appropriate header files and use the range-v3-specific namespaces:

```
#include "range/v3/view.hpp"
#include "range/v3/algorithm/sort.hpp"
#include "range/v3/algorithm/copy.hpp"
#include "range/v3/algorithm/reverse.hpp"
#include "range/v3/algorithm/count_if.hpp"
#include "range/v3/algorithm/max.hpp"

namespace rv = ranges::views;
namespace rg = ranges;
```

With these replacements, all the snippets from the *How to do it...* section will continue to work using a C++17 compliant compiler.

See also

- *Creating your own range view*, to see how to extend the ranges library's capabilities with user-defined range adaptors.
- *Specifying requirements on template arguments with concepts*, to explore the fundamentals of C++20 concepts.

Creating your own range view

The C++20 ranges library simplifies the handling of ranges of elements. The 16 range adaptors (views) defined in the library provide useful operations, as seen in the previous recipe. However, you can create your own view that can be used together with the standard ones. In this recipe, you will learn how to do that. We will create a view called `trim` that, given a range and a unary predicate, returns a new range without the front and back elements that satisfy the predicate.

Getting ready

In this recipe, we will use the same namespace aliases used in the previous one, with `rg` as an alias for `std::ranges` and `rv` as an alias for `std::ranges::views`.

How to do it...

To create a view, do the following:

- Create a class template, called `trim_view`, derived from `std::ranges::view_interface`:

```
template<rg::input_range R, typename P>
    requires rg::view<R>
class trim_view :
    public rg::view_interface<trim_view<R, P>>
{
};
```

- Define the internal state of the class, which, at a minimum, should include a begin and end iterator and the viewable range that is adapted by the view. For this adapter, we also need a predicate, and a Boolean variable to flag whether the iterators have been evaluated or not:

```
private:
  R base_ {};
  P pred_;
```

```
    mutable rg::iterator_t<R> begin_ {std::begin(base_)};
    mutable rg::iterator_t<R> end_   {std::end(base_)};
    mutable bool evaluated_ = false;

    void ensure_evaluated() const
    {
      if(!evaluated_)
      {
        while(begin_ != std::end(base_) && pred_(*begin_))
        {begin_ = std::next(begin_);}
        while(end_ != begin_ && pred_(*std::prev(end_)))
        {end_ = std::prev(end_);}
        evaluated_ = true;
      }
    }
```

- Define a default constructor (that can be defaulted) and a `constexpr` constructor with the required parameters. The first parameter is always the range. For this view, the other parameter is a predicate:

```
  public:
    trim_view() = default;

    constexpr trim_view(R base, P pred)
      : base_(std::move(base))
      , pred_(std::move(pred))
      , begin_(std::begin(base_))
      , end_(std::end(base_))
    {}
```

- Provide accessors to the internal data, such as the base range and the predicate:

```
    constexpr R base() const &       {return base_;}
    constexpr R base() &&            {return std::move(base_);}
    constexpr P const & pred() const { return pred_; }
```

- Provide functions to retrieve the begin and end iterators. To make sure the view is lazy, these iterators should only be evaluated by their first use:

```
    constexpr auto begin() const
    { ensure_evaluated(); return begin_; }
    constexpr auto end() const
    { ensure_evaluated(); return end_ ; }
```

- Provide other useful members, such as a function, to return the size of the range:

```
constexpr auto size() requires rg::sized_range<R>
{ return std::distance(begin_, end_); }
constexpr auto size() const requires rg::sized_range<const R>
{ return std::distance(begin_, end_); }
```

Put all together, the view appears as follows:

```
template<rg::input_range R, typename P> requires rg::view<R>
class trim_view : public rg::view_interface<trim_view<R, P>>
{
private:
  R base_ {};
  P pred_;
  mutable rg::iterator_t<R> begin_ {std::begin(base_)};
  mutable rg::iterator_t<R> end_   {std::end(base_)};
  mutable bool evaluated_ = false;

private:
  void ensure_evaluated() const
  {
    if(!evaluated_)
    {
      while(begin_ != std::end(base_) && pred_(*begin_))
      {begin_ = std::next(begin_);}
      while(end_ != begin_ && pred_(*std::prev(end_)))
      {end_ = std::prev(end_);}
      evaluated_ = true;
    }
  }

public:
  trim_view() = default;

  constexpr trim_view(R base, P pred)
    : base_(std::move(base))
    , pred_(std::move(pred))
    , begin_(std::begin(base_))
    , end_(std::end(base_))
  {}
```

```
    constexpr R base() const &        {return base_;}
    constexpr R base() &&             {return std::move(base_);}
    constexpr P const & pred() const { return pred_; }

    constexpr auto begin() const
    { ensure_evaluated(); return begin_; }
    constexpr auto end() const
    { ensure_evaluated(); return end_ ; }

    constexpr auto size() requires rg::sized_range<R>
    { return std::distance(begin_, end_); }
    constexpr auto size() const requires rg::sized_range<const R>
    { return std::distance(begin_, end_); }
};
```

To simplify the composability of this user-defined view with the standard ones and the simplicity of use, the following should also be done:

- Create a user-defined deduction guide for class template argument deduction of the `trim_view` class template:

```
template<class R, typename P>
trim_view(R&& base, P pred)
  -> trim_view<rg::views::all_t<R>, P>;
```

- Create function objects that can instantiate the `trim_view` adaptor with the proper arguments. These can be made available in a separate namespace because they represent implementation details:

```
namespace details
{
  template <typename P>
  struct trim_view_range_adaptor_closure
  {
    P pred_;
    constexpr trim_view_range_adaptor_closure(P pred)
      : pred_(pred)
    {}

    template <rg::viewable_range R>
    constexpr auto operator()(R && r) const
    {
      return trim_view(std::forward<R>(r), pred_);
    }
```

```
    };

    struct trim_view_range_adaptor
    {
      template<rg::viewable_range R, typename P>
      constexpr auto operator () (R && r, P pred)
      {
        return trim_view( std::forward<R>(r), pred ) ;
      }

      template <typename P>
      constexpr auto operator () (P pred)
      {
        return trim_view_range_adaptor_closure(pred);
      }
    };
  }
```

- Overload the pipe operator for the `trim_view_range_adaptor_closure` class defined previously:

```
namespace details
{
  template <rg::viewable_range R, typename P>
  constexpr auto operator | (
    R&& r,
    trim_view_range_adaptor_closure<P> const & a)
  {
    return a(std::forward<R>(r)) ;
  }
}
```

- Create an object of the `trim_view_range_adator` type that can be used to create `trim_view` instances. This can be done in a namespace called `views` to create a similarity with the namespaces of the ranges library:

```
namespace views
{
  inline static details::trim_view_range_adaptor trim;
}
```

How it works...

The `trim_view` class template we defined here is derived from the `std::ranges::view_interface` class template. This is a helper class in the ranges library for defining views, using the **curiously recurring template pattern** (CRTP). There are two template arguments for the `trim_view` class: the range type, which must satisfy the `std::ranges::input_range` concept, and the predicate type.

The `trim_view` class stores the base range and the predicate internally. Additionally, it requires a begin and end (sentinel) iterator. These iterators must point to the first element and the ones past the last element of the range that do not satisfy the trimming predicate. However, because the view is a lazy object, these iterators should not be resolved before they are needed to iterate over the range. The following diagram shows the positions of these iterators in a range of integers, for when the view must trim the odd numbers from the beginning and end of the range `{1,1,2,3,5,6,4,7,7,9}`:

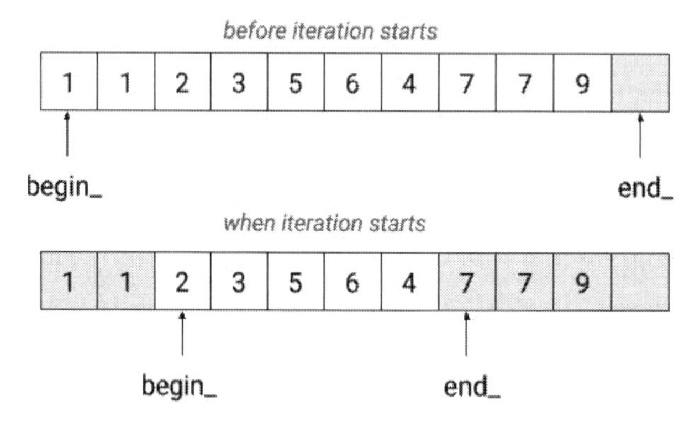

Figure 12.2: A visual conceptual representation of the range and the position of the start and end iterators before the iteration starts (above) and after (below)

We can use the `trim_view` class to write the following snippets:

```
auto is_odd = [](int const n){return n%2 == 1;};
std::vector<int> n { 1,1,2,3,5,6,4,7,7,9 };

auto v = trim_view(n, is_odd);
rg::copy(v, std::ostream_iterator<int>(std::cout, " "));
// prints 2 3 5 6 4

for(auto i : rv::reverse(trim_view(n, is_odd)))
  std::cout << i << ' ';
// prints 4 6 5 3 2
```

Using the `trim_view` class, as well as composition with other views, is simplified through the use of the function objects declared in the `details` namespace, which represent implementation details. However, these, together with the overloaded pipe operator (`|`), make it possible to rewrite the preceding code as follows:

```
auto v = n | views::trim(is_odd);
rg::copy(v, std::ostream_iterator<int>(std::cout, " "));

for(auto i : n | views::trim(is_odd) | rv::reverse)
  std::cout << i << ' ';
```

It should be mentioned that the **range-v3** library does contain a range view called `trim`, but it was not ported to the C++20 ranges library. This may happen in a future version of the standard.

See also

- *Iterating over collections with the ranges library*, to learn about the fundamentals of the C++ ranges library.
- *Specifying requirements on template arguments with concepts*, to explore the fundamentals of C++20 concepts.
- *Static polymorphism with the curiously recurring template pattern in Chapter 10, Implementing Patterns and Idioms,* to see how the CRTP works.

Creating a coroutine task type for asynchronous computations

A major component of the C++20 standard is represented by coroutines. Simply put, coroutines are functions that can be suspended and resumed. Coroutines are an alternative to writing asynchronous code. They help simplify asynchronous I/O code, lazy computations, or event-driven applications. When a coroutine is suspended, the execution returns to the caller and the data necessary to resume the coroutine is stored separately from the stack. For this reason, the C++20 coroutines are called *stackless*. Unfortunately, the C++20 standard does not define actual coroutines types, but only a framework for building them. This makes writing asynchronous code with coroutines difficult without relying on third-party components.

In this recipe, you will learn how to write a coroutine task type that represents an asynchronous computation that starts executing when the task is awaited.

Getting ready

The several standard library types and functions that define the coroutines framework are available in the `<coroutine>` header, in the `std` namespace. However, at the time of writing this book, not all compilers support coroutines other than as an experimental feature. Therefore, if you are using VC++ or Clang, you need to include the `<experimental/coroutine>` header and use the `std::experimental` namespace. In the samples shown in this recipe, `stdco` is an alias for either the `std` or the `std::experimental` namespace.

The goal of this recipe is to create a task type that enables us to write asynchronous functions, as follows:

```
task<int> get_answer()
{
  co_return 42;
}

task<> print_answer()
{
  auto t = co_await get_answer();
  std::cout << "the answer is " << t << '\n';
}

template <typename T>
void execute(T&& t)
{
  while (!t.is_ready()) t.resume();
};

int main()
{
  auto t = get_answer();
  execute(t);
  std::cout << "the answer is " << t.value() << '\n';

  execute(print_answer());
}
```

How to do it...

To create a task type that supports coroutines that return nothing (`task<>`), a value (`task<T>`), or a reference (`task<T&>`), you should do the following:

- Create a class called `promise_base` with the following content:

```
namespace details
{
  struct promise_base
  {
    auto initial_suspend() noexcept
    { return stdco::suspend_always{}; }

    auto final_suspend() noexcept
    { return stdco::suspend_always{}; }

    void unhandled_exception()
    { std::terminate(); }
  };
}
```

- Create a class template called `promise`, derived from `promise_base`, that adds the methods `get_return_object()` and `return_value()` and holds the value returned from the coroutine:

```
namespace details
{
  template <typename T>
  struct promise final : public promise_base
  {
    auto get_return_object()
    {
      return stdco::coroutine_handle<promise<T>>::
                 from_promise(*this);
    }

    template<typename V,
             typename = std::enable_if_t<
                std::is_convertible_v<V&&, T>>>
    auto return_value(V&& value)
    noexcept(std::is_nothrow_constructible_v<T, V&&>)
    {
      value_ = value;
```

```
      return stdco::suspend_always{};
    }

    T get_value() const noexcept { return value_; }
  private:
    T value_;
  };
}
```

- Specialize the `promise` class template for the `void` type, and provide implementations for the `get_return_object()` and `return_void()` methods:

```
namespace details
{
  template <>
  struct promise<void> final : public promise_base
  {
    auto get_return_object()
    {
      return stdco::coroutine_handle<promise<void>>::
                from_promise(*this);
    }

    void return_void() noexcept {}
  };
}
```

- Specialize the `promise` class template for `T&`. Provide implementations for `get_return_object()` and `return_value()` and store a pointer to the reference returned by the coroutine:

```
namespace details
{
  template <typename T>
  struct promise<T&> final : public promise_base
  {
    auto get_return_object()
    {
      return stdco::coroutine_handle<promise<T&>>::
                from_promise(*this);
    }

    void return_value(T& value) noexcept
    {
```

```
      value_ = std::addressof(value);
    }
    T& get_value() const noexcept { return *value_; }

  private:
    T* value_ = nullptr;
  };
}
```

- Create a class template called `task`, with the stub content shown below. This type must have an inner type called `promise_type`, and must hold a handle to the executing coroutine. The `task_awaiter` and the class members are listed here:

```
template <typename T = void>
struct task
{
  using promise_type = details::promise<T>;

  // task_awaiter

  // members

private:
  stdco::coroutine_handle<promise_type> handle_ = nullptr;
};
```

- Create an awaitable class called `task_awaiter` that implements the `await_ready()`, `await_suspend()`, and `await_resume()` methods:

```
struct task_awaiter
{
  task_awaiter(stdco::coroutine_handle<promise_type> coroutine)
  noexcept
    : handle_(coroutine)
  {}

  bool await_ready() const noexcept
  {
     return !handle_ || handle_.done();
  }

  void await_suspend(
    stdco::coroutine_handle<> continuation) noexcept
```

```
    {
      handle_.resume();
    }

    decltype(auto) await_resume()
    {
      if (!handle_)
        throw std::runtime_error{ "broken promise" };

      return handle_.promise().get_value();
    }

    friend class task<T>;
  private:
    stdco::coroutine_handle<promise_type> handle_;
  };
```

- Provide class members, including a conversion constructor, move constructor and move assignment operator, destructor, `co_await` operator, a method to check whether the coroutine has completed, a method to resume a suspended coroutine, and a method to get the value returned from the coroutine:

```
explicit task(stdco::coroutine_handle<promise_type> handle)
  : handle_(handle)
{
}

~task()
{
  if (handle_) handle_.destroy();
}

task(task&& t) noexcept : handle_(t.handle_)
{
  t.handle_ = nullptr;
}

task& operator=(task&& other) noexcept
{
  if (std::addressof(other) != this)
  {
    if (handle_) handle_.destroy();
```

```
    handle_ = other.handle_;
    other.handle_ = nullptr;
  }

  return *this;
}

task(task const &) = delete;
task& operator=(task const &) = delete;

T value() const noexcept
{ return handle_.promise().get_value(); }

void resume() noexcept
{ handle_.resume(); }

bool is_ready() noexcept
{ return !handle_ || handle_.done(); }

auto operator co_await() const& noexcept
{
  return task_awaiter{ handle_ };
}
```

How it works...

Functions are blocks of code that execute one or more statements. You can assign them to variables, pass them as arguments, take their address, and, of course, invoke them. These features make them first-class citizens in the C++ language. Functions are sometimes called *subroutines*. Coroutines, on the other hand, are functions that support two additional operations: suspending and resuming their execution.

In C++20, a function is a coroutine if it uses any of the following:

- The `co_await` operator, which suspends the execution until resumed
- The `co_return` keyword, to complete the execution and optionally return a value
- The `co_yield` keyword, to suspend the execution and return a value

Not every function, however, can be a coroutine. The following cannot be coroutines:

- Constructors and destructors
- Constexpr functions
- Functions with a variable number of arguments
- Functions that return `auto` or a concept type
- The `main()` function

A coroutine consists of the following three parts:

- A *promise object*, which is manipulated inside the coroutine and is used to pass the return value or an exception from the coroutine.
- A *coroutine handle*, which is manipulated outside the coroutine and is used to either resume the execution or destroy the coroutine frame.
- The *coroutine frame*, typically allocated on the heap and containing the promise object, the coroutine parameters copied by value, local variables, and temporaries whose lifetimes exceed the current suspension point, and a representation of the suspension point, so that resuming and destroying can be performed.

The promise object can be any type that implements the following interface, as expected by the compiler:

Default constructor	The promise must be default constructible
`initial_suspend()`	Indicates whether suspension happens at the initial suspend point
`final_suspend()`	Indicates whether suspension happens at the last suspend point
`unhandled_exception()`	Called when an exception propagates out of a coroutine block
`get_return_object()`	The return value of the function
`return_value(v)`	Enables the `co_return v` statement
`return_void()`	Enables the `co_return` statement
`yield_value(v)`	Enables the `co_yield v` statement

The implementation of `initial_suspend()` and `final_suspend()` we have seen for the `promise` type implemented here are returning an instance of `std::suspend_always`. This is one of the two trivial awaitables that the standard defines, the other being `std::suspend_never`. Their implementation is as follows:

```
struct suspend_always
{
  bool await_ready() noexcept { return false; }
  void await_suspend(coroutine_handle<>) noexcept {}
  void await_resume() noexcept {}
};

struct suspend_never
{
  bool await_ready() noexcept { return true; }
  void await_suspend(coroutine_handle<>) noexcept {}
  void await_resume() noexcept {}
};
```

These types implement the *awaitable* concept, which enables the use of the `co_await` operator. There are three functions required by this concept. These can be either free functions or class member functions. They are listed in the following table:

`await_ready()`	Indicates whether the result is ready. If the return value is `false` (or a value convertible to `false`), then `await_suspend()` is called.
`await_suspend()`	Schedules the coroutine to resume or to be destroyed.
`await_resume()`	Provides the result for the entire `co_await e` expression.

The `task<T>` type we built in this recipe has several members:

- An explicit constructor that takes an argument of the `std::coroutine_handle<T>` type, representing a non-owning handle to the coroutine.
- A destructor that destroys the coroutine frame.
- A move constructor and move assignment operator.
- A deleted copy constructor and copy assignment operator, making the class moveable-only.
- The `co_await` operator, which returns a `task_awaiter` value that implements the awaitable concept.
- `is_ready()`, a method that returns a Boolean value indicating whether the coroutine value is ready.
- `resume()`, a method that resumes the execution of the coroutine.
- `value()`, a method that returns the value held by the promise object.
- An inner promise type called `promise_type` (this name is mandatory).

If an exception occurs during the execution of the coroutine, and this exception leaves the coroutine without being handled, then the `unhandled_exception()` method of the promise is invoked. In this simple implementation, this situation is not handled and the program is abnormally terminated with a call to `std::terminate()`. In the following recipe, we will see an awaitable implementation that handles exceptions.

Let's take the following coroutine as an example to see how the compiler handles it:

```
task<> print_answer()
{
  auto t = co_await get_answer();
  std::cout << "the answer is " << t << '\n';
}
```

Because of all the mechanisms we built in this recipe, the compiler transforms this code into the following (this snippet is pseudocode):

```
task<> print_answer()
{
  __frame* context;

  task<>::task_awaiter t = operator co_await(get_answer());

  if(!t.await_ready())
  {
    coroutine_handle<> resume_co =
      coroutine_handle<>::from_address(context);

    y.await_suspend(resume_co);

    __suspend_resume_point_1:
  }

  auto value = t.await_resume();

  std::cout << "the answer is " << value << '\n';
}
```

As mentioned earlier, the `main()` function is one of the functions that cannot be a coroutine. For this reason, it is not possible to use the `co_await` operator in `main()`. This means that waiting for a coroutine to complete must be done differently in `main()`.

This is handled with the help of a function template called `execute()` that runs the following loop:

```
while (!t.is_ready()) t.resume();
```

This loop ensures that the coroutine is resumed after each suspension point, until its final completion.

There's more...

The C++20 standard does not provide any coroutine types, and writing your own is a cumbersome task. Fortunately, third-party libraries can offer these abstractions. Such a library is **cppcoro**, an open source experimental library that provides a set of general-purpose primitives for making use of the coroutines described in the C++20 standard. The library is available at `https://github.com/lewissbaker/cppcoro`. Among the components it provides is the `task<T>` coroutine type, similar to what we built in this recipe. Using the `cppcoro::task<T>` type, we can rewrite our examples as follows:

```
#include <iostream>
#include <cppcoro/task.hpp>
#include <cppcoro/sync_wait.hpp>

cppcoro::task<int> get_answer()
{
  co_return 42;
}

cppcoro::task<> print_answer()
{
  auto t = co_await get_answer();
  std::cout << "the answer is " << t << '\n';
}

cppcoro::task<> demo()
{
  auto t = co_await get_answer();
  std::cout << "the answer is " << t << '\n';

  co_await print_answer();
}
```

```
int main()
{
   cppcoro::sync_wait(demo());
}
```

As you can see, the code is very similar to what we wrote in the first part of this recipe. The changes are minimal. By using this **cppcoro** library or others that are similar, you do not need to be concerned with the details of implementing coroutine types and instead focus on their use.

See also

- *Creating a coroutine generator type for sequences of values*, to learn how to enable the use of `co_yield` to return multiple values from a coroutine.

Creating a coroutine generator type for sequences of values

In the previous recipe, we saw how to create a coroutine task that enables asynchronous computations. We used the `co_await` operator to suspend execution until resumed and the `co_return` keyword to complete execution and return a value. However, another keyword, `co_yield`, also defines a function as a coroutine. It suspends the execution of the coroutine and returns a value. It enables a coroutine to return multiple values, one each time it is resumed. To support this feature, another type of coroutine is required. This type is called a *generator*. Conceptually, it's like a stream that produces a sequence of values of a type `T` in a lazy manner (when iterated). In this recipe, we will see how we can implement a simple generator.

Getting ready

The goal of this recipe is to create a generator coroutine type that enables us to write code like the following:

```
generator<int> iota(int start = 0, int step = 1) noexcept
{
  auto value = start;
  for (int i = 0;; ++i)
  {
    co_yield value;
    value += step;
```

```
  }
}

generator<std::optional<int>> iota_n(
  int start = 0, int step = 1,
  int n = std::numeric_limits<int>::max()) noexcept
{
  auto value = start;
  for (int i = 0; i < n; ++i)
  {
    co_yield value;
    value += step;
  }
}

generator<int> fibonacci() noexcept
{
  int a = 0, b = 1;
  while (true)
  {
    co_yield b;
    auto tmp = a;
    a = b;
    b += tmp;
  }
}

int main()
{
  for (auto i : iota())
  {
    std::cout << i << ' ';
    if (i >= 10) break;
  }

  for (auto i : iota_n(0, 1, 10))
  {
    if (!i.has_value()) break;
    std::cout << i.value() << ' ';
  }

  int c = 1;
```

```
    for (auto i : fibonacci())
    {
      std::cout << i << ' ';
      if (++c > 10) break;
    }
  }
```

It is recommended that you follow the previous recipe, *Creating a coroutine task type for asynchronous computations*, before you continue with this one.

How to do it...

To create a generator coroutine type that supports synchronous lazy production of a sequence of values, you should do the following:

- Create a class template, called `generator`, with the following content (the details of each part are presented with the following bullets):

```
template <typename T>
struct generator
{
  // struct promise_type

  // struct iterator

  // member functions

  // iterators
private:
   stdco::coroutine_handle<promise_type> handle_ = nullptr;
};
```

- Create an inner class called `promise_type` (the name is mandatory) with the following content:

```
struct promise_type
{
  T const*             value_;
  std::exception_ptr   eptr_;

  auto get_return_object()
  { return generator{ *this }; }

  auto initial_suspend() noexcept
```

```
   { return stdco::suspend_always{}; }

   auto final_suspend() noexcept
   { return stdco::suspend_always{}; }

   void unhandled_exception() noexcept
   {
      eptr_ = std::current_exception();
   }

   void rethrow_if_exception()
   {
      if (eptr_)
      {
         std::rethrow_exception(eptr_);
      }
   }

   auto yield_value(T const& v)
   {
      value_ = std::addressof(v);
      return stdco::suspend_always{};
   }

   void return_void() {}

   template <typename U>
   U&& await_transform(U&& v)
   {
      return std::forward<U>(v);
   }
};
```

- Create an inner class called `iterator` with the following content:

```
struct iterator
{
  using iterator_category = std::input_iterator_tag;
  using difference_type   = ptrdiff_t;
  using value_type        = T;
  using reference         = T const&;
  using pointer           = T const*;
```

```
stdco::coroutine_handle<promise_type> handle_ = nullptr;

iterator() = default;
iterator(nullptr_t) : handle_(nullptr) {}

iterator(stdco::coroutine_handle<promise_type> arg)
  : handle_(arg)
{}

iterator& operator++()
{
   handle_.resume();
   if (handle_.done())
   {
      std::exchange(handle_, {}).promise()
                                .rethrow_if_exception();
   }

   return *this;
}

void operator++(int)
{
   ++* this;
}

bool operator==(iterator const& _Right) const
{
   return handle_ == _Right.handle_;
}

bool operator!=(iterator const& _Right) const
{
   return !(*this == _Right);
}

reference operator*() const
{
   return *handle_.promise().value_;
}
```

```
    pointer operator->() const
    {
        return std::addressof(handle_.promise().value_);
    }
};
```

- Provide a default constructor, an explicit constructor from a `promise_type` object, a move constructor and a move assignment operator, and a destructor. Delete the copy constructor and copy assignment operator so that the type is moveable-only:

```
explicit generator(promise_type& p)
  : handle_(
      stdco::coroutine_handle<promise_type>::from_promise(p))
{}

generator() = default;
generator(generator const&) = delete;
generator& operator=(generator const&) = delete;

generator(generator&& other) : handle_(other.handle_)
{
  other.handle_ = nullptr;
}

generator& operator=(generator&& other)
{
  if (this != std::addressof(other))
  {
     handle_ = other.handle_;
     other.handle_ = nullptr;
  }
  return *this;
}

~generator()
{
  if (handle_)
  {
     handle_.destroy();
  }
}
```

- Provide the `begin()` and `end()` functions to enable iterating over the generator sequence:

```
iterator begin()
{
  if (handle_)
  {
     handle_.resume();
     if (handle_.done())
     {
        handle_.promise().rethrow_if_exception();
        return { nullptr };
     }
  }

  return { handle_ };
}

iterator end()
{
  return { nullptr };
}
```

How it works...

The promise type implemented in this recipe is similar to the one from the previous recipe, although there are some differences:

- It is implemented as an inner type, so the name is `promise_type`, since the coroutine framework requires the coroutine type to have an inner promise type with this name.
- It supports handling exceptions that leave the coroutine block uncaught. In the previous recipe, this situation was not treated and `unhandled_exception()` called `std::terminate()` to abnormally terminate the process. This implementation, however, retries a pointer to the current exception and stores it in an `std::exception_ptr` object. This exception is rethrown when iterating through the generated sequence (either when calling `begin()` or when incrementing the iterator).
- The functions `return_value()` and `return_void()` are not present, but replaced with `yield_value()`, which is called when the `co_yield expr` expression is resolved.

The generator class also bears some similarities to the task class from the previous recipe:

- It is default constructible
- It can be constructed from a promise object
- It is not copy-constructible and copyable
- It is move-constructible and moveable
- Its destructor destroys the coroutine frame

This class does not overload the `co_await` operator, as it does not make sense to await on the generator, but provides the functions `begin()` and `end()`, which return iterator objects that enable iterating over the sequence of values. This generator is said to be lazy because it does not produce new values until the coroutine is resumed, either by calling `begin()` or incrementing an iterator. The coroutine is created suspended and its first execution begins only when calling the `begin()` function. The execution continues either until the first `co_yield` statement or until the coroutine completes its execution. Similarly, incrementing the iterator will resume the execution of the coroutine, which continues either until the next `co_yield` statement or until its completion.

The following example shows a coroutine that produces several integer values. It does so not by using a loop but by repeating `co_yield` statements:

```
generator<int> get_values() noexcept
{
  co_yield 1;
  co_yield 2;
  co_yield 3;
}

int main()
{
  for (auto i : get_values())
  {
    std::cout << i << ' ';
  }
}
```

An important thing to note is that the coroutine can only use the `co_yield` keyword and produce values synchronously. The use of the `co_await` operator within the coroutine is not supported with this particular implementation. To be able to suspend execution by using the `co_await` operator, a different implementation is required.

There's more...

The **cppcoro** library, mentioned in the previous recipe, has a `generator<T>` type that can be used instead of the one we created here. In fact, by replacing our `generator<T>` with `cppcoro::generator<T>`, the snippets of code shown previously will continue to work as expected. Moreover, the cppcoro library also features an `async_generator<T>` type, which supports the `co_await` operator and, therefore, producing values asynchronously, as well as a `recursive_generator<T>` type, which efficiently supports yielding the elements of a nested sequence as elements of an outer sequence.

See also

- *Creating a coroutine task type for asynchronous computations*, to get an introduction to the C++20 coroutines.

Bibliography

Websites

- C++ reference http://en.cppreference.com/w/
- ISO C++ https://isocpp.org/
- More C++ Idioms https://en.wikibooks.org/wiki/More_C%2B%2B_Idioms
- Boost http://www.boost.org/
- Catch2 https://github.com/catchorg/Catch2
- Google Test https://github.com/google/googletest
- CppCoro https://github.com/lewissbaker/cppcoro
- range-v3 https://github.com/ericniebler/range-v3

Articles and books

- David Abrahams, 2001. *Lessons Learned from Specifying Exception-Safety for the C++ Standard Library* http://www.boost.org/community/exception_safety.html
- Michael Afanasiev, 2016. *Combining Static and Dynamic Polymorphism with C++ Mixin classes* https://michael-afanasiev.github.io/2016/08/03/Combining-Static-and-Dynamic-Polymorphism-with-C++-Template-Mixins.html
- Alex Allain, 2011. *Constexpr - Generalized Constant Expressions in C++11* http://www.cprogramming.com/c++11/c++11-compile-time-processing-with-constexpr.html

- Matthew H. Austern, 2001. *The Standard Librarian: Defining a Facet* `http://www.drdobbs.com/the-standard-librarian-defining-a-facet/184403785`
- Thomas Badie, 2012. *C++11: A generic Singleton* `http://enki-tech.blogspot.ro/2012/08/c11-generic-singleton.html`
- Lewis Baker, 2019. *Coroutine Theory* `https://lewissbaker.github.io/2017/09/25/coroutine-theory`
- Lewis Baker, 2017. *C++ Coroutines: Understanding operator co_await* `https://lewissbaker.github.io/2017/11/17/understanding-operator-co-await`
- Eli Bendersky, 2016. *The promises and challenges of std::async task-based parallelism in C++11* `http://eli.thegreenplace.net/2016/the-promises-and-challenges-of-stdasync-task-based-parallelism-in-c11/`
- Eli Bendersky, 2011. *The Curiously Recurring Template Pattern in C++* `http://eli.thegreenplace.net/2011/05/17/the-curiously-recurring-template-pattern-in-c`
- Joshua Bloch, 2008. *Effective Java (2nd Edition)* Addison-Wesley
- Fernando Luis Cacciola Carballal, 2007. *Boost.Optional* `http://www.boost.org/doc/libs/1_63_0/libs/optional/doc/html/index.html`
- Bruce Dawson, 2012. *Comparing Floating Point Numbers, 2012 Edition* `https://randomascii.wordpress.com/2012/02/25/comparing-floating-point-numbers-2012-edition/`
- Kent Fagerjord. 2016. *How to build Boost 1.62 with Visual Studio 2015* `https://studiofreya.com/2016/09/29/how-to-build-boost-1-62-with-visual-studio-2015/`
- Bartlomiej Filipek, 2018. *The Amazing Performance of C++17 Parallel Algorithms, is it Possible?* `https://www.bfilipek.com/2018/11/parallel-alg-perf.html`
- Eric Friedman and Itay Maman, 2003. *Boost.Variant* `http://www.boost.org/doc/libs/1_63_0/doc/html/variant.html`
- Vanand Gasparyan, 2019. *A little bit of code [C++20 Ranges]* `https://itnext.io/a-little-bit-of-code-c-20-ranges-c6a6f7eae401`
- Wilfried Goesgens, 2015. *Comparison: Lockless programming with atomics in C++ 11 vs. mutex and RW-locks* `https://www.arangodb.com/2015/02/comparing-atomic-mutex-rwlocks/`
- Corentin Jabot, 2018. *A can of span* `https://cor3ntin.github.io/posts/span/`
- Corentin Jabot, 2020. *A Universal I/O Abstraction for C++* `https://cor3ntin.github.io/posts/iouring/`
- Kevlin Henney, 2001. *Boost.Any* `http://www.boost.org/doc/libs/1_63_0/doc/html/any.html`

- Howard Hinnant, *(library on GitHub)* `https://github.com/HowardHinnant/date`
- Nicolai M. Josuttis 2012. *The C++ Standard Library: Utilities* `http://www.informit.com/articles/article.aspx?p=1881386&seqNum=2`
- Nicolai Josutis, 2012. *The C++ Standard Library, 2nd Edition* Addison Wesley Danny Kalev, 2012. *Using constexpr to Improve Security, Performance and Encapsulation in C++* `http://blog.smartbear.com/c-plus-plus/using-constexpr-to-improve-security-performance-and-encapsulation-in-c/`
- Danny Kalev, 2012. *C++11 Tutorial: Introducing the Move Constructor and the Move Assignment Operator* `http://blog.smartbear.com/c-plus-plus/c11-tutorial-introducing-the-move-constructor-and-the-move-assignment-operator/`
- David Kieras, 2013. *Why std::binary_search of std::list Works, But You Shouldn't Use It!* EECS 381
- Matt Kline 2017. *Comparing Floating-Point Numbers Is Tricky,* `http://bitbashing.io/comparing-floats.html`
- Andrzej Krzemienski, 2016. *Another polymorphism* `https://akrzemi1.wordpress.com/2016/02/27/another-polymorphism/`
- Andrzej Krzemienski, 2011. *Using noexcept* `https://akrzemi1.wordpress.com/2011/06/10/using-noexcept/`
- Andrzej Krzemienski, 2014. *noexcept--what for?* `https://akrzemi1.wordpress.com/2014/04/24/noexcept-what-for/`
- Andrzej Krzemienski, 2013. *noexcept destructors* `https://akrzemi1.wordpress.com/2013/08/20/noexcept-destructors/`
- John Maddock and Steve Cleary, 2000. *C++ Type Traits* `http://www.drdobbs.com/cpp/c-type-traits/184404270`
- Arne Mertz, 2016. *Modern C++ Features – constexpr* `https://arne-mertz.de/2016/06/constexpr/`
- Scott Meyers, 2014. *Effective Modern C++, O'Reilly*
- Scott Meyers and Andrei Alexandrescu, 2004. *C++ and the Perils of Double-Checked Locking* `http://www.aristeia.com/Papers/DDJ_Jul_Aug_2004_revised.pdf`
- Bartosz Milewski, 2009. *Broken promises–C++0x futures* `https://bartoszmilewski.com/2009/03/03/broken-promises-c0x-futures/`
- Bartosz Milewski, 2008. *Who ordered sequential consistency?* `https://bartoszmilewski.com/2008/11/11/who-ordered-sequential-consistency/`

- Bartosz Milewski, 2008. *C++ atomics and memory ordering* `https://bartoszmilewski.com/2008/12/01/c-atomics-and-memory-ordering/`
- Oliver Mueller, 2014. *Testing C++ With A New Catch* `http://blog.coldflake.com/posts/Testing-C++-with-a-new-Catch/`
- Jonathan Müller, 2018. *Mathematics behind Comparison #1: Equality and Equivalence Relations* `https://foonathan.net/2018/06/equivalence-relations/`
- Ashwin Nanjappa, 2014. *How to build Boost using Visual Studio* `https://codeyarns.com/2014/06/06/how-to-build-boost-using-visual-studio/`
- Billy O'Neal, 2018. *Using C++17 Parallel Algorithms for Better Performance* `https://devblogs.microsoft.com/cppblog/using-c17-parallel-algorithms-for-better-performance/`
- M.E. O'Neill, 2015. *C++ Seeding Surprises* `http://www.pcg-random.org/posts/cpp-seeding-surprises.html`
- M.E. O'Neill, 2015. *Developing a seed_seq Alternative* `http://www.pcg-random.org/posts/developing-a-seed_seq-alternative.html`
- M.E. O'Neill, 2015. *Everything You Never Wanted to Know about C++'s random_device* `http://www.pcg-random.org/posts/cpps-random_device.html`
- M.E. O'Neill, 2015. *Simple Portable C++ Seed Entropy* `http://www.pcg-random.org/posts/simple-portable-cpp-seed-entropy.html`
- John Pearce, *Floating Point Numbers* `http://www.cs.sjsu.edu/~pearce/modules/lectures/co/ds/floats.htm`
- Jeff Preshing, 2013. *Double-Checked Locking is Fixed In C++11* `http://preshing.com/20130930/double-checked-locking-is-fixed-in-cpp11/`
- Rick Regan, 2010. *Hexadecimal Floating-Point Constants* `http://www.exploringbinary.com/hexadecimal-floating-point-constants/`
- Barry Revzin, 2019. *Comparisons in C++20* `https://brevzin.github.io/c++/2019/07/28/comparisons-cpp20/`
- Eugene Sadovoi, 2015. *Building and configuring boost in Visual Studio (MSBuild)* `https://www.codeproject.com/Articles/882581/Building-and-configuring-boost-in-Visual-Studio-MS`
- David Sankel, 2015. *A variant for the everyday Joe* `http://davidsankel.com/c/a-variant-for-the-everyday-joe/`
- Arpan Sen, 2010. *A quick introduction to the Google C++ Testing Framework* `http://www.ibm.com/developerworks/aix/library/au-googletestingframework.html`

- Bjarne Stroustrup, 2000. *Standard-Library Exception Safety* Addison Wesley `http://stroustrup.com/3rd_safe.pdf`
- Herb Sutter, 2013. *GotW #90 Solution: Factories* `https://herbsutter.com/2013/05/30/gotw-90-solution-factories/`
- Herb Sutter, 2002. *A Pragmatic Look at Exception Specifications* C/C++ Users Journal, 20(7) `http://www.gotw.ca/publications/mill22.htm`
- Herb Sutter, 2012. *GotW #102: Exception-Safe Function Calls* `https://herbsutter.com/gotw/_102/`
- Herb Sutter, 2013. *My Favorite C++ 10-Liner* `https://channel9.msdn.com/Events/GoingNative/2013/My-Favorite-Cpp-10-Liner`
- Herb Sutter, 2001. *Virtuality*, C/C++ Users Journal, 19(9) `http://www.gotw.ca/publications/mill18.htm`
- Andrey Upadyshev, 2015. *PIMPL, Rule of Zero and Scott Meyers* `http://oliora.github.io/2015/12/29/pimpl-and-rule-of-zero.html`
- Todd Veldhuizen, 2000. *Techniques for Scientific C++* `http://www.cs.indiana.edu/pub/techreports/TR542.pdf`
- Baptiste Wicht, 2014. *Catch: A powerful yet simple C++ test framework* `https://baptiste-wicht.com/posts/2014/07/catch-powerful-yet-simple-cpp-test-framework.html`
- Anthony Williams, 2009. *Multithreading in C++0x part 7: Locking multiple mutexes without deadlock* `https://www.justsoftwaresolutions.co.uk/threading/multithreading-in-c++0x-part-7-locking-multiple-mutexes.html`
- Anthony Williams, 2008. *Peterson's lock with C++0x atomics* `https://www.justsoftwaresolutions.co.uk/threading/petersons_lock_with_C++0x_atomics.html`
- Benjamin Wolsey, 2010. *C++ facets* `http://benjaminwolsey.de/node/78`
- Victor Zverovich, 2019. *std::format in C++20* `https://www.zverovich.net/2019/07/23/std-format-cpp20.html`

Other Books You May Enjoy

If you enjoyed this book, you may be interested in these other books by Packt:

Extreme C

Kamran Amini

ISBN: 9781789343625

- Build advanced C knowledge on strong foundations, rooted in first principles
- Understand memory structures and compilation pipeline and how they work, and how to make most out of them
- Apply object-oriented design principles to your procedural C code
- Write low-level code that's close to the hardware and squeezes maximum performance out of a computer system

- Master concurrency, multithreading, multi-processing, and integration with other languages
- Unit Testing and debugging, build systems, and inter-process communication for C programming

C# 8.0 and .NET Core 3.0 - Modern Cross-Platform Development

Mark J. Price

ISBN: 9781788478120

- Build cross-platform applications for Windows, macOS, Linux, iOS, and Android
- Explore application development with C# 8.0 and .NET Core 3.0
- Explore ASP.NET Core 3.0 and create professional web applications
- Learn object-oriented programming and C# multitasking
- Query and manipulate data using LINQ
- Use Entity Framework Core and work with relational databases
- Discover Windows app development using the Universal Windows Platform and XAML
- Build mobile applications for iOS and Android using Xamarin.Forms

Leave a review - let other readers know what you think

Please share your thoughts on this book with others by leaving a review on the site that you bought it from. If you purchased the book from Amazon, please leave us an honest review on this book's Amazon page. This is vital so that other potential readers can see and use your unbiased opinion to make purchasing decisions, we can understand what our customers think about our products, and our authors can see your feedback on the title that they have worked with Packt to create. It will only take a few minutes of your time, but is valuable to other potential customers, our authors, and Packt. Thank you!

Index

D

E

J

L

M

N

O

P

R

S

T

V

W

Made in United States
Orlando, FL
07 February 2022